T0338300

SHORT-MEMORY LINEAR PROCESSES AND ECONOMETRIC APPLICATIONS

SHORT-MEMORY LINEAR PROCESSES AND ECONOMETRIC APPLICATIONS

KAIRAT T. MYNBAEV

International School of Economics
Kazakh-British Technical University
Almaty, Kazakhstan

A JOHN WILEY & SONS, INC., PUBLICATION

Copyright © 2011 by John Wiley & Sons, Inc. All rights reserved

Published by John Wiley & Sons, Inc., Hoboken, New Jersey
Published simultaneously in Canada

No part of this publication may be reproduced, stored in a retrieval system, or transmitted in any form or by any means, electronic, mechanical, photocopying, recording, scanning, or otherwise, except as permitted under Sections 107 or 108 of the 1976 United States Copyright Act, without either the prior written permission of the Publisher, or authorization through payment of the appropriate per-copy fee to the Copyright Clearance Center, Inc., 222 Rosewood Drive, Danvers, MA 01923, (978) 750-8400, fax (978) 750-4470, or on the web at www.copyright.com. Requests to the Publisher for permission should be addressed to the Permissions Department, John Wiley & Sons, Inc., 111 River Street, Hoboken, NJ 07030, (201) 748-6011, fax (201) 748-6008, or online at http://www.wiley.com/go/permission.

Limit of Liability/Disclaimer of Warranty: While the publisher and author have used their best efforts in preparing this book, they make no representations or warranties with respect to the accuracy or completeness of the contents of this book and specifically disclaim any implied warranties of merchantability or fitness for a particular purpose. No warranty may be created or extended by sales representatives or written sales materials. The advice and strategies contained herein may not be suitable for your situation. You should consult with a professional where appropriate. Neither the publisher nor author shall be liable for any loss of profit or any other commercial damages, including but not limited to special, incidental, consequential, or other damages.

For general information on our other products and services or for technical support, please contact our Customer Care Department within the United States at (800) 762-2974, outside the United States at (317) 572-3993 or fax (317) 572-4002.

Wiley also publishes its books in variety of electronic formats. Some content that appears in print may not be available in electronic format. For more information about Wiley products, visit our web site at www.wiley.com.

Library of Congress Cataloging-in-Publication Data:

Mynbaev, K. T. (Kairat Turysbekovich)
  Short-memory linear processes and econometric applications / Kairat T. Mynbaev.
    p. cm.
  Includes bibliographical references and index.
  ISBN 978-0-470-92419-8
 1. Linear programming. 2. Econometric models. 3. Regression analysis.
4. Probabilities. I. Title.
  T57.74.M98 2011
  519.7'2—dc22

                                              2010040947

Printed in the United States of America
10 9 8 7 6 5 4 3 2 1

To my teacher Mukhtarbai Otelbaev,
from whom I learnt the best I know.

CONTENTS

LIST OF TABLES

PREFACE

1   RED LIGHT

There are no new econometric models in this book. You will not find real-life applications or tests of economic theories either.

2   GREEN LIGHT

The book concentrates on the methodology of asymptotic theory in econometrics. Specifically, central limit theorems (CLTs) for weighted sums of short-memory processes are obtained. They are applied to several well-known econometric models to demonstrate how their asymptotic behavior can be studied, what kind of assumptions are (in)appropriate and how probabilistic convergence statements are applied. Currently, no monographs or textbooks are devoted specifically to econometric models with deterministic regressors. The field is considered rather narrow by some specialists because the first thing they think about is polynomial trends. Indeed, polynomial trends are not widely used in econometrics. However, some other types of regressors fall into the classes of deterministic regressors considered in the literature; for example, some spatial matrices and seasonal dummies. This makes deterministic explanatory variables more important than commonly thought. Besides, on the level of CLTs deterministic weights are of interest in themselves. There is a monograph by Taylor (1978) devoted exclusively to such theorems.

3   THE ESSENCE

By and large, CLTs here are based on only one global idea: how sequences of discrete objects (vectors and matrices) can be approximated with functions of a continuous argument (defined on the segment [0, 1]). Stated in this general way, the idea is as old as calculus. The novelty here consists in application of the idea to weighted sums of linear processes

$$\sum_{t=1}^{n} w_{nt} u_t, \tag{0.1}$$

where $w_n = (w_{n1}, \ldots, w_{nn})$, $n = 1, 2, \ldots$ is a sequence of deterministic vector weights and

$$u_t = \sum_{j=-\infty}^{\infty} \psi_{t-j} e_j, \quad t = 0, \pm 1, \pm 2, \ldots \tag{0.2}$$

is a short-memory linear process. Anybody with a little experience in probabilities, statistics, and econometrics can confirm that statements on convergence in distribution of such weighted sums have many applications. As it turned out, the main difficulties in proving precise CLTs lay in the theory of functions. Hence, attempts to obtain general CLTs for sums of type Eq. (0.1) by researchers with backgrounds other than the theory of functions yielded results less satisfactory than those published in my paper (Mynbaev, 2001) on L_p-approximable sequences.

My interest in CLTs for Eq. (0.1) arose from the necessities of regression analysis. In the asymptotic theory of regressions with deterministic regressors, sequences of regressors can be approximated by functions of a continuous argument. The structure of the corresponding estimators allows for application of CLTs for Eq. (0.1). As I was developing applications, I needed various additional properties of L_p-approximable sequences. They are distributed throughout the book and, taken together, constitute a complete toolkit accompanying the main CLTs.

In the econometrics context, two other definitions of deterministic regressors are suggested in the literature. A purely algebraic definition (based on recursion) was proposed by Johansen (2000) and developed further by Nielsen (2005) to study strong consistency of ordinary least squares (OLS) estimators. Nielsen's result, given in Chapter 8, shows that such regressors are asymptotically polynomial functions multiplied by oscillating (trigonometric) functions. The Johansen–Nielsen approach and L_p-approximability complement each other.

Phillips (2007) has defined regressors in terms of slowly varying (SV) functions (which is a functional–theoretical construction). Slow variation is a limit property at infinity and, in general, has nothing to do with L_p-approximability, which is a limit property distributed over the segment [0, 1]. However, special sequences arising from SV functions in the regression context are all L_p-approximable.

4 STANDING PROBLEMS

About half of the results contained in the book were obtained after I started writing it. The theory has grown to the extent that no single person can embrace all the ramifications.

1. Linear processes (0.2), depending on the rate at which the numbers ψ_j vanish at infinity, are classified as follows. Processes for which

$$\sum_{j=-\infty}^{\infty} |\psi_j| < \infty \tag{0.3}$$

are called short-memory processes. Processes for which the series in Eq. (0.3) diverges, but

$$\sum_{j=-\infty}^{\infty} \psi_j^2 < \infty$$

are called long-memory processes. My CLT for weighted sums Eq. (0.1) holds in the case of short-memory processes. The existing CLTs for long-memory ones, as deep as they are, leave some questions open.

2. The main advantage of representing sequences of vectors with the help of functions of a continuous argument is that the limit expressions in asymptotic distributions involve integrals of those functions. Thus, they are amenable to further analysis, which I call analysis at infinity. For this reason alone, when my definition of L_p-approximability does not fit practical situations (and there is at least one, in spatial econometrics), developing a more suitable definition may be better than relinquishing the concept altogether.

3. The name of the book reflects its coverage rather than its potential. There are two important directions in which it can be extended. One is nonparametric and nonlinear estimation, where even my CLT will suffice for the beginning. Another is the case of stochastic regressors. In this case Anderson and Kunitomo (1992) impose conditions on separate parts of the OLS estimator that allow them to prove its convergence. As an alternative, I would embed enough structure in the stochastic regressors to be able to derive convergence of separate parts of the OLS estimator. The structure entailed by L_p-approximability in the deterministic case may guide the choice for the stochastic case.

5   REVIEW BY CHAPTERS

Chapter 1 is a collection of general ideas and preliminaries from probability theory and functional analysis. It also contains a discussion of L_p-approximability and its advantages. The first nontrivial application is to the convergence in distribution of the fitted value for the linear regression. This convergence looks to some econometricians so incredible that an anonymous referee of *Econometric Theory* said that my paper was "full of mistakes." Naturally, the paper was rejected and, not so naturally, the result was not published in journals. Thus this book was written. The discussion of issues related to normalization of regressors draws from folklore and should be in the core of any course on asymptotic theory in econometrics.

Chapter 2 covers the nonstochastic part of my paper (Mynbaev, 2001). Readers with taste for mathematical precision will find it illuminating that L_p-approximability (which relates sequences of vectors to functions defined on [0, 1]) can be characterized intrinsically (in terms of sequences of vectors themselves). This is evidence of a well-balanced definition. On a more practical note, such results and their by-products make sure that the ensuing CLTs are the most precise and general.

The main CLTs are proved in Chapter 3, which is based on Mynbaev (2001) but I would like to acknowledge the influence of Nabeya and Tanaka (1990) who paved the way to treating convergence of quadratic forms. This is where the theory of integral operators is needed and introduced first.

There are many CLTs and weak laws of large numbers (WLLN) out there. The reader will notice that when the innovations e_j in linear processes [Eq. (0.2)] are martingale differences (m.d.'s), the McLeish CLT (McLeish, 1974) and the Chow-Davidson WLLN (Davidson, 1994) are absolutely sufficient for the purposes of Chapter 3. I dare to suggest trying these tools first in all other problems with linear processes involving m.d.'s.

Serious applications (to static models) start in Chapter 4. Phillips (2007) developed a nice scheme of investigating asymptotic properties of regressions with regressors such as $\log s$, $\log(\log s)$, their reciprocals and so on. Chapter 4 follows this scheme, while the underlying central limit results are derived from my CLT. This is possible because Phillips' specification of the weights in Eq. (0.1) is a special case of L_p-approximable sequences. One of the methodological conclusions of this chapter is that direct derivation of a CLT given in Chapter 3 is better than recourse to Brownian motion used by Phillips.

Chapter 5 demonstrates what can be done with the help of L_p-approximability in the theory of spatial models. This research started with a joint paper (Mynbaev and Ullah, 2008) in which we showed that the OLS estimator for a purely spatial model is not asymptotically normal. In Mynbaev (2010), this result is extended to a mixed spatial model. Spatial models are peculiar in many respects, a full discussion of which would be too technical for a preface. It is worth stating here only the most general methodological conclusion. When studying the asymptotic behavior of a new model, never presume it is of a certain class. Otherwise, you will be bound to use specific techniques that will take you to a particular result so you will not see the general picture.

In the 1980s, Lai and Wei in a series of papers (Lai and Wei, 1982, 1983a, 1983b, 1985) obtained outstanding results on strong consistency of the OLS estimator for the linear model, with and without autoregressive terms. Reading those papers is a thankless task because the solution to a large problem is divided into publishable articles and the times of publication of the articles are not the best reflection of the logic of the solution. Chapter 6 is an attempt to expound Lai and Wei's theory coherently.

Chapter 7 contains a treatment of two nonlinear estimators: nonlinear least squares (NLS) and maximum likelihood (ML). The choice of the models is explained by the fact that in both cases the explanatory variables are deterministic. The first part of the chapter covers the Phillips (2007) result for the model $y_s = \beta s^\gamma + u_s$. The second part is my extension to unbounded explanatory variables of the approach to binary logit models suggested by Gouriéroux and Monfort (1981).

Finally, Chapter 8 contains a study of algebraic properties of L_p-approximable sequences of matrix-valued functions and a study of a different type of deterministic trends from Nielsen (2005). The applications to vector autoregressions (VARs) with deterministic trends are left out.

6 EXPOSITION

The book is analytical in nature, meaning that there is a lot of formula manipulation. Most calculations are detailed so they can be followed without a pen and paper. To simplify the reader's job, all meaningful parts of proofs are given in separate statements. Because of this, some proofs look longer than they are. Commuters who need to do their reading in buses and trains will benefit from such exposition.

Only the core theoretical results are collected in Chapters 2 and 3. All others are given immediately before they are applied (including some CLTs). Thus, application-specific properties of L_p-approximable sequences, as well as parts of the theory of integral operators, are scattered throughout the book.

If someone were to lecture using this book, I have imagined how clumsy it would be to say, "Let us recall the function defined by Eq. (9) in Lecture 3." For this reason I have tried to give names not only to final statements, but also to auxiliary objects, such as lemmas, functions and operators. In most cases the names reflect the roles performed by such objects. Thus, you will see βad and γood coefficients, a chain product, annihilation lemma, balancer, cutter and the like. However, in a couple of cases descriptive names would be too long, and the names I give reflect the look, not the role. There is a proξy and proXy, an awkward aggregate, genie (because of G_n) and so on.

No subsection contains more than one statement. Therefore statements are referred to by the section they are in. Thus, Lemma 3.1.2 means the statement from subsection 3.1.2, even though the name 'Lemma' may not be there. Equation numbering follows the Wiley standard: Eq. (7.1) means equation 1 from Chapter 7. To make the book self-contained, most preliminaries are given in the book. All calculations are detailed with extensive cross-referencing.

7 SUGGESTIONS FOR READING

The variety and depth of mathematical theories used by econometricians can be a serious obstacle for novices. Davidson (1994) has done an excellent job in gathering in one place the required minimum, from measure theory to stochastic processes. For me, this is the most important book I have read in the past 10 years, and I recommend it for preliminary or concurrent reading.

A partial excuse for the limited coverage of the existing literature is that during the four years that I was working on the book I did not receive any support, financial or otherwise, and did not have access to a good library, except when I traveled to international conferences. At the final stage, when the book was in production, I received useful references from some colleagues. Regarding weighted sums and their applications in econometrics, Jonathan B. Hill suggests reading Čížek (2008), Goldie and Smith (1987), Hahn et al. (1987), Hill (2010, 2011) and references therein. Jan Mielniczuk, who contributed a lot to the theory of long-memory processes not covered here, proposes reading Wu (2005) and Wu and Min (2005) for the most recent developments in the area. M. H. Pesaran was kind enough to provide references Chudik et al. (2010), Holly et al. (2008) and Pesaran and Chudik (2010) for spatial models, vector autoregressions and panel data models.

Personally, I find nothing more gratifying than reading applied econometric papers because they abound in new ideas. Sometimes they also show how things should not be done. See more about this in Chapter 1.

Kairat T. Mynbaev
Almaty, Kazakhstan

ACKNOWLEDGMENTS

I am grateful to Carlos Martins Filho for his encouragement for this book and many other projects. The folks at John Wiley & Sons have been highly efficient in preparing the book for publication. The production process surely involved many people of whom I would like to especially thank Susanne Steitz-Filler, Christine Punzo, Jacqueline Palmieri, and Nick Barber (Books Manager, Techset Composition Ltd).

CHAPTER 1

INTRODUCTION TO OPERATORS, PROBABILITIES AND THE LINEAR MODEL

THIS CHAPTER has a little bit of everything: normed and Hilbert spaces, linear operators, probabilities, including conditional expectations and different modes of convergence, and matrix algebra. Introduction to the OLS method is given along with a discussion of methodological issues, such as the choice of the format of the convergence statement, choice of the conditions sufficient for convergence and the use of L_2-approximability. The exposition presumes that the reader is versed more in the theory of probabilities than in functional analysis.

1.1 LINEAR SPACES

In this book basic notions of functional analysis are used more frequently than in most other econometric books. Here I explain these notions the way I understand them—omitting some formalities and emphasizing the intuition.

1.1.1 Linear Spaces

The Euclidean space $\mathbb{R}^n$ is a good point of departure when introducing linear spaces. An element $x = (x_1, \ldots, x_n) \in \mathbb{R}^n$ is called a *vector*. Two vectors x, y can be added coordinate by coordinate to obtain a new vector

$$x + y = (x_1 + y_1, \ldots, x_n + y_n). \tag{1.1}$$

A vector x can be multiplied by a number $a \in \mathbb{R}$, giving $ax = (ax_1, \ldots, ax_n)$. By combining these two operations we can form expressions like $ax + by$ or, more generally,

$$a_1 x^{(1)} + \cdots + a_m x^{(m)} \tag{1.2}$$

where $a_1, \ldots, a_n$ are numbers and $x^{(1)}, \ldots, x^{(m)}$ are vectors. Expression (1.2) is called a *linear combination of vectors* $x^{(1)}, \ldots, x^{(m)}$ with coefficients $a_1, \ldots, a_n$. Generally, multiplication of vectors is not defined.

Short-Memory Linear Processes and Econometric Applications. Kairat T. Mynbaev
© 2011 John Wiley & Sons, Inc. Published 2011 by John Wiley & Sons, Inc.

Here we observe the major difference between $\mathbb{R}$ and $\mathbb{R}^n$. In $\mathbb{R}$ both summation $a + b$ and multiplication ab can be performed. In $\mathbb{R}^n$ we can add two vectors, but to multiply them we use elements of another set – the set of real numbers (or scalars) $\mathbb{R}$.

Generalizing upon this situation we obtain abstract *linear* (or *vector*) *spaces*. The elements x, y of a linear space L are called *vectors*. They can be added to give another vector $x + y$. Summation is defined axiomatically and, in general, there is no coordinate representation of type (1.1) for summation. A vector x can be multiplied by a scalar $a \in \mathbb{R}$. As in $\mathbb{R}^n$, we can form linear combinations [Eq. (1.2)].

The generalization is pretty straightforward, so what's the big deal? You see, in functional analysis complex objects, such as functions and operators, are considered vectors or points in some space. Here is an example. Denote $C[0, 1]$ the set of continuous functions on the segment $[0, 1]$. The sum of two functions F, $G \in C[0, 1]$ is defined as the function $F + G$ with values $(F + G)(t) = F(t) + G(t)$, $t \in [0, 1]$ [this is an analog of Eq. (1.1)]. Continuity of F, G implies continuity of their sum and of the product aF, for a a scalar, so $C[0, 1]$ is a linear space.

1.1.2 Subspaces of Linear Spaces

A subset L_1 of a linear space L is called its *linear subspace* (or just a subspace, for simplicity) if all linear combinations $ax + by$ of any elements x, $y \in L_1$ belong to L_1. Obviously, the set $\{0\}$ and L itself are subspaces of L, called trivial subspaces. For example, in $\mathbb{R}^n$ the set $L_1 = \{x : c_1 x_1 + \cdots + c_n x_n = 0\}$ is a subspace because if x, $y \in L_1$, then $c_1(ax_1 + by_1) + \cdots + c_n(ax_n + by_n) = 0$. Thus, in $\mathbb{R}^3$ the usual straight lines and two-dimensional (2-D) planes containing the origin are subspaces. All intuition we get from our day-to-day experience with the space we live in applies to subspaces. Geometrically, summation $x + y$ is performed by the parallelogram rule. Multiplying x by a number $a \neq 0$ we obtain a vector ax of either the same ($a > 0$) or opposite ($a < 0$) direction. Multiplying x by all real numbers, we obtain a straight line $\{ax : a \in \mathbb{R}\}$ passing through the origin and parallel to x. This is a particular situation in which it may be convenient to call x a point rather than a vector. Then the previous sentence sounds like this: multiplying x by all real numbers we get a straight line passing through the origin and the given point x.

For a given $x_1, \ldots, x_n$ its *linear span* $\mathfrak{M}$ is, by definition, the least linear space of L containing those points. In the case $n = 2$ it can be constructed as follows. Draw a straight line $L_1 = \{ax_1 : a \in \mathbb{R}\}$ through the origin and x_1 and another straight line $L_2 = \{ax_2 : a \in \mathbb{R}\}$ through the origin and x_2. Then form $\mathfrak{M}$ by adding elements of L_1 and L_2 using the parallelogram rule: $\mathfrak{M} = \{x + y : x \in L_1, y \in L_2\}$.

1.1.3 Linear Independence

Vectors $x_1, \ldots, x_n$ are *linearly independent* if the linear combination $c_1 x_1 + \cdots + c_n x_n$ can be null only when all coefficients are null.

EXAMPLE 1.1. Denote by $e_j = (0, \ldots, 0, 1, 0, \ldots, 0)$ (unity in the jth place) the jth *unit vector* in $\mathbb{R}^n$. From the definition of vector operations in $\mathbb{R}^n$ we see that

$c_1 e_1 + \cdots + c_n e_n = (c_1, \ldots, c_n)$. Hence, the equation $c_1 e_1 + \cdots + c_n e_n = 0$ implies equality of all coefficients to zero and the unit vectors are linearly independent.

If in a linear space L there exist vectors $x_1, \ldots, x_n$ such that

1. $x_1, \ldots, x_n$ are linearly independent and
2. any other vector $x \in L$ is a linear combination of $x_1, \ldots, x_n$,

then L is called *n-dimensional* and the system $\{x_1, \ldots, x_n\}$ is called its *basis*. If, on the other hand, for any natural n, L contains n linearly independent vectors, then L is called *infinite-dimensional*.

EXAMPLE 1.2. The unit vectors in $\mathbb{R}^n$ form a basis because they are linearly independent and for any $x \in \mathbb{R}^n$ we can write $x = (x_1, \ldots, x_n) = x_1 e_1 + \cdots + x_n e_n$.

EXAMPLE 1.3. $C[0, 1]$ is infinite-dimensional. Consider monomials $x_j(t) = t^j$, $j = 0, \ldots, n$. By the main theorem of algebra, the equation $c_0 x_0(t) + \cdots + c_n x_n(t) = 0$ with nonzero coefficients can have at most n roots. Hence, if $c_0 x_0(t) + \cdots + c_n x_n(t)$ is identically zero on $[0, 1]$, the coefficients must be zero, so these monomials are linearly independent.

Functional analysis deals mainly with infinite-dimensional spaces. Together with the desire to do without coordinate representations of vectors this fact has led to the development of very powerful methods.

1.2 NORMED SPACES

1.2.1 Normed Spaces

The Pythagorean theorem gives rise to the Euclidean distance

$$\text{dist}(x, y) = \sqrt{\sum_i (x_i - y_i)^2} \tag{1.3}$$

between points $x, y \in \mathbb{R}^n$. In an abstract situation, we can first axiomatically define the distance $\text{dist}(x, 0)$ from x to the origin and then the distance between any two points will be $\text{dist}(x, y) = \text{dist}(x - y, 0)$ (this looks like tautology, but programmers use such definitions all the time). $\text{dist}(x, 0)$ is denoted $\|x\|$ and is called a norm.

Let X be a linear space. A real-valued function $\| \cdot \|$ defined on X is called a *norm* if

1. $\|x\| \geq 0$ (*nonnegativity*),
2. $\|ax\| = |a| \|x\|$ for all numbers a and vectors x (*homogeneity*),
3. $\|x + y\| \leq \|x\| + \|y\|$ (*triangle inequality*) and
4. $\|x\| = 0$ implies $x = 0$ (*nondegeneracy*).

By homogeneity the norm of the null vector is zero:

$$\left\| \begin{array}{c} 0 \\ \text{(vector)} \end{array} \right\| = \left\| \begin{array}{cc} 0 & \cdot \quad 0 \\ \text{(number)} & \text{(vector)} \end{array} \right\| = |0| \|0\| = 0.$$

Nondegeneracy makes sure that the null vector is the only vector whose norm is zero. If we omit the nondegeneracy requirement, the result is the definition of a *seminorm*.

Distance measurement is another context in which points and vectors can be used interchangeably. $\|x\|$ is a length of the vector x and a distance from point x to the origin.

In this book, the way norms are used for bounding various quantities is clear from the next two definitions. Let $\{X_i\}$ be a nested sequence of normed spaces, $X_1 \subseteq X_2 \subseteq \dots$. Take one element from each of these spaces, $x_i \in X_i$. We say that $\{x_i\}$ is a *bounded* sequence if $\sup_i \|x_i\|_{X_i} < \infty$ and *vanishing* if $\|x_i\|_{X_i} \to 0$.

1.2.2   Convergence in Normed Spaces

A linear space X provided with a norm $\| \cdot \|$ is denoted $(X, \| \cdot \|)$. This is often simplified to X. We say that a sequence $\{x_n\}$ *converges* to x if $\|x_n - x\| \to 0$. In this case we write $\lim x_n = x$.

Lemma

(i) *Vector operations are continuous: if* $\lim x_n = x$, $\lim y_n = y$ *and* $\lim a_n = a$, *then* $\lim a_n x_n = ax$, $\lim(x_n + y_n) = \lim x_n + \lim y_n$.

(ii) *If* $\lim x_n = x$, *then* $\lim \|x_n\| = \|x\|$ *(a norm is continuous in the topology it induces).*

Proof.

(i) Applying the triangle inequality and homogeneity,

$$\|a_n x_n - ax\| \le \|(a_n - a)x\| + \|a_n(x_n - x)\|$$
$$= |a_n - a| \|x\| + \|a_n\| \|x_n - x\| \to 0.$$

Here we remember that convergence of the sequence $\{a_n\}$ implies its boundedness: $\sup|a_n| < \infty$.

(ii) Let us prove that

$$\left| \|x\| - \|y\| \right| \le \|x - y\|. \tag{1.4}$$

The proof is modeled on a similar result for absolute values. By the triangle inequality, $\|x\| \le \|x - y\| + \|y\|$ and $\|x\| - \|y\| \le \|x - y\|$. Changing the places of x and y and using homogeneity we get $\|y\| - \|x\| \le \|y - x\| = \|x - y\|$. The latter two inequalities imply Eq. (1.4).

Equation (1.4) yields continuity of the norm: $|\|x_n\| - \|x\|| \le \|x_n - x\| \to 0$. ∎

We say that $\{x_n\}$ is a *Cauchy sequence* if $\lim_{n,m\to\infty}(x_n - x_m) = 0$. If $\{x_n\}$ converges to x, then it is a Cauchy sequence: $\|x_n - x_m\| \leq \|x_n - x\| + \|x - x_m\| \to 0$. If the converse is true (that is, every Cauchy sequence converges), then the space is called *complete*. All normed spaces considered in this book are complete, which ensures the existence of limits of Cauchy sequences.

1.2.3 Spaces l_p

A norm more general than (1.3) is obtained by replacing the index 2 by an arbitrary number $p \in [1, \infty)$. In other words, in $\mathbb{R}^n$ the function

$$\|x\|_p = \left(\sum_i |x_i|^p\right)^{1/p} \tag{1.5}$$

satisfies all axioms of a norm. For $p = \infty$, definition (1.5) is completed with

$$\|x\|_\infty = \sup_i |x_i| \tag{1.6}$$

because $\lim_{p\to\infty} \|x\|_p = \|x\|_\infty$. $\mathbb{R}^n$ provided with the norm $\|\cdot\|_p$ is denoted $\mathbb{R}^n_p$ ($1 \leq p \leq \infty$).

The most immediate generalization of $\mathbb{R}^n_p$ is the *space* l_p of infinite sequences of numbers $x = (x_1, x_2, \dots)$ that have a finite norm $\|x\|_p$ [defined by Eqs. (1.5) or (1.6), where i runs over the set of naturals $\mathbb{N}$]. More generally, the set of indices $I = \{i\}$ in Eq. (1.5) or Eq. (1.6) may depend on the context. In addition to $\mathbb{R}^n_p$ we use $\mathbb{M}_p$ (the set of matrices of all sizes).

The jth *unit vector* in l_p is an infinite sequence $e_j = (0, \dots, 0, 1, 0, \dots)$ with unity in the jth place and 0 in all others. It is immediate that the unit vectors are linearly independent and l_p is infinite-dimensional.

1.2.4 Inequalities in l_p

The triangle inequality in l_p $\|x + y\|_p \leq \|x\|_p + \|y\|_p$ is called the *Minkowski inequality*. Its proof can be found in many texts, which is not true with respect to another, less known, property that is natural to call *monotonicity* of l_p norms:

$$\|x\|_p \leq \|x\|_q \quad \text{for all } 1 \leq q \leq p \leq \infty. \tag{1.7}$$

If $x = 0$, there is nothing to prove. If $x \neq 0$, the general case can be reduced to the case $\|x\|_q = 1$ by considering the normalized vector $x/\|x\|_q$. $\|x\|_q = 1$ implies $|x_i| \leq 1$ for all i. Hence, if $p < \infty$, we have

$$\|x\|_p = \left(\sum_i |x_i|^p\right)^{1/p} \leq \left(\sum_i |x_i|^q\right)^{1/p} = \left(\sum_i |x_i|^q\right)^{1/q} = \|x\|_q.$$

If $p = \infty$, the inequality $\sup_i |x_i| \leq \|x\|_q$ is obvious.

In l_p there is no general inequality opposite to Eq. (1.7). In $\mathbb{R}_p^n$ there is one. For example, in the case $n = 2$ we can write

$$\max\{|x_1|, |x_2|\} \leq (|x_1|^p + |x_2|^p)^{1/p} \leq 2^{1/p}\max\{|x_1|, |x_2|\}.$$

All such inequalities are easy to remember under the general heading of equivalent norms. Two norms $\|\cdot\|_1$ and $\|\cdot\|_2$ defined on the same linear space X are called *equivalent* if there exist constants $0 < c_1 \leq c_2 < \infty$ such that $c_1\|x\|_1 \leq \|x\|_2 \leq c_2\|x\|_1$ for all x.

Theorem. (Trenogin, 1980, Section 3.3) *In a finite-dimensional space any two norms are equivalent.*

1.3   LINEAR OPERATORS

1.3.1   Linear Operators

A linear operator is a generalization of the mapping $A : \mathbb{R}^m \rightarrow \mathbb{R}^n$ induced by an $n \times m$ matrix A according to $y = Ax$. Let L_1, L_2 be linear spaces. A mapping $A : L_1 \rightarrow L_2$ is called a *linear operator* if

$$A(ax + by) = aAx + bAy \tag{1.8}$$

for all vectors $x, y \in L_1$ and numbers a, b.

A linear operator is a function in the first place, and the general definition of an *image* applies to it:

$$\text{Im}(A) = \{Ax : x \in L_1\} \subseteq L_2.$$

However, because of the linearity of A the image $\text{Im}(A)$ is a linear subspace of L_2. Indeed, if we take two elements y_1, y_2 of the image, then there exist $x_1, x_2 \in L_1$ such that $Ax_i = y_i$. Hence, a linear combination

$$a_1y_1 + a_2y_2 = a_1Ax_1 + a_2Ax_2 = A(ax_1 + bx_2)$$

belongs to the image. With a linear operator A we can associate another linear subspace

$$N(A) = \{x \in L_1 : Ax = 0\} \subseteq L_1,$$

called a *null space* of A. Its linearity easily follows from that of A: if x, y belong to the null space of A, then their linear combination belongs to it too: $A(ax + by) = aAx + bAy = 0$.

The set of linear operators acting from L_1 to L_2 can be considered a linear space. A *linear combination* of operators $aA + bB$ of operators A, B is an operator defined by $(aA + bB)x = aAx + bBx$. It is easy to check linearity of $aA + bB$.

If A is a linear operator from L_1 to L_2 and B is a linear operator from L_2 to L_3, then we can also define a *product* of operators BA by $(BA)x = B(Ax)$. Applying Eq. (1.8) twice we see that BA is linear:

$$(BA)(ax + by) = B(aAx + bAy) = a(BA)x + b(BA)y.$$

1.3.2   Bounded Linear Operators

Let X_1, X_2 be normed spaces and let $A : X_1 \to X_2$ be a linear operator. We can relate $\|Ax\|_2$ to $\|x\|_1$ by composing the ratio $\|Ax\|_2/\|x\|_1$ if $x \neq 0$. A is called a *bounded* operator if all such ratios are uniformly bounded, and the *norm* of an operator A is defined as the supremum of those ratios:

$$\|A\| = \sup_{x \neq 0} \frac{\|Ax\|_2}{\|x\|_1}. \tag{1.9}$$

An immediate consequence of this definition is the bound $\|Ax\|_2 \leq \|A\| \|x\|_1$ for all $x \in X_1$, from which we see that the images Ax of elements of the unit ball $b_1 = \{x \in X_1 : \|x\|_1 \leq 1\}$ are uniformly bounded:

$$\|Ax\|_2 \leq \|A\| \quad \text{for all } x \in b_1. \tag{1.10}$$

To save a word, a bounded linear operator is called simply a bounded operator. Let $B(X_1, X_2)$ denote the set of bounded operators acting from X_1 to X_2.

Lemma. $B(X_1, X_2)$ *with the norm (1.9) is a normed space.*

Proof.   We check the axioms from Section 1.2.1 one by one.

1. Nonnegativity is obvious.
2. Homogeneity of Eq. (1.9) follows from that of $\| \cdot \|_2$.
3. The inequality $\|(A + B)x\|_2 \leq \|Ax\|_2 + \|Bx\|_2$ implies

$$\|A + B\| = \sup_{x \neq 0} \frac{\|(A + B)x\|_2}{\|x\|_1} \leq \sup_{x \neq 0} \frac{\|Ax\|_2}{\|x\|_1} + \sup_{x \neq 0} \frac{\|Bx\|_2}{\|x\|_1} = \|A\| + \|B\|.$$

4. If $\|A\| = 0$, then $\|Ax\|_2 = 0$ for all x and, consequently, $A = 0$.   ∎

1.3.3   Isomorphism

Let X_1, X_2 be normed spaces. A linear operator $I : X_1 \to X_2$ is called an *isomorphism* if

1. $\|Ix\|_2 = \|x\|_1$ for all $x \in X_1$ (preservation of norms) and
2. $IX_1 = X_2$ (I is a surjection).

Item 1 implies that $\|I\| = 1$ and I is one-to-one (if $Ix_1 = Ix_2$, then $\|x_1 - x_2\|_1 = \|I(x_1 - x_2)\|_2 = 0$ and $x_1 = x_2$). Hence, the inverse of I exists and is an isomorphism from X_2 to X_1.

Normed spaces X_1 and X_2 are called *isomorphic* spaces if there exists an isomorphism $I : X_1 \to X_2$. Vector operations in X_1 are mirrored by those in X_2 and the norms are the same, so as normed spaces X_1 and X_2 are indistinguishable. However, a given operator in one of them may be easier to analyze than its isomorphic image in the other, because of special features. Let A be a bounded operator in X_1. It is easy to see that $\tilde{A} = IAI^{-1}$ is a linear operator in X_2. Moreover, the norms are preserved under this mapping:

$$\|\tilde{A}\| = \sup_{x \neq 0} \frac{\|IAI^{-1}x\|_2}{\|x\|_2} = \sup_{y \neq 0} \frac{\|IAy\|_2}{\|Iy\|_2} = \sup_{y \neq 0} \frac{\|Ay\|_1}{\|y\|_1} = \|A\|.$$

1.3.4 Convergence of Operators

Let $A, A_1, A_2, \ldots$ be bounded operators from a normed space X_1 to a normed space X_2. The sequence $\{A_n\}$ *converges to A uniformly* if $\|A_n - A\| \to 0$, where the norm is as defined in Eq. (1.9). This is convergence in a normed space $B(X_1, X_2)$. The word 'uniform' is pertinent because, as we can see from Eq. (1.10), when $\|A_n - A\| \to 0$, we also have the convergence $\|A_n x - Ax\|_2 \to 0$ uniformly in the unit ball b_1.

The sequence $\{A_n\}$ is said to *converge to A strongly*, or pointwise, if for each $x \in X_1$ we have $\|A_n x - Ax\|_2 \to 0$. Of course, uniform convergence implies strong convergence.

1.3.5 Projectors

Projectors are used (or implicitly present) in econometrics so often that it would be a sin to bypass them.

Let X be a normed space and let $P : X \to X$ be a bounded operator. P is called a *projector* if

$$P^2 = P. \tag{1.11}$$

Suppose y is a projection of x, $y = Px$. Then P doesn't change y: $Py = P^2 x = Px = y$. This property is the key to the intuition behind projectors.

Consider on the plane two coordinate axes, X and Y, intersecting at a positive, not necessarily straight, angle. Projection of points on the plane onto the axis X parallel to the axis Y has the following geometrical properties:

1. The projection of the whole plane is X.
2. Points on X stay the same.
3. Points on Y are projected to the origin.
4. Any vector on the plane is uniquely represented as a sum of two vectors, one from X and another from Y.

All these properties can be deduced from linearity of P and Eq. (1.11).

Lemma. *Let P be a projector and denote $Q = I - P$, where I is the identity operator in X. Then*

    (i) *Q is also a projector.*

    (ii) *Im(P) coincides with the set of fixed points of P: $\mathrm{Im}(P) = \{x : x = Px\}$.*

    (iii) *$\mathrm{Im}(Q) = N(P)$, $\mathrm{Im}(P) = N(Q)$.*

    (iv) *Any $x \in X$ can be uniquely represented as $x = y + z$ with $y \in \mathrm{Im}(P)$, $z \in \mathrm{Im}(Q)$.*

Proof.

    (i) $Q^2 = (I - P)^2 = I^2 - 2P + P^2 = I - P = Q$.

    (ii) If $x \in \mathrm{Im}(P)$, then $x = Py$ for some $y \in X$ and $Px = P^2 y = Py = x$, so that x is a fixed point of P. Conversely, if x is a fixed point of P, then $x = Px \in \mathrm{Im}(P)$.

    (iii) The equation $Px = 0$ is equivalent to $Qx = (I - P)x = x$, and the equation $\mathrm{Im}(Q) = N(P)$ follows. $\mathrm{Im}(P) = N(Q)$ is obtained similarly.

    (iv) The desired representation is obtained by writing $x = Px + (I - P)x = y + z$, where $y = Px \in \mathrm{Im}(P)$ and $z = (I - P)x = Qy \in \mathrm{Im}(Q)$. If $x = y_1 + z_1$ is another representation, then, subtracting one from another, we get $y - y_1 = -(z - z_1)$. Hence, $P(y - y_1) = -P(z - z_1)$. Here the right-hand side is null because $z, z_1 \in \mathrm{Im}(Q) = N(P)$. The left-hand side is $y - y_1$ because both y and y_1 are fixed points of P. Thus, $y = y_1$ and $z = z_1$. ∎

1.4 HILBERT SPACES

1.4.1 Scalar Products

A Hilbert space is another infinite-dimensional generalization of $\mathbb{R}^n$. Everything starts with noticing how useful a *scalar product*

$$\langle x, y \rangle = \sum_{i=1}^{n} x_i y_i \tag{1.12}$$

of two vectors $x, y \in \mathbb{R}^n$ is. In terms of it we can define the Euclidean norm, in $\mathbb{R}^n$:

$$\|x\|_2 = \left(\sum_{i=1}^{n} x_i^2 \right)^{1/2} = \langle x, x \rangle^{1/2}. \tag{1.13}$$

Most importantly, we can find the cosine of the angle between x, y by the formula

$$\cos(\widehat{x, y}) = \frac{\langle x, y \rangle}{\|x\|_2 \|y\|_2}. \tag{1.14}$$

To do without the coordinate representation, we observe algebraic properties of this scalar product. First of all, it is a *bilinear form*: it is linear with respect to one argument when the other is fixed:

$$\langle ax + by, z \rangle = a\langle x, z \rangle + b\langle y, z \rangle, \; \langle z, ax + by \rangle = a\langle z, x \rangle + b\langle z, y \rangle$$

for all vectors x, y, z and numbers a, b. Further, we notice that $\langle x, x \rangle$ is always nonnegative and $\langle x, x \rangle = 0$ is true only when $x = 0$.

Thus, on the abstract level, we start with the assumption that H is a linear space and $\langle x, y \rangle$ is a real function of arguments $x, y \in H$ having properties:

1. $\langle x, y \rangle$ is a bilinear form,
2. $\langle x, x \rangle \geq 0$ for all $x \in H$ and
3. $\langle x, x \rangle = 0$ implies $x = 0$.
4. $\langle x, y \rangle = \langle y, x \rangle$ for all x, y.

Such a function is called a *scalar product*. Put

$$\|x\| = \langle x, x \rangle^{1/2}. \tag{1.15}$$

Lemma.   *(Cauchy–Schwarz inequality)* $|\langle x, y \rangle| \leq \|x\| \|y\|$.

Proof.   The function $f(t) = \langle x + ty, x + ty \rangle$ of a real argument t is nonnegative by item 2. Using items 1 and 4 we see that it is a quadratic function:

$$f(t) = \langle x, x + ty \rangle + t\langle y, x + ty \rangle = \langle x, x \rangle + 2t\langle x, y \rangle + t^2 \langle y, y \rangle.$$

Its nonnegativity implies that its discriminant $\langle x, y \rangle^2 - \langle x, x \rangle\langle y, y \rangle$ is nonpositive. ∎

1.4.2   Continuity of Scalar Products

Notation (1.15) is justified by the following lemma.

Lemma

   (i) *Eq. (1.15) defines a norm on H and the associated convergence concept: $x_n \to x$ in H if $\|x_n - x\| \to 0$.*

   (ii) *The scalar product is continuous: if $x_n \to x$, $y_n \to y$, then $\langle x_n, y_n \rangle \to \langle x, y \rangle$.*

Proof.

   (i) By the Cauchy–Schwarz inequality

$$\|x + y\|^2 = \langle x + y, x + y \rangle = \|x\|^2 + 2\langle x, y \rangle + \|y\|^2$$
$$\leq \|x\|^2 + 2\|x\| \|y\| + \|y\|^2 = (\|x\| + \|y\|)^2,$$

which proves the triangle inequality in Section 1.2.1 (3). The other properties of a norm (nonnegativity, homogeneity and nondegeneracy) easily follow from the scalar product axioms.

(ii) Convergence $x_n \to x$ implies boundedness of the norms $\|x_n\|$. Therefore, by the Cauchy–Schwarz inequality,

$$\|\langle x_n, y_n \rangle - \langle x, y \rangle\| \leq \|\langle x_n, y_n - y \rangle\| + \|\langle x_n - x, y \rangle\|$$
$$\leq \|x_n\| \|y_n - y\| + \|x_n - x\| \|y\|. \qquad \blacksquare$$

A linear space H that is endowed with a scalar product and is complete in the norm generated by that scalar product is called a *Hilbert space*.

1.4.3 Discrete Hölder's Inequality

An interesting generalization of the Cauchy–Schwarz inequality is in terms of the spaces l_p from Section 1.2.3. Let p be a number from $[1, \infty)$ or the symbol ∞. Its *conjugate q* is defined from $1/p + 1/q = 1$. Explicitly,

$$q = \begin{cases} p/(p-1) \in (1, \infty), & 1 < p < \infty; \\ 1, & p = \infty; \\ \infty, & p = 1. \end{cases}$$

Hölder's inequality states that

$$\sum_{i=1}^{\infty} |x_i y_i| \leq \|x\|_p \|y\|_q . \qquad (1.16)$$

A way to understand it is by considering the bilinear form $\langle x, y \rangle = \sum_{i=1}^{\infty} x_i y_i$. It is defined on the Cartesian product $l_2 \times l_2$ and is continuous on it by Lemma 1.4.2 Hölder's inequality allows us to take arguments from different spaces: $\langle x, y \rangle$ is defined on $l_p \times l_q$ and is continuous on this product.

1.4.4 Symmetric Operators

Let A be a bounded operator in a Hilbert space H. Its *adjoint* is defined as the operator A^* that satisfies

$$\langle Ax, y \rangle = \langle x, A^* y \rangle \quad \text{for all } x, y \in H.$$

This definition arises from the property of the transpose matrix A',

$$\sum_{i=1}^{n} (Ax)_i y_i = \sum_{i=1}^{n} x_i (A' y)_i.$$

Existence of A^* is proved using the so-called Riesz theorem. We do not need the general proof of existence because in all the cases we need, the adjoint will be constructed explicitly. Boundedness of A^* will also be proved directly.

A is called *symmetric* if $A = A^*$. Symmetric operators stand out by having properties closest to those of real numbers.

1.4.5 Orthoprojectors

Cosines of angles between vectors from H can be defined using Eq. (1.14). We don't need this definition, but we do need its special case: vectors $x, y \in H$ are called *orthogonal* if $\langle x, y \rangle = 0$. For orthogonal vectors we have the Pythagorean theorem:

$$\|x + y\|^2 = \langle x + y, x + y \rangle = \|x\|^2 + 2\langle x, y \rangle + \|y\|^2 = \|x\|^2 + \|y\|^2.$$

Two subspaces $X, Y \subseteq H$ are called *orthogonal* if every element of X is orthogonal to every element of Y.

If a projector P in H ($P^2 = P$) is symmetric, $P = P^*$, then it is called an *orthoprojector*. In the situation described in Section 1.3.5, when points on the plane are projected onto one axis parallel to another, orthoprojectors correspond to the case when the axes are orthogonal.

Lemma. *Let P be an orthoprojector and let $Q = I - P$. Then*

(i) *Im(P) is orthogonal to Im(Q).*

(ii) *For any $x \in H$, $\|Px\|$ is the distance from x to Im(Q).*

Proof.

(i) Let $x \in \text{Im}(P)$ and $y \in \text{Im}(Q)$. By Lemma 1.3.5(ii), $x = Px$, $y = Qy$. Hence, x and y are orthogonal:

$$\langle x, y \rangle = \langle Px, Qy \rangle = \langle x, P(I - P)y \rangle = \langle x, (P - P^2)y \rangle = 0.$$

(ii) For an arbitrary element $x \in H$ and a set $A \subseteq H$ the *distance* from x to A is defined by

$$\text{dist}(x, A) = \inf_{y \in A} \|x - y\|.$$

Take any $y \in \text{Im}(Q)$. In the equation

$$x - y = Px + Qx - Qy = Px + Q(x - y)$$

the two terms at the right are orthogonal, so by the Pythagorean theorem

$$\|x - y\|^2 = \|Px\|^2 + \|Q(x - y)\|^2 \geq \|Px\|^2,$$

which implies the lower bound for the distance dist$(x, \text{Im}(Q)) \geq \|Px\|$. This lower bound is attained on $y = Qx \in \text{Im}(Q)$: $\|x - y\| = \|Px + Qx - Qx\| = \|Px\|$. Hence, dist$(x, \text{Im}(Q)) = \|Px\|$. ■

1.5 L_p SPACES

1.5.1 σ-Fields

Let Ω be some set and let $\mathcal{F}$ be a nonempty family of its subsets. $\mathcal{F}$ is called a *σ-field* if

1. unions, intersections, differences and complements of any two elements of $\mathcal{F}$ belong to $\mathcal{F}$,
2. the union of any sequence $\{A_n : n = 1, 2, \ldots\}$ of elements of $\mathcal{F}$ belongs to $\mathcal{F}$ and
3. Ω belongs to $\mathcal{F}$.

This definition contains sufficiently many requirements to serve most purposes of analysis. In probabilities, σ-fields play the role of information sets. The precise meaning of this sentence at times can be pretty complex. The following existence statement is used very often.

Lemma. *For any system S of subsets of Ω there exists a σ-field $\mathcal{F}$ that contains S and is contained in any other σ-field containing S.*

Proof. The set of σ-fields containing S is not empty. For example, the set of all subsets of Ω is a σ-field and contains S. Let σ be the intersection of all σ-fields containing S. It obviously satisfies 1–3 and hence is the σ-field we are looking for. ■

The σ-field whose existence is affirmed in this lemma is called the *least σ-field generated by S* and denoted $\sigma(S)$.

1.5.2 Borel σ-field in $\mathbb{R}^n$

A ball in $\mathbb{R}^n$ centered at $x \in \mathbb{R}^n$ of radius $\varepsilon > 0$,

$$b_\varepsilon(x) = \{y \in \mathbb{R}^n : \|x - y\|_2 < \varepsilon\},$$

is called an *ε-neighborhood* of x. We say that the set $A \subseteq \mathbb{R}^n$ is an *open* set if each point x belongs to A with its neighborhood $b_\varepsilon(x)$ (where ε depends on x). The *Borel σ-field* $\mathcal{B}_n$ in $\mathbb{R}^n$ is defined as the smallest σ-field that contains all open subsets of $\mathbb{R}^n$. It exists by Lemma 1.5.1. In more general situations, when open subsets of Ω are not defined, σ-fields of Ω are introduced axiomatically.

1.5.3 σ-Additive Measures

A pair $(\Omega, \mathcal{F})$, where Ω is some set and $\mathcal{F}$ is a σ-field of its subsets, is called a *measurable space*. A set function μ defined on elements of $\mathcal{F}$ with values in the extended half-line $[0, \infty]$ is called a *σ-additive measure* if for any disjoint sets $A_1, A_2, \ldots \in \mathcal{F}$ one has

$$\mu\left(\bigcup_{j=1}^{\infty} A_j\right) = \sum_{j=1}^{\infty} \mu(A_j).$$

EXAMPLE 1.4. On a plane, for any rectangle A define $\mu(A)$ to be its area. The extension procedure from the measure theory then leads to the *Lebesgue measure* μ with $\Omega = \mathbb{R}^2$ and $\mathcal{F} = \mathcal{B}_2$ (μ is defined on all Borel subsets of $\mathbb{R}^2$).

A *probabilistic measure* is a σ-additive measure that satisfies an additional requirement $\mu(\Omega) = 1$. In this case, following common practice, we write P instead of μ. Thus, a *probability space* (sometimes also called a *sample space*) is a triple $(\Omega, \mathcal{F}, P)$ where Ω is a set, $\mathcal{F}$ is a σ-field of its subsets and P is a σ-additive measure on $\mathcal{F}$ such that $P(\Omega) = 1$.

EXAMPLE 1.5. On a plane, take the square $[0, 1]^2$ as Ω and let P be the Lebesgue measure. Then $\mathcal{F}$ will be the set of Borel subsets of the square.

1.5.4 Measurable Functions

Let $(\Omega_1, \mathcal{F}_1)$ and $(\Omega_2, \mathcal{F}_2)$ be two measurable spaces. A function $f : \Omega_1 \to \Omega_2$ is called *measurable* if $f^{-1}(A) \in \mathcal{F}_1$ for any $A \in \mathcal{F}_2$. More precisely, it is said to be $(\mathcal{F}_1, \mathcal{F}_2)$-*measurable*. In particular, when $(\Omega_1, \mathcal{F}_1) = (\mathbb{R}^n, \mathcal{B}_n)$ and $(\Omega_2, \mathcal{F}_2) = (\mathbb{R}^m, \mathcal{B}_m)$, this definition gives the definition of *Borel-measurability*. Most of the time we deal with real-valued functions, when $\Omega_2 = \mathbb{R}$ and $\mathcal{F}_2 = \mathcal{B}_1$ is the Borel σ-field. In this case we simply say that f is $\mathcal{F}_1$-measurable. All analysis operations in the finite-dimensional case preserve measurability. The next theorem is often used implicitly.

Theorem. (Kolmogorov and Fomin, 1989, Chapter 5, Section 4)

1. *Let X, Y and Z be arbitrary sets with systems of subsets σ_X, σ_Y and σ_Z, respectively. Suppose the function $f : X \to Y$ is (σ_X, σ_Y)-measurable and $g : Y \to Z$ is (σ_Y, σ_Z)-measurable. Then the composition $z(x) = g(f(x))$ is (σ_X, σ_Z)-measurable.*

2. *Let f and g be defined on the same measurable space $(\Omega, \mathcal{F})$. Then a linear combination $af + bg$ and product fg are measurable. If g does not vanish, then the ratio f/g is also measurable.*

1.5.5 L_p Spaces

Let $(\Omega, \mathcal{F}, \mu)$ be any space with a σ-additive measure μ and let $1 \le p < \infty$. The set of measurable functions $f : \Omega \to \mathbb{R}$ provided with the norm

$$\|f\|_p = \left(\int_\Omega |f(x)|^p d\mu \right)^{1/p}, \ 1 \le p < \infty,$$

is denoted $L_p = L_p(\Omega)$. In the case $p = \infty$ this definition is completed with

$$\|f\|_\infty = \text{ess sup}_{x \in \Omega} |f(x)| = \inf_{\mu(A)=0} \sup_{x \in \Omega \backslash A} |f(x)|.$$

The term in the middle is, by definition, the quantity at the right and is called *essential supremum*. These definitions mean that values taken by functions on sets of measure zero don't matter. An equality $f(t) = 0$ is accompanied by the caveat "almost everywhere" (a.e.) or "almost surely" (a.s.) in the probabilistic setup, meaning that there is a set of measure zero outside which $f(t) = 0$.

1.5.6 Inequalities in L_p

Apparently, L_p spaces should have a lot in common with l_p spaces. The triangle inequality in L_p $\|F + G\|_p \le \|F\|_p + \|G\|_p$ is called a *Minkowski inequality*.

Hölder's inequality looks like this:

$$\int_\Omega |f(x)g(x)| \, d\mu \le \|f\|_p \, \|g\|_q,$$

where q is the conjugate of p. When $\mu(\Omega) < \infty$, we can use this inequality to show that for $1 \le p_1 < p_2 \le \infty$, L_{p_2} is a subset of L_{p_1}:

$$\int_\Omega |f(x)|^{p_1} \, d\mu \le \left(\int_\Omega |f(x)|^{p_1 p_2 / p_1} \, d\mu \right)^{p_1/p_2} \left(\int_\Omega d\mu \right)^{1 - p_1/p_2}$$

$$= \|f\|_{p_2}^{p_1} [\mu(\Omega)]^{1 - p_1/p_2}.$$

In particular, when $(\Omega, \mathcal{F}, P)$ is a probability space, we get

$$\|f\|_{p_1} \le \|f\|_{p_2} \quad \text{if } 1 \le p_1 < p_2 \le \infty.$$

This is the opposite of the monotonicity relation (1.7).

1.5.7 Covariance as a Scalar Product

Real-valued measurable functions on a probability space $(\Omega, \mathcal{F}, P)$ are called *random variables*. Let X, Y be integrable random variables (integrability is necessary for their means to exist). Denote $x = X - EX$, $y = Y - EY$. Then the *covariance* of X, Y is defined by

$$\text{cov}(X, Y) = E(X - EX)(Y - EY) = Exy, \tag{1.17}$$

the *standard deviation* of X is, by definition,

$$\sigma(X) = \sqrt{\text{cov}(X, X)} = \sqrt{Ex^2} = \sigma(x) \tag{1.18}$$

and the definition of *correlation* of X, Y is

$$\rho(X, Y) = \frac{\text{cov}(X, Y)}{\sigma(X)\sigma(Y)} = \frac{Exy}{\sigma(x)\sigma(y)}. \tag{1.19}$$

Comparison of Eqs. (1.17), (1.18) and (1.19) with Eqs. (1.12), (1.13) and (1.14) from Section 1.4.1 makes clear that definitions (1.17), (1.18) and (1.19) originate in Euclidean geometry. In particular, $\sigma(X)$ is the distance from X to EX and from x to 0. While this idea has been very fruitful, I often find it more useful to estimate $(EX^2)^{1/2}$, which is the distance from X to 0.

1.5.8   Dense Sets in L_p, $p < \infty$

Let us fix some space with measure $(\Omega, \mathcal{F}, \mu)$. A set $M \subseteq L_p$ is said to be *dense* in L_p if any function $f \in L_p$ can be approximated by some sequence $\{f_n\} \subseteq M$: $\| f_n - f \|_p \to 0$. By 1_A we denote the *indicator* of a set A:

$$1_A = \begin{cases} 1, & x \in A; \\ 0, & x \notin A. \end{cases}$$

A finite linear combination $\sum_i c_i 1_{A_i}$ of indicators of measurable sets $A_i \in \mathcal{F}$ is called a *step function*. We say that the measure μ is a *σ-finite* measure if Ω can be represented as a union of disjoint sets Ω_i,

$$\Omega = \bigcup_i \Omega_i, \tag{1.20}$$

of finite measure $\mu(\Omega_i) < \infty$. For example, $\mathbb{R}^n$ is a union of rectangles of finite Lebesgue measure.

Lemma.   *If $p < \infty$ and the measure μ is σ-finite, then the set M of step functions is dense in L_p.*

Proof.

Step 1.   Let $f \in L_p$. First we show that the general case of Ω of infinite measure can be reduced to the case $\mu(\Omega) < \infty$. Since for the sets from Eq. (1.20) we have

$$\int_\Omega |f(x)|^p d\mu = \sum_l \int_{\Omega_l} |f(x)|^p d\mu < \infty,$$

for any $\varepsilon > 0$ there exists $L > 0$ such that $\sum_{l > L} \int_{\Omega_l} |f(x)|^p d\mu < \varepsilon$. Denote $\widetilde{\Omega} = \bigcup_{l=1}^{L} \Omega_l$. Whatever step function $\widetilde{f}_\varepsilon$ we find to approximate f in $L_p(\widetilde{\Omega})$ in the sense that

$$\int_{\widetilde{\Omega}} |f(x) - \widetilde{f}_\varepsilon(x)|^p d\mu < \varepsilon,$$

we can extend it by zero,

$$f_\varepsilon(x) = \begin{cases} \widetilde{f}_\varepsilon(x), & x \in \widetilde{\Omega}; \\ 0, & x \in \Omega \setminus \widetilde{\Omega}, \end{cases}$$

to obtain an approximation to f in $L_p(\Omega)$:

$$\int_\Omega |f - f_\varepsilon|^p d\mu = \int_{\widetilde{\Omega}} |f - \widetilde{f}_\varepsilon|^p d\mu + \int_{\Omega \setminus \widetilde{\Omega}} |f|^p d\mu < 2\varepsilon.$$

f_ε will be a step function and $\mu(\widetilde{\Omega}) < \infty$.

Step 2. Now we show that f can be considered bounded. From

$$\int_\Omega |f|^p d\mu = \sum_{l=1}^{\infty} \int_{\{l-1 \le |f(x)| < l\}} |f(x)|^p d\mu < \infty$$

we see that for any $\varepsilon > 0$, L can be chosen so that $\int_{\{L \le |f(x)|\}} |f(x)|^p d\mu < \varepsilon$. Then f is bounded on $\widetilde{\Omega} = |f(x)| \le L$ and, as above, we see that approximating f by a simple function on $\widetilde{\Omega}$ is enough.

Step 3. Now we can assume that $\mu(\Omega) < \infty$ and $|f(x)| \le L$. Take a large k and partition $[-L, L]$ into k nonoverlapping (closed, semiclosed or open, it does not matter) intervals $\Delta_1, \ldots, \Delta_k$ of length $2L/k$. Let $l_1, \ldots, l_k$ denote the left ends of those intervals and put $A_m = f^{-1}(\Delta_m)$, $m = 1, \ldots, k$. Then the sets A_m are disjoint,

$$|l_m - f(x)| \le \frac{2L}{k} \quad \text{for } x \in A_m \text{ and } \Omega = \bigcup_{m=1}^{k} A_m.$$

This implies

$$\int_\Omega \left| \sum_m l_m 1_{A_m}(x) - f(x) \right|^p d\mu = \sum_m \int_{A_m} |l_m - f(x)|^p d\mu$$

$$\le \left(\frac{2L}{k} \right)^p \mu(\Omega) \to 0, \, k \to \infty. \qquad \blacksquare$$

1.6 CONDITIONING ON σ-FIELDS

1.6.1 Absolute Continuity of Measures

Let $(\Omega, \mathcal{F}, P)$ be a probability space and let f be an integrable function on Ω. Then the σ-*additivity* of Lebesgue integrals (Kolmogorov and Fomin, 1989, Chapter 5, Section 5.4)

$$\int_{\bigcup\limits_{m=1}^{\infty} A_m} f(x)dP = \sum_{m=1}^{\infty} \int_{A_m} f(x)dP \text{ for disjoint measurable } A_m$$

means that

$$v(A) = \int_A f(x)dP \tag{1.21}$$

is a σ-additive set function with the same domain $\mathcal{F}$ as that of P. Another property of Lebesgue integrals (see the same source) states that v is *absolutely continuous with respect to P*: $v(A) = 0$ for each measurable set A for which $P(A) = 0$. The Radon–Nikodym theorem affirms that the opposite is true: σ-additivity and absolute continuity are sufficient for a set function to be of form (1.21).

Theorem. (*Radon–Nikodym*) (Kolmogorov and Fomin, 1989, Chapter 6, Section 5.3) *If $(\Omega, \mathcal{F}, P)$ is a probability space and v is a set function defined on $\mathcal{F}$ that is σ-additive and absolutely continuous with respect to P, then there exists an integrable function f on Ω such that Eq. (1.21) is true. If g is another such function, then $f = g$ a.s.*

1.6.2 Conditional Expectation

Let $(\Omega, \mathcal{F}, P)$ be a probability space, X an integrable random variable and $\mathcal{G}$ a σ-field contained in $\mathcal{F}$. The *conditional expectation* $E(X|\mathcal{G})$ is defined as a $\mathcal{G}$-measurable function Y such that

$$\int_A YdP = \int_A XdP \quad \text{for all } A \in \mathcal{G}. \tag{1.22}$$

EXAMPLE 1.6. Let $\mathcal{G} = \{\emptyset, \Omega\}$ be the smallest σ-field. In the case $A = \emptyset$ (or, more generally, $P(A) = 0$) Eq. (1.22) turns into an equality of two zeros. In the case $A = \Omega$ we see that the means of Y and X should be the same. Since a constant is the only $\mathcal{G}$-measurable random variable, it follows that $E(X|\mathcal{G}) = EX$.

EXAMPLE 1.7. Let $\mathcal{G} = \mathcal{F}$ be the largest σ-field contained in $\mathcal{F}$. Since X is $\mathcal{G}$-measurable, $Y = X$ satisfies Eq. (1.22). Hence, $E(X|\mathcal{G}) = X$ by a.s. uniqueness.

$Y = X$ is an incorrect answer for Example 1.6 because inverse images $X^{-1}(B)$ of some Borel sets would not belong to $\{\emptyset, \Omega\}$ unless $\mathcal{F} = \{\emptyset, \Omega\}$. $Y = E(X|\mathcal{G})$ contains precisely as much information about X as is necessary to calculate the integrals in (1.22).

1.6.3   Conditioning as a Projector

Lemma.   *Let $(\Omega, \mathcal{F}, P)$ be a probability space and let $\mathcal{G}$ be a σ-field contained in $\mathcal{F}$.*

(i) *For any integrable X, $E(X|\mathcal{G})$ exists. Denote $P_\mathcal{G} X = E(X\mid\mathcal{G})$ for $X \in L_1(\Omega)$.*

(ii) *$P_\mathcal{G}$ is linear, $P_\mathcal{G}(aX + bY) = aP_\mathcal{G}X + bP_\mathcal{G}Y$, and bounded, $\|P_\mathcal{G}X\|_1 \le \|X\|_1$.*

(iii) *$P_\mathcal{G}$ is a projector.*

Proof.

(i) $v(A) = \int_A XdP$ defines a σ-additive set function on $\mathcal{G}$ that is absolutely continuous with respect to P. By the Radon–Nikodym theorem there exists a $\mathcal{G}$-measurable function Y such that Eq. (1.22) is true. This proves the existence of $Y = E(X\mid\mathcal{G})$.

(ii) We can use Eq. (1.22) repeatedly to obtain

$$\int_A P_\mathcal{G}(aX + bY)\, dP = \int_A (aX + bY)\, dP = a\int_A X dP + b\int_A Y\, dP$$

$$= a\int_A P_\mathcal{G}X\, dP + b\int_A P_\mathcal{G}Y\, dP$$

$$= \int_A (aP_\mathcal{G}X + bP_\mathcal{G}Y)\, dP, \quad A \in \mathcal{G}.$$

Since $aP_\mathcal{G}X + bP_\mathcal{G}Y$ is $\mathcal{G}$-measurable, it must coincide with $P_\mathcal{G}(aX + bY)$.

For any real-valued function f define its *positive part* by $f_+ = \max\{f, 0\}$ and *negative part* by $f_- = -\min\{f, 0\}$. Then it is geometrically obvious that $f = f_+ - f_-$ and $|f| = f_+ + f_-$. Decomposing $P_\mathcal{G}X$ into its positive and negative parts, $P_\mathcal{G}X = (P_\mathcal{G}X)_+ - (P_\mathcal{G}X)_-$, and remembering that both sets $\{P_\mathcal{G}X > 0\}$ and $\{P_\mathcal{G}X < 0\}$ are $\mathcal{G}$-measurable we have

$$\int_\Omega |P_\mathcal{G}X|\, dP = \int_\Omega [(P_\mathcal{G}X)_+ + (P_\mathcal{G}X)_-]\, dP$$

$$= \int_{P_\mathcal{G}X>0} P_\mathcal{G}X\, dP + \int_{P_\mathcal{G}X<0} P_\mathcal{G}X\, dP$$

$$= \int_{P_\mathcal{G}X>0} X\, dP + \int_{P_\mathcal{G}X<0} X\, dP \le \int_\Omega |X|\, dP.$$

This proves that $\|P_\mathcal{G}\| \le 1$.

(iii) $P_\mathcal{G}^2 X$ is defined as a $\mathcal{G}$-measurable function Y such that $\int_A Y\, dP = \int_A P_\mathcal{G}X\, dP$ for all $A \in \mathcal{G}$. Since $P_\mathcal{G}X$ itself is $\mathcal{G}$-measurable, we have $Y = P_\mathcal{G}X$ a.s.

■

1.6.4 The Law of Iterated Expectations

In a 3-D space, projecting first to a plane and then to a straight line in that plane gives the same result as projecting directly to the straight line. This is also true of conditioning (and projectors in general).

Lemma. *Let* $\mathcal{H} \subseteq \mathcal{G} \subseteq \mathcal{F}$ *be nested σ-fields and denote* $P_\mathcal{H}$ *and* $P_\mathcal{G}$ *as the conditioning projectors on* $\mathcal{H}$ *and* $\mathcal{G}$*, respectively. Then* $P_\mathcal{H} P_\mathcal{G} = P_\mathcal{G} P_\mathcal{H} = P_\mathcal{H}$*. Using the conditional expectation notation, this is the same as*

$$E[E(X|\mathcal{G})|\mathcal{H}] = E[E(X|\mathcal{H})|\mathcal{G}] = E(X|\mathcal{H}). \tag{1.23}$$

In particular, when $\mathcal{H} = \{\emptyset, \Omega\}$ *is the least σ-field, we get* $E[E(X|\mathcal{G})] = EX$ *for all integrable X.*

Proof. $\mathcal{H}$-measurability of $P_\mathcal{H} X$ implies its $\mathcal{G}$-measurability. Hence, by Lemma 1.6.3 (iii) $P_\mathcal{G}$ doesn't change it. This proves that $P_\mathcal{G} P_\mathcal{H} = P_\mathcal{H}$.

$P_\mathcal{G} X$ is $\mathcal{G}$-measurable and satisfies $\int_A P_\mathcal{G} X dP = \int_A X \, dP$ for all $A \in \mathcal{G}$. In particular, this is true for $A \in \mathcal{H}$: $\int_A P_\mathcal{G} X dP = \int_A X dP$, $A \in \mathcal{H}$. Confronting this with the definition of $P_\mathcal{H} P_\mathcal{G} X$,

$$\int_A P_\mathcal{H} P_\mathcal{G} X dP = \int_A P_\mathcal{G} X dP, \quad A \in \mathcal{H},$$

we see that $\int_A P_\mathcal{H} P_\mathcal{G} X dP = \int_A X dP$, $A \in \mathcal{H}$. But $P_\mathcal{H}$ satisfies the same equation with $P_\mathcal{H} X$ in place of $P_\mathcal{H} P_\mathcal{G} X$ and both are $\mathcal{H}$-measurable. Hence, $P_\mathcal{H} P_\mathcal{G} X = P_\mathcal{H} X$ a.s. ∎

1.6.5 Extended Homogeneity

In the usual homogeneity, $P_\mathcal{G}(aX) = aP_\mathcal{G}X$, a is a number. In the conditioning context, a can be any $\mathcal{G}$-measurable function, according to the next theorem. I call this property *extended homogeneity*.

Theorem. *If the variables X and XY are integrable and Y is* $\mathcal{G}$*-measurable, then* $P_\mathcal{G}(XY) = YP_\mathcal{G}X.$

The proof can be found, for example, in (Davidson 1994, Section 10.4).

1.6.6 Independence

σ-fields $\mathcal{H}$ and $\mathcal{G}$ are called *independent* σ-fields if any event $A \in \mathcal{H}$ is independent of any event $B \in \mathcal{G}$: $P(A \cap B) = P(A)P(B)$. Random variables X and Y are said to be *independent* if σ-fields $\sigma(X)$ and $\sigma(Y)$ are independent. Moreover, a family $\{X_i : i \in I\}$ of random variables is called *independent* if, for any two disjoint sets of indices J, K, σ-fields $\sigma(X_i : i \in J)$ and $\sigma(X_i : i \in K)$ are independent.

Theorem. (Davidson 1994, Section 10.5) *Suppose X is integrable and $\mathcal{H}$-measurable. If $\mathcal{G}$ is independent of $\mathcal{H}$, then conditioning X on $\mathcal{G}$ provides minimum information: $E(X|\mathcal{G}) = EX$.*

1.7 MATRIX ALGEBRA

Everywhere we follow the matrix algebra convention: all matrices and vectors in the same formula are compatible. All matrices in this section are assumed to be of size $n \times n$. The determinant of A is denoted as det A or $|A|$.

1.7.1 Orthogonal Matrices

A matrix T is called *orthogonal* if

$$T'T = I. \tag{1.24}$$

Since both $T'T$ and TT' have generic elements $\sum_l t_{il} t_{li}$, Eq. (1.24) is equivalent to $TT' = I$. Equation (1.24) means, by definition of the inverse, that $T^{-1} = T'$.

Geometrically, the mapping $y = Tx$ is rotation in $\mathbb{R}^n$. This is proved by noting that T preserves scalar products: $\langle Tx, Ty \rangle = \langle x, T'Ty \rangle = \langle x, y \rangle$. Hence, it preserves vector lengths and angles between vectors, see Equations (1.13) and (1.14) in Section 1.4.1. Rotation around the origin is the only mapping that has these properties.

1.7.2 Diagonalization of Symmetric Matrices

A number $\lambda \in \mathbb{R}$ is called an *eigenvalue* of a matrix A if there exists a nonzero vector x that satisfies $Ax = \lambda x$. Such a vector x is named an *eigenvector* corresponding to λ. From this definition it follows that A reduces to multiplication by λ along the straight line $\{ax : a \in \mathbb{R}\}$.

The set L of all eigenvectors corresponding to λ, completed with the null vector, is a subspace of $\mathbb{R}^n$, because $Ax = \lambda x$ and $Ay = \lambda y$ imply $A(ax + by) = \lambda(ax + by)$. This subspace is called a *characteristic subspace* of A corresponding to λ. The dimension of the characteristic subspace (see Section 1.1.3) is called *multiplicity* of λ. A reduces to multiplication by λ in L.

We say that a system of vectors $x_1, \ldots, x_k$ is *orthonormal* if

$$\langle x_i, x_j \rangle = \begin{cases} 1, & i = j; \\ 0, & i \neq j. \end{cases}$$

The system of unit vectors in $\mathbb{R}^n$ is an example of an orthonormal system. An orthonormal system is necessarily linearly independent because scalar multiplication of the equation $a_1 x_1 + \cdots + a_k x_k = 0$ by vectors $x_1, \ldots, x_k$ yields $a_1 = \cdots = a_k = 0$.

Theorem.   (Diagonalization theorem) (*Bellman 1995, Chapter 4, Section 7*). *If A is symmetric of size $n \times n$, then it has n real eigenvalues $\lambda_1, \ldots, \lambda_n$, repeated with their multiplicities. Further, there is an orthogonal matrix T such that*

$$A = T'\Lambda T, \tag{1.25}$$

where Λ is a diagonal matrix $\Lambda = \mathrm{diag}[\lambda_1, \ldots, \lambda_n]$. Finally, the eigenvectors $x_1, \ldots, x_n$ that correspond to $\lambda_1, \ldots, \lambda_n$ can be chosen orthonormal.

Equation (1.25) embodies the following geometry. In the original coordinate system with the unit vectors e_j (see Section 1.1.3) the matrix A has generic elements a_{ij}. The first transformation T in Eq. (1.25) rotates the coordinate system to a new position in which A is of simple diagonal form, the new axes being eigenvectors along which applying A amounts to multiplication by numbers. The final transformation by $T' = T^{-1}$ rotates the picture to the original position.

1.7.3   Finding and Applying Eigenvalues

Eigenvalues are the roots of the equation $\det(A - \lambda I) = 0$. Application of this matrix algebra rule is complicated as the left side of the equation is a polynomial of order n. Often it is possible to exploit the analytical structure of A to find its eigenvalues using the next lemma. A subspace L of $\mathbb{R}^n$ is called an *invariant subspace* of a matrix A if $AL \subseteq L$.

Lemma

   (i) λ *is an eigenvalue of A if and only if $\lambda - c$ is an eigenvalue of $A - cI$.*

   (ii) *Let L be an invariant subspace of a symmetric matrix A. Denote P an ortho-projector onto L, $Q = I - P$ and $M = \mathrm{Im}(Q)$. Then M is an invariant subspace of A and the analysis of A reduces to the analysis of its restrictions $A|_L$ and $A|_M$.*

Proof.   Statement

   (i) is obvious because the equation $Ax = \lambda x$ is equivalent to $(A - cI)x = (\lambda - c)x$.

   (ii) For any $x, y \in \mathbb{R}^n$ by symmetry of A, P,

$$\langle PAQx, y \rangle = \langle AQx, Py \rangle = \langle Qx, APy \rangle = 0.$$

The last equality follows from the facts that $Py \in L = \mathrm{Im}(P)$, $APy \in L$ and $\mathrm{Im}(P)$ is orthogonal to $\mathrm{Im}(Q)$ [see Lemma 1.4.5(i)]. Plugging in $y = PAQx$ we get $\|PAQx\| = 0$ and $PAQx = 0$. Since Qx runs over M when x runs over $\mathbb{R}^n$, we obtain $PAM = \{0\}$ or, by Lemma 1.4.5(ii), $AM \subseteq M$ and M is invariant with respect to A.

Now premultiply by A the identity $I = P + Q$ to get

$$A = AP + AQ = A|_L P + A|_M Q.$$ ∎

The second part of this lemma leads to the following practical rule. If you have managed to find the first eigenvalue λ and the corresponding characteristic subspace L of A, then consider the restriction $A|_M$ to find the rest of the eigenvalues. This process of "chipping off" characteristic subspaces can be repeated. While you do that, construct the orthonormal systems of eigenvectors until their total number reaches n.

Denoting $y = Tx$, from Theorem 1.7.2 we have

$$\langle Ax, x \rangle = \langle T'\Lambda Tx, x \rangle = \langle \Lambda Tx, Tx \rangle = \langle \Lambda y, y \rangle = \sum_{i=1}^{n} \lambda_i y_i^2.$$

Hence, A is nonnegative and $\langle Ax, x \rangle \geq 0$ for all x if and only if all eigenvalues of A are nonnegative. Therefore we can define the *square root* of a nonnegative symmetric matrix by

$$A^{1/2} = T'\text{diag}[\lambda_1^{1/2}, \ldots, \lambda_n^{1/2}]T.$$

1.7.4   Gram Matrices

In a Hilbert space H consider vectors $x_1, \ldots, x_k$. Their *Gram matrix* is defined by

$$G = \begin{pmatrix} \langle x_1, x_1 \rangle & \ldots & \langle x_1, x_k \rangle \\ \ldots & \ldots & \ldots \\ \langle x_k, x_1 \rangle & \ldots & \langle x_k, x_k \rangle \end{pmatrix}.$$

Theorem. (Gantmacher 1959, Chapter IX, Section 5) *Vectors $x_1, \ldots, x_k$ are linearly independent if and only if* $\det G > 0$.

1.7.5   Positive Definiteness of Gram Matrices

Lemma. *If vectors $x_1, \ldots, x_k \in \mathbb{R}^n$ are linearly independent, then G is positive definite:* $\langle Gx, x \rangle > 0$ *for all* $x \neq 0$.

Proof. According to the Silvester criterion (Bellman 1995, Chapter 5, Section 3), G is positive definite if and only if all determinants

$$\langle x_1, x_1 \rangle, \det \begin{pmatrix} \langle x_1, x_1 \rangle & \langle x_1, x_2 \rangle \\ \langle x_2, x_1 \rangle & \langle x_2, x_2 \rangle \end{pmatrix}, \ldots, \det G \qquad (1.26)$$

are positive. Linear independence of the system $\{x_1, \ldots, x_k\}$ implies that of all its subsystems $\{x_1\}, \{x_1, x_2\}, \ldots$. Thus all determinants are positive by Theorem 1.7.4. ∎

1.7.6 Partitioned Matrices: Determinant and Inverse

Lemma. (Lütkepohl 1991, Section A.10). *Let matrix A be partitioned as*

$$A = \begin{pmatrix} A_{11} & A_{12} \\ A_{21} & A_{22} \end{pmatrix}$$

where A_{11} and A_{22} are square. Then

(i) *If A_{11} is nonsingular, $|A| = |A_{11}| \cdot |A_{22} - A_{21}A_{11}^{-1}A_{12}|$.*

(ii) *If A_{11} and A_{22} are nonsingular,*

$$A^{-1} = \begin{pmatrix} D & -DA_{12}A_{22}^{-1} \\ -A_{22}^{-1}A_{21}D & A_{22}^{-1} + A_{22}^{-1}A_{21}DA_{12}A_{22}^{-1} \end{pmatrix}$$

$$= \begin{pmatrix} A_{11}^{-1} + A_{11}^{-1}A_{12}GA_{21}A_{11}^{-1} & -A_{11}^{-1}A_{12}G \\ -GA_{21}A_{11}^{-1} & G \end{pmatrix},$$

where $D = (A_{11} - A_{12}A_{22}^{-1}A_{21})^{-1}$ and $G = (A_{22} - A_{21}A_{11}^{-1}A_{12})^{-1}$.

1.8 CONVERGENCE OF RANDOM VARIABLES

A *random variable* is nothing but a $(\mathcal{F}, \mathcal{B})$-measurable function $X : \Omega \to \mathbb{R}$ where $(\Omega, \mathcal{F}, P)$ is a probability space and $\mathcal{B}$ is the Borel σ-field of $\mathbb{R}$. In the case of a *random vector* it suffices to replace $\mathbb{R}$ by $\mathbb{R}^n$ and $\mathcal{B}$ by $\mathcal{B}_n$, the Borel σ-field of $\mathbb{R}^n$.

1.8.1 Convergence in Probability

Let $X, X_1, X_2, \ldots$ be random vectors defined on the same probability space and with values in the same space $\mathbb{R}^n$. If

$$\lim_{n \to \infty} P(\|X_n - X\|_2 > \varepsilon) = 0 \text{ for any } \varepsilon > 0,$$

then $\{X_n\}$ is said to *converge in probability* to X. Convergence in probability is commonly denoted $X_n \overset{p}{\to} X$ or $\text{plim} X_n = X$. From the equivalent definition

$$\lim_{n \to \infty} P(\|X_n - X\|_2 \leq \varepsilon) = 1 \text{ for any } \varepsilon > 0$$

it may be easier to see that this notion is a natural generalization of convergence of numbers. A nice feature of convergence in probability is that it is preserved under arithmetic operations.

Lemma. *Let $\{X_i\}$ and $\{Y_i\}$ be sequences of $n \times 1$ random vectors and let $\{A_i\}$ be a sequence of random matrices such that* $\operatorname{plim} X_i$, $\operatorname{plim} Y_i$ *and* $\operatorname{plim} A_i$ *exist. Then*

(i) $\operatorname{plim}(X_i \pm Y_i) = \operatorname{plim} X_i \pm \operatorname{plim} Y_i$.

(ii) $\operatorname{plim} A_i X_i = \operatorname{plim} A_i \operatorname{plim} X_i$.

(iii) *Let* $g : \mathbb{R}^n \to \mathbb{R}$ *be a Borel-measurable function such that* $X = \operatorname{plim} X_i$ *takes values in the continuity set* C_g *of g with probability 1, $P(X \in C_g) = 1$. Then* $\operatorname{plim} g(X_i) = g(X)$.

(iv) *If* $\operatorname{plim} A_i = A$ *and* $P(\det A \neq 0) = 1$, *then* $\operatorname{plim} A_n^{-1} = A^{-1}$.

Proof. Statements (i) and (ii) are from (Lütkepohl 1991, Section C.1). (iii) is proved in (Davidson 1994, Theorem 18.8).

(iv) The real-valued function $1/\det A$ of a square matrix A of order n is continuous everywhere in the space $\mathbb{R}^{n^2}$ of its elements except for the set $\det A = 0$. Elements of A^{-1} are cofactors of elements of A divided by $\det A$. Hence, they are also continuous where $\det A \neq 0$. The statement follows on applying (iii) element by element. ∎

Part (iv) of this lemma does not imply invertibility of A_n a.e. It merely implies that the set on which A_n is not invertible has probability approaching zero.

1.8.2 Distribution Function of a Random Vector

Let X be a random vector with values in $\mathbb{R}^k$. Its *distribution function* is defined by

$$F_X(x) = P(X_1 \le x_1, \ldots, X_k \le x_k) = P\left(X^{-1}\left(\prod_{n=1}^{k}(-\infty, x_n]\right)\right), \quad x \in \mathbb{R}^k.$$

It is proved that F_X induces a probability measure on $\mathbb{R}^k$, also denoted by F_X. We say that X has *density* p_X if F_X is absolutely continuous with respect to the Lebesgue measure in $\mathbb{R}^k$, that is if

$$F_X(A) = \int_A p_X(t)\,dt$$

for any Borel set A. Random vectors X, Y are said to be *identically distributed* if their distribution functions are identical: $F_X(x) = F_Y(x)$ for all $x \in \mathbb{R}^k$. The original pair consisting of the vector X and probability space $(\Omega, \mathcal{F}, P)$ is distributed identically with the pair consisting of the identity mapping $X(t) = t$ on $\mathbb{R}^k$ and probability space $(\mathbb{R}^k, \mathcal{B}_k, F_X)$ where $\mathcal{B}_k$ is the Borel field of subsets of $\mathbb{R}^k$. Identically distributed vectors have equal moments. In particular, there are two different formulas for

$$EX = \int_\Omega X(\omega)\,dP(\omega) = \int_{\mathbb{R}^k} t\,dF_X(t)$$

(see Davidson 1994, Section 9.1).

1.8.3 Convergence in Distribution

We say that a sequence of random vectors $\{X_i\}$ *converges in distribution* to X if $F_{X_i}(t) \to F_X(t)$ at all continuity points t of the limit distribution F_X. For convergence in distribution we use the notation $X_i \xrightarrow{d} X$ or $\text{dlim}X_i = X$.

In econometrics, we are interested in convergence in distribution because confidence intervals for X in the one-dimensional (1-D) case can be expressed in terms of $F_X : P(a < X \le b) = F_X(b) - F_X(a)$. Here the right-hand side can be approximated by $F_{X_i}(b) - F_{X_i}(a)$ if $\text{dlim}X_i = X$ and a and b are continuity points of F_X (which is always the case if X is normal).

Convergence in distribution is so weak that it is not preserved under arithmetic operations. In expressions like $X_i + Y_i$ or $A_i X_i$ we can pass to the limit in distribution if one sequence converges in distribution and the other *in probability to a constant*.

Lemma. *Let $\{X_i\}$ and $\{Y_i\}$ be sequences of $n \times 1$ random vectors and let $\{A_i\}$ be a sequence of random matrices such that* $\text{dlim}X_i$, $\text{plim}Y_i$ *and* $\text{plim}A_i$ *exist.*

(i) If $c = \text{plim}Y_i$ is a constant, then $\text{dlim}(X_i + Y_i) = \text{dlim}X_i + c$.

(ii) If $A = \text{plim}A_i$ is constant, then $\text{dlim}A_i X_i = A\text{dlim}X_i$.

(iii) $\text{plim}X_i = X$ implies $\text{dlim}X_i = X$. If X is a constant, then the converse is true: $\text{dlim}X_i = c$ implies $\text{plim}X_i = c$.

(iv) (Dominance of convergence in probability to zero) If $\text{plim}A_i = 0$, then the same is true for the product: $\text{plim}A_i X_i = 0$.

(v) Suppose $X_n \xrightarrow{d} X$ where all random vectors take values in $\mathbb{R}^k$. Let $h : \mathbb{R}^k \to \mathbb{R}^m$ be measurable and denote D_h the set of discontinuities of h. If $F_X(D_h) = 0$, then $h(X_n) \xrightarrow{d} h(X)$.

Proof. For (i) and (ii) see (Davidson 1994, Theorem 22.14) (1-D case). The proof of (iii) can be found in (Davidson 1994, Theorems 22.4 and 22.5).

Statement (iv) is proved like this. If $\text{plim}A_i = 0$, then $\text{dlim}A_i X_i = 0$ by (ii), which implies $\text{plim}A_i X_i = 0$ by (iii).

The proof of (v) is contained in (Billingsley 1968, Chapter 1, Section 5). ∎

The case $c = 0$ of statement (i) is a perturbation result: adding to $\{X_i\}$ a sequence $\{Y_i\}$ such that $\text{plim}Y_i = 0$ does not change $\text{dlim}X_i$. A continuous h (for which D_h is empty) is a very special case of (v). This case is called a *continuous mapping theorem* (CMT). For (ii) "$\text{plim}A_i$" is not constant, the way around is to prove convergence in distribution of the pair $\{A_i, X_i\}$. Then CMT applied to $h(A_i, X_i) = A_i X_i$ does the job.

1.8.4 Boundedness in Probability

Let $\{X_n\}$ be a sequence of random variables. We know that a (proper) random variable X satisfies $P(|X| > M) \to 0$ as $M \to \infty$. Requiring this property to hold uniformly in n gives us the definition of *boundedness in probability*: $\sup_n P(|X_n| > M) \to 0$

as $M \to \infty$. We write $X_n = O_p(1)$ when $\{X_n\}$ is bounded in probability. This notation is justified by item (i) of the next lemma.

Lemma

(i) If $X_n = x_n = constant$, then $x_n = O(1)$ is equivalent to $X_n = O_p(1)$.

(ii) If $X_n = O_p(1)$ and $Y_n = O_p(1)$, then $X_n + Y_n = O_p(1)$ and $X_n Y_n = O_p(1)$.

Proof.

(i) It is easy to see that

$$\sup_n P(|x_n| > M) = \sup_n 1_{\{|x_n| > M\}} = 1_{\{\sup_n |x_n| > M\}}. \tag{1.27}$$

This implies that $\sup_n P(|X_n| > M) \to 0$ if and only if $\sup_n |x_n| \le M$.

(ii) Let us show that

$$\{|X_n + Y_n| > M\} \subseteq \{|X_n| > M/2\} \cup \{|Y_n| > M/2\}. \tag{1.28}$$

Suppose the opposite is true. Then there exists $\omega \in \Omega$ such that

$$M < |X_n(\omega) + Y_n(\omega)| \le |X_n(\omega)| + |Y_n(\omega)| \le M,$$

which is nonsense. Equation (1.28) implies

$$\sup_n P(|X_n + Y_n| > M) \le \sup_n P\left(|X_n| > \frac{M}{2}\right) + \sup_n P\left(|Y_n| > \frac{M}{2}\right)$$
$$\to 0, M \to \infty,$$

that is, $X_n + Y_n = O_p(1)$. Further, along with Eq. (1.28), we can prove

$$\{|X_n Y_n| > M\} \subseteq \left\{|X_n| > \sqrt{M}\right\} \cup \left\{|Y_n| > \sqrt{M}\right\}$$

and therefore

$$\sup_n P(|X_n Y_n| > M) \le \sup_n P\left(|X_n| > \sqrt{M}\right) + \sup_n P\left(|Y_n| > \sqrt{M}\right)$$
$$\to 0, M \to \infty, \tag{1.29}$$

which proves that $X_n Y_n = O_p(1)$.

■

1.8.5   Convergence in Probability to Zero

The definition of Section 1.8.1 in the special case when $\{X_n\}$ is a sequence of random variables gives the definition of *convergence in probability to zero*: $\lim_{n\to\infty} P(|X_n| > \varepsilon) = 0$ for any ε. In this case, instead of $X_n \overset{p}{\to} 0$ people often write $X_n = o_p(1)$.

Lemma

(i) *If $X_n = x_n = constant$, then $x_n = o(1)$ is equivalent to $X_n = o_p(1)$.*

(ii) *$X_n = o_p(1)$ implies $X_n = O_p(1)$.*

(iii) *If $X_n = o_p(1)$ and $Y_n = o_p(1)$, then $X_n \pm Y_n = o_p(1)$.*

(iv) *Suppose $X_n = o_p(1)$ or $X_n = O_p(1)$ and $Y_n = o_p(1)$. Then $X_n Y_n = o_p(1)$.*

(v) *If $X_n \overset{d}{\to} X$ and $Y_n = o_p(1)$, then $X_n Y_n = o_p(1)$.*

Proof.

(i) From an equation similar to Eq. (1.27):

$$\limsup_{n\to\infty} P(|x_n| > \varepsilon) = \limsup_{n\to\infty} 1_{\{|x_n|>\varepsilon\}} = 1_{\{\limsup_{n\to\infty} |x_n|>\varepsilon\}},$$

we see that $\lim_{n\to\infty} P(|X_n| > \varepsilon) = 0$ is equivalent to $\limsup_{n\to\infty} |x_n| \le \varepsilon$ and $X_n = o_p(1)$ is equivalent to $x_n = o(1)$.

(ii) If $X_n = o_p(1)$, then, for any given $\delta > 0$, there exists n_0 such that $P(|X_n| > M) \le \delta, n \ge n_0$. Increasing M, if necessary, we can make sure that $P(|X_n| > M) \le \delta, n < n_0$. Thus, $\sup_n P(|X_n| > M) \le \delta$. Since $\delta > 0$ is arbitrary, this proves $X_n = O_p(1)$.

(iii) This statement follows from Lemma 1.8.1(i).

(iv) By (ii) $X_n = O_p(1)$, modify Eq. (1.29) to get

$$\sup_{n\ge n_0} P(|X_n Y_n| > \varepsilon M) \le \sup_n P(|X_n| > M) + \sup_{n\ge n_0} P(|Y_n| > \varepsilon).$$

Taking an arbitrary $\delta > 0$, choose a sufficiently large M, define $\varepsilon = \delta/M$ and then select a sufficiently large n_0. The right-hand side will be small, which proves $X_n Y_n = o_p(1)$.

(v) This is just a different way of stating Lemma 1.8.3(iv).

■

1.8.6   Criterion of Convergence in Distribution of Normal Vectors

A normal vector is defined using its density. We don't need the formula for the density here. It suffices to know that the density of a normal vector e is completely determined by its *first moment* $Ee = \int_{\mathbb{R}^n} t \, dF_e(t)$ and *second moments* $Ee_i e_j = \int_{\mathbb{R}^n} t_i t_j \, dF_e(t)$.

Lemma.   *Convergence in distribution of a sequence $\{X_k\}$ of normal vectors takes place if and only if the limits $\lim EX_k$ and $\lim V(X_k)$ exist where $V(X) = E(X - EX)(X - EX)'$.*

Proof. This statement is obtained by combining two facts. The *characteristic function* ϕ_X of a random vector X is defined by

$$\phi_X(t) = Ee^{i\langle t, X\rangle}, \quad t \in \mathbb{R}^n.$$

Here $i = \sqrt{-1}$. The first fact is that convergence in distribution $\text{dlim} X_k = X$ is equivalent to the pointwise convergence

$$\lim \phi_{X_k}(t) = \phi_X(t) \quad \text{for all } t \in \mathbb{R}^n$$

(see Billingsley 1995, Theorem 26.3). The second fact is that the characteristic function of a normal vector X depends only on two parameters: its mean EX and variance $V(X)$ see (Rao 1965, Section 8a.2). ∎

1.9   THE LINEAR MODEL

1.9.1   The Classical Linear Model

The usual assumptions about the linear regression

$$y = X\beta + e \tag{1.30}$$

are the following:

1. y is an observed n-dimensional random vector,
2. the matrix of regressors (or independent variables) X of size $n \times k$ is assumed known,
3. $\beta \in \mathbb{R}^k$ is the parameter vector to be estimated from data (y and X),
4. e is an unobserved n-dimensional error vector with mean zero and
5. $n > k$ and $\det X'X \neq 0$.

The matrix X is assumed constant (deterministic). In dynamic models, with lags of the dependent variable at the right side, those lags are listed separately. I am in favor of separating deterministic regressors from stochastic ones from the very beginning, rather than piling them up together and later trying to specify the assumptions by sorting out the exogenous regressors.

1.9.2 Ordinary Least Squares Estimator

The least squares procedure first gives rise to the *normal equation*

$$X'X\hat{\beta} = X'y$$

for the OLS estimator $\hat{\beta}$ of β and then, subject to the condition det $X'X \neq 0$, to the formula of the estimator

$$\hat{\beta} = (X'X)^{-1}X'y.$$

This formula and model (1.30) itself lead to the representation

$$\hat{\beta} - \beta = (X'X)^{-1}X'e \qquad (1.31)$$

used to study the properties of $\hat{\beta}$. In particular, the assumption $Ee = 0$ implies that $\hat{\beta}$ is unbiased, $E\hat{\beta} = \beta$ and that its distribution is centered on β.

1.9.3 Normal Errors

$N(\mu, \Sigma)$ denotes the *class of normal vectors* with mean μ and variance Σ (which in general may be singular). Errors distributed as $N(0, \sigma^2 I)$ are assumed as the first approximation to reality. Components $e_1, \ldots, e_n$ of such errors satisfy

$$\text{cov}(e_i, e_j) = 0, \quad i \neq j, \quad Ee_i = 0, \quad Ee_i^2 = \sigma^2. \qquad (1.32)$$

The first equation here says that $e_1, \ldots, e_n$ are *uncorrelated*.

Lemma. *If $e \sim N(0, \sigma^2 I)$, then the components of e are independent identically distributed.*

Proof. By the theorem from (Rao 1965, Section 8a.2) uncorrelatedness of the components of e plus normality of e imply independence of the components. By Eq. (1.32) the first and second moments of the components coincide, therefore their densities and distribution functions coincide. ∎

1.9.4 Independent Identically Distributed Errors

We write $e \sim \text{IID}(0, \sigma^2 I)$ to mean that the components of e are independent identically distributed (i.i.d.), have mean zero and covariance $\sigma^2 I$. Lemma 1.9.3 means that $N(0, \sigma^2 I) \subseteq \text{IID}(0, \sigma^2 I)$.

Lemma. *Suppose $e \sim \text{IID}(0, \sigma^2 I)$ and put $\mathcal{F}_0 = \{\emptyset, \Omega\}$, $\mathcal{F}_t = \sigma(e_j : j \leq t)$, $t = 1, 2, \ldots$ Then e_t is $\mathcal{F}_t$-measurable, $E(e_t|\mathcal{F}_{t-1}) = 0$, $E(e_t^2|\mathcal{F}_{t-1}) = \sigma^2, t = 1, \ldots, n$.*

Proof. For $t = 1$, $E(e_1|\mathcal{F}_0) = Ee_1 = 0$ (see Example 1.6 in Section 1.6.2). Let $t > 1$. By definition, $\mathcal{F}_{t-1} = \sigma(e_j : j \leq t - 1)$ and $\sigma(e_t)$ are independent.

By Theorem 1.6.6, $E(e_t|\mathcal{F}_{t-1}) = Ee_t = 0$. Similarly, $E(e_t^2|\mathcal{F}_{t-1}) = Ee_t^2 = \sigma^2$ (see Theorem 1.5.4(i) about nonlinear transformations of measurable functions).   ∎

1.9.5 Martingale Differences

Let $\{\mathcal{F}_t : t = 1, 2, \ldots\}$ be an increasing sequence of σ-fields contained in $\mathcal{F}$: $\mathcal{F}_1 \subseteq \ldots \subseteq \mathcal{F}_n \subseteq \ldots \subset \mathcal{F}$. A sequence of random variables $\{e_t : t = 1, 2, \ldots\}$ is called *adapted* to $\{\mathcal{F}_t\}$ if e_t is $\mathcal{F}_t$-measurable for $t = 1, 2, \ldots$ If a sequence of integrable variables $\{e_t\}$ satisfies

  1. $\{e_t\}$ is adapted to $\{\mathcal{F}_t\}$ and
  2. $E(e_t|\mathcal{F}_{t-1}) = 0$ for $t = 1, 2, \ldots$, where $\mathcal{F}_0 = \{\varnothing, \Omega\}$,

then we say that $\{e_t, \mathcal{F}_t\}$ or, shorter, $\{e_t\}$ is a *martingale difference* (m.d.) sequence.

Lemma. *Square-integrable m.d. sequences are uncorrelated and have mean zero.*

Proof. By the law of iterated expectations (LIE) [Eq. (1.23)] and the m.d. property item 2 the means are zero:

$$Ee_t = E[E(e_t|\mathcal{F}_{t-1})|\mathcal{F}_0] = 0, t = 1, 2, \ldots$$

Let $s < t$. Since e_s is $\mathcal{F}_s$-measurable, it is $\mathcal{F}_{t-1}$-measurable. By extended homogeneity (Section 1.6.5) and the LIE

$$Ee_s e_t = E[E(e_s e_t|\mathcal{F}_{t-1})] = E[e_s E(e_t|\mathcal{F}_{t-1})] = 0.$$ ∎

The generality of the m.d. assumption is often reduced by the necessity to restrict the behavior of the second-order conditional moments by the condition

$$E(e_t^2|\mathcal{F}_{t-1}) = \sigma^2, t = 1, 2, \ldots \tag{1.33}$$

Owing to the LIE this condition implies $Ee_t^2 = \sigma^2, t = 1, 2, \ldots$ We denote by $MD(0, \sigma^2)$ the square-integrable m.d.'s that satisfy Eq. (1.33). By Lemma 1.9.4, $IID(0, \sigma^2 I) \subseteq MD(0, \sigma^2)$ if we put $\mathcal{F}_t = \sigma(e_j : j \leq t)$.

1.9.6 The Hierarchy of Errors

We have proved that

$$N(0, \sigma^2 I) \subseteq IID(0, \sigma^2 I) \subseteq MD(0, \sigma^2). \tag{1.34}$$

Members of any of these three classes have a mean of zero and are uncorrelated. Normal errors are in the core of all error classes considered in this book. This means that any asymptotic results should hold for normal errors and the class of normal errors can be used as litmus paper for tentative assumptions and proofs. The criterion of convergence in the distribution of normal vectors (Section 1.8.6) facilitates verifying convergence in this class.

Some results will be proved for linear processes as errors. Let $\{\psi_j : j \in \mathbb{Z}\}$ be a double-infinite summable sequence of numbers, $\sum_{j \in \mathbb{Z}} |\psi_j| < \infty$, and let $\{e_j : j \in \mathbb{Z}\}$ be a sequence of integrable zero-mean random variables, called *innovations*. A *linear process* is a sequence $\{v_j : j \in \mathbb{Z}\}$ defined by the convolution

$$v_t = \sum_{j \in \mathbb{Z}} \psi_j e_{t-j}, \quad t \in \mathbb{Z}. \tag{1.35}$$

Members of any of the above three classes may serve as the innovations. If $\psi_0 = 1$ and $\psi_j = 0$ for any $j \neq 0$, we get $v_t = e_t$, which shows that the class of linear processes includes any of the three classes of Eq. (1.34).

Linear processes with summable $\{\psi_j\}$ are called *short-memory processes*. If $\sup_j E|e_j| < \infty$ and $\sum_j |\psi_j| < \infty$, then v_t have uniformly bounded L_1-norms, $E|v_t| \leq \sup_j E|e_j| \sum_j |\psi_j| < \infty$, and zero means. More general processes with square-summable $\{\psi_j\}$, $\sum_{j \in \mathbb{Z}} \psi_j^2 < \infty$, are called *long-memory processes*. In this case, if the innovations are uncorrelated and have uniformly bounded L_2-norms, then v_t exist in the sense of L_2: $Ev_t^2 \leq \sup_j Ee_j^2 \sum_j \psi_j^2 < \infty$. There are also mixing processes, see (Davidson, 1994), which are more useful in nonlinear problems. Long-memory and mixing processes are not considered here. Long-memory processes do not fit Theorem 3.5.2, as discussed in Section 3. Conditions in terms of mixing processes do not look nice, perhaps because they are inherently complex or the theory is underdeveloped.

1.10 NORMALIZATION OF REGRESSORS

1.10.1 Normal Errors as the Touchstone of the Asymptotic Theory

Suppose we have a series of regressions $y = X\beta + e$ with the same β and n going to infinity (dependence of y, X and e on n is not reflected in the notation). We would like to know if the sequence of corresponding OLS estimators $\hat{\beta}$ converges in distribution to a normal vector. We shall see that, as a preliminary step, $\hat{\beta}$ should be centered on β and properly scaled, so that convergence takes place for $D_n(\hat{\beta} - \beta)$, where D_n is some matrix function of the regressors. The factor D_n is called a *normalizer* (it normalizes variances of components of the transformed errors in the OLS estimator formula to a constant). The choice of the normalizer is of crucial importance as it affects the conditions imposed later on X and e.

The classes of regressors and errors should be as wide as possible. The search for these classes is complicated if both regressors and errors are allowed to vary. However, under the hierarchy of errors described above the normal errors are the core of the theory. The implication is that, whatever the conditions imposed on X, they should work for the class of normal errors. The OLS estimator, being a linear transformation of e, is normal when e is normal. Therefore from the criterion of convergence in distribution of normal vectors (Section 1.8.6) we conclude that the choice of the normalizer and the class of regressors should satisfy the conditions

1. $\lim ED_n(\hat{\beta} - \beta)$ exists and

2. $\lim V(D_n(\hat{\beta} - \beta))$ exists

when $e \sim N(0, \sigma^2 I)$. For deterministic X, it is natural to stick to deterministic D_n, so condition 1 trivially holds because of unbiasedness of $\hat{\beta}$. The second condition can be called a *variance stabilization condition*.

1.10.2   Where Does the Square Root Come From?

Consider n independent observations on a normal variable with mean β and standard deviation σ. In terms of regression, we are dealing with $X = (1, \ldots, 1)'$ (n unities) and $e \sim N(0, \sigma^2 I)$. From the representation of the OLS estimator (1.31) $\hat{\beta} - \beta = (e_1 + \cdots + e_n)/n$. By independence of the components of e this implies

$$V(\hat{\beta} - \beta) = \frac{1}{n^2}[V(e_1) + \cdots + V(e_n)] = \frac{\sigma^2}{n}.$$

Now it is easy to see that with $D_n = \sqrt{n}$ the variance stabilization condition is satisfied and the criterion of convergence of normal variables gives $\sqrt{n}(\hat{\beta} - \beta) \xrightarrow{d} N(0, \sigma^2)$. The square root also works for stable autoregressive models (Hamilton, 1994).

1.10.3   One Nontrivial Regressor and Normal Errors

Consider a slightly more general case $y = x\beta + e$ with $x \in \mathbb{R}^n$ and a scalar β. The representation of the OLS estimator reduces to $\hat{\beta} - \beta = x'e/\|x\|_2^2$ and we easily find that

$$V(\|x\|_2 (\hat{\beta} - \beta)) = \frac{1}{\|x\|_2^2} \sum_{i=1}^{n} x_i^2 \sigma^2 = \sigma^2$$

under the same assumption $e \sim N(0, \sigma^2 I)$. It follows that

$$\|x\|_2 (\hat{\beta} - \beta) \xrightarrow{d} N(0, \sigma^2) \tag{1.36}$$

and $D_n = \|x\|_2$ is the right normalizer.

What if instead of D_n we use $\sqrt{n}$? Then $\sqrt{n}(\hat{\beta} - \beta) = \sqrt{n}x'e/\|x\|_2^2$ and the variance stabilization condition leads to

$$\frac{n}{\|x\|_2^2} \rightarrow constant.$$

This means that the $\sqrt{n}$-rule separates a narrow class of regressors for which $\|x\|_2$ is of order $\sqrt{n}$ for large n. In general, any function of n tending to ∞ as $n \to \infty$ can be used as a normalizer for some class of regressors, and there are as many classes as there are functions with different behavior at infinity.

The normalizer $D_n = \|x\|_2$ is better because it *adapts* to the regressor instead of separating some class. For example, for $x = (1, \ldots, 1)'$ (n unities) it gives the classical square root and for a *linear trend* $x_1 = 1, x_2 = 2, \ldots, x_n = n$ it grows as $n^{3/2}$. As D_n is self-adjusting, you don't need to know the rate of growth of $\|x\|_2$. This is especially important in applications where regressors don't have any particular analytical pattern. The decisive argument is that D_n is in some sense unique (see Section 1.11.3).

1.10.4   The Errors Contribution Negligibility Condition

Let us look again at $y = x\beta + e$ where $e_1, \ldots, e_n$ are now IID$(0, \sigma^2 I)$ and not necessarily normal. Having made up our mind regarding the normalizer we need to prove convergence in distribution of

$$\|x\|_2 (\hat{\beta} - \beta) = \frac{x_1}{\|x\|_2} e_1 + \cdots + \frac{x_n}{\|x\|_2} e_n.$$

Here is where CLTs step in. The CLTs we need affirm the asymptotic normality of weighted sums

$$\sum_{t=1}^{n} w_{nt} e_t$$

of random variables $e_1, \ldots, e_n$, which are not necessarily normal. Convergence in distribution of such sums is possible under two types of restrictions.

The first type limits dependence among the random variables and is satisfied in the case under consideration because we assume independence. The second type requires contribution of each term in the sum to vanish asymptotically where

$$\text{contribution} = \frac{\text{variance of a term}}{\text{variance of the sum}}.$$

Under our assumptions this type boils down to the condition

$$\lim_{n \to \infty} \max_{1 \leq t \leq n} \frac{|x_t|}{\|x\|_2} = 0, \tag{1.37}$$

often called an *errors contribution negligibility condition*. This condition in combination with $e \sim$ IID$(0, \sigma^2 I)$ is sufficient to prove Eq. (1.36).

1.11 GENERAL FRAMEWORK IN THE CASE OF *K* REGRESSORS

1.11.1 The Conventional Scheme

Now in the model $y = X\beta + e$ we allow X to have more than one column and assume $\det X'X \neq 0$, $e \sim \text{IID}(0, \sigma^2 I)$.

The rough approach consists in generalizing upon Section 1.10.2 (with a constant regressor) by relying on the identity

$$\sqrt{n}(\hat{\beta} - \beta) = \left(\frac{X'X}{n}\right)^{-1} \frac{X'e}{\sqrt{n}}. \tag{1.38}$$

Suppose that here

$$\text{limit } A = \lim_{n \to \infty} \frac{X'X}{n} \text{ exists and is nonsingular} \tag{1.39}$$

and that

$$\frac{X'e}{\sqrt{n}} \xrightarrow{d} N(0, B). \tag{1.40}$$

Then, by continuity of matrix inversion $(X'X/n)^{-1} \to A^{-1}$ and the rule for convergence in distribution [Lemma 1.8.3(ii)] implies

$$\left(\frac{X'X}{n}\right)^{-1} \frac{X'e}{\sqrt{n}} \xrightarrow{d} A^{-1}u, u \sim N(0, B).$$

As a result,

$$\sqrt{n}(\hat{\beta} - \beta) \xrightarrow{d} N(0, A^{-1}BA^{-1}). \tag{1.41}$$

As in case $k = 1$, the rough approach separates a narrow class of regressor matrices by virtue of conditions (1.39) and (1.40).

The refined approach is based on the variance stabilization idea.

Partitioning X into columns, $X = (X_1, \ldots, X_k)$, we see that the vector $u = X'e$ has components $u_j = X'_j e$ with variances $V(u_j) = \sigma^2 \|X_j\|_2^2$. Since $X'X$ is the Gram matrix of the system $\{X_1, \ldots, X_k\}$, the condition $\det X'X \neq 0$ is equivalent to linear independence of the columns (Section 1.7.4) and implies $\|X_j\|_2 \neq 0$ for all j and large n. If we define the normalizer by

$$D_n = \text{diag}[\|X_1\|_2, \ldots, \|X_k\|_2], \tag{1.42}$$

then the matrix

$$H = XD_n^{-1} = \left(\frac{X_1}{\|X_1\|_2}, \ \ldots, \ \frac{X_k}{\|X_k\|_2} \right) = (H_1, \ \ldots, \ H_k)$$

has normalized columns, $\|H_j\|_2 = 1$. This construction is simple yet so important that I would love to name it after the discoverer. Unfortunately, the historical evidence is not clear-cut, as is shown in Section 1.11.2. For this reason I call D_n a *variance-stabilizing (VS)* normalizer.

The analog of Eq. (1.38) is [see Eq. (1.31)]

$$D_n(\hat{\beta} - \beta) = D_n(X'X)^{-1}X'e$$
$$= (D_n^{-1}X'XD_n^{-1})^{-1}D_n^{-1}X'e = (H'H)^{-1}H'e. \tag{1.43}$$

Naturally, the place of Eqs. (1.39) and (1.40) is taken by

$$\text{limit } A = \lim_{n \to \infty} H'H \text{ exists and is nonsingular} \tag{1.44}$$

and

$$H'e \ \xrightarrow{d} \ N(0, B). \tag{1.45}$$

We call both the combinations of Eqs. (1.38) + (1.39) + (1.40) and Eqs. (1.43) + (1.44) + (1.45) a *conventional scheme* of derivation of the OLS asymptotics.

The result in Section 1.11.3 implies that, if we want to use Eq. (1.43), condition (1.44) is unavoidable. If Eq. (1.44) is not satisfied with any normalization, the conventional scheme itself should be modified (see in Chapter 4, how P.C.B. Phillips handles this issue).

1.11.2   History

The probabilists became aware of the variance stabilization principle a long time ago. It is realized in one or another form in all CLTs. It took some time for the idea to penetrate econometrics.

Eicker (1963) introduced the normalizer D_n, but considered convergence of components of the OLS estimator instead of convergence of the estimator in joint distribution. Anderson (1971) proved convergence in joint distribution using D_n and mentioned that the result "in a slightly different form was given by Eicker". Schmidt (1976), without reference to either Eicker or Anderson, established a result similar to Anderson's. None of these three authors compare D_n to the classical normalizer. Moreover, Schmidt's comments imply that he thinks of D_n as complementary to the square root.

Amemiya (1985) proved Anderson's result, without referring to the three authors just cited. Evidently, he was the first to show that D_n is superior to $\sqrt{n}$ in the sense that Eq. (1.44) is more general than Eq. (1.39). He also noticed that D_n-type normalization is applicable to maximum likelihood estimators.

Finally, Mynbaev and Castelar (2001) established that D_n is more general than *any other* normalizer, as long as the conventional scheme is employed. This result is the subject of Section 1.11.3.

1.11.3 Universality of D_n

Definition. A diagonal matrix (actually, a sequence of matrices) D_n is called a *conventional-scheme-compliant (CSC)* normalizer if $H = XD_n^{-1}$ satisfies Eqs. (1.44) and (1.45) for all errors $e \sim \text{IID}(0, \sigma^2 I)$.

If $\{M_n\}$ is any sequence of nonstochastic diagonal matrices satisfying the condition

$$\text{limit } M = \lim M_n \text{ exists and is nonsingular} \tag{1.46}$$

and D_n is a CSC normalizer, then it is easily checked that $\widetilde{D}_n = M_n D_n$ is also a CSC normalizer with

$$\widetilde{H} = HM_n^{-1}, \widetilde{A} = \lim \widetilde{H}' \widetilde{H} = M^{-1}AM^{-1}, \widetilde{B} = M^{-1}BM^{-1}.$$

Theorem.   (Mynbaev and Castelar 2001) *The VS normalizer (1.42) is unique in the class of CSC normalizers up to a factor satisfying Eq. (1.46). It follows that if with some normalizer the conventional scheme works, then D_n can also be used, while the converse may not be true.*

Proof.   Let $\overline{D}_n = \text{diag}[\,\overline{d}_{n1}, \ldots, \overline{d}_{nk}\,]$ be some CSC normalizer, $\overline{H} = X\overline{D}_n^{-1}$, and let $\overline{A}$ and $\overline{B}$ be the corresponding elements of the conventional scheme. The diagonal of the limit relation $\overline{H}' \overline{H} \to \overline{A}$ gives

$$\overline{H}_j' \overline{H}_j = \|X_j\|_2^2 / \overline{d}_{nj}^2 \longrightarrow \overline{a}_{jj}, \quad j = 1, \ldots, k, \tag{1.47}$$

where $\overline{H}_j$ denote the columns of $\overline{H}$, X_j the columns of X and $\overline{a}_{ij}$ the elements of $\overline{A}$. Recalling that D_n has $d_{nj} = \|X_j\|_2$ on its diagonal we deduce from Eq. (1.47) that

$$d_{nj} / \overline{d}_{nj} \longrightarrow \overline{a}_{jj}^{1/2}, \quad j = 1, \ldots, k. \tag{1.48}$$

By the Cauchy–Schwarz inequality the elements of $\overline{H}' \overline{H}$ satisfy the inequality $|\overline{H}_i' \overline{H}_j| \leq \|\overline{H}_i\|_2 \|\overline{H}_j\|_2$. Letting $n \to \infty$ here and using Eq. (1.47) we get $|\overline{a}_{ij}| \leq (\overline{a}_{ii} \overline{a}_{jj})^{1/2}$. This tells us that none of the diagonal elements can be zero because otherwise a whole cross in $\overline{A}$ would consist of zeros and $\overline{A}$ would be singular.

Now from Eq. (1.48) we see that $M_n = D_n \overline{D}_n^{-1}$ satisfies Eq. (1.46) and $D_n = M_n \overline{D}_n$ differs from $\overline{D}_n$ by an asymptotically constant diagonal factor. It follows that D_n is CSC with $A = M^{-1}\overline{A}M^{-1}$ and $B = M^{-1}\overline{B}M^{-1}$.

The square root is an example of a normalizer that has a narrower area of applicability than D_n.   ∎

1.11.4   The Moore–Penrose Inverse

Suppose A is a singular square matrix. According to (Rao 1965, Section 1b.5) the *Moore–Penrose inverse* A^+ of a matrix A is uniquely defined by the properties

$$AA^+A = A, \tag{1.49}$$

$$A^+AA^+ = A^+, \tag{1.50}$$

$$AA^+ \quad \text{and} \quad A^+A \text{ are symmetric.} \tag{1.51}$$

When A is symmetric, A^+ can be constructed explicitly using its diagonal representation. Let A be of order n and diagonalized as $A = P\Lambda P'$ where P is orthogonal, $P'P = I$ and Λ is a diagonal of eigenvalues of A (see Theorem 1.7.2). Denote

$$\left(\frac{1}{\lambda}\right)^+ = \begin{cases} \frac{1}{\lambda}, & \lambda \neq 0; \\ 0, & \lambda = 0. \end{cases} \quad (\Lambda^{-1})^+ = \text{diag}\left[\left(\frac{1}{\lambda_1}\right)^+, \ldots, \left(\frac{1}{\lambda_n}\right)^+\right],$$

$$A^+ = P(\Lambda^{-1})^+P'.$$

Lemma. A^+ *is the Moore–Penrose inverse of* A. *It is symmetric and the matrix* $Q = A^+A$ *is an orthoprojector:* $Q' = Q, Q^2 = Q$.

Proof. A^+ is symmetric by construction. It is easy to see that the product $\Delta = (\Lambda^{-1})^+\Lambda$ has zeros where Λ has zeros and unities where Λ has nonzero eigenvalues. Therefore $\Lambda\Delta = \Lambda$ and $\Delta\Lambda^+ = \Lambda^+$, so that Eqs. (1.49) and (1.50) are true:

$$AA^+A = P\Lambda\Delta P' = A, A^+AA^+ = P\Delta\Lambda^+P' = A^+.$$

Besides, the matrices $AA^+ = P\Lambda\Lambda^+P'$ and $A^+A = P\Lambda^+\Lambda P' = P\Delta P'$ are symmetric. By the uniqueness of the Moore–Penrose inverse, A^+ is that inverse.

The symmetry of $Q = A^+A$ has just been shown. Q is idempotent: $Q^2 = (A^+A)^2 = P\Delta^2P' = Q$.   ∎

Note that A^+ is not a continuous function of A. For example,

$$A_n = \begin{pmatrix} 1 & 0 \\ 0 & 1/n \end{pmatrix}$$

converges to

$$A = \begin{pmatrix} 1 & 0 \\ 0 & 0 \end{pmatrix} = A^+$$

but

$$A_n^+ = \begin{pmatrix} 1 & 0 \\ 0 & n \end{pmatrix}$$

does not converge to A^+.

1.11.5 What if the Limit of the Denominator Matrix is Singular?

Can the Moore–Penrose inverse save the situation? It is important to realize that convergence in distribution of $D_n(\hat{\beta} - \beta)$ in the conventional scheme is obtained as a consequence of Equations (1.43)–(1.45) from Section 1.11.1. Since the Moore–Penrose inversion is not continuous, the scheme does not work when the limit of the denominator matrix is singular. The next proposition shows that the Moore–Penrose inverse can be applied if outside (independent of the conventional scheme) information is available in the form

$$\text{limit } v = \text{dlim} D_n(\hat{\beta} - \beta) \text{ exists.} \tag{1.52}$$

Lemma.   *If instead of Eq. (1.44) we assume that*

$$\text{limit } A = \lim_{n \to \infty} H'H \text{ exists and is singular} \tag{1.53}$$

and if two pieces of information about convergence in distribution are available in the form of Eqs. (1.45) and (1.52), then

$$Qv \sim N(0, A^+BA^+)$$

where $Q = A^+A$ is an orthoprojector.

Proof.   The normal equation $X'X(\hat{\beta} - \beta) = X'e$ can be rewritten as

$$H'HD_n(\hat{\beta} - \beta) = H'e.$$

Denoting u the limit of the numerator and using Eqs. (1.53), (1.45) and (1.52) we get $Av = u$. Premultiply this by A^+ to obtain $Qv = A^+u$. Now the statement follows from Eq. (1.45). ∎

Thus, under the additional condition (1.52) some projection of v is normally distributed, with a degenerate variance A^+BA^+.

1.12 INTRODUCTION TO L_2-APPROXIMABILITY

1.12.1 Asymptotic Linear Independence

By Theorem 1.7.4 the Gram matrix

$$G = H'H = \begin{pmatrix} H_1'H_1 & \dots & H_1'H_k \\ \dots & \dots & \dots \\ H_k'H_1 & \dots & H_k'H_k \end{pmatrix}$$

is nonsingular if and only if the columns $H_1, \dots, H_k$ of H are linearly independent. Therefore condition (1.44) is termed the *asymptotic linear independence condition*. The question is: can the word "asymptotic" be removed from this name, that is, are there any vectors for which nonsingularity of the limit $A = \lim_{n \to \infty} H'H$ would mean simply linear independence? Imagine that for each j we have convergence of columns $H_j \to M_j$, as $n \to \infty$, in such a way that $H_k'H_l \to M_k'M_k$. Then existence of the limit $A = \lim_{n \to \infty} H'H$ would be guaranteed and $\det A \neq 0$ would mean linear independence of $M_1, \dots, M_k$.

Unfortunately, the sequences $\{H_j : n > k\}$ do not converge. Their elements belong to $\mathbb{R}_2^n$, which can be embedded naturally into $l_2(\mathbb{N})$. A necessary condition for convergence $x^{(n)} \to x$ in $l_2(\mathbb{N})$ is the coordinate-wise convergence $x_i^{(n)} \to x_i$, $n \to \infty$, for all $i = 1, 2, \dots$. But for Eq. (1.45) to be true we have to require the errors contribution negligibility condition (1.37) which in terms of the elements of H looks like this:

$$\lim_{n \to \infty} \max_{i,j} |h_{ij}| = 0.$$

Thus, convergence $H_j \to M_j$, as $n \to \infty$, implies $M_j = 0$, but this is impossible because $\|H_j\|_2 = 1$ for all n because of normalization.

1.12.2 Discretization

The general idea is to approximate sequences of vectors (functions of a discrete argument) with functions of a continuous argument.

For any natural n a function $f \in C[0, 1]$ generates a vector with coordinates $f(i/n)$, $i = 1, \dots, n$. A sequence of vectors $\{x^{(n)}\}$, with $x^{(n)} \in \mathbb{R}^n$ for all n, can be considered close to f if

$$\max_{1 \leq i \leq n} \left| x_i^{(n)} - f\left(\frac{i}{n}\right) \right| \to 0, \quad n \to \infty.$$

This kind of approximation was used by Nabeya and Tanaka (1988), see also, (Tanaka, 1996). A better idea is to use the class $L_2(0, 1)$, which is wider than $C[0, 1]$. However, the members of $L_2(0, 1)$ are defined only up to sets of Lebesgue measure 0, and it doesn't make sense to talk about values $f(i/n)$ for $f \in L_2(0, 1)$. Instead of values we can use integrals $\int_{(i-1)/n}^{i/n} f(t)\, dt$, $i = 1, \dots, n$. For convenience, the vector of integrals is multiplied by $\sqrt{n}$, which gives the definition of the *discretization operator* δ_n

$$(\delta_n f)_i = \sqrt{n} \int_{(i-1)/n}^{i/n} f(t)\,dt, \quad i = 1, \dots, n. \tag{1.54}$$

The sequence $\{\delta_n f : n \in \mathbb{N}\}$ is called L_2-*generated by* f. L_2-generated sequences were introduced by Moussatat (1976).

With the volatility of economic data, in econometrics it is unacceptable to require regressors to be L_2-generated or, in other words, to be exact images of some $f \in L_2(0, 1)$ under the mapping δ_n. To allow some deviation from exact images, in a conference presentation (Mynbaev 1997) I defined an L_2-*approximable* sequence as a sequence $\{x^{(n)}\}$ for which there is a function $f \in L_2(0, 1)$ satisfying

$$\|x^{(n)} - \delta_n f\|_2 \to 0.$$

If this is true, we also say that $\{x^{(n)}\}$ is L_2-*close* to $f \in L_2(0, 1)$.

It is worth emphasizing that the OLS estimator asymptotics can be proved without this condition. When the errors are independent, the asymptotic linear independence and errors contribution negligibility condition are sufficient for this purpose, see (Anderson 1971; Amemiya 1985). In 1997 I needed this notion to find the asymptotic behavior of the fitted value, which is a more advanced problem. Note also that (Pötscher and Prucha 1997) and Davidson (1994) used the term L_p-approximability in a different context.

L_2-approximable sequences and, more generally, L_p-approximable sequences defined in (Mynbaev 2000) possess some continuity properties when $p < \infty$. This is their main advantage over general sequences.

1.12.3 Ordinary Least Squares Asymptotics

Theorem.   *Consider a linear model* $y = X\beta + u$ *where*

   (i)   *the errors* $u_1, \dots, u_n$ *are defined by Eq. (1.35), the innovations* $\{e_j : j \in \mathbb{Z}\}$ *are IID$(0, \sigma^2 I)$,* $\sum_{j \in \mathbb{Z}} |\psi_j| < \infty$ *and* e_j^2 *are uniformly integrable;*

   (ii) *for each* $j = 1, \dots, k$, *the sequence of columns* $\{H_j : n > k\}$ *of the normalized regressor matrix* $H = XD_n^{-1}$ *is* L_2-*close to* $M_j \in L_2(0, 1)$;

   (iii) *the functions* $M_1, \dots, M_k$ *are linearly independent.*

Then the denominator matrix $H'H$ *converges to the Gram matrix* G *of the system* $M_1, \dots, M_k$ *and*

$$D_n(\hat{\beta} - \beta) \xrightarrow{d} N(0, (\sigma\beta_\psi)^2 G^{-1}). \tag{1.55}$$

Proof.   By Theorem 2.5.3 $\lim_{n\to\infty} H_i'H_j = \int_0^1 M_i M_j \, dt$ and, in consequence, $\lim H'H = G$. By Theorem 3.5.2 $H'u \xrightarrow{d} N(0, (\sigma\beta_\psi)^2 G)$ (this includes the case when $H'u$ converges in distribution and in probability to a null vector). Equation (1.55) follows from the conventional scheme.   ∎

In similar results with VS normalization (Anderson, 1971, Theorem 2.6.1; Schmidt, 1976, Section 2.7; Amemiya, 1985, Theorem 3.5.4) the errors are assumed independent. Assumptions on H vary from source to source. In Theorems 2.5.3 and 3.5.2 the necessary properties of H are derived from the L_2-approximability assumption. Instead, we could require them directly. When the errors are independent, these properties are: existence of the limit $A = \lim_{n\to\infty} H'H$, asymptotic linear independence $\det A \neq 0$ and the errors contribution negligibility condition $\lim_{n\to\infty} \max_{i,j}|h_{ij}| = 0$. Thus, as far as the OLS asymptotics for the classical model is concerned, the L_2-approximability condition is stronger than the minimum required. It becomes indispensable when deeper properties are needed, like convergence of the fitted value considered next.

1.12.4 Convergence of the Fitted Value

The *fitted value* is defined by $\hat{y} = X\hat{\beta}$. The need for its asymptotics may arise in the following way. Suppose we have to estimate stock $q(t)$ based on its known initial value $q(t_0)$ and flow (rate of change) $q'(t)$. By the Newton–Leibniz formula, $q(t) - q(t_0) = \int_{t_0}^{t} q'(s)\,ds$. If $q'(t)$ is measured at discrete points and regressed on, say, a polynomial of time, the interpolated fitted value approximates q' on the whole interval $[t_0, t]$ and integrating it gives an estimate of $q(t) - q(t_0)$.

As is the case with the OLS estimator, the fitted value has to be transformed to achieve convergence in distribution. Centering on $X\beta$ results in

$$\hat{y} - X\beta = X(\hat{\beta} - \beta) = XD_n^{-1}D_n(\hat{\beta} - \beta) = HD_n(\hat{\beta} - \beta). \tag{1.56}$$

Convergence of $D_n(\hat{\beta} - \beta)$ is available from Theorem 1.12.3, but H does not converge, as explained in Section 1.12.1. It happens, though, that interpolating H leads to a convergent sequence in $L_2(0, 1)$.

A vector x with n values is interpolated by constants to obtain a step function $\Delta_n x = \sum_{t=1}^{n} x_t 1_{it}$. The *interpolation operator* Δ_n is applied to columns of H. From Eq. (1.56) we get

$$\Delta_n(\hat{y} - X\beta) = \Delta_n \sum_{l=1}^{k} H_l[D_n(\hat{\beta} - \beta)]_l = \sum_{l=1}^{k} (\Delta_n H_l)[D_n(\hat{\beta} - \beta)]_l.$$

Theorem. *Under the assumptions of Theorem 1.12.3 the fitted value converges in distribution to a linear combination of the functions* $M_1, \ldots, M_k$,

$$\Delta_n(\hat{y} - X\beta) \xrightarrow{d} \sum_{l=1}^{k} M_l c_l,$$

where the random vector $c = (c, \ldots, c_k)'$ *is distributed as* $N(0, (\sigma\beta_\psi)^2 G^{-1})$.

Proof. By Lemma 2.5.1 the L_2-approximability condition $\|H_l - \delta_n M_l\| \to 0$ is equivalent to $\|\Delta_n H_l - M_l\| \to 0$. Convergence of $\{\Delta_n H_l\}$ to M_l in L_2 implies convergence in distribution of $\{\Delta_n H\}$ to the vector $M = (M_1, \ldots, M_k)'$. In the expression $\Delta_n(\hat{y} - X\beta) = [\Delta_n H'][D_n(\hat{\beta} - \beta)]$ both factors in brackets at the right converge in distribution. Since their limits M and $u = \text{dlim} D_n(\hat{\beta} - \beta)$ are independent and, for each n, $\Delta_n H$ and $D_n(\hat{\beta} - \beta)$ are independent, the relations $\Delta_n H \xrightarrow{d} M$ and $D_n(\hat{\beta} - \beta) \xrightarrow{d} u$ imply convergence of the pair $(\Delta_n H, D_n(\hat{\beta} - \beta)) \xrightarrow{d} (M, u)$ see (Billingsley 1968, pp. 26–27). By the continuous mapping theorem then $\Delta_n(\hat{y} - X\beta) \xrightarrow{d} M'u$. ∎

1.12.5 Convictions and Preconceptions

In econometrics too much depends on the views of the researcher. Apparently, a set of real-world data can be looked at from different angles. Unfortunately, theoretical studies also suffer from the subjectivity of their authors. Two different sets of assumptions for the same model may lead to quite different conclusions. The choice of the assumptions depends on the previous experience of the researcher, the method employed and the desired result. Assumptions made for and views drawn from a simple model are often taken to a higher level where they can be called convictions if justified or preconceptions if questionable.

A practitioner usually worries only about the qualitative side of the result. A highly technical paper about estimator asymptotics in his/her interpretation boils down to "under some regularity conditions the estimator is asymptotically normal". Hypotheses tests are conducted accordingly, the result is cited without proofs in expository monographs for applied specialists and, with time, becomes a part of folklore. The probability of a critical revision of the original paper declines exponentially.

Imagine that you are a security agent entrusted with the task of capturing an alien that is killing humans. If you presuppose that the beast is disguised like a human your course of actions will be quite different from what it would be if you were looking for a giant cockroach.

When you see a new estimator, its asymptotics is that alien. The best of all is not to presume that it is of a particular type. Make simplified assumptions and look at the finite-sample distributions in the case of normal disturbances. If they are normal, perhaps the asymptotics is also normal. If they are not, a suitable transformation of the estimator, such as centering and scaling, may result in normal asymptotics. Alternatively, you may have to apply a CLT in conjunction with the CMT to obtain nonnormal asymptotics. All these possibilities are illustrated in the book.

By choosing the format of the result you make a commitment. Normal asymptotics is usually proved using a CLT. Let us say it comes with conditions (A), (B) and (C). To satisfy them, you impose in terms of your model conditions (A'), (B') and (C'), respectively. These conditions determine the class of processes your result is applicable to. By selecting a different format you are bound to use different techniques and obtain a different class.

In the case of the conventional scheme an easy way to go is simply assume that X and e are such that either Eqs. (1.39) + (1.40) or Eqs. (1.44) + (1.45) are satisfied. I call such a "theorem" a *pig-in-a-poke* result. While this approach serves illustrative purposes in a university course well, its value in a research paper or monograph is doubtful. Eicker (1963) mentions that conditions should be imposed separately on the errors and regressors.

In this relation it is useful to distinguish between *low-level conditions*, stated directly in terms of the primary elements of the model, such as Eq. (1.44), and *high-level conditions*, expressed in terms of some complex combinations of the basic elements, such as Eq. (1.45). Of course, this distinction is relative. For instance, the L_2-approximability assumption about deterministic regressors made in the most part of this book is of a lower level than Eq. (1.44).

The *parsimony principle* in econometric modeling states that a model should contain as few parameters as possible or be simple otherwise and still describe the process in question well. A similar principle applies to the choice of conditions. If you have imposed several of them and are about to require a new one, make sure that it is not implied or contradicted by the previous conditions. My major professor, M. Otelbaev, used to say, "If I am allowed to impose many conditions, I can prove anything".

Transparency, simplicity and beauty are other subjective measures of the assumptions quality. A good taste is acquired by reading and comparing many sources. It is not a good idea to have a prospective user of your result prove a whole theorem to check whether your assumptions are satisfied. Nontransparent conditions appealing to *existence* of objects with certain properties are especially dangerous. It is quite possible to use the right theorems and comply with all the rules of formal logic and get a bad statement because the set of objects it applies to will be empty if the conditions are contradictory or existence requirements are infeasible. Contradictions are easy to avoid by using conditions with nonoverlapping responsibilities. In other words, beware of two different conditions governing the behavior of the same object.

Generalizations do not always work, as we have seen when going from constant to variable regressors. However, when studying a dynamic model, such as the mixed spatial model $Y = X\beta + \rho WY + e$ in Chapter 5, I choose the conditions and methods that work for its two submodels, $Y = X\beta + e$ and $Y = \rho WY + e$. In this sense, this book is not free from subjectivity.

Generalizations based on the conventional scheme can be as harmful as any others. The study of the purely spatial model in Chapter 5 shows that the said model violates the habitual notions in several ways:

1. the OLS asymptotics is not normal,
2. the limit of the numerator vector is not normal,
3. the limit of the denominator matrix is not constant,
4. the normalizer is identically 1 (that is, no scaling is necessary) and
5. there is no consistency.

These days requirements to econometric papers are very high. If you suggest a new model, you have to defend it by showing its theoretical advantages and testing its practical performance, preferably in the same paper. The author of a new model can be excused if he/she studies the model under simplified assumptions and leaves the generalizations and refinements to the followers. The way of modeling deterministic regressors advocated here allows us to combine simple assumptions with rigorous proofs.

CHAPTER 2

L_p-APPROXIMABLE
SEQUENCES OF VECTORS

IN THIS chapter we use some classical tools, the Haar projector and continuity modulus in the first place. With their help we can study the properties of discretization, interpolation and convolution operators. From there we go to L_p-approximable sequences and their properties, among which the criterion of L_p-approximability is the most advanced. The chapter ends with examples. Everywhere in this chapter L_p denotes the space $L_p(0, 1)$. Where necessary integration over subsets of $(0, 1)$ is indicated as in $\|F\|_{p,(a,b)} = \left(\int_a^b |F(x)|^p dx \right)^{1/p}$.

2.1 DISCRETIZATION, INTERPOLATION AND HAAR PROJECTOR IN L_p

2.1.1 Partitions and Coverings

For each natural n the set $\{t/n: t = 0, \ldots, n\}$ is called a *uniform partition*. The intervals $i_t = [(t - 1)/n, t/n)$ form a disjoint *covering* of $[0, 1)$ of equal length $1/n$. Denoting $[a]$ as the integer part of a real number a, we can see that the condition $x \in i_t$ is equivalent to $t - 1 \leq nx < t$, which, in turn, is equivalent to $t = [nx] + 1$. The function $[nx] + 1$ can be called a *locator* because $x \in i_{[nx]+1}$ for all $x \in [0, 1)$.

2.1.2 Discretization Operator Definition

For each natural n, we can define a *discretization operator* $\delta_{np}: L_p \to \mathbb{R}^n_p$ by

$$(\delta_{np}F)_t = n^{1/q} \int\limits_{i_t} F(x) \, dx, \, t = 1, \ldots, n, \, F \in L_p,$$

where q is the conjugate of p, $1/p + 1/q = 1$. Up to a scaling factor, the tth component of $\delta_{np}F$ is the average of F over the interval i_t. For a given $F \in L_p$, the sequence $\{\delta_{np}F: n \in \mathbb{N}\}$ is called L_p-*generated by* F.

Short-Memory Linear Processes and Econometric Applications. Kairat T. Mynbaev
© 2011 John Wiley & Sons, Inc. Published 2011 by John Wiley & Sons, Inc.

2.1.3 Discretization Operator Properties

Lemma. *If $F \in L_p$, $1 \le p \le \infty$, then*

(i) $|(\delta_{np}F)_t| \le \|F\|_{p,i_t}$,

(ii) $\|\delta_{np}F\|_p \le \|F\|_p$ *and*

(iii) $\lim_{n \to \infty} \max_{1 \le t \le n} |(\delta_{np}F)_t| = 0$ *in case $p < \infty$.*

Proof. Everywhere we assume $p < \infty$, the modification for $p = \infty$ being obvious.

(i) By Hölder's inequality

$$|(\delta_{np}F)_t| \le n^{1/q} \left(\int_{i_t} |F(x)|^p dx \right)^{1/p} \left(\int_{i_t} dx \right)^{1/q} = \|F\|_{p,i_t}.$$

(ii) If $p < \infty$, use part (i) to get by additivity of integrals

$$\left(\sum_{t=1}^{n} |(\delta_{np}F)_t|^p \right)^{1/p} \le \left(\sum_{t=1}^{n} \int_{i_t} |F(x)|^p dx \right)^{1/p} = \|F\|_p.$$

(iii) Since $|F(\cdot)|^p \in L_1$, we can use absolute continuity of the Lebesgue integral to find, for any $\varepsilon > 0$, a number $n(\varepsilon) > 0$ such that $n > n(\varepsilon)$ implies $\int_{i_t} |F(x)|^p dx < \varepsilon$ for $t = 1, \ldots, n$. Now the statement follows from (i). ∎

Statement (ii) means that the norms of δ_{np} from L_p to l_p do not exceed 1.

2.1.4 Continuity Modulus in L_p, $p < \infty$

Most properties of continuity moduli we need can be found in Zhuk and Natanson (2001).

For $y \in \mathbb{R}$, let τ_y be the *translation operator*, $(\tau_y F)(x) = F(x + y)$. If F is defined on (a, b), $\tau_y F$ is defined on $(a, b) - y = (a - y, b - y)$. As the domain of the difference $F - \tau_y F$ people take the intersection of these intervals, denoted

$$(a, b)_y = (a, b) \cap [(a, b) - y] = (\max\{a, a - y\}, \min\{b, b - y\}).$$

In particular, with $\Omega = (0, 1)$ the difference $F - \tau_y F$ is defined on Ω_y. The *continuity modulus* of $F \in L_p$ equals, by definition,

$$\omega_p(F, \delta) = \sup_{|y| \le \delta} \|F - \tau_y F\|_{p,\Omega_y}, \quad \delta > 0.$$

The continuity modulus is designed to measure how close $\tau_y F$ is to F for small y. This can be demonstrated using the indicator 1_A of a set A. Think of the function

$F = 1_A$ as an example, where A is some measurable subset of $(0, 1)$. Then $\tau_y 1_A = 1$ on $A - y$ and $\tau_y 1_A = 0$ outside $A - y$. The Venn diagram shows that $1_A - \tau_y 1_A$ is zero on the intersection $A \cap (A - y)$ and outside the union $A \cup (A - y)$ and it is unity on the symmetric difference $s_y = [A\backslash(A - y)] \cup [(A - y)\backslash A]$ of A and $A - y$. Therefore when $p < \infty$

$$\|1_A - \tau_y 1_A\|_{p,\Omega_y}^p = \int_{\Omega_y} |1_A - \tau_y 1_A|^p dx \leq \int_{s_y} dx = \text{mes}(s_y),$$

where mes denotes the Lebesgue measure. In the theory of the Lebesgue measure it is proved that $\text{mes}(s_y) \to 0$ when $y \to 0$, which implies

$$\|1_A - \tau_y 1_A\|_{p,\Omega_y} \to 0, \ y \to 0 \, (p < \infty). \tag{2.1}$$

However, if $p = \infty$, then

$$\|1_A - \tau_y 1_A\|_{\infty,\Omega_y} \geq \text{ess} \sup_{x \in s_y} 1_{s_y}(x). \tag{2.2}$$

Here the quantity at the right is 1 as long as $\text{mes}(s_y) > 0$.

2.1.5 Continuity of Elements of L_p

Lemma

    (i) *The continuity modulus is nondecreasing: $\delta \leq \gamma$ implies that $\omega_p(F, \delta) \leq \omega_p(F, \gamma)$.*

    (ii) *If $F \in L_p$, $p < \infty$, then $\lim_{\delta \to 0} \omega_p(F, \delta) = 0$.*

Proof. Part (i) follows directly from the definition: supremum over a larger set is larger.

    (ii) Since linear combinations of indicators of measurable sets are dense in L_p when $p < \infty$, Eq. (2.1) extends to all of L_p:

$$\|F - \tau_y F\|_{p,\Omega_y} \to 0, \ y \to 0 \, (F \in L_p, p < \infty). \tag{2.3}$$

This is described by saying that functions from L_p with finite p are *continuous in mean* (or *translation continuous*). To prove (ii), it remains to apply sup over $|y| \leq \delta$ to Eq. (2.3). ∎

    Equation (2.2) shows that elements of L_∞ are not translation continuous. When it is important to have this property, L_∞ is replaced by the set of continuous functions $C[0, 1]$. The *continuity modulus* of a continuous function on $[0, 1]$ is defined by

$$\omega_C(F, \delta) = \sup_{|x - y| \leq \delta, \, x,y \in [0,1]} |F(x) - F(y)|.$$

This tends to 0 when δ tends to zero because a continuous function on $[0, 1]$ is uniformly continuous.

2.1.6 Interpolation Operator and Haar Projector Definitions

The *interpolation operator* $\Delta_{np}\colon \mathbb{R}_p^n \to L_p$ takes a vector $f \in \mathbb{R}_p^n$ to a step function

$$\Delta_{np}f = n^{1/p} \sum_{t=1}^{n} f_t 1_{i_t}.$$

Here, the factor $n^{1/p}$ is introduced just for convenience. Interpolation by a piece-wise constant function is sufficient for our purposes.

The *Haar projector* P_n is defined on integrable functions on $[0, 1]$ by

$$P_nF = n \sum_{t=1}^{n} \int_{i_t} F(x)\, dx\, 1_{i_t}$$

(the value of P_nF on the interval i_t is the average of F on that interval). P_n is really a projector because for i_s in the above sum only one term can be different from zero and

$$P_n(P_nF) = n \sum_{s=1}^{n} \int_{i_s} (P_nF)(y)\, dy\, 1_{i_s}$$

$$= n \sum_{s=1}^{n} \int_{i_s} \left(n \int_{i_s} F(x)\, dx\, 1_{i_s}(y) \right) dy\, 1_{i_s} = P_nF.$$

2.1.7 Interpolation and Haar Projector Properties

Lemma. *Let $1 \le p \le \infty$.*

(i) Δ_{np} *preserves norms,* $\|\Delta_{np}f\|_p = \|f\|_p$ *for all $f \in \mathbb{R}_p^n$, and bilinear forms,*

$$\int_0^1 (\Delta_{np}f)\Delta_{nq}g\, dx = f'g \quad \text{for all } f, g \in \mathbb{R}^n. \tag{2.4}$$

(ii) *Discretizing and then interpolating is the same as projecting:* $\Delta_{np}\delta_{np} = P_n$. *Interpolation and subsequent discretization amount to applying the identity operator:* $\delta_{np}\Delta_{np} = I$ *on $\mathbb{R}_p^n$.*

(iii) *Norms of the projectors P_n do not exceed 1:* $\|P_nF\|_p \le \|F\|_p$.

Proof.

(i) If $p < \infty$, then

$$\int_0^1 |(\Delta_{np} f)(x)|^p dx = \sum_{t=1}^n \int_{i_t} |(\Delta_{np} f)(x)|^p dx$$

$$= n \sum_{t=1}^n \int_{i_t} |f_t|^p 1_{i_t}(x)\, dx = \sum_{t=1}^n |f_t|^p.$$

If $p = \infty$, then $\|\Delta_{n\infty} f\|_\infty = \max_{t=1,\ldots,n} |f_t|$. Further,

$$\int_0^1 (\Delta_{np} f)\Delta_{nq} g\, dx = \sum_{t=1}^n \int_{i_t} n^{1/p} f_t n^{1/q} g_t\, dx = \sum_{t=1}^n n f_t g_t \int_{i_t} dx = f'g.$$

(ii) For $F \in L_p$

$$\Delta_{np}(\delta_{np} F) = n^{1/p} \sum_{t=1}^n (\delta_{np} F)_t 1_{i_t} = n^{1/p+1/q} \sum_{t=1}^n \int_{i_t} F(x)\, dx\, 1_{i_t} = P_n F.$$

To see that $\delta_{np}\Delta_{np} f = f$ for all $f \in \mathbb{R}^n$ it suffices to check that $(\delta_{np}\Delta_{np} f)_t = f_t$ for all t. This is true because interpolating f_t generates a constant on i_t equal to $F = n^{1/p} f_t$. With this F, $(\delta_{np} F)_t$ gives f_t.

(iii) From boundedness of the discretization operator [Lemma 2.1.3(ii)] and items (i) and (ii) of this lemma

$$\|P_n F\|_p = \|\Delta_{np}\delta_{np} F\|_p = \|\delta_{np} F\|_p \le \|F\|_p. \qquad \blacksquare$$

2.2 CONVERGENCE OF BILINEAR FORMS

An expression of type $\int_0^1 F(x)G(x)\, dx$ is a bilinear form: it is linear in F when G is fixed,

$$\int_0^1 (aF + bH)G\, dx = a \int_0^1 FG\, dx + b \int_0^1 HG\, dx,$$

and similarly it is linear in G when F is fixed.

2.2.1   Convergence of Haar Projectors to the Identity Operator

Lemma.   *If $p < \infty$, then the sequence $\{P_n\}$ converges strongly to the identity operator with the next bound on the rate of convergence: $\|P_n F - F\|_p \leq 2^{1/p} \omega_p(F, 1/n)$.*

Proof.

Step 1.   Using additivity of integrals and the fact that the restriction of $P_n F$ on i_t equals $n \int_{i_t} F dx$ we have

$$\|P_n F - F\|_p^p = \sum_{t=1}^{n} \int_{i_t} |(P_n F)(y) - F(y)|^p dy$$

$$= \sum_{t=1}^{n} \int_{i_t} \left| n \int_{i_t} F(x)\, dx - n \int_{i_t} F(y)\, dx \right|^p dy$$

$$= n^p \sum_{t=1}^{n} \int_{i_t} \left| \int_{i_t} (F(x) - F(y))\, dx \right|^p dy.$$

Now we apply Hölder's inequality to $X(x) = F(x) - F(y)$ and $Y(x) \equiv 1$ and use the identity $p - p/q = 1$:

$$\|P_n F - F\|_p^p \leq n^p \sum_{t=1}^{n} \int_{i_t} \int_{i_t} |F(x) - F(y)|^p dx\, dy\, n^{-p/q}$$

$$= n \sum_{t=1}^{n} \int_{i_t} \int_{i_t} |F(x) - F(y)|^p dx\, dy.$$

As we can see, we need to estimate the integrals over the squares $i_t \times i_t$.

Step 2.   Let F be defined on $\Delta = (a, a + b)$. We want to reveal the translation operator in the integral

$$I = \int_{\Delta} \int_{\Delta} |F(x) - F(y)|^p\, dx\, dy$$

(change $x = y + z$ in the inner integral)

$$= \int_{a}^{a+b} \int_{a-y}^{a+b-y} |F(y + z) - F(y)|^p\, dz\, dy.$$

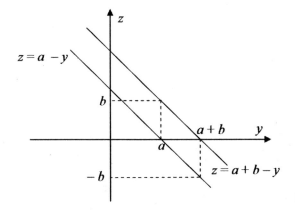

Figure 2.1   Change of variables.

The inner integral should be over y. To change the order of integration, we have to split $\{z: -b \leq z \leq b\}$ into $\{z: -b \leq z \leq 0\}$ and $\{z: 0 \leq z \leq b\}$ (Figure 2.1). Reading off the limits of integration from the diagram we write

$$I = \int_{-b}^{0} dz \int_{a-z}^{a+b} |F(y) - (\tau_z F)(y)|^p \, dy$$

$$+ \int_{0}^{b} dz \int_{a}^{a+b-z} |F(y) - (\tau_z F)(y)|^p \, dy.$$

Step 3.   Combining Steps 1 and 2 we get

$$\|P_n F - F\|_p^p \leq n \sum_{t=1}^{n} \left[\int_{-1/n}^{0} dz \int_{(i_t)_z} |F - \tau_z F|^p \, dy \right.$$

$$\left. + \int_{0}^{1/n} dz \int_{(i_t)_z} |F - \tau_z F|^p \, dy \right].$$

The intervals $(i_t)_z$ conveniently satisfy $\cup_{t=1}^{n} (i_t)_z \subseteq \Omega_z$. Therefore the definition of the continuity modulus gives

$$\|P_n F - F\|_p^p \leq n \left[\int_{-1/n}^{0} dz \int_{\Omega_z} |F - \tau_z F|^p dy \right.$$

$$\left. + \int_{0}^{1/n} dz \int_{\Omega_z} |F - \tau_z F|^p dy \right] \leq 2\omega_p^p(F, 1/n). \quad \blacksquare$$

2.2.2   Bilinear Forms Involving Haar Projectors and Discretizers

Here we prove a preliminary result that helps understand the main result from Section 2.2.3.

Lemma.   *(Convergence of bilinear forms) Let $1 < p < \infty$, $F \in L_p$, $G \in L_q$. Then*

$$\lim_{n \to \infty} (\delta_{np} F)' \delta_{nq} G = \lim_{n \to \infty} \int_0^1 (P_n F) P_n G \, dx = \int_0^1 FG \, dx. \tag{2.5}$$

Proof.   First we establish a variant of bilinear form preservation property. Plugging $f = \delta_{np} F$, $g = \delta_{nq} G$ in identity (2.4) and remembering that $\Delta_{np} \delta_{np} = P_n$ by Lemma 2.1.7(ii), we see that

$$\int_0^1 (P_n F) P_n G \, dx = (\delta_{np} F)' \delta_{nq} G, \tag{2.6}$$

which implies the first equation in Eq. (2.5).

Now we use the age-old trick of adding and subtracting members and Hölder's inequality to estimate

$$\left| \int_0^1 (P_n F) P_n G \, dx - \int_0^1 FG \, dx \right| = \left| \int_0^1 (P_n F)(P_n G - G) \, dx + \int_0^1 (P_n F - F) G \, dx \right|$$

$$\leq \| P_n F \|_p \| P_n G - G \|_q + \| P_n F - F \|_p \| G \|_q.$$

By Lemmas 2.1.7 and 2.2.1

$$\left| \int_0^1 (P_n F) P_n G \, dx - \int_0^1 FG \, dx \right|$$

$$\leq \max \{ 2^{3/(2p)}, 2^{3/(2q)} \} [\| F \|_p \omega_q(G, 1/n) + \omega_p(F, 1/n) \| G \|_q]. \tag{2.7}$$

This bound and Lemma 2.1.5 establish the second equation in Eq. (2.5).   ■

2.2.3   Bilinear Forms of L_p-Generated Sequences

Theorem.   (Mynbaev, 2000) *Let $1 < p < \infty$, $X \in L_p$, $Y \in L_q$ and let $[a, b] \subseteq [0, 1]$. Then*

$$\lim_{n \to \infty} [\delta_{np}(1_{[a,b]} X)]' \delta_{nq}(1_{[a,b]} Y) = \int_a^b X(x) Y(x) \, dx$$

uniformly with respect to the intervals $[a, b]$.

Proof.   After substituting $F = 1_{[a,b]}X$ and $G = 1_{[a,b]}Y$ in Eq. (2.7) and on account of Eq. (2.6) we conclude that the problem reduces to bounding $\|1_{[a,b]}X\|_p$ and $\omega_p(1_{[a,b]}X, \delta)$ for arbitrary $X \in L_p$, $1 < p < \infty$ and $[a, b] \subseteq [0, 1]$. It is easy to see that multiplication by $1_{[a,b]}$ is bounded in L_p uniformly in $[a, b]$:

$$\|1_{[a,b]}X\|_p \le \|X\|_p. \tag{2.8}$$

Bounding the continuity modulus is more involved. The beginning is suggested by the definition of $\omega_p(fX, \delta)$ where we put $f = 1_{[a,b]}$:

$$\|fX - \tau_y(fX)\|_{p,\Omega_y} \le \|fX - f\tau_yX\|_{p,\Omega_y} + \|f\tau_yX - (\tau_yf)\tau_yX\|_{p,\Omega_y}$$
$$= \|f(X - \tau_yX)\|_{p,\Omega_y} + \|(f - \tau_yf)\tau_yX\|_{p,\Omega_y}. \tag{2.9}$$

To the first term at the right apply Eq. (2.8):

$$\|f(X - \tau_yX)\|_{p,\Omega_y} \le \|X - \tau_yX\|_{p,\Omega_y}. \tag{2.10}$$

Note that the translation operator can be thrown over to the adjacent factor,

$$\|f\tau_yg\|_{p,\Omega_y}^p = \int_{\max\{0,-y\}}^{\min\{1,1-y\}} |f(x)g(x + y)|^p \, dx$$

(replace $x + y = t$)

$$= \int_{\max\{y,0\}}^{\min\{1+y,1\}} |f(t - y)g(t)|^p \, dt = \|(\tau_{-y}f)g\|_{p,\Omega_{-y}}^p.$$

Hence the second term at the right of Eq. (2.9) equals

$$\|(f - \tau_yf)\tau_yX\|_{p,\Omega_y} = \|(\tau_{-y}f - f)X\|_{p,\Omega_{-y}} \tag{2.11}$$

Consider the measure $\mu(A) = \int_A |X(x)|^p dx$ where X has been extended by zero outside $(0, 1)$. Let

$$s_y = \{[a, b]\setminus[a + y, b + y]\} \cup \{[a + y, b + y]\setminus[a, b]\}$$

denote the set on which $f - \tau_yf = 1$. With this notation, from Eq. (2.11) we see that

$$\|(f - \tau_yf)\tau_yX\|_{p,\Omega_y}^p = \int_{\Omega_{-y}} |f(x) - (\tau_{-y}f)(x)|^p d\mu(x)$$

$$= \mu(\Omega_{-y} \cap s_y) \le \mu(s_y). \tag{2.12}$$

Suppose $[a, b]$ and $[a, b] + y$ do not intersect. Then either $a + y > b$ or $b + y < a$. In both cases $b - a < y$. s_y is a union of two nonoverlapping segments of length $b - a$, so $\text{mes}(s_y) = 2(b - a) < 2|y|$. Suppose $[a, b]$ and $[a, b] + y$ do intersect. Then their symmetric difference s_y is a union of two disjoint intervals of length $|y|$ each, so $\text{mes}(s_y) = 2|y|$. In consequence, $\text{mes}(s_y) \leq 2|y|$ independently of $[a, b]$.

Since μ is absolutely continuous with respect to the Lebesgue measure, for any $\varepsilon > 0$ there exists $\delta > 0$ such that $\text{mes}(A) < \delta$ implies $\mu(A) < \varepsilon$. By choosing $|y| < \delta/2$ we satisfy $\mu(s_y) < \varepsilon$. Now Eqs. (2.9), (2.10) and (2.12) show that $\omega_p(fX, \delta/2) \leq \omega_p(X, \delta/2) + \varepsilon$. Since ε and δ are arbitrarily small, we have proved that

$$\lim_{\delta \to 0} \omega_p(fX, \delta) = 0$$

uniformly in $[a, b]$.   ∎

I claimed (Mynbaev, 2000) that this theorem holds for nonuniform partitions, but I failed to prove this generalization six years later when I was writing this chapter.

2.3   THE TRINITY AND ITS BOUNDEDNESS IN l_p

2.3.1   Motivation

Consider a linear process

$$v_t = \sum_{j \in \mathbb{Z}} \psi_{t-j} e_j, \, t \in \mathbb{Z},$$

where $\{\psi_j : j \in \mathbb{Z}\}$ is a summable sequence of real numbers and $\{e_j : j \in \mathbb{Z}\}$ is a sequence of centered ($Ee_j = 0$) integrable random variables (innovations).

Suppose that for each $n \in \mathbb{N}$ we are given a vector of weights $w_n \in \mathbb{R}^n$ and the question is about convergence in distribution of weighted sums

$$S_n = \sum_{t=1}^{n} w_{nt} v_t.$$

Changing the order of summation,

$$S_n = \sum_{t=1}^{n} w_{nt} \sum_{j \in \mathbb{Z}} \psi_{t-j} e_j = \sum_{j \in \mathbb{Z}} \left(\sum_{t=1}^{n} w_{nt} \psi_{t-j} \right) e_j,$$

we see that it makes sense to consider the convolution operator $T_n : \mathbb{R}_p^n \to l_p(\mathbb{Z})$ defined by

$$(T_n w)_j = \sum_{t=1}^{n} w_t \psi_{t-j}, \, j \in \mathbb{Z}.$$

Sometimes it is convenient to represent $T_n w$ as

$$T_n w = \begin{pmatrix} T_n^- w \\ T_n^0 w \\ T_n^+ w \end{pmatrix},$$

where $T_n^+: \mathbb{R}_p^n \to l_p(j > n)$, $T_n^0: \mathbb{R}_p^n \to \mathbb{R}_p^n$ and $T_n^-: \mathbb{R}_p^n \to l_p(j < 1)$ are defined by

$$(T_n^+ w)_j = (T_n w)_j, \quad j > n;$$
$$(T_n^0 w)_j = (T_n w)_j, \quad 1 \le j \le n;$$
$$(T_n^- w)_j = (T_n w)_j, \quad j < 1.$$

As a consequence of the exceptional role of T_n^+, T_n^0 and T_n^- in this theory, I call these three operators a *trinity*. Naturally, T_n is called a *T-operator*.

2.3.2   Boundedness of the Trinity in l_p

Lemma.   *If $\alpha_\psi < \infty$ and $1 \le p \le \infty$, then $\sup_n \|T_n\| \le \alpha_\psi$ and*

$$\sup_n \max\{\|T_n^+\|, \|T_n^0\|, \|T_n^-\|\} \le \alpha_\psi. \tag{2.13}$$

Proof.   Let $\mathcal{E}_n$ be the *embedding operator* of $\mathbb{R}_p^n$ into $l_p(\mathbb{Z})$:

$$(\mathcal{E}_n w)_t = \begin{cases} 0, & \text{if } t < 1 \text{ or } t > n; \\ w_t, & \text{if } 1 \le t \le n. \end{cases}$$

Denote τ_j the *translation operator* in $l_p(\mathbb{Z})$:

$$(\tau_j w)_t = w_{t+j}, j, t \in \mathbb{Z}.$$

Obviously, both operators preserve norms, $\|\mathcal{E}_n w\|_p = \|w\|_p$, $\|\tau_j w\|_p = \|w\|_p$ and, as a result, $\|\tau_j \mathcal{E}_n\| \le 1$.

From the definition of T_n we have

$$(T_n w)_j = \sum_{t \in \mathbb{Z}} (\mathcal{E}_n w)_t \psi_{t-j} = \sum_{s \in \mathbb{Z}} (\mathcal{E}_n w)_{j+s} \psi_s$$

$$= \sum_{s \in \mathbb{Z}} (\tau_s \mathcal{E}_n w)_j \psi_s = \left(\sum_{s \in \mathbb{Z}} \psi_s \tau_s \mathcal{E}_n w \right)_j.$$

Since this is true for all $j \in \mathbb{Z}$, we have proved the representation $T_n = \sum_{s \in \mathbb{Z}} \psi_s \tau_s \mathcal{E}_n$, which implies

$$\|T_n\| \le \sum_{s \in \mathbb{Z}} |\psi_s| \|\tau_s \mathcal{E}_n\| \le \alpha_\psi.$$

Now Eq. (2.13) follows from

$$\|T_n w\|_p = (\|T_n^+ w\|_p^p + \|T_n^0 w\|_p^p + \|T_n^- w\|_p^p)^{1/p}. \qquad \blacksquare$$

2.3.3 Matrix Representation of the Trinity

Correct me if I am wrong, but using matrix representations seems to be inevitable when studying the further properties of the trinity members contained in Theorem 2.4.9. These members can be identified with matrices

$$T_n^- = \begin{pmatrix} \cdots & \cdots & \cdots & \cdots \\ \psi_3 & \psi_4 & \cdots & \psi_{n+2} \\ \psi_2 & \psi_3 & \cdots & \psi_{n+1} \\ \psi_1 & \psi_2 & \cdots & \psi_n \end{pmatrix}, \quad T_n^0 = \begin{pmatrix} \psi_0 & \psi_1 & \cdots & \psi_{n-1} \\ \psi_{-1} & \psi_0 & \cdots & \psi_{n-2} \\ \cdots & \cdots & \cdots & \cdots \\ \psi_{1-n} & \psi_{-n} & \cdots & \psi_0 \end{pmatrix},$$

$$T_n^+ = \begin{pmatrix} \psi_{-n} & \psi_{1-n} & \cdots & \psi_{-1} \\ \psi_{-1-n} & \psi_{-n} & \cdots & \psi_{-2} \\ \psi_{-2-n} & \psi_{-1-n} & \cdots & \psi_{-3} \\ \cdots & \cdots & \cdots & \cdots \end{pmatrix}.$$

All of these matrices have n columns; T_n^- has an infinite number of rows stretching upward, and T_n^+ has an infinite number of rows stretching downward. Their structure suggests using diagonal matrices for analysis.

Let I_n and 0_n denote the $n \times n$ identity and null matrices. Then the matrices

$$A_0^0 = I_n; \; A_k^0 = \begin{pmatrix} 0_{(n-k) \times k} & I_{n-k} \\ 0_k & 0_{k \times (n-k)} \end{pmatrix}, \quad k = 1, \ldots, n-1;$$

$$A_k^0 = \begin{pmatrix} 0_{|k| \times (n-|k|)} & 0_{|k|} \\ I_{n-|k|} & 0_{(n-|k|) \times |k|} \end{pmatrix}, \qquad k = -1, \ldots, -n+1, \tag{2.14}$$

have the elements of their respective diagonals (main, sub or super) equal to 1 and all others equal to 0. The norms of all these operators do not exceed 1:

$$\|A_k^0 z\|_p = \|(z_{k+1}, \ldots, z_n, 0, \ldots, 0)'\|_p \le \|z\|_p, \quad k = 0, \ldots, n-1, \tag{2.15}$$

$$\|A_k^0 z\|_p = \|(0, \ldots, 0, z_1, \ldots, z_{n-|k|})'\|_p \le \|z\|_p, \quad k = -1, \ldots, -n+1. \tag{2.16}$$

From the matrix expression for T_n^0 it is directly seen that

$$T_n^0 = \sum_{k=-n+1}^{n-1} \psi_k A_k^0. \tag{2.17}$$

To obtain a similar representation for T_n^- put

$$A_k^- = \begin{pmatrix} 0_{\infty \times k} & 0_{\infty \times (n-k)} \\ I_k & 0_{k \times (n-k)} \end{pmatrix}_{\infty \times n}, \quad 1 \leq k \leq n;$$

$$A_k^- = \begin{pmatrix} 0_{\infty \times n} \\ I_n \\ 0_{(k-n) \times n} \end{pmatrix}_{\infty \times n}, \quad k > n.$$

Then

$$\|A_k^- z\|_p = \|(\ldots, 0, z_1, \ldots, z_k)'\|_p \leq \|z\|_p, \quad k \leq n;$$
$$\|A_k^- z\|_p = \|(\ldots, 0, z_1, \ldots, z_n, 0, \ldots, 0)'\|_p \leq \|z\|_p, \quad k > n; \tag{2.18}$$

$$T_n^- = \sum_{k=1}^{\infty} \psi_k A_k^-. \tag{2.19}$$

Following the same track, let

$$A_k^+ = \begin{pmatrix} 0_{k \times (n-k)} & I_k \\ 0_{\infty \times (n-k)} & 0_{\infty \times k} \end{pmatrix}_{\infty \times n}, \quad 1 \leq k \leq n;$$

$$A_k^+ = \begin{pmatrix} 0_{(k-n) \times n} \\ I_n \\ 0_{\infty \times n} \end{pmatrix}_{\infty \times n}, \quad k > n.$$

Quite similar to what we have for T_n^-, now we have

$$T_n^+ = \sum_{k=1}^{\infty} \psi_{-k} A_k^+, \|A_k^+ z\|_p \leq \|z\|_p, \quad k \geq 1. \tag{2.20}$$

By the way, the representations and bounds we have obtained allow us to improve upon Eq. (2.13):

$$\|T_n^0\| \leq \sum_{k=-n+1}^{n-1} |\psi_k|, \|T_n^-\| \leq \sum_{k=1}^{\infty} |\psi_k|, \|T_n^+\| \leq \sum_{k=1}^{\infty} |\psi_{-k}|.$$

2.4 CONVERGENCE OF THE TRINITY ON L_p-GENERATED SEQUENCES

2.4.1 Some Estimates for Images of Functions from L_p

Functions from L_p have two types of properties: magnitude properties, characterized by integrals $\int_A |F(x)|^p dx$ over measurable sets, and continuity properties, embodied mainly in the continuity modulus $\omega_p(F, \delta)$. In this terminology, functions from l_p have only magnitude properties and no continuity ones. We should expect discretizations $\delta_{np}F$ of elements of L_p to be better in some way than general elements of l_p. Here we obtain several estimates that confirm this surmise.

Lemma.   *If $F \in L_p, p < \infty$, then $f_n = \delta_{np}F$ satisfies*

(i) $\|A_k^0 f_n - f_n\|_p \le (\omega_p^p(F, k/n) + \|F\|_{p,(0,k/n)}^p)^{1/p}$, $k = -1, \ldots, -n+1$,

(ii) $\|A_k^0 f_n - f_n\|_p \le (\omega_p^p(F, k/n) + \|F\|_{p,(1-k/n,1)}^p)^{1/p}$, $k = 0, 1, \ldots, n-1$,

(iii) $\|A_k^0 f_n\|_p \le \|F\|_p$, $|k| \le n-1$,

(iv) $\|A_k^- f_n\|_p \le \|F\|_{p,(0,k/n)}$, $k \le n$,

(v) $\|A_k^- f_n\|_p \le \|F\|_p$ for all k,

(vi) $\|A_k^+ f_n\|_p \le \|F\|_{p,(1-k/n,1)}$, $k \le n$,

(vii) $\|A_k^+ f_n\|_p \le \|F\|_p$ for all k.

Proof.

(i) By Eq. (2.16) $A_k^0 f_n = (0, \ldots, 0, f_{n,1}, \ldots, f_{n,n-|k|})'$ (k zeros), so

$$\|A_k^0 f_n - f_n\|_p = \left(\sum_{t=1}^{|k|} |f_{nt}|^p + \sum_{t=|k|+1}^{n} |f_{n,t-|k|} - f_{nt}|^p \right)^{1/p}. \tag{2.21}$$

For $t \le |k|$ we use the bound on $|(\delta_{np}F)_t|$ from Lemma 2.1.3:

$$\sum_{t=1}^{|k|} |f_{nt}|^p \le \sum_{t=1}^{|k|} \int_{i_t}^{} |F(x)|^p \, dx = \int_0^{|k|/n} |F(x)|^p \, dx. \tag{2.22}$$

For $t > |k|$

$$|f_{n,t-|k|} - f_{nt}| = \left| n^{1/q} \int_{i_{t-|k|}}^{} F(x) \, dx - n^{1/q} \int_{i_t}^{} F(x) \, dx \right|$$

$$= n^{1/q} \left| \int_{i_{t-|k|}}^{} F(x) \, dx - \int_{i_t}^{} F(y + |k|/n) \, dy \right|.$$

Apply the change $x = y + |k|/n$ to map i_t to $i_{t-|k|}$:

$$|f_{n,t-|k|} - f_{nt}| = n^{1/q} \left| \int_{i_{t-|k|}}^{} [F(x) - (\tau_{|k|/n}F)(x)] \, dx \right|$$

$$\le \left(\int_{i_{t-|k|}}^{} |F(x) - (\tau_{|k|/n}F)(x)|^p \, dx \right)^{1/p}. \tag{2.23}$$

Summarizing,

$$\|A_k^0 f_n - f_n\|_p \le \left(\int_0^{|k|/n} |F|^p \, dx + \sum_{t=|k|+1}^n \int_{i_{t-|k|}} |F - \tau_{|k|/n} F|^p \, dx \right)^{1/p}$$

$$= (\|F\|_{p,(0,|k|/n)}^p + \|F - \tau_{|k|/n} F\|_{p,(0,1-|k|/n)}^p)^{1/p}$$

$$\le (\|F\|_{p,(0,|k|/n)}^p + \omega_p^p(F, |k|/n))^{1/p}. \tag{2.24}$$

The final inequality is by the definition of the continuity modulus.

(ii) For $k = 0$ both sides of the inequality are null. Let $k \ge 1$. By Eq. (2.15) $A_k^0 f_n = (f_{n,k+1}, \ldots, f_{n,n}, 0, \ldots, 0)'$ (k zeros), so instead of Eq. (2.21) we have

$$\|A_k^0 f_n - f_n\|_p = \left(\sum_{t=k+1}^n |f_{n,t} - f_{n,t-k}|^p + \sum_{t=n-k+1}^n |f_{nt}|^p \right)^{1/p}.$$

The place of Eq. (2.22) is taken by

$$\sum_{t=n-k+1}^n |f_{nt}|^p \le \sum_{t=n-k+1}^n \int_{i_t} |F(x)|^p dx = \int_{1-k/n}^1 |F(x)|^p \, dx.$$

Bound (2.23) is still applicable in the present situation. Equation (2.24) follows with $\|F\|_{p,(1-k/n,1)}$ in place of $\|F\|_{p,(0,k/n)}$.

Item (iii) follows from Eqs. (2.15)–(2.16) and Lemma 2.1.3. Item (iv) is a consequence of Eq. (2.22):

$$\|A_k^- f_n\|_p = \left(\sum_{t=1}^k |f_{nt}|^p \right)^{1/p} \le \|F\|_{p,(0,k/n)}, \quad k \le n.$$

Item (v) obtains from Eq. (2.18) and Lemma 2.1.3. The proofs of (vi) and (vii) mimic those of (iv) and (v).   ■

2.4.2 The Doubling Property of the Continuity Modulus

Lemma. $\omega_p(F, 2\delta) \le \omega_p(F, \delta)$.

Proof.   Let $|y| \leq 2\delta$. By the triangle inequality

$$\|F - \tau_y F\|_{p,\Omega_y} \leq \|F - \tau_{y/2} F\|_{p,\Omega_y} + \|\tau_{y/2} F - \tau_y F\|_{p,\Omega_y}$$
$$= \|F - \tau_{y/2} F\|_{p,\Omega_y} + \|F - \tau_{y/2} F\|_{p,(\Omega_y + y/2)}.$$

Here the end term results from the change $x + y/2 = t$. As it happens,

$$\Omega_y = (\max\{0, -y\}, \min\{1, 1 - y\}) \subseteq \Omega_{y/2}$$
$$\Omega_y + y/2 = (\max\{y/2, -y/2\}, \min\{1 + y/2, 1 - y/2\}) \subseteq \Omega_{y/2}.$$

Hence, increasing the domains in the above inequality and applying sup gives

$$\omega_p(F, 2\delta) = \sup_{|y| \leq 2\delta} \|F - \tau_y F\|_{p,\Omega_y}$$
$$\leq 2 \sup_{|y/2| \leq \delta} \|F - \tau_{y/2} F\|_{p,\Omega_{y/2}} = 2\omega_p(F, \delta). \qquad \blacksquare$$

2.4.3   The Continuity Modulus is Uniformly Continuous

Lemma.   *For $F \in L_p$, $p < \infty$, the continuity modulus $\omega_p(F, \delta)$ is a uniformly continuous function of $\delta > 0$.*

Proof.   Adapted from Zhuk and Natanson (2001).

Step 1.   Let us prove that $\delta_1 < \delta_2$ implies

$$\omega_p(F, \delta_2) - \omega_p(F, \delta_1) \leq \omega_p(F, \delta_2 - \delta_1). \qquad (2.25)$$

By definition, for any $\varepsilon > 0$ there exists y, $|y| \leq \delta_2$, such that

$$\omega_p(F, \delta_2) - \varepsilon \leq \|F - \tau_y F\|_{p,\Omega_y}. \qquad (2.26)$$

$|y|/\delta_2 \leq 1$ implies $|y|\delta_1/\delta_2 \leq \delta_1$, so for $h = y\delta_1/\delta_2$ by definition

$$\|F - \tau_h F\|_{p,\Omega_h} \leq \omega_p(F, \delta_1). \qquad (2.27)$$

Since $\delta_1/\delta_2 < 1$ by assumption, there is an inclusion

$$\Omega_h = \Omega_{y\delta_1/\delta_2} = (\max\{0, -y\delta_1/\delta_2\}, \min\{1, 1 - y\delta_1/\delta_2\}) \supseteq \Omega_y.$$

This, together with Eq. (2.27), implies

$$-\omega_p(F, \delta_1) \leq -\|F - \tau_h F\|_{p,\Omega_y}. \qquad (2.28)$$

Adding Eqs. (2.26) and (2.28) yields

$$\omega_p(F, \delta_2) - \omega_p(F, \delta_1) - \varepsilon \leq \|F - \tau_y F\|_{p,\Omega_y} - \|F - \tau_h F\|_{p,\Omega_y}$$

$$\leq \|\tau_h F - \tau_y F\|_{p,\Omega_y}, \tag{2.29}$$

where the final step is by the triangle inequality.

Now consider

$$I = \|\tau_h F - \tau_y F\|_{p,\Omega_y}^p = \int_{\Omega_y} \left| F\left(x + \frac{y\delta_1}{\delta_2}\right) - F(x + y)\right|^p dx.$$

Changing $x + y\delta_1/\delta_2 = z$ and denoting $u = y(1 - \delta_1/\delta_2)$ and $\tilde{\Omega} = \Omega_y + y\delta_1/\delta_2$, we have

$$I = \int_{\tilde{\Omega}} |F(z) - F(z + y(1 - \delta_1/\delta_2))|^p dz = \|F - \tau_u F\|_{p,\tilde{\Omega}}.$$

Note that $\tilde{\Omega}$ is a subset of Ω_u:

$$\tilde{\Omega} = \left(\max\left\{y\frac{\delta_1}{\delta_2}, -y\left(1 - \frac{\delta_1}{\delta_2}\right)\right\}, \min\left\{1 + y\frac{\delta_1}{\delta_2}, 1 - y\left(1 - \frac{\delta_1}{\delta_2}\right)\right\}\right)$$

$$= \left(\max\left\{y\frac{\delta_1}{\delta_2}, -u\right\}, \min\left\{1 + y\frac{\delta_1}{\delta_2}, 1 - u\right\}\right)$$

$$\subseteq (\max\{0, -u\}, \min\{1, 1 - u\}) \subseteq \Omega_u.$$

Now Eq. (2.29), the definition and the monotonicity of the continuity modulus give

$$\omega_p(F, \delta_2) - \omega_p(F, \delta_1) - \varepsilon \leq \|F - \tau_u F\|_{p,\Omega_u}$$

$$\leq \omega_p(F, |u|) \leq \omega_p(F, \delta_2(1 - \delta_1/\delta_2))$$

$$= \omega_p(F, \delta_2 - \delta_1).$$

Since ε is arbitrarily close to zero, Eq. (2.25) follows.

Step 2. By Lemma 2.1.5 the continuity modulus of $F \in L_p$, $p < \infty$, vanishes at zero. Hence, the right-hand side of Eq. (2.25) can be made arbitrarily small by choosing $\delta_2 - \delta_1$ small, regardless of where δ_1 is. The left side is nonnegative by monotonicity. Thus, the continuity modulus is, indeed, uniformly continuous. ∎

2.4.4   Major

For $F \in L_p, p < \infty$, put

$$\mu(\delta) = \mu(F, p, \delta) = \max\{\omega_p(F, \delta), \|F\|_{p,(0,\delta)}, \|F\|_{p,(1-\delta,1)}\}, \quad \delta \in (0, 1].$$

Since μ appears as a majorant in certain estimates, I call it just a *major* (luckily, the majors from matrix algebra do not play any role in this book).

Lemma.   *Let* $F \in L_p, p < \infty$. μ *is continuous on* $(0, 1]$ *and vanishes at zero*:

$$\lim_{\delta \to 0} \mu(\delta) = 0. \tag{2.30}$$

If $\|F\|_p \neq 0$, *then* $\mu(\delta)$ *is positive for positive* δ.

Proof.   Continuity of the major follows from continuity of $\omega_p(F, \delta)$ (Lemma 2.4.3) and absolute continuity of the Lebesgue integral (both norms $\|F\|_{p,(0,\delta)}$ and $\|F\|_{p,(1-\delta,1)}$ are continuous in δ). Equation (2.30) is a consequence of Lemma 2.1.5 and absolute continuity of the Lebesgue integral.

Suppose that $\mu(\delta) = 0$ for some $\delta \in (0, 1]$. If $\delta \geq 1/2$, then the intervals $(0, \delta)$ and $(1 - \delta, 1)$ cover $(0, 1)$ and $F = 0$ a.e. on $(0, 1)$, which contradicts the assumption $\|F\|_p \neq 0$. Let's assume $\delta < 1/2$. Then

$$F = 0 \text{ a.e. on } (0, \delta). \tag{2.31}$$

$\omega_p(F, \delta) = 0$ implies, in particular, $\int_0^{1-\delta} |F(x) - F(x + \delta)|^p dx = 0$, which, because of Eq. (2.31), reduces to $\int_0^{1-\delta} |F(x + \delta)|^p dx = 0$. That is, the vanishing behavior of F on $(0, \delta)$ extends to $(\delta, 2\delta)$. By the doubling property (Lemma 2.4.2) we have $\omega_p(F, 2\delta) = 0$. Hence, the above procedure of propagating the equality of F to zero can be repeated a finite number of times to cover the whole interval $(0, 1)$ (actually, covering $(0, 1 - \delta)$ is enough). The conclusion again contradicts $\|F\|_p \neq 0$. Thus, the assumption $\mu(\delta) = 0$ is wrong and μ is positive on $(0, 1]$.   ∎

2.4.5   Inverting the Major

Denote

$$\zeta(\varepsilon) = \zeta(F, P, \varepsilon) = \sup\{\delta \in (0, 1]: \mu(\delta) \leq \varepsilon\}, \quad \varepsilon \in (0, 1],$$

the *inverse* of the major. This is a usual way to obtain a generalized inverse of a function. If, for example, $\mu(\delta) = \sqrt{\delta}$, then $\zeta(\varepsilon) = \varepsilon^2$. The definition works when the theorem on inverses of continuous strictly monotone functions does not. If the graph of the major has a flat section at ε_0, $\mu(\delta) = \varepsilon_0$ for $\delta_1 \leq \delta \leq \delta_2$, the definition supplies the right end of that section: $\zeta(\varepsilon_0) = \delta_2$.

Lemma. *Let $F \in L_p$, $p < \infty$. Then ζ is positive on $(0, 1]$. For sufficiently small ε, $\zeta(\varepsilon)$ inverts μ:*

$$\mu(\zeta(\varepsilon)) = \varepsilon. \qquad (2.32)$$

It also vanishes at 0 if $\|F\|_p \neq 0$:

$$\lim_{\varepsilon \to 0} \zeta(\varepsilon) = 0. \qquad (2.33)$$

Proof. By Eq. (2.30), for any $\varepsilon \in (0, 1]$ there is $\delta \in (0, 1]$ such that $\mu(\delta) \leq \varepsilon$. Then $\zeta(\varepsilon) \geq \delta$ and ζ is positive on $(0, 1]$.

Let $\{\delta_n\}$ be a sequence such that $\delta_n \to \zeta(\varepsilon)$ and $\mu(\delta_n) \leq \varepsilon$. By continuity of μ, then $\mu(\zeta(\varepsilon)) \leq \varepsilon$. For sufficiently small ε a strict inequality here is impossible because if $\mu(\zeta(\varepsilon)) < \varepsilon$, then by continuity of μ we would have $\mu(\delta) \leq \varepsilon$ for some $\delta \in (\zeta(\varepsilon), 1]$, which is at variance with the definition of $\zeta(\varepsilon)$.

Equation (2.33) follows from Eq. (2.30) because in the case $\|F\|_p \neq 0$, by Lemma 2.4.4 $\delta = 0$ is the only point where μ vanishes. ∎

2.4.6 Zero-Tail and Nonzero-Tail Sequences of Weights

In principle, the bounds from Lemma 2.4.1 are sufficient to prove convergence of the trinity if we are willing to abuse the $\varepsilon - \delta$ language. The definitions in Sections 2.4.4 and 2.4.5, this section and Section 2.4.7 are aimed at making the things more beautiful by using just one ε in the main statement.

Everywhere it is assumed that

$$\alpha_\psi \equiv \sum_{j \in \mathbb{Z}} |\psi_j| < \infty, \ F \in L_p, \ \varepsilon \in (0, 1].$$

The objective is to study convergence of the trinity on images $\delta_{np} F$. This convergence is trivial if $\alpha_\psi = 0$ and/or $\|F\|_p = 0$. In Sections 2.4.4 and 2.4.5 we see the implications of $\|F\|_p \neq 0$. Here we combine them with those of the restriction $\alpha_\psi \neq 0$.

The sequence $\psi = \{\psi_j : j \in \mathbb{Z}\}$ with $\alpha_\psi \neq 0$ is called *zero-tail* if there exists a natural n such that $\sum_{|k| \geq n} |\psi_k| = 0$. By rejecting this condition we obtain *nonzero-tail sequences* for which $\sum_{|k| \geq n} |\psi_k| > 0$ for all $n > 0$. For a zero-tail nontrivial sequence the number

$$k_\psi = \min\left\{ n \in \mathbb{N}: \sum_{|k| \geq n} |\psi_k| = 0 \right\}$$

is defined.

2.4.7 Regulator Definition

The *regulator* $r: (0, 1] \to \mathbb{N}$ is used in a statement of type: for any $\varepsilon \in (0, 1]$ there exists a natural number $r(\varepsilon)$ such that a certain quantity (depending on n) does not exceed ε for $n \geq r(\varepsilon)$. In the trivial case $\alpha_\psi \|F\|_p = 0$ we put formally

$$r(\varepsilon) = 1 \ \text{for all } \varepsilon.$$

Consider the nontrivial case: $\alpha_\psi \|F\|_p \neq 0$.

1. If ψ is zero-tail, then k_ψ is a natural number and the set $\{n \in \mathbb{N}: \zeta(\varepsilon)n \geq k_\psi\}$ is nonempty because $\zeta(\varepsilon) > 0$ by Lemma 2.4.5. By definition

$$r(\varepsilon) = r(\psi, F, p, \varepsilon) = \min\{n \in \mathbb{N}: \zeta(\varepsilon)n \geq k_\psi\}.$$

2. If ψ is not zero-tail, then by summability of ψ for all sufficiently large n the inequality $\sum_{|k|>\zeta(\varepsilon)n} |\psi_k| \leq \varepsilon$ is true. In this case the regulator is defined by

$$r(\varepsilon) = r(\psi, F, p, \varepsilon) = \min\left\{n \in \mathbb{N}: \sum_{|k|>\zeta(\varepsilon)n} |\psi_k| \leq \varepsilon\right\}.$$

In both cases directly from the definition we see that

$$\sum_{|k|>\zeta(\varepsilon)r(\varepsilon)} |\psi_k| \leq \varepsilon. \tag{2.34}$$

From this property and Eq. (2.33) we also see that

$$\lim_{\varepsilon \to 0} r(\varepsilon) = \infty. \tag{2.35}$$

2.4.8   Cutter

Let $\alpha_\psi \|F\|_p \neq 0$. Put

$$c(n, \varepsilon) = [\zeta(\varepsilon)n], \quad n \in \mathbb{N}, \quad n \geq r(\varepsilon).$$

I call $c(n, \varepsilon)$ a *cutter* because it is used to cut sums and integrals.

Lemma.   *Suppose $\alpha_\psi \|F\|_p \neq 0$, $\varepsilon \in (0, 1]$ is sufficiently small and $n \geq r(\varepsilon)$.*

(i) *If $|k| \leq c(n, \varepsilon)$, then $|k|/n \leq \zeta(\varepsilon)$.*
(ii) $\sum_{|k|>c(n,\varepsilon)} |\psi_k| \leq \varepsilon$.
(iii) $c(n, \varepsilon) \leq n - 2$.

Proof.   From the definition of an integer part

$$c(n, \varepsilon) \leq \zeta(\varepsilon)n < c(n, \varepsilon) + 1. \tag{2.36}$$

By the condition of the lemma $\zeta(\varepsilon)n \geq \zeta(\varepsilon)r(\varepsilon)$, which, together with the right inequality in Eq. (2.36), leads to

$$c(n, \varepsilon) + 1 > \zeta(\varepsilon)r(\varepsilon). \tag{2.37}$$

Part (i) follows from the left side of Eq. (2.36).

Part (ii) results from Eqs. (2.34) and (2.37):

$$\sum_{|k|>c(n,\varepsilon)} |\psi_k| = \sum_{|k|\geq c(n,\varepsilon)+1} |\psi_k| \leq \sum_{|k|>\zeta(\varepsilon)r(\varepsilon)} |\psi_k| \leq \varepsilon.$$

(iii) By Eqs. (2.33) and (2.35) for small ε the expression $2/(1 - \zeta(\varepsilon))$ is close to 2 and $r(\varepsilon)$ is large, so for such ε we have $2/(1 - \zeta(\varepsilon)) \leq r(\varepsilon) \leq n$. Hence, $2 \leq n - n\zeta(\varepsilon)$ and $n\zeta(\varepsilon) \leq n - 2$. Combining this with the left inequality in Eq. (2.36) proves the statement. ∎

2.4.9 Convergence of the Trinity on L_p-Generated Sequences

In addition to the previous notation $\alpha_\psi = \sum_{j \in \mathbb{Z}} |\psi_j|$ we need

$$\beta_\psi = \sum_{j \in \mathbb{Z}} \psi_j.$$

Theorem. (Mynbaev, 2001) If $\alpha_\psi < \infty$, $F \in L_p$, $1 \leq p < \infty$, then for all sufficiently small ε

$$\max\{\|(T_n^0 - \beta_\psi)\delta_{np}F\|_p, \|T_n^-\delta_{np}F\|_p, \|T_n^+\delta_{np}F\|_p\}$$

$$\leq (2^{1/p}\alpha_\psi + 2\|F\|_p)\varepsilon \text{ for all } n \geq r(\varepsilon). \tag{2.38}$$

Proof. In the trivial case $\alpha_\psi\|F\|_p = 0$ the left side of Eq. (2.38) is zero and the inequality is true for all $n \geq 1 = r(\varepsilon)$, so we can assume $\alpha_\psi\|F\|_p \neq 0$. Denote $f_n = \delta_{np}F$.

The cutter determines what kind of estimate to use. For $0 > k \geq -c(n, \varepsilon)$ $(\geq -(n - 2))$ we use Lemma 2.4.1(i):

$$\|A_k^0 f_n - f_n\|_p \leq (\omega_p^p(F, |k|/n) + \|F\|_{p,(0,|k|/n)}^p)^{1/p}$$

[by Lemma 2.4.8(i) and monotonicity]

$$\leq (\omega_p^p(F, \zeta(\varepsilon)) + \|F\|_{p,(0,\zeta(\varepsilon))}^p)^{1/p}$$

[applying the major and Eq. (2.32)]

$$\leq 2^{1/p}\mu(\zeta(\varepsilon)) = 2^{1/p}\varepsilon. \tag{2.39}$$

Similarly, using item (ii) of Lemma 2.4.1, for $0 \leq k \leq c(n, \varepsilon)$ we have

$$\|A_k^0 f_n - f_n\|_p \leq (\omega_p^p(F, k/n) + \|F\|_{p,(1-k/n,1)}^p)^{1/p} \leq 2^{1/p}\varepsilon. \tag{2.40}$$

After subtracting $\beta_\psi f_n$ from Eq. (2.17) we can sort the terms as in

$$(T_n^0 - \beta_\psi)f_n = \sum_{k=0}^{n-1} \psi_k A_k^0 f_n + \sum_{k=-n+1}^{-1} \psi_k A_k^0 f_n - \sum_{k\in\mathbb{Z}} \psi_k f_n$$

$$= \underbrace{\sum_{k=0}^{c(n,\varepsilon)} \psi_k [A_k^0 f_n - f_n]}_{S_1} + \underbrace{\sum_{k=-c(n,\varepsilon)}^{-1} \psi_k [A_k^0 f_n - f_n]}_{S_2}$$

$$+ \underbrace{\sum_{|k|=c(n,\varepsilon)+1}^{n-1} \psi_k A_k^0 f_n}_{S_3} - \underbrace{\sum_{|k|>c(n,\varepsilon)} \psi_k f_n}_{S_4}.$$

Now estimate S_1 using Eq. (2.40) and S_2 using Eq. (2.39); for S_3 apply Lemma 2.4.1(iii) [the sum is not empty by Lemma 2.4.8(iii)], and for S_4 apply Lemmas 2.1.3 and 2.4.8(ii). The resulting bound is

$$\|(T_n^0 - \beta_\psi)f_n\|_p \leq \sum_{k=0}^{c(n,\varepsilon)} |\psi_k| 2^{1/p} \varepsilon + \sum_{k=-c(n,\varepsilon)}^{-1} |\psi_k| 2^{1/p} \varepsilon$$

$$+ \sum_{|k|>c(n,\varepsilon)}^{n-1} |\psi_k| \|F\|_p + \sum_{|k|>c(n,\varepsilon)} |\psi_k| \|F\|_p$$

$$\leq 2^{1/p} \varepsilon \sum_{|k|=0}^{c(n,\varepsilon)} |\psi_k| + 2\|F\|_p \sum_{|k|>c(n,\varepsilon)} |\psi_k|$$

$$\leq (2^{1/p} \alpha_\psi + 2\|F\|_p)\varepsilon. \tag{2.41}$$

Applying the cutter in representation (2.19) we get

$$\|T_n^- f_n\|_p \leq \underbrace{\sum_{k=1}^{c(n,\varepsilon)} |\psi_k| \|A_k^- f_n\|_p}_{S_1} + \underbrace{\sum_{k>c(n,\varepsilon)} |\psi_k| \|A_k^- f_n\|_p}_{S_2}.$$

For S_1 use Lemma 2.4.1(iv) and for S_2 Lemma 2.4.1(v). Next, apply parts (i) and (ii) of Lemma 2.4.8:

$$\|T_n^- f_n\|_p \leq \sum_{k=1}^{c(n,\varepsilon)} |\psi_k| \|F\|_{p,(0,k/n)} + \sum_{k>c(n,\varepsilon)} |\psi_k| \|F\|_p$$

$$\leq \alpha_\psi \|F\|_{p,(0,\zeta(\varepsilon))} + \varepsilon \|F\|_p$$

$$\leq \alpha_\psi \mu(\zeta(\varepsilon)) + \varepsilon\|F\|_p \leq \varepsilon(\alpha_\psi + \|F\|_p). \tag{2.42}$$

The final line follows from the property (2.32) of the major.

Similarly, for T_n^+ we use representation (2.30), Lemmas 2.4.1(vi) and 2.4.8(i) for $k \leq c(n, \varepsilon)$ and Lemmas 2.4.1(vii) and 2.4.8(ii) for $k > c(n, \varepsilon)$. The result is

$$\|T_n^+ f_n\|_p \leq \varepsilon(\alpha_\psi + \|F\|_p). \tag{2.43}$$

Equations (2.41), (2.42) and (2.43) prove the theorem.   ∎

2.4.10   Discussion

Components of $\delta_{np} F$ vanish in the limit [Lemma 2.1.3(iii)], so the terms $T_n^0 \delta_{np} F$ and $\beta_\psi \delta_{np} F$ in Eq. (2.38) do not converge separately in l_p. To understand why their difference converges to zero, it is useful to consider the operator

$$M_n F = \Delta_{np} T_n^0 \delta_{np} F = \Delta_{np} \left[\left(\sum_{t=1}^n (\delta_{np} F)_t \psi_{t-j} \right)_{j=1}^n \right]$$

$$= n^{1/p} \sum_{j=1}^n \sum_{t=1}^n (\delta_{np} F)_t \psi_{t-j} 1_{i_j}$$

$$= n^{1/p+1/q} \sum_{j=1}^n \sum_{t=1}^n \int_{i_t} F(x)\, dx\, \psi_{t-j} 1_{i_j}, \quad F \in L_p.$$

Thus, the restriction of $M_n F$ on i_j equals

$$M_n F|_{i_j} = \sum_{t=1}^n n \int_{i_t} F(x)\, dx\, \psi_{t-j}.$$

The averages of F over the covering intervals are multiplied by ψ_{t-j} and the results are summed to obtain $M_n F|_{i_j}$. As $n \to \infty$, the partition becomes finer and more and more of the numbers ψ_{t-j} are involved in the sum. The averages tend to values of F at points of $(0, 1)$. In the limit every value $F(x)$ is multiplied by the sum β_ψ of *all* numbers ψ_j. This intuitive explanation is substantiated by

$$\|M_n F - \beta_\psi F\|_p \leq \|\Delta_{np}(T_n^0 - \beta_\psi)\delta_{np} F\|_p + |\beta_\psi|\, \|\Delta_{np} \delta_{np} F - F\|_p$$

$$= \|(T_n^0 - \beta_\psi)\delta_{np} F\|_p + |\beta_\psi|\, \|P_n F - F\|_p \to 0, n \to \infty,$$

where we use Lemma 2.1.7, Eq. (2.38) and Lemma 2.2.1.

The limit $\lim_{n \to \infty} M_n$ is similar to the multiplier operator M in the Fourier analysis defined by

$$(MF)(x) = \sum_{k \in \mathbb{Z}} m_k c_k e^{ikx}$$

if the function F on the unit circumference is decomposed as

$$F(x) = \sum_{k \in \mathbb{Z}} c_k e^{ikx}$$

and $\{m_k\}$ is a given sequence of numbers. M is a composite of three mappings: first F is discretized to obtain its Fourier coefficients $\{c_k\}$, second the Fourier coefficients are multiplied by m_k to get $\{m_k c_k\}$ and, finally, the latter numbers are used as Fourier coefficients in the new series MF.

2.5   PROPERTIES OF L_p-APPROXIMABLE SEQUENCES

2.5.1   Definitions

Let $1 \leq p \leq \infty$ and let the sequence of vectors $\{f_n\}$ be such that $f_n \in \mathbb{R}^n$ for all $n \in \mathbb{N}$. $\{f_n\}$ is called L_p-approximable if there exists a function $F \in L_p$ such that

$$\| f_n - \delta_{np} F \|_p \to 0, \quad n \to \infty. \tag{2.44}$$

If such is the case, the sequence $\{f_n\}$ is said to be L_p-close to F. To make this definition work in the case $p = \infty$, it is necessary to assume additionally that F is continuous on $[0, 1]$, and I prefer to mention this condition each time rather than include it in the definition.

Lemma.   *If $p < \infty$, then Eq. (2.44) is equivalent to*

$$\| \Delta_{np} f_n - F \|_p \to 0, \quad n \to \infty. \tag{2.45}$$

Proof.   If Eq. (2.44) is true, then by Lemmas 2.1.7 and 2.2.1

$$\| \Delta_{np} f_n - F \|_p \leq \| \Delta_{np} f_n - \Delta_{np} \delta_{np} F \|_p + \| \Delta_{np} \delta_{np} F - F \|_p$$

$$= \| \Delta_{np} (f_n - \delta_{np} F) \|_p + \| P_n F - F \|_p \to 0, \quad n \to \infty.$$

Conversely, the same lemmas allow us to derive from Eq. (2.45) that

$$\| f_n - \delta_{np} F \|_p = \| \Delta_{np} (f_n - \delta_{np} F) \|_p$$

$$\leq \| \Delta_{np} f_n - F \|_p + \| F - P_n F \|_p \to 0, \quad n \to \infty. \qquad \blacksquare$$

2.5.2   M-Properties

The name *m-properties* is used for those properties of L_p-approximable sequences that stem mainly from magnitude properties of functions from L_p. Accordingly, *c-properties* reflect mainly the continuity characteristics of elements of L_p. They are more difficult to establish.

Lemma. *Let* $\{f_n\}$ *be* L_p-*approximable. Then*

(i) $\sup_n \|f_n\|_p < \infty.$

(ii) *If* $p < \infty,$ *then*

$$\lim_{n\to\infty} \max_{1\le t\le n} |f_{nt}| = 0.$$

Proof. (i) By Lemma 2.1.3(ii) L_p-approximability implies

$$\|f_n\|_p \le \|f_n - \delta_{np}F\|_p + \|\delta_{np}F\|_p \le \|f_n - \delta_{np}F\|_p + \|F\|_p \le c.$$

Part (ii) follows from Lemma 2.1.3(iii) and

$$\max_{1\le t\le n}|f_{nt}| \le \|f_n - \delta_{np}F\|_p + \max_{1\le t\le n}|(\delta_{np}F)_t|.\qquad\blacksquare$$

2.5.3 Bilinear Forms of L_p-Approximable Sequences

This section starts a series of c-properties.

Theorem. (Mynbaev, 2001) *If* $1 < p < \infty,$ $\{x_n\}$ *is* L_p-*close to* $X \in L_p$ *and* $\{y_n\}$ *is* L_q-*close to* $Y \in L_q,$ *then*

$$\lim_{n\to\infty} \sum_{t=[na]}^{[nb]} x_{nt}y_{nt} = \int_a^b X(s)Y(s)\,ds \quad \text{for all } [a,b] \subseteq [0,1]$$

uniformly with respect to the segments $[a,b].$ *Here we put* $x_{n0} = y_{n0} = 0$ *for the sum at the left to have meaning when* $a = 0.$

Proof. Denote $\{a,b\} = \{t \in \mathbb{N}: [na] \le t \le [nb]\}$ and apply Theorem 2.2.3. The locator (Section 2.1.1) makes sure that $a \in i_{[na]+1}, b \in i_{[nb]+1}.$ In consequence,

$$1_{[a,b]} = 1 \text{ on } \bigcup_{t=[na]+2}^{[nb]} i_t,\ 1_{[a,b]} = 0 \text{ on } \left(\bigcup_{t=1}^{[na]} i_t\right) \cup \left(\bigcup_{t=[nb]+2}^{n} i_t\right).$$

Therefore

$$[\delta_{np}(1_{[a,b]}X)]'\delta_{nq}(1_{[a,b]}Y) = \sum_{t=1}^{n} [\delta_{np}(1_{[a,b]}X)]_t [\delta_{nq}(1_{[a,b]}Y)]_t$$

$$= \sum_{t\in\{a,b\}} (\delta_{np}X)_t(\delta_{nq}Y)_t$$

$$+ \sum_{t=[na]+1,[nb]+1} [\delta_{np}(1_{[a,b]}X)]_t[\delta_{nq}(1_{[a,b]}Y)]_t$$

$$- \sum_{t=[na],[na]+1} (\delta_{np}X)_t(\delta_{nq}Y)_t. \qquad (2.46)$$

By $L_p(L_q)$-approximability and Hölder's inequality

$$\left| \sum_{t \in \{a,b\}} (\delta_{np}X)_t (\delta_{nq}Y)_t - \sum_{t \in \{a,b\}} x_{nt} y_{nt} \right|$$

$$\leq \left| \sum_{t \in \{a,b\}} [(\delta_{np}X)_t - x_{nt}](\delta_{nq}Y)_t \right| + \left| \sum_{t \in \{a,b\}} x_{nt}[(\delta_{nq}Y)_t - y_{nt}] \right|$$

$$\leq \|\delta_{np}X - x_n\|_p \|\delta_{nq}Y\|_q + \|x_n\|_p \|\delta_{nq}Y - y_n\|_q \to 0. \tag{2.47}$$

Here we used Lemmas 2.1.3(ii) and 2.5.2(i).

By Lemma 2.1.3(i)

$$\max \{ |[\delta_{np}(1_{[a,b]}X)]_t|, |(\delta_{np}X)_t| \}$$
$$\leq \max \{ \|1_{[a,b]}X\|_{p,i_t}, \|X\|_{p,i_t} \} = \|X\|_{p,i_t}.$$

A similar bound holds for Y. Hence, of the three sums at the right of Eq. (2.46), the last two tend to zero uniformly with respect to a, b. By Theorem 2.2.3, Eq. (2.46) and Eq. (2.47) we have uniformly in a, b

$$\lim_{n \to \infty} \sum_{t \in \{a,b\}} x_{nt} y_{nt} = \lim_{n \to \infty} \sum_{t \in \{a,b\}} (\delta_{np}X)_t (\delta_{nq}Y)_t$$

$$= \lim_{n \to \infty} [\delta_{np}(1_{[a,b]}X)]' \delta_{nq}(1_{[a,b]}Y) = \int_a^b X(s)Y(s)\,ds. \qquad \blacksquare$$

2.5.4   The Trinity and L_p-Approximable Sequences

In essence, statements for L_p-approximable sequences are obtained from those for L_p-generated ones by perturbation. Since the rate of convergence of $f_n - \delta_{np}F$ in Eq. (2.44) is not quantified, in the next theorem it is not possible to specify the rate of convergence of the trinity.

Theorem.   (Mynbaev, 2001) *If $p < \infty$, $\alpha_\psi < \infty$ and $\{f_n\}$ is L_p-approximable, then*

$$\lim_{n \to \infty} \max\{ \|(T_n^0 - B_\psi)f_n\|_p, \|T_n^- f_n\|_p, \|T_n^+ f_n\|_p \} = 0.$$

Proof.   By boundedness of T_n^0 in l_p (see Eq. (2.41)), convergence of the trinity on L_p-generated sequences (Theorem 2.4.9) and the L_p-approximability definition

$$\|(T_n^0 - B_\psi)f_n\|_p \leq \|(T_n^0 - B_\psi)(f_n - \delta_{np}F)\|_p + \|(T_n^0 - B_\psi)\delta_{np}F\|_p$$

$$\leq 2\alpha_\psi \|f_n - \delta_{np}F\|_p + \|(T_n^0 - B_\psi)\delta_{np}F\|_p \to 0.$$

The rest of the proof utilizes Eqs. (2.42) and (2.43) and is equally simple. $\blacksquare$

2.5.5 Bilinear Forms and *T* Operator Combined

Theorem. *If* $1 < p < \infty$, $\alpha_\psi < \infty$ *and* $\{f_n\}$ *is* L_p-close to F, $\{g_n\}$ *is* L_p-close to G, then

$$\lim_{n \to \infty} \sum_{t \in \mathbb{Z}} (T_n f_n)_t (T_n g_n)_t = \beta_\psi^2 \int_0^1 F(x) G(x)\, dx.$$

Proof. By Hölder's inequality

$$\left| \sum_{t=1}^n (T_n^0 f_n)_t (T_n^0 g_n)_t - \beta_\psi^2 \sum_{t=1}^n f_{nt} g_{nt} \right|$$

$$\leq \left| \sum_{t=1}^n (T_n^0 f_n - \beta_\psi f_n)_t (T_n^0 g_n)_t \right| + |\beta_\psi| \left| \sum_{t=1}^n f_{nt} (T_n^0 g_n - \beta_\psi g_n)_t \right|$$

$$\leq \|(T_n^0 - \beta_\psi) f_n\|_p \|T_n^0 g_n\|_q + |\beta_\psi| \|f_n\|_p \|(T_n^0 - \beta_\psi) g_n\|_q \to 0. \qquad (2.48)$$

The final line obtains by applying uniform boundedness of $\|T_n^0\|$, $\|f_n\|_p$ and $\|g_n\|_q$ and Theorem 2.5.4.

Hölder's inequality and Theorem 2.5.4 yield

$$\left| \sum_{t<1} (T_n^- f_n)_t (T_n^- g_n)_t \right| \leq \|T_n^- f_n\|_p \|T_n^- g_n\|_q \to 0.$$

Here T_n^- can be replaced with T_n^+. Therefore Eq. (2.48) implies

$$\sum_{t \in \mathbb{Z}} (T_n f_n)_t (T_n g_n)_t - \beta_\psi^2 \sum_{t=1}^n f_{nt} g_{nt} \to 0.$$

It remains to recall that by Theorem 2.5.3 $\sum_{t=1}^n f_{nt} g_{nt} \to \int_0^1 FG\, ds$. ∎

2.6 CRITERION OF L_p-APPROXIMABILITY

2.6.1 Statement of Problem

The definition of L_p-approximability appeals to the *existence* of a function $F \in L_p$ for which Eq. (2.44) would be true. Along with the question about what this entails it is natural to ask *when* such a function exists. Different answers are possible. Sufficient conditions and counter-examples are considered in Section 2.7. All of them rely on some external information about the sequence. Here we concentrate on what is called an *intrinsic characterization*, which should satisfy two conditions:

1. it should be equivalent to (that is, necessary and sufficient for) L_p-approximability and

2. it should be expressed in terms of just the sequence itself, without appealing to any other objects.

2.6.2   Continuity Modulus of a Step Function

Here is one of those technical calculations that look arbitrary—and therefore ugly— yet lead to a precise result.

Notation (2.14) conceals the fact that the matrices A_k^0 depend not only on k but also on n. Here it is more convenient to use the well-known fact that if $I_n^- = A_{-1}^0$ denotes the $n \times n$ matrix with the first subdiagonal filled with unities and all other cells with zeros, then all other matrices A_k^0 with negative k are its powers:

$$A_k^0 = (I_n^-)^{-k}, \ k = -1, \ldots, -n+1.$$

Lemma.   *For a natural n consider a step function*

$$F = \sum_{t=1}^{n} c_t 1_{i_t}$$

with some real coefficients and denote $c = (c_1, \ldots, c_n)'$. *If* $p < \infty$ *and* $\delta < 1$, *then*

$$\omega_p(F, \delta) \le (2/n)^{1/p} \left(2 \sup_{0 < y \le \delta} \|(I_n^-)^{[yn]} c - c\|_p + \|I_n^- c - c\|_p \right).$$

Proof.   Because of the symmetry

$$\|F - \tau_y F\|_{p, \Omega_y}^p = \int_{\max\{0, -y\}}^{\min\{1, 1-y\}} |F(x) - F(x+y)|^p dx$$

$$= \int_{\max\{y, 0\}}^{\min\{1+y, 1\}} |F(z-y) - F(z)|^p dz = \|F - \tau_{-y} F\|_{p, \Omega_{-y}}^p$$

the sup in the definition of the continuity modulus can be taken over only positive y:

$$\omega_p(F, \delta) = \sup_{0 < y \le \delta} \|F - \tau_y F\|_{p, \Omega_y}.$$

The condition $\delta < 1$ is not really a restriction because for $y \ge 1$ the set Ω_y is empty.

Fix $0 < y \le \delta < 1$ and denote $k = [yn] \le yn < n$. Because of the form of F we have to start with

$$\|F - \tau_y F\|^p_{p,\Omega_y} = \sum_{t=1}^{n} \int_{i_t \cap \Omega_y} |F - \tau_y F|^p \, dx.$$

Let's look at one term in this sum. Let $x \in i_t \cap \Omega_y$, that is,

$$(t-1)/n \le x < t/n, \, 0 < x < 1 - y.$$

From the definition of k

$$k/n \le y < (k+1)/n. \tag{2.49}$$

These inequalities imply $(t+k-1)/n \le x+y < (t+k+1)/n$ or $x+y \in i_{t+k} \cup i_{t+k+1}$. Hence $F(x+y)$ may take only values c_{t+k} (on $i_{t+k} - y$) and c_{t+k+1} (on $i_{t+k+1} - y$). It follows that

$$\int_{i_t \cap \Omega_y} |F - \tau_y F|^p \, dx = \int_{i_t \cap \Omega_y \cap (i_{t+k}-y)} |c_t - c_{t+k}|^p \, dx$$

$$+ \int_{i_t \cap \Omega_y \cap (i_{t+k+1}-y)} |c_t - c_{t+k+1}|^p dx$$

$$= |c_t - c_{t+k}|^p \, \text{mes}\,(i_t \cap \Omega_y \cap (i_{t+k} - y))$$
$$+ |c_t - c_{t+k+1}|^p \, \text{mes}(i_t \cap \Omega_y \cap (i_{t+k+1} - y)). \tag{2.50}$$

Obviously, with $\Omega_{y,t,k} = i_t \cap \Omega_y \cap (i_{t+k} - y)$ we have

$$\text{mes}(\Omega_{y,t,k}) \le \begin{cases} \text{mes}(i_{t+k} - y) = 1/n, & \text{if } \Omega_{y,t,k} \ne \emptyset; \\ 0, & \text{if } \Omega_{y,t,k} = \emptyset. \end{cases}$$

To avoid the headache of trying to figure out when $\Omega_{y,t,k}$ is nonempty we replace it by a weaker condition that $\Omega_y \cap (i_{t+k} - y)$ is nonempty (the upper bound may only increase). Since

$$i_{t+k} - y = [(t+k-1)/n, (t+k)/n - y), \, \Omega_y = (0, 1-y)$$

and by Eq. (2.49) $(t+k)/n - y > (k+1)/n - y > 0$, the intersection $\Omega_y \cap (i_{t+k} - y)$ is nonempty if $(t+k-1)/n - y < 1 - y$ or

$$t + k \le n.$$

Similarly, $\text{mes}(i_t \cap \Omega_y \cap (i_{t+k+1} - y)) \leq 1/n$ and we can count only those t that satisfy

$$t + k + 1 \leq n.$$

Summing Eq. (2.50) over the indicated t we get

$$\|F - \tau_y F\|_{p,\Omega_y}^p \leq \frac{1}{n}\left(\sum_{t=1}^{n-k} |c_t - c_{t+k}|^p + \sum_{t=1}^{n-k-1} |c_t - c_{t+k+1}|^p\right). \tag{2.51}$$

Consider, for example, the first sum at the right of Eq. (2.51),

$$\sum_{t=1}^{n-k} |c_t - c_{t+k}|^p = \sum_{j=k+1}^{n} |c_{j-k} - c_j|^p + \sum_{j=1}^{k} |c_j|^p.$$

From Eq. (2.16) we know that $(I_n^-)^k c = (0, \ldots, 0, c_1, \ldots, c_{n-k})'$ so the above sum equals

$$\sum_{t=1}^{n-k} |c_t - c_{t+k}|^p = \|(I_n^-)^k c - c\|_p^p$$

and similarly

$$\sum_{t=1}^{n-k-1} |c_t - c_{t+k+1}|^p = \|(I_n^-)^{k+1} c - c\|_p^p.$$

Thus, using also an elementary inequality $(a^p + b^p)^{1/p} \leq 2^{1/p}(a + b)$,

$$\|F - \tau_y F\|_{p,\Omega_y} \leq n^{-1/p}(\|(I_n^-)^k c - c\|_p^p + \|(I_n^-)^{k+1} c - c\|_p^p)^{1/p}$$

$$\leq (2/n)^{1/p}(\|(I_n^-)^k c - c\|_p + \|(I_n^-)^{k+1} c - c\|_p). \tag{2.52}$$

Here, by boundedness (2.16)

$$\|(I_n^-)^{k+1} c - c\|_p \leq \|(I_n^-)^{k+1} c - (I_n^-)^k c\|_p + \|(I_n^-)^k c - c\|_p$$

$$= \|(I_n^-)^k (I_n^- c - c)\|_p + \|(I_n^-)^k c - c\|_p$$

$$\leq \|I_n^- c - c\|_p + \|(I_n^-)^k c - c\|_p.$$

Thus,

$$\|F - \tau_y F\|_{p,\Omega_y} \leq (2/n)^{1/p}(2\|(I_n^-)^k c - c\|_p + \|I_n^- c - c\|_p),$$

which proves the lemma. ∎

2.6.3 Condition X: Discretizing the Continuity Modulus

The discretization operator δ_{np} takes us from L_p to l_p and the interpolation operator Δ_{np} takes us back. How does this two-way relationship extend to continuity moduli? In other words, what is, in terms of l_p, the equivalent of the property $\lim_{\delta \to 0} \omega_p(F, \delta) = 0, p < \infty$? This equivalent, let's call it *condition X*, is established in the next lemma taken from Mynbaev (2001). Denote

$$X(\{f_n\}) = \lim_{\delta \to 0, \, m \to \infty} \sup_{n \geq m, \, 0 < y \leq \delta} \|(I_n^-)^{[yn]} f_n - f_n\|_p \qquad (2.53)$$

for any sequence $\{f_n\} \subset l_p$. We say that $\{f_n\}$ *satisfies condition X* if $X(\{f_n\}) = 0$.

Lemma. *Let $p < \infty$.*

(i) *If $\{f_n\}$ is L_p-generated by $F \in L_p, f_n = \delta_{np} F$, then $\{f_n\}$ satisfies condition X.*

(ii) *Conversely, suppose that a sequence $\{f_n\}$, such that $f_n \in \mathbb{R}^n$ for all n, satisfies condition X. Then the step functions $F_n = \Delta_{np} f_n$ possess the property*

$$\lim_{\delta \to 0} \sup_{n \geq 1} \omega_p(F_n, \delta) = 0.$$

Proof.

(i) Let $0 < \delta < 1$ and $n \in \mathbb{N}$. Since $[yn] \leq yn$, Lemma 2.4.1(i) implies

$$\sup_{n \geq 1, \, 0 < y \leq \delta} \|(I_n^-)^{[yn]} f_n - f_n\|_p \leq (\omega_p^p(F, \delta) + \|F\|_{p,(0,\delta)}^p)^{1/p}.$$

Therefore

$$\lim_{\delta \to 0} \sup_{n \geq 1, \, 0 < y \leq \delta} \|(I_n^-)^{[yn]} f_n - f_n\|_p = 0,$$

which is stronger than $X(\{f_n\}) = 0$.

(ii) As a preliminary step, let's prove that $X(\{f_n\}) = 0$ implies

$$\lim_{n \to \infty} \|(I_n^-)^k f_n - f_n\|_p = 0 \text{ for any } k \in \mathbb{N}. \qquad (2.54)$$

From Eq. (2.53) we see that if $X(\{f_n\}) = 0$, then for any $\varepsilon > 0$ there exist $\delta > 0$ and $m \geq 1$ such that

$$\|(I_n^-)^{[yn]}f_n - f_n\|_p < \varepsilon \quad \text{for all } n \geq m \text{ and } y \in (0, \delta]. \tag{2.55}$$

For a natural k consider $n \geq m_0 \equiv \max\{m, k/\delta\}$ and put $y = k/n \leq \delta$. Then $[yn] = k$ and the preceding bound gives Eq. (2.54):

$$\|(I_n^-)^k f_n - f_n\|_p < \varepsilon \text{ for all } n \geq m_0. \tag{2.56}$$

Put $c = n^{1/p}f_n$ in Lemma 2.6.2. Then the function F from that lemma becomes $F_n = \Delta_{np}f_n$ and

$$\omega_p(F_n, \delta) \leq 2^{1/p}\left(2 \sup_{0 < y \leq \delta} \|(I_n^-)^{[yn]}f_n - f_n\|_p + \|I_n^- f_n - f_n\|_p\right).$$

Applying Eqs. (2.55) and (2.56) we get $\omega_p(F_n, \delta) \leq 2^{1/p}3\varepsilon$ for all $n \geq m_0$. The proof is complete. ∎

2.6.4   Precompactness in L_p

A set K in a normed space L is called *precompact* if every sequence $\{x_n\} \subset K$ contains a convergent subsequence $\{x_{n_m}\}$. Properties of precompact sets in infinite-dimensional spaces parallel those of bounded sets in finite-dimensional spaces. I give an example of how this notion works in Section 2.6.6.

Theorem (Frechet–Kolmogorov).   (Iosida, 1965, Section X.1) *A set $K \subset L_p$ is precompact if and only if*

$$\sup_{F \in K} \|F\|_p < \infty \text{ (uniform boundedness) and}$$

$$\lim_{\delta \to 0} \sup_{F \in K} \omega_p(F, \delta) = 0 \text{ (uniform equicontinuity in mean).}$$

2.6.5   Orthogonality

Lemma.   *Let $1 < p < \infty$. If a function $F \in L_p$ is orthogonal to indicators of all intervals,*

$$\int_0^1 F(x)1_{(a,b)}(x)\,dx = 0 \quad \text{for all } (a, b) \subseteq (0, 1), \tag{2.57}$$

then $F = 0$ a.e.

Proof.   By linearity, Eq. (2.57) extends to

$$\int_0^1 F(x)G(x)\,dx = 0 \quad \text{for all step functions } G. \tag{2.58}$$

If $G \in L_q$ is an arbitrary function, then the projections $P_n G$ are step functions. By Eq. (2.58), Hölder's inequality and Lemma 2.2.1

$$\left| \int_0^1 FG\,dx \right| = \left| \int_0^1 FG\,dx - \int_0^1 FP_n G\,dx \right|$$

$$\leq \|F\|_p \|G - P_n G\|_q \to 0.$$

This generalizes Eq. (2.58) to

$$\int_0^1 F(x)G(x)\,dx = 0 \quad \text{for all } G \in L_q. \tag{2.59}$$

It is easy to check that $H = |F|^{p-1}\operatorname{sgn}F$ belongs to L_q:

$$\int_0^1 |H(x)|^q\,dx = \int_0^1 |F(x)|^{(p-1)q}\,dx = \int_0^1 |F(x)|^p\,dx < \infty.$$

Then, by Eq. (2.59)

$$0 = \int_0^1 F(x)G(x)\,dx = \int_0^1 |F(x)||F(x)|^{p-1}\,dx = \|F\|_p^p$$

and $F = 0$ a.e.   ∎

2.6.6   Criterion of L_p-Approximability

Theorem.   (Mynbaev, 2001) *Let $1 < p < \infty$ and suppose $\{f_n\}$ is a sequence of vectors satisfying $f_n \in \mathbb{R}^n$ for all $n \in \mathbb{N}$. Then $\{f_n\}$ is L_p-approximable if and only if the following three conditions hold:*

(i) *$\sup_n \|f_n\|_p < \infty$ (uniform boundedness),*

(ii) *the limit $\lim_{n \to \infty} n^{-1/q} \sum_{t=[na]}^{[nb]} f_{nt}$ exists for any $0 \leq a < b \leq 1$ (here by definition $f_{n0} = 0$ for all n) and*

(iii) *$X(\{f_n\}) = 0$ (condition X).*

Proof.   **Necessity.** Let $\{f_n\}$ be L_p-close to $F \in L_p$. The necessity of uniform boundedness is proved in Lemma 2.5.2.

In the refined convergence theorem (Theorem 2.5.3) let $\{x_n\} = \{f_n\}$, $X = F$ and let $\{y_n\}$ be L_q-generated by $Y \equiv 1$. Then, by the definition from Section 2.1.2, $y_{nt} = n^{1/p-1} = n^{-1/q}, t = 1, \ldots, n$, and Theorem 2.5.3 gives

$$\lim_{n \to \infty} n^{-1/q} \sum_{t=[na]}^{[nb]} f_{nt} = \int_a^b F(s)\,ds \text{ uniformly in } [a, b] \subseteq [0, 1]. \tag{2.60}$$

This condition implies (ii). Later on in the proof we need a generalization of this property for subsequences: if some subsequence $\{f_{n_m}\}$ of $\{f_n\}$ is L_p-close to $F \in L_p$, meaning that $\|f_{n_m} - \delta_{n_m,p}F\|_p \to 0, m \to \infty$, then

$$\lim_{m \to \infty} n_m^{-1/q} \sum_{t=[n_m a]}^{[n_m b]} f_{n_m,t} = \int_a^b F(s)\,ds \text{ uniformly in } [a, b] \subseteq [0, 1]. \tag{2.61}$$

This is obtained from Eq. (2.60) simply by taking $\{f_{n_m}\}$ as the original sequence.

In Lemma 2.6.3(i) the necessity of condition X is proved for L_p-generated sequences, so for any $\varepsilon > 0$ there exist $\delta > 0$ and $m \geq 1$ such that

$$\sup_{n \geq m,\, 0 < y \leq \delta} \|(I_n^-)^{[yn]}\delta_{np}F - \delta_{np}F\|_p < \varepsilon.$$

Due to L_p-approximability, the choice of m can also be subjected to

$$\sup_{n \geq m} \|f_n - \delta_{np}F\|_p < \varepsilon.$$

By boundedness of $(I_n^-)^k$ [see Eq. (2.16)] for $n \geq m$ and $0 < y \leq \delta$

$$\|(I_n^-)^{[yn]}f_n - f_n\|_p \leq \|(I_n^-)^{[yn]}(f_n - \delta_{np}F)\|_p + \|(I_n^-)^{[yn]}\delta_{np}F - \delta_{np}F\|_p$$
$$+ \|\delta_{np}F - f_n\|_p$$
$$\leq 2\|f_n - \delta_{np}F\|_p + \|(I_n^-)^{[yn]}\delta_{np}F - \delta_{np}F\|_p \leq 3\varepsilon.$$

This proves necessity of condition X for L_p-approximable sequences.

Sufficiency. Put $F_n = \Delta_{np}f_n$. Since Δ_{np} is an isomorphism (Lemma 2.1.7), condition (i) implies uniform boundedness of F_n: $\sup_n \|F_n\|_p < \infty$. By Lemma 2.6.3(ii) condition X ensures uniform equicontinuity in the mean of the functions F_n: $\lim_{\delta \to 0} \sup_{n \geq 1} \omega_p(F_n, \delta) = 0$. In virtue of the Frechet–Kolmogorov theorem, the set $K = \{F_n\}$ is precompact in L_p. Hence, there exist a subsequence $\{F_{n_m}\}$ and a function $F \in L_p$ such that $\|F_{n_m} - F\|_p \to 0$. Then $\{f_{n_m}\}$ is L_p-close to F and Eq. (2.61) is true.

We need to show that the whole sequence $\{F_n\}$ converges to F. Suppose it does not. Then there exists another subsequence $\{F_{n_k}\}$ that is at a positive distance from F:

$$\|F_{n_k} - F\|_p \geq \varepsilon > 0. \tag{2.62}$$

By precompactness, $\{F_{n_k}\}$ has a convergent subsequence. Changing the notation, if necessary, we can think of $\{F_{n_k}\}$ itself as convergent to some $G \in L_p$:

$$\|F_{n_k} - G\|_p \to 0. \tag{2.63}$$

Note that $\{f_{n_k}\}$ is L_p-close to G because by Lemmas 2.1.7 and 2.2.1

$$\|f_{n_k} - \delta_{n_k,p}G\|_p = \|\Delta_{n_k,p}(f_{n_k} - \delta_{n_k,p}G)\|_p$$
$$= \|F_{n_k} - P_{n_k}G\|_p \leq \|F_{n_k} - G\|_p + \|G - P_{n_k}G\|_p \to 0.$$

This allows us to employ Eq. (2.61):

$$\lim_{k \to \infty} n_k^{-1/q} \sum_{t=[n_k a]}^{[n_k b]} f_{n_k,t} = \int_a^b G(s)\,ds \quad \text{for all } [a, b] \subseteq [0, 1]. \tag{2.64}$$

By condition (ii) the limits in Eqs. (2.61) and (2.64) should be the same. We write this conclusion as

$$\int_0^1 (F - G)1_{(a,b)}\,dx = 0 \quad \text{for all } (a, b) \subseteq (0, 1).$$

By the orthogonality Lemma 2.6.5, $F = G$ a.e., which contradicts Eqs. (2.62) and (2.63). Hence, the whole sequence $\{F_n\}$ converges to F and $\{f_n\}$ is L_p-close to F:

$$\|f_n - \delta_{np}F\|_p = \|\Delta_{np}(f_n - \delta_{np}F)\|_p$$
$$= \|F_n - P_nF\|_p \leq \|F_n - F\|_p + \|F - P_nF\|_p \to 0. \quad \blacksquare$$

2.6.7 Explicit Construction

Corollary. *If $1 < p < \infty$ and $\{f_n\}$ is L_p-approximable, then*

$$F(x) = \frac{d}{dx} \lim_{n \to \infty} n^{-1/q} \sum_{t=1}^{[nx]} f_{nt}, \quad x \in [0, 1],$$

is that function to which $\{f_n\}$ is L_p-close.

Proof. This follows from Eq. (2.60) where we can take $a = 0$, $b = x$ and use the Lebesgue differentiation theorem: if F is integrable, then $\frac{d}{dx} \int_0^x F(s)\, ds = F(x)$ a.e. (Kolmogorov and Fomin, 1989, Chapter VI, Section 3).   ∎

2.7   EXAMPLES AND COUNTEREXAMPLES

2.7.1   Definition of Trends

1. A *polynomial trend* equals, by definition, $x_n = (1^{k-1}, 2^{k-1}, \ldots, n^{k-1})'$ where k is natural.
2. A *logarithmic trend* is defined by $x_n = (\ln^k 1, \ldots, \ln^k n)'$ for a natural k.
3. A *geometric progression* is taken to be $x_n = (a^1, a^2, \ldots, a^n)'$ with a real $a \neq 0$.
4. Finally, an *exponential trend* is a vector $x_n = (e^a, \ldots, e^{na})'$.

Obviously, denoting $b = e^a$ we turn the exponential trend into a geometric progression $x_n = (b, \ldots, b^n)'$. A constant is a polynomial trend ($k = 1$), a geometric progression ($a = 1$) and an exponential trend ($a = 0$).

In the conventional scheme the regressors are normalized. This is why we are interested in L_p-approximability of the normalized trends $f_n = x_n / \|x_n\|_p$. The next theorem in the most important case $p = 2$ is proved in Mynbaev and Castelar (2001).

Theorem. *Let $p < \infty$.*

(i) *If $\{x_n\}$ is a polynomial trend, then the normalized sequence $\{f_n\}$ is L_p-close to $F(x) = ((k-1)p + 1)^{1/p} x^{k-1}$, $k \in \mathbb{N}$. When $p = \infty$, this statement is true with $F(x) = x^{k-1}$.*

(ii) *If $\{x_n\}$ is a logarithmic trend, then $\{f_n\}$ is L_p-close to $F \equiv 1$ for all $k \in \mathbb{N}$.*

(iii) *For a geometric progression, $\{f_n\}$ is not L_p-approximable, unless $a = 1$.*

(iv) *For an exponential trend, $\{f_n\}$ is not L_p-approximable, unless $a = 0$.*

Because exponential trends are a special case of geometric progressions, part (iv) follows from item (iii). The rest of the proof is split into sections. See Theorems 4.4.1, 4.4.8 and Lemma 7.2.3 for other examples of L_p-approximable sequences.

2.7.2   Simple Sufficient Conditions

Lemma. *Let $p \leq \infty$.*

(i) *Suppose that for a given $\{f_n\}$, with $f_n \in \mathbb{R}^n$ for all n, there exists $F \in L_\infty$ such that $\|\Delta_{np} f_n - F\|_\infty \to 0$. Then $\{f_n\}$ is L_p-close to F.*

(ii) *Let F be continuous on* [0, 1] *and suppose that a sequence* $\{p_n\}$, *with* $p_n \in \mathbb{R}^n$ *for all n, satisfies*

$$\max_{1 \leq t \leq n} |p_{nt} - F(t/n)| \to 0, \quad n \to \infty.$$

Denote $f_n = n^{-1/p} p_n$. *Then* $\{f_n\}$ *is* L_p-*close to F.*

Proof.

(i) By Hölder's inequality the equivalent definition of L_p-approximability [Eq. (2.45)] is satisfied:

$$\|\Delta_{np} f_n - F\|_p \leq \|\Delta_{np} f_n - F\|_\infty \to 0.$$

(ii) By uniform continuity of F

$$\max_{1 \leq t \leq n} \max_{x \in i_t} |F(t/n) - F(x)| \to 0, \quad n \to \infty.$$

Since $\Delta_{np} f_n = \sum_{t=1}^{n} p_{nt} 1_{i_t}$, we see that

$$\|\Delta_{np} f_n - F\|_\infty = \max_{1 \leq t \leq n} \max_{x \in i_t} |p_{nt} - F(x)|$$

$$\leq \max_{t} |p_{nt} - F(t/n)| + \max_{t} \max_{x \in i_t} |F(t/n) - F(x)| \to 0.$$

It remains to apply part (i). ∎

2.7.3 Proof of Theorem 2.7.1(i): Polynomial Trends

For a continuous function h on [0, 1] its integral $\int_0^1 h(t)\, dt$ is a limit of Riemann sums:

$$\frac{1}{n} \sum_{t=1}^{n} h(t/n) - \int_0^1 h(t)\, dt = o(1).$$

$o(1)$, as usual, denotes a sequence $\{\varepsilon_n\}$ satisfying $\lim \varepsilon_n = 0$. This notation is impersonal in the sense that the sequences $\{\varepsilon_n\}$ that appear in different places of the proof are not the same.

From

$$\|x_n\|_p^p = \sum_{t=1}^{n} t^{(k-1)p} = n^{(k-1)p+1} \frac{1}{n} \sum_{t=1}^{n} \left(\frac{t}{n}\right)^{(k-1)p}$$

we see that $h(t) = t^{(k-1)p}$ is the right choice to approximate $\|x_n\|_p^p$. Since

$$\int_0^1 t^{(k-1)p} dt = \frac{1}{(k-1)p+1},$$

(2.65)

we get

$$\|x_n\|_p = \left\{ n^{(k-1)p+1} \left[\frac{1}{(k-1)p+1} + \frac{1}{n} \sum_{t=1}^n h\left(\frac{t}{n}\right) - \int_0^1 h(t) dt \right] \right\}^{1/p}$$

$$= \left[\frac{n^{(k-1)p+1}}{(k-1)p+1} (1+o(1)) \right]^{1/p}$$

$$= \left(\frac{n^{(k-1)p+1}}{(k-1)p+1} \right)^{1/p} (1+o(1)).$$

(2.66)

The normalized trend is

$$f_n = \left(\frac{(k-1)p+1}{n} \right)^{1/p} \left(\left(\frac{1}{n}\right)^{k-1}, \ldots, \left(\frac{n}{n}\right)^{k-1} \right)' (1+o(1)).$$

(2.67)

Put $p_n = n^{1/p} f_n$, $F(x) = ((k-1)p+1)^{1/p} x^{p-1}$. From Eq. (2.67) we derive

$$|p_{nt} - F(t/n)| = ((k-1)p+1)^{1/p} (t/n)^{k-1} o(1).$$

Theorem 2.7.1(i) follows from this equation and Lemma 2.7.2(ii) because here $o(1)$ is a sequence that does not depend on t.

2.7.4   Proof of Theorem 2.7.1(ii): Logarithmic Trends

Denote, for any real m,

$$I_m(n) = \int_2^n \ln^m x\, dx.$$

Since no closed-form formula of type (2.65) exists, establishing an analog of (2.66) will be more difficult.

Step 1. Let us prove that

$$I_m(n) = n \ln^m n (1+o(1)).$$

(2.68)

Integration by parts yields

$$I_m(n) = x \ln^m x \big|_2^n - m \int_2^n x \frac{\ln^{m-1} x}{x} dx$$

$$= n \ln^m n - 2 \ln^m 2 - m I_{m-1}(n).$$

This recurrent relation can be used to prove by induction

$$I_m(n) = n \ln^m n + c_1 n \ln^{m-1} n + \cdots + c_{k-1} n \ln^{m-i+1} n$$

$$+ c_k + c_{k+1} I_{m-i}(n) \tag{2.69}$$

for any natural i. Here $c_1, \ldots, c_{k+1}$ depend on m. Now let $m > 0$ and consider two cases.

1. If m is integer, put $i = m$. The end term in Eq. (2.69) contains the integral $I_0(n) = \int_2^n dx = n - 2$ and Eq. (2.68) follows.

2. If m is not integer, put $i = [m] + 1$. From $[m] < m < [m] + 1 = i$ it follows that $-1 < m - i < 0$ and $0 < \ln^{m-i} x \le \ln^{m-i} 2$. Therefore the final integral in Eq. (2.69) is bounded as

$$I_{m-i}(n) = \int_2^n \ln^{m-i} x \, dx \le (n - 2) \ln^{m-i} 2.$$

Again, Eq. (2.69) implies Eq. (2.68).

Step 2. Now we show that

$$\|x_n\|_p = (1 + o(1)) n^{1/p} \ln^k n. \tag{2.70}$$

By monotonicity, for $t = 2, \ldots, n$

$$\int_{t-1}^t \ln^{kp} s \, ds \le \ln^{kp} t \le \int_t^{t+1} \ln^{kp} s \, ds.$$

Summing these inequalities and using the notation $I_m(n)$ we get

$$\int_1^2 \ln^{kp} s \, ds + I_{kp}(n) \le \|x_n\|_p^p = \sum_{t=2}^n \ln^{kp} t \le I_{kp}(n + 1). \tag{2.71}$$

In view of Eq. (2.68) the integrals at the left and right have the same asymptotics:

$$I_m(n+1) = (1 + o(1))(n+1)\ln^m(n+1)$$

$$= (1 + o(1))(n\ln^m n)\left(1 + \frac{1}{n}\right)\left(\frac{\ln n + \ln(1 + 1/n)}{\ln n}\right)^m$$

$$= (1 + o(1))n\ln^m n.$$

The conclusion is that Eq. (2.70) follows from Eqs. (2.68) and (2.71).

Step 3. Fix $\varepsilon \in (0, 1]$ and denote

$$\sigma_{\varepsilon,n} = \{t \in \mathbb{N}: 1 \le t \le [\varepsilon n]\}, \ \tau_{\varepsilon,n} = \{t \in \mathbb{N}: [\varepsilon n] + 1 \le t \le n\}.$$

If $t \in \sigma_{\varepsilon,n}$, then by monotonicity

$$\left|\left(\frac{\ln t}{\ln n}\right)^k - 1\right| \le \left(\frac{\ln n}{\ln n}\right)^k + 1 \le 2. \tag{2.72}$$

If $t \in \tau_{\varepsilon,n}$, then $\varepsilon n < [\varepsilon n] + 1 \le t$, the ratio t/n is bounded away from zero, $\varepsilon < t/n \le 1$, and there exists $c_1 = c_1(\varepsilon) > 0$ such that

$$\left|\ln\left(\frac{t}{n}\right)\right| \le c_1 \ \text{for all } t \in \tau_{\varepsilon,n}.$$

Hence, there is $n_1(\varepsilon)$ that satisfies, for all $t \in \tau_{\varepsilon,n}$,

$$\left|\left(\frac{\ln t}{\ln n}\right)^k - 1\right| = \left|\left(\frac{\ln n + \ln(t/n)}{\ln n}\right)^k - 1\right|$$

$$= \left|\left(1 + \frac{\ln(t/n)}{\ln n}\right)^k - 1\right| \le \varepsilon, \ n \ge n_1(\varepsilon). \tag{2.73}$$

Step 4. Eq. (2.70) implies

$$f_n = x_n/\|x_n\|_p = \frac{1 + o(1)}{n^{1/p}\ln^k n}(\ln^k 1, \dots, \ln^k n)'.$$

If we put $p_n = n^{1/p}f_n$, $F \equiv 1$, Lemma 2.7.2 is not applicable. The values p_{nt} for t close to n are close to 1 and those for t close to 1 are close to 0, so there is no uniform convergence $\max_{1 \le t \le n}|p_{nt} - F(t/n)| \to 0$. Instead, we show directly that $\|\Delta_{np}f_n - F\|_p \to 0$. The interpolated function can be represented as

$$\Delta_{np}f_n = \frac{1 + o(1)}{\ln^k n}\sum_{t=1}^{n} 1_{i_t}\ln^k t = g_n + h_n$$

where

$$g_n = \frac{1}{\ln^k n} \sum_{t=1}^n 1_{i_t} \ln^k t, \; h_n = \frac{o(1)}{\ln^k n} \sum_{t=1}^n 1_{i_t} \ln^k t.$$

$h_n \to 0$ in $C[0, 1]$ and therefore in L_p.

Decompose $g_n - F = S_{\varepsilon,n} + T_{\varepsilon,n}$ where

$$S_{\varepsilon,n} = \sum_{t \in \sigma_{\varepsilon,n}} \left[\left(\frac{\ln t}{\ln n} \right)^k - 1 \right] 1_{i_t}, \; T_{\varepsilon,n} = \sum_{t \in \tau_{\varepsilon,n}} \left[\left(\frac{\ln t}{\ln n} \right)^k - 1 \right] 1_{i_t}.$$

Using the inclusion $\cup_{t \in \sigma_{\varepsilon,n}} i_t = (0, [\varepsilon n]/n) \subseteq (0, \varepsilon)$ and Eq. (2.72) we get

$$\|S_{\varepsilon,n}\|_p \le 2[\mathrm{mes}(\cup_{t \in \sigma_{\varepsilon,n}} i_t)]^{1/p} \le 2\varepsilon^{1/p}.$$

Similarly, applying Eq. (2.73) and $\cup_{t \in \tau_{\varepsilon,n}} i_t \subset (0, 1)$,

$$\|T_{\varepsilon,n}\|_p \le \varepsilon[\mathrm{mes}(\cup_{t \in \tau_{\varepsilon,n}} i_t)]^{1/p} \le \varepsilon.$$

Thus,

$$\|g_n - F\|_p \le \|S_{\varepsilon,n}\|_p + \|T_{\varepsilon,n}\|_p \le 2\varepsilon^{1/p} + \varepsilon, \; n \ge n_1(\varepsilon),$$

which proves L_p-approximability of logarithmic trends. ∎

2.7.5 Proof of Theorem 2.7.1(iii): Geometric Progressions

Case $|a| < 1$. From

$$\|x_n\|_p = \left(\sum_{t=1}^n a^{tp} \right)^{1/p} = |a| \left(\frac{1 - |a|^{np}}{1 - |a|^p} \right)^{1/p} = \frac{|a|}{(1 - |a|^p)^{1/p}} (1 + o(1))$$

it follows that

$$f_n = (1 + o(1)) \frac{(1 - |a|^p)^{1/p}}{|a|} (a^1, \dots, a^n)$$

(recall that $a \ne 0$ by definition). We need to analyze

$$\Delta_{np} f_n = (1 + o(1)) \frac{(n(1 - |a|^p))^{1/p}}{|a|} \sum_{t=1}^n a^t 1_{i_t}.$$

For a fixed $\varepsilon \in (0, 1]$ denote $\tau_{\varepsilon,n} = \{t \in \mathbb{N}: [\varepsilon n] + 1 \le t \le n\}$. Since $[\varepsilon n] \le \varepsilon n$ and therefore $(0, \varepsilon) \subseteq \cup_{t \in \tau_{\varepsilon,n}} i_t$, we have

$$
\int_{\varepsilon}^{1} |\Delta_{np} f_n|^p dx \le \sum_{t \in \tau_{\varepsilon,n}} \int_{i_t} |\Delta_{np} f_n|^p dx
$$

$$
= (1 + o(1)) \frac{n(1 - |a|^p)}{|a|} \sum_{t \in \tau_{\varepsilon,n}} |a|^{tp} \frac{1}{n}
$$

$$
\le c_1 \frac{1 - |a|^p}{|a|} \sum_{t=[\varepsilon n]+1}^{\infty} |a|^{tp}
$$

$$
= c_2 |a|^{[\varepsilon n]p} \to 0, \quad n \to \infty. \tag{2.74}
$$

Suppose that $\{f_n\}$ is L_p-close to some $F \in L_p$. Then, by the triangle inequality, Eq. (2.74) implies

$$
\|F\|_{p,(\varepsilon,1)} \le \|F - \Delta_{np} f_n\|_p + \|\Delta_{np} f_n\|_{p,(\varepsilon,1)} \to 0, \quad n \to \infty.
$$

Since ε is arbitrarily close to zero, $F = 0$ a.e. However, the normalization of f_n implies normalization of F, $\|F\|_p = 1$. The contradiction finishes the proof in the case $|a| < 1$.

Case $|a| > 1$. Let $\bar{x}_n = (a^{-n}, \dots, a^{-1})'$, $\bar{f}_n = \bar{x}_n / \|\bar{x}_n\|_p$, $b = 1/a$. Then

$$
x_n = a^{1+n}(a^{-n}, \dots, a^{-1})' = a^{1+n}\bar{x}_n,
$$

$$
f_n = \frac{x_n}{\|x_n\|_p} = \frac{a^{1+n}\bar{x}_n}{|a|^{1+n}\|\bar{x}_n\|_p} = (\text{sgn}a)^{1+n}\bar{f}_n,
$$

$$
\Delta_{np}\bar{f}_n = (1 + o(1)) \frac{(n(1 - |b|^p))^{1/p}}{|b|} \sum_{t=1}^{n} b^{n-t+1} 1_{i_t},
$$

$$
\Delta_{np} f_n = (\text{sgn}a)^{1+n} \Delta_{np}\bar{f}_n.
$$

Since $|b| < 1$, the proof for the case $|a| < 1$ applies to $\bar{f}_n$, with the roles of the left and right endpoints of the interval $(0, 1)$ changed. Specifically, for $\varepsilon \in (0, 1)$ let $\sigma_{\varepsilon,n} = \{t \in \mathbb{N}: 1 \le t \le [(1 - \varepsilon)n] + 1\}$. By the definition of the integer part, $(1 - \varepsilon)n < [(1 - \varepsilon)n] + 1$, which implies $(1 - \varepsilon) < \{[(1 - \varepsilon)n] + 1\}/n$ and $(0, 1 - \varepsilon) \subseteq \cup_{t \in \sigma_{\varepsilon,n}} i_t$. Following the familiar line of reasoning,

$$
\int_{0}^{1-\varepsilon} |\Delta_{np}\bar{f}_n|^p dx \le \sum_{t \in \sigma_{\varepsilon,n}} \int_{i_t} |\Delta_{np}\bar{f}_n|^p dx
$$

$$
= (1 + o(1)) \frac{n(1 - |b|^p)}{|b|^p} \sum_{t \in \sigma_{\varepsilon,n}} |b|^{p(n-t+1)} \frac{1}{n}
$$

$$
\le c_1 \sum_{t=-\infty}^{[(1-\varepsilon)n]+1} |b|^{p(n-t+1)} = c_2 |b|^{p\{n-[(1-\varepsilon)n]\}}.
$$

Because $[(1 - \varepsilon)n] \leq (1 - \varepsilon)n$, we have $n - [(1 - \varepsilon)n] \geq \varepsilon n$ and, as a result,

$$\int_0^{1-\varepsilon} |\Delta_{np}\bar{f}_n|^p dx \leq c_2|b|^{p\varepsilon n} \to 0, \quad n \to \infty.$$

As in the previous case, the implication is that if $\{f_n\}$ is L_p-close to some $F \in L_p$, then by the triangle inequality

$$\|F\|_{p,(0,1-\varepsilon)} \leq \|F - \Delta_{np}\bar{f}_n\|_p + \|\Delta_{np}\bar{f}_n\|_{p,(0,1-\varepsilon)} \to 0, \quad n \to \infty.$$

The conclusion that $F = 0$ a.e. contradicts the normalization $\|F\|_p = 1$ and the proof of Theorem 2.7.1 is complete.

2.7.6 One Abstract Example

This example was suggested to me by participants of the Probabilities and Statistics Seminar of the Steklov Mathematical Institute in 2000. Is the sequence that results from normalization of

$$x_n = (\overbrace{\underbrace{1, \ldots, 1}_{[\ln n]}, 0, \ldots, 0}^{n})'$$

($[\ln n]$ unities in a sequence of n elements) L_p-approximable? Here

$$\|x_n\|_p = \left(\sum_{t=1}^{[\ln n]} 1\right)^{1/p} = ([\ln n])^{1/p}, \quad f_n = x_n([\ln n])^{-1/p}, \quad \|f_n\|_p = 1.$$

Suppose that $\{f_n\}$ is L_p-approximable. Then by the criterion of L_p-approximability [see, in particular, Eq. (2.60)], the limit of

$$n^{-1/q} \sum_{t=[na]}^{[nb]} f_{nt}$$

should exist for all $0 \leq a < b \leq 1$. However, for all sufficiently large n we have $[\ln n] \leq \ln n \leq \frac{1}{2}na < [na]$ and in the above sum there are no nonzero terms. Therefore the function F from Eq. (2.60) should vanish, which is impossible by its normalization. Thus, $\{f_n\}$ is not L_p-approximable.

CHAPTER **3**

CONVERGENCE OF LINEAR AND QUADRATIC FORMS

CONTINUING FROM Chapter 1, general tools from the theory of L_p spaces and probabilities are reviewed, up to martingale CLTs. This, together with the material of Chapter 2, provides us with a launch pad for CLTs for weighted sums of random variables, where those variables are initially m.d.'s and then short-memory linear processes. Next, the desire to obtain convergence statements for quadratic forms forces us to delve into the theory of integral operators. Certain classes of compact operators are studied, including Hilbert–Schmidt and nuclear ones. Both the final statements and some auxiliary results are important for later applications. For example, in Chapter 5 the gauge inequality is applied seven times.

In this chapter we deal with two types of L_p spaces: on the segment $[0, 1]$ or the square $[0, 1]^2$, for approximation purposes, and on a probability space $(\Omega, \mathcal{F}, P)$, for probabilistic results. To distinguish between these, the first two are denoted L_p, as in the previous chapter, and the latter $\mathcal{L}_p$. If X is a random vector, the norm in $\mathcal{L}_p$, $p < \infty$, is defined by $\|X\|_p = (E\|X(\cdot)\|_2^p)^{1/p}$ [the norm of X at the left is in the space $\mathcal{L}_p(\Omega)$ and at the right is in the finite-dimensional space $\mathbb{R}^{\dim X}$, with apologies for the confusion].

3.1 GENERAL INFORMATION

In this, some well-known facts from probability theory are reviewed.

3.1.1 Chebyshov Inequality

Lemma. *If X is a random vector and $\|X\|_p < \infty$, $p < \infty$, then*

$$P(\|X\|_2 \geq \varepsilon) \leq \varepsilon^{-p}\|X\|_p^p \quad \text{for all } \varepsilon > 0.$$

Proof. There are several versions of this inequality, but all of them are based on the same idea. Using an obvious fact that $1 \leq \|X\|_2/\varepsilon$ on the set $\{\|X\|_2 \geq \varepsilon\}$, we prove the

Short-Memory Linear Processes and Econometric Applications. Kairat T. Mynbaev
© 2011 John Wiley & Sons, Inc. Published 2011 by John Wiley & Sons, Inc.

inequality as

$$P(\|X\|_2 \geq \varepsilon) = \int\limits_{\|X\|_2 \geq \varepsilon} dP \leq \varepsilon^{-p} \int\limits_{\|X\|_2 \geq \varepsilon} \|X\|_2^p \, dP \leq \varepsilon^{-p} \|X\|_p^p.$$

∎

An obvious implication is that $\lim_{M \to \infty} P(\|X\|_2 \geq M) = 0$.

3.1.2 Convergence in L_p and in Probability

Lemma. If $p < \infty$ and $X_n \to X$ in $\mathcal{L}_p$, then $X_n \xrightarrow{p} X$.

Proof. This statement immediately follows from Chebyshov's inequality because for any fixed $\varepsilon > 0$

$$P(\|X - X_n\|_2 \geq \varepsilon) \leq \varepsilon^{-p} \|X - X_n\|_p^p \to 0.$$

∎

In our applications usually $p = 1$ or $p = 2$.

3.1.3 Convergence in Different $\mathcal{L}_p$ Spaces

Lemma. If $X_n \to X$ in $\mathcal{L}_p$, then $X_n \to X$ in all $\mathcal{L}_q$ with $q < p$.

Proof. Just apply Hölder's inequality to prove:

$$\int\limits_{\Omega} \|X_n - X\|_2^p \, dP \leq \left(\int\limits_{\Omega} \|X_n - X\|_2^{q\frac{p}{q}} dP \right)^{q/p} \left(\int\limits_{\Omega} dP \right)^{1-q/p}$$

$$= \|X_n - X\|_p^q \longrightarrow 0.$$

∎

One of the standard applications is when the difference $X_n - X$ is represented as a sum of terms each of which tends to zero in its own $\mathcal{L}_p$. In this situation $X_n \to X$ in $\mathcal{L}_p$ with the least p.

3.1.4 Uniform Integrability

A random variable is called *proper* if it is finite with probability 1. All random variables in this book are assumed proper, but this is not mentioned explicitly. For any integrable random variable we can write

$$E|X| = \sum_{t=0}^{\infty} E|X| 1_{\{t \leq |X| < t+1\}} < \infty.$$

The convergence of this series means its remainder should tend to zero:

$$\sum_{t=m}^{\infty} E|X| 1_{\{t \leq |X| < t+1\}} = E|X| 1_{\{|X| \geq m\}} \longrightarrow 0, \quad m \longrightarrow \infty.$$

Requiring this property uniformly for a family of random variables gives rise to the uniform integrability notion. A family $\{X_\tau: \tau \in T\}$ of random variables is called *uniformly integrable* if

$$\lim_{m \to \infty} \sup_{\tau \in T} E|X_\tau| 1_{\{|X_\tau| \geq m\}} = 0. \tag{3.1}$$

The next theorem (from Davidson, 1994) is extremely useful in establishing uniform integrability.

Theorem. (*Criterion of uniform integrability*) *A collection* $\{X_\tau: \tau \in T\}$ *of random variables is uniformly integrable if and only if the following two conditions are satisfied*

(i) $\sup_{\tau \in T} E|X_\tau| < \infty$ (*uniform* $\mathcal{L}_1$-*boundedness*) *and*

(ii) $\lim_{\delta \to 0} \sup_{P(A) \leq \delta} \sup_{\tau \in T} E|X_\tau| 1_A = 0$ (*uniform absolute continuity*)

where A are measurable subsets of Ω.

The advantage of condition (ii) over Eq. (3.1) is that in (ii), for a given δ, the set A can be chosen independently of X_τ.

3.1.5 Cramér–Wold Theorem

Theorem. *A sequence* $\{S_n: n \in \mathbb{N}\}$ *of k-dimensional random vectors converges in joint distribution to a random vector S if and only if a sequence of scalar variables* $\{a'S_n: n \in \mathbb{N}\}$ *converges in distribution to* $a'S$ *for every* $a \in \mathbb{R}^k$.

This theorem, also called a *Cramér–Wold device*, reduces the vector case to the scalar one. It is the main reason why many convergence statements in probabilities theory are given for random variables. In particular, when convergence in joint distribution to a normal vector S is sought and S is to be distributed as $N(0, V)$, the desired conclusion will follow if for all $a \in \mathbb{R}^k$

$$a'S_n \overset{d}{\to} N(0, a'Va). \tag{3.2}$$

This is because, taking $S \sim N(0, V)$, for its linear transformation we get $a'S \sim N(0, a'Va)$. Equation (3.2) is a shortcut for $a'S_n \overset{d}{\to} a'S$ with $S \sim N(0, V)$, so by the Cramér–Wold theorem $S_n \overset{d}{\to} S$.

3.1.6 Linear and Quadratic Forms in Independent Standard Normals

Let $\{u_n: n \in \mathbb{N}\}$ be a sequence of independent standard normal variables. The sequence $\{u_n^2: n \in \mathbb{N}\}$ consists of independent χ^2-variables with one degree of freedom. If a sequence of deterministic vectors $\{c_n: n \in \mathbb{N}\}$ is square-summable, $\sum_n \|c_n\|_2^2 < \infty$, then both series

$$L = \sum_n c_n u_n \quad \text{and} \quad Q = \sum_n c_n u_n^2$$

converge in $\mathcal{L}_2$ and, hence, in probability and distribution. We refer to L as a *linear form* and to Q as a *quadratic form* in independent standard normals. Such variables are convenient for characterizing limit distributions. In the case of convergence to a normal law they are just an equivalent way of expressing the same result, while in the more general cases (when the limit distribution contains both linear and quadratic parts) they become indispensable.

Lemma. *For a k-dimensional random vector S the condition $S \sim N(0, V)$ is equivalent to the representation*

$$S = \sum_n c_n u_n \quad with \quad \sum_n c_n c_n' = V, \quad \sum_n \|c_n\|_2^2 < \infty. \tag{3.3}$$

Proof. Suppose $S \sim N(0, V)$. Let C be the square root of V, partition C into columns, $C = (c_1, \ldots, c_k)$, denote $U = (u_1, \ldots, u_k)'$ and consider a normal vector $T = \sum_{n=1}^{k} c_n u_n = CU$. Then

$$ET = 0, \ V(T) = CEUU'C' = CC' = C^2 = \sum_n c_n c_n' = V.$$

Since a normal vector is completely determined by its mean and variance, we have $S = T$ (more precisely, T is distributed as S).

Conversely, if Eq. (3.3) is true, then S is a limit in distribution of normal vectors $S_n = \sum_{l \leq n} c_l u_l$. Here

$$ES = \lim_{n \to \infty} ES_n = 0,$$

$$V(S) = \lim_{n \to \infty} V(S_n) = \lim_{n \to \infty} E \left(\sum_{l \leq n} c_l u_l \right) \left(\sum_{l \leq n} c_l u_l \right)'$$

$$= \lim_{n \to \infty} \sum_{l,m \leq n} c_m c_l' E u_m u_l = \sum_n c_n c_n'. \qquad \blacksquare$$

3.1.7 Lindeberg–Lévy Theorem

From Davidson (1994, p. 336), *if $\{X_t\}_1^{\infty}$ is an i.i.d. sequence having zero mean and variance σ^2, then*

$$\frac{1}{\sqrt{n}} \sum_{t=1}^{n} X_t \xrightarrow{d} N(0, \sigma^2).$$

If X_t are not centered, the theorem can be applied to $X_t - EX_t$.

3.2 WEAK LAWS OF LARGE NUMBERS

3.2.1 Martingale Difference Arrays

Consider a family $\{\{X_{nt}, \mathcal{F}_{nt}: t = 1, \ldots, k_n\}: n = 1, 2, \ldots\}$, where $\{k_n\}$ is an increasing sequence of integers, X_{nt} are random variables and $\mathcal{F}_{nt}$ are nested sub-σ-fields of Ω, $\mathcal{F}_{n,t-1} \subseteq \mathcal{F}_{nt}$ for all n, t. Such a family is called a *martingale difference array* if

1. X_{nt} are $\mathcal{F}_{nt}$-measurable,
2. X_{nt} are integrable and
3. $E(X_{nt} \mid \mathcal{F}_{n,t-1}) = 0$ for all t, n.

An array can be visualized as a sequence of rows

$$
\begin{array}{ccccc}
X_{11} & \cdots & X_{1,k_1} & & \\
X_{21} & \cdots & X_{2,k_1} & \cdots & X_{2,k_2} \\
\cdots & \cdots & \cdots & \cdots & \cdots
\end{array}
$$

Convergence statements are usually given for row-wise sums $S_n = \sum_{t=1}^{k_n} X_{nt}$. Let $\{w_n\}$ be a sequence of scalar weights and let $\{e_n\}$ be a sequence of zero-mean fixed-variance random variables. Suppose we have to consider convergence of weighted sums $s_n = \sum_{t=1}^{n} w_t e_t$. Upon normalization these sums become $S_n = \left(\sum_{t=1}^{n} w_t^2\right)^{-1/2} \sum_{t=1}^{n} w_t e_t$. With $X_{nt} = \left(\sum_{t=1}^{n} w_t^2\right)^{-1/2} w_t e_t$ the task is cast in terms of arrays, which explains their necessity. In applications $k_n = n$ most of the time.

3.2.2 Martingale Weak Laws of Large Numbers

Statements about convergence in probability of weighted sums of random variables are called *weak laws of large numbers* (WLLN). The definition of *strong laws of large numbers* is obtained by replacing convergence in probability by almost sure convergence. In econometrics convergence in probability is used more often because it is easier to prove.

The next theorem was proved by Chow (1971) in the homogeneous case and generalized by Davidson (1994) to the heterogeneous case. J. Davidson calls it a *martingale WLLN*, even though it is actually about convergence in $\mathcal{L}_p$ (of which convergence in probability is a consequence).

Theorem. *Let $\{X_{nt}, \mathcal{F}_{nt}\}$ be a m.d. array, $\{c_{nt}\}$ a positive constant array and $\{k_n\}$ an increasing integer sequence with $k_n \to \infty$. Suppose $1 \le p \le 2$. If*

(i) $\{|X_{nt}/c_{nt}|^p\}$ is uniformly integrable,

(ii) $\limsup_{n \to \infty} \sum_{t=1}^{k_n} c_{nt} < \infty$, and

(iii) $\lim_{n \to \infty} \sum_{t=1}^{k_n} c_{nt}^2 = 0$,

then $S_n = \sum_{t=1}^{k_n} X_{nt} \to 0$ in $\mathcal{L}_p$.

The cases $p = 1$ and $p = 2$ are the main cases when verification of the conditions of this theorem is possible.

3.2.3   Weak Laws of Large Numbers for Uncorrelated Arrays

Theorem.   (Davidson, 1994, Corollary 19.10) *If $\{X_{nt}\}$ is a zero-mean stochastic array with $E(X_{nt}X_{ns}) = 0$ for $s \neq t$, and*

(i) $\{X_{nt}/c_{nt}\}$ *is L_2-bounded,* $\sup_{n,t} \|X_{nt}/c_{nt}\|_2 < \infty$,

(ii) $\lim_{n \to \infty} \sum_{t=1}^{k_n} c_{nt}^2 = 0$,

then $S_n = \sum_{t=1}^{k_n} X_{nt} \to 0$ in $\mathcal{L}_2$.

As compared to the martingale WLLN, here condition 3.2.2(ii) is not required, the m.d. assumption is weakened to uncorrelatedness and the uniform integrability to simple L_2-boundedness. This result is stated just for comparison purposes. It is not applied in this book.

3.3   CENTRAL LIMIT THEOREMS FOR MARTINGALE DIFFERENCES

CLTs are about convergence of sums of random variables in distribution. When I first started to study this theory, I was puzzled by the number of different CLTs. The variety is perhaps explained by the diversity of applications. Many papers on asymptotic theory in econometrics contain their own CLTs derived from more general CLTs established by probabilists. Here we look at two CLTs that are especially useful when working with m.d.'s.

3.3.1   Central Limit Theorems with Unconditional Normalization

Brown (1971) and McLeish (1974) established similar results (I leave it to historians to decide who did what). The next theorem is taken from Davidson (1994), who took it from McLeish:

Theorem.   *Let $\{X_{nt}, \mathcal{F}_{nt}\}$ be a m.d. array with finite unconditional variances $\sigma_{nt}^2 = EX_{nt}^2$ and let $\sum_{t=1}^{k_n} \sigma_{nt}^2 = 1$. If*

(i) $\sum_{t=1}^{k_n} X_{nt}^2 \overset{p}{\to} 1$ *(stabilization of the sum of squares condition) and*

(ii) $\max_{1 \leq t \leq k_n} |X_{nt}| \overset{p}{\to} 0$ *(terms asymptotic negligibility condition),*

then $S_n = \sum_{t=1}^{k_n} X_{nt} \overset{d}{\to} N(0, 1)$.

This is a good opportunity to comment on the way the theorem is applied. Most of the time the normalization $\sum_{t=1}^{k_n} \sigma_{nt}^2 = 1$ is not satisfied. We have to find the limit of $\sum_{t=1}^{k_n} \sigma_{nt}^2$ and then use it for normalization. If the limit turns out to be 0, we have to investigate the degenerate case. Verification of condition (i) calls for application of some WLLN. The surest way to prove (ii) is to try to derive it from $E \max_{1 \leq t \leq k_n} |X_{nt}| \to 0$.

3.3.2 Central Limit Theorems with Conditional Normalization

The following result from Hall and Heyde (1980, Corollary 3.1) corrects Dvoretzky (1972) who missed the requirement that σ-fields should be nested.

Theorem. *Let* $\{X_{nt}, \mathcal{F}_{nt}\}$ *be a m.d. array with finite unconditional variances* EX_{nt}^2. *Denote* $\sigma_{nt}^2 = E(X_{nt}^2 \mid \mathcal{F}_{n,t-1})$ *conditional variances. Suppose that*

(i) $\sum_{t=1}^{k_n} \sigma_{nt}^2 \xrightarrow{p} \sigma^2$ *(a constant)*,

(ii) *for all* $\varepsilon > 0$, $\sum_{t=1}^{k_n} E(X_{nt}^2 1_{\{|X_{nt}| > \varepsilon\}} \mid \mathcal{F}_{n,t-1}) \xrightarrow{p} 0$ *and*

(iii) *the* σ-*fields are nested over* n: $\mathcal{F}_{n,t} \subseteq \mathcal{F}_{n+1,t}$ *for* $t = 1, \ldots, k_n$, $n = 1, 2, \ldots$

Then $S_n = \sum_{t=1}^{k_n} X_{nt} \xrightarrow{d} N(0, \sigma^2)$.

Formally, in this theorem $\sigma^2 = 0$ is allowed. However, in applications the degenerate case still requires separate investigation. In most practical situations both this and the previous theorem can be applied. The small differences in the resulting assumptions on the error terms are indistinguishable from the practitioner's point of view.

3.4 CENTRAL LIMIT THEOREMS FOR WEIGHTED SUMS OF MARTINGALE DIFFERENCES

In econometric papers and books there are quite a few CLTs for weighted sums of random variables. Sometimes they are not even named CLTs. Anderson (1971), Anderson and Kunitomo (1992), and Hannan (1979) are the examples most relevant to the subject of this chapter. The CLTs obtained in this section are better for asymptotic theory of regressions because, owing to the L_p-approximability notion, they allow us to better trace the link between regressors and asymptotic properties of the estimator. The conditions on the linear processes are also weaker, except for Hannan's result (Hannan, 1979), which is about long-memory processes. Theorems on weighted sums of random elements in linear spaces collected in Taylor (1978) are not very useful in the econometric context. Theorems for mixing processes (Davidson, 1994) are a completely different area. See also Wu (2005) and Wu and Min (2005) regarding long-memory processes.

3.4.1 Weighted Sums of Martingale Differences

The format of the sums is dictated by applications to linear models. Let $\{e_{nt}, \mathcal{F}_{nt}\}$ be a m.d. array. Denote $e_n = (e_{n1}, \ldots, e_{nn})'$. Suppose we have L sequences of deterministic weights $\{w_n^l : n \in \mathbb{N}\}$, where $w_n^l \in \mathbb{R}^n$ for $n \in \mathbb{N}$ and $l = 1, \ldots, L$. Writing all vectors as column vectors and putting $w_n^1, \ldots, w_n^L$ side by side we obtain a matrix of weights

$$W_n = (w_n^1, \ldots, w_n^L)$$

of size $n \times L$. The L-dimensional random vector $W_n' e_n$ is the main attraction in this theme park. Assuming that the m.d.'s are square-integrable and variances of $e_{n1}, \ldots, e_{nn}$ are the same,

$$Ee_{n1}^2 = \cdots = Ee_{nn}^2 = \sigma^2 \quad \text{for all } n, \tag{3.4}$$

we have

$$EW_n' e_n = 0, \ V(W_n' e_n) = EW_n' e_n e_n' W_n = \sigma^2 W_n' W_n. \tag{3.5}$$

The simplifying assumption (3.4) makes comparison of the result for the linear model with those of Anderson (1971) and Amemiya (1985) easier. It can be relaxed by assuming $Ee_{nt}^2 = \sigma_{nt}^2$ where $\{\sigma_{n1}, \ldots, \sigma_{nn}\}$ is L_∞-close to a continuous function on $[0, 1]$.

3.4.2 Assumption on Weights and its Implications

For each l, it is assumed that $\{w_n^l : n \in \mathbb{N}\}$ is L_2-close to some $F_l \in L_2$. By the refined convergence theorem (see Section 2.5.3)

$$\lim_{n \to \infty} (w_n^k)' w_n^l = \int_0^1 F_k(x) F_l(x) \, dx \quad \text{for } 1 \leq k, l \leq L. \tag{3.6}$$

Denote

$$G_n = \begin{pmatrix} (w_n^1)' w_n^1 & \cdots & (w_n^1)' w_n^L \\ \cdots & \cdots & \cdots \\ (w_n^L)' w_n^1 & \cdots & (w_n^L)' w_n^L \end{pmatrix} = W_n' W_n$$

and

$$G = \begin{pmatrix} \int_0^1 F_1^2 \, dx & \cdots & \int_0^1 F_1 F_L \, dx \\ \cdots & \cdots & \cdots \\ \int_0^1 F_L F_1 \, dx & \cdots & \int_0^1 F_L^2 \, dx \end{pmatrix}$$

the Gram matrices of systems $\{w_n^1, \ldots, w_n^L\}$ and $\{F_1, \ldots, F_L\}$, respectively. Then Eq. (3.6) is equivalent to

$$\lim G_n = G. \tag{3.7}$$

By Lemma 2.5.2(ii) all elements of W_n asymptotically vanish:

$$\lim_{n\to\infty} \max_{t=1,\dots,n;\, l=1,\dots,L} |(w_n^l)_t| = 0. \tag{3.8}$$

3.4.3 Central Limit Theorems for Weighted Sums of Martingale Differences

Theorem. (Mynbaev, 2001) *Let $\{e_{nt}, \mathcal{F}_{nt}\}$ be a m.d. array and let $\{W_n\}$ be a sequence of $n \times L$ deterministic matrices with columns $w_n^1, \dots, w_n^L$. Suppose that*

(i) *e_{nt}^2 are uniformly integrable, $E(e_{nt}^2 | \mathcal{F}_{n,t-1}) = \sigma^2$ for all t and n, and*

(ii) *the sequence $\{w_n^l : n \in \mathbb{N}\}$ is L_2-close to $F_l \in L_2$, $l = 1, \dots, L$.*

Then

$$\lim_{n\to\infty} V(W_n'e_n) = \sigma^2 G \tag{3.9}$$

and

$$W_n'e_n \xrightarrow{d} N(0, \sigma^2 G), \tag{3.10}$$

where G is the Gram matrix of $F_1, \dots, F_L$.

By LIE, $Ee_{nt}^2 = E[E(e_{nt}^2 | \mathcal{F}_{n,t-1})] = \sigma^2$, so Eqs. (3.4) and (3.5) are true and Eq. (3.9) follows from Eq. (3.7).

The rest of the proof is split into several sections. Recall that the singularity of the Gram matrix of a system of vectors means that those vectors are linearly dependent. Sections 3.4.4–3.4.6 are about the nonsingular case (det $G \neq 0$) and Section 3.4.7 completes the proof by treating the singular case.

3.4.4 Reduction to One-Dimensional Case and Normalization (Nonsingular G)

Let det $G \neq 0$. By the Cramér–Wold theorem 3.1.5, Eq. (3.10) follows if we establish

$$a'W_n'e_n \xrightarrow{d} N(0, \sigma^2 a'Ga) \tag{3.11}$$

for any $a \in \mathbb{R}^L$, $a \neq 0$.

By Eq. (3.5)

$$V(a'W_n'e_n) = \sigma^2 a'G_n a.$$

Equation (3.7), $a \neq 0$ and linear independence of $F_1, \dots, F_L$ imply

$$\lim_{n\to\infty} a'G_n a = a'Ga \neq 0. \tag{3.12}$$

Hence, for all sufficiently large n we may define

$$S_n = a'W'_n e_n(\sigma^2 a' G_n a)^{-1/2}.$$

This variable is centered, $ES_n = 0$, and normalized:

$$ES_n^2 = a'W'_n Ee_n e'_n W_n a(\sigma^2 a' G_n a)^{-1} = 1. \tag{3.13}$$

It is convenient to work with coefficients

$$c_{nt} = \sum_{l=1}^{L} a_l(w_n^l)_t (\sigma^2 a' G_n a)^{-1}.$$

Then S_n becomes

$$S_n = \sum_{t=1}^{n} c_{nt} e_{nt}$$

and by uncorrelatedness of m.d.'s, Eq. (3.13) can be written

$$ES_n^2 = \sum_{s,t=1}^{n} c_{nt} c_{ns} Ee_{nt} e_{ns} = \sum_{t=1}^{n} E(c_{nt} e_{nt})^2 = 1. \tag{3.14}$$

Here $X_{nt} = c_{nt} e_{nt}$ are m.d.'s. Equation (3.14) shows that the normalization condition $\sum_{t=1}^{k_n} \sigma_{nt}^2 = 1$ from Theorem 3.3.1 is satisfied.

3.4.5   Proving that the Sum of Squares Stabilizes

Condition (i) from Theorem 3.3.1 takes the form

$$\operatorname{plim} \sum_{t=1}^{n} c_{nt}^2 e_{nt}^2 = 1. \tag{3.15}$$

To prove it, we apply the martingale WLLN 3.2.2 with $p = 1$. Denote $\bar{c}_{nt} = c_{nt}^2$ and $\bar{X}_{nt} = (e_{nt}^2 - \sigma^2)\bar{c}_{nt}$. $\bar{X}_{nt}$ are m.d.'s by the conditional second moment condition (i) of the theorem we are proving:

$$E(\bar{X}_{nt} \mid \mathcal{F}_{n,t-1}) = [E(e_{nt}^2 \mid \mathcal{F}_{n,t-1}) - \sigma^2]\bar{c}_{nt} = 0.$$

From the bound $|e_{nt}^2 - \sigma^2| \le e_{nt}^2 + \sigma^2$ we have

$$\{|e_{nt}^2 - \sigma^2| \ge m\} \subseteq \{e_{nt}^2 \ge m - \sigma^2\}, \quad 1_{\{|e_{nt}^2 - \sigma^2| \ge m\}} \le 1_{\{e_{nt}^2 \ge m - \sigma^2\}}.$$

Therefore uniform integrability of $\overline{X}_{nt}/\overline{c}_{nt} = e_{nt}^2 - \sigma^2$ follows from that of e_{nt}^2:

$$
\begin{aligned}
E|e_{nt}^2 - \sigma^2|1_{\{|e_{nt}^2-\sigma^2|\geq m\}} &\leq E(e_{nt}^2 + \sigma^2)1_{\{e_{nt}^2\geq m-\sigma^2\}} \\
&= Ee_{nt}^2 1_{\{e_{nt}^2\geq m-\sigma^2\}} \\
&\quad + \sigma^2 P(e_{nt}^2 \geq m - \sigma^2) \to 0, \quad m \to \infty,
\end{aligned}
$$

uniformly in n and t. Here we have used the Chebyshov inequality $P(e_{nt}^2 \geq m - \sigma^2) \leq 1/(m - \sigma^2)Ee_{nt}^2$.

By Eq. (3.14)

$$
\sum_{t=1}^{n} \overline{c}_{nt} = \sum_{t=1}^{n} c_{nt}^2 = \sigma^{-2}, \tag{3.16}
$$

so condition (ii) of Theorem 3.2.2 is satisfied.

By Eqs. (3.8) and (3.12) with some $c > 0$

$$
\max_{1\leq t\leq n} |c_{nt}| \leq c \max_{t=1,\ldots,n;\, l=1,\ldots,L} |(w_n^l)_t| \to 0, \quad n \to \infty. \tag{3.17}
$$

This fact and Eq. (3.16) show that condition (iii) of Theorem 3.2.2 also holds:

$$
\sum_{t=1}^{n} \overline{c}_{nt}^2 \leq \max_{1\leq t\leq n} c_{nt}^2 \sum_{t=1}^{n} c_{nt}^2 \to 0.
$$

Theorem 3.2.2 allows us to conclude that $\left\| \sum_{t=1}^{k_n} \overline{X}_{nt} \right\|_1 \to 0$, which implies Eq. (3.15).

3.4.6 Verifying the Terms Asymptotic Negligibility Condition

We need to check that

$$
\text{plim} \max_{1\leq t\leq n} |c_{nt}e_{nt}| = 0. \tag{3.18}
$$

Here the conditions on e_{nt} are weaker and the weights c_{nt} are more general than in (Tanaka, 1996, Chapter 3.5, Section 3.1, Problem 4.6).

By the assumed uniform integrability, for any $\varepsilon > 0$, we can choose $m > 0$ such that

$$
\sup_{n,t} Ee_{nt}^2 1_{\{|e_{nt}|>m\}} \leq \varepsilon\sigma^2
$$

which, together with Eq. (3.16), yields

$$
\sum_{t=1}^{n} c_{nt}^2 Ee_{nt}^2 1_{\{|e_{nt}|>m\}} \leq \varepsilon. \tag{3.19}
$$

From Eq. (3.17) we can see that there is a number n_0 such that

$$m^2 \max_{1 \leq t \leq n} c_{nt}^2 \leq \varepsilon, \quad n \geq n_0. \tag{3.20}$$

Denote

$$A_0 = \emptyset, \quad A_t = \{|c_{nt} e_{nt}| = \max_{1 \leq t \leq n} |c_{nt} e_{nt}|\} \setminus \bigcup_{j=0}^{t-1} A_j,$$

$$B_t = \{|e_{nt}| > m\}, \quad t = 1, \ldots, n.$$

Since $A_1, \ldots, A_n$ form a disjoint covering of Ω, we have

$$E \max_{1 \leq t \leq n} |c_{nt} e_{nt}|^2 = \sum_{s=1}^{n} E \max_{1 \leq t \leq n} |c_{nt} e_{nt}|^2 1_{A_s}$$

$(|c_{ns} e_{ns}|$ is the largest of $|c_{n1} e_{n1}|, \ldots, |c_{nn} e_{nn}|$ on $A_s)$

$$= \sum_{s=1}^{n} E |c_{ns} e_{ns}|^2 1_{A_s}.$$

Remembering that $|e_{ns}| \leq m$ on $A_s \setminus B_s$,

$$E \max_{1 \leq t \leq n} |c_{nt} e_{nt}|^2 = \sum_{s=1}^{n} c_{ns}^2 E e_{ns}^2 1_{A_s \cap B_s} + \sum_{s=1}^{n} c_{ns}^2 E e_{ns}^2 1_{A_s \setminus B_s}$$

$$\leq \sum_{s=1}^{n} c_{ns}^2 E e_{ns}^2 1_{B_s} + \max_{1 \leq t \leq n} c_{nt}^2 m^2 \sum_{s=1}^{n} E 1_{A_s} \leq 2\varepsilon, \quad n \geq n_0.$$

The end inequality follows from Eqs. (3.19) and (3.20). As we know, convergence in $\mathcal{L}_1$ implies that in probability 3.1.2. We have proved Eq. (3.18).

This section completes verification of conditions of Theorem 3.3.1 whose application proves Eqs. (3.11) and (3.10).

3.4.7 The Degenerate Case

Step 1. When $F_1, \ldots, F_L$ are linearly dependent, we can renumber them so that $F_1, \ldots, F_K$ are linearly independent and $F_{K+1}, \ldots, F_L$ are their linear combinations,

$$F_j = \sum_{i=1}^{K} c_{ji} F_i, \quad j = K+1, \ldots, L. \tag{3.21}$$

Denote

$$F = (F_1, \ldots, F_L)', \quad P = (F_1, \ldots, F_K)', \quad Q = (F_{K+1}, \ldots, F_L)',$$

with the view to partition F as $F = \begin{pmatrix} P \\ Q \end{pmatrix}$. With the matrix

$$C = \begin{pmatrix} c_{K+1,1} & \cdots & c_{K+1,K} \\ \cdots & \cdots & \cdots \\ c_{L,1} & \cdots & c_{L,K} \end{pmatrix}$$

Eq. (3.21) is just $Q = CP$. The next relationship is between the Gram matrix G_P of the system P and the Gram matrix G of F:

$$G = \int_0^1 FF' \, dx = \int_0^1 \begin{pmatrix} PP' & PQ' \\ QP' & QQ' \end{pmatrix} dx$$

$$= \begin{pmatrix} G_P & G_P C' \\ CG_P & CG_P C' \end{pmatrix}.$$

The proof is complete if we show that $W_n' e_n$ converges in distribution to a normal vector with variance of this structure.

Step 2. To prove convergence of an auxiliary vector, with

$$p_n = (w_n^1, \ldots, w_n^K), \quad q_n = (w_n^{K+1}, \ldots, w_n^L)$$

the matrix W_n is partitioned as $W_n = (p_n, \quad q_n)$. To parallel Eq. (3.21) define

$$\bar{w}_n^j = \sum_{i=1}^K c_{ji} w_n^i, \quad j = K+1, \ldots, L. \tag{3.22}$$

Note that Eq. (3.21) does not imply a similar dependence between q_n and p_n. It is easy to check that with $\bar{q}_n = (\bar{w}_n^{K+1}, \ldots, \bar{w}_n^L)$, Eq. (3.22) in matrix form looks like $\bar{q}_n = p_n C'$. Thus using $\overline{W}_n \equiv (p_n, \bar{q}_n)$ we can define an auxiliary vector:

$$\overline{W}_n' e_n = \begin{pmatrix} p_n' e_n \\ \bar{q}_n' e_n \end{pmatrix} = \begin{pmatrix} p_n' e_n \\ C p_n' e_n \end{pmatrix} = \begin{pmatrix} I \\ C \end{pmatrix} p_n' e_n.$$

From what is already proved in the nonsingular case, $p'_n e_n \xrightarrow{d} S$ where $S \sim N(0, G_P)$. Therefore

$$\overline{W}'_n e_n \xrightarrow{d} N\left(0, \begin{pmatrix} G_P & G_P C' \\ CG_P & CG_P C' \end{pmatrix}\right),$$

that is, $\overline{W}'_n e_n$ converges to the required vector.

Step 3. To prove convergence of the main vector,

$$\delta_{n2} F_j - \bar{w}_n^j = \sum_{i=1}^K c_{ji}(\delta_{n2} F_i - w_n^i)$$

is implied by Eqs. (3.21) and (3.22). Using this equation, orthogonality of m.d.'s and the definition of L_2-approximability, we get

$$\|(w_n^j)' e_n - (\bar{w}_n^j)' e_n\|_{2,\Omega} = \left[E\left(\sum_{t=1}^n (w_n^j - \bar{w}_n^j)_t e_{nt}\right)^2 \right]^{1/2}$$

$$= \sigma\left(\sum_{t=1}^n |(w_n^j)_t - (\bar{w}_n^j)_t|^2\right)^{1/2} = \sigma\|w_n^j - \bar{w}_n^j\|_2$$

$$\leq \sigma\|w_n^j - \delta_{n2} F_j\|_2 + \sigma\|\delta_{n2} F_j - \bar{w}_n^j\|_2$$

$$\leq \sigma\|w_n^j - \delta_{n2} F_j\|_2 + \sigma\sum_{i=1}^K |c_{ji}|\|\delta_{n2} F_i - w_n^i\|_2$$

$$\to 0.$$

We see that $\overline{W}'_n e_n$ and $W'_n e_n$ have the same limit in distribution because they differ by a vector whose probability limit is zero. This completes the proof of Theorem 3.4.3.

3.5   CENTRAL LIMIT THEOREMS FOR WEIGHTED SUMS OF LINEAR PROCESSES

3.5.1   Linear Processes with Short-Range Dependence

Let $\{\{e_{nt}, \mathcal{F}_{nt}: t \in \mathbb{Z}\}: n \in \mathbb{Z}\}$ be a double-infinite m.d. array. Except that the set of indices is wider, this satisfies the same requirements as a one-sided array $\{\{X_{nt}, \mathcal{F}_{nt}: t = 1, \ldots, k_n\}: n = 1, 2, \ldots\}$ from Section 3.2.1. Fixing a summable sequence of numbers $\{\psi_j: j \in \mathbb{Z}\}$, denote

$$v_{nt} = \sum_{j \in \mathbb{Z}} e_{n,t-j}\psi_j, \quad t \in \mathbb{Z}.$$

The array $\{v_{nt}: t, n \in \mathbb{Z}\}$ is called a *linear process* (with short-range dependence). This definition takes account of the array structure of $\{e_{nt}\}$ and is only marginally more general than the definition in Section 1.9.6.

3.5.2   Central Limit Theorems for Weighted Sums of Linear Processes

For each n, denote $v_n = (v_{n1}, \ldots, v_{nn})'$ and

$$\alpha_\psi = \sum_{j \in \mathbb{Z}} |\psi_j|, \quad \beta_\psi = \sum_{j \in \mathbb{Z}} \psi_j.$$

Theorem.   (Mynbaev, 2001) *Let $\{e_{nt}, \ \mathcal{F}_{nt}\}$ be a double-infinite m.d. array and let $\{W_n\}$ be a sequence of $n \times L$ matrices with columns $w_n^1, \ldots, w_n^L$. Suppose that*

(i) *e_{nt}^2 are uniformly integrable and $E(e_{nt}^2 | \mathcal{F}_{n,t-1}) = \sigma^2$ for all t and n,*

(ii) *the sequence $\{w_n^l : n \in \mathbb{N}\}$ is L_2-close to $F_l \in L_2, l = 1, \ldots, L$, and*

(iii) *$\alpha_\psi < \infty$.*

With the same W_n and G as in Section 3.4.3, the following statements are true:

(a) *If $\beta_\psi \neq 0$, then*

$$W_n' v_n \xrightarrow{d} N(0, (\sigma\beta_\psi)^2 G). \tag{3.23}$$

(b) *If $\beta_\psi = 0$, then*

$$\operatorname{plim} W_n' v_n = 0.$$

In both cases

$$\lim_{n \to \infty} V(W_n' v_n) = (\sigma\beta_\psi)^2 G. \tag{3.24}$$

3.5.2.1   A Word on Precision   Many parts of the proof rely on condition (iii), and long-memory processes are not covered by the present approach. In the case of equal weights $w_{nt} = n^{-1/2}$, $t = 1, \ldots, n$, there is a stronger result (Hall and Heyde, 1980, Corollary 5.2, in which the series β_ψ converges conditionally). Further, since G contains L_2-norms of F_l, the functions $F_1, \ldots, F_L$ cannot be taken from a wider class than L_2. See also Wu (2005) and Wu and Min (2005) regarding long-memory processes.

3.5.3   T-Decomposition for Linear Forms

Consider the convolution operator $T_n: \mathbb{R}_2^n \to l_2(\mathbb{Z})$ defined by

$$(T_n w)_j = \sum_{t=1}^n w_t \psi_{t-j}, \quad j \in \mathbb{Z}.$$

I call T_n a *T-operator*, alluding to the fact that it crowns the trinity of operators from Section 2.3.1. Changing the order of summation, it is easy to see that for any vector of weights $w_n \in \mathbb{R}_2^n$ the linear form $w_n' v_n$ is

$$w_n' v_n = \sum_{t=1}^{n} w_{nt} \sum_{j \in \mathbb{Z}} e_{n,t-j} \psi_j$$

$$= \sum_{i \in \mathbb{Z}} e_{ni} \sum_{t=1}^{n} w_{nt} \psi_{t-i} = \sum_{i \in \mathbb{Z}} e_{ni} (T_n w_n)_i. \tag{3.25}$$

Verbally, convolution of $\{\psi_j\}$ with $\{e_{nt}\}$ induces convolution of $\{\psi_j\}$ with the weights. When I was giving a seminar at Steklov Mathematical Institute in Moscow in December 2000, those present immediately guessed that I had thrown over the convolution from $\{e_{nt}\}$ to w_n, as done in Eq. (3.25). I call Eq. (3.25) a *T-decomposition* to mean two things: it involves the *T*-operator and, for some people, it is trivial.

If $\psi_j = 0$ for $j < 0$ and $w_{n1} = \cdots = w_{nn} = 1$, then

$$v_{nt} = \sum_{j=-\infty}^{t} e_{n,j} \psi_{t-j}, \quad (T_n w_n)_j = \sum_{t=\max\{1, j\}}^{n} \psi_{t-j}$$

and Eq. (3.25) becomes

$$\sum_{t=1}^{n} \sum_{j=-\infty}^{t} e_{n,j} \psi_{t-j} = \sum_{j \in \mathbb{Z}} e_{nj} \sum_{t=\max\{1, j\}}^{n} \psi_{t-j}.$$

This equation is known as the *Beveridge–Nelson decomposition* (Beveridge and Nelson, 1981). Ever since it was introduced it has been used to prove limit results by *perturbation argument*: the asymptotic statement is established first for uncorrelated innovations and then extended to linear processes by showing that the asymptotics is the same. See plenty of examples in (Tanaka 1996). Here Eq. (3.25) serves the same purpose.

3.5.4   Proving Convergence of $W_n' v_n$

Let us show that

$$\text{plim}(W_n' v_n - (B_\psi W_n)' e_n) = 0. \tag{3.26}$$

By Eq. (3.25) and the definition of the trinity (see Section 2.3.1), the lth component of the vector $u_n \equiv W_n' v_n - (B_\psi W_n)' e_n$ equals

$$u_{nl} = \sum_{i \in \mathbb{Z}} e_{ni} (T_n w_n^l)_i - B_\psi \sum_{t=1}^{n} (w_n^l)_t e_{nt}$$

$$= \sum_{t=1}^{n} e_{nt}((T_n^0 - B_\psi) w_n^l)_t + \sum_{t<1} e_{nt}(T_n^- w_n^l)_t + \sum_{t>n} e_{nt}(T_n^+ w_n^l)_t.$$

Hence, by orthogonality of m.d.'s and Theorem 2.5.4 (convergence of the trinity on L_p-approximable sequences)

$$Eu_{nl}^2 = \sigma^2[\|(T_n^0 - B_\psi)w_n^l\|_2^2 + \|T_n^- w_n^l\|_2^2 + \|T_n^+ w_n^l\|_2^2] \to 0, \quad n \to \infty.$$

Convergence in $\mathcal{L}_p$ implies that in probability. Thus Eq. (3.26) is true.

Now we can proceed with proving statements (a) and (b) in Theorem 3.5.2.

(a) Let $\beta_\psi \neq 0$. Since $\beta_\psi W_n$ and $\{e_{nt}, \mathcal{F}_{nt}\}$ satisfy the assumptions of Theorem 3.4.3 ($\{\beta_\psi w_n^l : n \in \mathbb{N}\}$ is L_2-close to $\beta_\psi F_l$, $l = 1, \ldots, L$), Eq. (3.10) gives

$$(\beta_\psi W_n)'e_n \xrightarrow{d} N(0, (\sigma\beta_\psi)^2 G).$$

Owing to Eq. (3.26), this equation proves (a).

Statement (b) follows directly from Eq. (3.26) if $\beta_\psi = 0$.

3.5.5 *T*-Decomposition for Means of Quadratic Forms

Applying Eq. (3.25) to w_n^k and w_n^l and multiplying the resulting equations we get

$$(w_n^k)'v_n(w_n^l)'v_n = (w_n^k)'v_n v_n' w_n^l$$

$$= \sum_{i \in \mathbb{Z}} e_{ni}(T_n w_n^k)_i \sum_{j \in \mathbb{Z}} e_{nj}(T_n w_n^l)_j, \quad k, l = 1, \ldots, L.$$

Now by the definition of the trinity and orthogonality of m.d.'s

$$E(w_n^k)'v_n v_n' w_n^l = \sigma^2 \sum_{j \in \mathbb{Z}} (T_n w_n^k)_j (T_n w_n^l)_j$$

$$= \sigma^2[(T_n^0 w_n^k, T_n^0 w_n^l) + (T_n^- w_n^k, T_n^- w_n^l)$$

$$+ (T_n^+ w_n^k, T_n^+ w_n^l)], \tag{3.27}$$

where $(\cdot, \cdot)$ denotes the scalar product in l_2.

3.5.6 Proving Convergence of Variances

To the elements of

$$V(W_n' v_n) = EW_n' v_n v_n' W_n = (E(w_n^k)'v_n v_n' w_n^l)_{k,l=1}^L$$

we apply Eq. (3.27). By the Cauchy–Schwarz inequality, boundedness of the trinity 2.3.2 and Theorem 2.5.4

$$|(T_n^0 w_n^k, T_n^0 w_n^l) - \beta_\psi^2(w_n^k, w_n^l)|$$

$$\leq |((T_n^0 - B_\psi)w_n^k, T_n^0 w_n^l)| + |(B_\psi w_n^k, (T_n^0 - B_\psi)w_n^l)|$$

$$\leq \|(T_n^0 - B_\psi)w_n^k\|_2 \|T_n^0 w_n^l\|_2 + \|B_\psi w_n^k\|_2 \|(T_n^0 - B_\psi)w_n^l\|_2$$

$$\leq \alpha_\psi \|(T_n^0 - B_\psi)w_n^k\|_2 \sup_n \|w_n^l\|_2 + |\beta_\psi| \|(T_n^0 - B_\psi)w_n^l\|_2 \sup_n \|w_n^k\|_2 \to 0.$$

The other two terms in Eq. (3.27) are easier to handle:

$$|(T_n^\pm w_n^k, T_n^\pm w_n^l)| \le \|T_n^\pm w_n^k\|_2 \, \|T_n^\pm w_n^l\|_2 \to 0.$$

The above estimates show that

$$\lim_{n \to \infty} E(w_n^k)' v_n v_n' w_n^l = \lim_{n \to \infty} E(\beta_\psi w_n^k)' e_n e_n' \beta_\psi w_n^l.$$

Thus, $V(W_n' v_n)$ is a perturbation of $V((\beta_\psi W_n)' e_n)$, which tends to $(\sigma \beta_\psi)^2 G$ by Eq. (3.9).

The proof of Theorem 3.5.2 is complete.

3.6 L_p-APPROXIMABLE SEQUENCES OF MATRICES

The theory in the preceding sections admits generalizations in different directions. This section develops some results necessary for spatial models. A different track is followed in Chapter 4.

3.6.1 Discretization and Interpolation in the Two-Dimensional Case

Corresponding to uniform coverings of $(0, 1)$ we can define uniform coverings of the square $Q = (0, 1)^2$ consisting of small squares

$$q_{st} = i_s \times i_t, \quad 1 \le s, t \le n,$$

of area n^{-2}. For a given $F \in L_p((0, 1)^2)$, $\delta_{np} F$ is defined by

$$(\delta_{np} F)_{st} = n^{2/q} \int_{q_{st}} F(x) \, dx, \quad 1 \le s, t \le n,$$

[here $x = (x_1, x_2)$ and dx is the Lebesgue measure on the plane]. If f is a matrix of size $n \times n$, the step function $\Delta_{np} f$ is, by definition,

$$\Delta_{np} f = n^{2/p} \sum_{s,t=1}^{n} f_{st} 1_{q_{st}}.$$

δ_{np} and Δ_{np} are called *discretization* and *interpolation operators*, respectively.

Lemma

(i) For all $F \in L_p((0, 1)^2)$ and $f \in l_p$

$$\|\delta_{np} F\|_p \le \|F\|_p, \quad \|\Delta_{np} f\|_p = \|f\|_p. \tag{3.28}$$

(ii) *If F is symmetric, $F(x, y) = F(y, x)$ for all $(x, y) \in (0, 1)^2$, then $\delta_{np}F$ is a symmetric matrix.*

(iii) *To distinguish the 2-D and 1-D cases, denote δ_{np}^2 as the operator defined here and δ_{np}^1 its 1-D cousin from Section 2.1.2. If $F(x, y) = G(x)H(y)$, then $(\delta_{np}^2 F)_{st} = (\delta_{np}^1 G)_s (\delta_{np}^1 H)_t$, for all s, t.*

Proof.

    (i) Equation (3.28) is proved as the corresponding properties in Sections 2.1.3 and 2.1.7.

    (ii) Observe that $(x, y) \in q_{st}$ if and only if $(y, x) \in q_{ts}$ and therefore by the symmetry of F

$$(\delta_{np}F)_{st} = n^{2/q} \int_{q_{st}} F(x, y)\, dx\, dy = n^{2/q} \int_{q_{ts}} F(x, y)\, dx\, dy = (\delta_{np}F)_{ts}.$$

    (x and y are real and dx and dy are linear Lebesgue measures).

    (iii) Obviously,

$$(\delta_{np}^2 F)_{st} = n^{1/q} \int_{i_s} G(x)\, dx \cdot n^{1/q} \int_{i_t} H(y)\, dy = (\delta_{np}^1 G)_s (\delta_{np}^1 H)_t.$$

∎

3.6.2   Continuity Modulus

Let τ_y be the *translation operator* by a vector $y \in \mathbb{R}^2$. Denote

$$Q = (0, 1)^2, \quad Q - y = \{x - y \colon x \in Q\}, \quad Q_y = Q \cap (Q - y).$$

If F is defined on Q, then $F - \tau_y F$ is defined on Q_y. With this notation, the definition of the *continuity modulus* is quite similar to that in the 1-D case:

$$\omega_p(F, \delta) = \sup_{\|y\|_2 \leq \delta} \|F - \tau_y F\|_{p, Q_y}, \quad \delta > 0.$$

Lemma.   *For all $F \in L_p(Q)$ and $1 \leq p < \infty$ we have $\lim_{\delta \to 0} \omega_p(F, \delta) = 0$.*
The proof is similar to the proof of Lemma 2.1.5.

3.6.3   The Haar Projector

The *Haar projector* P_n is defined on the integrable on Q functions F by

$$P_n F = n^2 \sum_{s,t=1}^{n} \int_{q_{st}} F(x)\, dx\, 1_{q_{st}}.$$

Lemma.   *For all $F \in L_p(Q)$ and $1 \le p \le \infty$*

(i) $P_n = \Delta_{np}\delta_{np}$.

(ii) $\|P_nF\|_p \le \|F\|_p$.

Proof.

(i) Directly from the definitions

$$\Delta_{np}(\delta_{np}F) = n^{2/p}\sum_{s,t=1}^{n}(\delta_{np}F)_{st}1_{q_{st}}$$

$$= n^{2/p+2/q}\sum_{s,t=1}^{n}\int_{q_{st}}F(x)\,dx1_{q_{st}} = P_nF.$$

(ii) Follows from (i) and Eq. (3.28). ∎

3.6.4   Convergence of Haar Projectors to the Identity Operator (Two-Dimensional Case)

Lemma.   *If $p < \infty$, then the sequence $\{P_n\}$ converges strongly to the identity operator with the next bound on the rate of convergence:*

$$\|P_nF - F\|_p \le (2\pi)^{1/p}\omega_p(F, \sqrt{2}/n).$$

Proof.

Step 1. Splitting the integral over Q into integrals over q_{st} we have

$$\|P_nF - F\|_p^p = \sum_{s,t=1}^{n}\int_{q_{st}}|P_nF - F|^p\,dy$$

(P_nF on q_{st} is just $n^2\int_{q_{st}}F\,dx$)

$$= \sum_{s,t=1}^{n}\int_{q_{st}}\left|n^2\int_{q_{st}}F(x)\,dx - n^2\int_{q_{st}}F(y)\,dx\right|^p dy.$$

Next, apply Hölder's inequality to the inner integral and use the identity $p - p/q = 1$

$$\|P_nF - F\|_p^p = n^{2p}\sum_{s,t=1}^{n}\int_{q_{st}}\left|\int_{q_{st}}(F(x) - F(y))\,dx\right|^p dy$$

$$\le n^2\sum_{s,t=1}^{n}\int_{q_{st}}\int_{q_{st}}|F(x) - F(y)|^p\,dx\,dy.$$

Step 2. To evaluate the small integrals that appear here, consider an integral over a square $\Delta = (a, a + b)^2$

$$I = \int\int_{\Delta\,\Delta} |F(x) - F(y)|^p dx\, dy$$

(change $x = y + z$ in the inner integral)

$$= \int\int_{\Delta\,\Delta - y} |F(y + z) - F(y)|^p dz\, dy.$$

Following exactly Step 2 of the proof of Lemma 2.2.1 would be difficult. Instead, we use the inclusion

$$A \equiv \{(y, z): y \in \Delta, \quad z \in \Delta - y\} \subseteq B \equiv \{(y, z): \|z\|_2 \leq \sqrt{2}b,$$
$$y \in \Delta_z\}. \tag{3.29}$$

This inclusion is proved by showing that each element of A belongs to B. Let $(y, z) \in A$. Then there is $x \in \Delta$ such that $z = x - y$. Since x and y belong to the same square with diagonal of length $\sqrt{2}$, we have $\|z\|_2 \leq \sqrt{2}b$. Further, $y \in \Delta$ and $y = x - z \in \Delta - z$ imply $y \in \Delta_z$. We have shown that $(y, z) \in B$.

Equation (3.29) allows us to estimate I as

$$I = \int_A |F(y) - F(y + z)|^p dz\, dy \leq \int_B |F(y) - F(y + z)|^p dz\, dy$$

$$= \int_{\|z\|_2 \leq \sqrt{2}b} \left(\int_{\Delta_z} |F(y) - (\tau_z F)(y)|^p dy \right) dz.$$

Step 3. Summarizing Steps 1 and 2

$$\|P_n F - F\|_p^p \leq n^2 \sum_{s,t=1}^n \int_{\|z\|_2 \leq \sqrt{2}/n} \left(\int_{(q_{st})_z} |F - \tau_z F|^p dy \right) dz$$

and noting that

$$\bigcup_{s,t} (q_{st})_z = \bigcup_{s,t} [q_{st} \cap (q_{st} - z)] \subseteq Q \cap (Q - z) = Q_z$$

we finally arrive at

$$\|P_n F - F\|_p^p \leq n^2 \int\limits_{\|z\|_2 \leq \sqrt{2}/n} \left(\int\limits_{Q_z} |F - \tau_z F|^p dy \right) dz$$

$$\leq \omega_p^p(F, \sqrt{2}/n) n^2 \int\limits_{\|z\|_2 \leq \sqrt{2}/n} dz = 2\pi \omega_p^p(F, \sqrt{2}/n).$$

∎

3.6.5 L_p-Approximable Sequences of Matrices

A sequence of matrices $\{f_n : n \in \mathbb{N}\}$, where f_n is of size $n \times n$ for all n, is called L_p-approximable if there exists a function $F \in L_p((0, 1)^2)$ satisfying the condition

$$\|f_n - \delta_{np} F\|_p \longrightarrow 0. \tag{3.30}$$

If this is true, we also say that $\{f_n\}$ is L_p-close to F.

Lemma. (Equivalent definition) If $p < \infty$, then Eq. (3.30) is equivalent to

$$\|\Delta_{np} f_n - F\|_p \longrightarrow 0.$$

The proof repeats that of Lemma 2.5.1, except that the references to Lemmas 2.1.7 and 2.2.1 should be replaced by references to the corresponding properties from Sections 3.6.1, 3.6.3 and 3.6.4.

3.6.6 Simple sufficient condition

Lemma. Let $\{B_n\}$ be a sequence of matrices such that B_n is of size $n \times n$ and there exists a continuous function $F \in C([0, 1]^2)$ satisfying

$$\max_{1 \leq s, t \leq n} |B_{nst} - F(s/n, t/n)| \longrightarrow 0. \tag{3.31}$$

Put $f_n = n^{-2/p} B_n$. If $p < \infty$, then $\{f_n\}$ is L_p-close to F.

The proof is obtained by making obvious changes in the proof of Lemma 2.7.2. Condition (3.31) was used in (Nabeya and Tanaka, 1988), see also (Tanaka, 1996, Section 5.6).

3.7   INTEGRAL OPERATORS

If in the definition of a matrix product

$$
\begin{pmatrix} a_{11} & \cdots & a_{1n} \\ \cdots & \cdots & \cdots \\ a_{n1} & \cdots & a_{nn} \end{pmatrix}
\begin{pmatrix} x_1 \\ \cdots \\ x_n \end{pmatrix}
= \begin{pmatrix} \sum_i a_{1i} x_i \\ \cdots \\ \sum_i a_{ni} x_i \end{pmatrix}
$$

we replace summation by integration, the definition of an integral operator emerges. Tracing the analogies between properties of integral operators and matrices makes one's life much easier, although infinite dimensionality certainly introduces a bit of adventure.

3.7.1   Integral Operators with Square-Integrable Kernels

Let K be a symmetric function from $L_2(Q)$, $Q = (0, 1)^2$. We can associate with it an *integral operator*

$$
(\mathcal{K}F)(x) = \int_0^1 K(x, y)F(y)dy, \ F \in L_2(0, 1).
$$

The function K is called a *kernel* of the operator $\mathcal{K}$. For the first pack of properties of $\mathcal{K}$ we need the notation

$$
(F, G) = \int_0^1 F(x)G(x)\, dx, \ (F, G) = \int_{(0,1)^2} F(x)G(x)\, dx
$$

of scalar products in $L_2(0, 1)$ and $L_2(Q)$. The norms these generate are denoted by the same symbol $\|F\|_2$.

Lemma.   *If K is symmetric and belongs to $L_2(Q)$, then*

   (i) $\mathcal{K}$ is linear, $\mathcal{K}(aF + bG) = a\mathcal{K}F + b\mathcal{K}G$ for all numbers a, b and elements $F, G \in L_2(0, 1)$,

   (ii) $\mathcal{K}$ is bounded, $\|\mathcal{K}\|_2 \le \|K\|_2$,

   (iii) $\mathcal{K}$ is symmetric, $(\mathcal{K}F, G) = (F, \mathcal{K}G)$.

Proof.

   (i) Linearity of $\mathcal{K}$ is obvious.

(ii) By the Hölder inequality

$$|(\mathcal{K}F)(x)| \leq \left(\int_0^1 K^2(x, y)\, dy \right)^{1/2} \|F\|_2$$

which implies

$$\|\mathcal{K}F\|_2 \leq \|K\|_2 \|F\|_2 . \tag{3.32}$$

This means that the domain of $\mathcal{K}$ is the whole $L_2(0, 1)$ and the norm of $\mathcal{K}$ is not larger than $\|K\|_2$.

(iii) Changing the order of integration,

$$(\mathcal{K}F, G) = \int_0^1 \left(\int_0^1 K(x, y)F(y)\, dy \right) G(x)\, dx$$

$$= \int_0^1 F(y) \left(\int_0^1 K(x, y)G(x)\, dx \right) dy$$

$$= \int_0^1 F(y) \left(\int_0^1 K(y, x)G(x)\, dx \right) dy = (F, \mathcal{K}G).$$

∎

3.7.2 Compactness of $\mathcal{K}$

A bounded linear operator A from one normed space, X, to another normed space, Y, is called *compact* if the image AB of the unit ball $B = \{y \in Y : \|y\| \leq 1\}$ is precompact (see the definition in Section 2.6.4).

Lemma. *If $K \in L_2(Q)$, then K is compact.*

Proof. To prove that the image $\mathcal{K}B$ of the ball $B = \{F : \|F\|_2 \leq 1\}$ is precompact we can use the Frechet–Kolmogorov theorem (Section 2.6.4). Eq. (3.32) shows that the elements of $\mathcal{K}B$ are uniformly bounded:

$$\sup_{\|F\|_2 \leq 1} \|\mathcal{K}F\|_2 \leq \|K\|_2 .$$

For an arbitrary $h \in \mathbb{R}$, estimate by Hölder's inequality that

$$|(\mathcal{K}F)(x) - (\tau_h \mathcal{K}F)(x)| \leq \left(\int_0^1 |K(x, y) - K(x + h, y)|^2 dy \right)^{1/2} \|F\|_2 .$$

If $|h| \leq \delta$, then by the definition of the 2-D continuity modulus the end bound implies

$$\int_{Q_h} |(\mathcal{K}F)(x) - (\tau_h \mathcal{K}F)(x)|^2 dx$$

$$\leq \int_{Q_h} \int_0^1 |K(x, y) - K(x + h, y)|^2 dy \, \|F\|_2^2 \leq \omega_2^2(K, \delta) \, \|F\|_2^2 \, .$$

Apply sup over $|h| \leq \delta$ to the left side:

$$\omega_2(\mathcal{K}F, \delta) \leq \omega_2(K, \delta) \, \|F\|_2 \leq \omega_2(K, \delta) \text{ for } F \in B.$$

Hence, by Lemma 3.6.2 the elements of $\mathcal{K}B$ are uniformly equicontinuous.

Thus, by the Frechet–Kolmogorov theorem $\mathcal{K}B$ is precompact and $\mathcal{K}$ is compact. ∎

3.7.3 Orthonormal Systems and Fourier Series

Let H be a Hilbert space. A system of vectors $\{x_n : n \in \mathbb{N}\} \subset H$ is called *orthonormal* if

   1. $(x_i, x_j) = 0$, $i \neq j$ (*orthogonality*) and
   2. $\|x_i\|_2 = 1$ (*normalization*).

With an orthonormal system at hand, we can consider *Fourier coefficients* $c_i = (y, x_i)$ and *Fourier series* $\sum_i c_i x_i$ for any $y \in H$. Here the infinite sum $\sum_{i=1}^{\infty} c_i x_i$ is defined as the limit in H of partial sums $\sum_{i=1}^{n} c_i x_i$.

Lemma

   (i) *y is representable by its Fourier series, $y = \sum_i c_i x_i$, if and only if* $\|y\|_2^2 = \sum_i c_i^2$.
   (ii) *If y and z are representable by their Fourier series, $y = \sum_i (y, x_i) x_i$ and $z = \sum_i (z, x_i) x_i$, then*

$$(y, z) = \sum_i (y, x_i)(z, x_i). \tag{3.33}$$

Proof.

   (i) For any natural n we can write

$$\left\| x - \sum_{i=1}^n c_i x_i \right\|_2^2 = \left(x - \sum_{i=1}^n c_i x_i, x - \sum_{i=1}^n c_i x_i \right)$$

(use linearity of scalar products)

$$= \|x\|_2^2 - \sum_{i=1}^{n} c_i(x_i, x) - \sum_{i=1}^{n} c_i(x, x_i) + \sum_{i,j=1}^{n} c_i c_j(x_i, x_j)$$

(apply orthonormality and plug in the coefficients)

$$= \|x\|_2^2 - \sum_{i=1}^{m} c_i^2.$$

Letting $n \to \infty$ yields $\left\|x - \sum_{i=1}^{\infty} c_i x_i\right\|_2^2 = \|x\|_2^2 - \sum_{i=1}^{\infty} c_i^2$, which proves statement (i).

(ii) Equation (3.33) is obtained by scalar multiplication of y and z with subsequent application of the linearity of scalar products and orthonormality. ∎

Equation (3.33) is called a *Parseval identity*.

3.7.4   Symmetric and Nonnegative Operators

Let A be a bounded linear operator in a Hilbert space H. Its *adjoint* A^* is defined as the operator that satisfies $(Ax, y) = (x, A^*y)$ for all $x, y \in H$. Further, A is called *symmetric* or *self-adjoint* if $A = A^*$. The thrust of Lemma 3.7.1 is that $\mathcal{K}$ is symmetric in this sense.

A symmetric operator A is called *nonnegative* if $(Ax, x) \geq 0$ for any $x \in H$.

Lemma

(i) *For any bounded operator A, the operator $B = A^*A$ is symmetric and nonnegative.*

(ii) *For any bounded operator A and compact operator B, the products AB and BA are compact.*

Proof.

(i) By the definition of the adjoint

$$(Bx, y) = (A^*Ax, y) = (Ax, Ay) = (x, A^*Ay) = (x, By) \quad \text{for all } x, y \in H.$$

This proves the symmetry of B. The proof of its nonnegativity is even simpler: $(Bx, x) = (A^*Ax, x) = (Ax, Ax) \geq 0$.

(ii) Consider, for example, the first product. We need to prove that if the vectors x_n satisfy $\|x_n\| \leq 1$, then the sequence $\{ABx_n\}$ contains a convergent subsequence. Indeed, since B is compact, there is a subsequence $\{x_{n_m}\} \subseteq \{x_n\}$ such that $\{Bx_{n_m}\}$ converges. But then by boundedness of A, the sequence $\{ABx_{n_m}\}$ also converges: $\|ABx_{n_m} - ABx_{n_k}\| \leq \|A\| \|Bx_{n_m} - Bx_{n_k}\| \to 0$. ∎

3.7.5 Hilbert–Schmidt Theorem

Let A be a bounded linear operator in a Hilbert space H. People say that x is an *eigenvector* of A that corresponds to its *eigenvalue* λ if $Ax = \lambda x$ and $x \neq 0$. Nonzero x is excluded here as an uninteresting case (with zero x, $Ax = \lambda x$ is true for any λ). However, a zero eigenvalue is a possibility.

If x is an eigenvector of A that corresponds to eigenvalue λ, then $Aax = \lambda ax$ for any number a. In other words, along the straight line $\{ax : a \in \mathbb{R}\}$ the action of A is simple: it multiplies vectors by λ. The dimension of the least linear subspace that contains all eigenvectors corresponding to the given eigenvalue λ is called *multiplicity* of that λ.

Theorem. (Hilbert–Schmidt). (Kolmogorov and Fomin, 1989, Chapter 4, Section 6) *If A is a symmetric, compact operator in H, then it possesses systems of eigenvalues $\{\lambda_n\}$ and corresponding eigenvectors $\{x_n\}$ such that*

(i) *the eigenvalues are real, repeated according to their multiplicities and λ_n converge to 0,*

(ii) *the system of eigenvectors is orthonormal and such that any $y \in H$ can be decomposed as*

$$y = \sum_i (y, x_i)x_i. \tag{3.34}$$

Since $Ax_i = \lambda_i x_i$, Eq. (3.34) obviously implies

$$Ay = \sum_i \lambda_i (y, x_i)x_i, \quad y \in H. \tag{3.35}$$

This representation, called a *spectral decomposition* of A, is the main purpose of the Hilbert–Schmidt theorem.

3.7.6 Functions of a Symmetric Compact Operator

The spectral decomposition (3.35) enables us to define *functions* of A. The idea is simple: define $f(A)$ by

$$f(A)y = \sum_i f(\lambda_i)(y, x_i)x_i \tag{3.36}$$

for any f for which $f(\lambda_i)$ exist and the series at the right converges. A simple sufficient condition is that f be defined and bounded on the real line, $\sup_{t \in \mathbb{R}} |f(t)| < \infty$, because then convergence of Eq. (3.36) trivially follows from convergence of Eq. (3.35).

Lemma. *Let A be a symmetric compact operator. It is nonnegative if and only if all its eigenvalues are nonnegative. Further, if it is nonnegative, then all its nonnegative powers A^t, $t \geq 0$, exist.*

Proof.   If A is nonnegative, then, selecting $y = x_i$ in Eq. (3.35), we get $0 \le (Ax_i, x_i) = \lambda_i(x_i, x_i) = \lambda_i$. Conversely, if all eigenvalues are nonnegative, Eqs. (3.34) and (3.35) give $(Ay, y) = \sum_i \lambda_i(y, x_i)^2 \ge 0$.

Suppose A is nonnegative. Then its eigenvalues are nonnegative and satisfy $\lambda_i \to 0$ by the Hilbert–Schmidt theorem. Hence, in the definition of powers

$$A^t y = \sum_i \lambda_i^t (y, x_i) x_i \tag{3.37}$$

the numbers λ_i^t are defined and bounded. Thus, A^t is correctly defined and bounded in H.   ∎

3.7.7   Fourier Decomposition of the Kernel

Lemma.   *If K is symmetric and square-integrable on Q, then it can be decomposed as*

$$K(x, y) = \sum_i \lambda_i F_i(x) F_i(y). \tag{3.38}$$

Besides,

$$\|K\|_2^2 = \sum_i \lambda_i^2. \tag{3.39}$$

Here eigenvalues $\{\lambda_n\}$ and eigenvectors $\{F_n\}$ are the result of the application of the Hilbert–Schmidt theorem to $\mathcal{K}$.

Proof.   By Fubini's theorem (Kolmogorov and Fomin, 1989, Chapter 5, Section 6), for almost all $x \in (0, 1)$ the kernel $K(x, \cdot)$ belongs to $L_2(0, 1)$ as a function of y. Hence, we can substitute it for y in Eq. (3.34) and thereby obtain

$$K(x, y) = \sum_i (K(x, \cdot), F_i) F_i(y).$$

Since F_i are eigenvectors, the Fourier coefficients here actually equal

$$(K(x, \cdot), F_i) = \int_0^1 K(x, y) F_i(y)\, dy = \lambda_i F_i(x).$$

This proves Eq. (3.38).

Equation (3.39) is a consequence of Eq. (3.38):

$$\|K\|_2^2 = \int_0^1 \int_0^1 \left(\sum_i \lambda_i F_i(x) F_i(y) \right)^2 dxdy$$

$$= \sum_{i,j} \lambda_i \lambda_j \int_0^1 F_i(x) F_j(x) dx \int_0^1 F_i(y) F_j(y) dy = \sum_i \lambda_i^2.$$

This shows, in particular, that the series in Eq. (3.38) converges in $L_2(Q)$. ∎

3.8 CLASSES σ_p

3.8.1 s-Numbers and Classes σ_p

Let A be a compact operator in H. By Lemma 3.7.4 the operator A^*A is compact, symmetric and nonnegative. By the Hilbert–Schmidt theorem its eigenvalues $\lambda_i(A^*A)$ tend to zero, while by Lemma 3.7.6 they are nonnegative. The numbers $s_i(A) = \sqrt{\lambda_i(A^*A)}$ are called *s-numbers* of A. A *class* σ_p, $1 \leq p \leq \infty$, is defined as the set of compact operators in H satisfying

$$\|A\|_{\sigma_p} = \|\{s_i(A)\}\|_{l_p} < \infty.$$

Note that the smaller p, the stronger is the requirement $A \in \sigma_p$. This is so because, by monotonicity of l_p norms,

$$\|A\|_{\sigma_q} \leq \|A\|_{\sigma_p} \quad \text{if } 1 \leq p \leq q \leq \infty. \tag{3.40}$$

The elements of σ_2 are called *Hilbert–Schmidt operators*. Equation (3.39) means that if K is symmetric and square-integrable on $(0, 1)^2$, then $\mathcal{K}$ is a Hilbert–Schmidt operator.

The elements of σ_1 are called *nuclear operators*. In the finite-dimensional case the trace of a symmetric matrix is, by definition, the sum of its diagonal elements. The trace is shown to be equal to the sum of the eigenvalues. In the infinite-dimensional case, when matrix representations, as a rule, don't work, it is natural to define the trace of a symmetric compact operator to be the sum of its eigenvalues. The nuclearity assumption ensures absolute convergence of the series $\sum_i \lambda_i$.

Lemma. *If A is symmetric and compact, then $s_i(A) = |\lambda_i(A)|$ and*

$$\left(\sum_i \lambda_i^2 \right)^{1/2} \leq \sum_i |\lambda_i|. \tag{3.41}$$

Proof. For a symmetric and compact A we have

$$s_i(A) = \sqrt{\lambda_i(A^*A)} = \sqrt{\lambda_i(A^2)} = \sqrt{\lambda_i^2(A)} = |\lambda_i(A)|.$$

Now Eq. (3.41) follows from Eq. (3.40). ∎

3.8.2 Discretizing an Integral Operator

Let P_n, Δ_n^1, δ_n^1 be the 1-D Haar projector, interpolation operator and discretization operator, respectively, obtained from Sections 2.1.2 and 2.1.6 by putting $p = 2$. Let δ_n^2 be the 2-D discretization operator from Section 3.6.1, also in case $p = 2$. Denote $\mathcal{K}_n = P_n \mathcal{K} P_n$.

Lemma. $\mathcal{K}_n = \Delta_n^1(\delta_n^2 K)\delta_n^1.$

Proof. Since $\Delta_n^1 \delta_n^1 = P_n$ (Lemma 2.1.7), we have $\mathcal{K}_n = \Delta_n^1(\delta_n^1 \mathcal{K} \Delta_n^1)\delta_n^1$ and the statement will follow if we establish

$$\delta_n^1 \mathcal{K} \Delta_n^1 = \delta_n^2 K. \tag{3.42}$$

Let us see what the application of $\mathcal{K}\Delta_n^1$ to $f \in \mathbb{R}^n$ gives:

$$(\mathcal{K}\Delta_n^1 f)(x) = \int_0^1 K(x, y)(\Delta_n^1 f)(y)\, dy = \sqrt{n} \sum_{t=1}^n \int_{i_t} K(x, y)\, dy\, f_t.$$

Multiply this by δ_n^1:

$$[\delta_n^1(\mathcal{K}\Delta_n^1 f)]_s = n \sum_{t=1}^n \int_{i_s}\left(\int_{i_t} K(x, y)\, dy\right) dx\, f_t$$

$$= n \sum_{t=1}^n \int_{i_s \times i_t} K(x, y)\, dx\, dy\, f_t = [(\delta_n^2 K)f]_s, \quad s = 1, \ldots, n.$$

Since f is arbitrary, this proves Eq. (3.42). ∎

3.8.3 Preservation of Spectra under Discretization

Lemma. *If K is symmetric and square-integrable on Q, then nonzero eigenvalues of $\mathcal{K}_n$, repeated according to their multiplicities, are the same as those of $\delta_n^2 K$.*

Proof. We know from Lemma 2.1.7(ii) that interpolating $f \in \mathbb{R}^n$ and discretizing the result $\Delta_n^1 f$ gives the original vector

$$\delta_n^1 \Delta_n^1 f = f, f \in \mathbb{R}^n. \tag{3.43}$$

Let λ be a nonzero eigenvalue of $\mathcal{K}_n$. $\mathcal{K}_n F = \lambda F$ by Lemma 3.8.2 and Eq. (3.43) implies

$$\lambda \delta_n^1 F = \delta_n^1 \mathcal{K}_n F = \delta_n^1 \Delta_n^1 (\delta_n^2 K) \delta_n^1 F = (\delta_n^2 K) \delta_n^1 F.$$

We need to satisfy ourselves that $f = \delta_n^1 F$ is not null. The image $\mathrm{Im}(\mathcal{K}_n)$ is contained in the image $\mathrm{Im}(P_n)$, which consists of functions constant on the elements of the covering $\{i_t\}$. Since F is not null and belongs to $\mathrm{Im}(\mathcal{K}_n)$, at least one of these constants is not zero and, hence, f is not null. We see that $f = \delta_n^1 F$ is an eigenvector of $\delta_n^2 K$ corresponding to the eigenvalue λ.

Now we prove that multiplicities are preserved. Multiplicity of λ equals the maximum number of orthogonal eigenvectors that correspond to λ. If G is another eigenvector that corresponds to the same eigenvalue λ and is orthogonal to F, then, denoting $g = \delta_n^1 G$, by Eq. (2.6) we have

$$f'g = (\delta_n F)' \delta_n G = \int_0^1 (P_n F) P_n G \, dx = \int_0^1 FG \, dx = 0.$$

Here we have used $P_n F = F$ (projectors don't change elements of their images). Thus, multiplicities are preserved.

Conversely, if $(\delta_n^2 K)f = \lambda f, f \neq 0$, then we multiply both sides by Δ_n^1 and use Eq. (3.43) to substitute f: $\Delta_n^1 (\delta_n^2 K) \delta_n^1 \Delta_n^1 f = \lambda \Delta_n^1 f$ or, by Lemma 3.8.2, $\mathcal{K}_n F = \lambda F$ where $F = \Delta_n^1 f$ is not null. Thus, nonzero eigenvalues of $\mathcal{K}_n$ and $\delta_n^2 K$ are the same. If g is another eigenvector that corresponds to the same eigenvalue λ of $\delta_n^2 K$ and is orthogonal to f, then with $G = \Delta_n^1 f$ Eq. (2.4) gives

$$\int_0^1 FG \, dx = \int_0^1 (\Delta_n f) \Delta_n g \, dx = f'g = 0.$$

Again, multiplicities are preserved.

In the case $\lambda = 0$ the above argument is not applicable because $\mathcal{K}_n F = \lambda F = 0$ does not imply $F = 0$. The subspace of eigenvectors of $\mathcal{K}_n$ that correspond to $\lambda = 0$ is infinite-dimensional. ∎

3.8.4 Integral Operators and Interpolation

Applying the 2-D interpolation operator Δ_n^2 to a symmetric matrix A of size $n \times n$ we get a function on Q

$$\Delta_n^2 A = n \sum_{i,j=1}^{n} a_{ij} 1_{q_{ij}}.$$

This function generates an integral operator

$$(\mathcal{A}F)(x) = \int_0^1 (\Delta_n^2 A)(x, y) F(y) \, dy.$$

Lemma. *There is a one-to-one correspondence between the set of nonzero eigenvalues of A and a similar set of $\mathcal{A}$.*

Proof. The image $\mathrm{Im}(P_n)$ of the 1-D Haar projector consists of functions constant on the elements of the covering $\{i_t\}$. Since $1_{q_{st}} = 1_{i_s} 1_{i_t}$, the image of $\mathcal{A}$ is contained in $\mathrm{Im}(P_n)$:

$$(\mathcal{A}F)(x) = n \sum_{s,t=1}^{n} a_{st} 1_{i_s}(x) \int_0^1 1_{i_t}(y) F(y) \, dy \in \mathrm{Im}(P_n).$$

P_n, being a projector, doesn't change elements of its image, so $P_n \mathcal{A} = \mathcal{A}$.

Suppose $\mathcal{A}F = \lambda F$, $\lambda \neq 0$. Since the left side belongs to $\mathrm{Im}(P_n)$, the right side also belongs to it. Therefore $P_n \mathcal{A} P_n F = \lambda F$. By Lemma 3.8.2 and $\delta_n^2 \Delta_n^2 = I$ this rewrites as

$$\Delta_n^1 (A \delta_n^1 F) = \Delta_n^1 (\delta_n^2 \Delta_n^2 A) \delta_n^1 F = \Delta_n^1 (\delta_n^2 K) \delta_n^1 F = \lambda F.$$

Multiply both sides by δ_n^1 and use the property $\delta_n^1 \Delta_n^1 = I$ and notation $f = \delta_n^1 F$ to get $Af = \delta_n^1 \Delta_n^1 (A \delta_n^1 F) = \lambda f$. Assumption $F \neq 0$ implies $f \neq 0$ because F is piece-wise constant. Thus, λ is an eigenvalue of F.

Conversely, let $Af = \lambda f$, $f \in \mathbb{R}^n$. Multiply both sides by Δ_n^1 and substitute $A = \delta_n^2 \Delta_n^2 A$, $f = \delta_n^1 \Delta_n^1 f$:

$$\Delta_n^1 (\delta_n^2 \Delta_n^2 A) \delta_n^1 \Delta_n^1 f = \lambda \Delta_n^1 f.$$

By Lemma 3.8.2 and denoting $F = \Delta_n^1 f$ we have $P_n \mathcal{A} P_n F = \lambda F$, which is actually the same as $\mathcal{A}F = \lambda F$.

In both parts of the proof multiplicities are preserved because of preservation of scalar products. ∎

3.8.5 Uniform Boundedness of σ_1-Norms of W_n

Here we need some facts from Gohberg and Kreĭn (1969):

1. The class σ_p is a normed space with the norm $\|\cdot\|_{\sigma_p}$. In particular, the triangle inequality $\|A + B\|_{\sigma_p} \leq \|A\|_{\sigma_p} + \|B\|_{\sigma_p}$ and its consequence

$$\left| \|A\|_{\sigma_p} - \|B\|_{\sigma_p} \right| \leq \|A - B\|_{\sigma_p} \tag{3.44}$$

   are true (Gohberg and Kreĭn, 1969, p. 92).

2. For any bounded operators B and C

$$\|BAC\|_{\sigma_p} \leq \|B\| \|A\|_{\sigma_p} \|C\| \tag{3.45}$$

   (Gohberg and Kreĭn, 1969, Section 2.1).

3. If for some orthonormal basis $\{\phi_j\}$ we have $\sum_j \|A\phi_j\| < \infty$, then $\|A\|_{\sigma_1} \leq \sum_j \|A\phi_j\|$ (Gohberg and Kreĭn, 1969, Section 7.8).

Let A be a square matrix of order n. Choosing $\phi_j = (0, \ldots, 0, 1, 0, \ldots, 0)$ (unity in the jth place) we have $A\phi_j = (a_{1j}, \ldots, a_{nj})'$ (jth column) and property 3 yields

$$\|A\|_{\sigma_1} \leq \sum_{j=1}^{n} \|(a_{1j}, \ldots, a_{nj})\|_2 \leq \sqrt{n} \|A\|_2. \tag{3.46}$$

Theorem. (Mynbaev, 2010) *Let $\{W_n\}$ be a sequence of symmetric matrices, W_n being of size $n \times n$. If K is a symmetric square-integrable function on Q, the operator $\mathcal{K}$ is nuclear and*

$$\|W_n - \delta_n^2 K\|_2 = o(1/\sqrt{n}), \tag{3.47}$$

then the eigenvalues $\lambda_{n1}, \ldots, \lambda_{nn}$ of W_n satisfy

$$\sup_n \sum_{j=1}^{n} |\lambda_{nj}| < \infty.$$

Proof. The operator $\mathcal{K}_n$ from Section 3.8.2 is symmetric because $\mathcal{K}$ and P_n are. By Lemma 3.8.3, $\|\mathcal{K}_n\|_{\sigma_1} = \|\delta_n^2 K\|_{\sigma_1}$ (zero eigenvalues do not affect the norms), while Lemma 3.8.4 implies $\sum_{j=1}^{n} |\lambda_{nj}| = \|W_n\|_{\sigma_1}$. Hence, from Eqs. (3.44), (3.47) and (3.46)

$$\left| \sum_{j=1}^{n} |\lambda_{nj}| - \|\mathcal{K}_n\|_{\sigma_1} \right| = \left| \|W_n\|_{\sigma_1} - \|\delta_n^2 K\|_{\sigma_1} \right|$$

$$\leq \|W_n - \delta_n^2 K\|_{\sigma_1} \leq \sqrt{n} \|W_n - \delta_n^2 K\|_2 \to 0.$$

Using $\|P_n\| \leq 1$, Eq. (3.45), Lemma 3.8.1 and the nuclearity assumption we see that

$$\|\mathcal{K}_n\|_{\sigma_1} = \sum_{j=1}^{\infty} s_j(P_n\mathcal{K}P_n) \leq \sum_{j=1}^{\infty} s_j(\mathcal{K}) = \sum_{j=1}^{\infty} |\lambda_j(\mathcal{K})| < \infty.$$

The two displayed equations immediately above prove the theorem. ∎

3.9 CONVERGENCE OF QUADRATIC FORMS OF RANDOM VARIABLES

Here we see how CMTs in combination with a CLT work to obtain convergence to a nonnormal distribution.

3.9.1 CLT for Quadratic Forms of Linear Processes: Version 1

Let the vector $\{v_n\}$ be the same as in Theorem 3.5.2 (a linear process, with m.d.'s e_{nt} as innovations, with coefficients ψ_j) and let $\{k_n: n \in \mathbb{N}\}$ be a sequence of nonstochastic matrices such that k_n is of size $n \times n$.

Theorem. (Mynbaev, 2001) *Suppose that*

(i) *e_{nt}^2 are uniformly integrable and $E(e_{nt}^2|\mathcal{F}_{n,t-1}) = \sigma^2$ for all t and n,*

(ii) *the sequence $\{\psi_j: j \in \mathbb{Z}\}$ is summable, $\alpha_\psi < \infty$,*

(iii) *the sequence $\{k_n: n \in \mathbb{N}\}$ is L_2-close to some symmetric function $K \in L_2((0,1)^2)$ with the next rate of approximation*

$$\|k_n - \delta_{n2}K\|_2 = o(1/n), \tag{3.48}$$

(iv) *the integral operator $\mathcal{K}$ with the kernel K is nuclear.*

Then we can assert that

1. *If $\beta_\psi \neq 0$, then the quadratic form*

$$Q_n(k_n) = v_n' k_n v_n$$

converges in distribution to $(\sigma\beta_\psi)^2 \sum_i \lambda_i u_i^2$ where u_i are independent standard normal and λ_i are the eigenvalues of $\mathcal{K}$.

2. *If $\beta_\psi = 0$, then $\mathrm{plim}Q_n(k_n) = 0$.*

This kind of a CLT appeared in Nabeya and Tanaka (1990). The important features of their approach include:

1. the link between the limit distribution of $Q_n(k_n)$ and the integral operator $\mathcal{K}$ through the eigenvalues of the latter;

2. approximation of $Q_n(k_n)$ by $Q_n(\delta_{n2}K)$ and of $Q_n(\delta_{n2}K)$ by $Q_n(\delta_{n2}K_L)$,

where

$$K_L(x, y) = \sum_{i=1}^{L} \lambda_i F_i(x) F_i(y) \tag{3.49}$$

is the initial segment of representation (3.35).

Adding to these features the properties of L_2-approximable sequences allowed me (Mynbaev, 2001) to replace their continuous kernels with square-integrable ones and consider double-infinite linear processes instead of one-sided processes ($\psi_j = 0$ for $j < 0$). [See in Tanaka (1996) the details regarding the so-called Fredholm approach.]

Prove the above theorem in Sections 3.9.2–3.9.6.

3.9.2 Approximation of $Q_n(k_n)$ by $Q_n(\delta_{n2}K)$

By the Cauchy–Schwarz inequality

$$|Q_n(k_n) - Q_n(\delta_{n2}K)| = \left| \sum_{s,t=1}^{n} v_{ns} v_{nt} (k_n - \delta_{n2}K)_{st} \right|$$

$$\leq \|k_n - \delta_{n2}K\|_2 \left(\sum_{s,t=1}^{n} v_{ns}^2 v_{nt}^2 \right)^{1/2}$$

$$= \|k_n - \delta_{n2}K\|_2 \sum_{t=1}^{n} v_{nt}^2.$$

Here, by orthogonality of m.d.'s,

$$E \sum_{t=1}^{n} v_{nt}^2 = \sum_{t=1}^{n} \sum_{i,j \in \mathbb{Z}} E e_{n,t-i} \psi_i e_{n,t-j} \psi_j$$

$$= \sigma^2 \sum_{t=1}^{n} \sum_{j \in \mathbb{Z}} \psi_j^2 = \sigma^2 n \sum_{j \in \mathbb{Z}} \psi_j^2.$$

As condition (ii) of Theorem 3.9.1 implies square-summability of $\{\psi_j : j \in \mathbb{Z}\}$, we can use Eq. (3.48) to conclude that

$$E|Q_n(k_n) - Q_n(\delta_{n2}K)| \leq cn\|k_n - \delta_{n2}K\|_2 \longrightarrow 0.$$

This proves that

$$\operatorname{plim}(Q_n(k_n) - Q_n(\delta_{n2}K)) = 0. \tag{3.50}$$

3.9.3   Approximation of $Q_n(\delta_{n2}K)$ by $Q_n(\delta_{n2}K_L)$

Subtracting from the representation of K [Eq. (3.35)] its initial segment [Eq. (3.49)] and applying Lemma 3.6.1(iii) we get

$$(\delta_{n2}^2 K - \delta_{n2}^2 K_L)_{st} = \sum_{i>L} \lambda_i (\delta_{n2}^1 F_i)_s (\delta_{n2}^1 F_i)_t.$$

Therefore

$$Q_n(\delta_{n2}^2 K) - Q_n(\delta_{n2}^2 K_L) = \sum_{i>L} \lambda_i \sum_{s,t=1}^n (\delta_{n2}^1 F_i)_s v_{ns} (\delta_{n2}^1 F_i)_t v_{nt}$$

$$= \sum_{i>L} \lambda_i \left(\sum_{t=1}^n (\delta_{n2}^1 F_i)_t v_{nt} \right)^2$$

$$= \sum_{i>L} \lambda_i [(\delta_{n2}^1 F_i)' v_n]^2. \tag{3.51}$$

By the T-decomposition for means of quadratic forms (3.27)

$$E[(\delta_{n2}^1 F_i)' v_n]^2 = \sigma^2 [\|T_n^0 \delta_{n2}^1 F_i\|_2^2 + \|T_n^- \delta_{n2}^1 F_i\|_2^2$$

$$+ \|T_n^+ \delta_{n2}^1 F_i\|_2^2] \le 3\sigma^2 \alpha_\psi^2 \|F_i\|_2^2 = 3\sigma^2 \alpha_\psi^2.$$

The passage is by boundedness of the trinity 2.3.2, of the discretization operator 2.1.3 and normalization of F_i.

From the two displayed equations immediately above by nuclearity of $\mathcal{K}$

$$E|Q_n(\delta_{n2}K) - Q_n(\delta_{n2}K_L)| \le 3\sigma^2 \alpha_\psi^2 \sum_{i>L} |\lambda_i| \to 0, \quad L \to \infty. \tag{3.52}$$

It is extremely important that the majorant here does not depend on n and, as a result,

$$\text{plim}_{L \to \infty} [Q_n(\delta_{n2}K) - Q_n(\delta_{n2}K_L)] = 0 \text{ uniformly in } n. \tag{3.53}$$

3.9.4   Convergence of the Cut-Off Quadratic Form

Case 1. Let $\beta_\psi \ne 0$. By selecting $w_n^l = \delta_{n2}F_l$, $l = 1, \ldots, L$, we satisfy condition (ii) of Theorem 3.5.2. All other conditions of that theorem also hold. By part (a) of Theorem 3.5.2

$$\begin{pmatrix} (\delta_{n2}F_1)' v_n \\ \cdots \\ (\delta_{n2}F_L)' v_n \end{pmatrix} \xrightarrow{d} N(0, (\sigma\beta_\psi)^2 G), \tag{3.54}$$

where by orthonormality of the system $F_l, l = 1, \ldots, L,$

$$G = ((F_i, F_j))_{i,j=1}^L = I.$$

It follows that Eq. (3.54) is equivalent to (see Section 3.1.6)

$$\begin{pmatrix} (\delta_{n2}F_1)'v_n \\ \ldots \\ (\delta_{n2}F_L)'v_n \end{pmatrix} \xrightarrow{d} |\sigma\beta_\psi| \begin{pmatrix} u_1 \\ \ldots \\ u_L \end{pmatrix}, \tag{3.55}$$

where $u_1, \ldots, u_L$ are independent standard normal. Similarly to Eq. (3.51)

$$Q_n(\delta_{n2}^2 K_L) = \sum_{i=1}^L \lambda_i [(\delta_{n2}^1 F_i)'v_n]^2.$$

Here at the right we have a continuous function of the vector at the left of Eq. (3.55). By CMT (Section 1.8.3) then

$$Q_n(\delta_{n2}^2 K_L) \xrightarrow{d} (\sigma\beta_\psi)^2 \sum_{i=1}^L \lambda_i u_i^2, \ n \to \infty. \tag{3.56}$$

Case 2. Let $\beta_\psi = 0$. By Theorem 3.5.2b

$$\begin{pmatrix} (\delta_{n2}F_1)'v_n \\ \ldots \\ (\delta_{n2}F_L)'v_n \end{pmatrix} \xrightarrow{p} 0, \ n \to \infty,$$

and by Lemma 1.8.1(iii)

$$Q_n(\delta_{n2}^2 K_L) \xrightarrow{p} 0, \ n \to \infty. \tag{3.57}$$

3.9.5 Theorem on a Double Limit

We are interested in the convergence in distribution of a sequence of random vectors $\{X_n: n \in \mathbb{N}\}$. Suppose that each of these vectors is approximated by a sequence $\{X_{nL}: L \in \mathbb{N}\}$, with the degree of approximation improving as $L \to \infty$. It is useful to visualize the situation as in the matrix:

$$\begin{array}{ccccccc}
X_{11} & X_{21} & \ldots & X_{n1} & \to & Y_1 \\
X_{12} & X_{22} & \ldots & X_{n2} & \to & Y_2 \\
\ldots & \ldots & \ldots & \ldots & \ldots & \ldots \\
X_{1L} & X_{2L} & \ldots & X_{nL} & \to & Y_L \\
\downarrow & \downarrow & & \downarrow & & \downarrow \\
X_1 & X_2 & \ldots & X_n & \to & Y
\end{array}$$

Theorem. (Billingsley, 1968) *Suppose there is convergence in distribution along the rows $X_{nL} \xrightarrow{d} Y_L, n \to \infty$, and that the vectors Y_L in the right margin converge* *in distribution themselves,* $Y_L \xrightarrow{d} Y$, $L \to \infty$. *Then we can conclude that* $X_n \xrightarrow{d} Y$, $n \to \infty$, *if*

$$\lim_{L \to \infty} \limsup_{n \to \infty} P(\|X_{nL} - X_n\|_2 \geq \varepsilon) = 0. \tag{3.58}$$

3.9.6   Culmination

Case 1. Let $\beta_\psi \neq 0$. Put $X_n = Q_n(\delta_{n2}K)$ and $X_{nL} = Q_n(\delta_{n2}K_L)$. By Eq. (3.56) we have row-wise convergence

$$X_{nL} \xrightarrow{d} Y_L \equiv (\sigma\beta_\psi)^2 \sum_{i=1}^{L} \lambda_i u_i^2, \, n \to \infty.$$

Summability of $\{\lambda_i\}$ implies convergence of Y_L to $Y \equiv (\sigma\beta_\psi)^2 \sum_{i=1}^{\infty} \lambda_i u_i^2$ in $\mathcal{L}_1$, probability and distribution. By Chebyshov's inequality and Eq. (3.52) for any $\varepsilon > 0$

$$\limsup_{n \to \infty} P(\|X_{nL} - X_n\|_2 \geq \varepsilon) \leq \frac{1}{\varepsilon} 3\sigma^2 \alpha_\psi^2 \sum_{i>L} |\lambda_i|,$$

which implies Eq. (3.58). This allows us to realize the double limit passage:

$$Q_n(\delta_{n2}K) \xrightarrow{d} (\sigma\beta_\psi)^2 \sum_{i=1}^{\infty} \lambda_i u_i^2.$$

It remains to apply Eq. (3.50) to complete the proof in the case under consideration.

Case 2. Let $\beta_\psi = 0$. Then we can use Eq. (3.57) instead of Eq. (3.56) in the above argument. With this change the conclusion is that $Q_n(k_n)$ converges in distribution to zero. But then we recall that convergence in distribution to a constant implies convergence in probability to that constant, see Lemma 1.8.3(iii).

3.9.7   CLT for Quadratic Forms of Linear Processes: Version 2

Here we show that by imposing a stronger condition on the m.d.'s (up to fourth moments) it is possible to relax the L_2-proximity requirement in Eq. (3.48) from $o(1/n)$ to $o(1/\sqrt{n})$. The next theorem derives from Mynbaev (2010).

Theorem.   *Suppose that*

(i) *the m.d. array* $\{e_{nt}, \mathcal{F}_{nt}\}$ *satisfies conditions:* $E(e_{nt}^2|\mathcal{F}_{n,t-1}) = \sigma^2$ *for all* t *and* n; *the third conditional moments are constant, but may depend on* n *and* t, $E(e_{nt}^3|\mathcal{F}_{n,t-1}) = a_{nt}$, *and the fourth moments are uniformly bounded,* $\mu_4 = \sup_{n,t} E e_{nt}^4 < \infty$;

(ii) the sequence $\{\psi_j: j \in \mathbb{Z}\}$ is summable, $\alpha_\psi < \infty$;

(iii) the sequence $\{k_n: n \in \mathbb{N}\}$ is L_2-close to some symmetric function $K \in L_2((0, 1)^2)$ with the next rate of approximation

$$\|k_n - \delta_{n2}K\|_2 = o(1/\sqrt{n}); \tag{3.59}$$

(iv) the integral operator $\mathcal{K}$ with the kernel K is nuclear.

Then we can assert that

1. If $\beta_\psi \neq 0$, then the quadratic form

$$Q_n(k_n) = v_n' k_n v_n$$

converges in distribution to $(\sigma\beta_\psi)^2 \sum_i \lambda_i u_i^2$, where u_i are independent standard normal and λ_i are the eigenvalues of $\mathcal{K}$.

2. If $\beta_\psi = 0$, then $\text{plim} Q_n(k_n) = 0$.

The proof is given in Sections 3.9.8–3.9.10.

3.9.8 Lemma on Mixed Fourth-Order Moments

The next lemma is close to that of (Lee, 2004b, Lemma A.11).

Lemma. *Denote $\mu_{pqrs} = Ee_{np}e_{nq}e_{nr}e_{ns}$ for integer $p, q, r, s \in \mathbb{Z}$. If the m.d. array $\{e_{nt}, \mathcal{F}_{nt}\}$ satisfies condition (i) of Theorem 3.9.7, then*

$$\mu_{pqrs} = \begin{cases} \sigma^4, & \text{if } [(p = q) \neq (r = s)] \text{ or } [(p = r) \neq (q = s)] \\ & \text{or } [(p = s) \neq (q = r)], \\ Ee_{np}^4, & \text{if } p = q = r = s. \end{cases}$$

In all other cases $\mu_{pqrs} = 0$.

Proof. Without loss of generality we can order the indices: $p \leq q \leq r \leq s$. Consider four situations.

1. $s > r$. By definition of m.d.'s

$$\mu_{pqrs} = E[e_{np}e_{nq}e_{nr}E(e_{ns}|\mathcal{F}_{n,s-1})] = 0.$$

2. $s = r > q$. By condition (i) of Theorem 3.9.7 and orthogonality of m.d.'s

$$\mu_{pqrs} = E[e_{np}e_{nq}E(e_{nr}^2|\mathcal{F}_{n,r-1})]$$

$$= \sigma^2 Ee_{np}e_{nq} = \begin{cases} 0, & \text{if } p < q, \\ \sigma^4, & \text{if } p = q. \end{cases}$$

3. $s = r = q > p$. By condition (i) of Theorem 3.9.7

$$\mu_{pqrs} = E[e_{np}E(e_{nq}^3|\mathcal{F}_{n,q-1})] = a_{nq}Ee_{np} = 0.$$

4. $s = r = q = p$. By definition $\mu_{pqrs} = Ee_{np}^4$.

As a result of the ordering the cases $[(p = r) \neq (q = s)]$ and $[(p = s) \neq (q = r)]$ are impossible. The case $[(p = q) \neq (r = s)]$ is covered in item 2, while $p = q = r = s$ is contained in item 4. In "all other cases" $s > r \geq q \geq p$ or $s \geq r \geq q > p$ should be true. The equality of μ_{pqrs} to zero then follows from items 1–3.   ■

3.9.9   The Gauge Inequality

For an $n \times n$ matrix A denote

$$g(A) = [E(v_n'Av_n)^2]^{1/2}. \tag{3.60}$$

This possesses the properties of a seminorm (homogeneity and triangle inequality), but I call it a *gauge* just to avoid the trite "norm" or "seminorm". After some experimenting with variance I understood that using the gauge for the problem at hand is better.

Lemma.   *Under conditions (i) and (ii) of Theorem 3.9.7 for any matrices A, B such that the product AB is of size $n \times n$*

$$g(AB) \leq (3\sigma^4 + \mu_4)^{1/2}\alpha_\psi^2\|A\|_2\|B\|_2.$$

Proof.   Denoting $a_1, \ldots, a_k$ the columns of A and $b^1, \ldots, b^k$ the rows of B, by the T-decomposition (3.25) we have

$$a_l'v_n = \sum_i e_{ni}(T_na_l)_i, \quad b^lv_n = \sum_j e_{nj}(T_nb^l)_j, \quad l = 1, \ldots, k.$$

Hence,

$$A'v_n = \begin{pmatrix} a_1'v_n \\ \cdots \\ a_k'v_n \end{pmatrix} = \sum_i e_{ni}\begin{pmatrix} (T_na_1)_i \\ \cdots \\ (T_na_k)_i \end{pmatrix},$$

$$Bv_n = \begin{pmatrix} b^1v_n \\ \cdots \\ b^kv_n \end{pmatrix} = \sum_j e_{nj}\begin{pmatrix} (T_nb^1)_j \\ \cdots \\ (T_nb^k)_j \end{pmatrix}.$$

This implies

$$v'_n ABv_n = (A'v_n)Bv_n = \sum_{i,j} e_{ni} e_{nj} \sum_{l=1}^{k} (T_n a_l)_i (T_n b^l)_j$$

and

$$E(v'_n ABv_n)^2 = \sum_{l,m=1}^{k} \sum_{i_1, i_2, j_1, j_2 \in \mathbb{Z}} E e_{ni_1} e_{ni_2} e_{nj_1} e_{nj_2}$$
$$\times (T_n a_l)_{i_1} (T_n b^l)_{j_1} (T_n a_m)_{i_2} (T_n b^m)_{j_2}.$$

By Lemma 3.9.8 many fourth-order moments vanish and those that don't are equal to either σ^4 or Ee_{np}^4:

$$E(v'_n ABv_n)^2 = \sum_{l,m=1}^{k} \sigma^4 \sum_{i,j \in \mathbb{Z}} [(T_n a_l)_i (T_n a_m)_i (T_n b^l)_j (T_n b^m)_j$$
$$+ (T_n a_l)_i (T_n b^l)_i (T_n a_m)_j (T_n b^m)_j$$
$$+ (T_n a_l)_i (T_n b^m)_i (T_n a_m)_j (T_n b^l)_j]$$
$$+ \sum_{l,m=1}^{k} \sum_{i \in \mathbb{Z}} E e_{ni}^4 (T_n a_l)_i (T_n b^l)_i (T_n a_m)_i (T_n b^m)_i.$$

The structure of this expression becomes much clearer if we use the notation $(\,\cdot\,,\,\cdot\,)_{l_2}$ for the scalar product in $l_2(\mathbb{Z})$:

$$E(v'_n ABv_n)^2 = \sum_{l,m=1}^{k} \sigma^4 [(T_n a_l, T_n a_m)_{l_2} (T_n b^l, T_n b^m)_{l_2}$$
$$+ (T_n a_l, T_n b^l)_{l_2} (T_n a_m, T_n b^m)_{l_2}$$
$$+ (T_n a_l, T_n b^m)_{l_2} (T_n a_m, T_n b^l)_{l_2}]$$
$$+ \sum_{l,m=1}^{k} \sum_{i \in \mathbb{Z}} E e_{ni}^4 (T_n a_l)_i (T_n b^l)_i (T_n a_m)_i (T_n b^m)_i.$$

By boundedness of the T-operator (2.13) and conditions (i) and (ii) of Theorem 3.9.7

$$|(T_n x, T_n y)_{l_2}| \le \|T_n x\|_2 \, \|T_n y\|_2 \le \alpha_\psi^2 \|x\|_2 \, \|y\|_2,$$
$$\|T_n x\|_\infty \le \|T_n x\|_2 \le \alpha_\psi \|x\|_2, \quad E e_{ni}^4 \le \mu_4.$$

Therefore

$$
E(v_n'ABv_n)^2 \leq 3\sigma^4 \alpha_\psi^4 \sum_{l,m=1}^{k} \|a_l\|_2 \|a_m\|_2 \|b^l\|_2 \|b^m\|_2
$$

$$
+ \mu_4 \sum_{l,m=1}^{k} \|T_n a_l\|_\infty \|T_n b^l\|_\infty \sum_{i \in \mathbb{Z}} |(T_n a_m)_i (T_n b^m)_i|
$$

$$
\leq 3\sigma^4 \alpha_\psi^4 \left(\sum_{l=1}^{k} \|a_l\|_2 \|b^l\|_2 \right)^2
$$

$$
+ \mu_4 \alpha_\psi^2 \sum_{l,m=1}^{k} \|a_l\|_2 \|b^l\|_2 \|T_n a_m\|_2 \|T_n b^m\|_2.
$$

Applying Hölder's inequality and, again, boundedness of T_n,

$$
E(v_n'ABv_n)^2 \leq (3\sigma^4 + \mu_4)\alpha_\psi^4 \left(\sum_{l=1}^{k} \|a_l\|_2^2 \right) \left(\sum_{l=1}^{k} \|b^l\|_2^2 \right)
$$

$$
= (3\sigma^4 + \mu_4)\alpha_\psi^4 \|A\|_2^2 \|B\|_2^2. \qquad \blacksquare
$$

3.9.10   Proof of Theorem 3.9.7

By the gauge inequality 3.9.9

$$
(E|Q_n(k_n) - Q_n(\delta_{n2}K)|^2)^{1/2} = (E[v_n'(k_n - \delta_{n2}K)v_n]^2)^{1/2}
$$
$$
= g(k_n - \delta_{n2}K) \leq c\|I\|_2 \|k_n - \delta_{n2}K\|_2
$$
$$
= c\sqrt{n} \|k_n - \delta_{n2}K\|_2 = o(1).
$$

Instead of bound 3.9.2 use this bound. All other steps of the proof of Theorem 3.9.1 do not change.

CHAPTER 4

REGRESSIONS WITH SLOWLY VARYING REGRESSORS

REGRESSIONS WITH asymptotically collinear regressors arise in a number of applications, both in linear and nonlinear settings. Examples are the log–periodogram analysis of long memory (see Robinson, 1995; Hurvich *et al.*, 1998; Phillips, 1999 and references therein), the study of growth convergence (Barro and Sala-i-Martin, 2003), and NLS estimation (Wu, 1981). This chapter is based on Phillips' 2007 paper. His contribution to the theory of regressions with asymptotically collinear regressors can be described as follows:

1. He used the properties of SV functions to develop asymptotic expansions of some nonstochastic expressions that arise in regression analysis.

2. Based on those asymptotic expansions, he employed Brownian motion to derive central limit results for weighted sums of linear processes where the weights are standardized SV regressors.

3. For the cases when the conventional scheme does not work (because of asymptotic collinearity of the regressors) he modified it so as to obtain convergence of the OLS estimator in a variety of practical situations.

This chapter is structured accordingly. The main results are contained in Sections 4.2, 4.4, 4.5, and 4.6. Section 4.2, called Phillips Gallery 1, covers his asymptotic expansions of nonstochastic expressions. Not all of them are applied later in the book, but I include them for two reasons: they may be useful in other applications and they have helped me to guess some facts related to L_p-approximability.

Section 4.4 is devoted to generalizations of the central limit results established by Phillips. The main point is that, for these sort of results, using L_p-approximability and my CLT 3.5.2 is preferable to recourse to Brownian motion. Here the reader will see that some expansions of nonstochastic expressions are also implied by L_p-approximability.

In Section 4.5, named Phillips Gallery 2, we return to Phillips' exposition by going over applications. Section 4.6, which is about regressions with two SV

Short-Memory Linear Processes and Econometric Applications. Kairat T. Mynbaev
© 2011 John Wiley & Sons, Inc. Published 2011 by John Wiley & Sons, Inc.

regressors, is a rigorous replacement for a heuristic argument given by Phillips in 2007. The analysis here reveals two important features of the model:

1. the asymptotic variance-covariance matrix jumps along certain rays in the parameter space and
2. there are infinitely many models with different asymptotic behavior of the functions of the sample size.

4.1   SLOWLY VARYING FUNCTIONS

4.1.1   Definition and Examples of Slowly Varying Functions

A positive measurable function on $[A, \infty)$, $A > 0$, is slowly varying (SV) if

$$\lim_{x \to \infty} \frac{L(rx)}{L(x)} = 1 \quad \text{for any } r > 0. \tag{4.1}$$

Examples of such functions are $L_1(x) = \log x$ and $L_2(x) = \log(\log x)$ because

$$\frac{L_1(rx)}{L_1(x)} = \frac{\log r + \log x}{\log x} \longrightarrow 1,$$

$$\frac{L_2(rx)}{L_2(x)} = \frac{\log(\log r + \log x)}{\log(\log x)} = \frac{\log(\log x) + \log(1 + (\log r/\log x))}{\log(\log x)} \longrightarrow 1.$$

Similarly, $L_3(x) = 1/\log x$ and $L_4(x) = 1/\log(\log x)$ are SV. The function $L_5(x) = x^a$, $a \neq 0$, is not SV because $(rx)^a/x^a = r^a$ does not tend to 1 unless $r = 1$. It turns out that condition (4.1) is very restrictive:

Theorem.   (Seneta, 1985, p. 25) *If L satisfies Eq. (4.1), then L^a for any real a also satisfies that condition. Further, if L and M satisfy it, then their product and sum also do.*

The statements regarding the power L^a and product LM are trivial.

4.1.2   Uniform Convergence Theorem

Theorem.   (Seneta, 1985, p. 10) *If L is SV, then, for any fixed interval $[a, b]$ with $0 < a < b < \infty$, Eq. (4.1) is true uniformly in $r \in [a, b]$.*

For the functions L_1 through L_4 this statement can be verified directly.

4.1.3   Representation Theorem

Theorem.   (Seneta, 1985, p. 10) *Let L be defined on $[A, \infty)$, $A > 0$. Then L is SV if and only if there exist a number $B \geq A$ and functions μ, ε on $[B, \infty)$ with properties:*

(i) $L(x) = \exp\left(\mu(x) + \int_B^x \varepsilon(t)\, dt/t\right)$,
(ii) μ *is bounded, measurable and the limit $c = \lim_{x \to \infty} \mu(x)$ exists ($c \in \mathbb{R}$),*
(iii) ε *is continuous on $[B, \infty)$ and $\lim_{x \to \infty} \varepsilon(x) = 0$.*

The equation in (i) is called *Karamata representation*. Dependence of L on B is not important and is therefore suppressed. However, it may surge in some bounds later, and I try to avoid using B for other purposes.

4.1.4   Growth Rates of Slowly Varying Functions

Theorem.   (Seneta, 1985, p. 24) *A SV function L grows or declines very slowly in comparison with the power scale: for any* $\gamma > 0$, $x^{\gamma}L(x) \to \infty$ *and* $x^{-\gamma}L(x) \to 0$ *as* $x \to \infty$.

4.1.5   Integrals of Slowly Varying Functions over Intervals Adjacent to the Origin

Theorem.   (Seneta, 1985, p. 65) *Let a number* $\eta > 0$ *and function f on* $(0, \infty)$ *be such that the integral* $\int_0^{\beta} t^{-\eta}f(t)\,dt$ *exists, where* $0 < \beta < \infty$. *Let L be SV and bounded on each finite subinterval of* $[0, \infty)$. *If* $\eta > 0$, *then*

$$\frac{1}{L(x)} \int_0^{\beta} f(t)L(xt)\,dt \longrightarrow \int_0^{\beta} f(t)\,dt, \quad x \to \infty.$$

In the case $\eta = 0$, *the same is true if L is nondecreasing.*

4.2   PHILLIPS GALLERY 1

Of the exhibits of this gallery, only Lemmas 4.2.6 and 4.2.7 are applied in later sections.

4.2.1   Phillips Simplifying Assumption and the Notation $L = K(\varepsilon)$

Phillips (2007) argues that, in the development of an asymptotic theory of regression, little seems to be lost if one considers $\mu \equiv constant$ because the asymptotic behavior of representation 4.1.3(i) is equivalent to that with $\mu \equiv constant$. Formally, this is justified as follows. If μ is continuously differentiable, then

$$L(x) = \exp\left(\mu(x) + \int_B^x \varepsilon(t)\,\frac{dt}{t} \right)$$

$$= \exp\left(\int_B^x \mu'(t)\,dt + \mu(B) + \int_B^x \varepsilon(t)\,\frac{dt}{t} \right)$$

$$= \exp\left(\mu(B) + \int_B^x (t\mu'(t) + \varepsilon(t))\,\frac{dt}{t} \right).$$

So, if additionally $\lim_{t \to \infty} t\mu'(t) = 0$, we have a new representation of the same function L with a constant μ. Thus, the suggestion is to use only SV functions with the representation $L(x) = c_L \exp\left(\int_B^x \varepsilon(t)\, dt/t\right)$ and write $L = K(\varepsilon)$ in this case, omitting the constant c_L from the notation. The function ε in this representation is called an *ε-function* of L.

Further, ε can be extended to the segment $[0, B]$ in such a way that the integral $\int_0^B \varepsilon(t)/t\, dt$ exists [e.g., one can set ε equal to 0 in the neighborhood of 0 and interpolate continuously between that neighborhood and $[B, \infty)$]. This will amount to redefining L on $[0, B]$, which does not matter asymptotically because only a finite number of regression equations is affected. In any case, L can be considered continuous and positive on $[0, \infty)$. From now on we assume that such adjustments are made.

For some expansions we need to assume that $|\varepsilon(x)|$ is also SV and ε has Karamata representation

$$\varepsilon(x) = c_\varepsilon \exp\left(\int_B^x \eta(t)\,\frac{dt}{t}\right) \quad \text{for } x \geq B,$$

for some (possibly negative) constant c_ε, where η is continuous and $\eta(x) \to 0$ as $x \to \infty$. In such cases we also write $\varepsilon = K(\eta)$, remembering that ε can be negative. The number of different conditions in this theory may be daunting. To reduce it, in some cases we assume a little more than is required by a puristic approach.

For $L = K(\varepsilon)$,

$$\varepsilon(x) = \frac{xL'(x)}{L(x)} \to 0 \quad \text{as } x \to \infty. \tag{4.2}$$

Using this formula we calculate and collect in Table 4.1 expressions for ε and η in the sequence $L = K(\varepsilon)$, $\varepsilon = K(\eta)$ (the role of the function

$$\mu(x) = \frac{1}{2}(\varepsilon(x) + \eta(x))$$

is disclosed in Section 4.2.7). In Table 4.1 we denote $l_1(x) = \log x$, $l_2(x) = \log(\log x)$ and assume $\gamma > 0$. The table contains the functions of most practical interest against which the plausibility of new assumptions should be checked.

TABLE 4.1 Basic SV Functions

L	ε	η	μ	$L\varepsilon\mu$
$L_1 = l_1^\gamma$	$\dfrac{\gamma}{l_1}$	$-\dfrac{1}{l_1}$	$\dfrac{1}{2}\dfrac{\gamma-1}{l_1}$	$\dfrac{\gamma(\gamma-1)}{2}l_1^{\gamma-2}$
$L_2 = l_2$	$\dfrac{1}{l_1 l_2}$	$-\dfrac{1+l_2}{l_1 l_2}$	$-\dfrac{1}{2l_1}$	$-\dfrac{1}{2l_1^2}$
$L_3 = \dfrac{1}{l_1}$	$-\dfrac{1}{l_1}$	$-\dfrac{1}{l_1}$	$-\dfrac{1}{l_1}$	$\dfrac{1}{l_1^3}$
$L_4 = \dfrac{1}{l_2}$	$-\dfrac{1}{l_1 l_2}$	$-\dfrac{1+l_2}{l_1 l_2}$	$-\dfrac{2+l_2}{2l_1 l_2}$	$\dfrac{2+l_2}{2l_1^2 l_2^3}$

4.2.2 Approximation of Sums by Integrals

To study sums that involve SV functions, Phillips' idea is to approximate the sums by integrals and then apply calculus to the integrals. The first step is realized here.

Lemma.   (Phillips, 2007, Lemma 7.1) *If $L = K(\varepsilon)$, then for integer $B \geq 1$*

$$\sum_{t=B}^{n} L(t) = \int_{B}^{n} L(t)\, dt + O(n^{\gamma}), \quad as\ n \to \infty,$$

where $\gamma > 0$ is arbitrarily small.

Proof.   For a natural k, integration by parts gives

$$\int_{k}^{k+1} \left\{ t - \underbrace{[t]}_{\text{(integer part of } t)} - \frac{1}{2} \right\} L'(t)\, dt$$

$$= \int_{k}^{k+1} t L'(t)\, dt - \left(k + \frac{1}{2} \right) \int_{k}^{k+1} L'(t)\, dt$$

$$= (k+1)L(k+1) - kL(k) - \int_{k}^{k+1} L(t)\, dt - \left(k + \frac{1}{2} \right)[L(k+1) - L(k)]$$

$$= \frac{1}{2}(L(k+1) + L(k)) - \int_{k}^{k+1} L(t)\, dt.$$

Summation of equations like this yields

$$\sum_{k=B}^{n} L(k) = \sum_{k=B}^{n-1} \frac{1}{2}(L(k+1) + L(k)) + \frac{1}{2}(L(B) + L(n))$$

$$= \frac{1}{2}(L(B) + L(n)) + \int_{B}^{n} L(t)\, dt + \int_{B}^{n} \left\{ t - [t] - \frac{1}{2} \right\} L'(t)\, dt. \quad (4.3)$$

Using $L'(t) = \varepsilon(t)L(t)/t$ [see Eq. (4.2)] and $|t - [t] - 1/2| \leq 1/2$ (this is the idea of the proof) we bound the last integral as

$$\left| \int_{B}^{n} \left\{ t - [t] - \frac{1}{2} \right\} L'(t)\, dt \right| \leq \frac{1}{2} \int_{B}^{n} \left| \frac{L(t)\varepsilon(t)}{t} \right| dt$$

$$= \frac{1}{2} \int_{B}^{c} \left| \frac{L(t)\varepsilon(t)}{t} \right| dt + \frac{1}{2} \int_{c}^{n} \left| \frac{L(t)}{t^{\gamma}} \varepsilon(t) t^{\gamma-1} \right| dt.$$

Here, by Theorems 4.1.3 and 4.1.4 the constant $c > B$ can be chosen so that $|t^{-\gamma}L(t)| \le 1$, $|\varepsilon(t)| \le 1$. On $[B, c]$ the function $|L(t)\varepsilon(t)/t|$ is bounded. Hence,

$$\left| \int_B^n \left\{ t - [t] - \frac{1}{2} \right\} L'(t)\, dt \right| \le c_1 + \frac{1}{2} \int_c^n t^{\gamma-1}\, dt = O(n^\gamma).$$

Since $\frac{1}{2}(L(B) + L(n)) = O(n^\gamma)$ by Theorem 4.1.4, the lemma follows from Eq. (4.3). ∎

4.2.3 Simple Integral Asymptotics

Lemma.   *If* $L = K(\varepsilon)$, *then* $\int_1^n L(t)\, dt = nL(n)(1 + o(1))$ *and* $\sum_{t=1}^n L(t) = nL(n)$ $(1 + o(1))$.

Proof.   Choosing $\beta = 1$, $\eta \in (0, 1)$, $f \equiv 1$ in Theorem 4.1.5 we get

$$\frac{1}{nL(n)} \int_0^n L(t)\, dt = \frac{1}{L(n)} \int_0^1 L(ns)\, ds \ \longrightarrow \ 1.$$

By continuity of L and Theorem 4.1.4

$$\frac{1}{nL(n)} \int_0^1 L(t)\, dt \ \longrightarrow \ 0.$$

From the above two equations

$$\frac{1}{nL(n)} \int_1^n L(t)\, dt \ \longrightarrow \ 1$$

and the first statement follows upon multiplication of this equation by $nL(n)$.
  By Lemma 4.2.2

$$\sum_{t=1}^n L(t) = \int_1^n L(t)\, dt + O(n^\gamma)$$

$$= nL(n) + nL(n)o(1) + nL(n)O\left(\frac{n^{\gamma-1}}{L(n)} \right).$$

$1/L(n)$ is SV and, with $\gamma \in (0, 1)$, Theorem 4.1.4 implies $O\left(\dfrac{n^{\gamma-1}}{L(n)} \right) = o(1)$. Hence, the second statement follows.   ∎

4.2.4 Things Get Complicated

Lemma. *Denote $M(n) = \dfrac{1}{nL^k(n)} \int_0^1 L^k(t)\, dt$.*

  (i) *If $L = K(\varepsilon)$, then $M(n) = 1 + o(1)$.*

 (ii) *If, in addition, $\varepsilon = K(\eta)$, then $M(n) = 1 - k\varepsilon(n) + o(\varepsilon(n))$.*

(iii) *If, along with the previous assumptions, we suppose that $\eta = K(\mu)$, then*

$$M(n) = 1 - k\varepsilon(n) + k^2\varepsilon^2(n) + k\varepsilon(n)\eta(n) + o(\varepsilon^2(n) + \varepsilon(n)\eta(n)).$$

(iv) (Phillips, 2007, Lemma 7.2) *Finally, if in addition $\mu = K(v)$, then*

$$\begin{aligned}
M(n) = {}& 1 - k\varepsilon(n) + k^2\varepsilon^2(n) + k\varepsilon(n)\eta(n) - k^3\varepsilon^3(n) \\
& - 3k^2\varepsilon^2(n)\eta(n) - k\varepsilon(n)\eta^2(n) - k\varepsilon(n)\eta(n)\mu(n) \\
& + o[\varepsilon^3(n) + \varepsilon^2(n)\eta(n) + \varepsilon(n)\eta^2(n) + \varepsilon(n)\eta(n)\mu(n)].
\end{aligned}$$

Proof. Since $L = K(\varepsilon)$ implies $L^k = K(k\varepsilon)$, statement

  (i) follows from Lemma 4.2.3.

 (ii) Below we use repeatedly $tL'(t) = L(t)\varepsilon(t)$ and similar equations for ε, η, μ. Integrating by parts,

$$\begin{aligned}
I_1 &\equiv \int_1^n L^k(t)\, dt = [tL^k(t)]\big|_1^n - k \int_1^n tL^{k-1}(t)L'(t)\, dt \\
&= nL^k(n) - L^k(1) - k \int_1^n L^k(t)\varepsilon(t)\, dt.
\end{aligned} \tag{4.4}$$

Since $L^k\varepsilon$ is SV, to the end integral we can apply Lemma 4.2.3:

$$\begin{aligned}
I_1 &= nL^k(n) + O(1) - knL^k(n)\varepsilon(n)[1 + o(1)] \\
&= nL^k(n) + nL^k(n)\varepsilon(n)O\!\left(\frac{1}{nL^k(n)\varepsilon(n)}\right) - knL^k(n)\varepsilon(n)[1 + o(1)] \\
&= nL^k(n) - knL^k(n)\varepsilon(n)[1 + o(1)]
\end{aligned}$$

because $nL^k(n)\varepsilon(n) \to \infty$. This proves the statement. Three elements of this proof are used below as a standard procedure:

  1. A term that results from substitution of the lower limit of integration, like $L^k(1)$, is $O(1)$.

  2. Since products and powers of SV functions are SV, Lemma 4.2.3 and Theorem 4.1.4 are applicable.

  3. $O(1)$ is subsumed by the remainder that results from application of Lemma 4.2.3.

(iii) For the integral at the right of Eq. (4.4) we have

$$I_2 \equiv \int_1^n L^k(t)\varepsilon(t)\,dt = nL^k(n)\varepsilon(n) - k\int_1^n tL^{k-1}(t)L'(t)\varepsilon(t)\,dt$$

$$- \int_1^n tL^k(t)\varepsilon'(t)\,dt + O(1)$$

$$= nL^k(n)\varepsilon(n) - k\int_1^n L^k(t)\varepsilon^2(t)\,dt - \int_1^n L^k(t)\varepsilon(t)\eta(t)\,dt + O(1)$$

$$= nL^k(n)\varepsilon(n) - kI_3 - I_4 + O(1), \tag{4.5}$$

where

$$I_3 = \int_1^n L^k(t)\varepsilon^2(t)\,dt, \quad I_4 = \int_1^n L^k(t)\varepsilon(t)\eta(t)\,dt.$$

By the standard procedure we can combine Eqs. (4.4) and (4.5) and jump directly to

$$I_1 = nL^k(n) + O(1) - knL^k(n)\varepsilon(n) + k^2\int_1^n L^k(t)\varepsilon^2(t)\,dt + k\int_1^n L^k(t)\varepsilon(t)\eta(t)\,dt$$

$$= nL^k(n) - knL^k(n)\varepsilon(n) + k^2 nL^k(n)\varepsilon^2(n) + knL^k(n)\varepsilon(n)\eta(n)$$

$$+ nL^k(n)o[\varepsilon^2(n) + \varepsilon(n)\eta(n)],$$

which proves the proposition.

(iv) For I_3 and I_4 the representations are

$$I_3 = nL^k(n)\varepsilon^2(n) + O(1) - k\int_1^n tL^{k-1}(t)L'(t)\varepsilon^2(t)\,dt - 2\int_1^n tL^k(t)\varepsilon(t)\varepsilon'(t)\,dt$$

$$= nL^k(n)\varepsilon^2(n) - k\int_1^n L^k(t)\varepsilon^3(t)\,dt - 2\int_1^n L^k(t)\varepsilon^2(t)\eta(t)\,dt + O(1), \tag{4.6}$$

$$I_4 = nL^k(n)\varepsilon(n)\eta(n) + O(1) - k\int_1^n tL^{k-1}(t)L'(t)\varepsilon(t)\eta(t)\,dt$$

$$- \int_1^n tL^k(t)\varepsilon'(t)\eta(t)\,dt - \int_1^n tL^k(t)\varepsilon(t)\eta'(t)\,dt$$

$$= nL^k(n)\varepsilon(n)\eta(n) - k\int_1^n L^k(t)\varepsilon^2(t)\eta(t)\,dt$$

$$- \int_1^n L^k(t)\varepsilon(t)\eta^2(t)\,dt - \int_1^n L^k(t)\varepsilon(t)\eta(t)\mu(t)\,dt + O(1). \qquad (4.7)$$

Equations (4.4) through (4.7) imply

$$I_1 = nL^k(n) + O(1) - knL^k(n)\varepsilon(n) + k^2 I_3 + kI_4$$

$$= nL^k(n) + O(1) - knL^k(n)\varepsilon(n) + k^2 nL^k(n)\varepsilon^2(n) - k^3 \int_1^n L^k(t)\varepsilon^3(t)\,dt$$

$$- 2k^2 \int_1^n L^k(t)\varepsilon^2(t)\eta(t)\,dt + knL^k(n)\varepsilon(n)\eta(n) - k^2 \int_1^n L^k(t)\varepsilon^2(t)\eta(t)\,dt$$

$$- k\int_1^n L^k(t)\varepsilon(t)\eta^2(t)\,dt - k\int_1^n L^k(t)\varepsilon(t)\eta(t)\mu(t)\,dt$$

or, applying the standard procedure,

$$\begin{aligned} I_1 = {} & nL^k(n) - knL^k(n)\varepsilon(n) + k^2 nL^k(n)\varepsilon^2(n) + knL^k(n)\varepsilon(n)\eta(n) \\ & - k^3 nL^k(n)\varepsilon^3(n) - 3k^2 nL^k(n)\varepsilon^2(n)\eta(n) - knL^k(n)\varepsilon(n)\eta^2(n) \\ & - knL^k(n)\varepsilon(n)\eta(n)\mu(n) + nL^k(n)o[\varepsilon^3(n) + \varepsilon^2(n)\eta(n) \\ & + \varepsilon(n)\eta^2(n) + \varepsilon(n)\eta(n)\mu(n)]. \end{aligned}$$

∎

EXAMPLE 4.1.   In the logarithmic case $L(t) = \log t$ we have

$$\varepsilon(t) = \frac{tL'(t)}{L(t)} = \frac{1}{\log t}, \quad \eta(t) = \frac{t\varepsilon'(t)}{\varepsilon(t)} = -\frac{1}{\log t}, \quad \mu(t) = \frac{t\eta'(t)}{\eta(t)} = \eta(t).$$

Part (iv) of the lemma then gives the expansion

$$\begin{aligned} \int_1^n \log^k t\,dt = {} & n\log^k n - kn\log^{k-1} n + k^2 n\log^{k-2} n - kn\log^{k-2} n - k^3 n\log^{k-3} n \\ & + 3k^2 n\log^{k-3} n - kn\log^{k-3} n - kn\log^{k-3} n + o(n\log^{k-3} n) \\ = {} & n\log^k n - kn\log^{k-1} n + k(k-1)n\log^{k-2} n \\ & - k(k-1)(k-2)n\log^{k-3} n + o(n\log^{k-3} n). \qquad (4.8) \end{aligned}$$

However, successive integration by parts gives the exact result

$$\int_1^n \log^k t \, dt = n \log^k n - k \int_1^n \log^{k-1} t \, dt = \cdots$$

$$= n \log^k n - kn \log^{k-1} n + k(k-1)n \log^{k-2} n + \cdots$$
$$+ k!(n-1).$$

The expansion in Eq. (4.8) is accurate to the fourth order.

4.2.5 Expansion Related to Simple Regression

For the simple regression

$$y_t = \alpha + \beta L(t) + u_t, \quad t = 1, \ldots, n,$$

one version of the formulas for the OLS estimates $\hat{\alpha}$ and $\hat{\beta}$ is (Theil, 1971, Section 3.1)

$$\hat{\beta} - \beta = \sum_{t=1}^n (L(t) - \bar{L}) u_t \left[\sum_{t=1}^n (L(t) - \bar{L})^2 \right]^{-1} \tag{4.9}$$

$$\hat{\alpha} - \alpha = \frac{1}{n} \sum_{t=1}^n u_t - \bar{L}(\hat{\beta} - \beta) \tag{4.10}$$

where

$$\bar{L} = \frac{1}{n} \sum_{t=1}^n L(t)$$

is the average. This explains the interest in the next proposition.

Lemma. (Phillips, 2007, Lemma 7.3) *If* $L = K(\varepsilon)$, $\varepsilon = K(\eta)$, $\eta = K(\mu)$, *and* $\eta(n) = o(\varepsilon(n))$, *then*

$$\frac{1}{n} \sum_{t=1}^n (L(t) - \bar{L})^2 = L^2(n) \varepsilon^2(n)(1 + o(1)).$$

Proof. We use Lemma 4.2.4(iii) with $k = 2$ and $k = 1$. The argument n is omitted everywhere.

$$\frac{1}{n} \sum_{t=1}^n (L(t) - \bar{L})^2 = \frac{1}{n} \sum_{t=1}^n L^2(t) - \left[\frac{1}{n} \sum_{t=1}^n L(t) \right]^2$$

$$= L^2 \{ 1 - 2\varepsilon + 4\varepsilon^2 + 2\varepsilon\eta + o(\varepsilon^2 + \varepsilon\eta)$$
$$- [1 - \varepsilon + \varepsilon^2 + \varepsilon\eta + o(\varepsilon^2 + \varepsilon\eta)]^2 \}$$

$$= L^2 [1 - 2\varepsilon + 4\varepsilon^2 + 2\varepsilon\eta - 1 - \varepsilon^2 - \varepsilon^4 - \varepsilon^2\eta^2 + 2\varepsilon$$
$$- 2\varepsilon^2 - 2\varepsilon\eta + 2\varepsilon^3 + 2\varepsilon^2\eta - 2\varepsilon^3\eta + o(\varepsilon^2 + \varepsilon\eta)]$$

$$= L^2 [\varepsilon^2 + o(\varepsilon^2)], \tag{4.11}$$

where we remember that $\eta(n) = o(\varepsilon(n))$. ∎

4.2.6   Second-Order Regular Variation (Point-wise Version)

Denote

$$G(t, n) = \frac{L(t) - L(n)}{L(n)\varepsilon(n)} \tag{4.12}$$

and call this function a *G-function* of *L*.

Lemma.   [Phillips, 2007, Eq. (60)] *If $L = K(\varepsilon)$ and ε is SV in the general sense of Section 4.1.1, then*

$$G(rn, n) = \log r[1 + o(1)] \text{ uniformly in } r \in [a, b],$$

for any $0 < a < b < \infty$.

Proof.   From Karamata representation

$$\log \frac{L(rn)}{L(n)} = -\int_{rn}^{n} \varepsilon(t)\frac{dt}{t} = -\varepsilon(n) \int_{r}^{1} \frac{\varepsilon(ns)}{\varepsilon(n)}\frac{ds}{s}.$$

The conditions

$$r \in [a, b] \quad \text{and} \quad s \in \begin{cases} [r, 1] & \text{if } r < 1; \\ [1, r] & \text{if } r > 1, \end{cases}$$

imply $s \in [\min\{1, a\}, \max\{1, b\}]$. By the uniform-convergence Theorem 4.1.2 $\varepsilon(ns)/\varepsilon(n) \to 1$ uniformly in s, so

$$\log \frac{L(rn)}{L(n)} = -\varepsilon(n)[1 + o(1)] \int_{r}^{1} \frac{ds}{s} = \varepsilon(n) \log r[1 + o(1)].$$

This implies

$$\frac{L(rn)}{L(n)} - 1 = \exp\{\varepsilon(n) \log r[1 + o(1)]\} - 1$$

$$= \varepsilon(n) \log r[1 + o(1)] \text{ uniformly in } r \in [a, b]. \quad \blacksquare$$

Note, in passing, that *L* is second-order regularly varying [see de Haan and Resnick (1996)] in the sense that $\lim_{n \to \infty} G(rn, n) = \log r$, $r > 0$. Equation (4.1) is a first-order regular variation (RV) in this terminology.

4.2.7   Third-Order Regular Variation

Lemma.   (Phillips, 2007, Lemma 7.5) *If* $L = K(\varepsilon)$, $\varepsilon = K(\eta)$, *and* η *is SV, then*

$$G(rn, n) - \log r = \mu(n) \log^2 r + o(\varepsilon(n) + \eta(n)) \text{ uniformly in } r \in [a, b],$$

for any $0 < a < b < \infty$. *Here* $\mu(n) = \frac{1}{2}[\varepsilon(n) + \eta(n)]$.

Proof.   By Lemma 4.2.6, applied to ε instead of L,

$$\frac{\varepsilon(rn)}{\varepsilon(n)} = 1 + \eta(n) \log r + o(\eta(n) \log r) \text{ uniformly in } r \in [\min\{a, 1\}, \max\{b, 1\}].$$

The cases $r < 1$ and $r > 1$ are similar, so we consider just $r < 1$. If $r \le t/n \le 1$ and $r \in [a, b]$, then $t/n \in [\min\{a, 1\}, \max\{b, 1\}]$ and the above equation can be applied in

$$\log \frac{L(rn)}{L(n)} = -\int_{rn}^{n} \varepsilon(t) \frac{dt}{t} = -\varepsilon(n) \int_{rn}^{n} \frac{\varepsilon(n(t/n))}{\varepsilon(n)} \frac{dt}{t}$$

$$= -\varepsilon(n) \int_{rn}^{n} \left[1 + \eta(n) \log \frac{t}{n} + o\left(\eta(n) \log \frac{t}{n}\right) \right] \frac{dt}{t}$$

$$= \varepsilon(n) \log r - \varepsilon(n)\eta(n)[1 + o(1)] \int_{r}^{1} \log s \frac{ds}{s}$$

$$= \varepsilon(n) \log r + \frac{1}{2}\varepsilon(n)\eta(n) \log^2 r [1 + o(1)].$$

This equation and the approximation $e^x - 1 = x + \frac{x^2}{2} + o(x^2)$, $x \to 0$, give

$$\frac{L(rn)}{L(n)} - 1 = \exp\left\{ \varepsilon(n) \log r + \frac{1}{2} \varepsilon(n)\eta(n) \log^2 r[1 + o(1)] \right\} - 1$$

$$= \varepsilon(n) \log r + \frac{1}{2} \varepsilon(n)\eta(n) \log^2 r + o(\varepsilon(n)\eta(n) \log^2 r)$$

$$+ \frac{1}{2} \varepsilon^2(n) \log^2 r + \frac{1}{2} \varepsilon^2(n)\eta(n)\log^3 r$$

$$= \varepsilon(n) \log r + \frac{1}{2} \varepsilon(n)[\varepsilon(n) + \eta(n)] \log^2 r + o(\varepsilon^2(n) + \varepsilon(n)\eta(n)). \quad \blacksquare$$

EXAMPLE 4.2.   For $L(n) = 1/\log n$ we have $\varepsilon(n) = -1/\log n$, $\eta(n) = -1/\log n$ and, by direct expansion,

$$\frac{L(rn)}{L(n)} - 1 = \frac{-\log r}{\log r + \log n} = -\frac{\log r}{\log n}\frac{1}{1 + \log r/\log n}$$

$$= -\frac{\log r}{\log n}\sum_{j=0}^{\infty}(-1)^j\left(\frac{\log r}{\log n}\right)^j \quad \text{if } |\log r| < \log n,$$

which agrees with the third-order expansion given in the lemma.

4.3   SLOWLY VARYING FUNCTIONS WITH REMAINDER

4.3.1   Definition and Notation $L = K(\varepsilon, \phi)$

Phillips (2007, Lemma 7.4) establishes an important property that

$$\int_0^1 \left(\frac{L(rn)}{L(n)} - 1\right)^k dr = (-1)^k k!\varepsilon^k(n)[1 + o(1)], \quad n \to \infty, \tag{4.13}$$

for any natural k, but its proof is incomplete. The full proof given in Section 4.3.7 relies on the theory of SV functions with remainder by Aljančić *et al.* (1955). We shall use the interpretation of that theory contained in the appendix of Shiganov in Seneta (1985).

Let us call a *remainder* a positive function ϕ on $[0, \infty)$ with properties:

1. ϕ is nondecreasing and $\phi(x) \to \infty$ as $x \to \infty$,
2. there exist positive numbers $\theta = \theta_\phi$, X such that $x^{-\theta}\phi(x)$ is nonincreasing on $[X, \infty)$.

A positive measurable function L defined on $[0, \infty)$ is called *SV with remainder* ϕ if for any $\lambda > 0$

$$L(\lambda x)/L(x) = 1 + O(1/\phi(x)), \quad x \to \infty$$

It is the same definition as before, with a makeweight in the form of a bound on the rate of convergence. For the examples considered in Section 4.2.1 the functions $L_i = K(\varepsilon_i)$ are SV with remainder $\phi_i(x) = 1/|\varepsilon_i(x)|$, and the number $\theta > 0$ can be taken arbitrarily close to 0. If $L = K(\varepsilon)$ and L is SV with remainder ϕ, we write $L = K(\varepsilon, \phi)$.

4.3.2   Basic Properties of Slowly Varying Functions with Remainder

Theorem. *(i) (Seneta, 1985, p. 100) For a SV function with remainder the Karamata representation (item 1 of Section 4.3.1) holds with the* *corresponding bounds on the rates*:

$$\mu(x) - c = O(1/\phi(x)), \quad \varepsilon(x) = O(1/\phi(x)). \tag{4.14}$$

(ii) (Seneta, 1985, p. 101) The uniform convergence theorem holds with the following bound on the rate of convergence: if L is SV with remainder ϕ, then

$$\sup\left\{\left|\left|\frac{L(\lambda x)}{L(x)} - 1\right|\right|:\lambda \in [a, b]\right\} = O(1/\phi(x)), \quad x \to \infty, \tag{4.15}$$

for any fixed $0 < a < b < \infty$.

4.3.3 Bounding the Log by the Power Function

We need bounds of type

$$2 + \log \lambda \le c_1 \lambda^a \quad \text{for } \lambda \ge 1 \tag{4.16}$$

and

$$2 - \log \lambda \le c_2 \lambda^{-a} \quad \text{for } 0 < \lambda \le 1, \tag{4.17}$$

where $a > 0$. Equation (4.17) is reduced to Eq. (4.16) by inverting λ. The precise value of c_1, c_2 does not matter much, and therefore in the next lemma bound (4.16) is obtained for all $\lambda > 0$.

Lemma. *Equations (4.16) and (4.17) are true with $c_1 = c_2 = \frac{1}{a}e^{2a-1}$.*

Proof. Consider $f(\lambda) = c_1\lambda^a - 2 - \log \lambda$. The first-order condition is

$$f'(\lambda) = c_1 a\lambda^{a-1} - \frac{1}{\lambda} = 0; \quad c_1 a\lambda^a = 1,$$

so the minimum point is $\lambda_0 = [1/(c_1 a)]^{1/a}$ (at 0 and ∞ the function goes to ∞). c_1 is determined from the tangency condition $f(\lambda_0) = 0$:

$$c_1 \frac{1}{c_1 a} - 2 - \frac{1}{a} \log \frac{1}{c_1 a} = 0; \quad \log \frac{1}{c_1 a} = 1 - 2a; \quad c_1 = \frac{1}{a}e^{2a-1}.$$

Substituting $1/\lambda$ for λ in Eq. (4.17) we get $2 + \log \lambda \le c_2 \lambda^a$. Hence, $c_2 = c_1$. ∎

4.3.4 The Case of Large λ

The purpose of this and Section 4.3.5 is to complement the uniform convergence theorem (4.15) with statements that cover large and small λ. Denote

$$r(\lambda, x) = L(\lambda x)/L(x), \quad U(\lambda, x) = \log r(\lambda, x).$$

Using an elementary bound $|e^x - 1| \leq |x|e^{|x|}$ we see that it suffices to estimate the right-hand side of

$$|r(\lambda, x) - 1| = |e^{U(\lambda, x)} - 1| \leq |U(\lambda, x)|e^{|U(\lambda, x)|}. \tag{4.18}$$

Lemma. (Seneta, 1985, p. 102) *If L is SV with remainder ϕ, then for any $a > 0$ there exist constants $M_a > 0$ and $B_a \geq B$ such that*

$$|r(\lambda, x) - 1| \leq M_a \lambda^a / \phi(x) \quad \text{for all } x \geq B_a \quad \text{and} \quad \lambda \geq 1.$$

Proof. Let $x \geq B$ and $\lambda \geq 1$. The Karamata representation 4.1.3(i) implies

$$U(\lambda, x) = \log L(\lambda x) - \log L(x) = \mu(\lambda x) - \mu(x) + \int_x^{\lambda x} \varepsilon(t) \frac{dt}{t}, \tag{4.19}$$

where $\lambda x \geq x$. By Eq. (4.14) there exists a constant $K > 0$ such that

$$|\mu(x) - c| \leq K/\phi(x), \quad |\varepsilon(x)| \leq K/\phi(x). \tag{4.20}$$

Since ϕ is nondecreasing, we can use Eqs. (4.19) and (4.20) to get

$$|U(\lambda, x)| \leq |\mu(\lambda x) - c| + |c - \mu(x)| + \int_x^{\lambda x} |\varepsilon(t)| \frac{dt}{t}$$

$$\leq \frac{K}{\phi(\lambda x)} + \frac{K}{\phi(x)} + K \int_x^{\lambda x} \frac{1}{\phi(t)} \frac{dt}{t}$$

$$\leq \frac{2K}{\phi(x)} + \frac{K}{\phi(x)} \int_x^{\lambda x} \frac{dt}{t} = K(2 + \log \lambda)/\phi(x). \tag{4.21}$$

Combining this with Eq. (4.18) we have

$$|r(\lambda, x) - 1| \leq \frac{K(2 + \log \lambda)}{\phi(x)} e^{2K/\phi(x)} \lambda^{K/\phi(x)}.$$

By Lemma 4.3.3 we can dominate the factor $2 + \log \lambda$ with $\lambda^{a/2}$:

$$|r(\lambda, x) - 1| \leq \frac{Kc_1}{\phi(x)} e^{2K/\phi(x)} \lambda^{K/\phi(x) + a/2}, \tag{4.22}$$

where $c_1 = c_1(a/2)$. Since $\phi(x) \to \infty$, there is $B_a \geq B$ (B is the lower limit of integration in the Karamata representation) such that $K/\phi(x) \leq a/2$ for $x \geq B_a$.

Therefore from Eq. (4.22) we finally obtain

$$|r(\lambda, x) - 1| \leq \frac{Kc_1}{\phi(x)} e^a \lambda^a = M_a \lambda^a / \phi(x) \quad \text{for} \quad x \geq B_a, \quad \lambda \geq 1,$$

where $M_a = Kc_1 e^a$. ∎

4.3.5   The Case of Small λ

Lemma 4.3.4 is given just for completeness and illustrative purposes. Only Lemma 4.3.5 is used subsequently. It means that the larger x, the closer λ is allowed to be to 0.

Lemma.   (Seneta, 1985, p. 102) *If L is SV with remainder ϕ, then for any $b > \theta$ [where θ is the number from item 2 of Section 4.3.1(ii)] there exist constants $M_b > 0$ and $B_b \geq B$ such that*

$$|r(\lambda, x) - 1| \leq M_b \lambda^{-b} / \phi(x) \quad \text{for all } x \geq B_b \quad \text{and} \quad B_b / x \leq \lambda \leq 1.$$

Proof.   In (Seneta, 1985, p. 102) there is a typo: this lemma is stated with $b > 0$ instead of $b > \theta$. Let $x \geq B$ and $B/x \leq \lambda \leq 1$. Since $\lambda x \leq x$, instead of Eq. (4.19) we have

$$U(\lambda, x) = \mu(\lambda x) - \mu(x) - \int_{\lambda x}^{x} \varepsilon(t) \frac{dt}{t}$$

and instead of Eq. (4.21)

$$|U(\lambda, x)| \leq \frac{2K}{\phi(\lambda x)} + \frac{K}{\phi(\lambda x)} \int_{\lambda x}^{x} \frac{dt}{t} = K(2 - \log \lambda)/\phi(\lambda x). \tag{4.23}$$

Fix some $b > \theta$. Using monotonicity of ϕ and that it increases to ∞ at ∞, from $B_b \leq x\lambda$ we have $K/\phi(\lambda x) \leq K/\phi(B_b) < (b - \theta)/2$ for a sufficiently large $B_b \geq B$. Then by Eq. (4.23)

$$|U(\lambda, x)| \leq \frac{b - \theta}{2}(2 - \log \lambda) = b - \theta - \frac{b - \theta}{2} \log \lambda. \tag{4.24}$$

However, by property 4.3.1(ii) of ϕ the inequality $\lambda x \leq x$ implies

$$(\lambda x)^{-\theta} \phi(\lambda x) \geq x^{-\theta} \phi(x) \quad \text{and} \quad 1/\phi(\lambda x) \leq \lambda^{-\theta}/\phi(x).$$

Hence, from Eq. (4.23)

$$|U(\lambda, x)| \leq K\lambda^{-\theta}(2 - \log \lambda)/\phi(x). \tag{4.25}$$

Using Eq. (4.25) for the first factor at the right of Eq. (4.18) and Eq. (4.24) for the second factor, we see that

$$|r(\lambda, x) - 1| \le \frac{K\lambda^{-\theta}}{\phi(x)}(2 - \log \lambda)e^{b-\theta}\lambda^{(-(b-\theta)/2)}.$$

To dominate $2 - \log \lambda$, in Eq. (4.17) put $a = (b - \theta)/2 > 0$. Then

$$|r(\lambda, x) - 1| \le \frac{K}{\phi(x)}e^{b-\theta}c_2\lambda^{-\theta-((b-\theta)/2)/((b-\theta)/2)} = M_b\lambda^{-b}/\phi(x),$$

where $M_b = Kc_2e^{b-\theta}$. ∎

Remark 4.1. Since in practical cases the number θ can be arbitrarily close to 0, the number $b > \theta$ can also be as close to 0 as desired.

4.3.6 Assumption 4.1 (for Second-Order Regular Variation)

The function L is SV with remainder and of form $L = K(\varepsilon)$ where ε is SV in the general sense of Section 4.1.1 and the remainder ϕ_ε (with properties 1 and 2 from Section 4.3.1) with some positive c satisfies

$$\frac{1}{c\phi_\varepsilon(x)} \le |\varepsilon(x)| \le \frac{c}{\phi_\varepsilon(x)} \qquad \text{for all } x \ge c. \tag{4.26}$$

As a result of the importance of this assumption, we write it out completely:

1. L has Karamata representation

$$L(x) = c_L \exp\left(\int_B^x \varepsilon(t)\frac{dt}{t}\right) \qquad \text{for } x \ge B$$

for some $B > 0$. Here $c_L > 0$ is a constant, ε is a continuous function and $\varepsilon(x) \to 0$ as $x \to \infty$. Further, L is continuous on $[0, \infty)$. [This part of the assumption is written as $L = K(\varepsilon)$ for short.]

2. ε is SV in the sense of the general definition in Section 4.1.1.

3. There exists a function ϕ_ε on $[0, \infty)$ with properties:

(3a) ϕ_ε is positive, nondecreasing on $[0, \infty)$, $\phi_\varepsilon(x) \to \infty$ as $x \to \infty$, and there exist positive numbers θ, X such that $x^{-\theta}\phi_\varepsilon(x)$ is nonincreasing on $[X, \infty)$;

(3b) $\varepsilon(x)$ is *quasi-monotone* for large x in the sense that with some positive constant c satisfies Eq. (4.26).

We write $L = K(\varepsilon, \phi_\varepsilon)$ for short to mean that L satisfies Assumption 4.1. In all practical examples from Section 4.2.1, Assumption 4.1 holds with $\phi_\varepsilon(x) = 1/|\varepsilon(x)|$.

4.3.7 Second-Order Regular Variation (Integral Version)

Lemma.   (Phillips, 2007, Lemma 7.4) *If Assumption 4.1 holds and $\theta = \theta_\phi \in (0, 1/k)$, then Eq. (4.13) is true.*

Proof.   Using the G-function (4.12) and the identity

$$\int_0^1 \log^k r \, dr = (-1)^k k! \tag{4.27}$$

we rewrite Eq. (4.13) as

$$\int_0^1 [G^k(rn, n) - \log^k r] \, dr \longrightarrow 0. \tag{4.28}$$

Let $0 < \delta < 1$.

Step 1.   Lemma 4.2.6 implies

$$G^k(rn, n) = \log^k r[1 + o(1)] \quad \text{uniformly in } r \in [a, b]. \tag{4.29}$$

Hence,

$$\int_\delta^1 [G^k(rn, n) - \log^k r] \, dr \longrightarrow 0, \quad n \longrightarrow \infty. \tag{4.30}$$

Step 2.   The right inequality in Eq. (4.26) means that L is SV with remainder ϕ_ε and allows us to apply Lemma 4.3.5. For $n > B_b/\delta$ the interval $(B_b/n, \delta)$ is not empty and

$$|G(rn, n)| \leq \frac{M_b r^{-b}}{\phi_\varepsilon(n)|\varepsilon(n)|} \quad \text{for } n \geq B_b/\delta \quad \text{and} \quad B_b/n \leq r \leq \delta.$$

Hence, using also the left inequality in Eq. (4.26), we have

$$\int_{B_b/n}^\delta |G^k(rn, n)| \, dr \leq \int_0^\delta \left(\frac{M_b r^{-b}}{\phi_\varepsilon(n)|\varepsilon(n)|} \right)^k dr$$

$$\leq \left(\frac{M_b}{c_1} \right)^k \int_0^\delta r^{-bk} \, dr = c_4 \delta^{1-bk}. \tag{4.31}$$

This tends to zero if $b \in (0, 1/k)$. This condition can be satisfied because b is arbitrarily close to θ.

Step 3. If $0 < r \le B_b/n$, then $rn \le B_b$ and $L(rn) \le c$ by continuity of L. As a result,

$$|G^k(rn, n)| \le \frac{1}{|\varepsilon(n)|^k} \left(\frac{c}{L(n)} + 1 \right)^k,$$

where the function on the right is SV. From Theorem 4.1.4 it follows that

$$\int_0^{B_b/n} |G^k(rn, n)| \, dr \le \frac{1}{|\varepsilon(n)|^k} \left(\frac{c}{L(n)} + 1 \right)^k \frac{B_b}{n} \longrightarrow 0, \quad n \longrightarrow \infty. \quad (4.32)$$

Equations (4.30), (4.31), and (4.32), together with

$$\left| \int_0^\delta \log^k r \, dr \right| \longrightarrow 0, \quad \delta \longrightarrow 0,$$

show that we can choose first a small δ and then a large n to make the left side of Eq. (4.28) as small as desired.   ■

4.4   RESULTS BASED ON L_P-APPROXIMABILITY

This section demonstrates that Assumption 4.1 (Section 4.3.6), coupled with an assumption on linear processes, is sufficient for all asymptotic results.

4.4.1   Theorem on L_p-Approximability of G

Theorem. (Mynbaev, 2009) *For $p \in [1, \infty)$ and integral $k \ge 0$ define a vector $w_n \in \mathbb{R}^n$ by*

$$w_{nt} = n^{-1/p} G^k(t, n), \quad t = 1, \ldots, n.$$

If $L = K(\varepsilon, \phi_\varepsilon)$ and $p\theta k < 1$, then $\{w_n\}$ is L_p-close to $f_k(x) = \log^k x$.

Proof.   The case $k = 0$ is trivial. The definitions of w_n and interpolation operator Δ_{np} (Section 2.1.6) give

$$\Delta_{np} w_n = \sum_{t=1}^n G^k(t, n) 1_{i_t}. \quad (4.33)$$

This is equivalent to n equations

$$(\Delta_{np} w_n)(u) = G^k(t, n) \quad \text{for } u \in i_t, \quad t = 1, \ldots, n.$$

The condition $u \in i_t$ is equivalent to the condition that t is an integer satisfying $t \leq nu + 1 < t + 1$ which, in turn, is equivalent to $t = [nu + 1]$. Hence, the above n equations take a compact form

$$(\Delta_{np} w_n)(u) = G^k([nu + 1], n), \quad 0 \leq u < 1. \tag{4.34}$$

Let $0 < \delta \leq 1/2$ and apply Lemma 4.3.5. With the number B_b from that lemma for $n > n_1 \equiv B_b/\delta$ the interval $(B_b/n, \delta)$ is not empty, and by the triangle inequality

$$\|\Delta_{np} w_n - f_k\|_{p,(0,1)} \leq \|\Delta_{np} w_n - f_k\|_{p,(\delta,1)} + \|f_k\|_{p,(0,\delta)}$$
$$+ \|\Delta_{np} w_n\|_{p,(0,B_b/n)} + \|\Delta_{np} w_n\|_{p,(B_b/n,\delta)}. \tag{4.35}$$

Obviously, $\|f_k\|_{p,(0,\delta)} \to 0$ as $\delta \to 0$. For the other three terms we consider three cases.

Case 1. $\delta \leq u < 1$. According to Eq. (4.29)

$$G^k(rn, n) = \log^k r[1 + o(1)] \text{ uniformly in } r \in \left[\delta, 1 + \frac{1}{2B_b}\right] \tag{4.36}$$

Defining $r = [nu + 1]/n$, from the inequality $nu < [nu + 1] \leq nu + 1$ we have

$$\delta \leq u < r \leq u + \frac{1}{n} < 1 + \frac{1}{n_1} \leq 1 + \frac{1}{2B_b}, \tag{4.37}$$

so that

$$r = u + o(1) \quad \text{and} \quad r \in \left[\delta, 1 + \frac{1}{2B_b}\right]. \tag{4.38}$$

Equations (4.36) and (4.38) lead to

$$G^k([nu + 1], n) - \log^k u = o(1) \text{ uniformly in } u \in (\delta, 1).$$

This proves that

$$\|\Delta_{np} w_n - f_k\|_{p,(\delta,1)} \to 0, \quad n \to \infty. \tag{4.39}$$

Case 2. $B_b/n \leq u < \delta$. Let $n > n_2 \equiv \max\{n_1, 2\}$. Then Eq. (4.37) and the conditions $u \in [B_b/n, \delta), n > n_2$ imply

$$\frac{B_b}{n} \leq u < r \leq u + \frac{1}{n} < \delta + \frac{1}{n_2} \leq 1.$$

This means we can apply Lemma 4.3.5, the left inequality of Eq. (4.26) and Eq. (4.37) to get

$$|G^k([nu+1],n)| \leq \left[\frac{M_b}{r^b \phi_\varepsilon(n)|\varepsilon(n)|}\right]^k \leq \left[\frac{M_b}{c_1}\right]^k u^{-bk} \quad \text{for } u \in \left[\frac{B_b}{n}, \delta\right).$$

Fixing $b \in (\theta, 1/(pk))$ we have, with a new constant c_2 (independent of n and δ),

$$\int_{B_b/n}^{\delta} |\Delta_{np} w_n|^p \, du \leq c_2 \int_0^{\delta} u^{-pbk} \, du = \frac{c_2}{1-pbk} \delta^{1-pbk}. \qquad (4.40)$$

Case 3. $0 < u < B_b/n$. In this case $[nu+1] \leq nu+1 < B_b+1$ and $L([nu+1]) \leq c$ by the assumed continuity of L. Hence,

$$|G([nu+1],n)| \leq (c/L(n)+1)/|\varepsilon(n)| \qquad (4.41)$$

and

$$\|\Delta_{np} w_n\|_{p,(0,B_b/n)} \leq \left[\left(\frac{c}{L(n)}+1\right)\frac{1}{|\varepsilon(n)|}\right]^k \left(\frac{B_b}{n}\right)^{1/p}. \qquad (4.42)$$

Here the expression on the right tends to zero because the expression in the square brackets is a SV function by Theorem 4.1.1, and Theorem 4.1.4 applies to the whole expression.

From Equations (4.39), (4.40), and (4.42) we see that we can choose first a small δ and then a large n to make the left side of Eq. (4.35) as small as desired. ∎

4.4.2 Second-Order Regular Variation (Discrete Version)

Corollary. If $L = K(\varepsilon, \phi_\varepsilon)$ and $\theta k < 1$, then

$$\lim_{n \to \infty} \frac{1}{n} \sum_{t=1}^{n} G^k(t,n) = (-1)^k k!$$

Proof. Put $p = 1$ in Theorem 4.4.1. Equations (4.27) and (4.33) imply

$$\left|\frac{1}{n}\sum_{t=1}^{n} G^k(t,n) - (-1)^k k!\right| = \left|\int_0^1 \Delta_{n1} w_n \, du - \int_0^1 \log^k u \, du\right|$$

$$\leq \|\Delta_{n1} w_n - f_k\|_{1,(0,1)} \longrightarrow 0. \qquad \blacksquare$$

4.4.3   Averages of Slowly Varying Functions

The next proposition is a discrete analog of Lemma 4.2.4(ii).

Corollary.   *If $L = K(\varepsilon, \phi_\varepsilon)$ and $\theta < 1$, then*

$$\frac{1}{nL^k(n)} \sum_{t=1}^{n} L^k(t) = 1 - k\varepsilon(n)[1 + o(1)].$$

Proof.   Letting $k = 1$ in the corollary in Section 4.4.2 yields

$$\frac{1}{n} \sum_{t=1}^{n} G(t, n) = -[1 + o(1)],$$

which can be rearranged to

$$\frac{1}{nL(n)} \sum_{t=1}^{n} L(t) = 1 - \varepsilon(n)[1 + o(1)]. \tag{4.43}$$

The ε-function of L^k is $x(L^k(x))'/L^k(x) = k\varepsilon(x)$ and $L(\lambda x)/L(x) = 1 + O(1/\phi_\varepsilon(x))$ implies $L^k(\lambda x)/L^k(x) = 1 + O(1/\phi_\varepsilon(x))$. Hence, $L^k = K(k\varepsilon, \phi_\varepsilon)$, so Eq. (4.43), applied to L^k, proves the corollary.   ∎

4.4.4   Averages of Squared Deviations from the Mean

The following proposition is an analog of Lemma 4.2.5.

Corollary.   *If $L = K(\varepsilon, \phi_\varepsilon)$ and $2\theta < 1$, then*

$$\frac{1}{n} \sum_{t=1}^{n} (L(t) - \bar{L})^2 = L^2(n)\varepsilon^2(n)[1 + o(1)].$$

Proof.   In the identity $E(Y - EY)^2 = EY^2 - (EY)^2$ take the random variable Y to be a discrete variable with values $Y_t = L(t)/L(n) - 1$, $t = 1, \ldots, n$, and uniform probability distribution $p_1 = \cdots = p_n = 1/n$. Then $EY = \bar{Y} = \bar{L}/L(n) - 1$ and $Y_t - EY = (L(t) - \bar{L})/L(n)$. The above identity gives

$$\frac{1}{n} \sum_{t=1}^{n} \left(\frac{L(t) - \bar{L}}{L(n)}\right)^2 = \frac{1}{n} \sum_{t=1}^{n} \left(\frac{L(t)}{L(n)} - 1\right)^2 - \left(\frac{1}{n} \sum_{t=1}^{n} \left(\frac{L(t)}{L(n)} - 1\right)\right)^2.$$

This implies

$$\frac{1}{nL^2(n)\varepsilon^2(n)} \sum_{t=1}^{n} (L(t) - \bar{L})^2 = \frac{1}{n} \sum_{t=1}^{n} G^2(t, n) - \left[\frac{1}{n} \sum_{t=1}^{n} G(t, n)\right]^2.$$

To finish the proof, it remains to apply Corollary 4.4.2 with $k = 1$ and $k = 2$.   ∎

4.4.5   Summary on Normalizing Factors

The main sequences of weights arising in the Phillips approach are (see Section 4.5)

$$x_n = (L(1), \dots, L(n)),$$

$$y_n = (L(1) - \bar{L}, \dots, L(n) - \bar{L}),$$

$$z_n = ((L(1) - L(n))^k, \dots, (L(n) - L(n))^k).$$

From Corollaries 4.4.3, 4.4.4, and 4.4.2, respectively, we see that

$$\|x_n\|_2 = \sqrt{n}L(n)[1 + o(1)],$$
$$\|y_n\|_2 = \sqrt{n}L(n)|\varepsilon(n)|[1 + o(1)],$$
$$\|z_n\|_2 = \sqrt{n}(L(n)|\varepsilon(n)|)^k\sqrt{(2k)!}[1 + o(1)].$$

Hence, instead of $\| \cdot \|_2$-norms we can use $\sqrt{n}L(n)$ for x_n, $\sqrt{n}L(n)\varepsilon(n)$ for y_n (the sign does not matter because of the symmetry of normal distributions) and $\sqrt{n}(L(n)\varepsilon(n))^k$ for z_n. This explains the choice of weights in Section 4.4.6.

4.4.6   Central Limit Results for Linear Regression

Here we need a new assumption.

4.4.6.1   Assumption 4.2 (On Linear Process) Let $\{\psi_j : j \in \mathbb{Z}\}$ be a sequence of numbers satisfying $\sum_{j \in \mathbb{Z}} |\psi_j| < \infty$, and let $\{e_j : j \in \mathbb{Z}\}$ be a *m.d.* such that e_t^2 are uniformly integrable and $E(e_t^2|\mathcal{F}_{t-1}) = \sigma_e^2$ for all t. Here $\{\mathcal{F}_t\}$ is an increasing sequence of σ-fields. A linear process $\{u_j : j \in \mathbb{Z}\}$ is defined by

$$u_t = \sum_{j \in \mathbb{Z}} \psi_j e_{t-j}, \quad t \in \mathbb{Z}.$$

(Phillips 2007, Lemma 2.1) makes a stronger assumption on the linear process than in the next lemma.

Lemma.   *Denote* $\sigma^2 = \left(\sigma_e \sum_{j \in \mathbb{Z}} \psi_j\right)^2$. *Under Assumptions 4.1 (Section 4.3.6) and 4.2 (Section 4.4.6.1) the following statements are true:*

(i) If $2\theta < 1$, *then* $\dfrac{1}{\sqrt{n}L(n)} \sum_{t=1}^{n} L(t)u_t \xrightarrow{d} N(0, \sigma^2)$.

(ii) If $2\theta < 1$, *then* $\dfrac{1}{\sqrt{n}L(n)\varepsilon(n)} \sum_{t=1}^{n} (L(t) - \bar{L})u_t \xrightarrow{d} N(0, \sigma^2)$.

(iii) If $2\theta k < 1$, *then* $\dfrac{1}{\sqrt{n}} \sum_{t=1}^{n} G^k(t, n)u_t \xrightarrow{d} N(0, \sigma^2(2k)!)$.

In the case $\sum_{j \in \mathbb{Z}} \psi_j = 0$, everywhere convergence in distribution can be replaced by convergence in probability to zero.

Proof. By Theorem 3.5.2 it is enough to establish L_2-approximability of the sequence of weights in question.

(i) Setting $p = 2$, $k = 1$ in Theorem 4.4.1 gives

$$\int_0^1 \left| \frac{L([nu+1]) - L(n)}{L(n)\varepsilon(n)} - \log u \right|^2 du \; \longrightarrow \; 0.$$

Multiply this relation by $\varepsilon^2(n) \to 0$ to obtain

$$\int_0^1 \left| \frac{L([nu+1])}{L(n)} - 1 \right|^2 du \; \longrightarrow \; 0.$$

In a similar way to the transition from Eq. (4.33) to Eq. (4.34) we have

$$\Delta_{n2} \left[\frac{1}{\sqrt{nL(n)}} (L(1), \ldots, L(n)) \right] = \frac{1}{L(n)} \sum_{t=1}^n L(t) 1_{i_t} = \frac{L([nu+1])}{L(n)}.$$

This shows that the sequence $\dfrac{1}{\sqrt{nL(n)}}(L(1), \ldots, L(n))$ is L_2-close to $g \equiv 1$.

(ii) From Eq. (4.43) we conclude that $\bar{L} = L(n) - L(n)\varepsilon(n)[1 + o(1)]$ and that the sequence of weights in statement (ii) is

$$w_n = \frac{1}{\sqrt{nL(n)}\varepsilon(n)} (L(1) - \bar{L}, \ldots, L(n) - \bar{L})$$

$$= \frac{1}{\sqrt{n}} (G(1, n), \ldots, G(n, n)) + \frac{1 + o(1)}{\sqrt{n}} (1, \ldots, 1).$$

It is easy to see that the second sequence on the right is L_2-close to $g \equiv 1$. The first sequence is L_2-close to f_1 by Theorem 4.4.1. Hence, w_n is L_2-close to $g_1(x) \equiv 1 + \log x$. The statement follows from the fact that $\int_0^1 g_1^2(x) \, dx = 1$.

Statement (iii) follows directly from Theorem 4.4.1 and Eq. (4.27). ∎

4.4.7 Controlling Small λ for Third-Order Regular Variation

To study higher-order expansions we need a condition that is stronger than Assumption 4.1 (Section 4.3.6).

4.4.7.1 Assumption 4.3

1. $L = K(\varepsilon, \phi_\varepsilon)$, $\varepsilon = K(\eta, \phi_\eta)$ where η is a general SV function (in particular, ε and η are quasi-monotone).

2. The function $\mu(x) = (\varepsilon(x) + \eta(x))/2$ is different from zero for all large x and satisfies the condition

$$\frac{1}{c}\max\{|\varepsilon(x)|, |\eta(x)|\} \leq |\mu(x)| \leq \max\{|\varepsilon(x)|, |\eta(x)|\}. \tag{4.44}$$

The constant c in Eqs. (4.26) and (4.44) is the same because, if these conditions hold with different constants, the constants can be replaced by the largest of them.

From Table 4.1 we see that $\mu(x)$ can be either identically zero or different from zero for all large x. When μ is not identically zero, $|\mu(x)|$ happens to be of order of the largest of $|\varepsilon(x)|$ and $|\eta(x)|$, and Eq. (4.44) is satisfied. Assumption 4.3 is designed to analyze the effects of expansion terms up to $\log^2 x$. Condition 2 excludes vanishing μ. If μ vanishes, $\log^2 x$ is not in the asymptotic expansion of $L(x)$, and higher-order approximations need to be considered.

There are different ways to characterize proximity of the G-function of L to $\log r$. Lemma 4.2.6 establishes the pointwise version

$$G(rn, n) = \log r[1 + o(1)] \text{ uniformly in } r \in [a, b].$$

Lemma 4.3.7 supplies the integral version:

$$\int_0^1 G^k(rn, n)\, dr = (-1)^k k![1 + o(1)], \quad n \longrightarrow \infty.$$

There is also an L_p-approximability relation (Theorem 4.4.1)

$$\left\| \sum_{t=1}^n G^k(t, n) 1_{i_t}(\cdot) - \log^k(\cdot) \right\|_{p,(0,1)}$$

and its discrete counterpart (Corollary 4.4.2)

$$\frac{1}{n}\sum_{t=1}^n G^k(t, n) = (-1)^k k![1 + o(1)], \quad n \longrightarrow \infty.$$

As we have seen, the L_p-approximability relation is the most useful. The purpose of this and the next few sections is to prove an L_p-approximability statement for

$$H(t, n) = \frac{G(t, n) - \log(t/n)}{\mu(n)},$$

which we call an *H-function*. By Lemma 4.2.7

$$H(rn, n) = \log^2 r[1 + o(1)], \quad n \longrightarrow \infty,$$

so $\sum_{t=1}^{n} H(t, n) 1_{i_t}(x)$ should be L_p-close to $\log^2 x$. The analysis of the proof of Theorem 4.4.1 shows that to prove this fact we need to bound $H(rn, n)$ for small r. This is done with the help of the next lemma.

Lemma. *If L satisfies Assumption 4.3 (Section 4.4.7.1), then for any $b > \max\{2\theta_\varepsilon, \theta_\eta\}$ there exist constants $M_b > 0$ and $B_b \geq B$ such that*

$$|G(\lambda x, x) - \log \lambda| \leq M_b \lambda^{-b} \left(\frac{1}{\phi_\varepsilon(x)} + \frac{1}{\phi_\eta(x)} \right) \quad \text{for } x \geq B_b \quad \text{and} \quad \frac{B_b}{x} \leq \lambda \leq 1.$$

Proof.   Denote $U(\lambda, x) = \log L(\lambda x)/L(x)$ and consider

$$L(\lambda x)/L(x) - 1 - \varepsilon(x) \log \lambda = e^{U(\lambda, x)} - 1 - U(\lambda, x) + U(\lambda, x)$$
$$- \varepsilon(x) \log \lambda. \tag{4.45}$$

By Lemma 4.3.5 applied to $\varepsilon = K(\eta, \phi_\eta)$

$$|\varepsilon(\lambda x)/\varepsilon(x) - 1| \leq c_1 \lambda^{-b_\eta}/\phi_\eta(x) \quad \text{for all } x \geq B_b \quad \text{and} \quad B_b/x \leq \lambda \leq 1 \tag{4.46}$$

where $b_\eta > \theta_\eta$ and c_1 depends on b_η.

Since $U(\lambda, x) = -\int_{\lambda x}^{x} \varepsilon(t)\, dt/t$, we have

$$|U(\lambda, x) - \varepsilon(x) \log \lambda| = \left| -\int_{\lambda x}^{x} \varepsilon(t) \frac{dt}{t} + \varepsilon(x) \int_{\lambda x}^{x} \frac{dt}{t} \right|$$

$$= \left| \varepsilon(x) \int_{\lambda x}^{x} \left(\frac{\varepsilon(t)}{\varepsilon(x)} - 1 \right) \frac{dt}{t} \right|$$

$$\leq |\varepsilon(x)| \int_{\lambda}^{1} \left| \frac{\varepsilon(sx)}{\varepsilon(x)} - 1 \right| \frac{ds}{s}.$$

The conditions $B_b \leq \lambda x \leq x$ and $\lambda \leq s \leq 1$ imply $B_b \leq sx \leq x$, so we can use Eq. (4.46) to get

$$|U(\lambda, x) - \varepsilon(x) \log \lambda| \leq |\varepsilon(x)| \frac{c_1}{\phi_\eta(x)} \int_{\lambda}^{1} s^{-b_\eta - 1}\, ds = |\varepsilon(x)| \frac{c_2}{\phi_\eta(x)} (\lambda^{-b_\eta} - 1)$$

$$\leq \frac{c_2 |\varepsilon(x)|}{\phi_\eta(x)} \lambda^{-b_\eta} \quad \text{for } x \geq B_b \quad \text{and} \quad \frac{B_b}{x} \leq \lambda \leq 1. \tag{4.47}$$

From bounds (4.24) and (4.25) and an elementary inequality $|e^x - 1 - x| \leq x^2 e^{|x|}$ we get

$$|e^{U(\lambda,x)} - 1 - U(\lambda, x)| \leq U^2(\lambda, x) e^{|U(\lambda,x)|} \leq c_3 \frac{\lambda^{-2\theta_\varepsilon}(2 - \log \lambda)^2}{\phi_\varepsilon^2(x)} \lambda^{-\frac{1}{2}(b_\varepsilon - \theta_\varepsilon)} \qquad (4.48)$$

where $b_\varepsilon > \theta_\varepsilon$. Now we combine Eqs. (4.45), (4.47), and (4.48) to obtain

$$\left| \frac{L(\lambda x)}{L(x)} - 1 - \varepsilon(x) \log \lambda \right| \leq c_4 \left[\frac{|\varepsilon(x)|}{\phi_\eta(x)} \lambda^{-b_\eta} + \frac{(2 - \log \lambda)^2}{\phi_\varepsilon^2(x)} \lambda^{-1/2 b_\varepsilon - 3/2\theta_\varepsilon} \right] \qquad (4.49)$$

By Lemma 4.3.3, $(2 - \log \lambda)^2$ can be dominated by $c_5 \lambda^{-\delta}$ with an arbitrary $\delta > 0$. Since the number $b_\varepsilon > \theta_\varepsilon$ is arbitrarily close to θ_ε, the number $-a_\varepsilon = -\frac{1}{2}b_\varepsilon - \frac{3}{2}\theta_\varepsilon - \delta$ is less than, and arbitrarily close to, $-2\theta_\varepsilon$. Hence, bounds (4.44) and (4.49) imply

$$|G(\lambda x, x) - \log \lambda| \leq c_6 \left(\frac{\lambda^{-b_\eta}}{\phi_\eta(x)} + \frac{\lambda^{-a_\varepsilon}}{\phi_\varepsilon^2(x)|\varepsilon(x)|} \right)$$

$$\leq c_7 \left(\frac{1}{\phi_\eta(x)} + \frac{1}{\phi_\varepsilon(x)} \right) \lambda^{-b}.$$

Here we take an arbitrary $b > \max\{2\theta_\varepsilon, \theta_\eta\}$ and put $a_\varepsilon = b_\eta = b$. c_7 depends on b. ∎

4.4.8 L_p-Approximability of H

Theorem. *(Mynbaev, 2011) Let Assumption 4.3 (Section 4.4.7.1) hold. For $p \in [1, \infty)$ define a vector $w_n \in \mathbb{R}^n$ by*

$$w_{nt} = n^{-1/p} H(t, n), \quad t = 1, \ldots, n.$$

If $\max\{2\theta_\varepsilon, \theta_\eta\} < 1/p$, *then* $\{w_n\}$ *is L_p-close to* $f(x) = \log^2 x$.

Proof. The proof follows that of Theorem 4.4.1. Similarly to the transition from Eq. (4.33) to Eq. (4.34) now we have

$$(\Delta_{np} w_n)(u) = H([nu + 1], n), \quad 0 \leq u < 1.$$

Let $0 < \delta \leq 1/2$. With the number B_b from Lemma 4.4.7 put $n_1 \equiv B_b/\delta$. For $n > n_1$ the interval $(B_b/n, \delta)$ is not empty and, by the triangle inequality,

$$\|\Delta_{np} w_n - f\|_{p,(0,1)} \leq \|\Delta_{np} w_n - f\|_{p,(\delta,1)} + \|f\|_{p,(0,\delta)}$$

$$+ \|\Delta_{np} w_n\|_{p,(0,B_b/n)} + \|\Delta_{np} w_n\|_{p,(B_b/n,\delta)}. \qquad (4.50)$$

Obviously, $\|f\|_{p,(0,\delta)} \to 0$ as $\delta \to 0$. Now we consider three cases.

Case 1. $\delta \leq u < 1$. Lemma 4.2.7 guarantees that

$$H(rn, n) = \log^2 r[1 + o(1)] \text{ uniformly in } r \in \left[\delta, 1 + \frac{1}{2B_b}\right]. \qquad (4.51)$$

Defining $r = [nu + 1]/n$, from the inequality $nu < [nu + 1] \leq nu + 1$ we have

$$\delta \leq u < r \leq u + \frac{1}{n} < 1 + \frac{1}{n_1} \leq 1 + \frac{1}{2B_b}. \qquad (4.52)$$

This leads to

$$r = u + o(1) \quad \text{and} \quad r \in \left[\delta, 1 + \frac{1}{2B_b}\right]. \qquad (4.53)$$

From Eqs. (4.51) and (4.53) we see that

$$H([nu + 1], n) - \log^2 u = o(1) \text{ uniformly in } u \in (\delta, 1),$$

which allows us to conclude that

$$\|\Delta_{np} w_n - f\|_{p,(\delta,1)} \longrightarrow 0, \quad n \longrightarrow \infty. \qquad (4.54)$$

Case 2. $B_b/n \leq u < \delta$. Let $n > n_2 \equiv \max\{n_1, 2\}$. Then Eq. (4.52) and the conditions $u \in [B_b/n, \delta)$, $n > n_2$ imply

$$\frac{B_b}{n} \leq u < r \leq u + \frac{1}{n} < \delta + \frac{1}{n_2} \leq 1.$$

This means we can successively apply Lemma 4.4.7, Eqs. (4.44) and (4.52) to get

$$
\begin{aligned}
|H([nu + 1], n)| &= \left|\frac{G(rn, n) - \log r}{\mu(n)}\right| \leq \frac{M_b r^{-b}}{|\mu(n)|}\left(\frac{1}{\phi_\eta(n)} + \frac{1}{\phi_\varepsilon(n)}\right) \\
&\leq \frac{c_1 r^{-b}}{|\mu(n)|} \max\left\{\frac{1}{\phi_\eta(n)}, \frac{1}{\phi_\varepsilon(n)}\right\} \\
&\leq \frac{c_2 r^{-b}}{|\mu(n)|} \max\{|\varepsilon(n)|, |\eta(n)|\} \\
&\leq c_3 r^{-b} \leq c_3 u^{-b} \quad \text{for } u \in \left[\frac{B_b}{n}, \delta\right].
\end{aligned}
$$

Hence,

$$\int_{B_b/n}^{\delta} |\Delta_{np} w_n|^p du \le c\delta^{1-pb}. \qquad (4.55)$$

Here the right-hand side tends to zero if $b < 1/p$. This is possible because of the inequality $\max\{2\theta_\varepsilon, \theta_\eta\} < 1/p$.

Case 3. $0 < u < B_b/n$. By monotonicity the inequality $[nu + 1]/n > u$ implies $|\log([nu + 1]/n)| \le |\log u|$. For $G([nu + 1], n)$ we can use Eq. (4.41). Then

$$|H([nu + 1], n)| \le \left| \frac{G([nu + 1], n)}{\mu(n)} \right| + \left| \frac{\log([nu + 1]/n)}{\mu(n)} \right|$$

$$\le \left| \frac{c + L(n)}{L(n)\varepsilon(n)\mu(n)} \right| + \left| \frac{\log u}{\mu(n)} \right|.$$

Since all functions of n here are SV and $|\log u|$ can be dominated by cu^{-a} with $0 < a < 1/p$, we see that

$$\|\Delta_{np} w_n\|_{p,(0,B_b/n)} \le \left| \frac{c + L(n)}{L(n)\varepsilon(n)\mu(n)} \right| \left(\frac{B_b}{n} \right)^{1/p} + \frac{c}{|\mu(n)|} \left(\frac{B_b}{n} \right)^{1-pa} \longrightarrow 0.$$

$$(4.56)$$

Equations (4.50), (4.54), (4.55), and (4.56) prove the theorem. ∎

Intuitively, L_p-approximability of H should be a stronger fact than L_p-approximability of G. Indeed, if we multiply

$$\left\| \frac{G([nu + 1], n) - \log([nu + 1]/n)}{\mu(n)} - \log^2 u \right\|_p \longrightarrow 0$$

by $\mu(n) \to 0$, we get

$$\left\| G([nu + 1], n) - \log\frac{[nu + 1]}{n} \right\|_p \longrightarrow 0.$$

Here $\frac{[nu+1]}{n} \to u$ uniformly on $(0, 1)$ by Eq. (4.37) and $\log\frac{[nu+1]}{n} \le |\log u|$. As a result of Eq. (4.34) the sequence $\{w_n\}$ from Theorem 4.4.1 with $k = 1$ is L_p-close to $\log x$.

4.5 PHILLIPS GALLERY 2

This whole Section is based on the paper of Phillips (2007), except that the asymptotic results are derived from L_p-approximability 4.4, rather than from 4.2.

These are the common features of the models considered in Phillips (2007):

1. the regressors are asymptotically collinear,
2. the (joint) limit distribution of the regression coefficients is one-dimensional, and
3. the usual regression formulas for asymptotic standard errors are valid, but rates of convergence are affected.

The reader is advised to review the properties of $o_p(1)$ and $O_p(1)$ from Sections 1.8.4 and 1.8.5. These are widely used in the rest of the book.

4.5.1 Simple Regression

In this and the next three sections we deal with the model

$$y_t = \alpha + \beta L(t) + u_t, \quad t = 1, \ldots, n, \tag{4.57}$$

where the errors u_t satisfy Assumption 4.2 (Section 4.4.6). In cases such as $L(s) = 1/\log s$ where $L(1)$ is undefined or, more generally, $L(1), \ldots, L(a)$ are undefined, $L(s)$ may be redefined as $L(s) = L(a + 1)$ for $1 \le s \le a$, with no effect on asymptotic results. Henceforth, it is assumed that such adjustments are made.

4.5.2 Problem with Estimation

The sequence $(L(1), \ldots, L(n))$ upon normalization becomes L_2-close to 1, as we have established in the proof of Lemma 4.4.6. This means that the regressors in Eq. (4.57) are asymptotically collinear and the normalized matrix of second moments $D_n^{-1}X'XD_n^{-1}$ is asymptotically singular.

With the expansions from Section 4.4 the above fact can be proved directly. Denote

$$X = \begin{pmatrix} 1 & L(1) \\ \cdots & \cdots \\ 1 & L(n) \end{pmatrix}$$

the matrix of regressors in Eq. (4.57). By Corollary 4.4.3 the normalizer for

$$X'X = \begin{pmatrix} n & \sum L(s) \\ \sum L(s) & \sum L^2(s) \end{pmatrix} \tag{4.58}$$

is

$$D_n = \begin{pmatrix} \sqrt{n} & 0 \\ 0 & \sqrt{n}L(n) \end{pmatrix},$$

so

$$D_n^{-1}X'XD_n^{-1} = \begin{pmatrix} 1 & \frac{1}{nL(n)}\sum L(s) \\ \frac{1}{nL(n)}\sum L(s) & \frac{1}{nL^2(n)}\sum L^2(s) \end{pmatrix} \rightarrow \begin{pmatrix} 1 & 1 \\ 1 & 1 \end{pmatrix}.$$

Thus, the conventional scheme is not applicable.

4.5.3 Way Around the Problem

Phillips' idea is to use the alternative formulas for OLS estimates from Section 4.2.5. $\sum_{t=1}^{n} (L(t) - \bar{L})^2$ can be normalized by $(nL^2(n)\varepsilon^2(n))^{-1}$, according to Corollary 4.4.4, and from Lemma 4.4.6 we know that $\sum_{t=1}^{n} (L(t) - \bar{L})u_t$ should be divided by $\sqrt{n}L(n)\varepsilon(n)$ to achieve convergence in distribution. Therefore Eq. (4.9) should be rearranged to

$$\sqrt{n}L(n)\varepsilon(n)(\hat{\beta} - \beta)$$

$$= \left[\frac{1}{nL^2(n)\varepsilon^2(n)} \sum_{t=1}^{n} (L(t) - \bar{L})^2 \right]^{-1} \frac{1}{\sqrt{n}L(n)\varepsilon(n)} \sum_{t=1}^{n} (L(t) - \bar{L})u_t. \quad (4.59)$$

Since $\bar{L} = L(n)(1 + o(1))$ [see Section (4.4.3)], to achieve convergence of the term involving $\hat{\beta} - \beta$ in Eq. (4.10), we have to multiply both sides by $\sqrt{n}\varepsilon(n)$ to get

$$\sqrt{n}\varepsilon(n)(\hat{\alpha} - \alpha) = \frac{\varepsilon(n)}{\sqrt{n}} \sum_{t=1}^{n} u_t - \frac{\bar{L}}{L(n)} \sqrt{n}L(n)\varepsilon(n)(\hat{\beta} - \beta).$$

Luckily, here $\frac{1}{\sqrt{n}}\sum_{t=1}^{n} u_t$ converges in distribution (correctly posed problems always have solutions), because the sequence of weights is L_2-close to 1. Therefore the first term is $o_p(1)$. The whole thing asymptotically is

$$\sqrt{n}\varepsilon(n)(\hat{\alpha} - \alpha) = -\sqrt{n}L(n)\varepsilon(n)(\hat{\beta} - \beta) + o_p(1). \quad (4.60)$$

Equations (4.59) and (4.60) and Lemma 4.4.6(ii) lead to the following conclusion.

Theorem. (Phillips, 2007, Theorem 3.1) *If L satisfies Assumption 4.1 (Section 4.3.6), $2\theta < 1$ and u_t satisfies Assumption 4.2 (Section 4.4.6.1), then*

$$\left(\begin{array}{c} \sqrt{n}\varepsilon(n)(\hat{\alpha} - \alpha) \\ \sqrt{n}L(n)\varepsilon(n)(\hat{\beta} - \beta) \end{array} \right) \xrightarrow{d} N\left(0, \sigma^2 \left(\begin{array}{cc} 1 & -1 \\ -1 & 1 \end{array} \right) \right). \quad (4.61)$$

4.5.4 Examples

EXAMPLE 4.3. $L(s) = \log^\gamma s$, $\gamma > 0$. This gives the semilogarithmic model. Here $\varepsilon(n) = \gamma/\log n$, $L(n)\varepsilon(n) = \gamma \log^{\gamma-1} n$ and the previous theorem gives

$$\left(\begin{array}{c} (\gamma\sqrt{n}/\log n)(\hat{\alpha} - \alpha) \\ \gamma\sqrt{n}\log^{\gamma-1} n(\hat{\beta} - \beta) \end{array} \right) \xrightarrow{d} N\left(0, \sigma^2 \left(\begin{array}{cc} 1 & -1 \\ -1 & 1 \end{array} \right) \right).$$

EXAMPLE 4.4. $L(s) = \log(\log s)$. Here

$$\varepsilon(n) = \frac{1}{(\log n)\log(\log n)}, \quad L(n)\varepsilon(n) = \frac{1}{\log n}$$

and convergence is described by

$$
\begin{pmatrix} \sqrt{n}/((\log n)\log(\log n))(\hat{\alpha} - \alpha) \\ \sqrt{n}/\log n(\hat{\beta} - \beta) \end{pmatrix} \xrightarrow{d} N\left(0, \sigma^2 \begin{pmatrix} 1 & -1 \\ -1 & 1 \end{pmatrix}\right).
$$

EXAMPLE 4.5. $L(s) = 1/\log s$. This example arises when the regressor decays slowly. Here $\varepsilon(n) = -1/\log n$, $L(n)\varepsilon(n) = -1/\log^2 n$, and the result is

$$
\begin{pmatrix} \sqrt{n}/\log n(\hat{\alpha} - \alpha) \\ \sqrt{n}/\log^2 n(\hat{\beta} - \beta) \end{pmatrix} \xrightarrow{d} N\left(0, \sigma^2 \begin{pmatrix} 1 & -1 \\ -1 & 1 \end{pmatrix}\right).
$$

EXAMPLE 4.6. $L(s) = 1/\log(\log s)$. Here

$$
\varepsilon(n) = -\frac{1}{(\log n)\log(\log n)}, \qquad L(n)\varepsilon(n) = -\frac{1}{(\log n)\log^2(\log n)},
$$

so that

$$
\begin{pmatrix} \sqrt{n}/((\log n)\log(\log n))(\hat{\alpha} - \alpha) \\ \sqrt{n}/((\log n)\log^2 n(\log n))(\hat{\beta} - \beta) \end{pmatrix} \xrightarrow{d} N\left(0, \sigma^2 \begin{pmatrix} 1 & -1 \\ -1 & 1 \end{pmatrix}\right).
$$

Some intuition that explains the results is as follows. When $L(n) \to \infty$ as $n \to \infty$, the convergence rate of the slope coefficient $\hat{\beta}$ exceeds that of the intercept $\hat{\alpha}$, because the signal from the regressor $L(s)$ is stronger than that of a constant regressor. When $L(n) \to 0$ as $n \to \infty$, the convergence rate of $\hat{\beta}$ is less than that of $\hat{\alpha}$, because the signal from the regressor $L(s)$ is weaker than that of a constant regressor.

4.5.5 Standard Errors

From the general equation

$$
V\left(\begin{pmatrix} \hat{\alpha} \\ \hat{\beta} \end{pmatrix}\right) = \sigma^2 (X'X)^{-1}
$$

we know how to find estimates of standard errors: they are computed by scaling square roots of diagonal elements of $(X'X)^{-1}$ with σ^2 (or estimate of σ^2). However, because of asymptotic singularity of $X'X$, its inverse behaves badly, as we see shortly.

Using the rule

$$
\begin{pmatrix} a & b \\ c & d \end{pmatrix} = \frac{1}{ad - bc} \begin{pmatrix} d & -b \\ -c & a \end{pmatrix} \tag{4.62}
$$

we have for the inverse of Eq. (4.58)

$$ad - bc = \left(\sum_t 1\right)\left(\sum_t L^2(t)\right) - \left(\sum_t L(t)\right)^2$$

$$= n\sum_t L^2(t) - \left(\sum_t L(t)\right)^2 = n\sum_t (L(t) - \bar{L})^2,$$

$$(X'X)^{-1} = \frac{1}{n\sum_t (L(t) - \bar{L})^2}\begin{pmatrix} \sum_t L^2(t) & -\sum_t L(t) \\ -\sum_t L(t) & n \end{pmatrix}.$$

Now apply expansions from Sections 4.4.3 and 4.4.4:

$$(X'X)^{-1} = \frac{1}{n^2 L^2(n)\varepsilon^2(n)[1 + o(1)]}\begin{pmatrix} nL^2(n) & -nL(n) \\ -nL(n) & n \end{pmatrix}[1 + o(1)]$$

$$= \begin{pmatrix} 1 & -\dfrac{1}{L(n)} \\ -\dfrac{1}{L(n)} & \dfrac{1}{L^2(n)} \end{pmatrix}\frac{[1 + o(1)]}{n\varepsilon^2(n)}.$$

Square roots of the elements on the main diagonal should be put on the diagonal of the normalizing matrix, denoted F_n, to obtain unities on the main diagonal of $F_n^{-1}(X'X)^{-1}F_n^{-1}$. Thus,

$$F_n = \text{diag}\left[\frac{1}{\sqrt{n}\varepsilon(n)}, \frac{1}{\sqrt{n}L(n)\varepsilon(n)}\right],$$

$$F_n^{-1}(X'X)^{-1}F_n^{-1} = \begin{pmatrix} 1 & -1 \\ -1 & 1 \end{pmatrix}[1 + o(1)].$$

It follows from these formulas that, in spite of the singularity in the limit matrix, the covariance matrix of the regression coefficients is consistently estimated as in conventional regression when an appropriate estimate s^2 of σ^2 is employed.

4.5.6 Lemma on a Linear Transformation of the Parameter

Lemma. *Let A be a nonsingular matrix. If the parameter vector in the linear model has been transformed as in*

$$y = X\beta + u = XA^{-1}A\beta + u = XA^{-1}\alpha + u,$$

then the linear relation between α and β, $\alpha = A\beta$, translates to a similar relation between the OLS estimators: $\hat{\alpha} = A\hat{\beta}$. Consequently, $\hat{\alpha} - \alpha = A(\hat{\beta} - \beta)$.

Proof.

$$\hat{\alpha} = ((XA^{-1})'XA^{-1})^{-1}(XA^{-1})'y = ((A^{-1})'X'XA^{-1})^{-1}(A^{-1})'X'y$$

$$= A(X'X)^{-1}A'(A^{-1})'X'y = A\hat{\beta}. \qquad \blacksquare$$

It is important that in asymptotic theory, where there is a sequence of linear models depending on n, the matrix A may also depend on n.

4.5.7   Polynomial Regression in *L(s)*

In this model the regressors are polynomials in the SV function L, and the data are generated by

$$y_t = \sum_{j=0}^{p} \beta_j L^j(t) + u_t = \beta' L_t + u_t \qquad (4.63)$$

where $L_t = (1, L(t), \ldots, L^p(t))'$ and the error u_t satisfies Assumption 4.2 (Section 4.4.6). This model may be analyzed using the approach applied to simple regression. But, as the degree p increases in Eq. (4.63), the analysis becomes complicated because high-order expansions of the sample moments of L are needed to develop a complete asymptotic theory. An alternate approach is to rewrite the model Eq. (4.63) in a form wherein the moment matrix of the regressors has a full-rank limit. The degeneracy in the new model, which has now an array format, then passes from the data matrix to the coefficients and is simpler to analyze.

The process is first illustrated with simple regression $y_t = \alpha + \beta L(t) + u_t$, which we can write in the form $y_t = \alpha + \beta L(n) + \beta(L(t) - L(n)) + u_t$ or, denoting $\alpha_n = \alpha + \beta L(n)$, as

$$y_t = \alpha_n + \beta(L(t) - L(n)) + u_t. \qquad (4.64)$$

The regressors $\{1, L(t) - L(n)\}$ in Eq. (4.64) are not collinear, and the OLS asymptotics is obtained by application of Theorem 1.12.3. The column of unities in the regressor matrix X is normalized by $\sqrt{n}$, giving $1/\sqrt{n}(1, \ldots, 1)'$, which is L_2-close to 1. The second column, in agreement with Corollary 4.4.4, is normalized by

$$\sqrt{n}L(n)\varepsilon(n) = \left(\sum_{t=1}^{n}(L(t) - \bar{L})^2\right)^{1/2}[1 + o(1)].$$

The normalized second column equals $1/\sqrt{n}(G(1, n), \ldots, G(n, n))$, which is L_2-close to $\log x$. Thus, by Theorem 1.12.3

$$\begin{pmatrix} \sqrt{n}(\hat{\alpha}_n - \alpha_n) \\ \sqrt{n}L(n)\varepsilon(n)(\hat{\beta} - \beta) \end{pmatrix} \xrightarrow{d} N(0, \sigma^2 G^{-1}) \qquad (4.65)$$

where G is the Gram matrix of the system $\{1, \log x\}$:

$$G = \int_0^1 \begin{pmatrix} 1 & \log x \\ \log x & \log^2 x \end{pmatrix} dx = \begin{pmatrix} 1 & -1 \\ -1 & 2 \end{pmatrix}.$$

By Lemma 4.5.6

$$\hat{\alpha}_n - \alpha_n = (\alpha + \widehat{\beta L(n)}) - (\alpha + \beta L(n)) = \hat{\alpha} - \alpha + (\hat{\beta} - \beta)L(n).$$

Since our purpose is to deduce convergence of $\hat{\alpha} - \alpha$, and we know the rates of convergence of $\hat{\beta} - \beta$ and $\hat{\alpha}_n - \alpha_n$ from Eq. (4.65), we have

$$\sqrt{n}\varepsilon(n)(\hat{\alpha} - \alpha) = -\sqrt{n}L(n)\varepsilon(n)(\hat{\beta} - \beta) + \sqrt{n}\varepsilon(n)(\hat{\alpha}_n - \alpha_n)$$
$$= -\sqrt{n}L(n)\varepsilon(n)(\hat{\beta} - \beta) + o_p(1).$$

This implies

$$\begin{pmatrix} \sqrt{n}\varepsilon(n)(\hat{\alpha} - \alpha) \\ \sqrt{n}L(n)\varepsilon(n)(\hat{\beta} - \beta) \end{pmatrix} \xrightarrow{d} N\left(0, \sigma^2 \begin{pmatrix} 1 & -1 \\ -1 & 1 \end{pmatrix}\right),$$

which is the same as Theorem 4.5.3.

4.5.8   General Case (Convergence for the Transformed Regression)

Extending the procedure devised for Eq. (4.64) to Eq. (4.63) gives the representation

$$y_t = \sum_{j=0}^p \beta_j \left[L(n)\left(\frac{L(t)}{L(n)} - 1\right) + L(n) \right]^j + u_t$$

$$= \sum_{j=0}^p \beta_j L^j(n) \sum_{i=0}^j \binom{j}{i}\left(\frac{L(t)}{L(n)} - 1\right)^j + u_t$$

(change the summation order)

$$= \sum_{i=0}^p \varepsilon^i(n) \sum_{j=i}^p \beta_j L^j(n) \binom{j}{i}\left(\frac{L(t) - L(n)}{L(n)\varepsilon(n)}\right)^j + u_t. \tag{4.66}$$

Here $\binom{j}{i} = j!/(i!(j-i)!)$ for $0 \le i \le j$. Denote

$$\alpha_{ni} = \sum_{j=i}^p \beta_j L^j(n) \binom{j}{i}, \quad i = 0, \ldots, p. \tag{4.67}$$

With the help of the G-function from Section 4.2.6 we rewrite Eq. (4.66) as

$$y_t = \sum_{i=0}^{p} \varepsilon^i(n)\alpha_{ni}G^i(t, n) + u_t \tag{4.68}$$

Further, introducing the vector

$$\alpha_n = (\alpha_{n0}, \ldots, \alpha_{np})'$$

and matrices

$$\mathcal{G} = \begin{pmatrix} G^0(1, n) & \cdots & G^p(1, n) \\ \cdots & \cdots & \cdots \\ G^0(n, n) & \cdots & G^p(n, n) \end{pmatrix}, \tag{4.69}$$

$$D_{n\varepsilon} = \mathrm{diag}[1, \varepsilon(n), \ldots, \varepsilon^p(n)]$$

we write Eq. (4.68) as

$$y = \mathcal{G}D_{n\varepsilon}\alpha_n + u. \tag{4.70}$$

By Corollary 4.4.2 the l_2-norm of the ith column of $\mathcal{G}$ is

$$\left(\sum_{t=1}^{n} G^{2(i-1)}(t, n)\right)^{1/2} = \sqrt{(2i - 2)!n}[1 + o(1)], \quad i = 1, \ldots, p+1.$$

For compatibility with Phillips (2007, Lemma 7.8) this is better normalized by $\sqrt{n}$. The normalized column

$$\frac{1}{\sqrt{n}}(G^{i-1}(1, n), \ldots, G^{i-1}(n, n))'$$

is L_2-close to $\log^{i-1} x$, $i = 1, \ldots, p+1$, by Theorem 4.4.1. Now we can apply Theorem 1.12.3 with $D_n = \sqrt{n}I$,

$$l_p(x) = (1, \log x, \ldots, \log^p x)'$$

to obtain the following statement.

Theorem.   (Phillips, 2007, Theorem 4.1) *If Assumptions 4.1 (Section 4.3.6) and 4.2 (Section 4.4.6.1) hold and $2\theta p < 1$, then*

$$\frac{1}{n}\mathcal{G}'\mathcal{G} \longrightarrow G \equiv \int_0^1 l_p(x)l_p'(x)\,dx, \quad \det G \neq 0, \tag{4.71}$$

$$\sqrt{n}D_{n\varepsilon}(\hat{\alpha}_n - \alpha_n) \xrightarrow{d} N\left(0, \left(\sigma_e \sum_{j\in\mathbb{Z}}\psi_j\right)^2 G^{-1}\right).$$

G has elements

$$g_{ij} = \int_0^1 \log^{i+j-2} dx = (-1)^{i+j-2}(i+j-2)!, \quad i, j = 1, \ldots, p+1.$$

4.5.9 Analysis of G

I think it is useful to know how one can guess a result like that reported here.

Triangular decompositions of matrices are convenient for calculating determinants and matrices because

1. the determinant of a triangular matrix equals the product of its diagonal elements and

2. the inverse of a lower (or upper) triangular matrix is again a lower (upper, respectively) triangular matrix.

The procedure for finding a lower triangular matrix B in the decomposition $S = BB'$ of a symmetric matrix S tells us that the elements on the main diagonal of B are completely determined by the values of major minors of S, (see Gantmacher, 1959, Chapter II, Section 4, Corollary 3). Once these has been found, other minors can be used to calculate the elements below the main diagonal. Both steps can be implemented in MathCAD. Then one can try to generalize from numbers to analytical expressions.

Lemma.   (Phillips, 2007, Lemma 7.8 corrected) *Put $F_p = \text{diag}[0!, 1!, \ldots, p!]$ and*

$$H_p = \begin{pmatrix} 1 & 0 & 0 & \cdots & 0 \\ -1 & 1 & 0 & \cdots & 0 \\ 1 & -2 & 1 & \cdots & 0 \\ \cdots & \cdots & \cdots & \cdots & \cdots \\ (-1)^p \binom{p}{0} & (-1)^{p+1} \binom{p}{1} & (-1)^{p+2} \binom{p}{2} & \cdots & 1 \end{pmatrix}$$

where the ith row consists of the coefficients in the binomial

$$(1 - 1)^{i-1} = \sum_{m=0}^{i-1} (-1)^{i-1+m} \binom{i-1}{m}.$$

Then

(i) $G = F_p H_p H_p' F_p,$

(ii) $\det G = \prod_{j=1}^p (j!)^2,$

(iii) $(G^{-1})_{p+1,p+1} = 1/(p!)^2.$

Proof.

(i) In the product F_pH_p the ith row of H_p gets multiplied by $(i-1)!$ The jth row of F_pH_p becomes the jth column of $(F_pH_p)' = H_p'F_p$. Therefore

$$(F_pH_pH_p'F_p)_{ij} = \sum_{m=0}^{\min\{i-1,j-1\}} (i-1)!(j-1)!(-1)^{i+j-2}\binom{i-1}{m}\binom{j-1}{m}.$$

Because of symmetry, we can assume, without loss of generality, that $i \leq j$ and then

$$(F_pH_pH_p'F_p)_{ij} = (-1)^{i+j-2}(i-1)!(j-1)!\sum_{m=0}^{i-1}\binom{i-1}{m}\binom{j-1}{m}.$$

According to [Vilenkin, 1969, Chapter II, Equation (25)], for $k \leq l$ there is an identity

$$\sum_{m=0}^{k}\binom{l}{m}\binom{k}{m} = \binom{k+l}{k}.$$

Application of this formula completes the proof:

$$(F_pH_pH_p'F_p)_{ij} = (-1)^{i+j-2}(i-1)!(j-1)!\frac{(i+j-2)!}{(i-1)!(j-1)!} = G_{ij}.$$

(ii) Obviously, $\det G = (\det F_p \det H_p)^2 = \prod_{j=1}^{p} (j!)^2$.

(iii) Part (i) implies

$$G^{-1} = [(F_pH_p)^{-1}]'(F_pH_p)^{-1}.$$

Direct calculation shows that

$$(G^{-1})_{ii} = \sum_{j=i}^{p+1} [(F_pH_p)^{-1}]_{ji}^2, \quad i = 1,\ldots,p+1.$$

In particular,

$$(G^{-1})_{p+1,p+1} = [(F_pH_p)^{-1}]_{p+1,p+1}^2 = 1/(p!)^2.$$

∎

4.5.10 An Equation with an Upper Triangular Matrix

Lemma. (Phillips, 2007, p. 601) *Denote* $e_{p+1} = (0, \ldots, 0, 1)'$ *((p + 1)th unit vector) and*

$$
A_{p+1} = \begin{pmatrix}
\binom{0}{0} & \binom{1}{0} & \binom{2}{0} & \cdots & \binom{p-1}{0} & \binom{p}{0} \\
0 & \binom{1}{1} & \binom{2}{1} & \cdots & \binom{p-1}{1} & \binom{p}{1} \\
0 & 0 & \binom{2}{2} & \cdots & \binom{p-1}{2} & \binom{p}{2} \\
\cdots & \cdots & \cdots & \cdots & \cdots & \cdots \\
0 & 0 & 0 & \cdots & \binom{p-1}{p-1} & \binom{p}{p-1} \\
0 & 0 & 0 & \cdots & 0 & \binom{p}{p}
\end{pmatrix},
$$

$$
\mu_{p+1} = \begin{pmatrix}
(-1)^p \binom{p}{0} \\
(-1)^{p-1} \binom{p}{1} \\
\cdots \\
(-1) \binom{p}{p-1} \\
1
\end{pmatrix}.
$$

The solution $x \in \mathbb{R}^{p+1}$ of the equation

$$
A_{p+1} x = c e_{p+1}, \tag{4.72}
$$

where c is a constant, is given by

$$
x = c \mu_{p+1}. \tag{4.73}
$$

Proof. The first p equations of Eq. (4.72) can be written as

$$
\sum_{j=k}^{p+1} \binom{j-1}{k-1} x_j = 0, \quad k = 1, \ldots, p. \tag{4.74}
$$

Equation (4.73) in a coordinate form is

$$
x_k = (-1)^{p-k+1} \binom{p}{k-1} c, \quad k = 1, \ldots, p+1. \tag{4.75}
$$

The statement is proved by induction in decreasing k. Equation (4.75) for $k = p + 1$ is just the right equation in Eq. (4.72). Equation (4.75) should be verified also for $k = p$ because the structure in Eq. (4.72) changes from $p + 1$ to p. The final two equations in Eq. (4.72) imply

$$x_p = -\binom{p}{p-1} x_{p+1} = -\binom{p}{p-1} c,$$

which agrees with Eq. (4.75). Suppose Eq. (4.75) is true for $k + 1, \ldots, p + 1$ and let us prove it for k. From Eqs. (4.74) and (4.75) we have

$$x_k = -\sum_{j=k+1}^{p+1} \binom{j-1}{k-1} x_j = -\sum_{j=k+1}^{p+1} (-1)^{p-j+1} \binom{j-1}{k-1} \binom{p}{j-1} c. \qquad (4.76)$$

Here the coefficient in front of c equals

$$(-1)^{p-k+1} \sum_{j=k+1}^{p+1} \frac{(-1)^{k-j+1}(j-1)!}{(k-1)!(j-k)!} \frac{p!}{(j-1)!(p-j+1)!} \frac{(p-k+1)!}{(p-k+1)!}$$

$$= (-1)^{p-k+1} \binom{p}{k-1} \sum_{j=k+1}^{p+1} (-1)^{j-k+1} \binom{p-k+1}{j-k}$$

(replace $j - k$ by i)

$$= (-1)^{p-k+1} \binom{p}{k-1} \left[\sum_{i=1}^{p-k+1} (-1)^{i+1} \binom{p-k+1}{i} - 1 + 1 \right]$$

$$= (-1)^{p-k+1} \binom{p}{k-1} [-(1-1)^{p-k+1} + 1]$$

$$= (-1)^{p-k+1} \binom{p}{k-1}. \qquad (4.77)$$

Equations (4.76) and (4.77) prove Eq. (4.75) and the lemma. ∎

4.5.11 From Convergence of $\hat{\alpha}_n$ to Convergence of $\hat{\beta}$

It transpires that only the final component, $\hat{\alpha}_{np}$, in $\hat{\alpha}_n$ (which translates to the component $\hat{\beta}_p$ in the original coordinates) determines the nondegenerate part of the limit theory for the full set of coefficients.

Theorem.   (Phillips, 2007, Theorem 4.2) *If Assumptions 4.1 (Section 4.3.6) and 4.2 (Section 4.4.6.1) hold and $2\theta p < 1$, then*

$$\sqrt{n}\varepsilon^p(n)D_{nL}(\hat{\beta} - \beta) = \mu_{p+1}\sqrt{n}L^p(n)\varepsilon^p(n)(\hat{\beta}_p - \beta_p) + o_p(1)$$

$$\xrightarrow{d} N\left(0, \frac{\sigma^2}{(p!)^2}\mu_{p+1}\mu'_{p+1}\right), \tag{4.78}$$

where μ_{p+1} is from Lemma 4.5.10 and

$$D_{nL} = \text{diag}[1, L(n), \dots, L^p(n)].$$

Proof.   By Lemma 4.5.6 the equation [see Eq. (4.67)]

$$\alpha_n = A_{p+1}D_{nL}\beta \tag{4.79}$$

implies

$$\hat{\alpha}_n - \alpha_n = A_{p+1}D_{nL}(\hat{\beta} - \beta). \tag{4.80}$$

First, we derive convergence of $\hat{\beta}_p$. The final equation in system (4.80) is $\hat{\alpha}_{np} - \alpha_{np} = L^p(n)(\hat{\beta}_p - \beta_p)$. Utilizing what we know about convergence of $\hat{\alpha}_{np}$ from Theorem 4.5.8 and Lemma 4.5.9(iii) we have

$$\sqrt{n}L^p(n)\varepsilon^p(n)(\hat{\beta}_p - \beta_p) = \sqrt{n}\varepsilon^p(n)(\hat{\alpha}_{np} - \alpha_{np}) \xrightarrow{d} N(0, \sigma^2/(p!)^2). \tag{4.81}$$

Now we are ready to derive convergence of the whole vector $\hat{\beta}$. On the right-hand side of Eq. (4.80) each equation contains the term $L^p(n)(\hat{\beta}_p - \beta_p)$ with a nonzero coefficient. From Eq. (4.81) we know that, to make this term convergent, we have to multiply each equation by $\sqrt{n}\varepsilon^p(n)$. In the resulting system

$$\sqrt{n}\varepsilon^p(n)(\hat{\alpha}_n - \alpha_n) = A_{p+1}\sqrt{n}\varepsilon^p(n)D_{nL}(\hat{\beta} - \beta), \tag{4.82}$$

the final equation is the same as Eq. (4.81). In the first p equations the left side is $o_p(1)$, as follows from Theorem 4.5.8 and that $\varepsilon(n) \to 0$. Letting $c = \sqrt{n}\varepsilon^p(n)(\hat{\alpha}_{np} - \alpha_{np})$ we rewrite Eq. (4.82) as

$$A_{p+1}\sqrt{n}\varepsilon^p(n)D_{nL}(\hat{\beta} - \beta) = ce_{p+1} + o_p(1),$$

which by Lemma 4.5.10 implies

$$\sqrt{n}\varepsilon^p(n)D_{nL}(\hat{\beta} - \beta) = A_{p+1}^{-1}ce_{p+1} + A_{p+1}^{-1}o_p(1)$$
$$= \mu_{p+1}\sqrt{n}\varepsilon^p(n)(\hat{\alpha}_{np} - \alpha_{np}) + o_p(1).$$

This equation and Eq. (4.81) prove Eq. (4.78).   ∎

4.5.12   Variance Matrix Estimation

The limit distribution of the expression $\sqrt{n}\varepsilon^p(n)D_{nL}(\hat{\beta} - \beta)$ has support given by the range of the vector μ_{p+1} and is therefore of dimension 1. The variance matrix of $\hat{\beta}$ is asymptotically

$$\frac{\sigma^2}{(p!)^2 n\varepsilon^{2p}(n)} D_{nL}^{-1}\mu_{p+1}\mu'_{p+1}D_{nL}^{-1}, \tag{4.83}$$

which, as we show now, is consistently estimated by the usual regression formula. The matrix of regressors X in the original regression (4.63) in terms of the vectors $L_t \equiv (1, L(t), \ldots, L^p(t))'$ satisfies $X' = (L_1, \ldots, L_n)$, so

$$X'X = \sum_{s=1}^{n} L_s L'_s. \tag{4.84}$$

This expression for $X'X$ has more of statistical flavor. The following result gives asymptotic expressions for both $X'X$ and its inverse. Those expressions show that, indeed, Eq. (4.83) is the asymptotic form of $(X'X)^{-1}$.

Theorem.   (Phillips, 2007, Theorem 4.3) *If L satisfies Assumption 4.1 (Section 4.3.6) and $2\theta p < 1$, then*

(i) $X'X = nD_{nL}i_{p+1}i'_{p+1}D_{nL}[1 + o(1)]$, *where* $i_{p+1} = (1, \ldots, 1)'$ *is a* $(p + 1)$-*vector with unity in each element.*

(ii) $(X'X)^{-1} = (1/((p!)^2 n\varepsilon^{2p}(n))) D_{nL}^{-1}\mu_{p+1}\mu'_{p+1}D_{nL}^{-1}[1 + o(1)]$, *where* μ_{p+1} *is from Lemma 4.5.10.*

Proof.

(i) **Step 1**. We need a working expression for L_t that would link $X'X$ to the matrix whose convergence is affirmed in Eq. (4.71). Let us take a closer look at the transformation that has led to Eq. (4.68):

$$\beta'L_t = \sum_{i=0}^{p} \varepsilon^i(n)\alpha_{ni}G^i(t, n).$$

Using representation Eq. (4.79) and denoting by

$$\mathcal{G}(t, n) = (G^0(t, n), \dots, G^p(t, n))'$$

the tth row of Eq. (4.69) we can continue as follows:

$$\beta' L_t = \alpha'_n D_{n\varepsilon} \mathcal{G}(t, n) = \beta' D_{nL} A'_{p+1} D_{n\varepsilon} \mathcal{G}(t, n).$$

Since this is true for any $\beta \in \mathbb{R}^{p+1}$, we obtain the desired representation

$$L_t = D_{nL} A'_{p+1} D_{n\varepsilon} \mathcal{G}(t, n).$$

Step 2. Equation (4.84), a similar identity

$$\mathcal{G}' \mathcal{G} = \sum_{t=1}^{n} \mathcal{G}(t, n) \mathcal{G}'(t, n),$$

the above representation and Eq. (4.71) lead to

$$X'X = \sum_t D_{nL} A'_{p+1} D_{n\varepsilon} \mathcal{G}(t, n) \mathcal{G}'(t, n) D_{n\varepsilon} A_{p+1} D_{nL}$$

$$= n D_{nL} A'_{p+1} D_{n\varepsilon} G D_{n\varepsilon} A_{p+1} D_{nL}[1 + o(1)]. \tag{4.85}$$

In $D_{n\varepsilon}$ all elements, except for the unity in the upper left corner, tend to zero. In G the element in the upper left corner is unity. Therefore $D_{n\varepsilon} G D_{n\varepsilon} = E + o(1)$, where E has 1 in the upper left corner and 0 elsewhere. Hence,

$$X'X = n D_{nL} A'_{p+1} E A_{p+1} D_{nL}[1 + o(1)]$$

$$= n D_{nL} i_{p+1} i'_{p+1} D_{nL}[1 + o(1)].$$

(**ii**) From Eq. (4.84) the inverse sample matrix is

$$(X'X)^{-1} = \frac{1}{n} D_{nL}^{-1} A_{p+1}^{-1} D_{n\varepsilon}^{-1} G^{-1} D_{n\varepsilon}^{-1} (A'_{p+1})^{-1} D_{nL}^{-1}[1 + o(1)]. \tag{4.86}$$

Now observe that $D_{n\varepsilon}^{-1}$ is dominated by its final diagonal element, and so we can write

$$D_{n\varepsilon}^{-1} = \frac{1}{\varepsilon^p(n)} e_{p+1} e'_{p+1}[1 + o(1)],$$

where $e_{p+1} = (0, \ldots, 0, 1)'$. Hence,

$$D_{n\varepsilon}^{-1} G^{-1} D_{n\varepsilon}^{-1} = \frac{1}{\varepsilon^{2p}(n)} e_{p+1} (e'_{p+1} G^{-1} e_{p+1}) e'_{p+1} = \frac{1}{(p!)^2 \varepsilon^{2p}(n)} e_{p+1} e'_{p+1}$$

and also, by Lemma 4.5.10, $A_{p+1}^{-1} e_{p+1} = \mu_{p+1}$. Thus, continuing Eq. (4.85),

$$(X'X)^{-1} = \frac{1}{(p!)^2 \varepsilon^{2p}(n)} \frac{1}{n} D_{nL}^{-1} (A_{p+1}^{-1} e_{p+1}) [e'_{p+1} (A'_{p+1})^{-1}] D_{nL}^{-1} [1 + o(1)]$$

$$= \frac{1}{(p!)^2 n \varepsilon^{2p}(n)} D_{nL}^{-1} \mu_{p+1} \mu'_{p+1} D_{nL}^{-1} [1 + o(1)]. \qquad \blacksquare$$

It follows from (ii) that, in spite of the singularity in the limit matrix, the covariance matrix of the regression coefficients is consistently estimated as in conventional regression by $s^2 (X'X)^{-1}$ whenever s^2 is a consistent estimate of σ^2.

4.6 REGRESSION WITH TWO SLOWLY VARYING REGRESSORS

Multiple regression with different SV regressors also appears in some applications, the case of two such regressors being of principal interest. One such formulation is given in Section 4.6.9.

4.6.1 Statement of Problem

It is convenient to call the product $\delta(x) = L(x)\varepsilon(x)\mu(x)$ a δ-function of L.

Our subject is the two-variable regression model

$$y_s = \beta_0 + \beta_1 L_1(s) + \beta_2 L_2(s) + u_s. \qquad (4.87)$$

The purpose is to develop its asymptotic theory general enough to include all pairs (L_i, L_j), $i < j$, of functions from Table 4.1, where in the case $L_1(x) = \log^\gamma x$ we assume $\gamma = 1$. This L_1 is special in that its μ- and δ-functions are identically zero. In all other cases ε, μ, and δ are nonzero for all large x. The following minimal assumptions are used implicitly:

1. To avoid multicollinearity, in the pair (L_1, L_2) only one function is allowed to be $\log x$ (and to have a vanishing δ-function). By changing the notation, if necessary, we can assume that if one of L_1, L_2 is $\log x$, then it is always L_1.

2. To exclude constant regressors, we also assume that none of ε_1 and ε_2 vanishes for all large n.

When $L_1(x) = \log x$, model (4.87) is called *semireduced*. When both δ_1 and δ_2 are nonzero, model (4.87) is called *nonreduced*.

The analysis in the subsequent sections shows that the asymptotic theory of model (4.87) depends on the asymptotic behavior of the ratios δ_1/δ_2 and $\varepsilon_1/\varepsilon_2$. In the next assumption L_1 and L_2 denote SV functions of form $K(\varepsilon_i, \phi_{\varepsilon_i})$, where $\varepsilon_i = K(\eta_i, \phi_{\eta_i})$, not necessarily those from Table 4.1.

4.6.1.1 Assumption 4.4

1. The limit $\lambda_\varepsilon = \lim_{n \to \infty} \varepsilon_1/\varepsilon_2$ (finite or infinite) exists and
2. in the nonreduced case we assume that the limit $\lambda_\delta = \lim_{n \to \infty} \delta_1/\delta_2$ (finite or infinite) exists.

4.6.2 Phillips' Transformation of the Regressor Space

Theorem 5.1 of Phillips (2007) is based on the following heuristic argument. Rewrite Eq. (4.87) as

$$y_s = \beta_0 + \beta_1 L_1(n) + \beta_2 L_2(n)$$
$$+ \beta_1 L_1(n)\left(\frac{L_1((s/n)n)}{L_1(n)} - 1\right) + \beta_2 L_2(n)\left(\frac{L_2((s/n)n)}{L_2(n)} - 1\right) + u_s. \qquad (4.88)$$

We note from Lemma 4.2.7 that L_2 has a higher-order representation

$$\frac{L_j(rn)}{L_j(n)} - 1 = \varepsilon_j(n)\log r + \varepsilon_j(n)\mu_j(n)\log^2 r[1 + o(1)], \quad r > 0. \qquad (4.89)$$

Letting $s = rn$ here we write (the argument n in L_j, ε_j, μ_j is suppressed):

$$y_s = \beta_0 + \beta_1 L_1 + \beta_2 L_2$$
$$+ \beta_1 L_1 \varepsilon_1 \log\frac{s}{n} + \beta_1 L_1 \varepsilon_1 \mu_1 \log^2\frac{s}{n}[1 + o(1)]$$
$$+ \beta_2 L_2 \varepsilon_2 \log\frac{s}{n} + \beta_2 L_2 \varepsilon_2 \mu_2 \log^2\frac{s}{n}[1 + o(1)] + u_s. \qquad (4.90)$$

Dropping here $o(1)$ produces an approximation

$$y_s = \beta_0 + \beta_1 L_1 + \beta_2 L_2 + (\beta_1 L_1 \varepsilon_1 + \beta_2 L_2 \varepsilon_2)\log\frac{s}{n}$$
$$+ (\beta_1 L_1 \varepsilon_1 \mu_1 + \beta_2 L_2 \varepsilon_2 \mu_2)\log^2\frac{s}{n} + u_s \qquad (4.91)$$

to Eq. (4.90). Denoting

$$\beta = \begin{pmatrix} \beta_0 \\ \beta_1 \\ \beta_2 \end{pmatrix}, \quad \gamma_n = \begin{pmatrix} \gamma_{n0} \\ \gamma_{n1} \\ \gamma_{n2} \end{pmatrix}, \quad A_n = \begin{pmatrix} 1 & L_1 & L_2 \\ 0 & L_1\varepsilon_1 & L_2\varepsilon_2 \\ 0 & \delta_1 & \delta_2 \end{pmatrix} \qquad (4.92)$$

we obtain

$$y_s = \gamma_{n0} + \gamma_{n1} \log \frac{s}{n} + \gamma_{n2} \log^2 \frac{s}{n} + u_s, \quad \gamma_n = A_n \beta. \tag{4.93}$$

We call the γ_i's *yood coefficients* and β_i's *βad coefficients*. The matrix A_n is called a *transition matrix*. Because of asymptotic collinearity of the regressors in Eq. (4.87), the asymptotic distribution of the βad coefficients is degenerate (one-dimensional) and is not possible to find directly by normalizing the OLS estimator. In Eq. (4.93) the regressors are not asymptotically collinear and therefore the asymptotic distribution of the OLS estimator $\hat{\gamma}_n$ is good (normal with a positive definite variance–covariance matrix). Phillips' idea is to extract the asymptotic distribution of the β's from that of the γ's using $\beta = A_n^{-1} \gamma_n$. A_n^{-1} is not well-behaved as $n \to \infty$. Thus, the study of the transition matrix is at the heart of the method.

The problem with this transformation is that it is impossible to prove that Eq. (4.91) approximates Eq. (4.90). Relationship Eq. (4.89) does not cover the segment $1 \le s < na$ whose length is proportional to the sample size. For such s the approximation cannot be good. For example, at $s = 2$ for functions L_1, L_3 from Table 4.1 we have $L_1(2)/L_1(n) = \log 2/\log n \to 0$, $L_3(2)/L_3(n) = \log n/\log 2 \to \infty$. Therefore Theorem 5.1 of Phillips (2007) is true for Eq. (4.91) and not for the original regression. Our main result shows that, indeed, replacing Eq. (4.90) by Eq. (4.91) results in loss of information in terms of the variety of different asymptotic types. We are able to show that the values of s for which there is no approximation are negligible because

1. we impose the condition of slow variation with remainder and
2. instead of the sup-norm used by Phillips we use the integral L_2-norm contained in the definition of L_2-approximability.

4.6.3   Precise Transformation

Now we describe a modification of the Phillips transformation that allows us to avoid dropping any terms. To explain the idea, we consider only a nonreduced model with

$$|\lambda_\delta| < \infty \quad \text{and} \quad \beta_1 \lambda_\delta + \beta_2 \neq 0. \tag{4.94}$$

For the nonreduced model both μ_1 and μ_2 are nonzero. Therefore we can write

$$L_j(s) = L_j(n) + (L_j(s) - L_j(n))$$

$$= L_j(n) + L_j(n)\varepsilon_j(n)\left(\frac{L_j(s) - L_j(n)}{L_j(n)\varepsilon_j(n)} - \log \frac{s}{n}\right) + L_j(n)\varepsilon_j(n) \log \frac{s}{n}$$

$$= L_j(n) + L_j(n)\varepsilon_j(n) \log \frac{s}{n} + \delta_j(n)H_j(s, n) \tag{4.95}$$

where

$$H_j(s, n) = \frac{1}{\mu_j(n)}\left(G_j(s, n) - \log \frac{s}{n}\right)$$

is the H-function of L_j. H_j is not equal to $\log^2(s/n)$, but by Theorem 4.4.8 under appropriate conditions the sequence $\{n^{-1/2}H_j(s, n) : s = 1, \ldots, n\}$, $n = 1, 2, \ldots$, is L_2-close to $\log^2 x$.

Substitution of Eq. (4.95) in Eq. (4.87) gives

$$y_s = \gamma_{n0} + \gamma_{n1} \log \frac{s}{n} + \Delta_n + u_s \tag{4.96}$$

where

$$\gamma_{n0} = \beta_0 + \beta_1 L_1 + \beta_2 L_2, \; \gamma_{n1} = \beta_1 L_1 \varepsilon_1 + \beta_2 L_2 \varepsilon_2 \tag{4.97}$$

and

$$\Delta_n = \beta_1 \delta_1(n) H_1(s, n) + \beta_2 \delta_2(n) H_2(s, n). \tag{4.98}$$

The crucial step is to define $\gamma_{n2} = a_{32}\beta_1 + a_{33}\beta_2$ and $\tilde{H}(s, n)$ in such a way that

$$\Delta_n = \gamma_{n2}\tilde{H}(s, n) \quad \text{and} \quad \{n^{-1/2}\tilde{H}(s, n)\} \text{ is } L_2\text{-close to } \log^2 x \tag{4.99}$$

where $\tilde{H}$ is a new function. Then Eq. (4.96) becomes

$$y_s = \gamma_{n0} + \gamma_{n1} \log \frac{s}{n} + \gamma_{n2}\tilde{H}(s, n) + u_s \tag{4.100}$$

and the transition matrix is

$$A_n = \begin{pmatrix} 1 & L_1 & L_2 \\ 0 & L_1\varepsilon_1 & L_2\varepsilon_2 \\ 0 & a_{32} & a_{33} \end{pmatrix}.$$

We show how this is done in the case of Eq. (4.94). Continuing Eq. (4.98) we get

$$\Delta_n = (\beta_1\delta_1 + \beta_2\delta_2)\left[\frac{\beta_1\delta_1 H_1(s, n)}{\beta_1\delta_1 + \beta_2\delta_2} + \frac{\beta_2\delta_2 H_2(s, n)}{\beta_1\delta_1 + \beta_2\delta_2}\right]$$

$$= (\beta_1\delta_1 + \beta_2\delta_2)\left[\frac{\beta_1\delta_1/\delta_2 H_1(s, n)}{\beta_1\delta_1/\delta_2 + \beta_2} + \frac{\beta_2 H_2(s, n)}{\beta_1\delta_1/\delta_2 + \beta_2}\right]. \tag{4.101}$$

Letting

$$\gamma_{n2} = \beta_1\delta_1 + \beta_2\delta_2, \; \tilde{H}(s, n) = \frac{\beta_1\delta_1/\delta_2 H_1(s, n)}{\beta_1\delta_1/\delta_2 + \beta_2} + \frac{\beta_2 H_2(s, n)}{\beta_1\delta_1/\delta_2 + \beta_2} \tag{4.102}$$

TABLE 4.2 Transition Matrix Summary

Case	Subcase	Coefficients
Nonreduced model, $|\lambda_\delta| < \infty$	$\beta_1 \lambda_\delta + \beta_2 \neq 0$	I. $a_{32} = \delta_1, a_{33} = \delta_2$
	$\beta_1 \lambda_\delta + \beta_2 = 0, \beta_2 \neq 0$	II. Indefinite
	$\beta_1 \lambda_\delta + \beta_2 = 0, \beta_2 = 0$	III. $a_{32} = \delta_1, a_{33} = 0$
Nonreduced model, $|\lambda_\delta| = \infty$	$\beta_1 \neq 0$	IV. $a_{32} = \delta_1, a_{33} = \delta_2$
	$\beta_1 = 0$	V. $a_{32} = 0, a_{33} = \delta_2$
Semireduced model,		VI. $a_{32} = 0, a_{33} = \delta_2$
$(L_1(x) = \log x, \delta_2 \neq 0)$		

we satisfy the first part of Eq. (4.99). By Assumption 4.4 (Section 4.6.1.1) and Eq. (4.94)

$$\frac{\beta_1 \delta_1/\delta_2}{\beta_1 \delta_1/\delta_2 + \beta_2} \rightarrow \frac{\beta_1 \lambda_\delta}{\beta_1 \lambda_\delta + \beta_2}, \quad \frac{\beta_2}{\beta_1 \delta_1/\delta_2 + \beta_2} \rightarrow \frac{\beta_2}{\beta_1 \lambda_\delta + \beta_2}. \tag{4.103}$$

It is shown in Section 4.6.5 that this implies the second part of Eq. (4.99). Note that $\tilde{H}(s, n)$ defined in Eq. (4.102) depends on β_1, β_2 in a nonlinear fashion, but in the limit that dependence disappears. The analysis in Section 4.6.5 shows that the elements a_{32}, a_{33} are as described in Table 4.2. The case in which the transition matrix is not defined and higher-order RV is necessary to determine it is marked as indefinite. The dependence of the transition matrix on the true β is not continuous.

4.6.4 Linearity of L_p-Approximable Sequences

Lemma. *If $\{v_n\}$ is L_p-close to V, $\{w_n\}$ is L_p-close to W and numerical sequences $\{a_n\}$ and $\{b_n\}$ converge to a and b, respectively, then $\{a_n v_n + b_n w_n\}$ is L_p-close to $aV + bW$.*

Proof. This property follows from

$$\|\Delta_{np}(a_n v_n + b_n w_n) - (aV + bW)\|_p \leq |a_n - a| \|\Delta_{np} v_n\|_p$$

$$+ |b_n - b| \|\Delta_{np} w_n\|_p + |a| \|\Delta_{np} v_n - V\|_p + |b| \|\Delta_{np} w_n - W\|_p \rightarrow 0,$$

where, by L_p-approximability, $\|\Delta_{np} v_n\|_p$ and $\|\Delta_{np} w_n\|_p$ are bounded. ∎

4.6.5 Derivation of the Transition Matrix

We consider one by one the six cases listed in the last column of Table 4.2.

4.6.5.1 Nonreduced Model
In the first five cases we assume that $\delta_1 \neq 0, \delta_2 \neq 0$ and L_1, L_2 satisfy Assumption 4.3 (Section 4.4.7.1). By Theorem 4.4.8, where we take $p = 2$, the sequences w_n^1, w_n^2 with components $w_{nt}^i = n^{-1/2} H_i(t, n), t = 1, \ldots, n, i = 1, 2$, are L_2-close to $\log^2 x$. By linearity we conclude that $\{a_n w_n^1 + b_n w_n^2\}$ is L_2-close to $(a + b) \log^2 x$ whenever $a_n \rightarrow a, b_n \rightarrow b$.

Case I Suppose $|\lambda_\delta| < \infty$, $\beta_1 \lambda_\delta + \beta_2 \neq 0$. This is exactly the model situation of Section 4.6.3. By Eq. (4.103) the second part of Eq. (4.99) is true and we can put $a_{32} = \delta_1$, $a_{33} = \delta_2$.

Case II $|\lambda_\delta| < \infty$, $\beta_1 \lambda_\delta + \beta_2 = 0$, $\beta_2 \neq 0$. This is the indefinite case discussed in Section 4.6.10.

Case III $|\lambda_\delta| < \infty$, $\beta_1 \lambda_\delta + \beta_2 = 0$, $\beta_2 = 0$. Obviously, from $\Delta_n = \beta_1 \delta_1 H_1(s, n)$ one has $a_{32} = \delta_1$, $a_{33} = 0$.

Case IV Assume that $|\lambda_\delta| = \infty$, $\beta_1 \neq 0$. From the first line of Eq. (4.101)

$$\Delta_n = (\beta_1 \delta_1 + \beta_2 \delta_2) \left[\frac{\beta_1}{\beta_1 + \beta_2 \delta_2 / \delta_1} H_1(s, n) + \frac{\beta_2 \delta_2 / \delta_1}{\beta_1 + \beta_2 \delta_2 / \delta_1} H_2(s, n) \right].$$

Here $\beta_1 / (\beta_1 + \beta_2 \delta_2 / \delta_1) \to 1$, $\beta_2 (\delta_2 / \delta_1) / (\beta_1 + \beta_2 \delta_2 / \delta_1) \to 0$. As above, by linearity Eq. (4.99) holds and the definition from Case I can be used again.

Case V Let $|\lambda_\delta| = \infty$, $\beta_1 = 0$. Obviously, $\Delta_n = \beta_2 \delta_2 H_2(s, n)$ and the choice $\gamma_{n2} = \beta_2 \delta_2$, $\tilde{H}(s, n) = H_2(s, n)$ satisfies Eq. (4.99) and gives $a_{32} = 0$, $a_{33} = \delta_2$.

4.6.5.2 Semireduced Model (Case VI) In this case by definition $L_1(s) = \log s$, $\delta_1 = 0$, $\delta_2 \neq 0$. We can still apply Eq. (4.95) to L_2. For L_1 we use simply $L_1(s) = L_1(n) + (L_1(s) - L_1(n)) = L_1(n) + \log(s/n)$. Since $L_1 \varepsilon_1 \equiv 1$, Eq. (4.97) is true and Eq. (4.98) formally holds with $\delta_1 = 0$. Therefore the choice is the same as in Case V: $\gamma_{n2} = \beta_2 \delta_2$, $\tilde{H}(s, n) = H_2(s, n)$.

4.6.6 Convergence of γood Coefficients

Denote G the Gram matrix of the system $f_j(x) = \log^{j-1} x$, $j = 1, 2, 3$, that is, the element g_{ij} of G equals

$$g_{ij} = \int_0^1 f_i(x) f_j(x) \, dx.$$

Theorem. (Phillips, 2007, Theorem 4.1) *Let Assumption 4.2 (Section 4.4.6.1) hold.*

(i) *In the nonreduced case suppose that both L_1, L_2 satisfy conditions of Theorem 4.4.8 (on L_p-approximability of H) with $p = 2$. In particular, assume that $\max\{2\theta_{\varepsilon_1}, \theta_{\eta_1}, 2\theta_{\varepsilon_2}, \theta_{\eta_2}\} < 1/2$. Then*

$$\sqrt{n}(\hat{\gamma}_n - \gamma_n) \xrightarrow{d} N(0, \sigma^2 G^{-1}). \tag{4.104}$$

(ii) *In the semi-reduced case suppose that $L_1(x) = \log x$ and that L_2 satisfies conditions of Theorem 4.4.8 with $p = 2$. In particular, assume that $\max\{2\theta_{\varepsilon_2}, \theta_{\eta_2}\} < 1/2$. Then Eq. (4.104) is true.*

Proof.

(i) **Nonreduced model.** Denote

$$
X_n = \begin{pmatrix} 1 & \log(1/n) & \tilde{H}(1, n) \\ \cdots & \cdots & \cdots \\ 1 & \log(n/n) & \tilde{H}(n, n) \end{pmatrix}
$$

the matrix of regressors in Eq. (4.100). The definition of $\tilde{H}$ is clear from 4.6.5.

Let us prove that the first, second and third columns of $W_n = (1/\sqrt{n})X_n$ are L_2-close to f_1, f_2, and f_3, respectively. For the first column this is obvious because if we denote it w_n, then $\Delta_{n2}w_n$ is identically 1 on $(0, 1)$. By Theorem 4.4.1 in which we put $p = 2$, $k = 1$,

$$
w_n = \frac{1}{\sqrt{n}}\left(\log\frac{1}{n}, \ldots, \log\frac{n}{n}\right)' \text{ is } L_2\text{-close to } f_2.
$$

For the third column the statement follows from Theorem 4.4.8 and linearity of L_p-approximability by construction of $\tilde{H}$.

Now Eq. (4.104) follows from Theorem 1.12.3 where $D_n = \sqrt{n}I$.

(ii) For the semi-reduced model the situation is simpler, since $\tilde{H}(s, n) = H_2(s, n)$, while the first two columns of W_n are the same. ∎

4.6.7 Convergence of βad Coefficients

It turns out that only $\hat{\gamma}_{n2}$ affects the limit distribution of $\hat{\beta}$. Lemma 4.5.9(iii) and convergence Eq. (4.104) imply

$$
\sqrt{n}(\hat{\gamma}_{n2} - \gamma_{n2}) \xrightarrow{d} N(0, \sigma^2/4). \tag{4.105}
$$

To describe the behavior of the βad coefficients denote

$$
B_n^{(i)} = \sqrt{n}\begin{pmatrix} \varepsilon_i(\hat{\beta}_0 - \beta_0) \\ L_1\varepsilon_1(\hat{\beta}_1 - \beta_1) \\ L_2\varepsilon_2(\hat{\beta}_2 - \beta_2) \end{pmatrix}, \quad i = 1, 2;
$$

$$
f(\lambda_\varepsilon) = \begin{pmatrix} \lambda_\varepsilon - 1 \\ 1 \\ -1 \end{pmatrix}, \quad g = \begin{pmatrix} 1 \\ 1 \\ -1 \end{pmatrix}.
$$

Let Γ be a normal variable distributed as $N(0, \sigma^2/4)$ [it arises from Eq. (4.105)].

Theorem. *(Classification theorem).* (Mynbaev, 2011) *Suppose conditions for convergence of the* γ*ood coefficients from Theorem 4.6.6 and Assumption 4.4 hold. Then the relation between the* β*ad coefficients [contained in* $B_n^{(i)}$*] and* γ*ood coefficients (represented by* Γ*) is as presented in Table 4.3. In the cases marked "indefinite" RV of orders higher than 3 is required to determine the type.*

This theorem reveals the distinction between the definite case, when the third-order RV is enough to determine the asymptotics, and the indefinite case, when higher-order RV is necessary. The situation is similar to the sufficient condition for optima in terms of the first- and second-order derivatives: if the second-order condition is not satisfied, we have to check higher-order derivatives. The most unexpected outcome is that the asymptotic variances jump along certain rays. The case of more than two different SV regressors should present an even larger number of different asymptotic types and Phillips (2007, Theorem 5.2) does not cover all possibilities.

4.6.8 Proof of the Classification Theorem

Repeating the main idea from Section 4.6.2, we use the information about convergence of the γood coefficients Eq. (4.104) in combination with the relation between the γood and βad coefficients to see what terms determine the limit distribution.
    By Lemma 4.5.6

$$\hat{\gamma}_n - \gamma_n = A_n(\hat{\beta} - \beta). \tag{4.106}$$

We now discuss the eight cases itemized in Table 4.3.

4.6.8.1   Case A   Let us restrict our attention to the nonreduced model and in the first two cases assume that either $(|\lambda_\delta| < \infty, \beta_1\lambda_\delta + \beta_2 \neq 0)$ or $(|\lambda_\delta| = \infty, \beta_1 \neq 0)$. In terms of Table 4.2, we are looking at Cases I and IV. In both cases the matrix A_n is the same as in the Phillips analysis. From Eq. (4.92) we have $\det A_n = L_1\varepsilon_1 L_2\varepsilon_2(\mu_2 - \mu_1)$. For A_n to be invertible, we have to require $\mu_1 \neq \mu_2$ for all large n. One can check that

$$A_n^{-1} = \begin{pmatrix} 1 & (1/(\mu_1 - \mu_2))(\mu_2/\varepsilon_1 - \mu_1/\varepsilon_2) & (1/(\mu_1 - \mu_2))(1/\varepsilon_2 - 1/\varepsilon_1) \\ 0 & -\mu_2/(L_1\varepsilon_1(\mu_1 - \mu_2)) & 1/(L_1\varepsilon_1(\mu_1 - \mu_2)) \\ 0 & \mu_1/(L_2\varepsilon_2(\mu_1 - \mu_2)) & -1/(L_2\varepsilon_2(\mu_1 - \mu_2)) \end{pmatrix} \tag{4.107}$$

satisfies $A_n^{-1}A_n = I$ and that

$$(\mu_1 - \mu_2)D_n^{(1)}A_n^{-1} = \begin{pmatrix} \mu_1 - \mu_2 & \mu_2 - \mu_1(\varepsilon_1/\varepsilon_2) & (\varepsilon_1/\varepsilon_2) - 1 \\ 0 & -\mu_2 & 1 \\ 0 & \mu_1 & -1 \end{pmatrix} \tag{4.108}$$

TABLE 4.3 Type-Wise OLS Asymptotics[*]

Case	Subcase	$|\lambda_\varepsilon| < \infty$	$|\lambda_\varepsilon| = \infty$	$|\lambda_\varepsilon| \leq \infty$
Nonreduced model $(\delta_1 \neq 0, \delta_2 \neq 0)$	$(|\lambda_\delta| < \infty, \beta_1\lambda_\delta + \beta_2 \neq 0)$ or $(|\lambda_\delta| = \infty, \beta_1 \neq 0)$	**A.** $(\mu_1 - \mu_2)B_n^{(1)} \xrightarrow{d} f(\lambda_\varepsilon)\Gamma$ if $\mu_1 \neq \mu_2$	**B.** $(\mu_1 - \mu_2)B_n^{(2)} \xrightarrow{d} g\Gamma$ if $\mu_1 \neq \mu_2$	Indefinite if $\mu_1 = \mu_2$
	$(|\lambda_\delta| < \infty, \beta_2 = 0, \beta_1\lambda_\delta + \beta_2 = 0)$	**C.** $\mu_1 B_n^{(1)} \xrightarrow{d} f(\lambda_\varepsilon)\Gamma$	**D.** $\mu_1 B_n^{(2)} \xrightarrow{d} g\Gamma$	
	$(|\lambda_\delta| = \infty, \beta_1 = 0)$	**E.** $\mu_2 B_n^{(1)} \xrightarrow{d} f(\lambda_\varepsilon)\Gamma$	**F.** $\mu_2 B_n^{(2)} \xrightarrow{d} g\Gamma$	
	$(|\lambda_\delta| < \infty, \beta_2 \neq 0, \beta_1\lambda_\delta + \beta_2 = 0)$	Indefinite	Indefinite	
Semireduced model, $(L_1(x) = \log x, \delta_2 \neq 0)$		**G.** $\mu_2 B_n^{(1)} \xrightarrow{d} f(\lambda_\varepsilon)\Gamma$	**H.** $\mu_2 B_n^{(2)} \xrightarrow{d} g\Gamma$	

[*]Cases **A–H** discussed in Section 4.6.8.

182

where $D_n^{(i)} = \text{diag}[\varepsilon_i, L_1\varepsilon_1, L_2\varepsilon_2]$, $i = 1, 2$. In the case under consideration $|\lambda_\varepsilon| < \infty$. From Eqs. (4.106), (4.107), and (4.108) we have

$$(\mu_1 - \mu_2)B_n^{(1)} = \sqrt{n}(\mu_1 - \mu_2)D_n^{(1)}(\hat{\beta} - \beta)$$

$$= \begin{pmatrix} \mu_1 - \mu_2 & \mu_2 - \mu_1(\varepsilon_1/\varepsilon_2) & (\varepsilon_1/\varepsilon_2) - 1 \\ 0 & -\mu_2 & 1 \\ 0 & \mu_1 & -1 \end{pmatrix} \sqrt{n}(\hat{\gamma}_n - \gamma_n).$$

Now take into account that ε_i and μ_i vanish at infinity by the Karamata theorem, that $\varepsilon_1/\varepsilon_2 \to \lambda_\varepsilon$ by assumption and that $\sqrt{n}(\hat{\gamma}_n - \gamma_n)$ converges in distribution by Theorem 4.6.6. Then the preceding equation and Eq. (4.105) imply

$$(\mu_1 - \mu_2)B_n^{(1)} = f(\lambda_\varepsilon)\sqrt{n}(\hat{\gamma}_{n2} - \gamma_{n2}) + o_p(1) \xrightarrow{d} f(\lambda_\varepsilon)\Gamma. \tag{4.109}$$

In the other cases the argument is similar, and we indicate only the analogs of Eqs. (4.107), (4.108), and (4.109).

4.6.8.2 Case B In this case $|\lambda_\varepsilon| = \infty$ and the other assumptions do not change, so we are still in Cases I and IV of Table 4.2. To obtain the fraction $\varepsilon_2/\varepsilon_1 \to 0$, we change the diagonal matrix in Eq. (4.108) to obtain

$$(\mu_1 - \mu_2)D_n^{(2)}A_n^{-1} = \begin{pmatrix} \mu_1 - \mu_2 & \mu_2(\varepsilon_2/\varepsilon_1) - \mu_1 & 1 - (\varepsilon_2/\varepsilon_1) \\ 0 & -\mu_2 & 1 \\ 0 & \mu_1 & -1 \end{pmatrix}.$$

Then

$$(\mu_1 - \mu_2)B_n^{(2)} = \sqrt{n}(\mu_1 - \mu_2)D_n^{(2)}A_n^{-1}(\hat{\gamma}_n - \gamma_n)$$

$$= g\sqrt{n}(\hat{\gamma}_{n2} - \gamma_{n2}) + o_p(1) \xrightarrow{d} g\Gamma.$$

4.6.8.3 Case C By Table 4.2, Case III, in the last row of A_n there is only one non-zero element,

$$A_n = \begin{pmatrix} 1 & L_1 & L_2 \\ 0 & L_1\varepsilon_1 & L_2\varepsilon_2 \\ 0 & \delta_1 & 0 \end{pmatrix}, \quad A_n^{-1} = \begin{pmatrix} 1 & -1/\varepsilon_2 & 1/\mu_1(1/\varepsilon_2 - 1/\varepsilon_1) \\ 0 & 0 & (1/\delta_1) \\ 0 & 1/(L_2\varepsilon_2) & -1/(L_2\varepsilon_2\mu_1) \end{pmatrix}.$$

Noting that

$$\mu_1 D_n^{(1)}A_n^{-1} = \begin{pmatrix} \mu_1\varepsilon_1 & -\mu_1(\varepsilon_1/\varepsilon_2) & (\varepsilon_1/\varepsilon_2) - 1 \\ 0 & 0 & 1 \\ 0 & \mu_1 & -1 \end{pmatrix}$$

we get

$$\mu_1 B_n^{(1)} = \sqrt{n}\mu_1 D_n^{(1)} A_n^{-1}(\hat{\gamma}_n - \gamma_n)$$

$$= f(\lambda_\varepsilon)\sqrt{n}(\hat{\gamma}_{n2} - \gamma_{n2}) + o_p(1) \xrightarrow{d} f(\lambda_\varepsilon)\Gamma.$$

4.6.8.4 Case D Here $|\lambda_\varepsilon| = \infty$ and all other assumptions are like in Case C (Table 4.2, Case III). So

$$\mu_1 D_n^{(2)} A_n^{-1} = \begin{pmatrix} \mu_1\varepsilon_2 & -\mu_1 & 1 - \varepsilon_2/\varepsilon_1 \\ 0 & 0 & 1 \\ 0 & \mu_1 & -1 \end{pmatrix}$$

and, as a result,

$$\mu_1 B_n^{(2)} = \sqrt{n}\mu_1 D_n^{(2)} A_n^{-1}(\hat{\gamma}_n - \gamma_n)$$

$$= g\sqrt{n}(\hat{\gamma}_{n2} - \gamma_{n2}) + o_p(1) \xrightarrow{d} g\Gamma.$$

4.6.8.5 Case E We continue looking at the nonreduced model and assume that $|\lambda_\delta| = \infty, \beta_1 = 0$. From Table 4.2, Case V, we see that A_n is triangular,

$$A_n = \begin{pmatrix} 1 & L_1 & L_2 \\ 0 & L_1\varepsilon_1 & L_2\varepsilon_2 \\ 0 & 0 & \delta_2 \end{pmatrix}, \quad A_n^{-1} = \begin{pmatrix} 1 & -1/\varepsilon_1 & 1/\mu_2(1/\varepsilon_1 - 1/\varepsilon_2) \\ 0 & 1/(L_1\varepsilon_1) & -1/(L_1\varepsilon_1\mu_2) \\ 0 & 0 & 1/\delta_2 \end{pmatrix}. \tag{4.110}$$

Suppose that $|\lambda_\varepsilon| < \infty$. To make use of this condition, consider

$$\mu_2 D_n^{(1)} A_n^{-1} = \begin{pmatrix} \mu_2\varepsilon_1 & -\mu_2 & 1 - \varepsilon_1/\varepsilon_2 \\ 0 & \mu_2 & -1 \\ 0 & 0 & 1 \end{pmatrix}.$$

It follows that

$$\mu_2 B_n^{(1)} = -f(\lambda_\varepsilon)\sqrt{n}(\hat{\gamma}_{n2} - \gamma_{n2}) + o_p(1) \xrightarrow{d} f(\lambda_\varepsilon)\Gamma. \tag{4.111}$$

4.6.8.6 Case F We are again in Table 4.2, Case V. Unlike Case E, now we have $|\lambda_\varepsilon| = \infty$ and use

$$\mu_2 D_n^{(2)} A_n^{-1} = \begin{pmatrix} \mu_2\varepsilon_2 & -\mu_2\varepsilon_2/\varepsilon_1 & \varepsilon_2/\varepsilon_1 - 1 \\ 0 & \mu_2 & -1 \\ 0 & 0 & 1 \end{pmatrix}.$$

Hence,

$$\mu_2 B_n^{(2)} = -g\sqrt{n}(\hat{\gamma}_{n2} - \gamma_{n2}) + o_p(1) \xrightarrow{d} g\Gamma. \tag{4.112}$$

4.6.8.7   Cases G and H   As is clear from Section 4.6.5.2 (Case VI), the transition matrix and its inverse are the same as in Eq. (4.110). Therefore the conclusions in Eqs. (4.111) and (4.112) apply.

The case $\mu_1 = \mu_2$ is marked as indefinite because, as mentioned in Case A, the matrix A_n is not invertible. Case II (Section 4.6.5.1) ($|\lambda_\delta| < \infty$, $\beta_1\lambda_\delta + \beta_2 = 0$, $\beta_2 \neq 0$) is also indefinite because the transition matrix is not defined.

4.6.9   Example

Since Phillips (2007, Theorem 5.1) is actually about regression with a quadratic form in $\log(s/n)$, no wonder its predictions are different from those of the classification theorem. In particular, the latter theorem captures a new effect that, within the same model, the rate of convergence and the asymptotic standard error depend on the true β_1 and β_2.

The following example from Phillips (2007) has iterated logarithmic growth, a trend decay component and a constant regressor:

$$y_s = \beta_0 + \beta_1/\log s + \beta_2 \log(\log s) + u_s.$$

Such a model is relevant in empirical research where we want to capture simultaneously two different opposing trends in the data. Here $L_1(s) = 1/\log s$, $L_2(s) = \log(\log s)$.

From Table 4.1

$$\varepsilon_1(n) = -\frac{1}{\log n}, \quad \mu_1(n) = -\frac{1}{\log n}, \quad \delta_1(n) = \frac{1}{\log^3 n},$$

$$\varepsilon_2(n) = \frac{1}{(\log n)\log(\log n)}, \quad \mu_2(n) = -\frac{1}{2\log n}, \quad \delta_2(n) = -\frac{1}{2\log^2 n}.$$

Since $\delta_1/\delta_2 \to 0$ and $\varepsilon_2/\varepsilon_1 \to 0$, we have from Table 4.3, Cases B and D,

$$\frac{\sqrt{n}}{\log^2 n}\begin{pmatrix} (1/\log(\log n))(\hat{\beta}_0 - \beta_0) \\ -(1/\log n)(\hat{\beta}_1 - \beta_1) \\ \hat{\beta}_2 - \beta_2 \end{pmatrix} \xrightarrow{d} \begin{cases} 2g\Gamma & \text{if } \beta_2 \neq 0; \\ g\Gamma & \text{if } \beta_2 = 0. \end{cases}$$

The formula from Phillips (2007, pp. 575–576), after correction of two typos, gives

$$\frac{\sqrt{n}}{\log^2 n}\begin{pmatrix} (1/\log(\log n))(\hat{\beta}_0 - \beta_0) \\ -(1/\log n)(\hat{\beta}_1 - \beta_1) \\ \hat{\beta}_2 - \beta_2 \end{pmatrix} \xrightarrow{d} g\Gamma,$$

regardless of β_2.

The comments by Phillips apply. The coefficient of the growth term converges fastest, but at less than an $\sqrt{n}$ rate. The intercept converges next fastest, and finally the coefficient of the evaporating trend. All of these outcomes relate to the strength of the signal from the respective regressor.

4.6.10 What Can be Done in the Indefinite Cases?

From the derivation of Table 4.2 and proof of Theorem 4.6.7 we can see that indefiniteness can occur when the rate of approximation is not good enough to define the transition matrix or when it is defined, but is not invertible. We use the first possibility as an example. To this end, basic notation related to approximation of SV functions is necessary.

Let

$$
L_i = K(\varepsilon_i^{(1)}, \phi_{\varepsilon_i^{(1)}}), \quad \varepsilon_i^{(1)} = K(\varepsilon_i^{(2)}, \phi_{\varepsilon_i^{(2)}}), \quad \varepsilon_i^{(2)} = K(\varepsilon_i^{(3)}, \phi_{\varepsilon_i^{(3)}});
$$

and suppose $\varepsilon_i^{(3)}$ is SV for $i = 1, 2$. One can then prove

$$
\frac{L_i(rn)}{L_i(n)} - 1 = \varepsilon_i^{(1)} \log r + \varepsilon_i^{(1)} \mu_i^{(1)} \log^2 r + \varepsilon_i^{(1)} \mu_i^{(1)} \mu_i^{(2)} \log^3 r
$$
$$
+ o(\varepsilon_i^{(1)} \mu_i^{(1)} \mu_i^{(2)}), \tag{4.113}
$$

where

$$
\mu_i^{(1)} = \frac{\varepsilon_i^{(1)} + \varepsilon_i^{(2)}}{2}, \quad \mu_i^{(2)} = \frac{\varepsilon_i^{(2)}(\varepsilon_i^{(2)} + \varepsilon_i^{(3)}) + 3\varepsilon_i^{(1)} \varepsilon_i^{(2)} + [\varepsilon_i^{(1)}]^2}{\varepsilon_i^{(1)} + \varepsilon_i^{(2)}}. \tag{4.114}
$$

Denoting $H^{(2)} = G$, $H^{(3)}(t, n) = [H^{(2)}(t, n) - \log^2(t/n)](1/\mu^{(2)}(n))$, from Eq. (4.113) we have the fourth-order RV $H_i^{(3)}(rn, n) = \log^3 r + o(1)$. With this information, an extension of Eq. (4.95) is

$$
L_j(s) = L_j(n) + L_j(n)\varepsilon_j^{(1)}(n)\log \frac{s}{n} + \delta_j(n)H_j^{(2)}(s, n)
$$
$$
= L_j(n) + L_j(n)\varepsilon_j^{(1)}(n)\log \frac{s}{n} + \delta_j(n)\log^2 \frac{s}{n} \tag{4.115}
$$
$$
+ \delta_j(n)\mu_j^{(2)} H_j^{(3)}(s, n).
$$

Equation (4.115) allows us to rewrite Eq. (4.98) as

$$
\Delta_n = \beta_1 \delta_1 \mu_1^{(2)} H_1^{(3)}(s, n) + \beta_2 \delta_2 \mu_2^{(2)} H_2^{(3)}(s, n) + (\beta_1 \delta_1 + \beta_2 \delta_2) \log^2 \frac{s}{n}. \tag{4.116}
$$

Denote $\kappa = (\beta_1 \delta_1 + \beta_2 \delta_2)/(\beta_1 \delta_1 \mu_1^{(2)} + \beta_2 \delta_2 \mu_2^{(2)})$.

TABLE 4.4 Transition Matrix Summary in Case II: $|\lambda_\delta| < \infty$, $\beta_1\lambda_\delta + \beta_2 = 0$, $\beta_2 \neq 0$

Case	Subcase		Transition matrix elements
$|\lambda_{\delta\mu}| < \infty$	$\beta_1\lambda_{\delta\mu} + \beta_2 = 0$		VII. Indefinite
	$\beta_1\lambda_{\delta\mu} + \beta_2 \neq 0$	$|\lambda_\kappa| < \infty$	VIII. $a_{32} = \delta_1\mu_1^{(2)}$, $a_{33} = \delta_2\mu_2^{(2)}$
		$|\lambda_\kappa| = \infty$	IX. $a_{32} = \delta_1$, $a_{33} = \delta_2$
$|\lambda_{\delta\mu}| = \infty$	$\beta_1 \neq 0$	$|\lambda_\kappa| < \infty$	X. $a_{32} = \delta_1\mu_1^{(2)}$, $a_{33} = \delta_2\mu_2^{(2)}$
		$|\lambda_\kappa| = \infty$	XI. $a_{32} = \delta_1$, $a_{33} = \delta_2$
	$\beta_1 = 0$	$|\lambda_\mu| < \infty$	XII. $a_{32} = 0$, $a_{33} = \delta_2$
		$|\lambda_\mu| = \infty$	XIII. $a_{32} = 0$, $a_{33} = \delta_2\mu_2^{(2)}$

4.6.10.1 Assumption 4.5

1. Let $\beta_1\delta_1\mu_1^{(2)} + \beta_2\delta_2\mu_2^{(2)} \neq 0$ for all large n.
2. Suppose the limits $\lambda_{\delta\mu} = \lim_{n\to\infty} \delta_1\mu_1^{(2)}/(\delta_2\mu_2^{(2)})$, $\lambda_\kappa = \lim \kappa$, $\lambda_\mu = \lim \mu_2^{(2)}$ (finite or infinite) exist.
3. $\{n^{-1/2}H_j^{(3)}\}$ is L_2-close to $\log^3 x, j = 1, 2$.

Under this assumption the last row of the transition matrix is described by Table 4.4, where the numbering continues that of Table 4.2. Case VII starts a new indefinite branch.

Equation (4.113) can be called a pointwise RV. The method requires establishing an integral version of the fourth-order RV in the form of Assumption 4.5(3) (Section 4.6.10.1). The proofs of second-order and third-order RV given in this chapter are pretty complex. The proof of the fourth-order RV must be even more complex given that the function $\mu^{(2)}$ in Eq. (4.114) depends nonlinearly on the ε-functions. Therefore, trying to obtain a general result is not recommended. If indefiniteness arises in an applied problem with specific L_1, L_2, it would be easier to prove Assumption 4.5(3) (Section 4.6.10.1) for those specific functions.

CHAPTER 5

SPATIAL MODELS

$\mathbf{U}$NLIKE AUTOREGRESSIVE models, which may contain only lags of the dependent variable, spatial models may contain all kinds of shifts: backward, forward and, in some problems, without any specific spatial or temporal direction. The reader can consult (Anselin, 1988), (Cliff and Ord, 1981), (Cressie, 1993) and (Anselin and Bera, 1998) about applications of spatial models. We concentrate on the mathematical side. Both the techniques and the asymptotic results in spatial models are quite different from those in Chapter 4. This chapter is based on (Mynbaev and Ullah, 2008) and (Mynbaev, 2010).

One of the major differences between the previous research and ours is that we do not impose any conditions on nonlinear matrix functions of the spatial matrix and derive their properties from low-level assumptions. Another difference is that the gauge inequality allows us to deal with autocorrelated errors using only low-level conditions. For the purely spatial model we prove convergence in distribution to a ratio of two quadratic forms in standard normal variables. This format of the asymptotic statement is justified by the finite-sample properties. As a by-product of the method, we show that the identification conditions for ML and method of moments (MM) developed by other authors fail under our conditions. Interestingly, the two-step procedure we suggest for correcting bias is a combination of least squares and ML estimators.

For the mixed spatial model we prove convergence in distribution to a nonstandard vector whose components contain both linear and quadratic forms in standard normal variables. For this we need to prove that the pair (denominator, numerator) converges in distribution because the denominator converges in distribution to a random matrix. This is the place where a parsimonious choice of assumptions and the normalizer is especially important. It is because of them that the asymptotic distribution automatically adjusts to the rates of growth of the exogenous regressors. Finally, the problem caused by randomness of the denominator matrix is addressed with the device called a multicollinearity detector.

Short-Memory Linear Processes and Econometric Applications. Kairat T. Mynbaev
© 2011 John Wiley & Sons, Inc. Published 2011 by John Wiley & Sons, Inc.

5.1   A MATH INTRODUCTION TO PURELY SPATIAL MODELS

5.1.1   The Model

To understand what a spatial model is, it is useful to start with a simple autoregression

$$y_t = \rho y_{t-1} + e_t, \quad t = 1, \dots, n.$$

Denoting

$$Y_n = (y_1, \dots, y_n)', \quad E_n = (e_1, \dots, e_n)', \quad Y_0 = (y_0, 0, \dots, 0)' \; (n \text{ coordinates}),$$

we can write the model as

$$Y_n = \rho \begin{pmatrix} 0 & 0 & \dots & 0 & 0 \\ 1 & 0 & \dots & 0 & 0 \\ 0 & 1 & \dots & 0 & 0 \\ \dots & \dots & \dots & \dots & \dots \\ 0 & 0 & \dots & 1 & 0 \end{pmatrix} Y_n + \rho Y_0 + E_n.$$

It is easy to see that in the case of a more general autoregression

$$y_t = \rho_1 y_{t-1} + \cdots + \rho_p y_{t-p} + e_t, \quad t = 1, \dots, n,$$

there will be more nonzero elements in the big matrix in front of Y_n, but all of them will be below the main diagonal.

In the *purely spatial model*

$$Y_n = \rho W_n Y_n + E_n, \tag{5.1}$$

Y_n and E_n have the same meaning as above. The *spatial matrix W_n*, however, can have nonzero elements anywhere and they don't have to be unities. If t is time, this means regressing y_t on scaled backward and forward shifts. If everything is happening in the 2-D space, one can add upward and downward shifts. However, in many applications there is no temporal, spatial or geographic connotation. The spatial matrix is assumed predetermined and its elements don't need to be estimated. It may or may not have a specific analytical structure. Finally, in the spatial model there is no reference to the initial vector Y_0. Members of Y_n form a closed community: they refer only to each other.

In most papers on spatial models the components of the error E_n in Eq. (5.1) are assumed to be independent or m.d.s, (see Lee, 2004a; Kelejian et al., 2004) and references therein. The method developed in (Mynbaev, 2010) works in case of linear processes with m.d.s as innovations. Therefore here we consider

$$Y_n = \rho W_n Y_n + v_n, \tag{5.2}$$

where the components of $v_n = (v_{n1}, \dots, v_{nn})'$ form a linear process.

5.1.2 OLS Estimator and Related Matrices

ρ is the parameter to be estimated. Since the regressor is $X_n = W_n Y_n$, the usual OLS estimator formula gives

$$\hat{\rho} = (X'_n X_n)^{-1} X'_n Y_n.$$

Its consequence

$$\hat{\rho} - \rho = (X'_n X_n)^{-1} X'_n v_n = \frac{(W_n Y_n)' v_n}{(W_n Y_n)' W_n Y_n}, \tag{5.3}$$

used in the conventional scheme here, is insufficient for analysis because of the presence of the dependent vector Y_n at the right-hand side.

Denote

$$S_n = S_n(\rho) = I - \rho W_n.$$

The matrix S_n^{-1}, when it exists, can be called a *solver* because it solves Eq. (5.2) for Y_n:

$$Y_n = S_n^{-1} v_n. \tag{5.4}$$

Equation (5.4) is the reduced form of Eq. (5.2) (the form in which there is no dependent variable at the right). It is convenient to put

$$G_n = W_n S_n^{-1}.$$

Substitution of Eq. (5.4) into Eq. (5.3) yields

$$\hat{\rho} - \rho = \frac{v'_n G'_n v_n}{v'_n G'_n G_n v_n}. \tag{5.5}$$

The analysis of the fraction at the right here is possible after we study S_n and G_n.

5.1.3 History

Kelejian and Prucha (1999) considered a generalized MM estimator for Eq. (5.1). Lee (2001) developed the theory of quasi-maximum likelihood (QML) estimation. Lee (2002) provided an example of inconsistency of the OLS estimator $\hat{\rho}$. These authors were looking for normal asymptotics

$$\sqrt{n}(\tilde{\rho} - \rho) \xrightarrow{d} N(0, V)$$

and imposed conditions accordingly. Here $\tilde{\rho}$ is any of MM, QML or OLS estimators and V is the variance of the limit distribution. The research in the above references moved towards relaxing the assumptions that underlie the asymptotic results. Along the way the conditions imposed and the results obtained became complex, to the point that it is hard to see whether a given condition can be satisfied or whether two different conditions imposed on the same sequence of matrices are compatible.

In (Mynbaev and Ullah, 2008) our main objective was to simplify and reduce the number of conditions, avoid assumptions with overlapping responsibilities and derive the characteristics of the limit distribution from the primary low-level conditions. We found that, under some conditions, the OLS estimator can be asymptotically a ratio of two infinite linear combinations of χ^2 variables.

5.1.4 Finite-Sample Expression

The intuition behind our result is explained as follows.

Lemma. *Suppose that W_n is symmetric with eigenvalues $\lambda_1, \ldots, \lambda_n$ and v_n is distributed as $N(0, \sigma^2 I)$. Then*

$$\hat{\rho} - \rho = \frac{\sum_{i=1}^n h(\lambda_i) u_i^2}{\sum_{i=1}^n h^2(\lambda_i) u_i^2}, \qquad (5.6)$$

where $u_1, \ldots, u_n$ are independent standard normal and $h(t) = t/(1 - \rho t)$.

Proof. By the diagonalization theorem (Theorem 1.7.2) W_n can be represented as $W_n = P'_n \Lambda_n P_n$, where P_n is an orthogonal matrix, $P'_n P_n = P_n P'_n = I$ and Λ_n is a diagonal matrix with $\lambda_1, \ldots, \lambda_n$ on the main diagonal. Then

$$S_n = I - \rho W_n = P'_n P_n - \rho P'_n \Lambda_n P_n = P'_n(I - \rho \Lambda_n) P_n,$$

$$G_n = W_n S_n^{-1} = P'_n \Lambda_n P_n P'_n (I - \rho \Lambda_n)^{-1} P_n = P'_n \Lambda_n (I - \rho \Lambda_n)^{-1} P_n,$$

$$v'_n G'_n v_n = v'_n P'_n \Lambda_n (I - \rho \Lambda_n)^{-1} P_n v_n = (P_n v_n)' \Lambda_n (I - \rho \Lambda_n)^{-1} P_n v_n,$$

$$v'_n G'_n G_n v_n = v'_n P'_n \Lambda_n (I - \rho \Lambda_n)^{-1} P_n P'_n \Lambda_n (I - \rho \Lambda_n)^{-1} P_n v_n$$

$$= (P_n v_n)' [\Lambda_n (I - \rho \Lambda_n)^{-1}] P_n v_n.$$

Here we remember that $\Lambda_n (I - \rho \Lambda_n)^{-1}$ is symmetric. Moreover,

$$\Lambda_n (I - \rho \Lambda_n)^{-1} = \operatorname{diag}[h(\lambda_1), \ldots, h(\lambda_n)].$$

Since

$$E P_n v_n = 0, \; V(P_n v_n) = P_n V(v_n) P'_n = \sigma^2 P_n P'_n = \sigma^2 I,$$

we see that $V_n = P_n v_n$ is distributed as $N(0, \sigma^2 I)$. Hence, it can be represented as $V_n = \sigma u$, where $u = (u_1, \ldots, u_n)'$. Substitution of this V_n in the above expressions yields

$$v'_n G'_n v_n = \sigma u' \operatorname{diag}[h(\lambda_1), \ldots, h(\lambda_n)] \sigma u = \sigma^2 \sum_{i=1}^n h(\lambda_i) u_i^2,$$

$$v'_n G'_n G_n v_n = \sigma u' \{\operatorname{diag}[h(\lambda_1), \ldots, h(\lambda_n)]\}^2 \sigma u = \sigma^2 \sum_{i=1}^n h^2(\lambda_i) u_i^2.$$

Now the statement follows from Eq. (5.5). ∎

As a result of this lemma we think that the asymptotics of the OLS estimator should be a ratio of two linear combinations of χ^2 variables rather than normal.

5.2 CONTINUITY OF NONLINEAR MATRIX FUNCTIONS

5.2.1 Elementary Algebraic Identities

Lemma. *Let A, B be square matrices of the same size. Then*

> *(i)* $A^{k+1} - B^{k+1} = A^k(A - B) + A^{k-1}(A - B)B + \cdots + (A - B)B^k$,
> $k = 1, 2, \ldots,$
> *(ii) If* $\|A\|_2 < 1$, *then* $\left(\sum_{k=0}^{\infty} A^k\right)^2 = \sum_{m=0}^{\infty} (m + 1)A^m$.

Proof.

> **(i)** The purpose here is to reveal the difference $A - B$ in
>
> $$A^{k+1} - B^{k+1} = A^{k+1} - A^k B + A^k B - A^{k-1}B^2 + A^{k-1}B^2 - \cdots$$
> $$+ AB^k - B^{k+1}$$
> $$= A^k(A - B) + A^{k-1}(A - B)B + \cdots + (A - B)B^k.$$

> **(ii)** It is easy to check that the $\| \cdot \|_2$-norm of matrices is *submultiplicative*:
>
> $$\|AB\|_2 \leq \|A\|_2 \|B\|_2.$$
>
> Therefore $\|A^k\|_2 \leq \|A\|_2^k$. $\|A\|_2 < 1$ implies that in the next equation all the series converge and rearranging the members is legitimate:
>
> $$\left(\sum_{k=0}^{\infty} A^k\right)^2 = \sum_{k,l=0}^{\infty} A^{k+l} = \sum_{m=0}^{\infty} \sum_{k+l=m} A^{k+l} = \sum_{m=0}^{\infty} (m + 1)A^m.$$
>
> The end equality obtains if we observe that there are $m + 1$ pairs (k, l) of nonnegative integers such that $k + l = m$. ∎

5.2.2 *h*-Function and *h*-Series

Functional calculus deals with applying functions of a real or complex argument to matrices and operators. We are interested in the function

$$h(t) = \frac{t}{1 - \rho t}$$

because $G_n = h(W_n)$. We call it an *h-function* because its graph is a hyperbola except for the case $\rho = 0$. This name gives rise to a series of related notions: *h*-series, *h*-continuity, etc.

Lemma. *If A is a square matrix satisfying $|\rho|\|A\|_2 < 1$, then*

$$h(A) = \sum_{k=0}^{\infty} \rho^k A^{k+1} \tag{5.7}$$

and

$$\|(I - \rho A)^{-1}\|_2 \leq \frac{1}{1 - |\rho|\|A\|_2}, \quad \|h(A)\|_2 \leq \frac{\|A\|_2}{1 - |\rho|\|A\|_2}. \tag{5.8}$$

Proof. If $\|A\|_2 < 1$, we can let $m \to \infty$ in the identity

$$(I - A) \sum_{k=0}^{m} A^k = A - A^{m+1}.$$

The resulting equation $(I - A) \sum_{k=0}^{\infty} A^k = I$ means that

$$(I - A)^{-1} = \sum_{k=0}^{\infty} A^k \text{ if } \|A\|_2 < 1.$$

Applying this well-known fact to ρA instead of A we see that

$$S_n^{-1}(\rho) = \sum_{k=0}^{\infty} \rho^k A^k, \tag{5.9}$$

which implies Eq. (5.7).

From Eqs. (5.9) and (5.7) we deduce

$$\|S_n^{-1}(\rho)\|_2 \leq \sum_{k=0}^{\infty} |\rho|^k \|A\|_2^k = \frac{1}{1 - |\rho|\|A\|_2},$$

$$\|h(A)\|_2 \leq \sum_{k=0}^{\infty} |\rho|^k \|A\|_2^{k+1} = \|A\|_2 \sum_{k=0}^{\infty} (|\rho|\|A\|_2)^k = \frac{\|A\|_2}{1 - |\rho|\|A\|_2}.$$

∎

We use the name *h-series* for the decomposition (5.7).

5.2.3 *h*-Continuity

Lemma. *For square matrices A, B such that*

$$\mu = |\rho|\max\{\|A\|_2, \|B\|_2\} < 1 \tag{5.10}$$

we have

$$\|h(A) - h(B)\|_2 \leq [1 + \phi(\rho, A, B)]\|A - B\|_2,$$

where

$$\phi(\rho, A, B) = \sum_{k=1}^{\infty} (k+1)\mu^k < \infty.$$

Proof. We need the bound

$$\|A^{k+1} - B^{k+1}\|_2 \leq \|A - B\|_2(k+1)(\max\{\|A\|_2, \|B\|_2\})^k, \quad k = 0, 1, \ldots \quad (5.11)$$

For $k = 0$ it is trivial. For $k > 0$ it follows from submultiplicativity and Lemma 5.2.1(i), where there are $k + 1$ terms at the right. This bound and the h-series lead to

$$\|h(A) - h(B)\|_2 \leq \sum_{k=0}^{\infty} |\rho|^k \|A^{k+1} - B^{k+1}\|_2$$

$$\leq \|A - B\|_2 \sum_{k=0}^{\infty} |\rho|^k(k+1)(\max\{\|A\|_2, \|B\|_2\})^k$$

$$= [1 + \phi(\rho, A, B)]\|A - B\|_2. \qquad \blacksquare$$

This lemma gives rise to the following property which can be termed *h-continuity*: if $\|A_n - B_n\|_2 \to 0$ and the numbers $\phi(\rho, A_n, B_n)$ are uniformly bounded,

$$\sup_n \phi(\rho, A_n, B_n) < \infty, \qquad (5.12)$$

then $\lim\|h(B_n) - h(A_n)\|_2 = 0$. I call condition (5.12) an *escort*, meaning that many convergence statements depend on its validity.

5.3 ASSUMPTION ON THE ERROR TERM AND IMPLICATIONS

5.3.1 Assumption on the Error Term

5.3.1.1 *Assumption 5.1*

1. $\{\{e_{nt}, \mathcal{F}_{nt} : n \in \mathbb{Z}\} : t \in \mathbb{Z}\}$ is a double-infinite m.d. array [e_{nt} is $\mathcal{F}_{nt}$-measurable, $\mathcal{F}_{n,t-1} \subset \mathcal{F}_{nt}$ and $E(e_{nt}|\mathcal{F}_{n,t-1}) = 0$].
2. $E(e_{nt}^2|\mathcal{F}_{n,t-1}) = \sigma^2$ for all t and n.
3. The third conditional moments are constant but may depend on n and t, that is, $E(e_{nt}^3|\mathcal{F}_{n,t-1}) = a_{nt}$, and the fourth moments are uniformly bounded, $\mu_4 = \sup_{n,t} E e_{nt}^4 < \infty$.

4. $\{\psi_j : j \in \mathbb{Z}\}$ is a summable sequence of numbers, $\alpha_\psi = \sum_{j\in\mathbb{Z}} |\psi_j| < \infty$.
5. Components of $v_n = (v_{n1}, \ldots, v_{nn})'$ are defined by

$$v_{nt} = \sum_{j\in\mathbb{Z}} e_{n,t-j}\psi_j, \quad t = 1, \ldots, n.$$

Conditions 1, 2, 4 and 5 are from Section 3.5.2. Condition 3 is from Section 3.9.7. Uniform integrability of e_{nt}^2 follows from Condition 3 and therefore is not included in Condition 2.

5.3.2 Gauge Version of h-Continuity

For an $n \times n$ matrix A

$$g(A) = [E(v_n' A v_n)^2]^{1/2}$$

denotes the gauge (Section 3.9.9). In the lemma below, $\sqrt{n}$ spoils the picture.

Lemma.   *If v_n satisfies Assumption 5.1 and A, B satisfy*

$$\mu = |\rho| \max\{\|A\|_2, \|B\|_2\} < 1,$$

then

$$g(h(A) - h(B)) \leq c\|A - B\|_2 [\sqrt{n} + \phi(\rho, A, B)], \tag{5.13}$$

where ϕ is the same as in Lemma 5.2.3.

Proof.   By the Minkowski inequality

$$g(h(A) - h(B)) = g\left(\sum_{k=0}^{\infty} \rho^k (A^{k+1} - B^{k+1})\right)$$

$$\leq g(A - B) + \sum_{k=1}^{\infty} |\rho|^k g(A^{k+1} - B^{k+1}). \tag{5.14}$$

By the gauge inequality (Section 3.9.9)

$$g(A - B) \leq c\|I\|_2 \|A - B\|_2 = c\sqrt{n}\|A - B\|_2. \tag{5.15}$$

For $k > 0$ we employ Lemma 5.2.1(i) and the gauge inequality to get

$$g(A^{k+1} - B^{k+1}) \leq g(A^k(A - B)) + g(A^{k-1}(A - B)B) + \cdots + g((A - B)B^k)$$

$$\leq c[\|A\|_2^k \|A - B\|_2 + \|A\|_2^{k-1}\|A - B\|_2\|B\|_2 + \cdots + \|A - B\|_2\|B\|_2^k]$$

$$\leq c(k + 1)(\max\{\|A\|_2, \|B\|_2\})^k \|A - B\|_2. \tag{5.16}$$

Summarizing,

$$g(h(A) - h(B)) \le c\|A - B\|_2\left[\sqrt{n} + \sum_{k=1}^{\infty}(k+1)\mu^k\right]. \qquad \blacksquare$$

5.3.3 Trace Version of *h*-Continuity

Lemma. *If v_n satisfies Assumption 5.1 (Section 5.3.1) and A, B satisfy Eq. (5.10), then*

$$|\mathrm{tr}h(A) - \mathrm{tr}h(B)| \le \|A - B\|_2\left[\sqrt{n} + \phi(\rho, A, B)\right] \qquad (5.17)$$

where ϕ is from Lemma 5.2.3.

Proof. Since a trace is a linear function of a matrix, $\mathrm{tr}(aA + bB) = a\mathrm{tr}A + b\mathrm{tr}B$, we have a trace analog of Eq. (5.14)

$$|\mathrm{tr}h(A) - \mathrm{tr}h(B)| = \left|\mathrm{tr}\left(\sum_{k=0}^{\infty}\rho^k(A^{k+1} - B^{k+1})\right)\right|$$

$$\le |\mathrm{tr}(A - B)| + \sum_{k=1}^{\infty}|\rho|^k|\mathrm{tr}(A^{k+1} - B^{k+1})|.$$

The trace of a single matrix gives rise to the nasty $\sqrt{n}$, as in

$$|\mathrm{tr}A| = \left|\sum_{i=1}^{n}a_{ii}\right| \le \sqrt{n}\|A\|_2,$$

while the trace of a product behaves better as long as the Euclidean norm is used:

$$|\mathrm{tr}AB| = \left|\sum_{i=1}^{n}\sum_{j=1}^{n}a_{ij}b_{ji}\right| \le \|A\|_2\|B\|_2. \qquad (5.18)$$

Bound (5.18) opens the door to the analog of Eq. (5.16):

$$|\mathrm{tr}(A^{k+1} - B^{k+1})| \le |\mathrm{tr}(A^k(A - B))| + \cdots + |\mathrm{tr}((A - B)B^k)|$$

$$\le (k+1)(\max\{\|A\|_2, \|B\|_2\})^k\|A - B\|_2.$$

The conclusion follows in the same way as for the gauge version. $\qquad \blacksquare$

5.4   ASSUMPTION ON THE SPATIAL MATRICES AND IMPLICATIONS

5.4.1   Assumption on the Spatial Matrices

5.4.1.1   *Assumption 5.2*   The sequence of matrices $\{W_n : n \in \mathbb{N}\}$ is such that W_n is of size $n \times n$ and there exists a function $K \in L_2((0, 1)^2)$ that satisfies

$$\|W_n - \delta_n K\|_2 = o\left(\frac{1}{\sqrt{n}}\right). \tag{5.19}$$

Here $\delta_n = \delta_{n2}$ is the 2-D discretization operator from Section 3.6.1. There are at least as many such classes of matrices as there are functions in $L_2((0, 1)^2)$. One can take any function $K \in L_2((0, 1)^2)$ and put $W_n = \delta_2 K$, in which case the left side of Eq. (5.19) is identically zero. Unfortunately, because of the presence of $\sqrt{n}$ in Eqs. (5.13) and (5.17) just L_2-approximability $\|W_n - \delta_n K\|_2 \to 0$ is insufficient for our purposes.

In Section 5.4.2 we show that L_2-approximability of W_n implies

$$\lim_{n \to \infty} \max_{i,j} |w_{nij}| = 0, \quad \lim_{n \to \infty} \sum_{i,j} |w_{nij}| = \infty. \tag{5.20}$$

The first equation means that the influence of a given economic unit on other units is weak. If the sum $\sum_{i,j} |w_{nij}|$ is adopted as a measure of total interaction among the units, the second equation shows that this interaction increases to infinity.

5.4.2   Simple Implications of Assumption 5.2

Lemma.   *Let $\{W_n\}$ satisfy Assumption 5.2. Then*

(i) *$\|W_n\|_2$ and $\|\delta_n K\|_2$ are asymptotically the same,*

$$\lim_{n \to \infty} \|W_n\|_2 = \lim_{n \to \infty} \|\delta_n K\|_2 = \|K\|_2. \tag{5.21}$$

(ii) *If K is symmetric, then W_n' approaches $\delta_n K$ with the same rate as W_n:*

$$\|W_n' - \delta_n K\|_2 = o\left(\frac{1}{\sqrt{n}}\right).$$

(iii) *Eq. (5.20) is true.*

Proof.

(i) Because of the convergence of $P_n K$ to K (see Section 2.2.1) and continuity of norms we have

$$\lim_{n \to \infty} \|P_n K\|_2 = \|K\|_2.$$

Also take into account that $P_n = \Delta_n \delta_n$ and that Δ_n preserves norms (see Section 2.1.7) so that

$$\|P_n K\|_2 = \|\Delta_n \delta_n K\|_2 = \|\delta_n K\|_2.$$

We have proved the second Eq. (5.21). The first equation follows directly from Eq. (5.19) and continuity of norms.

(ii) Note that $(x, y) \in q_{ij}$ if and only $(y, x) \in q_{ji}$ (see the definition of $\delta_n K$ in Section 3.6.1) and, hence, for a symmetric K, $\delta_n K$ is also symmetric. Now the statement follows from

$$\|W'_n - \delta_n K\|_2 = \|(W_n - \delta_n K)'\|_2 = \|W_n - \delta_n K\|_2. \qquad (5.22)$$

(iii) The first equation in Eq. (5.20) is established like Lemma 2.5.2 (ii): initially it is proved for L_p-generated sequences and then extended to L_p-approximable sequences. From the first equation in Eq. (5.20) and part (i) of this lemma

$$0 < c \le \|W_n\|_2^2 \le \|W_n\|_\infty \|W_n\|_1,$$

which implies the second equation of Eq. (5.20). ∎

5.4.3 Existence of the OLS Estimator

As is clear from Eq. (5.5), the OLS estimator exists whenever $S_n(\rho)$ is invertible. A good condition for the invertibility of $S_n(\rho)$ should be expressed in terms of the basic assumptions. Such a condition is provided in the lemma below. Fortunately, it is weaker than the condition on ρ imposed later for convergence of the estimator in distribution.

Lemma. *If $\{W_n\}$ satisfies Assumption 5.2 and ρ satisfies*

$$|\rho| < \frac{1}{\|K\|_2}, \qquad (5.23)$$

then there exists a natural n_0 such that

$$\sup_{n \ge n_0} \|G_n\|_2 < \infty \qquad (5.24)$$

and the OLS estimator Eq. (5.5) exists for all large n.

Proof. By condition Eq. (5.23) there exists $\varepsilon > 0$ satisfying $|\rho|\|K\|_2 \leq 1 - 2\varepsilon$. By Lemma 5.4.2 there is a natural n_0 such that

$$\sup_{n \geq n_0} |\rho|\|W_n\|_2 \leq 1 - \varepsilon, \quad \sup_{n \geq n_0} |\rho|\|\delta_n K\|_2 \leq 1 - \varepsilon. \tag{5.25}$$

Therefore Eq. (5.8) implies Eq. (5.24):

$$\|G_n\|_2 = \|h(W_n)\|_2 \leq \frac{\|W_n\|_2}{1 - |\rho|\|W_n\|_2} \leq \frac{1}{\varepsilon} \sup_{n \geq n_0} \|W_n\|_2 < \infty. \tag{5.26}$$

∎

5.4.4 Gauging $G'_n - h(\delta_n K)$

Lemma. *Under the conditions of Lemma 5.4.3*

$$g(G'_n - h(\delta_n K)) \to 0, \quad \|G_n - h(\delta_n K)\|_2 \to 0, \quad \|G'_n - h(\delta_n K)\|_2 \to 0.$$

Proof. Equation (5.25) implies

$$\mu_n = |\rho| \max \{ \|W'_n\|_2, \|\delta_n K\|_2 \} \leq 1 - \varepsilon$$

and therefore the escort is satisfied:

$$\phi(\rho, W'_n, \delta_n K) \leq \sum_{k=1}^{\infty} (k + 1)(1 - \varepsilon)^k \leq c, \quad \text{for } n \geq n_0.$$

By the gauge version of h-continuity and Lemma 5.4.2

$$\begin{aligned} g(G'_n - h(\delta_n K)) &= g(h(W'_n) - h(\delta_n K)) \\ &\leq c\|W'_n - \delta_n K\|_2 [\sqrt{n} + \phi(\rho, W'_n, \delta_n K)] \to 0. \end{aligned} \tag{5.27}$$

The other two statements of the lemma rely on Lemma 5.2.3 but the escort is the same. ∎

5.4.5 Gauging $G'_n G_n - h^2(\delta_n K)$

Lemma. *Under conditions of Lemma 5.4.3, $g(G'_n G_n - h^2(\delta_n K)) \to 0$.*

Proof. Replacing W_n by $\delta_n K$ in Eq. (5.26) we obtain

$$\sup_{n \geq n_0} \|h(\delta_n K)\|_2 < \infty. \tag{5.28}$$

By the Minkowski and gauge inequalities (Sections 1.2.4 and 3.9.9, respectively)

$$g(G'_n G_n - h^2(\delta_n K)) \leq g((G'_n - h(\delta_n K))G_n) + g(h(\delta_n K)(G_n - h(\delta_n K)))$$
$$\leq c[\|G'_n - h(\delta_n K)\|_2 \|G_n\|_2 + \|h(\delta_n K)\|_2 \|G_n - h(\delta_n K)\|_2].$$
$$(5.29)$$

The escort for $G'_n - h(\delta_n K)$ and $G_n - h(\delta_n K)$ is the same [this is proved like for Eq. (5.22)], and we have checked its validity in Lemma 5.4.4. Therefore both tend to zero in L_2. $\|G_n\|_2$ and $\|h(\delta_n K)\|_2$ are uniformly bounded by Eqs. (5.29) and (5.28). From Eq. (5.29) we see that the lemma is true. ∎

5.5 ASSUMPTION ON THE KERNEL AND IMPLICATIONS

5.5.1 Assumption on the Kernel

5.5.1.1 Assumption 5.3 The function K from Section 5.4.1 [Eq. (5.19)] is symmetric and the eigenvalues λ_i, $i = 1, 2, \ldots$, of the integral operator

$$(\mathcal{K}F)(x) = \int_0^1 K(x, y)F(y)dy, \quad F \in L_2(0, 1),$$

are summable:

$$\nu(\mathcal{K}) \equiv \sum_{j=1}^{\infty} |\lambda_j| < \infty, \tag{5.30}$$

Necessary and sufficient conditions (in terms of K) for summability of eigenvalues can be found in [Gohberg and Kreĭn (1969), Theorem 10.1]. Recall from Section 3.7.1 that K is called a kernel of $\mathcal{K}$ and the eigenvalues summability condition means that $\mathcal{K}$ is nuclear. The quantity $\nu(\mathcal{K})$ appears in many estimates. I call it a *nuke*. As proved in Section 3.7.2, $\mathcal{K}$ is compact and the Hilbert–Schmidt theorem (Theorem 3.7.5) is applicable. The eigenvalues $\{\lambda_n\}$ are counted with their multiplicities. From now on we denote by $\{F_n\}$ the orthonormal system of eigenvectors of $\mathcal{K}$.

5.5.2 Bounds for Segments of K

For any $1 \leq L < M \leq \infty$ consider a segment

$$K_{L,M}(x, y) = \sum_{j=L}^{M} \lambda_j F_j(x) F_j(x)$$

of decomposition (3.38). Note that in this notation the initial segment K_L becomes $K_{1,L}$.

Lemma.   *If K satisfies Assumption 5.3, then*

$$\|\delta_n K_{L,M}\|_2 \le \sum_{j=L}^{M} |\lambda_j| \quad \text{for any } L, M. \tag{5.31}$$

Proof.   We need the identity

$$(\delta_n^2 K_{L,M})_{s,t} = \sum_{j=L}^{M} \lambda_j (\delta_n^1 F_j)_s (\delta_n^1 F_j)_t, \quad s, t = 1, \ldots, n, \tag{5.32}$$

which follows from Lemma 3.6.1 (iii). Here δ_n^2 and δ_n^1 are 2-D and 1-D discretization operators, respectively. For any n, i, j by the Cauchy–Schwarz inequality and boundedness of δ_n

$$|(\delta_n F_i, \delta_n F_j)_{l_2}| \le \|\delta_n F_i\|_2 \|\delta_n F_j\|_2 \le \|F_i\|_2 \|F_j\|_2 = 1. \tag{5.33}$$

Hence, Eq. (5.32) gives

$$\|\delta_n K_{L,M}\|_2^2 = \sum_{s,t=1}^{n} \sum_{i,j=L}^{M} \lambda_i \lambda_j (\delta_n F_i)_s (\delta_n F_i)_t (\delta_n F_j)_s (\delta_n F_j)_t$$

$$= \sum_{i,j=L}^{M} \lambda_i \lambda_j (\delta_n F_i, \delta_n F_j)_{l_2}^2 \le \left(\sum_{j=L}^{M} |\lambda_j| \right)^2.$$

When $M = \infty$, this bound requires Eq. (5.30). ∎

5.5.3   *h*-Continuity for Segments of *K*

Lemma.   *Under Assumptions 5.1 and 5.3 and*

$$|\rho| < 1/v(\mathcal{K}), \tag{5.34}$$

the bound

$$\sup_{n \ge 1} \|h(\delta_n K) - h(\delta_n K_L)\|_2 \le c \|\delta_n K - \delta_n K_L\|_2 = c \sum_{j>L} |\lambda_j|$$

is true, where c does not depend on L.

Proof.   From Eqs. (5.34) and (5.31) we obtain a uniform bound

$$|\rho| \sup_{n,L,M} \|\delta_n K_{L,M}\|_2 \le |\rho| v(\mathcal{K}) < 1. \tag{5.35}$$

The quantity μ from Eq. (5.10) for the pair $(\delta_n K, \delta_n K_L)$ is also uniformly bounded away from 1:

$$\mu_{n,L} = |\rho| \max \{ \|\delta_n K\|_2, \|\delta_n K_L\|_2 \} \le |\rho| v(\mathcal{K}) < 1. \tag{5.36}$$

Hence, the escort condition holds,

$$\phi(\rho, \delta_n K, \delta_n K_L) = \sum_{k=1}^{\infty} (k+1)\mu_{n,L}^k \leq \sum_{k=1}^{\infty} (k+1)(|\rho|v(\mathcal{K}))^k = c < \infty.$$

Now, by Lemma 5.2.3 and Eq. (5.31)

$$\|h(\delta_n K) - h(\delta_n K_L)\|_2 \leq (1+c)\|\delta_n K - \delta_n K_L\|_2$$

$$= c_1\|\delta_n K_{L+1,\infty}\|_2 \leq c_1 \sum_{j=L+1}^{\infty} |\lambda_j|. \tag{5.37}$$

∎

5.5.4 Gauging $h(\delta_n K) - h(\delta_n K_L)$

This Lemma improves upon Lemma 5.3.2 thanks to the additional structure embedded in K. It is useful to follow the similarities in the proofs.

Lemma. *Under Assumptions 5.1 and 5.3 and Eq. (5.34) we have*

$$\sup_{n\geq 1} g(h(\delta_n K) - h(\delta_n K_L)) \leq c \sum_{j>L} |\lambda_j|,$$

where c does not depend on L.

Proof. We start with

$$g(h(\delta_n K) - h(\delta_n K_L))$$

$$\leq g(\delta_n K - \delta_n K_L) + \sum_{k=1}^{\infty} |\rho|^k g((\delta_n K)^{k+1} - (\delta_n K_L)^{k+1}). \tag{5.38}$$

By the gauge inequality (Section 3.9.9) with $A = \delta_n F_j$, $B = (\delta_n F_j)'$ and Eq. (5.33) write

$$g(\delta_n F_i(\delta_n F_j)') \leq c\|\delta_n F_i\|_2\|\delta_n F_j\|_2 \leq c. \tag{5.39}$$

The first term at the right of Eq. (5.38) is bounded like this:

$$g(\delta_n K - \delta_n K_L) = g\left(\left(\sum_{j>L} \lambda_j(\delta_n F_j)_s(\delta_n F_j)_t\right)_{s,t=1}^{n}\right)$$

$$= g\left(\sum_{j>L} \lambda_j \delta_n F_j(\delta_n F_j)'\right) \leq \sum_{j>L} |\lambda_j| g(\delta_n F_j(\delta_n F_j)')$$

$$\leq c \sum_{j>L} |\lambda_j|.$$

For the rest of the terms at the right of Eq. (5.38) successively apply Eq. (5.16), Eq. (5.36) and the last part of Eq. (5.37):

$$|\rho|^k g((\delta_n K)^{k+1} - (\delta_n K_L)^{k+1})$$

$$\leq c(k+1)(|\rho| \max\{\|\delta_n K\|_2, \|\delta_n K_L\|_2\})^k \|\delta_n K - \delta_n K_L\|_2$$

$$\leq c_1(k+1)(|\rho|v(\mathcal{K}))^k \sum_{j>L} |\lambda_j|.$$

Hence, collecting the terms gives

$$g(h(\delta_n K) - h(\delta_n K_L)) \leq c \sum_{j>L} |\lambda_j| + c_1 \sum_{k=1}^{\infty} (k+1)(|\rho|v(\mathcal{K}))^k \sum_{j>L} |\lambda_j|$$

$$= c_2 \sum_{j>L} |\lambda_j|,$$

where c_2 does not depend on n, L. ∎

5.5.5   Gauging $h^2(\delta_n K) - h^2(\delta_n K_L)$

Lemma.   *Under Assumptions 5.1 and 5.3 and Eq. (5.34) one has*

$$\sup_{n \geq 1} g(h^2(\delta_n K) - h^2(\delta_n K_L)) \leq c \sum_{j>L} |\lambda_j|,$$

where c does not depend on L.

Proof.   Equation (5.29) rewrites for the current situation as

$$g(h^2(\delta_n K) - h^2(\delta_n K_L))$$

$$\leq g([h(\delta_n K) - h(\delta_n K_L)]h(\delta_n K)) + g(h(\delta_n K)[h(\delta_n K) - h(\delta_n K_L)])$$

$$\leq c[\|h(\delta_n K_L)\|_2 + \|h(\delta_n K)\|_2]\|h(\delta_n K) - h(\delta_n K_L)\|_2.$$

Here, by Eqs. (5.8) and (5.35)

$$\|h(\delta_n K_L)\|_2 \leq \frac{\|\delta_n K_L\|_2}{1 - |\rho| \|\delta_n K_L\|_2} \leq \frac{\|\delta_n K_L\|_2}{1 - |\rho|v(\mathcal{K})} \leq c_1, \quad 1 \leq L \leq \infty. \tag{5.40}$$

Besides, by Lemma 5.5.3

$$\|h(\delta_n K) - h(\delta_n K_L)\|_2 \leq c \sum_{j>L} |\lambda_j|.$$

∎

5.6   LINEAR AND QUADRATIC FORMS INVOLVING SEGMENTS OF K

In the previous sections we have traced applications of the nuclearity assumption to nonlinear estimates of deterministic expressions. Here we show this assumption allows us to obtain closed-form expressions for a series of random variables.

5.6.1   Convergence of Chain Products

Consider any system $\{F_i : n \in \mathbb{N}\}$ in $L_2(0, 1)$ (in applications it is the system of eigenvectors of an integral operator). For a collection of indices $i = (i_1, \ldots, i_{k+1})$, where all $i_1, \ldots, i_{k+1}$ are natural, by a *chain product* we mean

$$c_{ni} = \begin{cases} (\delta_n F_{i_1}, \delta_n F_{i_2})_{l_2}(\delta_n F_{i_2}, \delta_n F_{i_3})_{l_2} \cdots (\delta_n F_{i_k}, \delta_n F_{i_{k+1}})_{l_2}, & \text{if } k > 0; \\ 1, & \text{if } k = 0. \end{cases}$$

Here $\delta_n = \delta_{n2}$ is the discretization operator from Section 2.1.2. One scalar product in the chain is called its *link*. Put

$$c_{\infty i} = \begin{cases} 1, & \text{if } (k > 0 \text{ and } i_1 = \cdots = i_{k+1}) \text{ or } (k = 0), \\ 0, & \text{otherwise.} \end{cases}$$

Lemma.   *If the system* $\{F_i : n \in \mathbb{N}\}$ *is orthonormal, then for all i with natural* $i_1, \ldots, i_{k+1}$

$$\lim_{n \to \infty} c_{ni} = c_{\infty i}.$$

Proof.   By Eq. (2.6)

$$\int_0^1 (P_n F_i) P_n F_j dx = (\delta_n F_i)' \delta_n F_j.$$

From Lemma 2.2.1 we know that $P_n F_i \to F_i$ in L_2. Therefore continuity of scalar products ensures that

$$\int_0^1 (P_n F_i) P_n F_j dx = (P_n F_i, P_n F_j)_{L_2} \to (F_i, F_j)_{L_2}, \quad n \to \infty.$$

From the above two equations we conclude that

$$\lim_{n \to \infty} (\delta_n F_i, \delta_n F_j)_{l_2} = (F_i, F_j)_{L_2} = \begin{cases} 1, & i = j, \\ 0, & i \neq j. \end{cases} \tag{5.41}$$

   In the case $k = 0$ there is nothing to prove. If $k > 0$ and among $i_1, \ldots, i_{k+1}$ there are at least two different indices, then at least two adjacent ones i_l, i_{l+1} must be unequal. In this case the corresponding link $(\delta_n F_{i_l}, \delta_n F_{i_{l+1}})_{l_2}$ in the chain product tends to zero and the product itself tends to zero. If $k > 0$ and $i_1 = \cdots = i_{k+1}$, then all links tend to 1. ∎

5.6.2 Powers of $\delta_n K_L$

Lemma. *If K satisfies Assumption 5.3, then the powers of $\delta_n K_L$ have elements*

$$(\delta_n K_L)_{st}^{k+1} = \sum_{i_1,\ldots,i_{k+1} \leq L} \prod_{j=1}^{k+1} \lambda_{i_j} c_{ni}(\delta_n F_{i_1})_s (\delta_n F_{i_{k+1}})_t. \tag{5.42}$$

Proof. The proof is by induction. By Eq. (5.32) and the definition of the chain products c_{ni} Eq. (5.42) is certainly true for $k = 0$:

$$(\delta_n K_L)_{st} = \sum_{i=1}^{L} \lambda_i (\delta_n F_i)_s (\delta_n F_i)_t. \tag{5.43}$$

Suppose Eq. (5.42) is true for some $k > 0$ and multiply it by Eq. (5.43):

$$((\delta_n K_L)^{k+1} \delta_n K_L)_{st} = \sum_{p=1}^{n} (\delta_n K_L)_{sp}^{k+1} (\delta_n K_L)_{pt}$$

$$= \sum_{p=1}^{n} \sum_{i_1,\ldots,i_{k+1} \leq L} \prod_{j=1}^{k+1} \lambda_{i_j} c_{ni} (\delta_n F_{i_1})_s (\delta_n F_{i_{k+1}})_p$$

$$\times \sum_{i_{k+2}=1}^{L} \lambda_{i_{k+2}} (\delta_n F_{i_{k+2}})_p (\delta_n F_{i_{k+2}})_t.$$

Rearranging,

$$((\delta_n K_L)^{k+1} \delta_n K_L)_{st}$$

$$= \sum_{i_1,\ldots,i_{k+2} \leq L} \prod_{j=1}^{k+2} \lambda_{i_j} c_{ni} \sum_{p=1}^{n} (\delta_n F_{i_{k+1}})_p (\delta_n F_{i_{k+2}})_p (\delta_n F_{i_1})_s (\delta_n F_{i_{k+2}})_t.$$

This coincides with Eq. (5.43) incremented by 1 because

$$c_{n(i_1,\ldots,i_{k+1})} \sum_{p=1}^{n} (\delta_n F_{i_{k+1}})_p (\delta_n F_{i_{k+2}})_p = c_{n(i_1,\ldots,i_{k+2})}.$$

∎

5.6.3 Double A Lemma

I call expressions at the right of Eqs. (5.44) and (5.45) below *awkward aggregates*. This explains the name of the lemma.

Lemma.   *Let a, b be two n-dimensional vectors (one or both may be random). Then*

$$a'h(\delta_n K_L)b = \sum_{k=0}^{\infty} \rho^k \sum_{i_1,\ldots,i_{k+1}\leq L} \prod_{j=1}^{k+1} \lambda_{i_j} c_{ni}(a'\delta_n F_{i_1})(b'\delta_n F_{i_{k+1}}) \quad (1^{st}\ AA) \qquad (5.44)$$

and

$$a'h^2(\delta_n K_L)b = \sum_{m=0}^{\infty} \rho^m(m+1) \sum_{i_1,\ldots,i_{m+2}\leq L} \prod_{j=1}^{m+2} \lambda_{i_j} c_{ni}(a'\delta_n F_{i_1})(b'\delta_n F_{i_{m+2}}) \quad (2^{nd}\ AA)$$

$$(5.45)$$

Proof.   To prove Eq. (5.44), plug Eq. (5.42) into Eq. (5.7)

$$h(\delta_n K_L) = \sum_{k=0}^{\infty} \rho^k(\delta_n K_L)_{st}^{k+1}$$

$$= \sum_{k=0}^{\infty} \rho^k \sum_{i_1,\ldots,i_{k+1}\leq L} \prod_{j=1}^{k+1} \lambda_{i_j} c_{ni}(\delta_n F_{i_1})_s(\delta_n F_{i_{k+1}})_t. \qquad (5.46)$$

Multiplying this by $a_s b_t$ and summing over $s, t = 1,\ldots, n$ we get Eq. (5.44). From Eq. (5.7) and Lemma 5.2.1(ii) we get

$$h^2(A) = \left(\sum_{k=0}^{\infty} \rho^k A^k\right)^2 A^2 = \sum_{m=0}^{\infty} (m+1)\rho^m A^{m+2}. \qquad (5.47)$$

Use this identity together with Eq. (5.42) to prove an analog of Eq. (5.46):

$$h^2(\delta_n K_L) = \sum_{m=0}^{\infty} (m+1)\rho^m(\delta_n K_L)_{st}^{m+2}$$

$$= \sum_{m=0}^{\infty} \rho^m(m+1) \sum_{i_1,\ldots,i_{m+2}\leq L} \prod_{j=1}^{m+2} \lambda_{i_j} c_{ni}(\delta_n F_{i_1})_s(\delta_n F_{i_{m+2}})_t. \qquad (5.48)$$

This implies Eq. (5.45).   ∎

5.7   THE ROUNDABOUT ROAD

We need to study the behavior of the numerator and denominator of Eq. (5.5). The distinctive feature of spatial models is that, at least under our conditions, both converge to nontrivial random variables. To be able to pass from their convergence to convergence of their ratio, we need to prove their convergence in joint distribution.

5.7.1 Basic Definitions

The numerator and denominator are considered coordinates of a new vector $\mathcal{P}_n$ (for *pair*),

$$\mathcal{P}_n = \begin{pmatrix} v_n' G_n' v_n \\ v_n' G_n' G_n v_n \end{pmatrix} = \begin{pmatrix} v_n' h(W_n)' v_n \\ v_n' h(W_n)' h(W_n) v_n \end{pmatrix}.$$

$\mathcal{P}_n$ is approximated by another vector with $h(\delta_n K)$ in place of $G_n = h(W_n)$

$$\begin{pmatrix} v_n' h(\delta_n K) v_n \\ v_n' h^2(\delta_n K) v_n \end{pmatrix}.$$

That second vector, in turn, is approximated by yet another vector with $h(\delta_n K_L)$ instead of $h(\delta_n K)$,

$$\begin{pmatrix} v_n' h(\delta_n K_L) v_n \\ v_n' h^2(\delta_n K_L) v_n \end{pmatrix},$$

where K_L is the initial segment of K. (The primes are omitted because $\delta_n K$ and $\delta_n K_L$ are symmetric.) The third approximation is a continuous function of the weighted sum of linear processes from Chapter 3. To this last vector we are able to apply Billingsley's theorem on a double limit (Section 3.9.5). A special notation for the intermediate vectors is not introduced because what we actually need is the initial vector $\mathcal{P}_n$, final vector X_{nL} and the differences between successive approximations.

This scheme is realized in the representation

$$\mathcal{P}_n = \alpha_n + \beta_{nL} + \gamma_{nL} + X_{nL},$$

where

$$\alpha_n = \begin{pmatrix} v_n' [G_n' - h(\delta_n K)] v_n \\ v_n' [G_n' G_n - h^2(\delta_n K)] v_n \end{pmatrix}, \tag{5.49}$$

$$\beta_{nL} = \begin{pmatrix} v_n' [h(\delta_n K) - h(\delta_n K_L)] v_n \\ v_n' [h^2(\delta_n K) - h^2(\delta_n K_L)] v_n \end{pmatrix} \tag{5.50}$$

and

$$\gamma_{nL} = \begin{pmatrix} v_n' h(\delta_n K_L) v_n \\ v_n' h^2(\delta_n K_L) v_n \end{pmatrix} - X_{nL}. \tag{5.51}$$

The vector X_{nL} carries all the essential information about $\mathcal{P}_n$ to the extent that its double limit $\mathrm{dlim}_{L \to \infty} \mathrm{dlim}_{n \to \infty} X_{nL}$ describes the limit of $\mathcal{P}_n$. Therefore X_{nL} is called a *proXy*. Its first limit

$$\xi_L = \mathrm{dlim}_{n \to \infty} X_{nL} \tag{5.52}$$

is also representative of $\mathcal{P}_n$ and is called a *proξy*. The proXy is defined as follows. With the system of eigenvalues $\{\lambda_i\}$ and eigenfunctions $\{F_i\}$ of the operator $\mathcal{K}$ put for any $n, L \in \mathbb{N}$

$$U_{nL} = \begin{pmatrix} v'_n \delta_n F_1 \\ \cdots \\ v'_n \delta_n F_L \end{pmatrix}, \quad X_{nL} = \sum_{j=1}^{L} U_{nLj}^2 \left(\frac{h(\lambda_j)}{h^2(\lambda_j)} \right). \tag{5.53}$$

The goal is to show that α_n, β_{nL} and γ_{nL} are negligible in some sense.

5.7.2 Convergence of the Proxies

Lemma. *Let Assumption 5.1 hold and let the sequence $\{h(\lambda_j)\}$ be summable. Denote*

$$\xi_L = (\sigma \beta_\psi)^2 \sum_{j=1}^{L} u_j^2 \left(\frac{h(\lambda_j)}{h^2(\lambda_j)} \right), \quad \Xi = (\sigma \beta_\psi)^2 \sum_{j=1}^{\infty} u_j^2 \left(\frac{h(\lambda_j)}{h^2(\lambda_j)} \right)$$

where $u_1, u_2, \ldots$ are independent standard normal. Then

(i) *Eq. (5.52) is true,*

(ii) *ξ_L converges to Ξ in $\mathcal{L}_1$.*

Proof.

(i) Assumption 5.1 on the error term is stronger than in Theorem 3.5.2. The Gram matrix G of the system $\{F_1, \ldots, F_L\}$ equals I_L. Disposing $\delta_n F_1, \ldots, \delta_n F_L$ into rows of W_n, by Theorem 3.5.2 we have

$$U_{nL} = W'_n v_n \overset{d}{\to} N(0, (\sigma \beta_\psi)^2 I_L) \text{ as } n \to \infty,$$

including the case $\beta_\psi = 0$. By Lemma 3.1.6 we can equivalently write

$$U_{nL} \overset{d}{\to} |\sigma \beta_\psi| \begin{pmatrix} u_1 \\ \cdots \\ u_L \end{pmatrix}. \tag{5.54}$$

The proXy is a continuous function of U_{nL}. Equation (5.52) follows by CMT from Eq. (5.54).

(ii) Convergence of ξ_L to Ξ in $\mathcal{L}_1$ follows from the summability of $\{h(\lambda_j)\}$ and integrability of u_i^2 [recall that summability of $\{h(\lambda_j)\}$ implies its square-summability].

One can prove that the means and variances of X_{nL} tend to those of ξ_L, see (Mynbaev and Ullah, 2008). ∎

5.7.3 Bounding Alphas and Betas

Lemma. *If Assumptions 5.1 and 5.3 hold and $|\rho| v(\mathcal{K}) < 1$, then the coordinates of vectors α_n and β_{nL} satisfy*

$$\|\alpha_{n1}\|_{2,\Omega} + \|\alpha_{n2}\|_{2,\Omega} = o(1) \tag{5.55}$$

and

$$\|\beta_{nL1}\|_{2,\Omega} + \|\beta_{nL2}\|_{2,\Omega} \le c \sum_{j>L} |\lambda_j|, \tag{5.56}$$

where c does not depend on n and L.

Proof. Equation (5.34) implies $|\rho| \|K\|_2 < 1$ because $\|K\|_2 = \left(\sum_{j=1}^{\infty} \lambda_j^2\right)^{1/2} \le v(\mathcal{K})$ [see Eq. (3.39)]. By definitions (3.60) and (5.49)

$$\|\alpha_{n1}\|_{2,\Omega} = [E(v_n'[G_n' - h(\delta_n K)]v_n)^2]^{1/2} = g(G_n' - h(\delta_n K)).$$

By Lemma 5.4.4 $\|\alpha_{n1}\|_{2,\Omega} \to 0$. Since

$$\|\alpha_{n2}\|_{2,\Omega} = g(G_n' G_n - h^2(\delta_n K)),$$

Lemma 5.4.5 gives $\|\alpha_{n2}\|_{2,\Omega} \to 0$.
    Similarly, because

$$\|\beta_{nL1}\|_{2,\Omega} = [E(v_n'[h(\delta_n K) - h(\delta_n K_L)]v_n)^2]^{1/2} = g(h(\delta_n K) - h(\delta_n K_L))$$

we can use Lemma 5.5.4 to conclude that $\|\beta_{nL1}\|_{2,\Omega} \le c \sum_{j>L} |\lambda_j|$ where c does not depend on n and L. For

$$\|\beta_{nL2}\|_{2,\Omega} = g(h^2(\delta_n K) - h^2(\delta_n K_L))$$

Lemma 5.5.5 leads to the same result.   ∎

5.7.4 Representation of Gammas

Lemma. *If Assumption 5.3 holds and*

$$|\rho| \max_j |\lambda_j| < 1, \tag{5.57}$$

then

$$\gamma_{nL1} = \sum_{k=0}^{\infty} \rho^k \sum_{i_1,\ldots,i_{k+1}\leq L} \prod_{j=1}^{k+1} \lambda_{i_j}(c_{ni} - c_{\infty i})U_{nLi_1} U_{nLi_{k+1}}, \tag{5.58}$$

$$\gamma_{nL2} = \sum_{m=0}^{\infty} \rho^m(m+1) \sum_{i_1,\ldots,i_{m+2}\leq L} \prod_{j=1}^{m+2} \lambda_{i_j}(c_{ni} - c_{\infty i})U_{nLi_1} U_{nLi_{m+2}}. \tag{5.59}$$

See Section 5.6.1 and Eq. (5.53) for the definitions of c_{ni}, $c_{\infty i}$ and U_{nL}.

Proof. Letting $a = b = v_n$ in the Double A Lemma (Section 5.6.3) we get

$$v_n' h(\delta_n K_L)v_n = \sum_{k=0}^{\infty} \rho^k \sum_{i_1,\ldots,i_{k+1}\leq L} \prod_{j=1}^{k+1} \lambda_{i_j} c_{ni}(v_n' \delta_n F_{i_1})(v_n' \delta_n F_{i_{k+1}})$$

$$= \sum_{k=0}^{\infty} \rho^k \sum_{i_1,\ldots,i_{k+1}\leq L} \prod_{j=1}^{k+1} \lambda_{i_j} c_{ni} U_{nLi_1} U_{nLi_{k+1}}. \tag{5.60}$$

We need to express the first component of the proXy in similar terms. Condition (5.57) allows us to replace $h(\lambda_j)$ in its definition [Eq. (5.53)] by

$$h(\lambda_j) = \sum_{k=0}^{\infty} \rho^k \lambda_j^{k+1}, \tag{5.61}$$

thus obtaining

$$X_{nL1} = \sum_{j=1}^{L} U_{nLj}^2 \sum_{k=0}^{\infty} \rho^k \lambda_j^{k+1} = \sum_{k=0}^{\infty} \rho^k \sum_{j=1}^{L} \lambda_j^{k+1} U_{nLj}^2.$$

Since the chain product $c_{\infty i}$ vanishes for i with different components, this is the same as

$$X_{nL1} = \sum_{k=0}^{\infty} \rho^k \sum_{i_1,\ldots,i_{k+1}\leq L} \prod_{j=1}^{k+1} \lambda_{i_j} c_{\infty i} U_{nLi_1} U_{nLi_{k+1}}.$$

Equation (5.58) is a consequence of this formula and Eq. (5.60).

Letting $a = b = v_n$ in Eq. (5.45) we get

$$v_n' h^2(\delta_n K_L)v_n = \sum_{m=0}^{\infty} \rho^m(m+1) \sum_{i_1,\ldots,i_{m+2}\leq L} \prod_{j=1}^{m+2} \lambda_{i_j} c_{ni} U_{nLi_1} U_{nLi_{m+2}}. \tag{5.62}$$

By Lemma 5.2.1(ii)

$$h^2(\lambda_j) = \left(\sum_{k=0}^{\infty} \rho^k \lambda_j^k\right)^2 \lambda_j^2 = \sum_{m=0}^{\infty} (m+1)\rho^m \lambda_j^{m+2}.$$

Hence, the proXy's second component is

$$X_{nL2} = \sum_{j=1}^{L} U_{nLj}^2 h^2(\lambda_j) = \sum_{m=0}^{\infty} \rho^m (m+1) \sum_{j=1}^{L} \lambda_j^{m+2} U_{nLj}^2.$$

As above, we can insert here $c_{\infty i}$ because these chain products vanish outside the diagonal $i_1 = \cdots = i_{m+2}$:

$$X_{nL2} = \sum_{m=0}^{\infty} \rho^m (m+1) \sum_{i_1,\ldots,i_{m+2} \leq L} \prod_{j=1}^{m+2} \lambda_{i_j} c_{\infty i} U_{nLi_1} U_{nLi_{m+2}}.$$

Combining this equation with Eq. (5.62) we obtain the representation for γ_{nL2}. ∎

5.7.5 Bounding Gammas

Lemma. *For any positive (small) ε and (large) L there exists $n_0 = n_0(\varepsilon, L)$ such that*

$$E(|\gamma_{nL1}| + |\gamma_{nL2}|) \leq c\varepsilon \text{ for all } n \geq n_0,$$

where c does not depend on n and L.

Proof. By Hölder's inequality and Eq. (5.39)

$$E|U_{nLi} U_{nLj}| \leq \{E[v_n' \delta_n F_i(\delta_n F_j)' v_n]^2\}^{1/2} = g(\delta_n F_i(\delta_n F_j)') \leq c. \tag{5.63}$$

By Lemma 5.6.1, for any ε, L from the statement of this lemma we can choose $n_0 = n_0(\varepsilon, L)$ so large that

$$|c_{ni} - c_{\infty i}| \leq \varepsilon \text{ for all } n \geq n_0 \text{ and } i_1, \ldots, i_{k+1} \leq L. \tag{5.64}$$

Now Eqs. (5.58), (5.63) and (5.64) give

$$E|\gamma_{nL1}| \leq \sum_{k=0}^{\infty} |\rho|^k \sum_{i_1,\ldots,i_{k+1} \leq L} \prod_{j=1}^{k+1} |\lambda_{i_j}| |c_{ni} - c_{\infty i}| E|U_{nLi_1} U_{nLi_{k+1}}|$$

$$\leq c\varepsilon \sum_{k=0}^{\infty} |\rho|^k \sum_{i_1,\ldots,i_{k+1} \leq L} \prod_{j=1}^{k+1} |\lambda_{i_j}| \leq c\varepsilon \sum_{k=0}^{\infty} |\rho|^k (v(\mathcal{K}))^{k+1} = c_1 \varepsilon,$$

where c_1 does not depend on n and L, as claimed.

The proof for γ_{nL2} is identical. ∎

5.8   ASYMPTOTICS OF THE OLS ESTIMATOR FOR PURELY SPATIAL MODEL

For the reader's convenience all major assumptions made so far are repeated in this section.

5.8.1   Main Assumptions and Statement

Denote $\alpha_\psi = \sum_{j\in\mathbb{Z}} |\psi_j|$, $\beta_\psi = \sum_{j\in\mathbb{Z}} \psi_j$.

5.8.1.1   Assumption 5.1 on the Error Term

1. $\{\{e_{nt}, \mathcal{F}_{nt} : n \in \mathbb{Z}\} : n \in \mathbb{Z}\}$ is a double-infinite m.d. array.
2. $E(e_{nt}^2|\mathcal{F}_{n,t-1}) = \sigma^2$ for all t and n.
3. The third conditional moments are constant, $E(e_{nt}^3|\mathcal{F}_{n,t-1}) = a_{nt}$, and the fourth moments are uniformly bounded, $\mu_4 = \sup_{n,t} Ee_{nt}^4 < \infty$.
4. $\{\psi_j : j \in \mathbb{Z}\}$ is a summable sequence of numbers, $\alpha_\psi < \infty$.
5. Components of $v_n = (v_{n1}, \ldots, v_{nn})'$ are defined by

$$v_{nt} = \sum_{j\in\mathbb{Z}} e_{n,t-j}\psi_j, \quad t = 1, \ldots, n.$$

For simplicity, one can think of a double-infinite sequence $\{e_j : j \in \mathbb{Z}\}$ of i.i.d. random variables with finite fourth moments and put $v_t = \sum_{j\in\mathbb{Z}} e_{t-j}\psi_j$.

5.8.1.2   Assumption 5.2 on the Spatial Matrices
The sequence of matrices $\{W_n : n \in \mathbb{N}\}$ is such that W_n is of size $n \times n$ and there exists a function $K \in L_2((0, 1)^2)$ that satisfies

$$\|W_n - \delta_n K\|_2 = o\left(\frac{1}{\sqrt{n}}\right).$$

5.8.1.3   Assumption 5.3 on the Function K
The function K is symmetric and the eigenvalues λ_i, $i = 1, 2, \ldots$ of the integral operator

$$(KF)(x) = \int_0^1 K(x, y)F(y)\,dy, \quad F \in L_2(0, 1),$$

are summable:

$$v(K) \equiv \sum_{j=1}^{\infty} |\lambda_j| < \infty. \tag{5.65}$$

Assumption 5.3 implies $\sum_{j=1}^{\infty} \lambda_j^2 < \infty$. The inequality

$$|\rho| < \left(\sum_{j=1}^{\infty} \lambda_j^2 \right)^{-1/2} \tag{5.66}$$

is sufficient for existence of the OLS estimator and representation (5.5) for all large n. To analyze $\hat{\rho}$, the pair $\mathcal{P}_n = (v_n' G_n v_n, \ v_n' G_n' G_n v_n)'$ was composed and represented as

$$\mathcal{P}_n = \alpha_n + \beta_{nL} + \gamma_{nL} + X_{nL}. \tag{5.67}$$

To be able to estimate β_{nL} and γ_{nl}, we have imposed the condition

$$|\rho| < 1/v(\mathcal{K}), \tag{5.68}$$

which is stronger than Eq. (5.66).

Theorem. *Let Assumptions 5.1–5.3 hold and let ρ satisfy Eq. (5.68). If $\beta_\psi \neq 0$, then*

$$\text{dlim}\,(\hat{\rho} - \rho) = \frac{\sum_{j=1}^{\infty} h(\lambda_j) u_j^2}{\sum_{j=1}^{\infty} h^2(\lambda_j) u_j^2}, \tag{5.69}$$

where u_j are independent standard normal, $h(\lambda_j) = \lambda_j / (1 - \rho \lambda_j)$ and

$$\sum_{j=1}^{\infty} |h(\lambda_j)| < \infty. \tag{5.70}$$

5.8.2 Discussion

Theorem 5.8.1 was proved in Mynbaev and Ullah (2008) in the case of i.i.d. errors and in Mynbaev (2010) when the errors are linear processes. The gauge inequality (Section 3.9.9) plays the key role in the generalization from the i.i.d. case to linear processes. It replaces Lemma A.11 [used in Mynbaev and Ullah (2008)] of Lee's supplement (Lee, 2004a). Lemma 5.1.4 about the finite-sample distribution of the OLS estimator explains why Eq. (5.69) is a better reflection of reality than convergence to a normal vector. Kelejian and Prucha (2001) and Lee (2004a) noticed that the finite-sample distribution of the OLS estimator contains quadratic forms. They developed CLTs for linear-quadratic forms. However, under their assumptions the quadratic part disappears in the limit.

   In addition to being nonnormal, the asymptotics (5.69) is special in other respects. Both the numerator and denominator of the fraction at the right are nontrivial random variables, unlike many other econometric problems in which the numerator is nontrivial and the denominator is constant. The mean of the fraction in general is not zero. We don't know if $\hat{\rho} - \rho$ converges in probability but if it does, the mean of

$\hat{\rho}$ may not be zero. This is the true reason for the inconsistency of $\hat{\rho}$ previously mentioned in several other sources. No scaling by $\sqrt{n}$ or any other nontrivial normalizer is necessary to achieve convergence in distribution. The limit distribution does not depend on the second moments of the innovations.

By Lemma 5.7.2 the top and bottom of the fraction in Eq. (5.69) converge in $\mathcal{L}_1$ and, hence, in probability. This can be used for approximate calculations by truncating the sums.

5.8.3 Proof of Theorem 5.8.1

Let us check that under condition (5.68) the nuclearity condition (5.65) is equivalent to the summability of $h(\lambda_j)$ [Eq. (5.70)]. Using Eq. (5.68)

$$0 < c_1 = 1 - |\rho| \sum_{j=1}^{\infty} |\lambda_j| \leq 1 - |\rho\lambda_j| \leq |1 - \rho\lambda_j|$$

$$\leq 1 + |\rho\lambda_j| \leq 1 + |\rho| \sum_{j=1}^{\infty} |\lambda_j| = c_2 < \infty \text{ for all } j.$$

Hence,

$$\frac{|\lambda_j|}{c_2} \leq |h(\lambda_j)| \leq \frac{|\lambda_j|}{c_1} \text{ for all } j, \tag{5.71}$$

which proves the equivalence.

By Eq. (5.55) $\operatorname{plim} \alpha_n = 0$. Combining Eq. (5.56) with the Chebyshov and Hölder inequalities gives

$$P(|\beta_{nL1}| + |\beta_{nL2}| > \varepsilon) \leq \frac{1}{\varepsilon} \|\|\beta_{nL1}| + |\beta_{nL2}\|\|_{2,\Omega} \leq \frac{c}{\varepsilon} \sum_{j>L} |\lambda_j|,$$

where c does not depend on n and L. From Lemma 5.7.5 we conclude that for any fixed L, $\operatorname{plim}_{n \to \infty} \gamma_{nL} = 0$. Equation (5.67) then implies, for any fixed L,

$$P(\|\mathcal{P}_n - X_{nL}\|_1 > \varepsilon) \leq P(\|\alpha_n\|_1 + \|\beta_{nL}\|_1 + \|\gamma_{nL}\|_1 > \varepsilon)$$

$$\leq P\left(\|\alpha_n\|_1 > \frac{\varepsilon}{3}\right) + P\left(\|\beta_{nL}\|_1 > \frac{\varepsilon}{3}\right)$$

$$+ P\left(\|\gamma_{nL}\|_1 > \frac{\varepsilon}{3}\right)$$

so that

$$\limsup_{n \to \infty} P(\|\mathcal{P}_n - X_{nL}\|_1 > \varepsilon) \leq 3\frac{c}{\varepsilon} \sum_{j>L} |\lambda_j|.$$

Since c does not depend on L, all conditions of Billingsley's theorem on a double limit (Section 3.9.5) are satisfied with $Y = \Xi$ (see Lemma 5.7.2). Consequently,

$$\operatorname*{dlim}_{n \to \infty} \mathcal{P}_n = \Xi. \tag{5.72}$$

Remembering that $\beta_\psi \neq 0$ and $\Xi_2 > 0$ a.s., by CMT

$$\operatorname*{dlim}_{n \to \infty} (\hat{\rho} - \rho) = \operatorname*{dlim}_{n \to \infty} \frac{\mathcal{P}_{n1}}{\mathcal{P}_{n2}} = \frac{\Xi_1}{\Xi_2}.$$

5.8.4   Convergence in Distribution of the Estimator of σ^2

Let

$$\hat{\sigma}^2 = \frac{1}{n-1}(Y_n - \hat{\rho} W_n Y_n)'(Y_n - \hat{\rho} W_n Y_n)$$

be the OLS estimator of σ^2.

Corollary. (Mynbaev and Ullah, 2008) *In addition to the conditions of Theorem 5.8.1 assume that the errors $v_{nt} = e_t, t = 1, \ldots, n$, are i.i.d. Then*

$$\operatorname*{dlim}_{n \to \infty} \sqrt{n}(\hat{\sigma}^2 - \sigma^2) \in N(0, \mu_4 - \sigma^2),$$

where $\mu_4 = E e_t^4$. In particular, $\hat{\sigma}^2$ is consistent.

Proof.   For convenience, in the definition of $\hat{\sigma}^2$ we put n instead of $n - 1$ because the result is asymptotically the same. Substituting

$$S_n(\hat{\rho})S_n^{-1}(\rho) = [(I - \rho W_n) + (\rho - \hat{\rho})W_n]S_n^{-1} = I + (\rho - \hat{\rho})G_n \tag{5.73}$$

we have

$$
\begin{aligned}
(Y_n - \hat{\rho} W_n Y_n)'(Y_n - \hat{\rho} W_n Y_n) &= (S_n(\hat{\rho})S_n^{-1}(\rho)v_n)S_n(\hat{\rho})S_n^{-1}(\rho)v_n \\
&= v_n'(I + (\rho - \hat{\rho})G_n)'(I + (\rho - \hat{\rho})G_n)v_n \\
&= v_n'v_n + (\rho - \hat{\rho})v_n'G_n'v_n \\
&\quad + (\rho - \hat{\rho})v_n'G_nv_n + (\rho - \hat{\rho})^2 v_n'G_n'G_nv_n \\
&= v_n'v_n + 2(\rho - \hat{\rho})\mathcal{P}_{n1} + (\rho - \hat{\rho})^2 \mathcal{P}_{n2}.
\end{aligned}
$$

Taking an arbitrary $\varepsilon \in (0, 1/2)$ we can write

$$\sqrt{n}(\hat{\sigma}^2 - \sigma^2) = \frac{(Y_n - \hat{\rho}W_nY_n)'(Y_n - \hat{\rho}W_nY_n) - n\sigma^2}{n^{1/2}}$$

$$= \frac{v_n'v_n - n\sigma^2}{n^{1/2}} + \frac{2(\rho - \hat{\rho})}{n^\varepsilon}\frac{\mathcal{P}_{n1}}{n^{1/2-\varepsilon}} + \frac{(\rho - \hat{\rho})^2}{n^\varepsilon}\frac{\mathcal{P}_{n2}}{n^{1/2-\varepsilon}}.$$

From the proof of Theorem 5.8.1 we know that $\mathcal{P}_{n1}$, $\mathcal{P}_{n2}$, $(\rho - \hat{\rho})$ and $(\rho - \hat{\rho})^2$ converge in distribution. Therefore

$$\sqrt{n}(\hat{\sigma}^2 - \sigma^2) = \frac{v_n'v_n - n\sigma^2}{\sqrt{n}} + o_p(1).$$

The term

$$\frac{v_n'v_n - n\sigma^2}{\sqrt{n}} = \frac{\sum_{t=1}^n(e_t^2 - \sigma^2)}{\sqrt{n}}$$

is known to converge in distribution to $N(0, \mu_4 - \sigma^2)$. This follows from the Lindeberg-Lévy Theorem 3.1.7: $e_t^2 - \sigma^2$ are i.i.d., have mean zero and variance

$$V(e_t^2 - \sigma^2) = V(e_t^2) = Ee_t^4 - (Ee_t^2)^2 = \mu_4 - \sigma^4. \qquad \blacksquare$$

5.9 METHOD OF MOMENTS AND MAXIMUM LIKELIHOOD

The method used in the previous sections to study the OLS estimator allows us to calculate some limits that play an important role in the theory of other two methods: MM and ML. Everywhere the assumptions of Theorem 5.8.1 are maintained.

5.9.1 Identification Conditions for ML

In ML estimation random variables are assumed to be normal and the ML estimator is obtained by maximizing the log-likelihood function. If the same estimator is used in case of nonnormal variables, it is a QML estimator. For a purely autoregressive spatial model the QML estimator was studied by Lee (2001). One of key elements in his proof consists in applying the identification uniqueness condition (White, 1994, Chapter 3). Lee worked out conditions sufficient for local and global identification. They involve a special parameter h_n designed to accommodate different asymptotics of W_n at infinity. Under our conditions, the only meaningful choice is $h_n = 1$ for all n. This is why this parameter is omitted, and the conditions look as follows.

5.9.1.1   Condition 1 – Local Identification (ID) Condition   The limit

$$\lim_{n \to \infty} \frac{1}{n} \left[\text{tr}(G_n' G_n) + \text{tr}(G_n^2) - \frac{2}{n} \text{tr}^2(G_n) \right] \tag{5.74}$$

exists and is positive.

In ML estimation it is customary to denote the true parameters by ρ_0 and σ_0^2 and use ρ and σ^2 for any other parameter values.

5.9.1.2   Condition 2 – Global ID Condition   For any ρ different from the true value ρ_0 the limit

$$\lim_{n \to \infty} \frac{1}{n} (\ln |\sigma_0^2 S_n^{-1} S_n^{-1'}| - \ln |\sigma_n^2(\rho) S_n^{-1}(\rho) S_n^{-1'}(\rho)|) \tag{5.75}$$

exists and is not zero.

Here $S_n(\rho) = I - \rho W_n$ and $S_n = I - \rho_0 W_n$. $|A|$ denotes the determinant of A. An expression like $\ln |A|$ presumes that $|A| > 0$. By definition

$$\sigma_n^2(\rho) = \frac{\sigma_0^2}{n} \text{tr}(S_n^{-1'} S_n'(\rho) S_n(\rho) S_n^{-1}). \tag{5.76}$$

5.9.2   ML Identification Conditions Failure

Theorem.   (Mynbaev and Ullah, 2008) *Under the assumptions of Theorem 5.8.1 identification conditions 1 and 2 fail.*

The proof is divided into several sections. We need the notation that reflects dependence of $h(\lambda_j)$ and G_n on ρ:

$$h(\rho, \lambda_j) = \frac{\lambda_j}{1 - \rho \lambda_j}, \quad G_n(\rho) = W_n S_n^{-1}(\rho) = h(\rho, W_n).$$

5.9.3   Calculating the Limit of $\text{tr}(G_n(\rho))$

Lemma.   *Uniformly on any compact subset s of* $\{\rho : |\rho| < 1/v(\mathcal{K})\}$

$$\lim_{n \to \infty} \text{tr}(G_n(\rho)) = \sum_{j=1}^{\infty} h(\rho, \lambda_j).$$

Here the series at the right converges uniformly on the set s.

Proof.   We approximate $\text{tr}(G_n(\rho))$ by $\text{tr}(h(\delta_n K))$ and then find the limit of $\text{tr}(h(\delta_n K))$.

By the trace version of h-continuity (Section 5.3.3)

$$|\text{tr}(G_n(\rho)) - \text{tr}(h(\delta_n K))| = |\text{tr}(h(W_n)) - \text{tr}(h(\delta_n K))|$$
$$\leq \|W_n - \delta_n K\|_2 \left[\sqrt{n} + \phi(\rho, W_n, \delta_n K) \right] \to 0, \tag{5.77}$$

where the escort condition of type Eq. (5.27) is applied. Moreover, from Eq. (5.25) we see that the numbers $\phi(\rho, W_n, \delta_n K)$ are uniformly bounded with respect to $\rho \in s$.

The nuke is finite, [see Eq. (5.65)] so we can use Eq. (5.46) with $L = \infty$, $s = t$ to calculate

$$\mathrm{tr}(h(\delta_n K)) = \sum_{k=0}^{\infty} \rho^k \mathrm{tr}(\delta_n K)^{k+1}$$

$$= \sum_{k=0}^{\infty} \rho^k \sum_{i_1,\dots,i_{k+1}=1}^{\infty} \prod_{j=1}^{k+1} \lambda_{i_j} c_{ni}(\delta_n F_{i_1}, \delta_n F_{i_{k+1}})_{l_2}.$$

Sending $n \to \infty$ and taking into account Lemma 5.6.1 and Eq. (5.41) we have

$$\mathrm{tr}(h(\delta_n K)) \to \sum_{k=0}^{\infty} \rho^k \sum_{i_1,\dots,i_{k+1}=1}^{\infty} \prod_{j=1}^{k+1} \lambda_{i_j} c_{\infty i}(F_{i_1}, F_{i_{k+1}})_{l_2}$$

$$= \sum_{k=0}^{\infty} \rho^k \sum_{i=1}^{\infty} \lambda_i^{k+1} = \sum_{i=1}^{\infty} h(\rho, \lambda_i). \tag{5.78}$$

We may pass to the limit because all series converge uniformly in n and ρ. Equations (5.77) and (5.78) prove the lemma. ∎

5.9.4   Calculating Traces of Products

Lemma.   *Uniformly on any compact subset s of $|\rho| < 1/v(\mathcal{K})$*

$$\lim_{n\to\infty} \mathrm{tr}(G_n' G_n) = \sum_{j=1}^{\infty} h^2(\rho, \lambda_j) = \lim_{n\to\infty} \mathrm{tr}(G_n^2).$$

Proof.   Ideally, $\mathrm{tr}(G_n' G_n) = \mathrm{tr}(h(W_n')h(W_n))$ should be close to $\mathrm{tr}(h^2(\delta_n K))$. By Eq. (5.18)

$$|\mathrm{tr}(G_n' G_n) - \mathrm{tr}(h^2(\delta_n K))| \le |\mathrm{tr}(G_n' - h(\delta_n K))G_n]|$$
$$+ |\mathrm{tr}[h(\delta_n K)(G_n - h(\delta_n K))]|$$
$$\le \|G_n' - h(\delta_n K)\|_2 \|G_n\|_2$$
$$+ \|h(\delta_n K)\|_2 \|G_n - h(\delta_n K)\|_2 = o(1).$$

The concluding piece here is based on Eqs. (5.24), (5.27) and (5.28).

Now we repeat Eq. (5.78) using Eq. (5.48) where appropriate

$$
\begin{aligned}
\operatorname{tr}(h^2(\delta_n K)) &= \sum_{m=0}^{\infty} \rho^m (m+1) \sum_{i_1,\dots,i_{m+2}=1}^{\infty} \prod_{j=1}^{m+2} \lambda_{ij} c_{ni}(\delta_n F_{i_1}, \delta_n F_{i_{m+2}})_{l_2} \\
&\rightarrow \sum_{m=0}^{\infty} \rho^m (m+1) \sum_{i_1,\dots,i_{m+2}=1}^{\infty} \prod_{j=1}^{m+2} \lambda_{ij} c_{\infty i}(F_{i_1}, F_{i_{m+2}})_{l_2} \\
&= \sum_{m=0}^{\infty} \rho^m (m+1) \sum_{i=1}^{\infty} \lambda_i^{m+2} = \sum_{i=1}^{\infty} h^2(\rho, \lambda_i).
\end{aligned}
$$

We have proved the left equation. Replacing G'_n by G_n everywhere we get the right one. ∎

5.9.5 Essential Formula of the ML Theory of Spatial Models

Lemma. *If ρ is such that $|S_n(\rho)|$ is positive, then*

$$
\frac{\partial \ln |S_n(\rho)|}{\partial \rho} = -\operatorname{tr}[W_n S_n^{-1}(\rho)].
$$

Proof. By definition, if $f(A)$ is a scalar function of a matrix A, then

$$
\left(\frac{\partial f}{\partial A} \right)_{ij} = \frac{\partial f}{\partial a_{ij}}.
$$

Lütkepohl (1991, p. 473) has the equation

$$
\frac{\partial \ln |A|}{\partial A} = (A')^{-1}
$$

for a nonsingular matrix with $|A| > 0$. Combining it with $(A')^{-1} = (A^{-1})'$ we have

$$
\frac{\partial \ln |S_n(\rho)|}{\partial S_n(\rho)} = (S_n^{-1}(\rho))'.
$$

Obviously,

$$
\frac{\partial (S_n(\rho))_{ij}}{\partial \rho} = \frac{\partial}{\partial \rho}(\delta_{ij} - \rho w_{nij}) = -w_{nij},
$$

where $\delta_{ij} = 1$ if $i = j$ and $\delta_{ij} = 0$ if $i \neq j$. These equations imply

$$\frac{\partial \ln|S_n(\rho)|}{\partial \rho} = \sum_{i,j=1}^{n} \frac{\partial \ln|S_n(\rho)|}{\partial (S_n(\rho))_{ij}} \frac{\partial (S_n(\rho))_{ij}}{\partial \rho}$$

$$= -\sum_{i,j=1}^{n} (S_n^{-1}(\rho))_{ji} (W_n)_{ij} = -\text{tr}[W_n S_n^{-1}(\rho)]. \qquad \blacksquare$$

5.9.6   Limit of the Newton–Leibniz Equation

Lemma.   *Recall that the true parameter ρ_0 satisfies Eq. (5.68). If ρ is in a small neighborhood of ρ_0, then*

$$\lim_{n \to \infty} (\ln|S_n(\rho)| - \ln|S_n|) = -\int_{\rho_0}^{\rho} \sum_{i=1}^{\infty} h(t, \lambda_i) dt.$$

Proof.   By the *Newton–Leibniz formula* and Lemma 5.9.5

$$\ln|S_n(\rho)| - \ln|S_n| = \int_{\rho_0}^{\rho} \frac{\partial \ln|S_n(t)|}{\partial t} dt = -\int_{\rho_0}^{\rho} \text{tr}[W_n S_n^{-1}(t)] dt.$$

By Lemma 5.9.3

$$\lim_{n \to \infty} \text{tr}[W_n S_n^{-1}(t)] = \text{tr}(G_n(t)) = \sum_{j=1}^{\infty} h(t, \lambda_j).$$

Since convergence here is uniform in a small neighborhood of ρ_0, term-wise integration of this equation is possible. $\blacksquare$

5.9.7   Proof of Theorem 5.9.2

For the local ID condition [Eq. (5.74)] we apply Lemmas 5.9.3 and 5.9.4:

$$\lim_{n \to \infty} \frac{1}{n} \left[\text{tr}(G_n' G_n) + \text{tr}(G_n^2) - \frac{2}{n} \text{tr}^2(G_n) \right]$$

$$= \lim_{n \to \infty} \frac{1}{n} \left[2 \sum_{j=1}^{\infty} h^2(\lambda_j) - \frac{2}{n} \left(\sum_{j=1}^{\infty} h(\lambda_j) \right)^2 \right] = 0.$$

The expression (5.75) used in the global ID condition is rearranged into a more transparent form using properties of logs, determinants and the fact that $S_n(\rho)$, S_n and their inverses commute:

$$\ln|\sigma_0^2 S_n^{-1} S_n^{-1'}| - \ln|\sigma_n^2(\rho) S_n^{-1}(\rho) S_n^{-1'}(\rho)|$$
$$= \ln|\sigma_0^2/\sigma_n^2(\rho)| + \ln|S_n^{-1}| + \ln|S_n^{-1'}| - \ln|S_n^{-1}(\rho)| - \ln|S_n^{-1'}(\rho)|$$
$$= \ln|\sigma_0^2/\sigma_n^2(\rho)| + 2(\ln|S_n(\rho)| - \ln|S_n|). \tag{5.79}$$

Lemma 5.9.6 gives for the second part of this aggregate

$$\lim_{n\to\infty} \frac{1}{n}(\ln|S_n(\rho)| - \ln|S_n|) = 0. \tag{5.80}$$

For the first part Eqs. (5.76) and (5.73) imply

$$\sigma_n^2(\rho) = \frac{\sigma_0^2}{n} \mathrm{tr}[(I + (\rho_0 - \rho)G_n)'\,(I + (\rho_0 - \rho)G_n)]$$
$$= \frac{\sigma_0^2}{n} \mathrm{tr}[I + 2(\rho_0 - \rho)G_n + (\rho_0 - \rho)^2 G_n' G_n]$$
$$= \sigma_0^2 \left[1 + 2(\rho_0 - \rho)\frac{\mathrm{tr}G_n}{n} + (\rho_0 - \rho)^2 \frac{\mathrm{tr}G_n' G_n}{n}\right].$$

Now it is clear from Lemmas 5.9.3 and 5.9.4 that

$$\lim_{n\to\infty} \sigma_0^2/\sigma_n^2(\rho) = 1 \text{ for any } \rho \text{ that satisfies (5.68)}. \tag{5.81}$$

Equations (5.79), (5.80) and (5.81) prove that the global ID condition fails.

5.9.8   Identification Condition for Method of Moments

For the purely spatial model Kelejian and Prucha (1999) studied a generalized moments estimator. Lee (2001) simplified their approach and worked out an ID condition in terms of a 2×2 matrix A_n with elements

$$a_{n11} = 2\left[Y_n' W_n'^2 W_n Y_n - \mathrm{tr}(W_n' W_n)\frac{1}{n} Y_n' W_n Y_n\right],$$

$$a_{n12} = -Y_n' W_n'^2 W_n^2 Y_n + \mathrm{tr}(W_n' W_n)\frac{1}{n} Y_n' W_n' W_n Y_n,$$

$$a_{n21} = Y_n' W_n^2 Y_n + Y_n' W_n' W_n Y_n,$$

$$a_{n22} = -Y_n' W_n'^2 W_n Y_n.$$

5.9.8.1   Condition 3 – Identification Condition for Method of Moments
The Limit

$$\operatorname*{plim}_{n\to\infty} \frac{1}{n} A_n \tag{5.82}$$

exists and is nonsingular.

5.9.9   Method of Moments Identification Condition Failure

Theorem.   (Mynbaev and Ullah, 2008) *Under the assumptions of Theorem 5.8.1 the limit (5.82) is zero.*

Proof.   The desired result follows if we show that $\mathcal{L}_2$-norms of all elements of A_n are uniformly bounded. Those elements have some common parts which we bound first. Since $Y_n = S_n^{-1} v_n$, we have, by Lemma 3.9.9,

$$[E(Y_n' W_n'^2 W_n Y_n)^2]^{1/2} = g(S_n'^{-1} W_n'^2 W_n S_n^{-1}) = g(G_n' W_n' G_n)$$

$$\leq c_1 \|G_n'\|_2 \|W_n'\|_2 \|G_n\|_2 = c_1 \|W_n\|_2 \|G_n\|_2^2 \leq c_2,$$

where Lemma 5.4.2(i) and Eq. (5.24) have been applied.
Similarly, by Lemma 5.2.2

$$[E(Y_n' W_n Y_n)^2]^{1/2} = g(S_n'^{-1} G_n) \leq c_1 \|S_n^{-1}\|_2 \|G_n\|_2 \leq c_2.$$

By Eq. (5.18) and Lemma 5.4.2(i)

$$\|\operatorname{tr}(W_n' W_n)\| \leq \|W_n\|_2^2 \leq c.$$

The three estimates above imply plim $a_{n11}/n = 0$ and plim $a_{n22}/n = 0$.
A similar conclusion for a_{n12} is reached if we note additionally that

$$[E(Y_n' W_n'^2 W_n^2 Y_n)^2]^{1/2} = g(G_n' W_n' W_n G_n) \leq c_1 \|G_n\|_2^2 \|W_n\|_2^2 \leq c_2,$$

$$[E(Y_n' W_n' W_n Y_n)^2]^{1/2} = g(G_n' G_n) \leq c_1 \|G_n\|_2^2 \leq c_2.$$

a_{n21} contains one new term for which

$$[E(Y_n' W_n^2 Y_n)^2]^{1/2} = g(S_n'^{-1} W_n G_n) \leq c_1 \|S_n^{-1}\|_2 \|W_n\|_2 \|G_n\|_2 \leq c_2. \qquad \blacksquare$$

5.10   TWO-STEP PROCEDURE

5.10.1   Maximum Likelihood Estimators

I am not a big specialist in ML and MM estimation and can't say whether in the situation of Theorem 5.8.1 these methods work without the conditions whose failure is reported in Theorems 5.9.2 and 5.9.9. In Mynbaev and Ullah (2008) we decided to revert to the analysis of the OLS estimator, instead of trying to revive the ML or MM procedures. The OLS estimator seemed to be more amenable to analysis, but the outcome turned out to be a hybrid of OLS and ML estimators. It also incorporates precise (finite-sample) results on ratios of quadratic forms of normal variables.

Unlike most two-stage least squares (2SLS) estimators, where the least squares is used in both stages, in our procedure the first step is the OLS, whereas the second step is a correction to it based on a construct that mimics the ML estimator. In view of Theorem 5.8.1, correcting the OLS estimator means trying to obtain a zero-mean variable from a nonzero-mean variable with *an unknown mean*.

The expression of the ML estimator will help the reader understand the idea behind our construction. The ML estimator was derived in a more general situation by Ord (1975), among others. In our case the log-likelihood function is

$$\ln L_n(\theta) = -\frac{n}{2}\ln(2\pi) - \frac{n}{2}\ln\sigma^2 + \ln|S_n(\rho)| - \frac{1}{2\sigma^2}\|Y_n - \rho W_n Y_n\|_2^2, \qquad (5.83)$$

where $\theta = (\rho, \sigma^2)$. By the essential formula of the ML theory (Section 5.9.5)

$$\frac{\partial \ln L_n(\theta)}{\partial \rho} = -\mathrm{tr}(W_n S_n^{-1}(\rho)) - \frac{1}{2\sigma^2}(-Y_n' W_n Y_n - Y_n' W_n' Y_n + 2\rho\|W_n Y_n\|_2^2)$$

$$= -\mathrm{tr}(W_n S_n^{-1}(\rho)) + \frac{1}{\sigma^2}(Y_n' W_n Y_n - \rho\|W_n Y_n\|_2^2),$$

$$\frac{\partial \ln L_n(\theta)}{\partial \sigma^2} = -\frac{n}{2}\frac{1}{\sigma^2} + \frac{1}{2\sigma^4}\|Y_n - \rho W_n Y_n\|_2^2.$$

The first-order conditions for maximization of $\ln L_n(\theta)$ give the estimators

$$\hat{\rho}_{ML} = \frac{Y_n' W_n Y_n - \hat{\sigma}_{ML}^2 \mathrm{tr}(W_n S_n^{-1}(\rho))}{\|W_n Y_n\|_2^2},$$

$$\hat{\sigma}_{ML}^2 = \frac{1}{n}\|Y_n - \rho W_n Y_n\|_2^2.$$

Of course, these estimators are not feasible as they contain an unknown ρ.

5.10.2 Annihilation of Means of Quadratic Forms of Normal Variables

The material of this section is another piece of information that is necessary to understand the two-step procedure definition.

In the theory of normal variables there are many nice finite-sample results. Mathai and Provost (1992) serves as a good introduction and guide to the literature. The *annihilation lemma* (the name is mine) below answers the question: how can a ratio of quadratic forms

$$\sum_{i=1}^{n} h_i u_i^2 \left(\sum_{i=1}^{n} h_i^2 u_i^2 \right)^{-1}$$

be combined with an inverse of a quadratic form

$$\left(\sum_{i=1}^{n} h_i^2 u_i^2\right)^{-1}$$

in such a way that the resulting expression has mean zero? Here $h_1, \ldots, h_n$ are some nonzero real numbers.

Denote

$$\pi_n(t) = \left[\prod_{i=1}^{n}(1 + 2th_i^2)\right]^{1/2},$$

$$I_n = \int_0^{\infty} \frac{dt}{\pi_n(t)}, \quad I_{ni} = \int_0^{\infty} \frac{dt}{\pi_n(t)(1 + 2th_i^2)}, \quad i = 1, \ldots, n. \tag{5.84}$$

Since $\pi_n(t)$ is of order $t^{n/2}$ at infinity, the integral I_n converges when $n > 2$, and for such n

$$0 < I_{ni} < I_n < \infty. \tag{5.85}$$

Lemma. If $n > 2$, $h_1^2 > 0, \ldots, h_n^2 > 0$ and $u \sim N(0, \sigma^2 I)$, then

$$E\left(\frac{\sum_{i=1}^{n} h_i u_i^2}{\sum_{i=1}^{n} h_i^2 u_i^2} - \frac{\sigma^2}{I_n}\sum_{i=1}^{n} I_{ni} h_i \frac{1}{\sum_{i=1}^{n} h_i^2 u_i^2}\right) = 0.$$

Proof. Hoque (1985) proved that if S and B are symmetric matrices, B is positive definite and $u \sim N(0, \Omega)$, then

$$E\left(\frac{u'Su}{u'Bu}\right) = \int_0^{\infty} |I + 2t\Omega B|^{-1/2}\mathrm{tr}[(I + 2t\Omega B)^{-1}\Omega S]dt.$$

We apply this result to

$$S = \mathrm{diag}[h_1, \ldots, h_n], \quad B = \mathrm{diag}[h_1^2, \ldots, h_n^2],$$

$$\Omega = \sigma^2 I, I + 2t\Omega B = \mathrm{diag}[1 + 2t\sigma^2 h_1^2, \ldots, 1 + 2t\sigma^2 h_n^2],$$

$$(I + 2t\Omega B)^{-1}\Omega S = \mathrm{diag}\left[\frac{\sigma^2 h_1}{1 + 2t\sigma^2 h_1^2}, \ldots, \frac{\sigma^2 h_n}{1 + 2t\sigma^2 h_n^2}\right].$$

Then

$$E\left(\frac{\sum_{i=1}^{n} u_i^2 h_i}{\sum_{i=1}^{n} u_i^2 h_i^2}\right) = \int_0^{\infty}\sum_{i=1}^{n} \frac{\sigma^2 h_i}{1 + 2t\sigma^2 h_i^2}\frac{dt}{\pi_n(\sigma^2 t)} = \sum_{i=1}^{n} I_{ni} h_i. \tag{5.86}$$

However, formula (10) from (Jones, 1986) yields

$$E\left(\frac{1}{\sum_{i=1}^{n} u_i^2 h_i^2}\right) = \frac{1}{\sigma^2} \int_0^\infty \frac{dt}{\pi_n(t)} = \frac{I_n}{\sigma^2}. \tag{5.87}$$

To annihilate Eq. (5.86) we have to multiply Eq. (5.87) by $\sigma^2/I_n \sum_{i=1}^{n} I_{ni}h_i$.   ∎

5.10.3   Modification Factor Definition

Since the OLS estimator and the two-step estimator from Section 5.10.4 do not change if W_n is replaced by its symmetric derivative $(W_n + W_n')/2$, from now on we assume without loss of generality that W_n is symmetric. Then W_n can be represented as

$$W_n = P_n \text{diag}[\lambda_{n1}, \ldots, \lambda_{nn}]P_n', \tag{5.88}$$

where $\lambda_{n1}, \ldots, \lambda_{nn}$ are eigenvalues of W_n and P_n is an orthogonal matrix: $P_n P_n' = I$. In the definition of integrals (5.84) put

$$h_i = h(\lambda_{ni}), \ i = 1, \ldots, n.$$

The *modification factor* is defined by

$$M_n = P_n \text{diag}[I_{n1}/I_n, \ldots, I_{nn}/I_n]P_n'. \tag{5.89}$$

5.10.4   Correction Term and Two-Step Estimator Definition

Step 1. Estimate ρ and σ^2 by OLS.

Step 2. Calculate *the correction term* and *two-step estimator* using formulas

$$\rho_{corr} = \frac{Y_n' W_n Y_n - \hat{\sigma}^2 \text{tr}(M_n W_n S_n^{-1}(\hat{\rho}))}{\|W_n Y_n\|_2^2}, \quad \rho_{2S} = \frac{\hat{\rho} + \rho_{corr}}{2}.$$

Notice that Step 2 does not require additional estimation. For analytical purposes we rewrite the correction term as

$$\rho_{corr} = \frac{e_n' S_n'^{-1} G_n e_n - \hat{\sigma}^2 \text{tr}(M_n W_n S_n^{-1}(\hat{\rho}))}{\|G_n e_n\|_2^2}. \tag{5.90}$$

Here, e_n appears in place of v_n because the errors will be assumed independent normal.

5.10.5   Properties of the Correction Term

Instead of Assumption 5.1 here we make a stronger assumption about the error term: $e_n \sim N(0, \sigma^2 I)$. The next theorem under an additional condition that with some $p < 2$

$$\sup_n \sum_{i=1}^n |\lambda_{ni}|^p < \infty$$

has been established in [Mynbaev and Ullah, 2008]. Theorem 3.8.5 shows that this condition with $p = 1$ is implied by Assumptions 5.2 and 5.3.

Theorem. [Mynbaev, 2010] *Suppose Assumptions* 5.2 *and* 5.3 *hold and* $e_n \sim N(0, \sigma^2 I)$. *If the true* ρ *satisfies* $|\rho|v(\mathcal{K}) < 1$, *then there exist random variables* $\kappa_{n1}, \kappa_{n2}, \kappa_{n3}$ *and a deterministic function* ψ_n *such that*

$$\rho_{corr} = \rho + \kappa_{n1} + \kappa_{n2} + \kappa_{n3} \int_{\hat{\rho}}^{\rho} \psi_n(t)dt, \tag{5.91}$$

$$E\kappa_{n1} = 0 \ \text{for all } n, \quad \text{plim } \kappa_{n2} = 0, \tag{5.92}$$

$$\text{dlim } \kappa_{n3} = \frac{1}{\sum_{i=1}^{\infty} u_i^2 h^2(\lambda_i)}, \tag{5.93}$$

where u_i *are independent standard normal and* κ_{n3} *and* ψ_n *are positive a.e.*

5.10.6   Discussion

Theorem 5.8.1 suggests replacing the usual consistency definition plim $\hat{\rho} = \rho$ by

$$\text{plim } \hat{\rho} = \rho + \kappa \text{ where } E\kappa = 0.$$

Equation (5.92) shows to what extent we have been able to satisfy this definition.

Intuitively, the definition of ρ_{2S} can be explained as follows. By the mean value theorem Eqs. (5.91) and (5.92) imply $\rho_{corr} \approx \rho + \kappa_{n3}\psi_n(t^*)(\rho - \hat{\rho})$, so that the true parameter is a weighted sum of ρ_{corr} and $\hat{\rho}$:

$$\rho \approx \frac{\rho_{corr} + \kappa_{n3}\psi_n(t^*)\hat{\rho}}{1 + \kappa_{n3}\psi_n(t^*)}. \tag{5.94}$$

Here t^* is some point between the true value and the OLS estimate. Since the weights are unknown we choose one half for each, which seems to work pretty well.

As a result of the positivity of κ_{n3} and ψ_n, overshooting of $\hat{\rho}$ ($\hat{\rho} > \rho$) results in negativity of the end term in the Eq. (5.91) and undershooting of the correction term ($\rho_{corr} < \rho$). This is why their average is closer to ρ than to $\hat{\rho}$. Our attempt to use more correction terms in Monte Carlo simulations did not improve upon ρ_{2S}.

5.10.7   Deriving the Correction Term Representation [Equation (5.91)]

Using the diagonalization of W_n [Eq. (5.88)] and the definition of M_n [Eq. (5.89)] we have the expressions

$$S_n(\hat{\rho}) = I - \hat{\rho}W_n = P_n \text{diag}[1 - \hat{\rho}\lambda_{n1}, \ldots, 1 - \hat{\rho}\lambda_{nn}]P_n',$$

$$G_n = W_n S_n^{-1} = P_n \text{diag}[h(\lambda_{n1}), \ldots, h(\lambda_{nn})]P_n',$$

$$\text{tr}(M_n W_n S_n^{-1}(\hat{\rho})) = \frac{1}{I_n}\sum_{i=1}^{n} I_{ni} h(\hat{\rho}, \lambda_{ni}).$$

It is easy to see that the vector $\tilde{e}_n = P_n' e_n$ is distributed as $N(0, \sigma^2 I)$. By properties of trace

$$e_n' S_n^{-1} G_n e_n = \tilde{e}_n' P_n' P_n \text{diag}\left[\frac{1}{1 - \rho\lambda_{n1}}, \ldots, \frac{1}{1 - \rho\lambda_{nn}}\right]P_n'$$

$$\times P_n \text{diag}[h(\lambda_{n1}), \ldots, h(\lambda_{nn})]P_n' P_n \tilde{e}_n$$

$$= \sum_{i=1}^{n} \tilde{e}_i^2 \frac{h(\lambda_{ni})}{1 - \rho\lambda_{ni}}$$

and similarly

$$\|G_n e_n\|_2^2 = e_n' G_n' G_n e_n = \sum_{i=1}^{n} \tilde{e}_i^2 h^2(\lambda_{ni}).$$

Equation (5.90) becomes

$$\rho_{corr} = \frac{\sum_{i=1}^{n} \tilde{e}_i^2 h(\lambda_{ni})/(1 - \rho\lambda_{ni}) - \hat{\sigma}^2/I_n \sum_{i=1}^{n} I_{ni} h(\hat{\rho}, \lambda_{ni})}{\sum_{i=1}^{n} \tilde{e}_i^2 h^2(\lambda_{ni})}. \tag{5.95}$$

Rearrange the numerator to reveal $\rho \sum_{i=1}^{n} \tilde{e}_i^2 h^2(\lambda_{ni})$ and $\sigma^2 - \hat{\sigma}^2$:

$$\sum_{i=1}^{n} \tilde{e}_i^2 \frac{h(\lambda_{ni})}{1 - \rho\lambda_{ni}} - \frac{\hat{\sigma}^2}{I_n}\sum_{i=1}^{n} I_{ni} h(\hat{\rho}, \lambda_{ni}) = \sum_{i=1}^{n} \tilde{e}_i^2 \left(\frac{h(\lambda_{ni})}{1 - \rho\lambda_{ni}} - h(\lambda_{ni})\right)$$

$$+ \sum_{i=1}^{n}\left(\tilde{e}_i^2 - \frac{\sigma^2 I_{ni}}{I_n}\right)h(\lambda_{ni}) + \frac{\sigma^2 - \hat{\sigma}^2}{I_n}\sum_{i=1}^{n} I_{ni} h(\lambda_{ni})$$

$$+ \frac{\hat{\sigma}^2}{I_n}\sum_{i=1}^{n} I_{ni}[h(\lambda_{ni}) - h(\hat{\rho}, \lambda_{ni})].$$

Here the first term actually is $\rho \sum_{i=1}^{n} \tilde{e}_i^2 \, h^2(\lambda_{ni})$. Hence, if we denote

$$\kappa_{n0} = \sum_{i=1}^{n} \tilde{e}_i^2 \, h^2(\lambda_{ni}), \quad \kappa_{n1} = \frac{1}{\kappa_{n0}} \sum_{i=1}^{n} \left(\tilde{e}_i^2 - \frac{\sigma^2 I_{ni}}{I_n} \right) h(\lambda_{ni}),$$

$$\kappa_{n2} = \frac{\sigma^2 - \hat{\sigma}^2}{\kappa_{n0} I_n} \sum_{i=1}^{n} I_{ni} h(\lambda_{ni}), \quad \kappa_{n3} = \frac{\hat{\sigma}^2}{\kappa_{n0}}, \tag{5.96}$$

then Eq. (5.95) becomes

$$\rho_{corr} = \rho + \kappa_{n1} + \kappa_{n2} + \kappa_{n3} \sum_{i=1}^{n} \frac{I_{ni}}{I_n} (h(\lambda_{ni}) - h(\hat{\rho}, \lambda_{ni})). \tag{5.97}$$

If we also take into account that

$$h(\lambda_{ni}) - h(\hat{\rho}, \lambda_{ni}) = h(\rho, \lambda_{ni}) - h(\hat{\rho}, \lambda_{ni})$$

$$= \int_{\hat{\rho}}^{\rho} \frac{\partial h(t, \lambda_{ni})}{\partial t} \, dt = \int_{\hat{\rho}}^{\rho} h^2(t, \lambda_{ni}) \, dt$$

and denote

$$\psi_n(t) = \sum_{i=1}^{n} \frac{I_{ni}}{I_n} h^2(t, \lambda_{ni}),$$

then Eq. (5.97) gives Eq. (5.91).

5.10.8   Establishing the Properties of Components of ρ_{corr}

By Eq. (5.96) and the annihilation Lemma 5.10.2

$$E\kappa_{n1} = E \frac{\sum_{i=1}^{n} \tilde{e}_i^2 \, h(\lambda_{ni}) - \sigma^2/I_n \sum_{i=1}^{n} I_{ni} h(\lambda_{ni})}{\sum_{i=1}^{n} \tilde{e}_i^2 \, h^2(\lambda_{ni})} = 0.$$

Lemma 5.10.2 is applicable because zero $h(\lambda_{ni})$ can be left out of all sums. We have proved the first part of Eq. (5.92).

Since κ_{n0} is the second component of the vector $\mathcal{P}_n$ from Section 5.7.1, $\kappa_{n0} = \mathcal{P}_{n1} = e_n' G_n' G_n e_n$, and $\mathcal{P}_n$ converges to the proξy, see [Eqs. (5.72) and Section 5.7.2], we have

$$\underset{n \to \infty}{\text{dlim}} \, \kappa_{n0} = \Xi_2 = (\sigma \beta_\psi)^2 \sum_{i=1}^{\infty} u_i^2 \, h^2(\lambda_i). \tag{5.98}$$

Assumption 5.3, Eqs. (5.71) and (5.85), and Theorem 3.8.5 imply

$$\left|\sum_{i=1}^{n}\frac{I_{ni}}{I_n}h(\lambda_{ni})\right| \le \sum_{i=1}^{n}|h(\lambda_{ni})| \le c \text{ for all } n. \tag{5.99}$$

Hence, factorizing κ_{n2} as

$$\kappa_{n2} = \frac{1}{n^{1/2}}\left[\sqrt{n}(\sigma^2 - \hat{\sigma}^2)\right]\left[\frac{1}{\kappa_{n0}}\right]\left[\sum_{i=1}^{n}\frac{I_{ni}}{I_n}h(\lambda_{ni})\right]$$

we see that by Corollary 5.8.4 and Eqs. (5.98) and (5.99) the factors in all brackets are $O_p(1)$, so that $\kappa_{n2} = o_p(1)$. We have proved the second relation in Eq. (5.92).

Equation (5.93) follows from Eq. (5.98) and consistency of $\hat{\sigma}^2$ by CMT:

$$\operatorname*{dlim}_{n\to\infty}\kappa_{n3} = \operatorname{plim}\hat{\sigma}^2\frac{1}{\operatorname*{dlim}_{n\to\infty}\kappa_{n0}} = \frac{\sigma^2}{(\sigma\beta_\psi)^2\sum_{i=1}^{\infty}u_i^2\,h^2(\lambda_i)}.$$

Nonnegativity of κ_{n3} and ψ_n is obvious. ∎

5.11 EXAMPLES AND COMPUTER SIMULATION

The exposition here follows Mynbaev and Ullah (2008).

5.11.1 Definition of the Case Spatial Matrices

Conditions in the asymptotic theory usually involve infinite sequences of matrices. In our case we need a link between the function K and sequence of spatial matrices. Other authors in the area have advanced more complex conditions. Those that involve S_n^{-1}, G_n and random vectors (involving the error directly or through Y_n) are especially difficult to verify, (see Kelejian and Prucha, 1999, Assumption 5; Kelejian and Prucha, 2001, Assumption 7; Kelejian and Prucha, 2002, Assumption 7; Lee, 2002, Assumptions 5,7,9; Lee, 2003, Assumption 5; Lee, 2004a, Assumptions 9,10; Theorem 3.2).

Going from a function $K \in L_2((0, 1)^2)$ to spatial matrices is easy: just discretize K, and the approximation condition trivially holds. Going back, that is finding a function K that approximates a given sequence $\{W_n\}$ of practical interest, is more difficult. Here we take a look at one practical example of spatial matrices considered by Case (1991). We prove L_2-approximability, but the rate of approximation is slower than $o(1/\sqrt{n})$. Despite this slower rate, we think that Monte Carlo simulations can still be useful if they support the corollary of Theorem 5.8.1 that the asymptotics of $\hat{\rho}$ is not normal and provide evidence that the two-step procedure from Section 5.10.4 improves the OLS estimator. Besides, the model can be reformulated as one with an exogenous regressor and a pseudo-Case matrix (see the definition and lemma in Section 5.11.3) and then the result for the mixed spatial model will apply.

In the Case (1991) framework there are r districts and m farmers in each district. Denote $l_m = (1, \ldots, 1)'$ (m unities), $B_m = (l_m l_m' - I_m)/(m - 1)$ and $n = rm$. The Case spatial matrix equals

$$W_n = I_r \otimes B_m.$$

Here the blocks B_m are put along the diagonal. All elements of the blocks except those on the diagonal are equal to $1/(m - 1)$. The diagonal elements are null.

5.11.2   Eigenvalues of the Case Matrices

Lemma. W_n *has* r *eigenvalues equal to 1 and* $(r - 1)m$ *eigenvalues equal to* $1/(1 - m)$.

Proof.   From $(l_m l_m') l_m = l_m (l_m' l_m) = m l_m$ we see that $\lambda_1 = m$ is an eigenvalue and $e_1 = l_m$ is the corresponding eigenvector of the matrix $l_m l_m'$. Denote X_m the $(m - 1)$-dimensional subspace of $\mathbb{R}^m$ of vectors orthogonal to e_2:

$$X_m = \{x \in \mathbb{R}^m : l_m' x = x_1 + \cdots + x_m = 0\}.$$

For any $x \in X_m$, $l_m l_m' x = 0$. Selecting in X_m a set $e_2, \ldots, e_m$ of pairwise orthogonal vectors we see that they are eigenvectors that correspond to eigenvalues $\lambda_2 = \cdots = \lambda_m = 0$. Since the system $e_1, \ldots, e_m$ is complete in $\mathbb{R}^m$, we have found all eigenvalues of $l_m l_m'$.

$\det(l_m l_m' - \lambda I) = 0$ is equivalent to $\det(B_m - (\lambda - 1)/(m - 1)I) = 0$. Therefore each eigenvalue λ of $l_m l_m'$ generates an eigenvalue $(\lambda - 1)/(m - 1)$ of B_m. The eigenvalues of B_m then are $\lambda_1 = 1$ and $\lambda_2 = \cdots = \lambda_m = 1/(1 - m)$. Since I_r has r eigenvalues equal to 1, the statement follows from the following property of the Kronecker products (Lütkepohl, 1991, p. 464): the eigenvalues $\lambda_{ij}(A \otimes B)$ of $A \otimes B$ are obtained by multiplying all possible eigenvalues $\lambda_i(A)$ of A by all possible eigenvalues $\lambda_j(B)$ of B.   ∎

5.11.3 L_2-Approximability of the Case Matrices

The Case matrix W_n has r blocks on the main diagonal equal to B_m and all other blocks null. If $\{W_n\}$ is to be L_2-close to some function K, the blocks on the main diagonal must be modeled by the behavior of K along the 45° line. L_2-approximability requires some stabilization of these blocks. If m is fixed and r tends to infinity, then K would have to be zero outside an arbitrary neighborhood of the 45° line and in that case K would have to simply vanish. Since B_m has zeros on the main diagonal and all other elements equal to $1/(m - 1)$, we have

$$\|W_n\|_2^2 = \left(\sum_{j=1}^{r} \|B_m\|_2^2\right)^{1/2} = \left(\sum_{j=1}^{r} \frac{m^2 - m}{m - 1}\right)^{1/2} = \left(r \frac{m}{m - 1}\right)^{1/2} \to \infty,$$

so that $\{W_n\}$ is not L_2-close to $K \equiv 0$.

In the lemma below we see that $\{W_n\}$ is L_2-approximable in the other extreme case, when r is fixed and m tends to infinity. Define *pseudo-Case matrices* by

$$\widetilde{W}_n = I_r \otimes l_m l'_m/(m-1).$$

The rate of approximation for the Case matrices is slower than required in Theorem 5.8.1, so we mention in passing that the pseudo-Case matrices satisfy Assumption 5.2 of Theorem 5.8.1. However, for the computer simulations only the proper Case matrices were used.

Denote by

$$q_{uv}^{(n)} = \left\{ (s,t): \frac{u-1}{n} < s < \frac{u}{n}, \frac{v-1}{n} < t < \frac{v}{n} \right\}, \quad 1 \le u, v \le n,$$

squares with sides of length $1/n$. They cover $(0,1)^2$. We define K to be r on the union q of diagonal squares of side $1/r$ and 0 outside that union:

$$q = \bigcup_{u=1}^{r} q_{uu}^{(r)}, \quad K = r1_q.$$

Lemma

(i) *For any fixed r, the sequence $\{W_n : m = 1, 2, \dots\}$ of the Case matrices is L_2-close to K and $\|W_n - \delta_n K\|_2 = O\!\left(1/\sqrt{n}\right)$.*

(ii) *For any fixed r, the sequence $\{\widetilde{W}_n : m = 1, 2, \dots\}$ of the pseudo-Case matrices satisfies $\|\widetilde{W}_n - \delta_n K\|_2 = o\!\left(1/\sqrt{n}\right)$.*

Proof.

(i) Consider the terms in

$$\|W_n - \delta_n K\|_2^2 = \sum_{i,j=1}^{n} [w_{nij} - (\delta_n K)_{ij}]^2.$$

Let

$$b_{uv} = \{(i,j): (u-1)m+1 \le i \le um, (v-1)m+1 \le j \le vm\}, \quad 1 \le u, v \le r,$$

be the batches of indices that correspond to blocks of W_n of size $m \times m$. The diagonal blocks are all B_m and the others are null matrices.

1. Let $(i,j) \in b_{uu}$. From inequalities

$$1 \le i - (u-1)m \le m, \quad 1 \le j - (u-1)m \le m$$

we see that

$$w_{nij} = \begin{cases} 1/(m-1), & \text{if } i \ne j, \\ 0, & \text{if } i = j. \end{cases}$$

However,

$$q_{ij}^{(n)} \subset q_{uu}^{(r)} \subset q, \quad (\delta_n K)_{ij} = n \int_{q_{ij}^{(n)}} r \, dx \, dy = \frac{1}{m}.$$

2. Let $(i, j) \in b_{uv}$ with $u \neq v$. Then

$$w_{nij} = 0.$$

Since $q_{ij}^{(n)} \subset ((0, 1)^2 \backslash q)$, we have

$$(\delta_n K)_{ij} = 0.$$

The equations we have derived imply

$$\sum_{i,j=1}^{n} [w_{nij} - (\delta_n K)_{ij}]^2$$

$$= \left(\sum_{u,v=1, u \neq v}^{r} \sum_{(i,j) \in b_{uv}} + \sum_{u=1}^{r} \sum_{(i,j) \in b_{uu}} \right) [w_{nij} - (\delta_n K)_{ij}]^2$$

$$= \sum_{i=1}^{n} \frac{1}{m^2} + \sum_{u=1}^{r} \sum_{(i,j) \in b_{uu}, i \neq j} \left(\frac{1}{m-1} - \frac{1}{m} \right)^2$$

$$= \frac{r}{m} + \frac{1}{m^2(m-1)^2} \sum_{u=1}^{r} (m^2 - m) = \frac{r}{m} + \frac{r}{m(m-1)} = O\left(\frac{1}{n} \right).$$

(ii) From the above proof one can see that it is the diagonal elements $-I_n/(m-1)$ in B_m that prevent the norm $\|W_n - \delta_n K\|_2$ from being of order better than $O(1/\sqrt{n})$. By removing them we get statement (ii). ■

5.11.4   Monte Carlo Simulations for Theorem 5.8.1

In a finite-sample framework, there is no sequence of spatial matrices and we cannot know the function K that approximates that sequence. Applying the interpolation operator to W_n, we can define K and regard it as the function that approximates the given and all subsequent (unknown) spatial matrices. With this definition, W_n for the given sample becomes an exact image of K under discretization. As Lemma 3.8.4 shows, nonzero eigenvalues of W_n and $\mathcal{K}$ coincide. Simulation of the asymptotic result of Theorem 5.8.1 becomes, effectively, a comparison of simulation results for the finite-sample deviation from the true value [Eq. (5.5)] and its eigenvalue representation [Eq. (5.6)] in the case of a symmetric W_n. In this sense the simulation of Theorem 5.8.1 is trivial. However, it can be useful if evidence is sought against the null hypothesis of normal asymptotics.

Lee (2004a) studied the performance of the QML estimator for r ranging from 30 to 120 and m from 3 to 100. Our values for r, m are roughly the same. Unlike Lee, who investigated only convergence properties, we also checked the empirical distribution and found evidence that it is not normal.

We find the empirical distribution function of the OLS estimator with 1000 repetitions. As Lemma 5.11.2 shows, W_n has a large number of equal negative eigenvalues, denoted λ_{min}, and a small number of equal positive eigenvalues, denoted λ_{max}. Recall that Theorem 5.8.1 guarantees convergence of $\hat{\rho}$ for ρ in a small neighborhood of 0, called here a *convergence neighborhood*. The combinations of r and m considered are:

   (a) $m = 10$, $r = 100$ ($|\rho| < 0.0047$);
   (b) $m = 100$, $r = 10$ ($|\rho| < 0.0524$);
   (c) $m = 50$, $r = 50$ ($|\rho| < 0.01$).

(The intervals in parentheses are convergence neighborhoods). For each of the cases (a), (b) and (c) we take three different values of ρ: one in a small neighborhood of 0, another close to λ_{min} and the third close to λ_{max}. Thus, we do nine simulations and for each of them:

   (i) test for normality the distributions of the OLS estimator and its "eigenvalue"-counterpart (5.6),
   (ii) find sample means and standard deviations of the OLS estimator $\hat{\rho}$ and its expression in terms of eigenvalues.

Table 5.1 shows that, in many cases, bias is large and comparable in absolute value with the parameter being estimated. This should not come as a surprise because a ratio of quadratic forms in general does not have mean zero. The main calculations were made in GAUSS and the empirical distributions were fed to Minitab to test for

TABLE 5.1   Simulations for Theorem 5.8.1

Values of m, r	True ρ	OLS estimator mean (s.d.)	"Eigenvalue" formula mean (s.d.)
(a) $m = 10$, $r = 100$	(a1) -0.105	-0.2445 (0.1648)	-0.2350 (0.1712)
	(a2) 0.1	0.1789 (0.1085)	0.1781 (0.1189)
	(a3) 0.95	0.9976 (0.0003)	0.9976 (0.0003)
(b) $m = 100$, $r = 10$	(b1) -0.095	-0.4972 (0.8410)	-0.4503 (0.7753)
	(b2) 0.1	0.0165 (0.5512)	0.0212 (0.5461)
	(b3) 0.95	0.9969 (0.0016)	0.9969 (0.0016)
(c) $m = 50$, $r = 50$	(c1) -0.015	-0.0707 (0.2175)	-0.0685 (0.2193)
	(c2) 0.1	0.1728 (0.1662)	0.1605 (0.1669)
	(c3) 0.95	1.0129 (0.1694)	1.0015 (0.0005)

Mynbaev and Ullah (2008). (s.d.) standard deviation.

normality. In all cases the null hypothesis that the distribution is normal is rejected (the p-value of the Anderson–Darling statistic is less than 0.005 in all cases).

When m is small relative to r ($m = 10$, $r = 200$) and ρ is close to zero, the sample distribution of $\hat{\rho}$ for the purely spatial model is closer to the normal. When, on the contrary, m is large relative to r ($m = 200$, $r = 10$) and ρ is the same, the sample distribution of $\hat{\rho}$ is positively skewed. Thus, if nonzero entries of W_n are concentrated around the main diagonal, we should expect asymptotic normality. To a lesser extent, this effect is observed in case of the mixed model. For the purely spatial model, as ρ approaches the right end of the theoretical interval of convergence, the sample distribution collapses to a spike.

5.11.5 Monte Carlo Simulations for the Two-Step Procedure

The second part of the computer simulations is related to Theorem 5.10.5. The two-step procedure from Section 5.10.4 is computationally intensive. GAUSS' internal code for calculating integrals is unreliable and we had to use MathCAD to find the coefficients I_n and I_{ni}. For moderate values of n (10 and 100) we have to take values from $a = 100$ to $a = 1000$ to approximate improper integrals over the half-line by integrals over $[0, a]$. For $n = 1000$ the function $1/\pi_n$ declines very quickly and it is sufficient to take $a = 10$. With I_n and I_{ni} at hand we used GAUSS to realize the two-step procedure. In cases (a) and (b) from Section 5.11.4 it took about half an hour on a computer with a processor speed 2.4 MHZ to simulate 100 procedures and the total time for each of the six subcases was about 50 minutes. Therefore we did not attempt to simulate 1000 times and in case (c) the combination $m = 50$, $r = 50$ was replaced with $m = 40$, $r = 40$ (the convergence neighborhood being $|\rho| < 0.0125$). The results are presented in Table 5.2. Some of them are not particularly illuminating [see, for example, cases (a3), where the approximation is not very good, and (b1), where the standard error is comparable with the bias]. This is why it is better to compare the errors of the OLS and our procedure.

TABLE 5.2   Simulations for Two-Step Estimator

Values of m, r	True ρ	Two-step estimator mean (s.d.)
(a) $m = 10$, $r = 100$	(a1) -0.105	-0.0950 (0.0051)
	(a2) 0.1	0.1017 (0.0027)
	(a3) 0.95	0.5070 (3.2e-008)
(b) $m = 100$, $r = 10$	(b1) -0.095	-0.1884 (0.1918)
	(b2) 0.1	0.0888 (0.0586)
	(b3) 0.95	0.9467 (1.3e-006)
(c) $m = 40$, $r = 40$	(c1) -0.015	-0.0721 (0.0525)
	(c2) 0.1	0.1556 (0.0483)
	(c3) 0.95	0.9974 (3.7e-007)

Mynbaev and Ullah (2008).

TABLE 5.3 Comparison of Percentage Errors

Values of m, r	True ρ	OLS error %	"Eigenvalue" formula error%	Two-step estimator error
(a) $m = 10, r = 100$	(a1) −0.105	132.86	123.81	9.52
	(a2) 0.1	78.90	78.10	1.70
	(a3) 0.95	5.01	5.01	46.63
(b) $m = 100, r = 10$	(b1) −0.095	423.37	374.00	98.32
	(b2) 0.1	83.50	78.80	11.20
	(b3) 0.95	4.94	4.94	0.35
(c) $m = 40, r = 40$	**(c1) −0.015**	371.33	356.67	380.67
	(c2) 0.1	72.80	60.50	55.60
	(c3) 0.95	6.62	5.42	4.99

Mynbaev and Ullah (2008).

Comparison of errors is given in Table 5.3. As we can see, for ρ close to zero the two-step procedure improves the OLS estimator in all cases. For ρ close to one of the eigenvalues of W_n the evidence is mixed: in two cases (shown in bold) the error has increased.

5.12 MIXED SPATIAL MODEL

5.12.1 Statement of Problem

Here we study the model

$$Y_n = X_n\beta + \rho W_n Y_n + v_n, \tag{5.100}$$

where ρ, W_n and v_n are the same as in the purely spatial model, X_n is an $n \times k$ matrix of deterministic exogenous regressors and β is a k-dimensional parameter vector. A range of estimation techniques for this model has been investigated in the literature: ML and QML, MM and generalized MM, the least squares and 2SLS and the instrumental variables estimator (see Ord, 1975; Kelejian and Prucha, 1998,1999; Smirnov and Anselin, 2001; Lee, 2001, 2002, 2003, 2004a). Despite the conceptual and technical differences in approaches, all these authors have been looking for a normal asymptotics.

The goal in the rest of this chapter is to extend to the mixed spatial model the method developed in the previous sections for the purely spatial model. Corresponding to two particular cases $\beta = 0$ and $\rho = 0$ we have two submodels

$$\text{Submodel 1: } Y_n = \rho W_n Y_n + v_n,$$
$$\text{Submodel 2: } Y_n = X_n\beta + v_n.$$

Theorem 5.8.1 supplies a set of conditions sufficient for convergence in distribution of the OLS estimator $\hat{\rho}$ for Submodel 1. Let's call this set Set 1. The corresponding set for

Submodel 2 is provided in Chapter 1. When considering the combined model (5.100) it is natural to join Sets 1 and 2 into one Set C (comprehensive or combined) and try to impose on top of Set C as few conditions as possible to obtain convergence in distribution of the OLS estimator $\hat{\theta}$ of $\theta = (\beta', \rho)'$. Not only should the conditions be combined, but also the knowledge of the elements of the conventional scheme, for the submodels should contribute to the construction of the conventional scheme for the combined model.

Inspection of the conditions of Theorems 1.12.3 and 5.8.1 shows that Set C consists of Assumptions 5.1–5.3 plus just one condition on the columns $H_{n1}, \ldots, H_{nk}$ of the normalized regressor matrix $H_n = X_n D_n^{-1}$ where

$$D_n = \text{diag}[\|X_{n1}\|_2, \ldots, \|X_{nk}\|_2]$$

is the VS normalizer (see Section 1.11.1 for the definition) and X_{n1} through X_{nk} are columns of X_n. The condition looks like this:

5.12.1.1   *Assumption 5.4 on the normalized regressors*

1. The sequence of columns $\{H_{nl} : n \in \mathbb{N}\}$ is L_2-close to $M_l \in L_2(0, 1)$, $l = 1, \ldots, k$.

2. $M_1, \ldots, M_k$ are linearly independent or, equivalently, the Gram matrix

$$\Gamma_0 = \begin{pmatrix} (M_1, M_1)_{L_2} & \cdots & (M_1, M_k)_{L_2} \\ \cdots & \cdots & \cdots \\ (M_k, M_1)_{L_2} & \cdots & (M_k, M_k)_{L_2} \end{pmatrix}$$

is positive definite (see Section 1.7.5).

Item 2 of this assumption can be called *asymptotic linear independence of normalized regressors*. We need to analyze the elements of the conventional scheme for the mixed model and get the most out of Assumptions 5.1–5.4.

5.12.2   The Conventional Scheme for the Mixed Model

Denoting $\theta = (\beta', \rho)'$ the parameter vector and $Z_n = (X_n, W_n Y_n)$ the regressor matrix we rewrite Eq. (5.100) as $Y_n = Z_n \theta + v_n$. Until we work out the condition for nonsingularity of $Z_n' Z_n$ it is safer to work with the normal equation $Z_n' Z_n (\hat{\theta} - \theta) = Z_n' v_n$. Following the discussion in Section 1.11.1 the suggestion is to put

$$\mathcal{D}_n = \begin{pmatrix} D_n & 0 \\ 0 & d_n \end{pmatrix}$$

with $d_n > 0$ to be defined later. The normal equation is easily rearranged to

$$\mathcal{D}_n^{-1} Z_n' Z_n \mathcal{D}_n^{-1} \mathcal{D}_n (\hat{\theta} - \theta) = \mathcal{D}_n^{-1} Z_n' v_n.$$

Here

$$\zeta_n = \mathcal{D}_n^{-1} Z_n' v_n \quad \text{and} \quad \Omega_n = \mathcal{D}_n^{-1} Z_n' Z_n \mathcal{D}_n^{-1}$$

are called *numerator* and *denominator*, respectively. Recalling the notation

$$S_n = I - \rho W_n, \quad G_n = W_n S_n^{-1},$$

and assuming that S_n^{-1} exists we get the reduced form $Y_n = S_n^{-1} X_n \beta + S_n^{-1} v_n$ of Eq. (5.100) so that

$$W_n Y_n = G_n X_n \beta + G_n v_n = G_n H_n D_n \beta + G_n v_n.$$

Therefore the normalized regressor matrix is

$$Z_n \mathcal{D}_n^{-1} = (X_n, W_n Y_n) \begin{pmatrix} D_n^{-1} & 0 \\ 0 & d_n^{-1} \end{pmatrix} = \left(H_n, \frac{1}{d_n} G_n H_n D_n \beta + \frac{1}{d_n} G_n v_n \right) \quad (5.101)$$

and the numerator is

$$\zeta_n = \mathcal{D}_n^{-1} Z_n' v_n = \begin{pmatrix} H_n' v_n \\ \frac{1}{d_n} (D_n \beta)' H_n' G_n' v_n + \frac{1}{d_n} v_n' G_n' v_n \end{pmatrix}. \quad (5.102)$$

From our experience with Submodels 1 and 2 (Section 5.12.1) we can surmise that perhaps the behavior of the terms involving H_n', G_n' and v_n can be deduced from Assumptions 5.1–5.4. However, the vector

$$b_n = \frac{1}{d_n} D_n \beta = \frac{1}{d_n} (\|X_{n1}\|_2 \beta_1, \ldots, \|X_{nk}\|_2 \beta_k)$$

involves both d_n and D_n and its behavior may present problems; b_n is called a *balancer*.

With the help of Eq. (5.101) it is easy to establish the working expressions for the blocks of the denominator

$$\Omega_{n11} = H_n' H_n,$$

$$\Omega_{n12} = H_n' G_n H_n b_n + \frac{1}{d_n} H_n' G_n v_n,$$

$$\Omega_{n21} = \Omega_{n12}',$$

$$\Omega_{n22} = b_n' H_n' G_n' G_n H_n b_n + \frac{2}{d_n} b_n' H_n' G_n' G_n v_n + \frac{1}{d_n^2} v_n' G_n' G_n v_n. \quad (5.103)$$

As we see in the next few sections, all parts of ζ_n and Ω_n not involving d_n and b_n converge under Assumptions 5.1–5.4. Everywhere these assumptions are assumed to hold and only additional conditions are listed.

5.12.3 Infinite-Dimensional Matrices

We use infinite-dimensional matrices A of size $l \times m$, where one or both dimensions can be infinite. Matrices can extend downward or rightward, but not upward or leftward. We consider only matrices with finite l_2-norms. Summation, transposition and multiplication are performed as usual and preserve this property because

$$\|A + B\|_2 \leq \|A\|_2 + \|B\|_2, \ \|A'\|_2 = \|A\|_2, \ \|AB\|_2 \leq \|A\|_2\|B\|_2.$$

The above inequality ensures the validity of the associativity law for multiplication and the transposition law for products

$$(AB)C = A(BC), \ (AB)' = B'A'. \tag{5.104}$$

This may be the only fact that is not evident, so here is the proof for multiplication. Formally, for the ijth element of the products $(AB)C$ and $A(BC)$ we have

$$((AB)C)_{ij} = \sum_l (AB)_{il}c_{lj} = \sum_{k,l} a_{ik}b_{kl}c_{lj}$$

$$= \sum_k a_{ik}\left(\sum_l b_{kl}c_{lj}\right) = \sum_k a_{ik}(BC)_{kj} = (A(BC))_{ij}.$$

These formal manipulations are justified by absolute convergence of all the series. For example, for one of the terms in the middle

$$\sum_k |a_{ik}|\left(\sum_l |b_{kl}c_{lj}|\right) \leq \sum_k |a_{ik}|\left(\sum_l b_{kl}^2\right)^{1/2}\left(\sum_l c_{lj}^2\right)^{1/2}$$

$$\leq \left(\sum_k a_{ik}^2\right)^{1/2}\left(\sum_{k,l} b_{kl}^2\right)^{1/2}\left(\sum_l c_{lj}^2\right)^{1/2} < \infty.$$

Elements of l_2 are written as column-vectors. A matrix A with $\|A\|_2 < \infty$ induces a bounded linear operator $\mathcal{A}$ in l_2 by the formula

$$\mathcal{A}x = \begin{pmatrix} \sum_j a_{1j}x_j \\ \cdots \\ \sum_j a_{lj}x_j \\ \cdots \end{pmatrix}$$

because $\|\mathcal{A}x\|_2 \leq \|A\|_2\|x\|_2$. Henceforth for the operator we use the same notation A as for the matrix.

Denote B the set of bounded operators in l_2 and BM the set of bounded operators in l_2 having a matrix representation A with $\|A\|_2 < \infty$. BM is a proper subset of B (for example, for the diagonal matrix representing the identity operator one has $\|I\|_2 = \infty$).

Therefore some care is necessary when in one formula there are operators from both B and BM.

5.12.4 EXtender and eXtended M

Let $\{F_i\}$ be the orthonormal system of eigenfunctions of the operator $\mathcal{K}$ from Assumption 5.3 (Section 5.3.1). With a function $F \in L_2(0, 1)$ decomposed as

$$F = \sum_{j \geq 1} (F, F_j)_{L_2} F_j$$

we associate a vector $\mathcal{X}F \in l_2$ of its Fourier coefficients

$$\mathcal{X}F = ((F, F_1)_{L_2}, (F, F_2)_{L_2}, \ldots)'.$$

By Parseval's identity (3.33)

$$(\mathcal{X}F)'\mathcal{X}G = \sum_i (F, F_i)(G, F_i) = (F, G)_{L_2}$$

for any functions $F, G \in L_2(0, 1)$. In particular, $\mathcal{X}$ preserves norms and $\|\mathcal{X}F\|_2 = \|F\|_2$. Hence, $\mathcal{X}$ is an isomorphism from $L_2(0, 1)$ to l_2. Denote

$$M = (M_1, \ldots, M_k)'.$$

I call $\mathcal{X}$ an *eXtender* because its application to M' gives a matrix

$$\mathcal{M} = (\mathcal{X}M_1, \ldots, \mathcal{X}M_k) = \mathcal{X}M'$$

of size $\infty \times k$. $\mathcal{M}$ is named an *eXtended M*. The linear span of $M_1, \ldots, M_k$ is denoted $\mathfrak{M}$.

Lemma. *If Assumption 5.4 (Section 5.12.1.1) holds, then the columns of $\mathcal{M}$ are linearly independent and $\|\mathcal{M}\|_2 < \infty$.*

Proof. By Assumption 5.4 the functions M_i are linearly independent. The columns of $\mathcal{M}$ are linearly independent because, by isomorphism, $\sum_i c_i M_i = 0$ is equivalent to $\sum_i c_i \mathcal{X}M_i = 0$.

Assumption 5.4 also guarantees square-summability of columns of $\mathcal{M}$. Since the number of the columns is finite, we have $\|\mathcal{M}\|_2 < \infty$. $\blacksquare$

5.12.5 Double P Lemma

Denote

$$\begin{aligned} P &= \mathcal{M}(\mathcal{M}'\mathcal{M})^{-1}\mathcal{M}', &&(1^{st}PP), \\ Q &= I - P, &&(2^{nd}PP). \end{aligned} \qquad (5.105)$$

P and Q are referred to as *principal projectors* of the theory of mixed spatial models.

Lemma. *If Assumption 5.4 (Section 5.12.1) holds, then*

(i) *P and Q are symmetric and idempotent.*

(ii) *P projects l_2 onto the image $\mathcal{X}\mathfrak{M}$ of $\mathfrak{M}$ under $\mathcal{X}: L_2(0, 1) \to l_2$.*

Proof.

(i) Like in linear algebra, we use Eq. (5.104) to check that

$$P' = \mathcal{M}''[(\mathcal{M}'\mathcal{M})^{-1}]'\mathcal{M}' = \mathcal{M}[(\mathcal{M}'\mathcal{M})']^{-1}\mathcal{M}' = \mathcal{M}[\mathcal{M}'\mathcal{M}'']^{-1}\mathcal{M}' = P,$$
$$P^2 = \mathcal{M}(\mathcal{M}'\mathcal{M})^{-1}\mathcal{M}'\mathcal{M}(\mathcal{M}'\mathcal{M})^{-1}\mathcal{M}' = \mathcal{M}(\mathcal{M}'\mathcal{M})^{-1}\mathcal{M}' = P.$$

Since $\mathcal{M}'\mathcal{M}$ is finite-dimensional, we can change the order of inversion and transposition without worrying about generalization of linear algebra rules.

To prove that Q is an orthoprojector we need to treat P as an operator, not a matrix, because with the identity operator, matrix calculus doesn't work:

$$Q' = I - P' = I - P, \ Q^2 = (I - P)^2 = I - P - P + P^2 = I - P = Q.$$

(ii) The image of P coincides with $\mathcal{X}\mathfrak{M}$ because for any $x \in l_2$ the vector Px is a linear combination of $\mathcal{X}M_1, \ldots, \mathcal{X}M_k$ with coefficients $(\Gamma^{-1}\mathcal{M}'x)_l$, $l = 1, \ldots, k$:

$$Px = \mathcal{M}(\mathcal{M}'\mathcal{M})^{-1}\mathcal{M}'x = (\mathcal{X}M_1, \ldots, \mathcal{X}M_k)\Gamma^{-1}\mathcal{M}'x$$
$$= \sum_{l=1}^{k}(\Gamma^{-1}\mathcal{M}'x)_l\mathcal{X}M_l.$$

∎

5.12.6 The Genie

The eXtender generates an isomorphism between two sets of operators: any bounded operator A in $L_2(0, 1)$ induces a bounded operator $\tilde{A} = \mathcal{X}A\mathcal{X}^{-1}$ in l_2.

Let

$$h_\mathcal{X} = \text{diag}[h(\lambda_1), h(\lambda_2), \ldots]$$

be an infinite-dimensional diagonal matrix. It is shown in Section 5.8.3 that Eq. (5.68) implies $\sum_{i\geq 1}|h(\lambda_i)| < \infty$, so $\|h_\mathcal{X}\|_2 < \infty$. I call $h_\mathcal{X}$ a *genie* because, ultimately, it is a reflection of the limit of $G_n = h(W_n)$. The significance of $h_\mathcal{X}$ is explained by the following fact.

Lemma. *The genie is the operator induced in l_2 by $h(\mathcal{K})$:*

$$\mathcal{X}h(\mathcal{K}) = h_\mathcal{X}\mathcal{X}. \tag{5.106}$$

Proof. According to the general definition of functions of operators [Eq. (3.36)]

$$h(\mathcal{K})F = \sum_i h(\lambda_i)(F, F_i)F_i.$$

By definition of the eXtender,

$$\mathcal{X}h(\mathcal{K})F = (h(\lambda_1)(F, F_1), h(\lambda_2)(F, F_2), \dots)'$$
$$= h_\mathcal{X}((F, F_1), (F, F_2), \dots)' = h_\mathcal{X}\mathcal{X}F.$$

Since F is arbitrary, this proves the lemma.   ∎

5.12.7   Convergence of Quadratic Forms in H_n

Denote

$$\Gamma_i = \mathcal{M}'h_\mathcal{X}^i\mathcal{M}, \ i = 0, 1, 2. \tag{5.107}$$

By Parseval's identity, the Γ_0 defined here is the same as the Gram matrix from Assumption 5.4 (Section 5.12.1):

$$\Gamma_0 = \mathcal{X}M \cdot \mathcal{X}M' = \left(\sum_i (M_l, F_i)_{L_2}(M_m, F_i)_{L_2}\right)_{l,m=1}^k = \int_0^1 M(x)M'(x)dx.$$

Lemma. *If $|\rho|\nu(\mathcal{K}) < 1$, then*

(i) $\lim_{n \to \infty} H_n'H_n = \Gamma_0,$

(ii) $\lim_{n \to \infty} H_n'G_nH_n = \Gamma_1 = \lim_{n \to \infty} H_n'G_n'H_n,$

(iii) $\lim_{n \to \infty} H_n'G_n'G_nH_n = \Gamma_2.$

Proof. Statement (i) follows directly from Assumption 5.4, Theorem 2.5.3 and the definition of $\mathcal{M}$:

$$\lim_{n \to \infty} (H_n'H_n)_{lm} = \lim_{n \to \infty} H_{nl}'H_{nm} = \int_0^1 M_l(x)M_m(x)dx$$

$$= \sum_{j=1}^\infty (M_l, F_j)_{L_2}(M_m, F_j)_{L_2} = (\mathcal{M}'\mathcal{M})_{lm}.$$

The proofs of the other statements are given in separate sections.   ∎

5.12.8   Proving Convergence of $H_n'G_nH_n$ and $H_n'G_n'H_n$

The elements of the matrix $H_n'G_nH_n$ are $H_{nl}'G_nH_{nm}$, $1 \le l, m \le k$. For any l, m

$$H_{nl}'G_nH_{nm} = H_{nl}'[h(W_n) - h(\delta_nK)]H_{nm} + H_{nl}'h(\delta_nK)H_{nm}.$$

Here the first term tends to zero by Eq. (5.19) and boundedness of $\|H_{nl}\|_2$:

$$|H'_{nl}[h(W_n) - h(\delta_n K)]H_{nm}| \leq c\|H_{nl}\|_2\|W_n - \delta_n K\|_2\|H_{nm}\|_2 \to 0.$$

For the second term, Lemma 5.6.3 with $L = \infty$ gives

$$H'_{nl}h(\delta_n K)H_{nm} = \sum_{p=0}^{\infty} \rho^p \sum_{i_1,\ldots,i_{p+1}=1}^{\infty} \prod_{j=1}^{p+1} \lambda_{i_j} c_{ni}(\delta_n F_{i_1}, H_{nl})_{l_2}(\delta_n F_{i_{p+1}}, H_{nm})_{l_2}.$$

The series converge uniformly in l, m, n because the scalar and chain products c_{ni} are uniformly bounded and

$$|H'_{nl}h(\delta_n K)H_{nm}| \leq c \sum_{p=0}^{\infty} |\rho|^p \sum_{i_1,\ldots,i_{p+1}=1}^{\infty} |\lambda_{i_1} \cdots \lambda_{i_{p+1}}|$$

$$= c \sum_{p=0}^{\infty} (|\rho| v(K))^p v(K) < \infty.$$

Besides, there is convergence of the chain products (Lemma 5.6.1) and scalar products [Eq. (5.41)], with an obvious modification for H_{nm}, so

$$H'_{nl}h(\delta_n K)H_{nm} \to \sum_{p=0}^{\infty} \rho^p \sum_{i_1,\ldots,i_{p+1}=1}^{\infty} \prod_{j=1}^{p+1} \lambda_{i_j} c_{\infty i}(F_{i_1}, M_l)_{L_2}(F_{i_{p+1}}, M_m)_{L_2}$$

($c_{\infty i}$ vanishes outside the diagonal $i_1 = \cdots = i_{p+1}$)

$$= \sum_{p=0}^{\infty} \rho^p \sum_{i=1}^{\infty} \lambda_i^{p+1}(F_i, M_l)_{L_2}(F_i, M_m)_{L_2}$$

[using Eq. (5.61) and the definition of $\mathcal{M}$]

$$= \sum_{i=1}^{\infty} h(\lambda_i)(F_i, M_l)_{L_2}(F_i, M_m)_{L_2} = (\mathcal{M}'h_\chi\mathcal{M})_{lm}.$$

We have proved that $H'_{nl}G_nH_{nm} \to (\mathcal{M}'h_\chi\mathcal{M})_{lm}$. The second equation in Lemma 5.12.7(ii) follows from the first and Lemma 5.4.4:

$$|H'_{nl}(G_n - G'_n)H_{nm}| \leq \|H_{nl}\|_2(\|G_n - h(\delta_n K)\|_2$$
$$+ \|G'_n - h(\delta_n K)\|_2)\|H_{nm}\|_2 \to 0.$$

5.12.9 Proving Convergence of $H'_nG'_nG_nH_n$

As in Section 5.12.8, note that $H'_nG'_nG_nH_n$ has $H'_{nl}G'_nG_nH_{nm}$ as its elements and

$$H'_{nl}G'_nG_nH_{nm} = H'_{nl}[G'_nG_n - h^2(\delta_n K)]H_{nm} + H'_{nl}h^2(\delta_n K)H_{nm}.$$

The first term on the right is estimated using Lemma 5.4.5 and Eqs. (5.24) and (5.28):

$$
\begin{aligned}
|H'_{nl}[G'_n G_n - h^2(\delta_n K)]H_{nm}| &\leq \|H_{nl}\|_2 (\|G'_n - h(\delta_n K)\|_2 \|G_n\|_2 \\
&\quad + \|h(\delta_n K)\|_2 \|G_n - h(\delta_n K)\|_2)\|H_{nm}\|_2 \\
&\leq c\|W_n - \delta_n K\|_2 \;\to\; 0.
\end{aligned}
$$

By Lemma 5.6.3 the second term can be re-written as

$$
H'_{nl} h^2(\delta_n K) H_{nm}
$$

$$
= \sum_{p=0}^{\infty} \rho^p (p+1) \sum_{i_1,\dots,i_{p+2}=1}^{\infty} \prod_{j=1}^{p+2} \lambda_{i_j} c_{ni}(\delta_n F_{i_1}, H_{nl})_{l_2} (\delta_n F_{i_{p+2}}, H_{nm})_{l_2}
$$

with the series converging uniformly, as in Section 5.12.8. After letting $n \to \infty$ and applying Lemma 5.6.1 and Eqs. (5.41) and (5.47) we obtain

$$
H'_{nl} h^2(\delta_n K) H_{nm}
$$

$$
\to \sum_{p=0}^{\infty} \rho^p (p+1) \sum_{i_1,\dots,i_{p+2}=1}^{\infty} \prod_{j=1}^{p+2} \lambda_{i_j} c_{\infty i}(F_{i_1}, M_l)_{L_2}(F_{i_{p+2}}, M_m)_{L_2}
$$

$$
= \sum_{i=1}^{\infty} \left(\sum_{p=0}^{\infty} \rho^p (p+1) \lambda_i^{p+2} \right)(F_i, M_l)_{L_2}(F_i, M_m)_{L_2}
$$

$$
= \sum_{i=1}^{\infty} h^2(\lambda_i)(F_i, M_l)_{L_2}(F_i, M_m)_{L_2} = (\mathcal{M}' h_{\mathcal{X}}^2 \mathcal{M})_{lm}.
$$

Thus, for any l, m $H'_{nl} G'_n G_n H_{nm} \to (\mathcal{M}' h_{\mathcal{X}}^2 \mathcal{M})_{lm}$.

5.13 THE ROUNDABOUT ROAD (MIXED MODEL)

The idea here generalizes Section 5.7.1. Before explaining it I report an unsuccessful attempt to realize a customary way of proving convergence of the OLS estimator. By writing

$$
\Omega_n^{-1} \zeta_n = [E\Omega_n + (\Omega_n - E\Omega_n)]^{-1} \zeta_n
$$

we see that convergence of $\Omega_n^{-1} \zeta_n$ will take place if

1. ζ_n converges in distribution,
2. $E\Omega_n$ converges to a nonsingular deterministic matrix,
3. $\Omega_n - E\Omega_n$ converges in probability to a null matrix.

I failed to implement steps (2) and (3) because Ω_n converges in distribution to a stochastic matrix.

5.13.1 Definition of the Proxies (Mixed Model)

For any natural n, L denote

$$
U_{nL} = \begin{pmatrix} H'_n v_n \\ (\delta_n F_1)' v_n \\ \cdots \\ (\delta_n F_L)' v_n \end{pmatrix}
\tag{5.108}
$$

a random vector with $k + L$ components. The previous U_{nL} [from Eq. (5.53)] represents the final two components of this one.

Now we define the *proXy* by

$$
X_{nL} = \begin{pmatrix} H'_n v_n \\ \sum_{i=1}^{L} h(\lambda_i)(M, F_i)_{L_2} U_{nL,k+i} \\ \sum_{i=1}^{L} h^2(\lambda_i)(M, F_i)_{L_2} U_{nL,k+i} \\ \sum_{i=1}^{L} h(\lambda_i) U_{nL,k+i}^2 \\ \sum_{i=1}^{L} h^2(\lambda_i) U_{nL,k+i}^2 \end{pmatrix}.
\tag{5.109}
$$

Its last two components give the old X_{nL} from Section 5.7.1. The limiting behavior of X_{nL}, as $n \to \infty$, is described in terms of the *proξy*

$$
\xi_L = |\sigma\beta_\psi| \begin{pmatrix} \sum_{i=1}^{\infty} (M, F_i)_{L_2} u_i \\ \sum_{i=1}^{L} h(\lambda_i)(M, F_i)_{L_2} u_i \\ \sum_{i=1}^{L} h^2(\lambda_i)(M, F_i)_{L_2} u_i \\ |\sigma\beta_\psi| \sum_{i=1}^{L} h(\lambda_i) u_i^2 \\ |\sigma\beta_\psi| \sum_{i=1}^{L} h^2(\lambda_i) u_i^2 \end{pmatrix}, \quad 1 \le L < \infty,
\tag{5.110}
$$

where $u_1, u_2, \ldots$ are independent standard normal. Once again, the final two components of this proξy give the earlier proξy. Both proxies carry the essential information about the auxiliary vector from the next section.

5.13.2 Auxiliary Vector, Alphas, Betas and Gammas

All random components contained in the numerator ζ_n [Eq. (5.102)] and denominator Ω_n [Eq. (5.103)] are dumped into one *auxiliary vector* (now it is not a pair)

$$
\mathcal{A}_n = \begin{pmatrix} \mathcal{A}_{n1} \\ \mathcal{A}_{n2} \\ \mathcal{A}_{n3} \\ \mathcal{A}_{n4} \\ \mathcal{A}_{n5} \end{pmatrix} = \begin{pmatrix} H'_n v_n \\ H'_n G_n v_n \\ H'_n G'_n G_n v_n \\ v'_n G'_n v_n \\ v'_n G'_n G_n v_n \end{pmatrix}.
$$

$H'_n G'_n V_n$ (which is a part of ζ_n) is not included because plim $(H'_n G_n V_n - H'_n G'_n V_n) = 0$ (see Lemma 5.13.6). The first three components of $\mathcal{A}_n$ are $k \times 1$ and linear in v_n, whereas the final two are (scalar) quadratic forms of v_n. The ordering of components of $\mathcal{A}_n$ does not matter. The final two components of $\mathcal{A}_n$ coincide with $\mathcal{P}_n$ from Section 5.7.1. Therefore in the representation

$$\mathcal{A}_n = \alpha_n + \beta_{nL} + \gamma_{nL} + X_{nL} \tag{5.111}$$

the terms at the right will have the final two components equal to the corresponding vectors from Section 5.7.1. Naturally, the vectors at the right-hand side of Eq. (5.111) have blocks conformable with those of $\mathcal{A}_n$.

X_{nL} is defined in Eq. (5.109) and represents the main part of $\mathcal{A}_n$. The other three vectors are defined by

$$\alpha_n = \begin{pmatrix} 0 \\ H'_n[G_n - h(\delta_n K)]v_n \\ H'_n[G'_n G_n - h^2(\delta_n K)]v_n \\ v'_n[G'_n - h(\delta_n K)]v_n \\ v'_n[G'_n G_n - h^2(\delta_n K)]v_n \end{pmatrix},$$

$$\beta_{nL} = \begin{pmatrix} 0 \\ H'_n[h(\delta_n K) - h(\delta_n K_L)]v_n \\ H'_n[h^2(\delta_n K) - h^2(\delta_n K_L)]v_n \\ v'_n[h(\delta_n K) - h(\delta_n K_L)]v_n \\ v'_n[h^2(\delta_n K) - h^2(\delta_n K_L)]v_n \end{pmatrix}$$

and

$$\gamma_{nL} = \begin{pmatrix} 0 \\ H'_n h(\delta_n K_L)v_n \\ H'_n h^2(\delta_n K_L)v_n \\ v'_n h(\delta_n K_L)v_n \\ v'_n h^2(\delta_n K_L)v_n \end{pmatrix} - \begin{pmatrix} 0 \\ X_{nL2} \\ X_{nL3} \\ X_{nL4} \\ X_{nL5} \end{pmatrix}. \tag{5.112}$$

In α_n, β_{nL} and γ_{nL} the first blocks are null because the CLT for weighted sums of linear processes from Chapter 3 is directly applicable to the first block of $\mathcal{A}_n$.

$\alpha_{nj}, j = 1, \ldots, 5$, mean the five blocks in α_n, not its scalar coordinates. A similar convention applies to all other vectors defined here. The proof of convergence of $\mathcal{A}_n$ consists of three steps.

Step 1. α_n, β_{nL}, γ_{nL} are negligible in some sense. For their final two components this is shown in Sections 5.7.3 and 5.7.5. For the first three we show it in Lemmas 5.13.6–5.13.8.

Step 2. The limit of X_{nL}, as $n \to \infty$, is ξ_L, which, in turn, converges to Ξ defined in Eq. (5.115).

Step 3. Apply Billingsley's theorem on a double limit and the CLT.

5.13.3   Convergence of the proXy

Lemma.   *If*

$$\sum_{i\geq 1} |h(\lambda_i)| < \infty, \tag{5.113}$$

then $\operatorname*{dlim}_{n \to \infty} X_{nL} = \xi_L$ *for all natural L.*

Proof.   In Theorem 3.5.2 put $W_n = (H_n, \delta_n F_1, \ldots, \delta_n F_L)$. By that theorem $U_{nL} = W'_n v_n$ converges in distribution to a normal vector with zero mean and variance equal to $(\sigma \beta_\psi)^2$ multiplied by the Gram matrix G of the system $\{M_1, \ldots, M_k, F_1, \ldots, F_L\}$:

$$U_{nL} \xrightarrow{d} N(0, (\sigma \beta_\psi)^2 G). \tag{5.114}$$

Denoting $F^{(L)} = (F_1, \ldots, F_L)'$ and applying the usual vector operations we write G in the form

$$G = \begin{pmatrix} (M, M')_{L_2} & (M, F^{(L)\prime})_{L_2} \\ (F^{(L)}, M')_{L_2} & (F^{(L)}, F^{(L)\prime})_{L_2} \end{pmatrix}$$

$$= \begin{pmatrix} \sum_{i=1}^{\infty} (M, F_i)_{L_2} (M', F_i)_{L_2} & (M, F_1)_{L_2} & \cdots & (M, F_L)_{L_2} \\ (M', F_1)_{L_2} & 1 & \cdots & 0 \\ \cdots & \cdots & \cdots & \cdots \\ (M', F_L)_{L_2} & 0 & \cdots & 1 \end{pmatrix}.$$

Here the upper left block is the Parseval identity. The lower right block is the result of orthonormality of $F_1, \ldots, F_L$.

If we take a sequence of independent standard normals and define U_L by

$$U_L = |\sigma \beta_\psi| \begin{pmatrix} \sum_{i=1}^{\infty} (M, F_i)_{L_2} u_i \\ u_1 \\ \cdots \\ u_L \end{pmatrix},$$

then it will be normal, have zero mean and variance

$$E U_L U'_L = (\sigma \beta_\psi)^2 \begin{pmatrix} V_{11} & V'_{21} \\ V_{21} & V_{22} \end{pmatrix},$$

where

$$V_{11} = \sum_{i,j} (M, F_i)_{L_2} (M', F_j)_{L_2} E u_i u_j = (M, M')_{L_2},$$

$$V_{21} = \begin{pmatrix} \sum (M', F_i)_{L_2} E u_1 u_i \\ \cdots \\ \sum (M', F_i)_{L_2} E u_L u_i \end{pmatrix} = \begin{pmatrix} (M', F_1)_{L_2} \\ \cdots \\ (M', F_L)_{L_2} \end{pmatrix},$$

$$V_{22} = \begin{pmatrix} E u_1^2 & \cdots & E u_1 u_L \\ \cdots & \cdots & \cdots \\ E u_L u_1 & \cdots & E u_L^2 \end{pmatrix} = I.$$

Hence, $E U_L U_L' = (\sigma \beta_\psi)^2 G$ and, in consequence, $U_{nL} \overset{d}{\to} U_L$ as $n \to \infty$.

X_{nL}, being a continuous function of U_{nL}, converges in distribution to the same function of U_L. When comparing the expressions of X_{nL} and its limit in distribution ξ_L, keep in mind two corollaries of Eq. (5.114). First, the relationship $H_n' v_n \overset{d}{\to} N(0, (\sigma \beta_\psi)^2 (M, M')_{L_2})$ is equivalent to

$$H_n' v_n \overset{d}{\to} |\sigma \beta_\psi| \sum_{i=1}^\infty (M, F_i)_{L_2} u_i$$

and, second,

$$U_{nL,k+i} \overset{d}{\to} |\sigma \beta_\psi| u_i, \quad U_{nL,k+i}^2 \overset{d}{\to} (\sigma \beta_\psi)^2 u_i^2. \qquad \blacksquare$$

5.13.4   Convergence of the Proξy

Denote

$$\Xi = \begin{pmatrix} \Xi_1 \\ \Xi_2 \\ \Xi_3 \\ \Xi_4 \\ \Xi_5 \end{pmatrix} = |\sigma \beta_\psi| \begin{pmatrix} \mathcal{M}'u \\ \mathcal{M}'h_\chi u \\ \mathcal{M}'h_\chi^2 u \\ |\sigma \beta_\psi| u' h_\chi u \\ |\sigma \beta_\psi| u' h_\chi^2 u \end{pmatrix}, \quad u = \begin{pmatrix} u_1 \\ u_2 \\ \cdots \end{pmatrix} \qquad (5.115)$$

(see Sections 5.12.4 and 5.12.6 for the definitions of the eXtended M and genie). Note that Ξ_1, Ξ_2, Ξ_3 are linear in standard normal variables and Ξ_4, Ξ_5 are quadratic.

Lemma

(i) $\mathcal{L}_1$-$\lim \xi_L = \Xi,$

(ii) components of Ξ converge in $\mathcal{L}_2$.

Proof.

(i) This part follows from the fact that Eq. (5.113) implies $\sum_{i \geq 1} h^2(\lambda_i) < \infty$ and that $Eu_i^2 = 1$.

(ii) This proposition is equivalently expressed by saying that the vectors

$$\Xi_L = |\sigma\beta_\psi| \sum_{i=1}^{L} \begin{pmatrix} (M, F_i)_{L_2} u_i \\ h(\lambda_i)(M, F_i)_{L_2} u_i \\ h^2(\lambda_i)(M, F_i)_{L_2} u_i \\ |\sigma\beta_\psi| h(\lambda_i) u_i^2 \\ |\sigma\beta_\psi| h^2(\lambda_i) u_i^2 \end{pmatrix} \tag{5.116}$$

converge to Ξ in $\mathcal{L}_2$. We can't be sure that $M'u$ belongs to l_2 for every point in the sample space Ω. However, components of $M'u$ converge in $\mathcal{L}_2$:

$$E \sum_i (\mathcal{X}M_l)_i^2 u_i^2 = \|\mathcal{X}M_l\|_2^2 = \|M_l\|_2^2 < \infty.$$

For the fourth component, by independence of u_i^2

$$E\left(\sum_i |h(\lambda_i)u_i^2|\right)^2 = \sum_{i,j} |h(\lambda_i)h(\lambda_j)| Eu_i^2 u_j^2 = \left(\sum_i |h(\lambda_i)| Eu_i^2\right)^2 < \infty.$$

The second, third and fifth components of Ξ converge even faster because of multiplication by $h(\lambda_i)$ and $h^2(\lambda_i)$.   ∎

5.13.5   Bounding Linear Forms in v_n

Lemma.   *For any $n \times n$ matrix A*

$$(E\|H_n'Av_n\|^2)^{1/2} \leq c\|H_n\|_2\|A\|_2.$$

Proof.   Use the partition of H_n into its columns:

$$E\|H_n'Av_n\|_2^2 = E \sum_{l=1}^{k} (H_{nl}'Av_n)^2 = \sum_{l=1}^{k} Ev_n'A'H_{nl}H_{nl}'Av_n$$

(apply Hölder's inequality and Lemma 3.9.9)

$$\leq \sum_{l=1}^{k} [E(v_n'A'H_{nl}H_{nl}'Av_n)^2]^{1/2} = \sum_{l=1}^{k} g(A'H_{nl}H_{nl}'A)$$

$$\leq c \sum_{l=1}^{k} \|A'H_{nl}\|_2 \|H_{nl}'A\|_2 \leq c \sum_{l=1}^{k} \|A\|_2^2 \|H_{nl}\|_2^2$$

$$= c\|H_n\|_2^2\|A_n\|_2^2.$$ ∎

5.13.6 Estimating Alphas

Lemma. *If* $|\rho|\left(\sum_{j=1}^{\infty}\lambda_j^2\right)^{1/2} < 1,$ *then*

$$\lim_{n \to \infty} E\|\alpha_{nj}\|_2^2 = 0, j = 1, \ldots, 5, \qquad (5.117)$$

and

$$\operatorname{plim}(H_n'G_nV_n - H_n'G_n'V_n) = 0. \qquad (5.118)$$

Proof. For $j = 4, 5$, Eq. (5.117) is proved in Section 5.7.3. The case $j = 1$ is trivial, for $\alpha_{n1} = 0$.

By Assumption 5.4 (Section 5.12.1.1) and Theorem 2.5.3

$$\lim_{n \to \infty} \|H_n\|_2^2 = \sum_{l=1}^{k} \|M_l\|_2^2. \qquad (5.119)$$

The assumptions of this lemma allow us to use Lemma 5.4.4. By Lemma 5.13.5

$$
\begin{aligned}
(E\|\alpha_{n2}\|_2^2)^{1/2} &= (E\|H_n'[G_n - h(\delta_n K)]v_n\|_2^2)^{1/2} \\
&\leq c\|H_n\|_2\|G_n - h(\delta_n K)\|_2 \to 0.
\end{aligned}
\qquad (5.120)
$$

Similarly, by Lemmas 5.4.5 and 5.13.5 and bounds (5.24) and (5.28)

$$
\begin{aligned}
(E\|\alpha_{n3}\|_2^2)^{1/2} &= (E\|H_n'[G_n'G_n - h^2(\delta_n K)]v_n\|_2^2)^{1/2} \\
&\leq c\|H_n\|_2[\|G_n' - h(\delta_n K)\|_2\|G_n\|_2 + \|h(\delta_n K)\|_2 \\
&\quad \times \|G_n - h(\delta_n K)\|_2] \to 0.
\end{aligned}
$$

Replacing G_n by G_n' in Eq. (5.120)

$$(E\|H_n'[G_n' - h(\delta_n K)]v_n\|^2)^{1/2} \leq c\|H_n\|_2 \|G_n - h(\delta_n K)\|_2 \to 0.$$

This equation and Eq. (5.120) imply Eq. (5.118):

$$
\begin{aligned}
&(E\|H_n'(G_n - G_n')v_n\|_2^2)^{1/2} \\
&\leq (E\|H_n'[G_n - h(\delta_n K)]v_n\|_2^2)^{1/2} + (E\|H_n'[h(\delta_n K) - G_n']v_n\|_2^2)^{1/2} \to 0. \qquad \blacksquare
\end{aligned}
$$

5.13.7 Estimating Betas

Lemma. *If* $|\rho|v(K) < 1,$ *then*

$$(E\|\beta_{nLj}\|_2^2)^{1/2} \leq c\sum_{i>L} |\lambda_i|, j = 1, \ldots, 5,$$

where c does not depend on n, L.

Proof. As in Lemma 5.13.6, we need to consider only β_{nL2} and β_{nL3}. By Lemmas 5.13.5 and 5.5.3 and Eq. (5.119)

$$
\begin{aligned}
(E\|\beta_{nL2}\|_2^2)^{1/2} &= \{E\|H_n'[h(\delta_n K) - h(\delta_n K_L)]v_n\|_2^2\}^{1/2} \\
&\leq c\|H_n\|_2\|h(\delta_n K) - h(\delta_n K_L)\|_2 \leq c_1 \sum_{i>L} |\lambda_i|.
\end{aligned}
$$

For β_{nL3} we also use Eq. (5.40):

$$
\begin{aligned}
(E\|\beta_{nL3}\|_2^2)^{1/2} &= (E\|H_n'[h^2(\delta_n K) - h^2(\delta_n K_L)]v_n\|_2^2)^{1/2} \\
&\leq c\|h^2(\delta_n K) - h^2(\delta_n K_L)\|_2 \\
&\leq c(\|h(\delta_n K)\|_2 + \|h(\delta_n K_L)\|_2)\|h(\delta_n K) - h(\delta_n K_L)\|_2 \\
&\leq c_1 \sum_{i>L} |\lambda_i|. \qquad\blacksquare
\end{aligned}
$$

5.13.8 Estimating Gammas

Lemma. *If $|\rho|v(\mathcal{K}) < 1$, then for any positive (small) ε and (large) L there exists $n_0 = n_0(\varepsilon, L)$ such that*

$$
E\|\gamma_{nLj}\|_1 \leq c\varepsilon \text{ for all } n \geq n_0, j = 1, \dots, 5,
$$

where c does not depend on n and L.

Proof. Recall definitions (5.109) and (5.112). For the first component, we need to consider:

$$
\gamma_{nL2} = H_n' h(\delta_n K_L) v_n - \sum_{i=1}^{L} h(\lambda_i)(M, F_i)_{L_2} U_{nL,k+i}. \tag{5.121}
$$

By the Double A Lemma 5.6.3 we write the lth component of $H_n' h(\delta_n K_L)v_n$ as

$$
\begin{aligned}
&H_{nl}' h(\delta_n K_L) v_n \\
&= \sum_{p=0}^{\infty} \rho^p \sum_{i_1,\dots,i_{p+1} \leq L} \prod_{j=1}^{p+1} \lambda_{i_j} c_{ni} \sum_{s,t=1}^{n} (\delta_n F_{i_1})_s (H_{nl})_s (\delta_n F_{i_{p+1}})_t v_{nt} \\
&= \sum_{p=0}^{\infty} \rho^p \sum_{i_1,\dots,i_{p+1} \leq L} \prod_{j=1}^{p+1} \lambda_{i_j} c_{ni} (H_{nl}, \delta_n F_{i_1})_{l_2} U_{nL,k+i_{p+1}}. \tag{5.122}
\end{aligned}
$$

However, the lth component of the sum in Eq. (5.121) is

$$\sum_{i=1}^{L} h(\lambda_i)(M_l, F_i)_{L_2} U_{nL,k+i}$$

$$= \sum_{p=0}^{\infty} \rho^p \sum_{i=1}^{L} \lambda_i^{p+1}(M_l, F_i)_{L_2} U_{nL,k+i}$$

$$= \sum_{p=0}^{\infty} \rho^p \sum_{i_1,\dots,i_{p+1} \leq L} \prod_{j=1}^{p+1} \lambda_{i_j} c_{\infty i}(M_l, F_{i_1})_{L_2} U_{nL,k+i_{p+1}} \qquad (5.123)$$

(in the end sum all those terms with unequal $i_1, \dots, i_{p+1}$ actually vanish). The last two equations give the next expression for the lth component of γ_{nL2}:

$$(\gamma_{nL2})_l = \sum_{p=0}^{\infty} \rho^p \sum_{i_1,\dots,i_{p+1} \leq L} \prod_{j=1}^{p+1} \lambda_{i_j} [c_{ni}(H_{nl}, \delta_n F_{i_1})_{l_2}$$

$$- c_{\infty i}(M_l, F_{i_1})_{L_2}] U_{nL,k+i_{p+1}}. \qquad (5.124)$$

By Theorem 2.5.3 $(H_{nl}, \delta_n F_{i_1})_{l_2} \to (M_l, F_{i_1})_{L_2}$ and by Lemma 5.6.1 $c_{ni} \to c_{\infty i}$ as $n \to \infty$. Hence, for any $\varepsilon, L > 0$ there exists $n_0 = n_0(\varepsilon, L)$ such that

$$|c_{ni}(H_{nl}, \delta_n F_{i_1})_{l_2} - c_{\infty i}(M_l, F_{i_1})_{L_2}| < \varepsilon, n \geq n_0, \qquad (5.125)$$

for all i that appear in $(\gamma_{nL2})_l$. Besides, similarly to Eq. (5.63)

$$E|U_{nL,k+i_{p+1}}| \leq (E|U_{nL,k+i_{p+1}}|^2)^{1/2} = [E(v_n' \delta_n F_{i_{p+1}}(\delta_n F_{i_{p+1}})' v_n)]^{1/2}$$

$$\leq \{E[v_n' \delta_n F_{i_{p+1}}(\delta_n F_{i_{p+1}})' v_n]^2\}^{1/4}$$

$$= g(\delta_n F_{i_{p+1}}(\delta_n F_{i_{p+1}})')^{1/2} \leq c\|\delta_n F_{i_{p+1}}\|_2 \leq c. \qquad (5.126)$$

The result of Eqs. (5.124), (5.125) and (5.126) is the desired estimate for $(\gamma_{nL2})_l$:

$$E\|\gamma_{nL2}\|_1 \leq \sum_{l=1}^{k} E|(\gamma_{nL2})_l| \leq c\varepsilon \sum_{p=0}^{\infty} |\rho|^p \sum_{i_1,\dots,i_{p+1} \leq L} \prod_{j=1}^{p+1} |\lambda_{i_j}|$$

$$\leq c\varepsilon \sum_{p=0}^{\infty} (|\rho|\nu(\mathcal{K}))^p \nu(\mathcal{K}) = c_1 \varepsilon.$$

The definitions from Sections 5.13.1 and 5.13.2 imply

$$\gamma_{nL3} = H_n' h^2(\delta_n K_L) v_n - \sum_{i=1}^{L} h^2(\lambda_i)(M, F_i)_{L_2} U_{nL,k+i}.$$

By Lemma 5.6.3

$$H'_{nl}h^2(\delta_n K_L)v_n$$

$$= \sum_{m=0}^{\infty} \rho^m(m+1) \sum_{i_1,\ldots,i_{m+2}\leq L} \prod_{j=1}^{m+2} \lambda_{i_j} c_{ni}(H_{nl}, \delta_n F_{i_1})_{l_2} U_{nL,k+i_{m+2}}$$

because $v'_n\delta_n F_{i_{m+2}} = U_{nL,k+i_{m+2}}$. The next calculation is analogous to that for (5.123)

$$\sum_{i=1}^{L} h^2(\lambda_i)(M_l, F_i)_{L_2} U_{nL,k+i}$$

$$= \sum_{m=0}^{\infty} \rho^m(m+1) \sum_{i=1}^{L} \lambda_i^{m+2}(M_l, F_i)_{L_2} U_{nL,k+i}$$

$$= \sum_{m=0}^{\infty} \rho^m(m+1) \sum_{i_1,\ldots,i_{m+2}\leq L} \prod_{j=1}^{m+2} \lambda_{i_j} c_{\infty i}(M_l, F_{i_1})_{L_2} U_{nL,k+i_{m+2}}.$$

For the lth component of γ_{nL3} we get:

$$(\gamma_{nL3})_l = \sum_{m=0}^{\infty} \rho^m(m+1) \sum_{i_1,\ldots,i_{m+2}\leq L} \prod_{j=1}^{m+2} \lambda_{i_j} [c_{ni}(H_{nl}, \delta_n F_{i_1})_{l_2}$$

$$- c_{\infty i}(M_l, F_{i_1})_{L_2}] U_{nL,k+i_{m+2}}.$$

The rest of the proof is exactly the same as that for γ_{nL2}.   ■

5.13.9 Convergence of the Auxiliary Vector

Lemma. *If $|\rho|v(\mathcal{K}) < 1$, then $\operatorname{dlim}A_n = \Xi$.*

Proof. The condition of the lemma implies $|\rho|\left(\sum_{j=1}^{\infty}\lambda_j^2\right)^{1/2} < 1$. By the Chebyshov inequality and Lemmas 5.7.3 and 5.13.6

$$\operatorname{plim} \alpha_n = 0.$$

From Lemmas 5.7.3 and 5.13.7 we infer that

$$P\left(\|\beta_{nL}\|_1 > \varepsilon\right) \leq \frac{1}{\varepsilon}E\|\beta_{nL}\|_1 \leq \frac{c}{\varepsilon}E\|\beta_{nL}\|_2$$

$$\leq \frac{c}{\varepsilon}\left(E\|\beta_{nL}\|_2^2\right)^{1/2} \leq \frac{c}{\varepsilon}\sum_{i>L}|\lambda_i|,$$

where c does not depend on ε, n, L. Lemmas 5.7.5 and 5.13.8 show that

$$\operatorname{plim}_{n\to\infty} \gamma_{nL} = 0$$

for any fixed L.

The facts we have just listed and Eq. (5.111) ensure that for any fixed L

$$\lim \sup_{n \to \infty} P(\|\mathcal{A}_n - X_{nL}\|_1 > \varepsilon) \le \frac{c}{\varepsilon} \sum_{i > L} |\lambda_i|.$$

Equivalence (5.71) allows us to use Lemmas 5.13.3 and 5.13.4. Application of Billingsley's theorem (Theorem 3.9.5) completes the proof.   ∎

5.14   ASYMPTOTICS OF THE OLS ESTIMATOR FOR MIXED SPATIAL MODEL

5.14.1   Crucial Choice and Assumption

From Lemmas 5.12.7 and 5.13.9 we know that all elements in Eqs. (5.102) and (5.103) converge, except for b_n and $1/d_n$. It is tempting to leave the choice of d_n to the user and make an assumption such as that below.

5.14.1.1 *Tentative Assumption* The sequence $\{d_n\}$ of positive constants is such that the limits $\lim 1/d_n$ and $B = \lim b_n$ exist.

I don't like such a "thing in itself" and prefer d_n governed by the elements of the model. However, the issue is not just a matter of taste. With this tentative assumption it is easy to run into problems. The simplest choice is to select d_n quickly growing to make both $\lim 1/d_n$ and B zero. In that case the inverse of

$$\text{dlim } \Omega_n = \begin{pmatrix} \lim H_n' H_n & 0 \\ 0 & 0 \end{pmatrix} = \Omega$$

does not exist.

Three requirements to the choice of d_n make sense:

1. It should be such that the existence of the limits $\lim 1/d_n$ and B is a plausible but not very restrictive condition.
2. The cases $\lim 1/d_n = 0$ and $B = 0$ should be mutually exclusive, otherwise $|\Omega| = 0$.
3. The components of the numerator and denominator due to Submodels 1 and 2 (Section 5.12.1) should be retained in the mixed model.

5.14.1.2 *Definition*

$$d_n = \max \{\|X_{n1}\|_2 |\beta_1|, \ldots, \|X_{nk}\|_2 |\beta_k|, 1\}.$$

The idea here is the same as that with the time series autoregressive model of (Mynbaev 2006a). The normalizer for Submodel 1 is identically 1, as we know from Theorem 5.8.1. The autoregressive term in the mixed model is subordinate to the exogenous term in the following sense. If the exogenous regressors are bounded, normalizing by unity the autoregressive term in the estimator is sufficient. If the exogenous regressors grow quickly, they pull the dependent variable to the extent that the autoregressive term should be normalized more heavily,

d_n is equivalent to $\tilde{d}_n = \sum_{j=1}^{k} |\beta_j| \|X_{nj}\|_2 + 1: d_n \le \tilde{d}_n \le (k+1)d_n$. Therefore

$$\lim d_n = \infty \text{ is equivalent to } \lim \sum_{j=1}^{k} |\beta_j| \|X_{nj}\|_2 = \infty. \qquad (5.127)$$

Obviously,

$$d_n \ge 1, \ |\beta_j| \|X_{nj}\|_2 / d_n \le 1.$$

The vector b_n with coordinates

$$b_{nj} = \beta_j \|X_{nj}\|_2 / d_n \in [-1, 1], j = 1, \ldots, k$$

is called a balancer in 5.12.2.

5.14.1.3 *Assumption 5.5*   The limits

$$d = \lim d_n \in [1, \infty] \text{ and } B_j = \lim b_{nj} \in [-1, 1], j = 1, \ldots, k$$

exist.

Lemma 5.14.2 partially answers the question of what this assumption means in terms of the regressors and β.

5.14.2 Balancer Properties

Lemma.   *If Assumption 5.5 holds, then the following is true.*

(i) *If $\beta_j = 0$, then X_{nj} is arbitrary and $B_j = 0$.*

(ii) *Let $\beta_j \ne 0$. Then*

(ii$_a$) *$B_j = 0$ is equivalent to $\|X_{nj}\|_2 = o(d_n)$.*

(ii$_b$) *$B_j \ne 0$ is equivalent to $\|X_{nj}\|_2 / d_n \to c_j > 0$.*

(iii) *Conditions*

$$\max_j |B_j| < 1 \text{ and } d > 1 \qquad (5.128)$$

are mutually exclusive. In particular, conditions $B = 0$ and $d = \infty$ are mutually exclusive.

(iv) *$B = 0$ if and only if either*

(iv$_a$) *$\beta = 0$*

  or

(iv$_b$) *$\beta \ne 0$ and $\lim_{n \to \infty} \|X_{nj}\|_2 = 0$ for any j such that $\beta_j \ne 0$.*

In either case $d_n = 1$ for all large n and $d = 1$.

Proof.

(i) is obvious.

(ii) If $\beta_j \neq 0$, then $\|X_{nj}\|_2 = b_{nj}d_n/\beta_j$. This equation implies (ii_a) and (ii_b).

(iii) Suppose that Eq. (5.128) is true and denote $\varepsilon = 1 - \max_i |B_i|$. $d > 1$ implies

$$d_n = \max\{\|X_{n1}\|_2|\beta_1|, \dots, \|X_{nk}\|_2|\beta_k|\} > 1 \quad \text{for all large } n. \quad (5.129)$$

$\max_j |B_j| < 1$ implies

$$|b_{nj}| = \|X_{nj}\|_2|\beta_j|/d_n \leq 1 - \varepsilon/2 \quad \text{for all large } n. \quad (5.130)$$

Equations (5.129) and (5.130) lead to a contradiction: $d_n \leq (1 - \varepsilon/2)d_n$.

(iv) Let $B = 0$. If $\beta = 0$, there is nothing to prove. If $\beta \neq 0$, then consider any j such that $\beta_j \neq 0$. By (ii_a) for any such j we have $\|X_{nj}\|_2 = o(d_n)$. By (iii) the assumption $B = 0$ excludes the possibility $d = \infty$. Hence, $d < \infty$ and $\|X_{nj}\|_2 = o(d_n)$ is equivalent to $\|X_{nj}\|_2 = o(1)$. Since this is true for any j with $\beta_j \neq 0$, we have $d_n = 1$ for all large n and, consequently, $d = 1$. We have proved (iv_b).

Conversely, if (iv_a) is true, then trivially $B = 0$. If (iv_b) is true, then $d_n = 1$ for all large n and $b_{nj} = \|X_{nj}\|_2\beta_j \to 0$ for any j such that $\beta_j \neq 0$. Hence, $B = 0$. ∎

5.14.3 Convergence of the Pair (Ω_n, ζ_n)

It is useful to summarize what we can say about convergence of the elements of the conventional scheme, to see the problem with convergence of the OLS estimator $\hat{\theta}$.

Lemma. *Under Assumptions 5.1–5.5 and $|\rho|v(\mathcal{K}) < 1$ we have*

$$\text{dlim}\,(\Omega_n, \zeta_n) = (\Omega, \zeta),$$

where

$$\zeta = \begin{pmatrix} \Xi_1 \\ B'\Xi_2 + \frac{1}{d}\Xi_4 \end{pmatrix}, \quad (5.131)$$

$$\Omega = \begin{pmatrix} \Gamma_0 & \Gamma_1 B + \frac{1}{d}\Xi_2 \\ B'\Gamma_1 + \frac{1}{d}\Xi_2' & B'\Gamma_2 B + \frac{2}{d}B'\Xi_3 + \frac{1}{d^2}\Xi_5 \end{pmatrix}; \quad (5.132)$$

the matrices Γ_j are defined in Eq. (5.107) and the vector Ξ in Eq. (5.115).

Proof. The expressions for Γ_j are established in Lemma 5.12.7. Convergence in distribution of the auxiliary vector of random components of Ω_n and ζ_n is supplied by Lemma 5.13.9. The expressions of Ω and ζ are obtained by replacing various parts in formulas (5.103) and (5.102) by their respective limits from Lemma 5.12.7,

Eq. (5.115) and Assumption 5.5 (Section 5.14.1.3). The correspondence between components of $\mathcal{A}_n$ and Ξ is seen by comparison of Eqs. (5.111) and (5.115). ∎

The problem with Eq. (5.132) is that it is stochastic and contains both linear (Ξ_2 and Ξ_3) and quadratic (Ξ_5) forms in standard normals.

5.14.4   Multicollinearity Detector

It is curious that infinite-dimensional matrices are helpful in the study of finite-dimensional matrices. Denote

$$\Phi = \left\| Qh_\chi \left(MB + \frac{|\sigma\beta_\psi|}{d} u \right) \right\|_{l_2}^2, \quad \text{where } u = (u_1, u_2, \dots)'. \tag{5.133}$$

Due to the lemma below,

$$|\Omega| > 0 \text{ a.e.} \iff \Phi > 0 \text{ a.e.}$$

This is why we call Φ a *multicollinearity detector* (the notation comes from Φinesse).

Lemma

(i) $\Phi = \mathcal{L}_1\text{-lim}\,\Phi_L$, where

$$\Phi_L = \left\| Qh_\chi \left(MB + \frac{|\sigma\beta_\psi|}{d} u^{(L)} \right) \right\|_{l_2}^2, \quad u^{(L)} = (u_1, u_2, \dots, u_L, 0, \dots)'.$$

(ii) $|\Omega| = |\Gamma_0|\Phi$.

Proof. We start with part (ii) which will help us prove (i). In the determinant of a partitioned matrix rule [Lemma 1.7.6 (i)] put $\Omega_{11} = \Gamma_0$. Then the second determinant at the right of Lemma 1.7.6 (i) is just a number [see Eq. (5.132)]

$$number = \Omega_{22} - \Omega_{21}\Omega_{11}^{-1}\Omega_{12} = B'\Gamma_2 B + \frac{2}{d}B'\Xi_3 + \frac{1}{d^2}\Xi_5$$

$$- \left(B'\Gamma_1 + \frac{1}{d}\Xi_2' \right)\Gamma_0^{-1}\left(\Gamma_1 B + \frac{1}{d}\Xi_2 \right)$$

$$= B'\Gamma_2 B + \frac{2}{d}\underline{B'\Xi_3} + \frac{1}{d^2}\underline{\Xi_5} - \underline{B'\Gamma_1\Gamma_0^{-1}\Gamma_1 B}$$

$$- \frac{1}{d}\underbrace{B'\Gamma_1\Gamma_0^{-1}\Xi_2} - \frac{1}{d}\underbrace{\Xi_2'\Gamma_0^{-1}\Gamma_1 B} - \frac{1}{d^2}\underline{\Xi_2'\Gamma_0^{-1}\Xi_2}.$$

Collect similarly underlined terms,

$$number = B'(\Gamma_2 - \Gamma_1\Gamma_0^{-1}\Gamma_1)B + \frac{1}{d^2}(\Xi_5 - \Xi_2'\Gamma_0^{-1}\Xi_2)$$

$$+ \frac{2}{d}B'(\Xi_3 - \Gamma_1\Gamma_0^{-1}\Xi_2).$$

Now replace the matrices Γ_j by their expressions from Eq. (5.107) and recall the definitions of Ξ_i given in Eq. (5.115):

$$number = B'[\mathcal{M}'h_\chi^2\mathcal{M} - \mathcal{M}'h_\chi\mathcal{M}(\mathcal{M}'\mathcal{M})^{-1}\mathcal{M}'h_\chi\mathcal{M}]B$$

$$+ \frac{(\sigma\beta_\psi)^2}{d^2}[u'h_\chi^2 u - (\mathcal{M}'h_\chi u)'(\mathcal{M}'\mathcal{M})^{-1}\mathcal{M}'h_\chi u]$$

$$+ \frac{2}{d}|\sigma\beta_\psi|B'[\mathcal{M}'h_\chi^2 u - \mathcal{M}'h_\chi\mathcal{M}(\mathcal{M}'\mathcal{M})^{-1}\mathcal{M}'h_\chi u]. \qquad (5.134)$$

Next, employ the principal projectors of Lemma 5.12.5:

$$number = (h_\chi\mathcal{M}B)'(I - P)h_\chi\mathcal{M}B + \frac{(\sigma\beta_\psi)^2}{d^2}(h_\chi u)'(I - P)h_\chi u$$

$$+ \frac{2}{d}|\sigma\beta_\psi|(h_\chi\mathcal{M}B)'(I - P)h_\chi u$$

$$= (h_\chi\mathcal{M}B)'Q^2 h_\chi\mathcal{M}B + \frac{(\sigma\beta_\psi)^2}{d^2}(h_\chi u)'Q^2 h_\chi u$$

$$+ \frac{|\sigma\beta_\psi|}{d}(h_\chi\mathcal{M}B)'Q^2 h_\chi u + \frac{|\sigma\beta_\psi|}{d}(h_\chi u)'Q^2 h_\chi\mathcal{M}B$$

$$= \left\|Qh_\chi\left(\mathcal{M}B + \frac{|\sigma\beta_\psi|}{d}u\right)\right\|_{l_2}^2.$$

Thus,

$$\Omega_{22} - \Omega_{21}\Omega_{11}^{-1}\Omega_{12} = \Phi. \qquad (5.135)$$

Equation (5.134) is particularly convenient to see that statement (i) is true. It can also be deduced from Lemma 5.13.4(ii). ∎

5.14.5 Multicollinearity Detector and Exogenous Regressors Domination

From Eq. (5.127) we know that $d = \infty$ only when at least one of the exogenous regressors grows to infinity. In this case we say that *the exogenous regressors dominate*, and by Lemma 5.14.2(iii) $B \neq 0$. If, however, $B = 0$, then by Lemma 5.14.2(iv) all exogenous regressors are negligible in some sense and $d = 1$. In this situation it is natural to say that *the autoregressive term dominates*.

Lemma. *If the exogenous regressors dominate, then* Φ *is the squared distance from the image of* $B'\mathcal{M}$ *under the mapping* $h(\mathcal{K})$ *to the linear span* $\mathfrak{M}$ *of functions* $M_1, \ldots, M_k$:

$$\Phi = \mathrm{dist}^2(h(\mathcal{K})B'\mathcal{M}, \mathfrak{M}).$$

Proof. The image of P is characterized in Lemma 5.12.5. It equals $\mathcal{X}\mathfrak{M}$. Q projects onto the subspace of l_2 orthogonal to $\mathcal{X}\mathfrak{M}$ and $\|Qx\|_2^2$ is the squared distance from x to $\mathcal{X}\mathcal{M}$. Thus, putting $d = \infty$ in Eq. (5.133) we have

$$\Phi = \|Qh_{\mathcal{X}}\mathcal{M}B\|_{l_2}^2 = \mathrm{dist}^2(h_{\mathcal{X}}\mathcal{M}B, \mathcal{X}\mathfrak{M}). \tag{5.136}$$

Using the main property of the genie Eq. (5.106) we have

$$h_{\mathcal{X}}\mathcal{M}B = h_{\mathcal{X}} \sum_{l=1}^{k} B_l \mathcal{X}M_l = h_{\mathcal{X}}\mathcal{X}B'M = \mathcal{X}h(\mathcal{K})B'M. \tag{5.137}$$

Since $\mathcal{X}$ is an isomorphism, Eq. (5.136) and (5.137) imply

$$\Phi = \mathrm{dist}^2(\mathcal{X}h(\mathcal{K})B'\mathcal{M}, \mathcal{X}\mathfrak{M}) = \mathrm{dist}^2(h(\mathcal{K})B'\mathcal{M}, \mathfrak{M}). \qquad\blacksquare$$

5.14.6 Main Theorem

Theorem. *Let Assumptions 5.1–5.5 and* $|\rho|v(\mathcal{K}) < 1$ *hold. Then the following statements are true.*

(i) $|\Omega| > 0$ *a.e. if and only if*

$$\Phi > 0\, a.e. \tag{5.138}$$

If condition (5.138) holds, then the OLS estimator $\hat{\theta}$ *for the mixed spatial model converges in distribution,*

$$\mathcal{D}_n(\hat{\theta} - \theta) \xrightarrow{d} \Omega^{-1}\zeta, \tag{5.139}$$

where

$$\Omega^{-1} = \frac{1}{\Phi}\Lambda\Psi\Lambda, \ \Lambda = \begin{pmatrix} \Gamma_0^{-1} & 0 \\ 0 & 1 \end{pmatrix},$$

$$\Psi = \begin{pmatrix} \Gamma_0 + \Omega_{12}\Omega_{21} & -\Omega_{12} \\ -\Omega_{21} & 1 \end{pmatrix}. \tag{5.140}$$

(ii) *In particular, when the autoregressive term dominates, ζ, Ψ and Φ simplify to*

$$\zeta = \begin{pmatrix} \Xi_1 \\ \Xi_4 \end{pmatrix}, \quad \Psi = \begin{pmatrix} \Gamma_0 + \frac{1}{d^2}\Xi_2\Xi_2' & -\Xi_2 \\ -\Xi_2' & 1 \end{pmatrix},$$

$$\Phi = (\sigma\beta_\psi)^2 \|Qh_\chi u\|_2^2.$$

(5.141)

As we see, $\beta_\psi \neq 0$ is necessary for Eq. (5.138) in this case.

(iii) *In the other special case, when the exogenous regressors dominate, ζ, Ψ and Φ become*

$$\zeta = \begin{pmatrix} \Xi_1 \\ B'\Xi_2 \end{pmatrix}, \quad \Psi = \begin{pmatrix} \Gamma_0 + \Gamma_1 BB'\Gamma_1 & -\Gamma_1 B \\ -B'\Gamma_1 & 1 \end{pmatrix}, B \neq 0, \quad (5.142)$$

$$\Phi = \text{dist}^2(h(\mathcal{K})B'M, \mathfrak{M}).$$

(5.143)

This means that linear independence of $h(\mathcal{K})B'M$ and $M_1, \ldots, M_k$ is necessary and sufficient for Eq. (5.138). Moreover, if the constant Φ is positive, then the convergence relation has a more familiar format

$$\mathcal{D}_n(\hat{\theta} - \theta) \overset{d}{\to} N(0, (\sigma\beta_\psi)^2\Omega^{-1})$$

(5.144)

where

$$\Omega = \begin{pmatrix} \Gamma_0 & \Gamma_1 B \\ B'\Gamma_1 & B'\Gamma_2 B \end{pmatrix}.$$

Recall that Ξ_1, Ξ_2 and Ξ_3 are linear in standard normals, while Ξ_4 and Ξ_5 are quadratic forms of standard normals. In the case of domination by the exogenous regressors, the quadratic parts disappear from ζ and Ω and Ω is nonstochastic. If the autoregressive term dominates, the linear part vanishes in ζ_2 and Ω_{22}. These are the traces of features of Submodels 1 and 2 (Section 5.12.1). None of these extreme cases involves Ξ_3, which reflects interaction between the exogenous regressors and the spatial matrix. Condition Eq. (5.138) is called an *invertibility criterion*.

Proof.

(i) Equivalence of the invertibility criterion to the absence of multicollinearity follows from Lemma 5.14.4. Equation (5.139) is a consequence of Lemma 5.14.3 and CTM. It remains to prove expression (5.140) for Ω^{-1}. In terms of the partition of Ω we use the formula for the inverse of Lemma 1.7.6(ii), which looks like this:

$$\Omega^{-1} = \begin{pmatrix} \Omega_{11}^{-1} + \Omega_{11}^{-1}\Omega_{12}G\Omega_{21}\Omega_{11}^{-1} & -\Omega_{11}^{-1}\Omega_{12}G \\ -G\Omega_{21}\Omega_{11}^{-1} & G \end{pmatrix},$$

where $G = (\Omega_{22} - \Omega_{21}\Omega_{11}^{-1}\Omega_{12})^{-1}$. From Eq. (135) we know that $G = 1/\Phi$. Hence,

$$\Omega^{-1} = \frac{1}{\Phi} \begin{pmatrix} \Gamma_0^{-1} + \Gamma_0^{-1}\Omega_{12}\Omega_{21}\Gamma_0^{-1} & -\Gamma_0^{-1}\Omega_{12} \\ -\Omega_{21}\Gamma_0^{-1} & 1 \end{pmatrix}$$

$$= \frac{1}{\Phi} \begin{pmatrix} \Gamma_0^{-1} & 0 \\ 0 & 1 \end{pmatrix} \begin{pmatrix} \Gamma_0 + \Omega_{12}\Omega_{21} & -\Omega_{12} \\ -\Omega_{21} & 1 \end{pmatrix} \begin{pmatrix} \Gamma_0^{-1} & 0 \\ 0 & 1 \end{pmatrix},$$

which proves Eq. (5.140).

(ii) Eq. (5.141) obtains from Equations (5.140), (5.131), (5.133) and (5.132) on putting $B = 0$, $d = 1$.

(iii) Similarly, Eq. (5.142) follows from Eqs. (5.140), (5.131) and (5.132), with $d = \infty$. $B \neq 0$ by Lemma 5.14.2(iii). Equation (5.143) is proved in Lemma 5.14.5.

Now we prove Eq. (5.144). In the case under consideration directly from Eq. (5.132)

$$\Omega = \begin{pmatrix} \Gamma_0 & \Gamma_1 B \\ B'\Gamma_1 & B'\Gamma_2 B \end{pmatrix}.$$

However, by definitions Eq. (5.107) and Eq. (5.115)

$$V(\zeta) = E \begin{pmatrix} \Xi_1 \\ B'\Xi_2 \end{pmatrix} \begin{pmatrix} \Xi_1' & \Xi_2'B \end{pmatrix}$$

$$= (\sigma\beta_\psi)^2 \begin{pmatrix} EM'uu'M & EM'uu'h_\chi MB \\ EB'M'h_\chi uu'M & EB'M'h_\chi uu'h_\chi MB \end{pmatrix}$$

$$= (\sigma\beta_\psi)^2 \begin{pmatrix} M'M & M'h_\chi MB \\ B'M'h_\chi M & B'M'h_\chi^2 MB \end{pmatrix} = (\sigma\beta_\psi)^2 \Omega.$$

These equations imply Eq. (5.144). ■

5.14.7 Example

In the model $Y_n = \beta l_n + \rho W_n Y_n + v_n$ with a constant term and Case matrix W_n the regressors are collinear because $W_n l_n = l_n$ and $Z_n = W_n(l_n, Y_n)$ is of rank at most 2. Therefore we consider $Y_n = \beta l_n + \rho \widetilde{W}_n Y_n + v_n$. The pseudo-Case matrix $\widetilde{W}_n$ satisfies the assumptions of Theorem 5.14.6 with $\sum_{i \geq 1} |\lambda_i| \sim 2r - 1$, if r is fixed and $m \to \infty$. For simplicity, the components of the error vector v_n are assumed i.i.d. with mean 0 and variance σ^2. Application of Theorem 5.14.6 leads to the following conclusions. The conditions $d = \infty$ (exogenous regressors domination) and $B = 0$ (autoregressive term domination) are mutually exclusive and together cover all possible β. The theoretical statements combined with long and dull calculations result in Table 5.4. In this example ζ and Φ contain quadratic forms of standard normal variables, but those

TABLE 5.4   Asymptotic Distribution with a Constant Term and Case Matrix

$\beta = 0$	$\beta \neq 0$
$d = 1, B = 0$ (autoregressive term domination)	$d = \infty, \max |B_j| = 1$ (exogenous regressor domination)
If $r = 1$, there is asymptotic multicollinearity.	For any natural r, there is asymptotic multicollinearity
If $r \geq 2$, then $(\sqrt{n}(\hat{\beta} - \beta), \hat{\rho} - \rho) \xrightarrow{p} (0, 1 - \rho)$.	

Mynbaev (2010).

forms cancel out in $\Phi^{-1}\zeta$. Still, the asymptotic distribution, when it exists, is not normal. In particular, $\hat{\beta}$ is consistent and $\hat{\rho}$ is not when $\beta = 0$, $r \geq 2$.

Computer simulations confirm the theoretical results. For pseudo-Case matrices the values of m, r were fixed at $m = 200$, $r = 10$ giving $n = 1000$. Each of the values $\beta = -1, 0, 1$ was combined with 20 values of ρ from the segment $[-0.2, 0.2]$, to see if there is deterioration of convergence at the boundary of the theoretical interval of convergence $\rho \in (-1/19, 1/19)$. For each combination (β, ρ) 100 simulations were run. The ranges of sample means and sample standard deviations for the samples of size 100 are reported in Table 5.5 (for small values we indicate just the order of magnitude). As we see, the estimate of $\beta = 0$ is good, as predicted, and the estimates of $\beta = \pm 1$ are not. As a result of inconsistency, the estimate of ρ is always bad (closer to 1 than to the true ρ). To see the dynamics of $\hat{\rho}$ as m increases we combined $\beta = 0$, $\rho = -0.2$ with $m = 200, 300, \ldots, 1000$. The corresponding values of $\hat{\rho}$ approach 1, starting from 0.9966 and monotonically increasing to 0.999. These simulations did not reveal any deterioration of convergence outside the theoretical interval, which suggests that the convergence may hold in a wider interval. For combinations $\beta = -1, 0, 1$ with $\rho = 0.2$ the null hypothesis of normal distribution for $\hat{\beta}$ and $\hat{\rho}$ is rejected (the p-value of the Anderson-Darling statistic is less than 0.0001). Recall that a similar worrisome evidence was found in the case of a purely autoregressive spatial model.

The results for the Case matrices are reported in Table 5.6. Owing to multicollinearity, there is no definite pattern in these numbers, and for the combination $\beta = 0$, $\rho = -0.2$ an increase in m from 200 to 1000 did not improve the estimates. Finally, in cases $\beta = \pm 1$ for both the Case and pseudo-Case matrices the sample

TABLE 5.5   Simulation Results for Pseudo-Case Matrices

Statistic	$\beta = -1$	$\beta = 0$	$\beta = 1$
mean β	10^{-12}	10^{-12}	10^{-16}
st.d. β	10^{-11}	10^{-11}	10^{-15}
mean ρ	0.995	0.995	0.995
st.d. ρ	10^{-11}	10^{-11}	10^{-14}

Mynbaev (2010).

TABLE 5.6 Simulation Results for Case Matrices

Statistic	$\beta = -1$	$\beta = 0$	$\beta = 1$
mean β	$[-1.7, -1.02]$	$[-0.92, -0.17]$	$[-0.008, 0.014]$
s.d. β	$[0.54, 1.15]$	$[0.57, 1.63]$	$[0.02, 0.05]$
mean $\hat{\rho} - \rho$	$[-0.82, -0.02]$	$[-0.95, -0.06]$	$[-0.79, -0.03]$
s.d. ρ	$[0.43, 1.34]$	$[0.49, 1.95]$	$[0.46, 2.35]$

Mynbaev (2010).

correlation between the estimates of β and ρ was at least 0.99 in absolute value. For the GAUSS code see (Mynbaev, 2006b).

We also verified that the distinction made in Theorem 5.14.6 between the autoregressive term and exogenous term domination reflects the reality. The first column of Table 5.4 shows that Theorem 5.14.6 correctly works in the case of the autoregressive term domination. Column 2 of that table is not satisfactory because of the asymptotic multicollinearity. To make the exogenous regressor dominant and stay within the same example, we set $m = 10, r = 200$ and choose β large relative to ρ ($\rho = 10^{-5}$; $\beta = 10^5$). Then, despite the asymptotic multicollinearity, the distributions of both $\hat{\rho}$ and $\hat{\beta}$ are approximately normal (the p-value of the Anderson–Darling statistics is higher than 0.9). Both estimates are still biased.

5.14.8 Conclusions

Estimation for the mixed spatial model is the subject of quite a few papers and books. Among the estimation techniques are the ML, MM, instrumental variables, least squares and two-stage least squares (see Ord, 1975; Anselin, 1988; Kelejian and Prucha, 1998, 1999; Lee, 2002, 2003, 2004a).

In the context of the ML estimation (Lee, 2004a) lists several problems that arise in spatial models:

1. The estimators may have rates of convergence lower than the customary $\sqrt{n}$.

2. Different components of the estimator may converge at different rates.

3. Under some circumstances, the estimator may be inconsistent.

4. The asymptotic behavior of the estimator depends on the degree of collinearity of the exogenous regressors with the spatial term.

The impression I get from the cited literature is that the same problems arise with any other estimation procedure. I am in favor of intelligent formulas which think for you and provide the necessary rates of convergence or address the multicollinearity issue without you having to sort the things out by selecting the appropriate conditions. Theorem 5.14.6 does just that. The normalizer $\mathcal{D}_n$ adjusts to the rate of growth of the regressors, including the spatially lagged term. It does not matter whether the exogenous regressors grow, like polynomial trends, or are bounded. The invertibility criterion covers all possible cases, from $B = 0$ to $d = \infty$. Most importantly, the asymptotic distribution includes linear combinations of χ^2 variables discovered, in the case of Submodel 1 (Section 5.12.1), in Mynbaev and Ullah (2008), (Theorem 5.8.1).

The present theory is far from being complete. Three important issues have not been considered here because of their complexity.

1. For the purposes of statistical inference, we need to estimate the variance − covariance matrix of the vector $\Phi^{-1}\zeta$. The situation is relatively simple in the case of exogenous regressors domination, when Φ is constant, $\Phi_n = \overline{H}'_n \overline{H}_n$ converges to Φ in probability and, hence, Φ_n^{-1} estimates Φ^{-1}. $(\sigma \beta_\psi)^2$ can be estimated by $\Phi_n^{-1} V(\zeta_n)$ (see the end of the proof of Theorem 5.14.6). Even in this case there is a problem because $\Phi_n = \overline{H}'_n \overline{H}_n$ depends, through d_n, on unknown β. This problem is partially alleviated by the fact that ζ_n depends on β in the same way. Therefore if some of $\|x_n^{(1)}\|_2, \ldots, \|x_n^{(k)}\|_2$ tend to infinity and, for example, $\|x_n^{(1)}\|_2$ is the largest of these quantities and $\beta_1 \neq 0$, then $d_n = \|x_n^{(1)}\|_2 |\beta_1|$ for all large n and the quantities that depend on β_1 in Φ_n and $V(\zeta_n)$ cancel out. If, however, all of $\|x_n^{(1)}\|_2, \ldots, \|x_n^{(k)}\|_2$ are bounded, then $1 \leq d_n \leq$ constant, so that dependence on β is weak. In the general case, when Φ is stochastic, there is no simple link between estimates of Φ, $V(\zeta)$ and $V(\Phi^{-1}\zeta)$. At the moment I can suggest no constructive ideas on the matter and invite the profession to think about it.

2. The second issue is consistency of the OLS estimator. Again, the problem deserves a separate study, and only general considerations are offered here. First, for a purely spatial model we have shown that, because of the presence of quadratic forms in standard normals in the asymptotic distribution, the consistency notion itself should be modified, from $\text{plim}\,\hat{\rho} = \rho$ to $\text{plim}\,\hat{\rho} = \rho + X$ where $EX = 0$. Since the mixed spatial model inherits those quadratic forms, the situation for the problem at hand must be even more complex. Second, what is known for Submodel 2 (Section 5.12.1), about consistency (Amemiya, 1985, Theorem 3.5.1) and asymptotic normality (Amemiya, 1985, Theorem 3.5.4) of the OLS estimator, indicates that consistency and convergence in distribution are two essentially different problems that require different approaches and conditions (also see Chapter 6). That is to say, trying to extract from Theorem 5.14.6 conditions sufficient for consistency may not be the best idea. Still, if we wish to realize it, this is how. The components of $\hat{\theta} - \theta$ converge with different rates. This can be written as $m_{ni}(\hat{\theta}_i - \theta_i) \xrightarrow{d} \phi_i, i = 1, \ldots, k+1$, where m_{ni} are normalizing multipliers and ϕ_i are random variables. $m_{ni} \to 0$ means a swelling distribution, so in such cases $\hat{\theta}_i - \theta_i$ does not converge in probability. If $m_{ni} \to \infty$, then $\hat{\theta}_i - \theta_i$ behaves as $1/m_{ni}\phi_i$, which goes to 0 in probability. Finally, for i with $m_{ni} \equiv 1$ it suffices to impose conditions providing $\phi_i = 0$.

3. Finally, because of nontransparent conditions in papers listed in Section 5.11.1 it is desirable to reconsider asymptotic results for other estimation methods.

CHAPTER 6

CONVERGENCE ALMOST EVERYWHERE

T HIS CHAPTER is based on a series of papers by Tze Leung Lai and Ching Zong Wei published in the 1980s. Let $\{\mathcal{F}_n: n \geq 1\}$ be a sequence of increasing $(\mathcal{F}_n \subseteq \mathcal{F}_{n+1})$ σ-fields. It is convenient to call a sequence of random variables $\{w_n\}$ *premeasurable* (relative to $\{\mathcal{F}_n\}$) if w_n is $\mathcal{F}_{n-1}$-measurable for every $n \geq 1$. Lai and Wei first investigated the convergence of the series $\sum_1^\infty w_i e_i$ with a m.d. sequence $\{e_n, \mathcal{F}_n\}$ and premeasurable coefficients $\{w_n\}$ and then applied the statements obtained to the study of stochastic regression models. Even though their models contain no deterministic regressors, there are two reasons to include the results by Lai and Wei in this book. First, their approach was extended later by Nielsen (2005) to include deterministic regressors, in addition to the lags of the dependent variable, and that extension is impossible to understand without going through the results by Lai and Wei. The second reason is that one of their results is applied in Chapter 7.

Unlike in Chapters 4 and 5, here only strong convergence is used. Therefore we have to go through a range of related technical tools, from conditional versions of the Borel–Cantelli lemma, Jensen's inequality, and so on, to the martingale convergence theorem.

6.1 THEORETICAL BACKGROUND

6.1.1 Borel–Cantelli Lemma

Let $\{A_n\}$ be an arbitrary sequence of measurable sets. We say that the event $\omega \in A_n$ occurs *infinitely often* (notation: A_n i.o.) if there is a sequence $n_1 < n_2 < \cdots < n_k \to \infty$ such that $\omega \in A_{n_i}$ for all i (the sequence $\{n_i\}$ depends on ω).

Lemma. *For any measurable events A_i the implication*

$$\sum_{i=1}^\infty P(A_i) < \infty \quad \Rightarrow \quad P(A_n \, i.o.) = 0 \tag{6.1}$$

is true.

Short-Memory Linear Processes and Econometric Applications. Kairat T. Mynbaev
© 2011 John Wiley & Sons, Inc. Published 2011 by John Wiley & Sons, Inc.

Proof. The verbal definition given above immediately translates to $\{A_n \text{ i.o.}\} = \bigcap_{n=1}^{\infty} \bigcup_{m=n}^{\infty} A_m$. The traditional proof of the lemma is based on this equation. A more transparent proof employs the *counting functions* of $\{A_n\}$ defined by $C = \sum_{1}^{\infty} 1(A_i)$. For each ω, the value $C(\omega)$ shows the number of those sets A_i that contain ω, and $\{C = \infty\} = \{A_n \text{ i.o. }\}$. If $\sum_{i=1}^{\infty} P(A_i) < \infty$, then by the monotone convergence theorem (Davidson, 1994, p. 60)

$$EC \leq \lim_{n \to \infty} \sup E \sum_{1}^{n} 1(A_i) = \lim_{n \to \infty} \sup \sum_{1}^{n} P(A_i) < \infty.$$

This implies $C < \infty$ a.s. and $P(A_n \text{ i.o.}) = 0$. ∎

6.1.2   Conditional Borel–Cantelli Lemma

Lemma.   (Hall and Heyde, 1980, p. 32) *Let* $\{Z_n\}$ *be a sequence of random variables adapted to an increasing sequence of σ-fields* $\{\mathcal{F}_n\}$ *and such that* $0 \leq Z_n \leq 1$. *Then* $\sum_{i=1}^{\infty} Z_i < \infty$ *a.s. if and only if* $\sum_{i=1}^{\infty} E(Z_i \mid \mathcal{F}_{i-1}) < \infty$ *a.s.*

Just to digest this statement, consider a sequence of events $\{A_n\}$ adapted to $\{\mathcal{F}_n\}$. By the definition of conditional probability of events

$$\sum_{i=1}^{\infty} P(A_i \mid \mathcal{F}_{i-1}) = \sum_{i=1}^{\infty} E(1(A_i) \mid \mathcal{F}_{i-1}).$$

If the premise of the Borel–Cantelli lemma holds and, hence, $C < \infty$ a.s., then from

$$\infty > \sum_{i=1}^{\infty} P(A_i) = \sum_{i=1}^{\infty} E1(A_i)$$

$$= \sum_{i=1}^{\infty} E[E(1(A_i) \mid \mathcal{F}_{i-1})] \geq E\left[\sum_{i=1}^{\infty} P(A_i \mid \mathcal{F}_{i-1})\right]$$

we see that $\sum_{i=1}^{\infty} P(A_i) < \infty \Rightarrow \sum_{i=1}^{\infty} P(A_i \mid \mathcal{F}_{i-1}) < \infty$ a.s. Since the variables $Z_n = 1(A_n)$ satisfy the assumptions of the conditional Borel–Cantelli lemma, we have a related proposition $P(A_n \text{ i.o.}) = 0 \Longleftrightarrow \sum_{i=1}^{\infty} P(A_i \mid \mathcal{F}_{i-1}) < \infty$ a.s.

6.1.3   Martingale Convergence Theorem

Theorem.   (Chow, 1965; Hall and Heyde, 1980, Theorem 2.16) *Let* $\{X_n, \mathcal{F}_n : n \geq 1\}$ *be a m.d. sequence with* $E|X_n|^p < \infty$ *for each* n *and some* $p \in [1, 2]$. *Then* $S_n = \sum_{1}^{n} X_i$ *converges a.s. on the set* $\{\sum_{i=1}^{\infty} E(|X_i|^p \mid \mathcal{F}_{i-1}) < \infty\}$.

This theorem is used herein as often as Theorem 6.1.4, which is its consequence. Chow's contribution was to extend the known result from $p = 2$ to $p < 2$. The importance of this extension is seen in later applications.

6.1.4   Martingale Strong Law (Convergence of Normed Sums)

Instead of convergence of $\{S_n\}$ itself we may be interested in convergence of normed sums S_n/U_n, where the norming sequence $\{U_n\}$ is a nondecreasing sequence of positive random variables. To this end, Theorem 6.1.3 can be applied to obtain the following proposition.

Theorem.   (Hall and Heyde, 1980) *Let* $\{X_n, \mathcal{F}_n: n \geq 1\}$ *be a m.d. sequence and let* $\{U_n\}$ *be a premeasurable nondecreasing sequence of positive random variables. Suppose* $1 \leq p \leq 2$ *and* $E|X_n|^p < \infty$ *for each* n. *Then* $\lim_{n \to \infty} S_n/U_n = 0$ *a.s. on the set*

$$\left\{ \lim_{n \to \infty} U_n = \infty, \ \sum_{i=1}^{\infty} U_i^{-p} E(|X_i|^p \mid \mathcal{F}_{i-1}) < \infty \right\}$$

where $S_n = \sum_1^n X_i$.

6.1.5   Conditional Hölder Inequality

(Long, 1993, p. 3) *Let* $p, q \in [1, \infty]$ *be Hölder conjugates, as in the usual Hölder inequality,* $1/p + 1/q = 1$, *and let* $\mathcal{G}$ *be a sub-σ-field of* $\mathcal{F}$. *Then*

$$|E(fg|\mathcal{G})| \leq [E(|f|^p|\mathcal{G})]^{1/p}[E(|g|^q|\mathcal{G})]^{1/q}.$$

6.1.6   Conditional Jensen Inequality

(Long, 1993, p. 5) *Let* ϕ *be a convex function defined on* (a, b). *Suppose that* $f \in L_1(\Omega)$ *is real with values in* (a, b) *for almost all* ω *and such that* $\phi(f) \in L_1(\Omega)$ *or* $\phi(f)$ *is nonnegative [definition 1.1.2 from (Long, 1993) extends* $E(f|\mathcal{G})$ *from* $f \in L_1$ *to nonnegative* f]. *Then* $\phi(E(f|\mathcal{G})) \leq E(\phi(f)|\mathcal{G})$ *a.s.*

6.1.7   Conditional Chebyshov Inequality

Lemma.   *For* $p \geq 1$ *and* $\mathcal{G}$-*measurable* g *such that* $g > 0$ *a.s. one has* $P(f > g|\mathcal{G}) \leq g^{-p}E(|f|^p|\mathcal{G})$.

Proof.

$$P(f > g|\mathcal{G}) = E(1(f/g > 1)|\mathcal{G}) \leq E(|f/g|^p 1(f/g > 1)|\mathcal{G}) \leq g^{-p}E(|f|^p|\mathcal{G}). \ \blacksquare$$

6.1.8   Paley–Zygmund Inequality

This statement and its proof are taken from Burkholder (1968, Lemma 1).

Lemma.   *Let* $\alpha > \beta \geq 0$. *If a real random variable* X *satisfies* $EX \geq \alpha$ *and* $EX^2 = 1$, *then* $P(X \geq \beta) \geq (\alpha - \beta)^2$.

Proof.   Let $Y = 1(X \geq \beta)$. Then

$$\alpha \leq EX = EXY + EX(1 - Y) \leq (EY^2)^{1/2} + \beta = [P(X \geq \beta)]^{1/2} + \beta$$

and the desired inequality follows.   ∎

6.1.9   Conditional Paley–Zygmund Inequality

For a random variable d let us call the variable $v = [E(d^2 | \mathcal{G})]^{1/2}$ its *variation*. The following lemma, taken from Chow (1969, Lemmas 1 and 1′), roughly means that if the conditional mean $m = E(d | \mathcal{G})$ of a random variable d is not very small relative to its variation v, then d itself is not very small relative to v either.

Lemma.   *Let d be a nonnegative random variable and let $\mathcal{G} \subseteq \mathcal{F}$ be a σ-field. If $P(3\lambda v \leq m < \infty) = 1$ for some constant $\lambda > 0$, then*

$$P(d > \lambda v | \mathcal{G}) \geq \lambda^2. \tag{6.2}$$

Proof.   First we prove an auxiliary statement: if $\lambda \geq 0$ is a $\mathcal{G}$-measurable random variable and $P(m < \infty) = 1$, then

$$vP(d > \lambda v | \mathcal{G}) \geq \lambda(m - 2\lambda v). \tag{6.3}$$

We can assume that $\lambda > 0$ a.s. because if $\lambda \geq 0$, we can prove Eq. (6.3) for $\lambda + \varepsilon$ with a positive constant ε and then let $\varepsilon \to 0$. Let us split Ω in three sets: $A = \{d \leq \lambda v\}$, $B = \{\lambda v < d \leq v/\lambda\}$ and $C = \{d > v/\lambda\}$. On A, d is bounded by λv, which is $\mathcal{G}$-measurable; on B the lower bound we need for d is available, and on C the variation v helps to dominate d. The estimation on A is the easiest:

$$\begin{aligned} m = E(d | \mathcal{G}) &= E[d1(A) + d1(B) + d1(C) | \mathcal{G}] \\ &\leq \lambda v + E(d1(B) | \mathcal{G}) + E(d1(C) | \mathcal{G}). \end{aligned} \tag{6.4}$$

By the definition of conditional probability

$$E(d1(B) | \mathcal{G}) \leq (v/\lambda)E(1(\lambda v < d) | \mathcal{G}) = (v/\lambda)P(d > \lambda v) | \mathcal{G}). \tag{6.5}$$

By the conditional Hölder and Chebyshov inequalities with $p = 2$

$$\begin{aligned} E(d1(C) | \mathcal{G}) &\leq [E(d^2 | \mathcal{G})]^{1/2}[P(d > v/\lambda) | \mathcal{G})]^{1/2} \\ &\leq v[(\lambda/v)^2 E(d^2 | \mathcal{G})]^{1/2} = \lambda v. \end{aligned} \tag{6.6}$$

From Eqs. (6.4), (6.5) and (6.6) we get $m \leq 2\lambda v + (v/\lambda)P(d > \lambda v) | \mathcal{G})$, which proves Eq. (6.3).

Now we treat λ as a positive constant. From the assumption $3\lambda v \leq m$ a.s. we have $m - 2\lambda v \geq \lambda v$, so Eq. (6.3) gives Eq. (6.2).[1]   ∎

---

[1] Here and in a couple more places I am going to be honest. When v is positive in $vP(d > \lambda v | G) \geq \lambda^2 v$, we can divide both sides by v to get Eq. (6.2). What Chow does when $v = 0$ I have no idea.

6.1.10 Lemma on Convex Combinations of Nonnegative Random Variables

Lemma. (Burkholder, 1968, Lemma 2) *Let* $Y_1, \ldots, Y_n$ *be nonnegative random variables that are bounded away from zero on sets of positive probability:* $P(Y_i \geq \delta) \geq \varepsilon$, $1 \leq i \leq n$, *with some constants* $\varepsilon, \delta > 0$. *Denote* S *the simplex*

$$S = \left\{ a \in \mathbb{R}^n : a_i > 0, \ \sum_{i=1}^{n} a_i = 1 \right\}.$$

Then any convex combination $\sum_{i=1}^{n} a_i Y_i$ *with coefficients* $a \in S$ *is bounded away from zero on a set of positive probability:* $P\left(\sum_{i=1}^{n} a_i Y_i \geq \gamma \delta \varepsilon\right) \geq (1 - \gamma)^2 \varepsilon$ *for any* $\gamma \in (0, 1)$ *and* $a \in S$.

Proof. It may and will be assumed that the probability space is nonatomic[2]: for any A with $P(A) > 0$ there is $B \subseteq A$ such that $0 < P(B) < P(A)$. Then there exist measurable sets $A_i \subseteq \{Y_i \geq \delta\}$ such that $P(A_i) = \varepsilon$. Let $X_i = \delta 1(A_i)$ and $X = \sum_{i=1}^{n} a_i X_i$, $a \in S$. Then $EX = \varepsilon \delta$ and, by Hölder's inequality,

$$EX^2 = E\left(\sum_{i=1}^{n} a_i^{1/2} a_i^{1/2} X_i \right)^2 \leq E \sum_{i=1}^{n} a_i X_i^2 = \delta^2 \sum_{i=1}^{n} a_i P(A_i) = \varepsilon \delta^2.$$

Therefore α defined by $\alpha = EX(EX^2)^{-1/2}$ satisfies $\alpha^2 \geq \varepsilon$. Letting $\beta = \alpha \gamma$ we have $\alpha > \beta$. Now by Lemma 6.1.8 applied to $X(EX^2)^{-1/2}$ we get from the inequality $X = \sum_{i=1}^{n} a_i X_i \leq \sum_{i=1}^{n} a_i Y_i$ that

$$P\left(\sum_{i=1}^{n} a_i Y_i \geq \gamma \delta \varepsilon \right) \geq P(X \geq \gamma EX) = P(X \geq \alpha \gamma (EX^2)^{1/2})$$

$$= P(X(EX^2)^{-1/2} \geq \beta) \geq (\alpha - \beta)^2$$

$$= (1 - \gamma)^2 \alpha^2 = (1 - \gamma)^2 \varepsilon. \qquad \blacksquare$$

6.1.11 Egorov's Theorem

(Davidson, 1994, Theorem 18.4) *For a.s. convergence* $X_n \to X$ *the following condition is necessary and sufficient: there exists for every* $\delta > 0$ *a set* $C(\delta)$, *with* $P(C(\delta)) \geq 1 - \delta$, *such that* $X_n(\omega) \to X(\omega)$ *uniformly on* $C(\delta)$.

---

[2]I do not understand this, I am just following the principle that great guys do not err, and when they do it can always be fixed.

6.1.12   Kronecker's Lemma

Lemma.   (Davidson, 1994, Lemma 2.35), *Let $\{x_i: i \geq 1\}$ be a sequence of real numbers and let $\{a_i: i \geq 1\}$ be a nondecreasing sequence of positive numbers such that $a_i \to \infty$. If $\sum_{i=1}^{n} x_i/a_i$ converges to a real number, as $n \to \infty$, then $1/a_n \sum_{i=1}^{n} x_i \to 0$.*

The essence of the lemma is that if in the convergent sum $x_1/a_1 + \cdots + x_n/a_n$ the weights are replaced by the smallest, $1/a_n$, then the resulting sum tends to zero. Davidson assumes positivity of x_i, but this condition is not used in the proof.

6.2   VARIOUS BOUNDS ON MARTINGALE TRANSFORMS

Sections 6.2–6.4 are based mainly on Lai and Wei (1982, 1983b).

6.2.1   Truncation Argument

When $\{e_n, \mathcal{F}_n\}$ is a m.d. sequence and $\{w_n\}$ is premeasurable, we may need to consider expressions such as $E(w_n e_n | \mathcal{F}_{n-1})$ or $E((w_n e_n)^2 | \mathcal{F}_{n-1})$. The product $w_n e_n$ may not satisfy the necessary integrability requirements. To avoid imposing conditions of type $E|w_n e_n| < \infty$ or $E(w_n e_n)^2 < \infty$, the following *truncation argument* is used.

Let a_n be so large that $P(|w_n| > a_n) \leq n^{-2}$ and put $w_n^* = w_n 1(|w_n| \leq a_n)$. Then

$$E|w_n^* e_n| \leq a_n E|e_n| < \infty, \quad E(w_n^* e_n | \mathcal{F}_{n-1}) = w_n^* E(e_n | \mathcal{F}_{n-1}).$$

Thus, w_n^* are bounded, $w_n^* e_n$ are integrable and $\{w_n^* e_n\}$ is a m.d. sequence. The sets $A_n = \{|w_n| > a_n\} = \{w_n^* = w_n\}$ satisfy $\sum_{i=1}^{\infty} P(A_i) < \infty$. By the Borel–Cantelli lemma (Section 6.1.1) $P(A_n \text{ i.o.}) = 0$ or, equivalently,

$$P(w_n^* = w_n \text{ for all large } n) = 1 \text{ a.s.} \tag{6.7}$$

The conclusion is that when we need to prove a.s. convergence of the series $\sum_{i=1}^{\infty} w_n e_n$ or the like, we can consider w_n bounded, without loss of generality.

6.2.2   Convergence of Normed Martingale Transforms

When $\{e_n, \mathcal{F}_n\}$ is a m.d. sequence and the sequence of weights $\{w_n\}$ is premeasurable, the sum $S_n = \sum_{i=1}^{n} w_i e_i$ is called a *martingale transform*. The next lemma shows what happens if S_n is normed by $U_n = \sum_{1}^{n} w_i^2$.

Lemma.   *Let d_n be square-integrable m.d.'s such that*

$$\sup_n E(d_n^2 | \mathcal{F}_{n-1}) < \infty \text{ a.s.} \tag{6.8}$$

and let $\{w_n\}$ be premeasurable. Then

$$\sum_{i=1}^{n} w_i d_i \left(\sum_{1}^{n} w_i^2\right)^{-1} \to 0 \ a.s. \ on \ U = \left\{\sum_{1}^{\infty} w_i^2 = \infty\right\}. \tag{6.9}$$

Proof. In Theorem 6.1.4 put $X_i = w_i d_i$, $p = 2$ and $U_n = \sum_{1}^{n} w_i^2$. (To make U_n positive, we can replace it by max $\{\sum_{1}^{n} w_i^2, 1\}$, which does not affect asymptotic statements.) Condition (6.8) implies

$$\sum_{i=1}^{\infty} \frac{E(X_i^2 \mid \mathcal{F}_{i-1})}{U_i^2} = \sum_{i=1}^{\infty} \frac{w_i^2 E(d_i^2 \mid \mathcal{F}_{i-1})}{U_i^2} \leq \sup_n E(d_n^2 \mid \mathcal{F}_{n-1}) \sum_{i=1}^{\infty} \frac{w_i^2}{U_i^2}. \tag{6.10}$$

By monotonicity of the function $f(x) = x^{-2}$ we have

$$\sum_{i=m}^{n} \frac{w_i^2}{U_i^2} = \sum_{i=m}^{n} \frac{U_i - U_{i-1}}{U_i^2} = \sum_{i=m}^{n} \frac{1}{U_i^2} \int_{U_{i-1}}^{U_i} dx$$

$$\leq \sum_{i=m}^{n} \int_{U_{i-1}}^{U_i} \frac{dx}{x^2} = \int_{U_{m-1}}^{U_n} \frac{dx}{x^2} = O(1) \ a.s. \ on \ U \tag{6.11}$$

if $U_{m-1} > 0$. From Eqs. (6.10) and (6.11) we see that

$$\left\{\lim_{n \to \infty} U_n = \infty, \ \sum_{i=1}^{\infty} U_i^{-2} E(X_i^2 \mid \mathcal{F}_{i-1}) < \infty\right\} = U$$

and Eq. (6.9) follows from Theorem 6.1.4. ∎

6.2.3 The Local Marcinkiewicz–Zygmund condition

Marcinkiewicz and Zygmund (1937) showed that if e_n are independent random variables with zero mean and satisfy

$$\sup_n Ee_n^2 < \infty, \ \liminf_{n \to \infty} E\,|\,e_n\,| > 0, \tag{6.12}$$

then for every sequence of constants $\{a_n\}$ an a.s. convergence of the series $\sum_{i=1}^{\infty} a_i e_i$ is equivalent to convergence of the numerical series $\sum_{i=1}^{\infty} a_i^2$.

Gundy (1967) proved an alternative result that sounds as follows: if a m.d. sequence $\{e_n, \mathcal{F}_n\}$ satisfies

$$E(e_n^2 \mid \mathcal{F}_{n-1}) = 1, \ \inf_n E(|e_n| \mid \mathcal{F}_{n-1}) \geq \delta \tag{6.13}$$

with some constant $\delta > 0$ and if $\{w_n\}$ is premeasurable, then, except on a null set, the conditions $\sum_{i=1}^{\infty} w_i^2 < \infty$, $\sum_{i=1}^{\infty} (w_i e_i)^2 < \infty$ and the convergence of $\sum_{i=1}^{\infty} w_i e_i$ are equivalent. Alternative proofs of Gundy's theorem are given by Chow (1969) and Burkholder and Gundy (1970).

Following Lai and Wei (1983b) we say that the m.d. sequence $\{e_n, \mathcal{F}_n\}$ satisfies a *local Marcinkiewicz–Zygmund condition (M–Z condition)* if

$$\sup_n E(e_n^2 | \mathcal{F}_{n-1}) < \infty \text{ and } \liminf_{n \to \infty} E(|e_n| \| \mathcal{F}_{n-1}) > 0 \text{ a.s.} \quad (6.14)$$

Clearly, Eq. (6.14) is weaker than both Eq. (6.12) and Eq. (6.13). The purpose of the next several sections is to investigate the convergence properties of the series $\sum_{i=1}^{\infty} w_i e_i$. For convenience we introduce Assumption L-W.

6.2.3.1   Assumption L-W   The m.d. sequence $\{e_n, \mathcal{F}_n\}$ satisfies the local M–Z condition and the sequence of random weights $\{w_n\}$ is premeasurable.

6.2.4   Convergence of Centered Modules of Martingale Differences (Norming by $\sum_{i=1}^{n} w_i^2$)

Lemma.   *Under Assumption L-W*

$$\sum_{i=1}^{n} w_i[|e_i| - E(|e_i| \| \mathcal{F}_{i-1})] = o\left(\sum_{i=1}^{n} w_i^2\right) \text{ a.s. on } U = \left\{\sum_{i=1}^{\infty} w_i^2 = \infty\right\} \quad (6.15)$$

and

$$\sum_{i=1}^{n} w_i[|e_i| - E(|e_i| \| \mathcal{F}_{i-1})] \text{ converges a.s. on } \Omega \backslash U = \left\{\sum_{i=1}^{\infty} w_i^2 < \infty\right\}. \quad (6.16)$$

Proof.   The centered modules $d_i = |e_i| - E(|e_i| \| \mathcal{F}_{i-1})$ are, obviously, m.d.'s. Since $E(|e_i| \| \mathcal{F}_{i-1})$ is $\mathcal{F}_{i-1}$-measurable, we have

$$E(d_i^2 | \mathcal{F}_{i-1}) = E\{e_i^2 - 2|e_i| E(|e_i| \| \mathcal{F}_{i-1}) + [E(|e_i| \| \mathcal{F}_{i-1})]^2 | \mathcal{F}_{i-1}\}$$
$$= E(e_i^2 | \mathcal{F}_{i-1}) - 2[E(|e_i| \| \mathcal{F}_{i-1})]^2 + [E(|e_i| \| \mathcal{F}_{i-1})]^2$$
$$\leq E(e_i^2 | \mathcal{F}_{i-1}). \quad (6.17)$$

Now we see that by the local M–Z condition, Lemma 6.2.2 is applicable and Eq. (6.9) rewrites as Eq. (6.15).

On $\Omega \backslash U$ for $X_n = w_n d_n$ we have, by Eq. (6.17)

$$\sum_{i=1}^{\infty} E(X_i^2 | \mathcal{F}_{i-1}) = \sum_{i=1}^{\infty} w_i^2 E(d_i^2 | \mathcal{F}_{i-1}) \leq \sup_n E(e_n^2 | F_{i-1}) \sum_{i=1}^{\infty} w_i^2 < \infty.$$

Hence, $\Omega \backslash U \subset \left\{\sum_{i=1}^{\infty} E(X_i^2 | \mathcal{F}_{i-1}) < \infty\right\}$ and Eq. (6.16) follows from Theorem 6.1.3.   ∎

6.2.5 Norming by $\sum_{i=1}^{n} w_i$

The difference between this and Lemma 6.2.4 is that the norming by $\sum_{i=1}^{n} w_i^2$ is replaced by the norming by $\sum_{i=1}^{n} w_i$. Assuming that w_i are nonnegative, denote

$$V = \left\{ \sum_{i=1}^{\infty} w_i = \infty, \ \sup_i w_i < \infty \right\} \tag{6.18}$$

the set where the series $\sum_{i=1}^{\infty} w_i$ diverges and w_i are uniformly (in i) bounded.

Lemma.   *If w_i are nonnegative and Assumption L-W holds, then*

$$\sum_{i=1}^{n} w_i[|e_i| - E(|e_i| \| \mathcal{F}_{i-1})] = o\left(\sum_{i=1}^{n} w_i \right) \quad a.s \ on \ V. \tag{6.19}$$

Proof.   From the definition of V

$$\sum_{1}^{n} w_i = \sup_j w_j \sum_{i=1}^{n} \frac{w_i}{\sup_j w_j} \geq \sup_j w_j \sum_{i=1}^{n} \left(\frac{w_i}{\sup_j w_j} \right)^2 \quad \text{on } V$$

and with the notation $d_i = |e_i| - E(|e_i| \| \mathcal{F}_{i-1})$ Eq. (6.15) implies

$$\left| \sum_{1}^{n} w_i d_i \left(\sum_{1}^{n} w_i \right)^{-1} \right| \leq \sup_j w_j \left| \sum_{1}^{n} w_i d_i \left(\sum_{1}^{n} w_i^2 \right)^{-1} \right| \to 0 \text{ a.s. on } V \cap U.$$

$$\tag{6.20}$$

However, if $\omega \in V \cap (\Omega \backslash U)$, then $\sum_{i=1}^{\infty} w_i(\omega) d_i(\omega)$ converges by Eq. (6.16), while $\sum_{1}^{n} w_i(\omega) \to \infty$ by the definition of V, so

$$\sum_{1}^{n} w_i d_i \left(\sum_{1}^{n} w_i \right)^{-1} \to 0 \text{ a.s. on } V \cap (\Omega \backslash U). \tag{6.21}$$

Equations (6.20) and (6.21) prove Eq. (6.19).   ∎

6.2.6 A Lower Bound for Weighted Sums of Modules of Martingale Differences

Lemma.   *If w_i are nonnegative and Assumption L-W holds, then with the same V as in Eq. (6.18) one has*

$$\liminf_{n \to \infty} \sum_{1}^{n} w_i |e_i| \left(\sum_{1}^{n} w_i \right)^{-1} \geq \liminf_{n \to \infty} E(|e_n| \| \mathcal{F}_{n-1}) \quad a.s. \ on \ V. \tag{6.22}$$

Proof.   Obviously, with $d_i = |e_i| - E(|e_i|\|\mathcal{F}_{i-1})$

$$\frac{\sum_1^n w_i|e_i|}{\sum_1^n w_i} = \frac{\sum_1^n w_i E(|e_i|\|\mathcal{F}_{i-1})}{\sum_1^n w_i} + \frac{\sum_1^n w_i d_i}{\sum_1^n w_i}.$$

By Eq. (6.19) on V, the last term is asymptotically negligible. Denoting $\alpha = \lim\inf_{n\to\infty} E(|e_n|\|\mathcal{F}_{n-1})$, for any $\varepsilon \in (0, \alpha/2)$ we can find $N > 0$ such that $E(|e_n|\|\mathcal{F}_{n-1}) \geq \alpha - \varepsilon$ for $n > N$. In

$$\frac{\sum_1^n w_i E(|e_i|\|\mathcal{F}_{i-1})}{\sum_1^n w_i} = \frac{\sum_1^N w_i E(|e_i|\|\mathcal{F}_{i-1})}{\sum_1^n w_i} + \frac{\sum_{N+1}^n w_i E(|e_i|\|\mathcal{F}_{i-1})}{\sum_1^n w_i} \tag{6.23}$$

the first term on the right tends to 0 as $n \to \infty$, on V. The second term is not less than

$$\frac{\sum_{i=N+1}^n w_i}{\sum_1^N w_i + \sum_{N+1}^n w_i}(\alpha - \varepsilon) = \frac{\alpha - \varepsilon}{\sum_1^N w_i / \sum_{N+1}^n w_i + 1} \geq \alpha - 2\varepsilon, \tag{6.24}$$

say, for all n sufficiently large. Equations (6.23) and (6.24) prove Eq. (6.22).   ∎

6.2.7   A Lower Bound for Weighted Sums of Powers of Martingale Differences

Lemma.   [Lai and Wei, 1983b Lemma 1(i)] *If w_i are nonnegative and Assumption L-W holds, then for every $r \geq 1$*

$$\lim_{n\to\infty}\inf \sum_1^n w_i|e_i|^r \left(\sum_1^n w_i\right)^{-1} > 0 \; a.s. \; on \; V = \left\{\sum_{i=1}^\infty w_i = \infty, \; \sup_i w_i < \infty\right\}.$$

Proof.   Viewing $\{w_i \left(\sum_1^n w_i\right)^{-1} : i = 1, \ldots, n\}$ as a probability density function on $\{1, \ldots, n\}$, by Hölder's inequality we have

$$\left[\sum_1^n w_i|e_i|^r \left(\sum_1^n w_i\right)^{-1}\right]^{1/r} \geq \sum_1^n w_i|e_i| \left(\sum_1^n w_i\right)^{-1}.$$

Hence, the statement follows from the local M–Z condition Eq. (6.14) and Eq. (6.22).   ∎

6.2.8   Uniform Boundedness of Weights

Lemma.   [Lai and Wei, 1983b, Lemma 1(ii)] *If w_i are nonnegative and Assumption L-W holds, then w_n are uniformly (in n) bounded on the set $A = \{\sup_n w_n|e_n| < \infty\}$:*

$$P(\sup_n w_n = \infty, \; \sup_n w_n|e_n| < \infty) = 0. \tag{6.25}$$

Proof.   Let

$$d_n = w_n|e_n|, \quad m_n = E(d_n|\mathcal{F}_{n-1}), \quad v_n = [E(d_n^2|\mathcal{F}_{n-1})]^{1/2}$$

and, for a natural $K \geq 1$, define

$$A_K = \{\sup_n d_n < K\} \cap \{m_n \geq 3K^{-1}v_n \text{ for all large } n\}.$$

In the definition of A_K, "for all large n" means "for $n \geq N(\omega)$, where $N(\omega)$ is large enough".

Step 1. To prove boundedness of w_n, it suffices to prove boundedness of the variations v_n. Indeed, by the conditional Hölder inequality and the local M–Z condition

$$0 < \liminf_{n \to \infty} E(|e_n||\mathcal{F}_{n-1}) \leq \liminf_{n \to \infty} [E(e_n^2|\mathcal{F}_{n-1})]^{1/2}.$$

Therefore from $w_n = v_n/[E(e_n^2|\mathcal{F}_{n-1})]^{1/2}$ it follows that

$$\limsup_{n \to \infty} w_n \leq \frac{\limsup_{n \to \infty} v_n}{\liminf_{n \to \infty} [E(e_n^2|\mathcal{F}_{n-1})]^{1/2}}$$

and we have the implication $\sup_n v_n < \infty \Rightarrow \sup_n w_n < \infty$.

Step 2. Now we reduce the problem further by showing that

$$\sup_n v_n < \infty \text{ on } A_K \text{ for all } K \Rightarrow \sup_n v_n < \infty \text{ on } A. \qquad (6.26)$$

The local M–Z condition implies

$$E(|e_n||\mathcal{F}_{n-1}) = \frac{E(|e_n||\mathcal{F}_{n-1})}{[E(e_n^2|\mathcal{F}_{n-1})]^{1/2}} [E(e_n^2|\mathcal{F}_{n-1})]^{1/2}$$

$$\geq \frac{1/2 \liminf_{n \to \infty} E(|e_n||\mathcal{F}_{n-1})}{\sup_n [E(e_n^2|\mathcal{F}_{n-1})]^{1/2}} [E(e_n^2|\mathcal{F}_{n-1})]^{1/2}, \text{ all large } n.$$

Multiplying this by w_n (which is $\mathcal{F}_{n-1}$-measurable), we get $m_n \geq cv_n$ for all large n, where c depends on ω. Hence, for almost any ω there exists K such that $m_n \geq 3K^{-1}v_n$ for all large n. As a result, $\Omega = \bigcup_{K=1}^{\infty} \{m_n \geq 3K^{-1}v_n \text{ for all large } n\}$, up to a set of probability zero. Besides, $A = \bigcup_{K=1}^{\infty} \{\sup_n d_n < K\}$. Hence, $A = \bigcup_{K=1}^{\infty} A_K$, which proves Eq. (6.26).

Step 3. The variable $Z_n = 1(d_n \geq K)$ is $\mathcal{F}_n$-measurable and satisfies $0 \leq Z_n \leq 1$, so by the conditional Borel-Cantelli lemma (Lemma 6.1.2) the conditions $\sum_{i=1}^{\infty} E(Z_i|\mathcal{F}_{i-1}) < \infty$ and $\sum_{i=1}^{\infty} Z_i < \infty$ are a.s. equivalent. The sum $\sum_{i=1}^{\infty} Z_i$ equals the number of times the inequality $d_n \geq K$ is true. On A_K this number is zero and therefore

$$\sum_{i=1}^{\infty} E(Z_i|\mathcal{F}_{i-1}) = \sum_{i=1}^{\infty} P(d_i \geq K|\mathcal{F}_{i-1}) < \infty \text{ on } A_K. \qquad (6.27)$$

Step 4. Put

$$\chi_n = 1(m_n \geq 3K^{-1}v_n), \quad \bar{d}_n = d_n\chi_n,$$

$$\bar{m}_n = E(\bar{d}_n \mid \mathcal{F}_{n-1}), \quad \bar{v}_n = [E(\bar{d}_n^2 \mid \mathcal{F}_{n-1})]^{1/2}.$$

As χ_n is $\mathcal{F}_{n-1}$-measurable, we have $\bar{m}_n = m_n\chi_n$ and $\bar{v}_n = v_n\chi_n$. Obviously, $\bar{m}_n \geq 3K^{-1}\bar{v}_n$ a.s. Hence, by the conditional Paley–Zygmund inequality (Lemma 6.1.9)

$$P(\bar{d}_n > K^{-1}\bar{v}_n \mid \mathcal{F}_{n-1}) \geq K^{-2}. \tag{6.28}$$

Noting that

$$P(\bar{d}_n > K^{-1}\bar{v}_n \mid \mathcal{F}_{n-1}) = E(1(\bar{d}_n > K^{-1}\bar{v}_n) \mid \mathcal{F}_{n-1})$$

$$= E(1(d_n > K^{-1}v_n)\chi_n \mid \mathcal{F}_{n-1})$$

$$= P(d_n > K^{-1}v_n \mid \mathcal{F}_{n-1})\chi_n$$

we get from Eq. (6.28)

$$P(d_n > K^{-1}v_n \mid \mathcal{F}_{n-1}) \geq K^{-2} \text{ on } A_K. \tag{6.29}$$

Step 5. The resulting Eqs. (6.27) and (6.29) can be combined as follows. The inequalities $d_n > K^{-1}v_n$, $K^{-1}v_n \geq K$ imply $d_n \geq K$ and therefore

$$1(d_n > K^{-1}v_n)1(K^{-1}v_n \geq K) \leq 1(d_n \geq K). \tag{6.30}$$

Equations (6.29) and (6.30) lead to

$$K^{-2}\sum_n 1(K^{-1}v_n \geq K) \leq \sum_n 1(K^{-1}v_n \geq K)P(d_n > K^{-1}v_n \mid \mathcal{F}_{n-1})$$

$$= \sum_n E[1(K^{-1}v_n \geq K)1(d_n > K^{-1}v_n) \mid \mathcal{F}_{n-1}]$$

$$\leq \sum_n P(d_n \geq K \mid \mathcal{F}_{n-1}) \text{ on } A_K.$$

Recalling that by Eq. (6.27) the right-hand side is a.s. finite, we see that the inequality $K^{-1}v_n \geq K$ may be true on A_K only for a finite number of indices n. Hence, $\sup_n v_n < \infty$ on A_K for all K. As we know from Steps 1 and 2, this completes the proof. ∎

6.2.9   Implication of Uniform Boundedness of Partial Sums

Lemma.   *If Assumption L-W holds, then*

$$\sup_n w_n^2 = \infty \ a.s. \ on \ B = \left\{ \sup_n S_n^2 < \infty, \ \sum_{i=1}^{\infty} w_i^2 = \infty \right\},$$

where $S_n = \sum_1^n w_i e_i$.

Proof.   Putting $S_0 = 0$ and summing the identity

$$S_i^2 = (S_{i-1} + w_i e_i)^2 = S_{i-1}^2 + 2S_{i-1}w_i e_i + w_i^2 e_i^2$$

we get

$$S_n^2 = \sum_1^n S_i^2 - \sum_1^n S_{i-1}^2 = 2 \sum_1^n S_{i-1}w_i e_i + \sum_1^n w_i^2 e_i^2. \tag{6.31}$$

In Theorem 6.1.4 put $X_n = S_{n-1}w_n e_n$, $U_n = \sum_{i=1}^{n} w_i^2$, $p = 2$. On the set B by the local M–Z condition

$$\sum_{i=1}^{\infty} \frac{E(X_i^2 \mid \mathcal{F}_{i-1})}{U_i^2} = \sum_{i=1}^{\infty} \frac{S_{i-1}^2 w_i^2 E(e_i^2 \mid \mathcal{F}_{i-1})}{U_i^2}$$

$$\leq \left(\sup_n S_n^2 \right) \left(\sup_n E(e_n^2 \mid \mathcal{F}_{n-1}) \right) \sum_{i=1}^{\infty} \frac{w_i^2}{U_i^2} < \infty$$

[see Eq. (6.11) for the proof of convergence of the above series]. Hence, by Theorem 6.1.4

$$\sum_1^n S_{i-1}w_i e_i = o\left(\sum_{i=1}^{n} w_i^2 \right) \ \text{a.s. on } B. \tag{6.32}$$

Since, obviously, $S_n^2 = o\left(\sum_{i=1}^{n} w_i^2 \right)$ on B, Eqs. (6.31) and (6.32) show that

$$\sum_1^n w_i^2 e_i^2 = o\left(\sum_{i=1}^{n} w_i^2 \right) \ \text{a.s. on } B.$$

However, by Lemma 6.2.7

$$\liminf_{n \to \infty} \sum_1^n w_i^2 e_i^2 \left(\sum_1^n w_i^2 \right)^{-1} > 0 \ \text{a.s. on } V$$

$$= \left\{ \sum_{i=1}^{\infty} w_i^2 = \infty, \ \sup_i w_i^2 < \infty \right\}. \tag{6.33}$$

Thus, the assumption that $\sup_i w_i^2 < \infty$ on B leads to a contradiction. ∎

6.3 MARCINKIEWICZ–ZYGMUND THEOREMS AND RELATED RESULTS

6.3.1 Generalized Marcinkiewicz–Zygmund Theorem I

Theorem. (Lai and Wei, 1983b, Corollary 1) *Suppose Assumption L-W holds (Section 6.2.3). Then, except on a null set, the following statements are equivalent:*

(i) $\sum_{i=1}^{\infty} w_i^2 < \infty$,

(ii) $\sum_1^{\infty} w_i e_i$ *converges*,

(iii) $\sup_n \left| \sum_1^n w_i e_i \right| < \infty$,

(iv) $\sum_1^{\infty} w_i^2 e_i^2 < \infty$.

Proof. Denote $S_n = \sum_1^n w_i e_i$. The implication symbols below denote implications outside some null set.

(i) $\Rightarrow$ (ii). From (i) and the local M–Z condition (Section 6.2.3) we see that with $X_n = w_n e_n$

$$\sum_{i=1}^{\infty} E(X_i^2 \mid \mathcal{F}_{i-1}) \leq \sup_n E(e_n^2 \mid \mathcal{F}_{n-1}) \sum_{i=1}^{\infty} w_i^2 < \infty \text{ a.s.}$$

Therefore, by the martingale strong law (Section 6.1.4) S_n converges a.s. on Ω and (ii) holds. For future reference, notice that this argument can be summarized as follows: if the m.d. sequence $\{e_n\}$ satisfies $\sup_n E(e_n^2 \mid \mathcal{F}_{n-1}) < \infty$ and $\{w_n\}$ is premeasurable, then $\sum_1^n w_i e_i$ converges a.s. on $W = \{\sum_{i=1}^{\infty} w_i^2 < \infty\}$.

The implication (ii) $\Rightarrow$ (iii) is trivial.

(iii) $\Rightarrow$ (i). (iii) implies

$$\sup_n |w_n e_n| = \sup_n |S_n - S_{n-1}| \leq \sup_n (|S_n| + |S_{n-1}|) < \infty.$$

As $|w_n|$ is nonnegative and $\mathcal{F}_{n-1}$-measurable, it follows by Lemma 6.2.8 that $\sup_n w_n^2 < \infty$. This would not be true by Lemma 6.2.9 if we had $\sum_{i=1}^{\infty} w_i^2 = \infty$.

(i) $\Rightarrow$ (iv). Since we have established that (i) implies (iii), it suffices to show that

$$\sum_1^{\infty} w_i^2 e_i^2 < \infty \text{ a.s. on } A = \left\{ \sup_n S_n^2 < \infty, \sum_{i=1}^{\infty} w_i^2 < \infty \right\}. \tag{6.34}$$

As a result of the bound

$$\sum_{i=1}^{\infty} E\big((S_{i-1} w_i e_i)^2 \mid \mathcal{F}_{i-1}\big) \leq \left(\sup_n S_n^2\right)\left(\sup_n E(e_n^2 \mid \mathcal{F}_{i-1})\right) \sum_{i=1}^{\infty} w_i^2 < \infty,$$

the martingale strong law (Section 6.1.4) provides convergence of the series $\sum_1^{\infty} S_{i-1} w_i e_i$ on A. It remains to apply identity (6.31) and that $\sup_n S_n^2 < \infty$ on A to see that Eq. (6.34) holds.

(iv) $\Rightarrow$ **(i).** From (iv) $\sup_n |w_n e_n| < \infty$, which implies $\sup_n |w_n| < \infty$ by Lemma 6.2.8. Therefore to prove (i) it suffices to show that

$$P\left(\sum_1^\infty w_i^2 e_i^2 < \infty, \ \sup_n w_n^2 < \infty, \ \sum_{i=1}^\infty w_i^2 = \infty\right) = 0. \tag{6.35}$$

By Lemma 6.2.7, Eq. (6.33) holds and $\sum_1^\infty w_i^2 e_i^2 = \infty$ on V. Thus, Eq. (6.35) is true. $\blacksquare$

6.3.2 Approximation Lemma

Lemma. *Let $\{e_n, \mathcal{F}_n\}$ be a m.d. sequence satisfying the local M–Z condition from Section 6.2.3. Then for every given $\eta \in (0, 1)$, there exist positive integers m and K and a m.d. sequence $\{\tilde{e}_n, \tilde{\mathcal{F}}_n\}$ satisfying*

$$E(\tilde{e}_n^2 \mid \tilde{\mathcal{F}}_{n-1}) \le K^2 \ \text{and} \ E(|\tilde{e}_n| \| \tilde{\mathcal{F}}_{n-1}) \le K^{-1} \ \text{a.s. for all } n \ge m \tag{6.36}$$

and such that $\mathcal{F}_n \subseteq \tilde{\mathcal{F}}_n$ for all n and

$$P(e_n = \tilde{e}_n \ \text{for all } n \ge m) \ge 1 - \eta. \tag{6.37}$$

Proof. Enlarging the probability space, if necessary, let $\{d_n\}$ be a sequence of i.i.d. symmetric Bernoulli variables such that $P(d_n = 1) = P(d_n = -1) = 1/2$ and $\{d_n\}$ is independent of $\sigma(\bigcup_1^\infty \mathcal{F}_n)$. Denote $\mathcal{B}_n = \sigma(d_1, \ldots, d_n)$, $\tilde{\mathcal{F}}_n = \sigma(\mathcal{F}_n \cup \mathcal{B}_n)$. By independence of d_n we have

$$E(d_n | \mathcal{B}_{n-1}) = Ed_n = 0, \ E(d_n^2 | \mathcal{B}_{n-1}) = Ed_n^2 = 1,$$
$$E(|d_n| \| \mathcal{B}_{n-1}) = E|d_n| = 1. \tag{6.38}$$

Denote $A_{K,n} = \{E(e_n^2|\mathcal{F}_{n-1}) \le K^2, \ E(|e_n| \| \mathcal{F}_{n-1}) \ge K^{-1}\}$. By the local M–Z condition, $\Omega = \bigcup_{m,K=1}^\infty \bigcap_{n \ge m} A_{K,n}$, up to a set of probability zero. Since the event $\bigcap_{n \ge m} A_{K,n}$ increases with K and m, this implies

$$\lim_{m,K \to \infty} P\left(\bigcap_{n \ge m} A_{K,n}\right) = 1.$$

This means that for any $\eta \in (0, 1)$ there exist positive integers m and K such that

$$P\left(\bigcap_{n \ge m} A_{K,n}\right) \ge 1 - \eta. \tag{6.39}$$

Define $\tilde{e}_n = e_n 1(A_{K,n}) + d_n 1(\Omega \backslash A_{K,n})$ for $n \ge 1$.

The functions $1(A_{K,n})$ and $1(\Omega \backslash A_{K,n})$ are $\mathcal{F}_{n-1}$- and $\tilde{\mathcal{F}}_{n-1}$-measurable. Hence, by Eq. (6.38) and LIE

$$
\begin{aligned}
E(\tilde{e}_n \mid \tilde{\mathcal{F}}_{n-1}) &= 1(A_{K,n})E(e_n \mid \tilde{\mathcal{F}}_{n-1}) + 1(\Omega \backslash A_{K,n})E(d_n \mid \tilde{\mathcal{F}}_{n-1}) \\
&= 1(A_{K,n})E[E(e_n \mid \mathcal{F}_{n-1}) \mid \tilde{\mathcal{F}}_{n-1}] \\
&\quad + 1(\Omega \backslash A_{K,n})E[E(d_n \mid \mathcal{B}_{n-1}) \mid \tilde{\mathcal{F}}_{n-1}] = 0.
\end{aligned}
$$

Thus, $\{\tilde{e}_n, \tilde{\mathcal{F}}_n\}$ is a m.d. sequence.

Now we show that the first of the conditions (6.36) is met:

$$
\begin{aligned}
E(\tilde{e}_n^2 \mid \tilde{\mathcal{F}}_{n-1}) &= 1(A_{K,n})E(e_n^2 \mid \tilde{\mathcal{F}}_{n-1}) + 1(\Omega \backslash A_{K,n})E(d_n^2 \mid \tilde{\mathcal{F}}_{n-1}) \\
&= 1(A_{K,n})E[E(e_n^2 \mid \mathcal{F}_{n-1}) \mid \tilde{\mathcal{F}}_{n-1}] \\
&\quad + 1(\Omega \backslash A_{K,n})E[E(d_n^2 \mid \mathcal{B}_{n-1}) \mid \tilde{\mathcal{F}}_{n-1}] \\
&\leq K^2 1(A_{K,n}) + 1(\Omega \backslash A_{K,n}) \leq K^2.
\end{aligned}
$$

Similarly,

$$
\begin{aligned}
E(|\tilde{e}_n| \mid \tilde{\mathcal{F}}_{n-1}) &= 1(A_{K,n})E[E(|e_n| \mid \mathcal{F}_{n-1}) \mid \tilde{\mathcal{F}}_{n-1}] \\
&\quad + 1(\Omega \backslash A_{K,n})E[E(|d_n| \mid \mathcal{F}_{n-1}) \mid \tilde{\mathcal{F}}_{n-1}] \\
&\geq K^{-1} 1(A_{K,n}) + 1(\Omega \backslash A_{K,n}) \geq K^{-1}.
\end{aligned}
$$

Finally, Eq. (6.37) follows from Eq. (6.39):

$$
P(e_n = \tilde{e}_n \text{ for all } n \geq m) = P\left(\bigcap_{n \geq m} \{e_n = \tilde{e}_n\} \right) \geq 1 - \eta.
$$

$\blacksquare$

6.3.3   Generalized Marcinkiewicz–Zygmund Theorem II

Lemma. (Burkholder, 1968, Lemma 4) *To each $\delta \in (0, 1)$ corresponds an $\alpha \in (0, 1)$ with the following property: if d_i, $i \geq 1$, are m.d.'s satisfying $E|d_i| \geq \delta(Ed_i^2)^{1/2}$, $i \geq 1$, then the martingale $f_n = \sum_{i=1}^n d_i$ satisfies $E|f_n| \geq \alpha(Ef_n^2)^{1/2}$ for all n.*

For the original Marcinkiewicz–Zygmund result see Marcinkiewicz and Zygmund (1937). The restrictions α, $\delta \leq 1$ are necessary by Hölder's inequality.

Proof. The numbers $c_i = (Ed_i^2)^{1/2}$ can be assumed positive because those d_i that vanish a.s. can be omitted from the sequence. Geometrically, it is obvious that we can choose β to satisfy the $0 < \beta < \delta$ and $\beta = (\delta - \beta)^2$. Application of the Paley–Zygmund inequality (Section 6.1.8) to $d_i(Ed_i^2)^{-1/2}$ yields $P(d_i \geq \beta c_i) \geq (\delta - \beta)^2 = \beta$. The numbers $a_i = c_i^2 / \sum_1^n c_j^2$ and variables $Y_i = (d_i/c_i)^2$ satisfy the assumptions of Lemma 6.1.10 with $\delta = \beta^2$, $\varepsilon = \beta$ and $\gamma = \beta \in (0, 1)$. Hence,

$$P\left(\sum_{i=1}^{n} a_i Y_i \geq \beta^4\right) \geq (1 - \beta)^2 \beta \geq (\delta - \beta)^2 \beta = \beta^2. \tag{6.40}$$

Let $S_n(f) = \left(\sum_{i=1}^{n} d_i^2\right)^{1/2}$. As $Ef_n^2 = \sum_{i=1}^{n} Ed_i^2 = \sum_{i=1}^{n} c_i^2$, we have

$$P(S_n(f) \geq \beta^2(Ef_n^2)^{1/2}) = P\left(\sum_{i=1}^{n} c_i^2(d_i/c_i)^2 \geq \beta^4 \sum_{i=1}^{n} c_i^2\right). \tag{6.41}$$

Equations (6.40) and (6.41) lead to the bound

$$\beta^2 [\beta^2(Ef_n^2)^{1/2}]^{3/2} \leq P\left(\sum_{i=1}^{n} c_i^2(d_i/c_i)^2 \left(\sum_{j=1}^{n} c_j^2\right)^{-1} \geq \beta^4\right)[\beta^2(Ef_n^2)^{1/2}]^{3/2}$$

$$= P(S_n(f) \geq \beta^2(Ef_n^2)^{1/2})[\beta^2(Ef_n^2)^{1/2}]^{3/2}$$

$$= \int_{\{S_n(f) \geq \beta^2(Ef_n^2)^{1/2}\}} [\beta^2(Ef_n^2)^{1/2}]^{3/2} dP$$

$$\leq E(S_n(f))^{3/2}. \tag{6.42}$$

By Burkholder's inequality (Long, 1993, Theorem 5.5.7) for $1 < p < \infty$ the norms $(E|f_n|^p)^{1/p}$ and $[E(S_n(f)^p)]^{1/p}$ are equivalent. In particular, with some constant $c > 0$, and also applying Hölder's inequality, we have

$$E(S_n(f))^{3/2} \leq cE|f_n|^{3/2} \leq c(E|f_n|)^{1/2}(Ef_n^2)^{1/2}. \tag{6.43}$$

Combining Eqs. (6.42) and (6.43) yields $\beta^5(Ef_n^2)^{1/2}(Ef_n^2)^{1/4} \leq c(E|f_n|)^{1/2}(Ef_n^2)^{1/2}$ or $E|f_n| \geq \alpha(Ef_n^2)^{1/2}$ with $\alpha = (\beta^5/c)^2$. ∎

6.3.4 Lemma on Probing Martingale Differences

Lemma. [Lai and Wei, 1983b, Lemma 2 (ii)] *Let $\{\tilde{e}_n, \tilde{\mathcal{F}}_n\}$ be a m.d. sequence satisfying*

$$E(\tilde{e}_n^2 \mid \tilde{\mathcal{F}}_{n-1}) \leq K^2 \text{ and } E(|\tilde{e}_n| \| \tilde{\mathcal{F}}_{n-1}) \geq K^{-1} \text{ a.s. for all } n \geq m \tag{6.44}$$

with m, K sufficiently large. Let $\{a_n\}$ be a sequence of constants and $m = n_0 < n_1 < \ldots$ a sequence of nonrandom positive integers such that

$$\sum_{n \in b_i} a_n^2 > 0 \text{ for all } i, \tag{6.45}$$

where the batch b_i is defined by $b_i = \{n_{i-1} < n \leq n_i\}$. Further, define

$$u_i = \left(\sum_{n \in b_i} a_n \tilde{e}_n\right)\left(\sum_{n \in b_i} a_n^2\right)^{-1/2}, \quad \mathcal{G}_i = \tilde{\mathcal{F}}_{n_i}. \tag{6.46}$$

Then $\{u_i, \mathcal{G}_i: i \geq 1\}$ is a m.d. sequence and

$$\sup_n E(u_n^2|\mathcal{G}_{n-1}) \leq K^2, \quad \inf_n E(|u_n| \| \mathcal{G}_{n-1}) \geq c_K \ a.s. \tag{6.47}$$

where c_K is a positive constant that depends only on K.

Proof. u_i form a m.d. sequence because, up to a constant factor, $E(u_n|\mathcal{G}_{n-1})$ is $\sum_{n \in b_i} a_n E(\tilde{e}_n | \tilde{\mathcal{F}}_{n_{i-1}}) = 0$.

From the first inequality in Eq. (6.44) we see that the first condition in Eq. (6.47) is met:

$$E\left[\left(\sum_{n \in b_i} a_n \tilde{e}_n\right)^2 \Big| \tilde{\mathcal{F}}_{n_{i-1}}\right] = \sum_{n \in b_i} a_n^2 E[E(\tilde{e}_n^2 | \tilde{\mathcal{F}}_{n-1})| \tilde{\mathcal{F}}_{n_{i-1}}]$$

$$\leq K^2 \sum_{n \in b_i} a_n^2$$

Let us prove the lower bound in Eq. (6.47). Lai and Wei (1983b) modeled this argument on (Barlow, 1975, p. 845). Take $A \in \tilde{\mathcal{F}}_{n_{i-1}}$ with $P(A) > 0$ and consider the stochastic sequence $\{a_n \tilde{e}_n 1(A), \tilde{\mathcal{F}}_n: n > n_{i-1}\}$ on the probability space with the probability measure P_A defined by $P_A(B) = P(B \cap A)/P(A)$. This sequence is a m.d. sequence under P_A: $E(a_n \tilde{e}_n 1(A)| \tilde{\mathcal{F}}_{n-1}) = a_n 1(A) E(\tilde{e}_n | \tilde{\mathcal{F}}_{n-1}) = 0$. Denoting $E_A X = E1(A)X/P(A)$, from condition (6.44) we have

$$E_A|\tilde{e}_n 1(A)| = E_A[1(A)E(|\tilde{e}_n| \| \tilde{\mathcal{F}}_{n-1})] \geq E_A K^{-1} = K^{-1},$$

$$E_A(\tilde{e}_n 1(A))^2 = E_A[1(A)E(\tilde{e}_n^2 | \tilde{\mathcal{F}}_{n-1})] \leq K^2$$

and the consequence is that

$$E_A|a_n \tilde{e}_n 1(A)| \geq |a_n|K^{-1} \geq K^{-2}[E_A(a_n \tilde{e}_n 1(A))^2]^{1/2}, \quad n > n_{i-1}.$$

By M–Z Theorem II (Section 6.3.3) it follows that there exists a constant $d_K \in (0,1)$ depending only on K and such that for $n > n_{i-1}$:

$$E_A\left|\sum_{n_{i-1} < j \leq n} a_j \tilde{e}_j 1(A)\right| \geq d_K\left[E_A\left(\sum_{n_{i-1} < j \leq n} a_j \tilde{e}_j 1(A)\right)^2\right]^{1/2}. \tag{6.48}$$

We note that for $n > n_{i-1}$

$$E_A \left(\sum_{n_{i-1} < j \le n} a_j \tilde{e}_j \, 1(A) \right)^2 = E\left[\left(\sum_{n_{i-1} < j \le n} a_j \tilde{e}_j \right)^2 1(A) \right] \Big/ P(A)$$

$$= \sum_{n_{i-1} < j \le n} a_j^2 E[E(\tilde{e}_j^2 \mid \tilde{\mathcal{F}}_{j-1}) 1(A)] \Big/ P(A)$$

[applying the conditional Jensen inequality (Section 6.1.6)]

$$\ge \sum_{n_{i-1} < j \le n} a_j^2 E\left[E(|\tilde{e}_j| \, \| \, \tilde{\mathcal{F}}_{j-1}) \right]^2 1(A)/P(A)$$

[using the second inequality in Eq. (6.44)]

$$\ge K^{-2} \sum_{n_{i-1} < j \le n} a_j^2 E1(A)/P(A)$$

$$= K^{-2} \sum_{n_{i-1} < j \le n} a_j^2. \tag{6.49}$$

The conclusion from Eqs. (6.48) and (6.49) is that

$$E \left| \sum_{j \in b_i} a_j \tilde{e}_j \right| 1(A)/P(A) \ge d_K K^{-1} \left(\sum_{j \in b_i} a_j^2 \right)^{1/2}.$$

Since this inequality holds for all $A \in \tilde{F}_{n_{i-1}}$ with $P(A) > 0$, it follows from the definition of conditional expectation that $E(|u_i| \| \mathcal{G}_{i-1}) \ge d_K K^{-1}$ a.s. So, the second condition in Eq. (6.47) is satisfied. ∎

6.3.5 Lemma on Leading Terms

Lemma. *Let $\{ \tilde{e}_n, \tilde{\mathcal{F}}_n \}$ be a m.d. sequence and let $\{a_n\}$ be a sequence of constants satisfying the condition of nontriviality of batches (6.45). Define $S_n = \sum_{i=1}^{n} a_i \tilde{e}_i$,*

$$A_i = \left(\sum_{n \in b_i} a_n^2 \right)^{1/2} \ne 0 \tag{6.50}$$

and let u_i, $\mathcal{G}_i$ be as in Eq. (6.46). Then the leading terms in $\sum_{i=1}^{k} S_{n_i}^2 / A_i^2$ are given by the expression

$$\sum_{i=1}^{k} \frac{S_{n_i}^2}{A_i^2} = \begin{cases} \sum_{i=1}^{k} u_i^2 + O(1) \ on \ \left\{ \sum_{i=1}^{\infty} \frac{S_{n_{i-1}}^2}{A_i^2} < \infty \right\} \\ (1 + o(1)) \sum_{i=1}^{k} \frac{S_{n_{i-1}}^2}{A_i^2} + \sum_{i=1}^{k} u_i^2 \ on \ \left\{ \sum_{i=1}^{\infty} \frac{S_{n_{i-1}}^2}{A_i^2} = \infty \right\} \end{cases} \tag{6.51}$$

Proof.   Start with the identity

$$\frac{S_{n_i}^2}{A_i^2} = \left(S_{n_{i-1}} + \sum_{n\in b_i} a_n \tilde{e}_n\right)^2 A_i^{-2}$$

$$= \left[S_{n_{i-1}}^2 + 2S_{n_{i-1}}\sum_{n\in b_i} a_n \tilde{e}_n + \left(\sum_{n\in b_i} a_n \tilde{e}_n\right)^2\right]A_i^{-2}$$

$$= S_{n_{i-1}}^2 A_i^{-2} + 2(S_{n_{i-1}}A_i^{-1})u_i + u_i^2.$$

Summation over i gives

$$\sum_{i=1}^{k} S_{n_i}^2/A_i^2 = \sum_{i=1}^{k} S_{n_{i-1}}^2 A_i^{-2} + 2\sum_{i=1}^{k}(S_{n_{i-1}}A_i^{-1})u_i + \sum_{i=1}^{k} u_i^2. \tag{6.52}$$

Since $S_{n_{i-1}}A_i^{-1}$ is $\mathcal{G}_{i-1}$-measurable, we can put $p = 2$, $X_i = (S_{n_{i-1}}A_i^{-1})u_i$, $\mathcal{F}_i = \mathcal{G}_i$ in the martingale convergence theorem (Section 6.1.3) and use Eq. (6.47) to conclude that

$$\sum_{i=1}^{k}(S_{n_{i-1}}A_i^{-1})u_i \text{ converges on } \left\{\sum_{i=1}^{\infty} S_{n_{i-1}}^2 A_i^{-2} < \infty\right\}. \tag{6.53}$$

In the martingale strong law (Section 6.1.4), in addition to the above choice, let us take $U_n = \sum_{i=1}^{n} S_{n_{i-1}}^2 A_i^{-2}$. On the set $U = \{\lim_{n\to\infty} U_n = \infty\}$ we have

$$\sum_{i=1}^{\infty} U_i^{-2}E(X_i^2|\mathcal{F}_{i-1}) \leq \sup_n E(u_n^2|\mathcal{F}_{n-1})\sum_{i=1}^{\infty}(S_{n_{i-1}}A_i^{-1})^2 U_i^{-2} < \infty$$

[see Eq. (6.11) for the proof of convergence of the last series]. By Theorem 6.1.4 $\lim_{n\to\infty} S_n/U_n = 0$ on U, that is,

$$\sum_{i=1}^{k}(S_{n_{i-1}}A_i^{-1})u_i = o\left(\sum_{i=1}^{k} S_{n_{i-1}}^2 A_i^{-2}\right) \text{ on } \left\{\sum_{i=1}^{\infty} S_{n_{i-1}}^2 A_i^{-2} = \infty\right\}. \tag{6.54}$$

Equations (6.52), (6.53) and (6.54) prove Eq. (6.51).   ∎

6.3.6 Theorem on Almost Sure Convergence of a Series with Square-Summable Coefficients (One-Dimensional Case)

Theorem.   (Lai and Wei, 1983b, Corollary 2) *Let $\{e_n, \mathcal{F}_n\}$ be a m.d. sequence satisfying the local M−Z condition (6.14). Let $\{a_n\}$ be a sequence of constants such that*

$$\sum_{i=1}^{\infty} a_i^2 < \infty \text{ and } a_i \neq 0 \text{ for infinitely many } i. \tag{6.55}$$

Then the series $\sum_{i=1}^{\infty} a_i e_i$ converges a.s. and

$$P\left(\sum_{i=1}^{\infty} a_i e_i = Y\right) = 0 \qquad (6.56)$$

for every random variable Y that is $\mathcal{F}_p$-measurable for some $p \geq 1$. Hence, in particular, $\sum_{i=1}^{\infty} a_i e_i$ has a nonatomic distribution and $P(\sum_{i=1}^{\infty} a_i e_i = c) = 0$ for any constant c.

When the m.d. sequence $\{e_n, \mathcal{F}_n\}$ satisfies the stronger condition (6.13), that $\sum_{i=1}^{\infty} a_i e_i$ has a nonatomic distribution for constants a_n satisfying Eq. (6.55) was established by Barlow (1975).

Proof. The a.s. convergence of $\sum_{i=1}^{\infty} a_i e_i$ follows from the generalized M–Z theorem I (Section 6.3.1).

To prove Eq. (6.56), assume the contrary that

$$P\left(\sum_{i=1}^{\infty} a_i e_i - Y = 0\right) = 3\eta > 0 \qquad (6.57)$$

for some $\mathcal{F}_p$-measurable Y. By Egorov's theorem there exists an event Ω_0 such that

$$P(\Omega_0) \geq 1 - \eta \text{ and } \sum_{i=1}^{\infty} a_i e_i(\omega) \text{ converges uniformly for } \omega \in \Omega_0. \qquad (6.58)$$

By the approximation lemma (Lemma 6.3.2), for the given η there exist positive integers m and K and a m.d. sequence $\{\tilde{e}_n, \tilde{\mathcal{F}}_n\}$ satisfying conditions (6.36) and (6.37) and such that $\mathcal{F}_n \subseteq \tilde{\mathcal{F}}_n$ for all n. Moreover, m can be taken larger than p.

Let

$$S_n = \left(\sum_{i=1}^{m-1} a_i e_i - Y\right) + \sum_{i=m}^{n} a_i \tilde{e}_i, \quad n \geq m. \qquad (6.59)$$

As the term in the parentheses is $\mathcal{F}_{m-1}$-measurable and $\mathcal{F}_n \subseteq \tilde{\mathcal{F}}_n$, $\{S_n, \tilde{\mathcal{F}}_n : n \geq m\}$ is a martingale:

$$E(S_n | \tilde{\mathcal{F}}_{n-1}) = \left(\sum_{i=1}^{m-1} a_i e_i - Y\right) + \sum_{i=m}^{n-1} a_i \tilde{e}_i + a_n E(\tilde{e}_n | \tilde{\mathcal{F}}_{n-1}) = S_{n-1}.$$

Denote

$$\Omega_1 = \left\{\sum_{i=1}^{\infty} a_i e_i - Y = 0\right\}, \quad \Omega_2 = \bigcap_{n \geq m} \{e_n = \tilde{e}_n\}, \quad \Omega_3 = \Omega_0 \cap \Omega_1 \cap \Omega_2.$$

From Eqs. (6.57), (6.58) and (6.59) we see that

$$S_n = \sum_{i=1}^{n} a_i e_i - Y \text{ converges uniformly to } 0 \text{ on } \Omega_3. \tag{6.60}$$

By Eq. (6.37), (6.57) and (6.58) we have $P(\overline{\Omega}_2) \le \eta$, $P(\overline{\Omega}_1) = 1 - 3\eta$ and $P(\overline{\Omega}_0) \le \eta$ (the bars stand for complements). Hence,

$$\begin{aligned} P(\Omega_3) &= 1 - P(\overline{\Omega}_3) = 1 - P(\overline{\Omega}_0 \cup \overline{\Omega}_1 \cup \overline{\Omega}_2) \\ &= 1 - P(\overline{\Omega}_0) - P(\overline{\Omega}_1) - P(\overline{\Omega}_2) \\ &\quad + P(\overline{\Omega}_0 \cap \overline{\Omega}_1) + P(\overline{\Omega}_0 \cap \overline{\Omega}_2) + P(\overline{\Omega}_1 \cap \overline{\Omega}_2) - P(\overline{\Omega}_0 \cap \overline{\Omega}_1 \cap \overline{\Omega}_2) \\ &\ge 1 - P(\overline{\Omega}_0) - P(\overline{\Omega}_1) - P(\overline{\Omega}_2) \ge \eta. \end{aligned}$$

We now define nonrandom positive integers $m = n_0 < n_1 < \cdots$ inductively as follows. Having defined n_{i-1}, we can choose by Eq. (6.55) an index $v > n_{i-1}$ such that $a_v \ne 0$. By Eq. (6.60), we can then choose $n_i > v$ in such a way that $\sup_{\omega \in \Omega_3} |S_{n_i}(\omega)| \le |a_v|/i$. With the numbers A_i defined in Eq. (6.50) this choice ensures that $S_{n_i}^2(\omega) \le A_i^2/i^2$ for all $\omega \in \Omega_3$ and that $A_i > 0$ for all i, so that

$$\sum_{i=1}^{\infty} S_{n_i}^2 A_i^{-2} \le \sum_{1}^{\infty} i^{-2} < \infty \text{ on } \Omega_3 \text{ with } P(\Omega_3) > 0. \tag{6.61}$$

Having defined the integers n_i, we then define u_i and $\mathcal{G}_i$ as in Eq. (6.46) and obtain by Lemma 6.3.4 that $\{u_i, \mathcal{G}_i\}$ is a m.d. sequence satisfying the local M−Z condition Eq. (6.47). Taking in Lemma 6.2.7 $w_i = 1$ for all i and $r = 2$ we see that the set V from that lemma equals Ω and

$$\liminf_{n \to \infty} \frac{1}{n} \sum_{1}^{n} u_i^2 > 0 \text{ a.s.} \tag{6.62}$$

The S_n defined in Eq. (6.59) differs from the S_n defined in Lemma 6.3.5 by the term Y which is $\mathcal{F}_p$-measurable and does not affect the proof of Lemma 6.3.5. Hence, Eq. (6.51) is applicable in the current situation. Equations (6.51) and (6.62) lead to the conclusion $\sum_{i=1}^{k} S_{n_i}^2/A_i^2 \to \infty$ a.s., which contradicts Eq. (6.61). ∎

6.3.7 Multivariate Local Marcinkiewicz−Zygmund Condition

The assumption to be made in the multivariate case is stronger than the local M−Z condition [Eq. (6.14)] in that in the first part of Eq. (6.14) higher powers of the m.d.'s are used:

$$\sup_n E(|e_n|^\alpha | \mathcal{F}_{n-1}) < \infty \text{ a.s. with some } \alpha > 2. \tag{6.63}$$

Besides, under this condition the second part of Eq. (6.14) becomes equivalent to

$$\liminf_{n\to\infty} E(e_n^2|\mathcal{F}_{n-1}) > 0 \text{ a.s.} \tag{6.64}$$

Indeed, if $\liminf_{n\to\infty} E(|e_n||\mathcal{F}_{n-1}) > 0$ a.s., then Eq. (6.64) holds because of the inequality $E(|e_n||\mathcal{F}_{n-1}) \leq [E(e_n^2|\mathcal{F}_{n-1})]^{1/2}$. Conversely, if Eq. (6.64) is true, then by the conditional Hölder inequality with $p = (\alpha-1)/(\alpha-2)$, $q = \alpha-1$ we have $1/p + 1/q = 1$, $1/p + \alpha/q = 2$ and

$$E(e_n^2|\mathcal{F}_{n-1}) = E(e_n^{1/p+\alpha/2}|\mathcal{F}_{n-1})$$

$$\leq [E(|e_n||\mathcal{F}_{n-1})]^{1/p} [\sup_n E(|e_n|^\alpha|\mathcal{F}_{n-1})]^{1/q}.$$

Hence, $\liminf_{n\to\infty} E(|e_n||\mathcal{F}_{n-1}) > 0$ follows.

If $e_n = (e_{n1}, \ldots, e_{nd})'$ is a column vector in $\mathbb{R}^d$, we replace the positivity of $E(e_n^2|\mathcal{F}_{n-1})$ in Eq. (6.64) by the positive definiteness of the covariance matrix $E(e_n e_n'|\mathcal{F}_{n-1})$ or, equivalently, by the positivity of its least eigenvalue $\lambda_{\min}[E(e_n e_n'|\mathcal{F}_{n-1})]$. Thus, by a *multivariate local M–Z condition* we mean

$$\left.\begin{array}{c} \sup_n E(\|e_n\|^\alpha |\mathcal{F}_{n-1}) < \infty \text{ a.s. with some } \alpha > 2 \\[6pt] \text{and} \\[6pt] \liminf_{n\to\infty} \lambda_{\min}[E(e_n e_n'|\mathcal{F}_{n-1})] > 0. \end{array}\right\} \tag{6.65}$$

6.3.8 Generalized Marcinkiewicz–Zygmund Theorem, Multivariate Case

Theorem. (Lai and Wei, 1983b, Corollary 3) *Let $\{e_n, \mathcal{F}_n\}$ be a vector m.d. sequence satisfying Eq. (6.65). Let $\{w_n\}$ be a premeasurable sequence of vectors $w_n = (w_{n1}, \ldots, w_{nd})'$ of the same dimension as e_n. Then, except for a null set, the following statements are equivalent*:

(i) $\sum_1^\infty \|w_i\|^2 < \infty$,

(ii) $\sum_1^\infty w_i' e_i$ *converges,*

(iii) $\sup_n|\sum_1^n w_i' e_i| < \infty$,

(iv) $\sum_1^\infty |w_i' e_i|^2 < \infty$.

Proof. The idea is to reduce the multivariate case to the scalar case considered in Section 6.3.1. Put

$$u_i = \frac{w_i' e_i}{\|w_i\|} 1(w_i \neq 0) + e_{i1} 1(w_i = 0). \tag{6.66}$$

Then

$$\sup_n E(|u_n|^\alpha|\mathcal{F}_{n-1}) \leq \sup_n E(\|e_n\|^\alpha |\mathcal{F}_{n-1}) < \infty \text{ a.s.} \tag{6.67}$$

Moreover, if $w_n \neq 0$, then

$$E(u_n^2|\mathcal{F}_{n-1}) = w_n' E(e_n e_n'|\mathcal{F}_{n-1}) w_n / \|w_n\|^2$$
$$\geq \lambda_{\min}[E(e_n e_n'|\mathcal{F}_{n-1})].$$

When $w_n = 0$, a similar inequality is true with w_n replaced by $(1, 0, \ldots, 0)' \in \mathbb{R}^d$. Therefore

$$\liminf_{n \to \infty} E(u_n^2|\mathcal{F}_{n-1}) \geq \liminf_{n \to \infty} \lambda_{\min}[E(e_n e_n'|\mathcal{F}_{n-1})] > 0 \text{ a.s.} \qquad (6.68)$$

By the argument in Section 6.3.7 it follows from Eqs. (6.67) and (6.68) that $\{u_n\}$ satisfies the local M–Z condition. That it is a m.d. sequence is easily seen from Eq. (6.66). Since $w_i' e_i = \|w_i\| u_i$ and $\|w_i\|$ is $\mathcal{F}_{i-1}$-measurable, items (i)–(iv) from Section 6.3.1 rewrite as items (i)–(iv) from this section. ∎

6.3.9   Convergence of a Series with Constant Vector Coefficients

Theorem.   (Lai and Wei, 1983b, Corollary 4) *Let $\{e_n, \mathcal{F}_n\}$ be a m.d. sequence satisfying the multivariate local M–Z condition Eq. (6.65). Suppose $\{A_n\}$ is a sequence of nonrandom vectors from $\mathbb{R}^d$ such that*

$$\sum_{i=1}^{\infty} \|A_i\|^2 < \infty \text{ and } A_i \neq 0 \text{ for infinitely many } i. \qquad (6.69)$$

Then the series $\sum_{i=1}^{\infty} A_i' e_i$ converges a.s. and $P(\sum_{i=1}^{\infty} A_i' e_i = Y) = 0$ for every random variable Y that is $\mathcal{F}_p$-measurable for some $p \geq 1$.

Proof.   In the definitions of Section 6.3.8 replace w_i by A_i to see that $\{u_i\}$ is a m.d. sequence satisfying the univariate local M–Z condition. As a result of the equality $A_i' e_i = \|A_i\| u_i$ we can put $a_i = \|A_i\|$. Then condition of Eq. (6.69) translates into Eq. (6.55) and the statement follows from Theorem 6.3.6. ∎

6.3.10   Wei's Bound on Martingale Transforms

Theorem.   (Wei, 1985, Lemma 2) *Let $\{e_n, \mathcal{F}_n\}$ be a m.d. sequence such that, with some $\alpha > 2$, $\sup_n E(|e_n|^\alpha|\mathcal{F}_{n-1}) < \infty$ a.s. and let $\{w_n\}$ be a premeasurable sequence of random variables. Define $s_n = \left(\sum_1^n w_i^2\right)^{1/2}$. Then for any $\delta > 1/\min\{\alpha, 4\}$*

$$\sum_1^n w_i e_i = O(s_n(\log s_n)^\delta) \text{ a.s.} \qquad (6.70)$$

Furthermore, if

$$|w_n| = o(s_n^c) \text{ for some } 0 < c < 1, \qquad (6.71)$$

then

$$\sum_{1}^{n} w_i e_i = O(s_n (\log \log s_n)^{1/2}) \text{ a.s.} \tag{6.72}$$

The proof is omitted because it uses stochastic processes in continuous time. Instead, in Section 6.3.11 we give a simpler statement from Lai and Wei (1982) with a proof. Note that this theorem covers both cases $\{\sum_{1}^{\infty} w_i^2 = \infty\}$ and $\{\sum_{1}^{\infty} w_i^2 < \infty\}$. In the latter case Eqs. (6.70) and (6.72) become $\sum_{1}^{n} w_i e_i = O(1)$. Eq. (6.71) becomes $w_n = o(1)$ and trivially follows from $\sum_{1}^{\infty} w_i^2 < \infty$.

6.3.11 A Simple Bound on Martingale Transforms

The following statement is stronger than Lemma 6.2.2.

Lemma.   *If the m.d. sequence* $\{e_n, \mathcal{F}_n\}$ *satisfies*

$$\sup_{n} E(e_n^2 | \mathcal{F}_{n-1}) < \infty \tag{6.73}$$

and $\{w_n\}$ *is premeasurable, then*

(i) $\sum_{1}^{\infty} w_i e_i$ *converges a.s. on* $U = \{\sum_{1}^{\infty} w_i^2 < \infty\}$;

(ii) *For every* $\eta > 1/2$ *with* $s_n = \left(\sum_{1}^{n} w_i^2\right)^{1/2}$ *we have*

$$\sum_{1}^{n} w_i e_i = o(s_n (\log s_n)^{\eta}) \text{ a.s. on } \Omega \backslash U = \left\{ \sum_{1}^{\infty} w_i^2 = \infty \right\}.$$

Proof.   By the truncation argument from Section 6.2.1 $w_n^* e_n$ can be considered square-integrable, and Eq. (6.7) ensures that $U = U^* = \{\sum_{1}^{\infty} (w_i^*)^2 < \infty\}$. In the proof we omit the stars.

Statement (i) was actually obtained in the course of the proof of Theorem 6.3.1, see implication (i) $\Rightarrow$ (ii) in the proof of that theorem.

(ii) $\{w_n e_n\}$ is a m.d. sequence. $U_n = s_n (\log s_n)^{1/2}$ is nondecreasing, positive and $\mathcal{F}_{n-1}$-measurable. Obviously,

$$\sum_{i=1}^{\infty} E((w_i e_i)^2 | \mathcal{F}_{i-1}) U_i^{-2} \leq \sum_{i=1}^{\infty} w_i^2 U_i^{-2} \sup_{n} E(e_n^2 | \mathcal{F}_{n-1}).$$

Replace the function $f(x) = x^{-2}$ in the proof of Lemma 6.2.2 by $f(x) = [x(\log x)^{2\eta}]^{-1}$, to get with sufficiently large m

$$\sum_{i=m}^{\infty} \frac{w_i^2}{U_i^2} = \sum_{i=m}^{\infty} \frac{1}{U_i^2} \int_{U_{i-1}}^{U_i} dx \leq \int_{U_{m-1}}^{\infty} \frac{dx}{x(\log x)^{2\eta}} < \infty \text{ on } U$$

because $2\eta > 1$. Now the statement follows from Theorem 6.1.4.   ∎

6.3.12   Bounds for Weighted Sums of Squared Martingale Differences

Lemma.   *Assume the conditions of Lemma 6.3.11. Then*

(i) $\sum_1^\infty |w_i| e_i^2 < \infty$ *a.s. on* $T = \{\sum_1^\infty |w_i| < \infty\}$;

(ii) For every $\rho > 1$

$$\sum_1^n |w_i| e_i^2 = o\left(\left(\sum_1^n |w_i|\right)^\rho\right) \quad \text{a.s. on } \Omega \backslash T. \tag{6.74}$$

Proof

(i) The centered squares $d_i = e_i^2 - E(e_i^2|\mathcal{F}_{i-1})$ are m.d.'s and satisfy $E(|d_i|\,||\,\mathcal{F}_{i-1}) \le 2 \sup_n E(e_n^2|\mathcal{F}_{n-1})$. In the identity

$$\sum_1^\infty |w_i| e_i^2 = \sum_1^\infty |w_i|\, d_i + \sum_1^\infty |w_i| E(e_i^2|\mathcal{F}_{i-1})$$

the second series on the right clearly converges on T. The first series converges by the martingale convergence theorem (Theorem 6.1.3) because $\{|w_i| d_i\}$ is a m.d. sequence and

$$\sum_1^\infty E(|w_i d_i|\,||\,\mathcal{F}_{i-1}) \le \sup_n E(|d_n|\,||\,\mathcal{F}_{n-1}) \sum_1^\infty |w_i| < \infty$$

on T.

(ii) As a first step we prove

$$\sum_1^\infty |w_i| e_i^2 c_i^{-\rho} < \infty \text{ a.s. on } \Omega \backslash T, \tag{6.75}$$

where $c_i = \sum_1^i |w_j|$ and, by definition, $0/0 = 0$. The assumption $\rho > 1$ implies

$$\sum_{i=1}^\infty \frac{|w_i|}{c_i^\rho} = \sum_{i=1}^\infty \frac{c_i - c_{i-1}}{c_i^\rho} \le \int_{c_1}^\infty \frac{dx}{x^\rho} < \infty \text{ a.s. on } \Omega \backslash T.$$

Applying statement (i) with $|w_i| c_i^{-\rho}$ in place of $|w_i|$ we obtain Eq. (6.75).

To apply Kronecker's lemma (Lemma 6.1.12), denote $x_i = |w_i| e_i^2$, $a_i = c_i^\rho$. $\sum_{i=1}^n x_i/a_i$ converges by Eq. (6.75) and $\{a_n\}$ monotonically increases to ∞ on $\Omega \backslash T$. Hence,

$$\sum_1^n |w_i| e_i^2 c_n^{-\rho} = 1/a_n \sum_{i=1}^n x_i \longrightarrow 0.$$

■

6.3.13 Precise Order of Weighted Squares of Martingale Differences

Lemma. *If the m.d. sequence $\{e_n, \mathcal{F}_n\}$ satisfies the M-Z condition Eq. (6.65) (in the 1-D case) and $\{w_n\}$ is premeasurable, then*

$$0 < \liminf_{n \to \infty} \frac{\sum_1^n |w_i| e_i^2}{\sum_1^n |w_i|} \leq \limsup_{n \to \infty} \frac{\sum_1^n |w_i| e_i^2}{\sum_1^n |w_i|} < \infty$$

$$on \ V = \left\{ \sum_{i=1}^\infty |w_i| = \infty, \ \sup_i |w_i| < \infty \right\}. \tag{6.76}$$

Proof. The left inequality in Eq. (6.76) is proved in Lemma 6.2.7. Note that the right inequality strengthens Eq. (6.74) by allowing $\rho = 1$. Let us prove it.

Take some $r \in (1, \min\{2, \alpha/2\})$ and denote $d_i = e_i^2 - E(e_i^2 | \mathcal{F}_{i-1})$. From the elementary inequality $|a - b|^r \leq c_r(a^r + b^r)$, conditional Jensen's inequality (Section 6.1.6) and M-Z condition [Eq. (6.65)] we get

$$E(|d_i|^r | \mathcal{F}_{i-1}) \leq c_r E\{|e_i|^{2r} + [E(e_i^2 | \mathcal{F}_{i-1})]^r | \mathcal{F}_{i-1}\}$$

$$\leq 2c_r \sup_n E(|e_n|^{2r} | \mathcal{F}_{n-1}) < \infty \ \text{a.s.} \tag{6.77}$$

The products $|w_i| d_i$ are m.d.'s. Now consider two cases:

1. Suppose

$$\sum_1^\infty |w_i|^r = \infty. \tag{6.78}$$

Denoting $U_i = \sum_1^i |w_j|^r$, by Eqs. (6.77) and (6.78) we have

$$\sum_{i=m}^\infty \frac{E(|w_i d_i|^r | \mathcal{F}_{i-1})}{U_i^r} \leq c \sum_{i=m}^\infty \frac{|w_i|^r}{U_i^r} = c \sum_{i=m}^\infty \frac{U_i - U_{i-1}}{U_i^r}$$

$$\leq c \sum_{i=m}^\infty \int_{U_{i-1}}^{U_i} \frac{dx}{x^r} = c \int_{U_{m-1}}^\infty \frac{dx}{x^r} < \infty \ \text{a.s.},$$

where c depends on ω and $U_{m-1} > 0$. By the martingale strong law (Section 6.1.4)

$$\text{Eq. (6.78)} \implies \sum_{i=1}^n |w_i| d_i = o\left(\sum_{i=1}^n |w_i|^r \right) \ \text{a.s.} \tag{6.79}$$

2. Next assume the opposite of Eq. (6.78):

$$\sum_1^\infty |w_i|^r < \infty. \tag{6.80}$$

Since by Eq. (6.77) $\sum_{i=1}^{\infty} E(|w_i d_i|^r | \mathcal{F}_{i-1}) \leq c \sum_{1}^{\infty} |w_i|^r < \infty$ in this case, the martingale convergence theorem (Theorem 6.1.3) shows that

$$\text{Eq. (6.80)} \quad \Rightarrow \quad \sum_{i=1}^{n} |w_i| \, d_i = O(1) \text{ a.s.} \tag{6.81}$$

Now we are able to prove

$$\sum_{i=1}^{n} |w_i| \, d_i = o\left(\sum_{i=1}^{n} |w_i| \right) \text{ a.s.} \tag{6.82}$$

From the bound

$$\sum_{1}^{n} |w_i| = \sup_j |w_j| \sum_{i=1}^{n} \frac{|w_i|}{\sup_j |w_j|} \geq \sup_j |w_j|^{1-r} \sum_{i=1}^{n} |w_i|^r$$

we see that

$$\sum_{i=1}^{n} |w_i|^r = O\left(\sum_{i=1}^{n} |w_i| \right) \text{ on } V. \tag{6.83}$$

Take $\omega \in V$. If Eq. (6.78) is true, then Eq. (6.82) follows from Eqs. (6.79) and (6.83). If Eq. (6.80) is true, then Eq. (6.82) is a consequence of Eq. (6.81) and $\sum_{1}^{\infty} |w_i| = \infty$.

Finally, Eq. (6.82) and the M-Z condition (Section 6.2.3) imply

$$\sum_{1}^{n} |w_i| e_i^2 = \sum_{i=1}^{n} |w_i| \, d_i + \sum_{i=1}^{n} |w_i| E(e_i^2 | \mathcal{F}_{i-1}) = O\left(\sum_{i=1}^{n} |w_i| \right) \text{ on } V. \quad \blacksquare$$

6.4   STRONG CONSISTENCY FOR MULTIPLE REGRESSION

6.4.1   Notation

In the multiple regression model

$$y_n = X_n \beta + \varepsilon_n, \; n = 1, 2, \ldots, \text{ where } \varepsilon_n = (e_1, \ldots, e_n)'$$

we assume that $\{e_n, \mathcal{F}_n\}$ is a m.d. sequence, the parameter vector is $p \times 1$ and the matrix X_n is of size $n \times p$. It is assumed that, as n grows, new equations are appended to the system and the previous equations are not changed. Further, for each n the nth row $(x_{n1}, \ldots, x_{np})$ is $\mathcal{F}_{n-1}$-measurable. The nth row is written as the transpose of $x_n = (x_{n1}, \ldots, x_{np})'$ and, therefore, if $X_n' X_n$ is nonsingular, the least squares estimate

b_n of β becomes

$$b_n = (X_n'X_n)^{-1}X_n'y_n = \beta + \left(\sum_1^n x_ix_i'\right)^{-1}\sum_1^n x_ie_i.$$

It is seen that the statistical properties of b_n are related to the martingale transform $\sum_1^n x_ie_i$ and the random matrix

$$A_n = \sum_1^n x_ix_i'.$$

That this matrix is a sum of nonnegative definite matrices x_ix_i' is one of the leading ideas in Section 6.4. In particular, some important properties of the sequence $\{A_n\}$ depend on quadratic forms $x_k'A_k^{-1}x_k$, which we call *increments*. All statements in Section 6.4 are taken from Lai and Wei (1982).

For a $p \times p$ symmetric matrix A we denote by

$$\lambda_{\min}(A) = \lambda_1(A) \leq \cdots \leq \lambda_p(A) = \lambda_{\max}(A) \qquad (6.84)$$

its eigenvalues. $|A|$ stands for the determinant of A.

6.4.2   Lemma on Increments

Lemma.   *Let B be a $p \times p$ matrix and let w be a $p \times 1$ vector. If $A = B + ww'$ is nonsingular, then $w'A^{-1}w = 1 - |B|/|A|$.*

Proof.   By the partitioned matrix rule [Lemma 1.7.6(i)]

$$|B| = |A - ww'| = \begin{vmatrix} 1 & w' \\ w & A \end{vmatrix} = |A|(1 - w'A^{-1}w),$$

which gives the desired result.   ∎

6.4.3   The Link between Increments and $\lambda_{\max}$ (A_n)

Lemma.   *Let $x_1, x_2, \ldots$ be $p \times 1$ vectors and let $A_n = \sum_1^n x_ix_i'$. Suppose that A_N is nonsingular for some N. Then*

   (i) $\lambda_{\max}(A_n)$ *is nondecreasing and A_n is nonsingular for all $n \geq N$.*
   (ii) *If $\lim_{n\to\infty} \lambda_{\max}(A_n) < \infty$, then $\sum_{k=N}^{\infty} x_k'A_k^{-1}x_k < \infty$.*
   (iii) *If $\lim_{n\to\infty} \lambda_{\max}(A_n) = \infty$, then $\sum_{k=N}^n x_k'A_k^{-1}x_k = O(\log \lambda_{\max}(A_n))$.*

Proof.

   (i) By (Gohberg and Kreǐn (1969), Lemma 1.1) the inequality $A_k \geq A_{k-1}$ implies

$$\lambda_j(A_k) \geq \lambda_j(A_{k-1}), \quad j = 1, \ldots, p. \qquad (6.85)$$

In particular, $\lambda_{\max}(A_n)$ is nondecreasing. If A_N is nonsingular, then $\lambda_{\min}(A_N)$ is positive and all A_n with $n \geq N$ are nonsingular.

(ii) The equation $A_k = A_{k-1} + x_k x'_k$ and Lemma 6.4.2 imply

$$\sum_{k=N+1}^{n} x'_k A_k^{-1} x_k = \sum_{k=N+1}^{n} (1 - |A_{k-1}|/|A_k|), \quad n \geq N + 1. \tag{6.86}$$

Obviously, Eq. (6.85) implies

$$[\lambda_{\max}(A_n)]^p \geq |A_n| = \prod_{j=1}^{p} \lambda_j(A_n) \geq [\lambda_{\min}(A_n)]^p, \quad n \geq N + 1. \tag{6.87}$$

If $\lim_{n \to \infty} \lambda_{\max}(A_n) < \infty$, then Eqs. (6.86) and (6.87) give

$$\sum_{k=N+1}^{n} x'_k A_k^{-1} x_k = \sum_{k=N+1}^{n} (|A_k| - |A_{k-1}|)/|A_k|$$

$$\leq \lambda_{\min}^{-p}(A_{N+1}) \sum_{k=N+1}^{n} (|A_k| - |A_{k-1}|)$$

$$= \lambda_{\min}^{-p}(A_{N+1})(|A_n| - |A_N|)$$

$$\leq [\lambda_{\max}(A_n)/\lambda_{\min}(A_{N+1})]^p \leq c, \quad n \geq N + 1.$$

(iii) As a result of Eq. (6.85) we have $|A_k| \geq |A_{k-1}|$ and

$$\frac{|A_k| - |A_{k-1}|}{|A_k|} = \int_{|A_{k-1}|}^{|A_k|} \frac{dx}{|A_k|} \leq \int_{|A_{k-1}|}^{|A_k|} \frac{dx}{x} = \ln|A_k| - \ln|A_{k-1}|.$$

Summing these inequalities and applying Eqs. (6.86) and (6.87) we get

$$\sum_{k=N+1}^{n} x'_k A_k^{-1} x_k \leq \sum_{k=N+1}^{n} (\ln|A_k| - \ln|A_{k-1}|)$$

$$= \ln|A_n| - \ln|A_N| = O(\ln|A_n|) = O\{\log[\lambda_{\max}(A_n)]\}. \quad \blacksquare$$

6.4.4   Lemma on Recursions

Define

$$N = \inf\{n : X'_n X_n \text{ is nonsingular}\}, \quad \inf \phi = \infty,$$

and for $n \geq N$ consider the quadratic form

$$Q_n = \varepsilon'_n X_n (X'_n X_n)^{-1} X'_n \varepsilon_n = \varepsilon'_n X_n A_n^{-1} X'_n \varepsilon_n.$$

Lemma. *Let us partition X_n into rows, $X_n = (x_1, \ldots, x_n)'$, and denote $q_k = x_k' A_{k-1}^{-1} x_k$. Then*

$$A_k^{-1} = A_{k-1}^{-1} - A_{k-1}^{-1} x_k x_k' A_{k-1}^{-1}/(1 + q_k), \tag{6.88}$$

$$Q_k = Q_{k-1} - \frac{\left(x_k' A_{k-1}^{-1} \sum_1^{k-1} x_i e_i\right)^2}{1 + q_k} + 2 \frac{\left(x_k' A_{k-1}^{-1} \sum_1^{k-1} x_i e_i\right) e_k}{1 + q_k}$$

$$+ x_k' A_k^{-1} x_k e_k^2, \tag{6.89}$$

and for $n > N$

$$Q_n - Q_N + \sum_{k=N+1}^{n} \frac{\left(x_k' A_{k-1}^{-1} \sum_1^{k-1} x_i e_i\right)^2}{1 + q_k}$$

$$= 2 \sum_{k=N+1}^{n} \frac{\left(x_k' A_{k-1}^{-1} \sum_1^{k-1} x_i e_i\right) e_k}{1 + q_k} + \sum_{k=N+1}^{n} x_k' A_k^{-1} x_k e_k^2. \tag{6.90}$$

Proof. To prove Eq. (6.88), it is enough to check that premultiplication of the matrix at the right of Eq. (6.88) by $A_k = X_{k-1}' X_{k-1} + x_k x_k'$ gives the identity matrix. Remembering that $X_k' X_k A_k^{-1} = I$ we have

$$(X_{k-1}' X_{k-1} + x_k x_k')\left(A_{k-1}^{-1} - \frac{A_{k-1}^{-1} x_k x_k' A_{k-1}^{-1}}{1 + q_k}\right)$$

$$= I - \frac{x_k x_k' A_{k-1}^{-1}}{1 + q_k} + x_k x_k' A_{k-1}^{-1} - \frac{x_k (x_k' A_{k-1}^{-1} x_k) x_k' A_{k-1}^{-1}}{1 + q_k}$$

$$= I + \left(1 - \frac{1}{1 + q_k}\right) x_k x_k' A_{k-1}^{-1} - \frac{q_k x_k x_k' A_{k-1}^{-1}}{1 + q_k}$$

$$= I + \left(\frac{q_k}{1 + q_k} - \frac{q_k}{1 + q_k}\right) x_k x_k' A_{k-1}^{-1} = I.$$

Now we prove Eq. (6.89). By Eq. (6.88) for $k > N$

$$x_k' A_k^{-1} = x_k' A_{k-1}^{-1} - \frac{(x_k' A_{k-1}^{-1} x_k) x_k' A_{k-1}^{-1}}{1 + x_k' A_{k-1}^{-1} x_k} = \frac{x_k' A_{k-1}^{-1}}{1 + q_k}. \tag{6.91}$$

For $k > N$ the definition of Q_n, and Eqs. (6.88) and (6.91) give

$$Q_k = \left(\sum_1^{k-1} x_i' e_i + x_k' e_k\right) A_k^{-1} \left(\sum_1^{k-1} x_i e_i + x_k e_k\right)$$

$$= \sum_1^{k-1} x_i' e_i A_k^{-1} \sum_1^{k-1} x_i e_i + 2\left(x_k' A_k^{-1} \sum_1^{k-1} x_i e_i\right) e_k + x_k' A_k^{-1} x_k e_k^2$$

$$= \sum_{1}^{k-1} x_i' e_i \left(A_{k-1}^{-1} - \frac{A_{k-1}^{-1} x_k x_k' A_{k-1}^{-1}}{1 + q_k} \right) \sum_{1}^{k-1} x_i e_i$$

$$+ 2 \left(\frac{x_k' A_{k-1}^{-1}}{1 + q_k} \sum_{1}^{k-1} x_i e_i \right) e_k + x_k' A_k^{-1} x_k e_k^2$$

$$= Q_{k-1} - \frac{\left(x_k' A_{k-1}^{-1} \sum_{1}^{k-1} x_i e_i \right)^2}{1 + q_k} + 2 \frac{\left(x_k' A_{k-1}^{-1} \sum_{1}^{k-1} x_i e_i \right) e_k}{1 + q_k}$$

$$+ x_k' A_k^{-1} x_k e_k^2,$$

which proves Eq. (6.89).

Sending the first two terms at the right of Eq. (6.89) to the left side and summing over $k = N + 1, \ldots, n$ we get Eq. (6.90). ∎

6.4.5   Bounding Q_n

Lemma.   *Let the m.d. sequence $\{e_n, \mathcal{F}_n\}$ satisfy*

$$\sup_n E(e_n^2 | \mathcal{F}_{n-1}) < \infty \, a.s. \tag{6.92}$$

and let $\{x_n\}$ be premeasurable. Put

$$\Lambda_{<\infty} = \{ N < \infty, \; \lim_{n \to \infty} \lambda_{max}(A_n) < \infty \},$$

$$\Lambda_{=\infty} = \{ N < \infty, \; \lim_{n \to \infty} \lambda_{max}(A_n) = \infty \}.$$

The following statements are true:

(i) $Q_n = O(1)$ a.s. on $\Lambda_{<\infty}$.

(ii) For every $\delta > 0$

$$Q_n = o([\log \lambda_{max}(A_n)]^{1+\delta}) \, a.s. \, on \, \Lambda_{=\infty}. \tag{6.93}$$

(iii) If Eq. (6.92) is replaced by

$$\sup_n E(|e_n|^\alpha | \mathcal{F}_{n-1}) < \infty \, a.s. \, for \, some \, \alpha > 2, \tag{6.94}$$

then Eq. (6.93) can be strengthened into

$$Q_n = O(\log \lambda_{max}(A_n)) \, a.s. \, on \, \Lambda_{=\infty}. \tag{6.95}$$

Proof.

(i) Let $w_k = x_k' A_{k-1}^{-1} \sum_1^{k-1} x_i e_i / (1 + q_k)$ if $k > N$ and $w_k = 0$ if $k \le N$. Since $\{w_n\}$ is premeasurable, it follows from Lemma 6.3.11(ii) that

$$\sum_{k=N+1}^{n} w_k e_k = o\left[\left(\sum_{k=N+1}^{n} w_k^2 \right)^{1/2} \left(\log \sum_{k=N+1}^{n} w_k^2 \right)^{\eta} \right]$$

$$= o\left(\sum_{k=N+1}^{n} w_k^2 \right) \text{ on } \left\{ \sum_{N+1}^{\infty} w_k^2 = \infty \right\}.$$

However, by Lemma 6.3.11(i)

$$\sum_{k=N+1}^{n} w_k e_k = O(1) \text{ on } \left\{ \sum_{N+1}^{\infty} w_k^2 < \infty \right\}.$$

The two bounds above imply

$$\sum_{k=N+1}^{n} \frac{x_k' A_{k-1}^{-1} \sum_1^{k-1} x_i e_i}{1 + q_k} e_k = o\left(\sum_{k=N+1}^{n} w_k^2 \right) + O(1)$$

$$= o\left(\sum_{k=N+1}^{n} \left(\frac{x_k' A_{k-1}^{-1} \sum_1^{k-1} x_i e_i}{1 + q_k} \right)^2 \right) + O(1)$$

$$= o\left(\sum_{k=N+1}^{n} \frac{\left(x_k' A_{k-1}^{-1} \sum_1^{k-1} x_i e_i \right)^2}{1 + q_k} \right) + O(1). \tag{6.96}$$

By Lemma 6.4.3(ii) $\sum_{k=N+1}^{\infty} x_k' A_k^{-1} x_k < \infty$ on $\Lambda_{<\infty}$. Because $x_k' A_k^{-1} x_k$ is $\mathcal{F}_{k-1}$-measurable, by Lemma 6.3.12(i)

$$\sum_{k=N+1}^{\infty} x_k' A_k^{-1} x_k e_k^2 < \infty \text{ on } \Lambda_{<\infty}. \tag{6.97}$$

Equations (6.96) and (6.97) allow us to use Eq. (6.90) to conclude that

$$Q_n + \sum_{k=N+1}^{n} \frac{\left(x_k' A_{k-1}^{-1} \sum_1^{k-1} x_i e_i \right)^2}{1 + q_k} (1 + o(1)) = O(1) \text{ a.s. on } \Lambda_{<\infty}. \tag{6.98}$$

This proves statement (i).

(ii) In the event $\Lambda_{=\infty}$, by Lemmas 6.4.3(iii) and 6.3.12(ii) for every $\delta > 0$

$$\sum_{k=N+1}^{n} x_k' A_k^{-1} x_k e_k^2 = o\left[\left(\sum_{k=N+1}^{n} x_k' A_k^{-1} x_k\right)^{1+\delta}\right]$$

$$= o[(\log \lambda_{\max}(A_n))^{1+\delta}] \text{ if } \sum_{k=N+1}^{\infty} x_k' A_k^{-1} x_k = \infty$$

and by Lemma 6.3.12(i)

$$\sum_{k=N+1}^{n} x_k' A_k^{-1} x_k e_k^2 = O(1) = o(\log \lambda_{\max}(A_n)) \text{ if } \sum_{k=N+1}^{\infty} x_k' A_k^{-1} x_k < \infty.$$

Consequently, for every $\delta > 0$

$$\sum_{k=N+1}^{n} x_k' A_k^{-1} x_k e_k^2 = o[(\log \lambda_{\max}(A_n))^{1+\delta}] \text{ on } \Lambda_{=\infty}. \qquad (6.99)$$

As above, we apply Eqs. (6.96), (6.99) and (6.90) to derive

$$Q_n + \sum_{k=N+1}^{n} \frac{\left(x_k' A_{k-1}^{-1} \sum_1^{k-1} x_i e_i\right)^2}{1 + q_k} (1 + o(1))$$

$$= o[(\log \lambda_{\max}(A_n))^{1+\delta}] \text{ on } \Lambda_{=\infty} \qquad (6.100)$$

for every $\delta > 0$. The proof of Eq. (6.93) is complete.

(iii) Suppose Eq. (6.94) holds. By Lemma 6.4.2 $x_k' A_k^{-1} x_k = 1 - |A_{k-1}|/|A_k| \le 1$ and therefore

$$\left\{\sup_k x_k' A_k^{-1} x_k < \infty, \ \sum_{k=N+1}^{\infty} x_k' A_k^{-1} x_k = \infty\right\} = \left\{\sum_{k=N+1}^{\infty} x_k' A_k^{-1} x_k = \infty\right\}.$$

By Lemmas 6.3.13 and 6.4.3(iii)

$$\sum_{k=N+1}^{n} x_k' A_k^{-1} x_k e_k^2 = O\left(\sum_{k=N+1}^{n} x_k' A_k^{-1} x_k\right) = O(\log \lambda_{\max}(A_n)).$$

Using this relationship instead of Eq. (6.99) in the proof of Eq. (6.100) we finish the proof of Eq. (6.95). ∎

6.4.6 Case of One Regressor

The beauty of Lemma 6.4.5 is that the convergence properties established in Lemma 6.3.11 are extended to the multiple regression case without deterioration of the rates of convergence. More importantly, Lemma 6.4.5 in the case of one regressor ($p = 1$)

provides an improvement of Lemma 6.3.11(ii) under the assumption (6.94). This is the content of the next corollary.

Corollary.   *Let the m.d. sequence $\{e_n, \mathcal{F}_n\}$ satisfy Eq. (6.94) and suppose that the sequence of random weights $\{w_n\}$ is premeasurable. Then in the event $\left\{\sum_1^\infty w_i^2 = \infty\right\}$*

$$\sum_1^n w_i e_i = O\left(\left[\sum_1^n w_i^2\left(\log \sum_1^n w_i^2\right)\right]^{1/2}\right) \ a.s.$$

Proof.   Set $X_n = (w_1, \ldots, w_n)'$ in Lemma 6.4.5 to obtain

$$A_n = X_n'X_n = \sum_1^n w_i^2, \ \lambda_{\max}(A_n) = \sum_1^n w_i^2, \ X_n'\varepsilon_n = \sum_1^n w_i e_i,$$

$$Q_n = \varepsilon_n'X_n(X_n'X_n)^{-1}X_n'\varepsilon_n = \left(\sum_1^n w_i e_i\right)^2\left(\sum_1^n w_i^2\right)^{-1}.$$

Then by Eq. (6.95)

$$\left(\sum_1^n w_i e_i\right)^2\left(\sum_1^n w_i^2\right)^{-1} = O\left(\log \sum_1^n w_i^2\right) \text{ on } \left\{\sum_1^\infty w_i^2 = \infty\right\}. \qquad \blacksquare$$

6.4.7   Strong Consistency of the Ordinary Least Squares Estimator in Stochastic Regression Models

Consider the regression model $y_n = X_n\beta + \varepsilon_n$, where $\varepsilon_n = (e_1, \ldots, e_n)'$, and denote $A_n = X_n'X_n$. For nonrandom x_{ij}, Lai et al. (1978, 1979) proved that the condition $A_n^{-1} \to 0$ is necessary and sufficient for the strong consistency of the OLS estimator b_n.[3] This condition is equivalent to $\lambda_{\min}(A_n) \to \infty$. Now suppose that x_{ij} are random and $\lambda_{\min}(A_n) \to \infty$ a.s. Anderson and Taylor (1979) established the strong consistency of b_n under the condition $\lambda_{\max}(A_n) = O(\lambda_{\min}(A_n))$, while Christopeit and Helmes (1980) weakened that condition to $[\lambda_{\max}(A_n)]^r = O(\lambda_{\min}(A_n))$ a.s. for some $r > 1/2$. The following theorem by Lai and Wei (1982) is a substantial improvement of those results.

Theorem.   *Suppose that in the above regression model, $\{e_n, \mathcal{F}_n\}$ is a m.d. sequence such that Eq. (6.94) holds. Further, assume that the nth row x_n of X_n is $\mathcal{F}_{n-1}$-measurable, for all n, and that*

$$\lambda_{\min}(A_n) \to \infty \ a.s. \ and \ \log \lambda_{\max}(A_n) = o(\lambda_{\min}(A_n)) \ a.s. \qquad (6.101)$$

---

[3]It would be good to include this result in the book but I could not find the complete proof.

Then the least-squares estimator b_n converges a.s. to β; in fact,

$$\|b_n - \beta\| = O\left(\left[\frac{\log \lambda_{\max}(A_n)}{\lambda_{\min}(A_n)}\right]^{1/2}\right) \text{ a.s.} \tag{6.102}$$

Proof. Since $\lambda_{\min}(A_n) \to \infty$ a.s., we have $N < \infty$ a.s. Note the identity

$$\left\|A_n^{-1/2}\sum_1^n x_i e_i\right\|^2 = (A_n^{-1/2}X_n'\varepsilon_n)'A_n^{-1/2}X_n'\varepsilon_n = \varepsilon_n'X_nA_n^{-1}X_n'\varepsilon_n = Q_n.$$

It allows us to apply Lemma 6.4.5(iii) and condition (6.101) in writing

$$\|b_n - \beta\|^2 = \left\|A_n^{-1}\sum_1^n x_i e_i\right\|^2 \leq \|A_n^{-1/2}\|^2\left\|A_n^{-1/2}\sum_1^n x_i e_i\right\|^2$$

$$= [\lambda_{\min}(A_n)]^{-1}Q_n = O([\log \lambda_{\max}(A_n)]/\lambda_{\min}(A_n)) = o(1). \qquad \blacksquare$$

6.4.8 Another Version of the Strong Consistency Statement

In Chapter 7 on nonlinear models there is a situation where condition (6.94) is too tough. To this end, the theorem below is useful.

Theorem. *If in Theorem 6.4.7 condition (6.94) is replaced by a weaker condition Eq. (6.92) and condition (6.101) is replaced by a stronger one*

$$\lambda_{\min}(A_n) \to \infty \text{ a.s. and } [\log \lambda_{\max}(A_n)]^{1+\delta} = o(\lambda_{\min}(A_n)) \text{ for some } \delta > 0, \tag{6.103}$$

then the conclusion [Eq. (6.102)] is true.

This follows from Lemma 6.4.5(ii).

6.5 SOME ALGEBRA RELATED TO VECTOR AUTOREGRESSION

6.5.1 The Model and History

Consider the vector autoregressive model

$$Y_n = BY_{n-1} + e_n, \quad n = 1, 2, \ldots \tag{6.104}$$

where B is a $p \times p$ nonrandom matrix with real elements and $\{e_n, \mathcal{F}_n\}$ is a vector m.d. sequence satisfying

$$\sup_n E(\|e_n\|^\alpha | \mathcal{F}_{n-1}) < \infty \text{ a.s. with some } \alpha > 2. \tag{6.105}$$

Equation (6.104) is equivalent to

$$Y_n = B^n Y_0 + \sum_{i=1}^{n} B^{n-i} e_i, \qquad (6.106)$$

where Y_0 is assumed to be $\mathcal{F}_0$-measurable. We denote

$$Y_n = (Y_{n1}, \ldots, Y_{np})', \; e_n = (e_{n1}, \ldots, e_{np})',$$
$$B = (b_{ij})_{1 \le i, j \le p}, \; b_i = (b_{i1}, \ldots, b_{ip})' \qquad (6.107)$$

(B is partitioned into rows). The least-squares estimate of b_i based on observed $Y_1, \ldots, Y_{n+1}$ is

$$\hat{b}_k(n+1) = \left(\sum_{i=1}^{n} Y_i Y_i' \right)^{-1} \sum_{i=1}^{n} Y_i Y_{i+1,k} = b_k + \left(\sum_{i=1}^{n} Y_i Y_i' \right)^{-1} \sum_{i=1}^{n} Y_i e_{i+1,k}, \quad (6.108)$$

where the inverse sign denotes the Moore–Penrose generalized inverse. In view of Eq. (6.108) the least-squares estimate is strongly consistent if and only if

$$\left(\sum_{i=1}^{n} Y_i Y_i' \right)^{-1} \sum_{i=1}^{n} Y_i e_{i+1}' \to 0 \text{ a.s.} \qquad (6.109)$$

The autoregressive $AR(p)$ model

$$y_n = \beta_1 y_{n-1} + \cdots + \beta_p y_{n-p} + \varepsilon_n \qquad (6.110)$$

can be written in the vector form [Eq. (6.104)] with

$$Y_n = (y_n, y_{n-1}, \ldots, y_{n-p+1})', \; e_n = (\varepsilon_n, 0, \ldots, 0)',$$
$$B = \begin{pmatrix} \beta_1 & \cdots & \beta_{p-1} & \beta_p \\ I_{p-1} & & & 0 \end{pmatrix}. \qquad (6.111)$$

This B is called a *companion matrix* for Eq. (6.110).

Everywhere we denote $z_1, \ldots, z_p$ the eigenvalues of B (the roots of its characteristic polynomial) and put $M = \max |z_j|$, $m = \min |z_j|$. If $m > 1$, the process $\{Y_n\}$ is called *purely explosive*. If $M \le 1$, we say that it is *nonexplosive*. Section 6.5 is based on the paper Lai and Wei (1985). Table 6.1 describes the contributions of various authors prior to that paper. All these authors considered weak consistency. Lai and Wei established strong consistency for Eq. (6.110) in (Lai and Wei, 1983a) and for Eq. (6.104) in (Lai and Wei, 1985). Nielsen (2005) added a deterministic term (see the definition in Chapter 8) in Eq. (6.104). In Nielsen, (2008) he discovered that the least-squares estimator for a vector autoregression (VAR) of dimension larger than 1 may be inconsistent. To achieve consistency, we have to decompose Y_n into stationary, unit root and explosive processes and require the unit root component to be of dimension 1, [see (Nielsen, 2008, pp. 3-4) for the decomposition

TABLE 6.1   **Contributions to the Consistency Theory of Autoregressions**

Author(s)	Case(s) considered
Mann and Wald (1943)	$M < 1$
Rubin (1950), Anderson (1959)	$m > 1$
Rao (1961)	$p = 2,\ |z_1| < 1,\ |z_2| < 1$
White (1958)	$p = 1,\ |z_1| = 1$
Muench(1974), Stigum(1974)	Roots anywhere

and Assumption E that ensures consistency]. He mentions that Lai and Wei (1985) and Nielsen (2005) overlooked the possibility of singularity. Giving complete proofs is not an option here, and we just require the unit root component to be of dimension 1, remembering that this makes the argument by Lai and Wei correct.

6.5.2   Growth Rate of Natural Powers of B

For $x \in \mathbb{R}^p$ denote $\|x\| = (x'x)^{1/2}$ and for a $p \times p$ matrix A denote $\|A\| = \sup_{\|x\|=1} \|Ax\|$. Let $\lambda_1, \ldots, \lambda_q$, $q \leq p$, denote all the distinct eigenvalues of B, and express it in its Jordan form,

$$B = C^{-1}DC, \quad \text{where} \quad D = \text{diag}[D_1, \ldots, D_q], \tag{6.112}$$

$$D_j = \begin{pmatrix} \lambda_j & 1 & 0 & \cdots & 0 \\ 0 & \lambda_j & 1 & \cdots & 0 \\ 0 & 0 & \lambda_j & \cdots & \cdots \\ \vdots & \vdots & \vdots & \ddots & \vdots \\ 0 & 0 & 0 & \cdots & \lambda_j \end{pmatrix} \quad \text{is an } m_j \times m_j \text{ matrix,}$$

m_j is the multiplicity of λ_j $\left(\sum_{j=1}^q m_j = p\right)$, and C is a nonsingular $p \times p$ matrix (over the complex field). Denote

$$M = \max|\lambda_j|, \quad \mu = \max\{m_j : |\lambda_j| = M\}. \tag{6.113}$$

μ is the multiplicity of the largest (in absolute value) eigenvalue of B.

Lemma

(i) *There exists a constant $c = c(\mu, M) > 0$ such that*

$$\|B^n\| \leq cn^{\mu-1}M^n \text{ for all natural } n. \tag{6.114}$$

(ii) $\frac{1}{n}\log\|B^n\| = (1 + o(1))\log M$.

(iii) $\frac{1}{n}\log\|B^{-n}\| = -(1 + o(1))\log m$.

Proof.

(i) [Varga, 1962, p. 65] proved that

$$\|B^n\| = (1 + o(1))cC_{\mu-1}^n[\lambda_{\max}(B)]^{n-(\mu-1)}, \qquad (6.115)$$

where c does not depend on B. The quantity

$$C_{\mu-1}^n M^{n-(\mu-1)} = \frac{n(n-1)\cdots(n-\mu+2)}{(\mu-1)!} \frac{M^n}{M^{\mu-1}}$$

$$= \frac{(1-\frac{1}{n})\cdots(1-\frac{\mu-2}{n})}{(\mu-1)!M^{\mu-1}} n^{\mu-1} M^n \qquad (6.116)$$

is of order $n^{\mu-1}M^n$, which proves (i).

(ii) From Eqs. (6.115) and (6.116) it follows that with

$$c(n) = \frac{\left(1-\frac{1}{n}\right)\cdots\left(1-\frac{\mu-2}{n}\right)}{[(\mu-1)!M^{\mu-1}]}$$

we have

$$\frac{1}{n}\log\|B^n\| = \frac{1}{n}\log\left[(1 + o(1))cc(n)\right] + \frac{\mu-1}{n}\log n + \log M.$$

This proves (ii).

(iii) is a consequence of (ii) because $\lambda_{\max}(B^{-1}) = 1/\lambda_{\min}(B) = m^{-1}$. ∎

6.5.3 The Meddling Middle Factor

This lemma is used to show that in some situations for the estimation of $\lambda_{\max}(A_n C_n A_n')$ the factor in the middle, C_n, is asymptotically negligible.

Lemma. *Let A, C be $p \times p$ matrices such that C is symmetric and nonnegative definite. Then*

$$\lambda_{\max}(C)\lambda_{\max}(AA') \geq \lambda_{\max}(ACA') \geq \lambda_{\min}(C)\lambda_{\max}(AA'). \qquad (6.117)$$

Proof. In the proof we use the fact that for any symmetric nonnegative definite matrix C

$$\lambda_{\max}(C) = \sup_{\|x\|=1} x'Cx = \sup_{\|x\|=1} \|Cx\|. \qquad (6.118)$$

Together with the equation $\|A\| = \|A'\|$ this leads to

$$\|A\|^2 = \sup_{\|x\|=1} \|A'x\|^2 = \sup_{\|x\|=1} x'AA'x = \lambda_{\max}(AA'). \qquad (6.119)$$

Using the diagonalization $C = U'\Lambda U$, where U is an orthogonal matrix, $U'U = I$, and Λ is a diagonal matrix with the eigenvalues $\lambda_j(C)$ on the main diagonal, we have a two-sided bound on the quadratic form $x'Cx$:

$$\lambda_{\min}(C)\|x\|^2 \le x'Cx = (Ux)'\Lambda Ux \le \lambda_{\max}(C)\|x\|^2.$$

The left inequality in Eq. (6.117) is proved as follows:

$$\lambda_{\max}(ACA') = \sup_{\|x\|=1} x'ACA'x = \sup_{\|x\|=1} (A'x)'C(A'x)$$

$$\le \lambda_{\max}(C) \sup_{\|x\|=1} \|A'x\|^2 = \lambda_{\max}(C)\lambda_{\max}(AA').$$

The right inequality follows from

$$\sup_{\|x\|=1} x'ACA'x \ge \sup_{\|x\|=1} \{\lambda_{\min}(C)\|A'x\|^2\} = \lambda_{\min}(C)\lambda_{\max}(AA').$$ ∎

6.5.4   Lemma on an Enveloping Resolvent

Let us call

$$\mathcal{B}F = \sum_{i=0}^{\infty} B^i F(B^i)'$$

an *enveloping resolvent* (see related definitions in Section 8.4.1). Here F is a $p \times p$ matrix.

Lemma.   *If $M < 1$, then the equation $X - BXB' = F$ has a unique solution $X = \mathcal{B}F$ for any right-hand side F.*

Proof.   If there are two different solutions, X_1 and X_2, then the difference $X = X_1 - X_2$ satisfies $X - BXB' = 0$. Since $\|B\| < 1$, we arrive at a contradiction: $0 < \|X\| \le \|B\|^2\|X\| < \|X\|$. Further, $X = \mathcal{B}F$ is really a solution:

$$X - BXB' = \sum_{i=0}^{\infty} B^i F(B^i)' - \sum_{i=0}^{\infty} B^{i+1} F(B^{i+1})' = F.$$ ∎

6.5.5   Lemma on the Same Order

Lemma.   *Denote $V_n = \sum_{i=1}^{n} Y_i Y_i'$. $\lambda_{\max}(V_n)$ and $\sum_{i=1}^{n} \|Y_i\|^2$ are of the same order.*

Proof. Denoting λ_j the eigenvalues of V_n and using properties of trace we have

$$\lambda_{\max}(V_n) \le \sum_{i=1}^{p} \lambda_i(V_n) = \operatorname{tr} V_n = \operatorname{tr} \sum_{i=1}^{n} Y_i Y_i'$$

$$= \sum_{i=1}^{n} \operatorname{tr} Y_i' Y_i = \sum_{i=1}^{n} \|Y_i\|^2 \le p\lambda_{\max}(V_n). \tag{6.120}$$

∎

6.5.6 Towards the Lower Bound

Let $\varphi(\lambda) = |B - \lambda I_p| = \lambda^p + a_1 \lambda^{p-1} + \cdots + a_p$ be the characteristic polynomial of B and let $a_0 = 1$. The variables

$$Z_n = Y_n + \sum_{j=1}^{p} a_j Y_{n-j} = \sum_{j=0}^{p} a_j Y_{n-j}, \quad n \ge p, \tag{6.121}$$

are instrumental in the estimation of $\lambda_{\min}(V_n)$ from below.

Lemma. $\lambda_{\min}\left(\sum_{i=p}^{n} Z_i Z_i'\right) \le p\left(\sum_{j=0}^{p} a_j^2\right)\lambda_{\min}\left(\sum_{i=0}^{n} Y_i Y_i'\right).$

Proof. Let u be a unit vector, $\|u\| = 1$. By Eq. (6.121) and Hölder's inequality

$$u' Z_i Z_i' u = \left(\sum_{j=0}^{p} a_j u' Y_{i-j}\right)^2 \le \sum_{j=0}^{p} a_j^2 \sum_{j=0}^{p} (u' Y_{i-j})^2$$

and therefore

$$\sum_{i=p}^{n} u' Z_i Z_i' u \le \left(\sum_{j=0}^{p} a_j^2\right) \sum_{i=p}^{n} \sum_{j=0}^{p} (u' Y_{i-j})^2$$

(in the inner sum replace $i - j = k$)

$$= \left(\sum_{j=0}^{p} a_j^2\right) \sum_{i=p}^{n} \sum_{k=i}^{i-p} (u' Y_k)^2$$

(changing summation order)

$$= \left(\sum_{j=0}^{p} a_j^2\right) \sum_{k=0}^{n} \sum_{i=k}^{k+p} (u' Y_k)^2 = p\left(\sum_{j=0}^{p} a_j^2\right) \sum_{k=0}^{n} u' Y_k Y_k' u.$$

The lemma follows from this inequality and that for any symmetric matrix A the equation $\lambda_{\min}(A) = \inf_{\|u\|=1} u' A u$ is true. ∎

6.5.7 Representation in Terms of Errors

Denote

$$C_j = \sum_{i=0}^{j} a_i B^{j-i}, \quad j = 0, \ldots, p-1. \tag{6.122}$$

Lemma

(i) *Along with Eq. (6.121) there is the representation*

$$Z_k = \sum_{j=0}^{p-1} C_j e_{k-j}. \tag{6.123}$$

(ii) *Denoting*

$$A_{k,l} = \sum_{j=k-l+1}^{p-1} e'_{k-j} C'_j = \sum_{m=k-p+1}^{l-1} e'_m C'_{k-m}, \tag{6.124}$$

$$R_n = \sum_{l=2}^{n} \sum_{k=l}^{l+p-2} (A'_{k,l} e'_i C'_{k-l} + C_{k-l} e_l A_{k,l}), \tag{6.125}$$

we have

$$\sum_{i=p}^{n} Z_i Z'_i = \sum_{j=0}^{p-1} C_j \left(\sum_{k=p}^{n} e_{k-j} e'_{k-j} \right) C'_j + R_n. \tag{6.126}$$

Proof.

(i) The recursion Eq. (6.106), applied to $Y_{k-j}, j \le p$, is used to reveal its dependence on Y_{k-p}:

$$Y_{k-j} = B^{k-j} Y_0 + \sum_{i=1}^{k-p} B^{k-j-i} e_i + \sum_{i=k-p+1}^{k-j} B^{k-j-i} e_i$$

$$= B^{p-j} \left(B^{k-p} Y_0 + \sum_{i=1}^{k-p} B^{k-p-i} e_i \right) + \sum_{i=k-p+1}^{k-j} B^{k-j-i} e_i$$

$$= B^{p-j} Y_{k-p} + \sum_{i=k-p+1}^{k-j} B^{k-j-i} e_i$$

(the sum in the expression above is empty when $j = p$).

Now we plug these expressions in Eq. (6.121) and use the fact that B satisfies its determinantal equation $\varphi(B) = 0$ by the Caley–Hamilton theorem (see Herstein, 1975). For $p \leq k \leq n$

$$Z_i = \sum_{j=0}^{p} a_j Y_{i-j} = \left(\sum_{j=0}^{p} a_j B^{p-j} \right) Y_{i-p} + \sum_{j=0}^{p} a_j \sum_{h=i-p+1}^{i-j} B^{i-j-h} e_h$$

[the first sum is null; in the second one change the summation order and apply notation Eq. (6.122)]

$$= \sum_{h=i-p+1}^{i} \left(\sum_{j=0}^{i-h} a_j B^{i-j-h} \right) e_h = \sum_{h=i-p+1}^{i} C_{i-h} e_h = \sum_{j=0}^{p-1} C_j e_{i-j}.$$

This is Eq. (6.123).

(ii) We substitute Eq. (6.123) in $\sum_{k=p}^{n} Z_k Z_k'$, multiply through the inner sums and sort out the terms into groups with $i = j$, $i < j$ and $i > j$:

$$\sum_{k=p}^{n} Z_k Z_k' = \sum_{k=p}^{n} \left(\sum_{i=0}^{p-1} C_i e_{k-i} \right) \left(\sum_{j=0}^{p-1} e_{k-j}' C_j' \right) = S_{i=j} + S_{i<j} + S_{i>j}. \quad (6.127)$$

The terms at the right-hand side are rearranged as below:

$$S_{i=j} = \sum_{k=p}^{n} \sum_{i=0}^{p-1} C_i e_{k-i} e_{k-i}' C_i' = \sum_{i=0}^{p-1} C_i \left(\sum_{k=p}^{n} e_{k-i} e_{k-i}' \right) C_i', \quad (6.128)$$

$$S_{i<j} = \sum_{k=p}^{n} \sum_{i=0}^{p-2} \sum_{j=i+1}^{p-1} C_i e_{k-i} e_{k-j}' C_j'$$

(replacing i according to $k - i = l$)

$$= \sum_{k=p}^{n} \sum_{l=k-p+2}^{k} C_{k-l} e_l \left(\sum_{j=k-l+1}^{p-1} e_{k-j}' C_j' \right)$$

$$= \sum_{l=2}^{n} \sum_{k=l}^{l+p-2} C_{k-l} e_l \left(\sum_{j=k-l+1}^{p-1} e_{k-j}' C_j' \right), \quad (6.129)$$

and

$$S_{i>j} = \sum_{k=p}^{n} \sum_{j=0}^{p-2} \sum_{i=j+1}^{p-1} C_i e_{k-i} e_{k-j}' C_j'$$

(replacing j according to $k - j = l$)

$$= \sum_{k=p}^{n} \sum_{l=k-p+2}^{k} \left(\sum_{i=k-l+1}^{p-1} C_i e_{k-i} \right) e_l' C_{k-l}'$$

$$= \sum_{l=2}^{n} \sum_{k=l}^{l+p-2} \left(\sum_{j=k-l+1}^{p-1} C_j e_{k-j} \right) e_l' C_{k-l}'. \tag{6.130}$$

Collecting Eqs. (6.127)–(6.130) and using notations (6.124) and (6.125) we finish the proof of Eq. (6.126). ∎

6.5.8 Spectrum-Separating Decomposition

Let $M > 1 \geq m$. From the rational canonical form (over the real field) of the real matrix B (see Herstein, 1975, p. 307) it follows that there exists a nonsingular real matrix M such that

$$B = M^{-1} \begin{pmatrix} B_1 & 0 \\ 0 & B_2 \end{pmatrix} M, \tag{6.131}$$

where

$$\left. \begin{array}{c} B_1 \text{ and } B_2 \text{ are real square matrices such that} \\ \min |\lambda_j(B_1)| > 1, \quad \max |\lambda_j(B_2)| \leq 1. \end{array} \right\} \tag{6.132}$$

Substituting Eq. (6.131) in $Y_n = B Y_{n-1} + e_n$ and premultiplying the resulting equation by M we obtain

$$M Y_n = \begin{pmatrix} B_1 & 0 \\ 0 & B_2 \end{pmatrix} M Y_{n-1} + M e_n.$$

With conformal partitioning

$$M Y_n = \begin{pmatrix} S_n \\ T_n \end{pmatrix}, \quad M e_n = \begin{pmatrix} \xi_n \\ \zeta_n \end{pmatrix} \tag{6.133}$$

the system breaks up into

$$S_n = B_1 S_{n-1} + \xi_n, \quad T_n = B_2 T_{n-1} + \zeta_n. \tag{6.134}$$

The first of the processes in Eq. (6.134) is purely explosive and the second one is non-explosive. As a result of nonsingularity of M estimating V_n is the same as estimating

$$M V_n M' = \sum_1^n (M Y_i)(M Y_i)' = \begin{pmatrix} \sum_1^n S_i S_i' & \sum_1^n S_i T_i' \\ \sum_1^n T_i S_i' & \sum_1^n T_i T_i' \end{pmatrix}. \tag{6.135}$$

6.5.9   Exploiting Order Properties of Symmetric Matrices

Lemma.   *Let A be a $p \times p$ symmetric positive definite matrix*

(i) *If $A^{-1} = I_p + B + C$, where B, C are symmetric, B is nonnegative definite and $\|C\| < 1$, then*

$$\|A\| \leq 1/(1 - \|C\|). \tag{6.136}$$

(ii) *If A is partitioned as*

$$A = \begin{pmatrix} P & H \\ H' & Q \end{pmatrix},$$

where P and Q are, respectively, $r \times r$ and $s \times s$ matrices such that $p = r + s$, then for $u \in \mathbb{R}^r$

$$\begin{pmatrix} u \\ 0 \end{pmatrix}' A^{-1} \begin{pmatrix} u \\ 0 \end{pmatrix} \leq u'P^{-1}u(1 + \|A^{-1}\|\mathrm{tr}Q). \tag{6.137}$$

Proof.

(i) Note that

$$\lambda_{\min}(A^{-1}) = \inf_{\|x\|=1} x'A^{-1}x = \inf_{\|x\|=1} (x'x + x'Bx + x'Cx)$$

$$\geq \inf_{\|x\|=1} x'x - \sup_{\|x\|=1} |x'Cx| \geq 1 - \|C\|.$$

Since $\|A\| = \lambda_{\max}(A) = 1/\lambda_{\min}(A^{-1})$, Eq. (6.136) follows.

(ii) By the partitioned matrix inversion rule [Lemma 1.7.6(ii)]

$$A^{-1} = \begin{pmatrix} P^{-1} + P^{-1}H\Gamma H'P^{-1} & -P^{-1}H\Gamma \\ -\Gamma H'P^{-1} & \Gamma \end{pmatrix}, \tag{6.138}$$

where

$$\Gamma^{-1} = Q - H'P^{-1}H \text{ is positive definite} \tag{6.139}$$

because $\Gamma = (0 \ I)A^{-1}\begin{pmatrix} 0 \\ I \end{pmatrix}$ is positive definite. Taking $x_2 \in \mathbb{R}^s, 0 \in \mathbb{R}^r$ and letting $y = \begin{pmatrix} 0 \\ x_2 \end{pmatrix}$ we have from Eq. (6.138)

$$\|\Gamma\| = \sup_{\|x_2\|=1} x_2'\Gamma x_2 = \sup_{\|x_2\|=1} y'A^{-1}y$$

$$\leq \sup_{x \in \mathbb{R}^p, \|x\|=1} x'A^{-1}x = \|A^{-1}\|. \tag{6.140}$$

By Eq. (6.139) $\operatorname{tr}(H'P^{-1}H) = \operatorname{tr}Q - \operatorname{tr}\Gamma^{-1} \leq \operatorname{tr}Q$. Therefore

$$\lambda_{\max}(P^{-1/2}HH'P^{-1/2}) \leq \operatorname{tr}(P^{-1/2}HH'P^{-1/2}) = \operatorname{tr}(H'P^{-1}H) \leq \operatorname{tr}Q. \tag{6.141}$$

In the equation

$$\begin{pmatrix} u \\ 0 \end{pmatrix}' A^{-1} \begin{pmatrix} u \\ 0 \end{pmatrix} = u'P^{-1}u + u'P^{-1}H\Gamma H'P^{-1}u \tag{6.142}$$

we need to estimate only the end term. Using the inequality $v'Cv \leq \|C\| \|v\|^2$ (C is symmetric) twice we get

$$\begin{aligned}
u'P^{-1}H\Gamma H'P^{-1}u &= (H'P^{-1}u)'\Gamma(H'P^{-1}u) \leq \|\Gamma\| \|H'P^{-1}u\|^2 \\
&= \|\Gamma\| u'P^{-1}HH'P^{-1}u \\
&= \|\Gamma\| (P^{-1/2}u)'P^{-1/2}HH'P^{-1/2}(P^{-1/2}u) \\
&\leq \|\Gamma\| \|P^{-1/2}HH'P^{-1/2}\| \|P^{-1/2}u\|^2 \\
&= \|\Gamma\| \lambda_{\max}(P^{-1/2}HH'P^{-1/2})u'P^{-1}u. \tag{6.143}
\end{aligned}$$

Combining Eqs. (6.140)–(6.143) we obtain Eq. (6.137). ∎

6.6 PRELIMINARY ANALYSIS

6.6.1 Bound on the Error Norm

Lemma. *If the m.d. $\{e_n, \mathcal{F}_n\}$ satisfies Eq. (6.105), then for any $\beta > 1/\alpha$*

$$\|e_n\| = o(n^\beta). \tag{6.144}$$

Proof. By the conditional Chebyshov inequality (Lemma 6.1.7) for any $\delta > 0$

$$P(\|e_i\|^\alpha > \delta i^{\alpha\beta} | \mathcal{F}_{i-1}) \leq \frac{1}{\delta i^{\alpha\beta}} E(\|e_i\|^\alpha | \mathcal{F}_{i-1}) \leq \frac{c}{\delta i^{\alpha\beta}}.$$

As $\alpha\beta > 1$, we get

$$\sum_{i=1}^\infty P(\|e_i\|^\alpha > \delta i^{\alpha\beta} | \mathcal{F}_{i-1}) \leq \frac{c}{\delta} \sum_{i=1}^\infty i^{-\alpha\beta} < \infty.$$

Letting $Z_i = 1(\|e_i\|^\alpha > \delta i^{\alpha\beta})$ in the conditional Borel–Cantelli lemma (Lemma 6.1.2) we see that $\sum_{i=1}^\infty Z_i < \infty$ a.s. This means that $\|e_i\|^\alpha \leq \delta i^{\alpha\beta}$ for all large i. Since this is true for any $\delta > 0$, we obtain Eq. (6.144). ∎

6.6.2 Laws of Iterated Logarithm-Type Upper Bound

The bound (6.145) below and, more generally, Eq. (6.72) is the same rate as is seen in the so-called laws of iterated logarithm; see Stout (1974).

Lemma. *Suppose that the (real-valued) m.d. sequence $\{e_n, \mathcal{F}_n\}$ satisfies Eq. (6.105) and that λ is a complex number with $|\lambda| = 1$. Denote $\mathcal{R}(a)$ and $\mathcal{I}(a)$ the real and imaginary parts of a complex number a and put*

$$R_n = \sum_{j=1}^{n} \mathcal{R}(\lambda^{-j} e_{jk}), \quad I_n = \sum_{j=1}^{n} \mathcal{I}(\lambda^{-j} e_{jk}), \quad k = 1, \ldots, p.$$

Then

$$R_n = O((n \log \log n)^{1/2}), \quad I_n = O((n \log \log n)^{1/2}) \ a.s. \qquad (6.145)$$

Proof. By the Euler formula $\lambda = e^{i\varphi}$, $i = \sqrt{-1}$, implies $\lambda^{-j} = e^{-ij\varphi} = \cos j\varphi - i \sin j\varphi$ and $R_n = \sum_{j=1}^{n} e_{jk} \cos j\varphi$. $\{e_{jk} \cos j\varphi, \mathcal{F}_j\}$ is a m.d. sequence such that

$$\sup_j E(|e_{jk} \cos j\varphi|^\alpha \mid \mathcal{F}_{j-1}) \le \sup_j E(\|e_j\|^\alpha \mid \mathcal{F}_{j-1}) < \infty.$$

Putting $w_n = 1$ for all n, we satisfy all conditions required for Wei's bound (Section 6.3.10), where $s_n = n^{1/2}$ and $|w_n| = 1 = o(s_n^c) = o(n^{c/2})$ for all $0 < c < 1$. Therefore

$$R_n = O(n^{1/2}(\log \log n^{1/2})^{1/2}) = O((n \log \log n)^{1/2}).$$

Obviously, such a proof works for I_n too. ∎

6.6.3 Case of One Jordan Cell

Lemma. *Let λ be a complex number with $|\lambda| = 1$. Define a $p \times p$ matrix*

$$D = \begin{pmatrix} \lambda & 1 & 0 & \cdots & 0 \\ 0 & \lambda & 1 & \cdots & 0 \\ 0 & 0 & \lambda & \cdots & \cdots \\ \vdots & \vdots & \vdots & \ddots & \vdots \\ 0 & 0 & 0 & \cdots & \lambda \end{pmatrix}.$$

If the m.d. sequence $\{e_n, \mathcal{F}_n\}$ satisfies Eq. (6.105), then

$$\left\| \sum_{i=1}^{n} D^{n-i} e_i \right\| = O(n^{p-1/2}(\log \log n)^{1/2}) \, a.s.$$

Proof.   We begin with the expression for the powers of D:

$$
D^k = \begin{pmatrix} \lambda^k & \binom{k}{1}\lambda^{k-1} & \cdots & \binom{k}{p-1}\lambda^{k-p+1} \\ 0 & \lambda^k & \cdots & \binom{k}{p-2}\lambda^{k-p+2} \\ \vdots & \vdots & \ddots & \vdots \\ 0 & 0 & \cdots & \lambda^k \end{pmatrix}, \quad k = 0, 1, \ldots \quad (6.146)
$$

Here we set $\binom{0}{0} = 1$, $\binom{a}{b} = 0$ if $a < b$ and $\binom{a}{b} = \dfrac{a!}{b!(a-b)!}$ if $a \geq b$. Therefore

$$
D^{n-i}e_i = \left(\sum_{v=0}^{p-1} \lambda^{n-i-v} \binom{n-i}{v} e_{i,v+1}, \ldots, \sum_{v=0}^{0} \lambda^{n-i-v} \binom{n-i}{v} e_{i,v+p} \right)'.
$$

Introducing for $v = 0, 1, \ldots, p-1$ and $k = v+1, \ldots, p$ the sum

$$
S_n(v, k) = \lambda^{n-v} \sum_{i=1}^{n} \binom{n-i}{v} \lambda^{-i} e_{ik}, \quad (6.147)
$$

we have

$$
\sum_{i=1}^{n} D^{n-i}e_i = \left(\sum_{v=0}^{p-1} \sum_{i=1}^{n} \lambda^{n-i-v} \binom{n-i}{v} e_{i,v+1}, \ldots, \sum_{v=0}^{0} \sum_{i=1}^{n} \lambda^{n-i-v} \binom{n-i}{v} e_{i,v+p} \right)'
$$

$$
= \left(\sum_{v=0}^{p-1} S_n(v, v+1), \ldots, \sum_{v=0}^{0} S_n(v, v+p) \right)'. \quad (6.148)
$$

By partial summation, $\sum_{i=1}^{n} a_i b_i = \sum_{j=1}^{n-1} (a_j - a_{j+1}) \sum_{i=1}^{j} b_i$, we have

$$
\sum_{i=1}^{n} \binom{n-i}{v} \mathcal{R}(\lambda^{-i} e_{ik}) = \sum_{j=1}^{n-1} \left[\binom{n-j}{v} - \binom{n-j-1}{v} \right] R_j, \quad (6.149)
$$

where R_j and $\mathcal{R}(\lambda^{-i} e_{ik})$ are from Lemma 6.6.2. Note that, as $m \to \infty$,

$$
\binom{m}{v} - \binom{m-1}{v} = \frac{(m-1)!}{v!(m-1-v)!} \left(\frac{m}{m-v} - 1 \right) = \binom{m-1}{v-1}
$$

$$
= \frac{(m-1)\cdots(m-(v-1))}{(v-1)!} \sim \frac{m^{v-1}}{(v-1)!}. \quad (6.150)
$$

(The equivalence relation "$\sim$" between two sequences a_n and b_n means $c_1 a_n \leq b_n \leq c_2 a_n$ with constants independent of n.) For moderate m the left side is bounded. Lemma 6.6.2 and Eqs. (6.149) and (6.150) lead to the bound

$$\sum_{i=1}^{n} \binom{n-i}{\nu} \mathcal{R}(\lambda^{-i} e_{ik}) = \sum_{j=1}^{n-1} O((n-j)^{\nu-1}) O((j \log \log j)^{1/2})$$

$$= \sum_{j=1}^{n-1} O(n^{\nu-1/2}(\log \log n)^{1/2})$$

$$= O(n^{\nu+1/2}(\log \log n)^{1/2}) \text{ a.s.} \qquad (6.151)$$

Likewise,

$$\sum_{i=1}^{n} \binom{n-i}{\nu} \mathcal{I}(\lambda^{-i} e_{ik}) = O(n^{\nu+1/2}(\log \log n)^{1/2}) \text{ a.s.} \qquad (6.152)$$

Since $\nu \le p - 1$ and $|\lambda| = 1$, Eqs. (6.151) and (6.152) imply, in view of Eq. (6.147), that $S_n(\nu, k) = O(n^{p-1/2}(\log \log n)^{1/2})$ a.s. Therefore the lemma follows from Eq. (6.148). ∎

6.6.4 Order of Magnitude of $\|Y_n\|$ in Case $M < 1$

Lemma. *Let the m.d. sequence $\{e_n, \mathcal{F}_n\}$ satisfy Eq. (6.105) and let $M < 1$. Then $\|Y_n\| = o(n^\beta)$ a.s. for every $\beta > 1/\alpha$.*

Proof. As $M < 1$, we can simplify Eq. (6.114) as

$$\|B^n\| \le c n^{\mu-1} M^n = c(n^{\mu-1} M^{n/2}) M^{n/2} \le c_1 M^{n/2}. \qquad (6.153)$$

By Lemma 6.6.1 for any $\varepsilon > 0$ there exists $I(\varepsilon) > 0$ such that

$$\|e_i\| \le \varepsilon i^\beta, \quad i \ge I(\varepsilon). \qquad (6.154)$$

We can extend this bound by writing

$$\|e_i\| \le c_2, \quad i < I(\varepsilon). \qquad (6.155)$$

Apply Eq. (6.106) and Eqs. (6.153)–(6.155) to get

$$\|Y_n\| \le \|B^n\| \|Y_0\| + \sum_{i=1}^{n} \|B^{n-i}\| \|e_i\|$$

$$\le c_1 \|Y_0\| M^{n/2} + c_1 c_2 \sum_{i=1}^{I(\varepsilon)-1} M^{(n-i)/2} + c_1 \varepsilon \sum_{i=I(\varepsilon)}^{n} M^{(n-i)/2} i^\beta$$

$$= o(n^\beta) + c_3 M^{(n-I(\varepsilon))/2} + c_1 \varepsilon n^\beta \sum_{i=I(\varepsilon)}^{n} M^{(n-i)/2} \left(\frac{i}{n}\right)^\beta$$

$$= o(n^\beta) + c_1 \varepsilon n^\beta \sum_{i=0}^{\infty} M^{i/2}.$$

Since $\varepsilon > 0$ is arbitrary, the lemma is proved.   ∎

6.6.5   Order of Magnitude of $\|Y_n\|$ in Case $M = 1$

Lemma.   *Let the m.d. sequence $\{e_n, \mathcal{F}_n\}$ satisfy Eq. (6.105) and let $M = 1$. Then $\|Y_n\| = O(n^{\mu-1/2}(\log \log n)^{1/2})$ a.s.*

Proof.   Plugging the Jordan representation (6.112) in autoregression (6.104) and pre-multiplying the resulting equation by C we obtain

$$CY_n = DCY_{n-1} + Ce_n. \tag{6.156}$$

Partition the vectors CY_n and Ce_n conformably with D as

$$CY_n = \begin{pmatrix} z_n^{(1)} \\ \cdots \\ z_n^{(q)} \end{pmatrix}, \quad Ce_n = \begin{pmatrix} u_n^{(1)} \\ \cdots \\ u_n^{(q)} \end{pmatrix}, \tag{6.157}$$

where $z_n^{(j)}$ and $u_n^{(j)}$ are $m_j \times 1$ vectors, $j = 1, \ldots, q$. The properties of e_n imply $\sup_{j,n} E(\|u_n^{(j)}\|^\alpha \mid \mathcal{F}_{n-1}) < \infty$. Then, because D is diagonal, system (6.156) breaks up into q equations

$$z_n^{(j)} = D_j z_{n-1}^{(j)} + u_n^{(j)} = D_j^n z_0^{(j)} + \sum_{i=1}^{n} D_j^{n-i} u_i^{(j)}. \tag{6.158}$$

For j with $|\lambda_j| = 1$ from Eq. (6.158) and Lemmas 6.5.2 and 6.6.3 we obtain

$$\|z_n^{(j)}\| = O(n^{m_j-1}) + O(n^{m_j-1/2}(\log \log n)^{1/2}) = O(n^{m_j-1/2}(\log \log n)^{1/2}). \tag{6.159}$$

For j with $|\lambda_j| = 1$ by part (i) of Lemma 6.5.2 $\|z_n^{(j)}\| = o(n^{1/2})$. Hence, Eq. (6.159) holds for every j. This proves the statement because C is nonsingular.   ∎

6.6.6   Order of Magnitude of $\|Y_n\|$ in Case $M > 1$

Lemma.   *Let $\{e_n, \mathcal{F}_n\}$ be a m.d. sequence satisfying Eq. (6.105). If $M > 1$, then $\|Y_n\| = O(n^{\mu-1}M^n)$ a.s. where μ and M are as defined in Eq. (6.113).*

Proof.   We use Eq. (6.156) with CY_n and Ce_n partitioned as in Eq. (6.157). Equations (6.154) and (6.155) imply $\|u_i^{(j)}\| \leq c \max\{1, \varepsilon i^\beta\}$. Using this bound, Eq. (6.158) and

Eq. (6.114) we estimate one component of CY_n as follows:

$$\|z_n^{(j)}\| \leq \|D_j^n\|\|z_0^{(j)}\| + \sum_{i=1}^{n} \|D_j^{n-i}\|\|u_i^{(j)}\|$$

$$\leq c_1 n^{m_j-1}|\lambda_j|^n + c_2 \sum_{i=1}^{n} (n-i)^{m_j-1}|\lambda_j|^{n-i} \max\{1, \varepsilon i^\beta\}$$

$$= c_1 n^{m_j-1}|\lambda_j|^n \left[1 + c_3 \sum_{i=1}^{n} \left(1 - \frac{i}{n}\right)^{m_j-1} |\lambda_j|^{-i} \max\{1, \varepsilon i^\beta\} \right]$$

$$\leq c_4 n^{m_j-1}|\lambda_j|^n.$$

This implies the required bound on Y_n. ∎

6.6.7 Generalization of Rubin's Theorem

For purely explosive systems (i.e. $m = \min|\lambda_j| > 1$), Rubin (1950) showed in the 1-D case that if the e_n are i.i.d. random variables with $Ee_1 = 0$ and $Ee_1^2 = \sigma^2 > 0$, then Y_n diverges exponentially fast so that

$$P(B^{-n}Y_n \text{ converges to nonzero limit}) = 1.$$

The theorem below is a multivariate generalization of Rubin's result.

Theorem. *Let the m.d. sequence $\{e_n, \mathcal{F}_n\}$ satisfy Eq. (6.105) and let Y_n be defined by Eq. (6.106). If $m > 1$, then B is invertible and*

$$B^{-n}Y_n \text{ converges a.s. to } Y = Y_0 + \sum_{i=1}^{\infty} B^{-i}e_i. \tag{6.160}$$

If, furthermore,

$$\liminf_{n\to\infty} \lambda_{\min}\left(E\left[\sum_{k=1}^{r} B^{r-k} e_{nr+k} e'_{nr+k} (B^{r-k})' \Big| \mathcal{F}_{nr} \right] \right) > 0 \tag{6.161}$$

for some $r \geq 1$, then the limit Y in Eq. (6.160) has the property that

$$a'Y \text{ has a continuous distribution for all } a \neq 0. \tag{6.162}$$

Proof. Let $Z_n = Y_0 + \sum_{i=1}^{n} B^{-i}e_i$ be the initial segment of Eq. (6.160). By Eq. (6.106) $B^{-n}Y_n = Z_n$. By Lemma 6.5.2 $\|B^{-n}\| \leq cm^{-n}$. This bound and Eq. (6.105) imply

$$\sum_{i=1}^{\infty} E(\|B^{-i}e_i\|^2 \mid \mathcal{F}_{i-1}) \leq \sum_{i=1}^{\infty} \|B^{-i}\|^2 \sup_n E(\|e_n\|^2 \mid \mathcal{F}_{n-1}) < \infty \text{ a.s.}$$

By the martingale convergence theorem (Theorem 6.1.3) $Z_n \to Y$ a.s.

Now we turn to the proof of Eq. (6.162). Note that, since B^{-i} is nonsingular, the vectors $(B^{-i})'a$, $i = 1, 2, \ldots$, are nonzero for $a \neq 0$. Let us write the series in Eq. (6.160) in batches of r terms:

$$\sum_{i=1}^{\infty} B^{-i} e_i = \sum_{n=0}^{\infty} \sum_{k=1}^{r} B^{-nr-k} e_{nr+k} = \sum_{n=0}^{\infty} B^{-(n+1)r} \sum_{k=1}^{r} B^{r-k} e_{nr+k}.$$

Denote

$$u_n = \sum_{k=1}^{r} B^{r-k} e_{nr+k}, \quad \tilde{\mathcal{F}}_n = \mathcal{F}_{(n+1)r}.$$

The sequence $\{u_n, \tilde{\mathcal{F}}_n\}$ is a m.d. sequence,

$$E(u_n \mid \tilde{\mathcal{F}}_{n-1}) = \sum_{k=1}^{r} B^{r-k} E(e_{nr+k} \mid \mathcal{F}_{nr}) = 0,$$

with conditional second moments

$$E(u_n u_n' \mid \tilde{\mathcal{F}}_{n-1}) = E\left(\sum_{k,l=1}^{r} B^{r-k} e_{nr+k} e_{nr+l}' (B^{r-l})' \mid \mathcal{F}_{nr} \right).$$

Here for $k < l$

$$E(e_{nr+k} e_{nr+l}' \mid \mathcal{F}_{nr}) = E[E(e_{nr+k} e_{nr+l}' \mid \mathcal{F}_{nr+l-1}) \mid \mathcal{F}_{nr}]$$
$$= E[e_{nr+k} E(e_{nr+l}' \mid \mathcal{F}_{nr+l-1}) \mid \mathcal{F}_{nr}] = 0$$

and similarly for $l < k$ $E(e_{nr+k} e_{nr+l}' \mid \mathcal{F}_{nr}) = 0$. Hence,

$$E(u_n u_n' \mid \tilde{\mathcal{F}}_{n-1}) = E\left(\sum_{k=1}^{r} B^{r-k} e_{nr+k} e_{nr+k}' (B^{r-k})' \mid \mathcal{F}_{nr} \right)$$

and condition Eq. (6.161) rewrites as

$$\liminf_{n \to \infty} \lambda_{\min} E(u_n u_n' \mid \tilde{\mathcal{F}}_{n-1}) > 0.$$

As $\{u_n, \tilde{\mathcal{F}}_n\}$ satisfies the multivariate local M–Z condition [Eq. (6.65)] and the coefficients $A_n = (B^{-(n+1)r})'a$ satisfy Eq. (6.69), Theorem 6.3.9 yields

$$P(a'Y = c) = P\left(a'Y_0 + \sum_{n=0}^{\infty} A_n' u_n = c \right) = 0$$

for every constant c. ∎

6.6.8 $\|F_n\|$ is Bounded

Lemma. *If the m.d. sequence $\{e_n, \mathcal{F}_n\}$ satisfies Eq. (6.105), then the expression $F_n = n^{-1} \sum_{i=1}^{n} e_i e_i'$ satisfies $\|F_n\| = O(1)$.*

Proof. Let $d_i = \|e_i\|^2 - E(\|e_i\|^2 \mid \mathcal{F}_{i-1})$. Taking some $r \in (1, \min\{2, \alpha/2\})$, in a way similar to Eq. (6.77) we have $\sup_i E(|d_i|^r \mid \mathcal{F}_{i-1}) < \infty$. Letting $U_n = n$ in Theorem 6.1.4 we see that

$$\sum_{1}^{\infty} E(|d_i|^r \mid \mathcal{F}_{i-1}) U_i^{-r} \le c \sum_{1}^{\infty} i^{-r} < \infty \text{ a.s.}$$

and therefore $\sum_{i=1}^{n} d_i = o(n)$. Hence,

$$\sum_{i=1}^{n} \|e_i\|^2 = \sum_{i=1}^{n} d_i + \sum_{i=1}^{n} E(\|e_i\|^2 \mid \mathcal{F}_{i-1}) = o(n) + O(n) = O(n) \text{ a.s.} \quad (6.163)$$

Since F_n is nonnegative definite, by Lemma 6.5.5 it is true that

$$\|F_n\| = \lambda_{\max}(F_n) \sim \sum_{i=1}^{p} \lambda_i(F_n) = \text{tr}\left(\frac{1}{n} \sum_{i=1}^{n} e_i e_i'\right) = \frac{1}{n} \sum_{i=1}^{n} \|e_i\|^2. \quad (6.164)$$

Equations (6.163) and (6.164) prove the lemma. ∎

6.6.9 $\|X_n\|$ is Bounded

Lemma. *If $M < 1$ and Eq. (6.105) holds, then $X_n = \frac{1}{n} \sum_{i=1}^{n} Y_i Y_i'$ satisfies*

$$\|X_n\| \sim \frac{1}{n} \sum_{i=1}^{n} \|Y_i\|^2 = O(1). \quad (6.165)$$

Proof. By the recursion (6.106)

$$\left(\sum_{k=1}^{n} \|Y_k\|^2\right)^{1/2} \le \left[\sum_{k=1}^{n} \left(\|B^k\| \|Y_0\| + \sum_{i=1}^{k} \|B^{k-i}\| \|e_i\|\right)^2\right]^{1/2}$$

$$\le \left[\sum_{k=1}^{n} (\|B^k\| \|Y_0\|)^2\right]^{1/2}$$

$$+ \left[\sum_{k=1}^{n} \left(\sum_{i=1}^{k} \|B^{k-i}\| \|e_i\|\right)^2\right]^{1/2}. \quad (6.166)$$

The first term on the right causes no trouble as $M < 1$. The second term is bounded using Eq. (6.163):

$$\sum_{k=1}^{n} \left(\sum_{i=1}^{k} \|B^{k-i}\| \|e_i\| \right)^2 \leq \sum_{k=1}^{n} \left(\sum_{i=1}^{k} \|B^{k-i}\| \right) \left(\sum_{i=1}^{k} \|B^{k-i}\| \|e_i\|^2 \right)$$

$$\leq \left(\sum_{i=0}^{\infty} \|B^i\| \right) \sum_{i=1}^{n} \left(\sum_{k=i}^{n} \|B^{k-i}\| \right) \|e_i\|^2$$

$$\leq \left(\sum_{i=0}^{\infty} \|B^i\| \right)^2 \sum_{i=1}^{n} \|e_i\|^2 = O(n) \text{ a.s.} \tag{6.167}$$

For X_n a relationship of type Eq. (6.164) is true. Therefore Eqs. (6.166) and (6.167) give Eq. (6.165). ∎

6.6.10 Lemma on Almost Decreasing Sequences

Lemma. (Nielsen, 2005, Lemma 8.5) *If a numerical nonnegative sequence $\{a_t\}$ is almost decreasing, in the sense that there exist constants $c > 0$ and $\kappa > 0$ such that $a_{t+1} \leq a_t + ct^{-\kappa}$ for all large t, and the numbers $a_1, \ldots, a_T$ are jointly bounded as*

$$\sum_{t=1}^{T} a_t = o(T^\delta) \tag{6.168}$$

for all $\delta > 0$, then these numbers tend to zero at the rate $a_T = o(T^{-\rho})$ for all $\rho < \min\{1, \kappa/2\}$.

Proof. By the "almost decreasing" condition, there exists T_0 such that $a_{t+1} \leq a_t + ct^{-\kappa}$ for all $t \geq T_0$. Suppose $T > T_0$ and consider $T_0 \leq t \leq T$. Inductively,

$$a_t \geq a_{t+1} - ct^{-\kappa} \geq a_{t+2} - ct^{-\kappa} - c(t+1)^{-\kappa} \geq \cdots$$
$$\geq a_T - [ct^{-\kappa} + c(t+1)^{-\kappa} + \cdots + c(T-1)^{-\kappa}]. \tag{6.169}$$

Now let $0 < \rho < 1$. For large enough T, Eq. (6.169) is applicable to $t \in [T - T^\rho, T] \subseteq [T_0, T]$. The sum in the brackets at the right of Eq. (6.169) contains at most T^ρ terms, and each of these does not exceed $c(T - T^\rho)^{-\kappa} \leq 2cT^{-\kappa}$ for large T. Therefore

$$\min_{T \geq t \geq T - T^\rho} a_t \geq a_T - 2cT^{\rho - \kappa}.$$

Restricting ρ to $\rho \in (0, \min\{1, \kappa/2\})$ it is seen that

$$\sum_{t=1}^{T} a_t \geq \sum_{t=T-T^\rho}^{T} a_t \geq T^\rho (a_T - 2cT^{\rho-\kappa})$$

$$= T^\rho a_T - 2cT^{2\rho-\kappa} \geq T^\rho a_T - 2c$$

for large T. Combining this with Eq. (6.168) gives $a_T \leq T^{-p}\left(\sum_{t=1}^{T} a_t + 2c\right) = o(T^{\delta-p})$. As δ can be chosen arbitrarily small, this proves the lemma. ∎

6.7 STRONG CONSISTENCY FOR VECTOR AUTOREGRESSION AND RELATED RESULTS

6.7.1 Theorem on Relative Compactness

Recall that a sequence of vectors $\{a_k\} \subseteq \mathbb{R}^p$ is called *relatively compact* if any subsequence $\{b_k\}$ of it contains a further subsequence $\{c_k\}$ that is convergent. We say that a sequence of random matrices $\{X_n\}$ is *relatively compact with probability* 1 if for almost any $\omega \in \Omega$ the sequence $\{X_n(\omega)\}$ is relatively compact. In this situation it is convenient to denote $\mathrm{Lim}\{X_n\}$ the set of limit points of $\{X_n\}$. The purpose here is to establish the relationship between

$$X_n = \frac{1}{n}\sum_{i=1}^{n} Y_i Y_i' \quad \text{and} \quad F_n = n^{-1}\sum_{i=1}^{n} e_i e_i'.$$

The relative compactness notion is required because $\{X_n\}$ and $\{F_n\}$ do not converge.

Theorem. *Let the m.d. sequence $\{e_n, \mathcal{F}_n\}$ satisfy Eq. (6.105) and let Y_n be defined by*

$$Y_n = BY_{n-1} + e_n, \tag{6.170}$$

where B satisfies $M = \max|\lambda_j| < 1$. Then with probability 1 the matrix sequence $\{X_n\}$ is relatively compact and its set of limit points is $\mathcal{B}F$, where $\mathcal{B}$ is the enveloping resolvent from Lemma 6.5.4 and F is the set of limit points of $\{F_n\}$ (which is also relatively compact): $\mathrm{Lim}\{X_n\} = \mathcal{B}\,\mathrm{Lim}\{F_n\}$.

Proof. In a finite-dimensional space relative compactness is equivalent to boundedness, so the statements about relative compactness of $\{X_n\}$ and $\{F_n\}$ follow from Lemmas 6.6.8 and 6.6.9.

From Eq. (6.170) we get

$$\sum_{i=1}^{n} Y_i Y_i' = \sum_{i=1}^{n} (BY_{i-1} + e_i)(Y_{i-1}'B' + e_i') = B\sum_{i=1}^{n} Y_{i-1}Y_{i-1}'B'$$

$$+ \sum_{i=1}^{n} (BY_{i-1}e_i' + e_i Y_{i-1}'B') + \sum_{i=1}^{n} e_i e_i'$$

or, using X_n and F_n,

$$X_n = BX_nB' + \frac{1}{n}B(Y_0Y_0' - Y_nY_n')B' + \frac{1}{n}\sum_{i=1}^{n}(BY_{i-1}e_i' + e_iY_{i-1}'B') + F_n. \tag{6.171}$$

Because Y_{i-1} is $\mathcal{F}_{i-1}$-measurable, $\{BY_{i-1}e_i'\}$ is a m.d. sequence. Let us bound

$$\sum_1^n E(\|BY_{i-1}e_i'\|^2 \,|\mathcal{F}_{i-1})/i^2 \leq \sum_1^n \|B\|^2 \|Y_{i-1}\|^2 E(\|e_i\|^2 \,|\mathcal{F}_{i-1})/i^2$$

$$\leq c \sum_1^n \|Y_{i-1}\|^2 /i^2. \tag{6.172}$$

Denote $S_n = \sum_1^n \|Y_{i-1}\|^2$, $a_i = i^{-2}$. From Lemma 6.6.9 we see that

$$\sum_1^n \|Y_{i-1}\|^2 /i^2 = \sum_1^n (S_i - S_{i-1})a_i$$

$$= -S_0 a_1 + S_n a_n + \sum_1^{n-1} S_j(a_j - a_{j+1})$$

$$= O(1) + O(n)\frac{1}{n^2} + \sum_1^{n-1} O(j)\left(\frac{1}{j^2} - \frac{1}{(j+1)^2}\right)$$

$$= O(1) + \sum_1^{n-1} O\left(\frac{1}{j^2}\right) = O(1). \tag{6.173}$$

Now Eqs. (6.172), (6.173) and the martingale strong law (Section 6.1.4) with $p = 2$, $X_n = BY_{n-1}e_n'$ and $U_n = n$ imply

$$\frac{1}{n}\sum_{i=1}^n (BY_{i-1}e_i' + e_iY_{i-1}'B') = o(1) \text{ a.s.} \tag{6.174}$$

Besides, by Lemma 6.6.4 with $\beta = 1/2 > 1/\alpha$

$$\frac{1}{n}B(Y_0Y_0' - Y_nY_n')B' = o(1). \tag{6.175}$$

The consequence of Eqs. (6.171), (6.174) and (6.175) is that $X_n - BX_nB' = F_n + o(1)$ or, in terms of the operator $\mathcal{B}$,

$$X_n = \mathcal{B}(F_n + o(1)). \tag{6.176}$$

By Lemma 6.6.8 $\{F_n\}$ is relatively compact. If $\{F_n(\omega): n \geq 1\}$ is convergent for some $\omega \in \Omega$, then, because of boundedness of $\mathcal{B}$, $\{X_n(\omega): n \geq 1\}$ is also convergent. The set of limit points of $\{X_n\}$ is an image under $\mathcal{B}$ of the set of limit points of $\{F_n\}$. ∎

6.7.2 Bounding $\lambda_{\max}(V_n)$

Theorem. *If the m.d. sequence $\{e_n, \mathcal{F}_n\}$ satisfies Eq. (6.105), then for $V_n = \sum_{i=1}^{n} Y_i Y_i'$ the following is true:*

(i) $\lambda_{\max}(V_n) = O(n^{2\mu-2} M^{2n})$ a.s. if $M > 1$;

(ii) $\lambda_{\max}(V_n) = O(n^{2\mu} \log \log n)$ a.s. if $M = 1$;

(iii) $\lambda_{\max}(V_n) = O(n)$ a.s. if $M < 1$.

Proof.

(i) From Eq. (6.120) and Lemma 6.6.6 we derive

$$\lambda_{\max}(V_n) \leq \sum_{i=1}^{n} \|Y_i\|^2 \leq c \sum_{i=1}^{n} i^{2\mu-2} M^{2i}$$

$$= cn^{2\mu-2} M^{2n} \sum_{i=1}^{n} \left(\frac{i}{n}\right)^{2\mu-2} (M^2)^{i-n}$$

$$\leq cn^{2\mu-2} M^{2n} \sum_{i=0}^{\infty} (M^2)^{-i}.$$

(ii) Similarly, by Lemma 6.6.5, excluding i for which $\log \log i$ is not defined,

$$\lambda_{\max}(V_n) \leq \|Y_1\|^2 + c \sum_{i=2}^{n} i^{2\mu-1} \log \log i$$

$$\leq c_1 + cn^{2\mu-1} (\log \log n)(n - 2) = O(n^{2\mu} \log \log n).$$

Statement (iii) follows from Eq. (6.165). ∎

6.7.3 Bounding $\lambda_{\min}(V_n)$ from Below in the Stable Case

The importance of the theorem on relative compactness (Section 6.7.1) is demonstrated by the following application. For the notations $\mathcal{B}, F_n, X_n$ and V_n see Sections 6.5.4, 6.7.1 and 6.7.2, respectively.

Lemma. *If the m.d. sequence $\{e_n, \mathcal{F}_n\}$ satisfies Eq. (6.105), then the condition*

$$\liminf_{n \to \infty} \lambda_{\min}(\mathcal{B}F_n) > 0 \text{ a.s.} \tag{6.177}$$

is necessary and sufficient for

$$\liminf_{n \to \infty} \frac{1}{n} \lambda_{\min}(V_n) = \liminf_{n \to \infty} \lambda_{\min}(X_n) > 0 \text{ a.s.} \tag{6.178}$$

Proof. Suppose Eq. (6.177) is true and denote $\alpha = \liminf_{n \to \infty} \lambda_{\min}(X_n)$. Then there exists a subsequence $\{X_{n_k}\} \subseteq \{X_n\}$ such that $\alpha = \lim_{n \to \infty} \lambda_{\min}(X_{n_k})$. By Lemma 6.6.9

$\{X_n\}$ is relatively precompact. To simplify the notation, we can assume that $\{X_{n_k}\}$ converges. Similarly, by Lemma 6.6.8 we may assume that $\{F_{n_k}\}$ converges. By Theorem 6.7.1 the respective limit points satisfy $\text{Lim}\{X_n\} = \mathcal{B}\text{Lim}\{F_n\}$ and almost sure positivity of α follows from Eq. (6.177). The proof of (6.178) $\Rightarrow$ (6.177) is absolutely analogous. ∎

To extend this result to unstable systems, we need to modify Eq. (6.177) because the operator $\mathcal{B}$ is not defined in the case $M > 1$. This is the subject of Sections 6.7.4 and 6.7.5, the final result being Theorem 6.7.5.

6.7.4 Conditions Equivalent to Equation (6.177)

Denote

$$H_k(L) = (I, B, \ldots, B^{k-1})L^{1/2} = (L^{1/2}, BL^{1/2}, \ldots, B^{k-1}L^{1/2}), \quad k = 1, 2, \ldots$$

The matrices H_k, H_p and $H_p H_p'$ are of sizes $p \times (kp)$, $p \times p^2$ and $p \times p$, respectively.

Lemma. *Under the conditions of Lemma 6.7.3, condition (6.177) of that lemma is equivalent to each of the next two conditions:*

$$P(\text{rank} H_p(L) = p) \quad \text{for all } L \in \text{Lim}\{F_n\} \tag{6.179}$$

and

$$\liminf_{n \to \infty} \lambda_{\min}(H_p(F_n)[H_p(F_n)]') > 0 \ a.s. \tag{6.180}$$

Proof.

Step 1. We prove that for any L the following three conditions are equivalent

$$\lambda_{\min}(H_k(L)[H_k(L)]') > 0 \quad \text{for some } k \geq p, \tag{6.181}$$
$$\text{rank} H_p(L) = p \tag{6.182}$$

and

$$\lambda_{\min}(H_p(L)[H_p(L)]') > 0 \tag{6.183}$$

(see Kushner, 1971, p. 264). With the identity and null matrices of appropriate sizes we can define $A = \begin{pmatrix} I \\ 0 \end{pmatrix}$ to obtain

$$(I, B, \ldots, B^{k-1-p})L^{1/2} = (I, B, \ldots, B^{p-1})L^{1/2}A = H_p(L)A,$$
$$H_k(L) = (I, \ldots, B^{p-1}, B^p, \ldots, B^{k-1})L^{1/2}$$
$$= (H_p(L), B^p(I, \ldots, B^{k-1-p})L^{1/2})$$
$$= (H_p(L), B^p H_p(L)A). \tag{6.184}$$

This implies $H_k(L)[H_k(L)]' = H_p(L)[H_p(L)]' + B^p H_p(L)AA'[H_p(L)]'(B^p)'$ and

$$\lambda_{\min}(H_k(L)[H_k(L)]') \geq \lambda_{\min}(H_p(L)[H_p(L)]'). \tag{6.185}$$

Furthermore, with appropriately sized matrices we can define $S = (I, B^p)$ and $T = \text{diag}[I, A]$ to obtain from Eq. (6.184)

$$SH_p(L)T = (H_p(L), B^p H_p(L))\begin{pmatrix} I & 0 \\ 0 & A \end{pmatrix} = H_k(L). \tag{6.186}$$

If $\text{rank}\, H_p(L) < p$, then $\text{rank}\, H_k(L) \leq \min\{\text{rank}\, S,\ \text{rank}\, H_p(L),\ \text{rank}\, T\} < p$ by Eq. (6.186) and $\text{rank}\, H_k(L)[H_k(L)]' < p$. Since $H_k(L)[H_k(L)]'$ is of size $p \times p$ and nonnegative definite, we can use

$$|H_k(L)[H_k(L)]'| = \prod_{j=1}^{p} \lambda_j(H_k(L)[H_k(L)]') \tag{6.187}$$

to conclude that $\lambda_{\min}(H_k(L)[H_k(L)]') = 0$. Thus, $(6.181) \Rightarrow (6.182)$. By Eq. (6.187), the implication $(6.182) \Rightarrow (6.183)$ is true. And, finally, according to Eq. (6.185), (6.183) implies $\lambda_{\min}(H_k(L)[H_k(L)]') > 0$ for all $k \geq p$.

Step 2. As we know from Lemma 6.6.8, $\{F_n(\omega): n \geq 1\}$ is relatively compact for almost every ω. Suppose that Eq. (6.177) holds. Then there is a subsequence $\{F_{n_k}\} \subseteq \{F_n\}$ such that $\lim_{n \to \infty} \lambda_{\min}(\mathcal{B}F_{n_k}(\omega)) > 0$. By relative compactness we can assume that $\{F_{n_k}(\omega)\}$ converges to some $L(\omega)$. Then $\lambda_{\min}(\mathcal{B}L(\omega)) > 0$ and we can choose $k = k(\omega) \geq p$ such that

$$\lambda_{\min}(H_k(L(\omega))[H_k(L(\omega))]') = \lambda_{\min}\left(\sum_{i=0}^{k-1} B^i L(\omega)(B^i)'\right) > 0.$$

From Step 1, this is equivalent to Eqs. (6.182) and (6.183) for the given $L = L(\omega)$. For the reason that this proof applies to each limit point L of $\{F_n\}$, we have proved that $(6.177) \Rightarrow (6.179)$. Since Eq. (6.183) is just an equivalent way of writing Eq. (6.180), we have also proved $(6.179) \Longleftrightarrow (6.180)$. The implication $(6.180) \Rightarrow (6.177)$ is obvious because $H_p(F_n)[H_p(F_n)]' = \sum_{i=0}^{p-1} B^i F_n(B^i)'$. ∎

6.7.5 A General Lower Bound on $\lambda_{\min}(V_n)$

The theorem here, unlike Lemma 6.7.3, does not require the assumption $M < 1$.

Theorem. *Let the m.d. sequence $\{e_n, \mathcal{F}_n\}$ satisfy Eq. (6.105) and define Y_n by Eq. (6.106). Suppose that condition (6.179) or, equivalently, (6.180) holds. Then $\liminf_{n \to \infty} n^{-1}\lambda_{\min}(V_n) > 0$ a.s.*

Proof.

Step 1. Let us show that the residual R_n in Eq. (6.126) satisfies $R_n = o(n)$. Obviously, the matrices from Eq. (6.122) satisfy

$$c = \max_j \|C_j\| < \infty. \tag{6.188}$$

Denote $X_l = \sum_{k=l}^{l+p-2} C_{k-l} e_l A_{k,l}$. As we can see from Eq. (6.124), $A_{k,l}$ is $\mathcal{F}_{l-1}$-measurable and $\{X_l\}$ is a m.d. sequence. By Eq. (6.188),

$$\|A_{k,l}\| \le c \sum_{m=k-p+1}^{l-1} \|e_m\|$$

and

$$\|X_l\| \le c \sum_{k=l}^{l+p-2} \|e_l\| \|A_{k,l}\| \le c_1 \|e_l\| \sum_{k=l}^{l+p-2} \sum_{m=k-p+1}^{l-1} \|e_m\|$$

$$= c_1 \|e_l\| \sum_{m=l-p+1}^{l-1} \sum_{k=l}^{m+p-1} \|e_m\| \le c_1(p-1)\|e_l\| \sum_{m=l-p+1}^{l-1} \|e_m\|$$

$$\le c_2 \|e_l\| \left(\sum_{m=l-p+1}^{l-1} \|e_m\|^2 \right)^{1/2}.$$

With this bound at hand, we can estimate

$$\sum_{l=2}^{n} E(\|X_l\|^2 \mid \mathcal{F}_{l-1}) l^{-2} \le c_3 \sum_{l=2}^{n} \sum_{m=l-p+1}^{l-1} \|e_m\|^2 E(\|e_l\|^2 \mid \mathcal{F}_{l-1}) l^{-2}$$

$$\le c_3 \sup_n E(\|e_n\|^2 \mid \mathcal{F}_{n-1}) \sum_{m=3-p}^{n-1} \|e_m\|^2 \sum_{l=m+1}^{m+p-1} l^{-2}$$

$$\le c_4 \sup_n E(\|e_n\|^2 \mid \mathcal{F}_{n-1}) \sum_{m=3-p}^{n-1} \|e_m\|^2 m^{-2}. \tag{6.189}$$

As we know from Eq. (6.163), $\sum_1^n \|e_m\|^2 = O(n)$. Therefore the right side of Eq. (6.189) is bounded uniformly in n [see a similar argument in Section 6.7.1, in particular, Eq. (6.173)]. By Theorem 6.1.4 $R_n = \sum_{l=2}^{n} (X_l + X_l') = o(n)$.

Step 2. In view of Eq. (6.126) we have proved that

$$\frac{1}{n} \sum_{i=p}^{n} Z_i Z_i' = \sum_{j=0}^{p-1} C_j \left(\frac{1}{n} \sum_{k=p}^{n} e_{k-j} e_{k-j}' \right) C_j' + o(1).$$

This equation and Lemma 6.6.8 show that the sequence $\left\{ \frac{1}{n} \sum_{i=p}^{n} Z_i Z_i' \right\}$ is relatively compact with probability 1. Moreover, its set of limit points is $\{\Phi(F): F \in \text{Lim}\{F_n\}\}$, where

$$\Phi(F) = \sum_{j=0}^{p-1} C_j F C_j'.$$

All terms in this expression are nonnegative definite. Therefore if $x'\Phi(F)x = 0$, then $F^{1/2}x = 0$, $F^{1/2}(B + a_1 I_p)'x = 0, \ldots, F^{1/2}(B^{p-1} + \cdots + a_{p-1}I_p)'x = 0$ which, in turn, implies $F^{1/2}x = 0$, $F^{1/2}B'x = 0, \ldots,$ $F^{1/2}(B^{p-1})'x = 0$. Hence, if $\lambda_{\min}\left(\sum_{i=0}^{p-1} B^i F(B^i)'\right) > 0$, then $\Phi(F)$ is non-singular. Therefore $\liminf_{n \to \infty} \lambda_{\min}\left(\frac{1}{n} \sum_{i=p}^{n} Z_i Z_i'\right) > 0$ a.s. by assumption (6.180). Lemma 6.5.6 and this relation prove the theorem. ∎

6.7.6   Application to Scalar Autoregression

Consider an autoregressive model (6.110), which can be written as Eq. (6.104) if notation (6.111) is adopted.

Theorem.   *If the m.d. sequence $\{\varepsilon_n, \mathcal{F}_n\}$ satisfies*

$$\sup_n E(|\varepsilon_n|^\alpha \mid \mathcal{F}_{n-1}) < \infty \text{ a.s. with some } \alpha > 2 \tag{6.190}$$

and

$$\liminf_{n \to \infty} \frac{1}{n} \sum_{i=1}^{n} E(\varepsilon_i^2 \mid \mathcal{F}_{i-1}) > 0 \text{ a.s.} \tag{6.191}$$

then $\liminf_{n \to \infty} \lambda_{\min}(V_n) > 0$ a.s.

Proof.   Obviously, Eq. (6.190) implies Eq. (6.105). We need to verify Eq. (6.179). With $u = (1, 0, \ldots, 0)'$ we have $e_n = \varepsilon_n u$ and

$$F_n = n^{-1} \sum_{i=1}^{n} e_i e_i' = n^{-1} \sum_{i=1}^{n} \varepsilon_i u u' \varepsilon_i = n^{-1} \sum_{i=1}^{n} \varepsilon_i^2 u u',$$

$$\sum_{i=0}^{p-1} B^i F_n (B^i)' = n^{-1} \sum_{i=1}^{n} \varepsilon_i^2 \left[\sum_{i=0}^{p-1} B^i u u' (B^i)' \right]. \tag{6.192}$$

From

$$
Bu = \begin{pmatrix} \beta_1 & \cdots & \beta_{p-1} & \beta_p \\ & I_{p-1} & & 0 \end{pmatrix} \begin{pmatrix} 1 \\ 0 \\ \cdots \\ 0 \end{pmatrix} = \begin{pmatrix} \beta_1 \\ 1 \\ 0 \\ \cdots \\ 0 \end{pmatrix},
$$

$$
B^2 u = \begin{pmatrix} \beta_1 & \cdots & \beta_{p-1} & \beta_p \\ & I_{p-1} & & 0 \end{pmatrix} \begin{pmatrix} \beta_1 \\ 1 \\ 0 \\ \cdots \\ 0 \end{pmatrix} = \begin{pmatrix} \beta_1^2 + \beta_2 \\ \beta_1 \\ 1 \\ 0 \\ \cdots \\ 0 \end{pmatrix}
$$

and similar expressions for other powers of B we observe that the matrix $(u, Bu, \ldots, B^{p-1}u)$ is upper triangular with unities on the main diagonal and is therefore nonsingular. It follows that in Eq. (6.192) the matrix in the brackets is nonsingular:

$$
\det\left(\sum_{i=0}^{p-1} B^i u u'(B^i)' \right) = \det\left[(u, Bu, \ldots, B^{p-1}u) \begin{pmatrix} u' \\ (Bu)' \\ \cdots \\ (B^{p-1}u)' \end{pmatrix} \right] > 0.
$$

Theorem 6.7.5 is applicable.   ∎

6.7.7   Purely Explosive Case

Here we establish that in the purely explosive case ($m = \min|\lambda_j| > 1$) both $\lambda_{\min}(V_n)$ and $\lambda_{\max}(V_n)$ grow exponentially fast under assumption (6.161).

Theorem.   Let $\{e_n, \mathcal{F}_n\}$ be a m.d. sequence satisfying Eqs. (6.105) and (6.161), and define Y_n by Eq. (6.106). Suppose $m > 1$. Then

(i) The product $B^{-n}V_n(B^{-n})'$ converges a.s. to $G = \sum_{i=0}^{\infty} B^{-i} YY'(B^{-i})'$, where $V_n = \sum_{i=1}^{n} Y_i Y_i'$ and $Y = \lim_{n \to \infty} B^{-n}Y_n$.

(ii) G is positive definite with probability 1.

(iii) With probability 1

$$
\lim_{n \to \infty} n^{-1} \log \lambda_{\max}(V_n) = 2\log M,
$$

$$
\lim_{n \to \infty} n^{-1}\log \lambda_{\min}(V_n) = 2\log m.
$$

Proof.

(i) As for the existence of the limit $Y = \lim_{n\to\infty} B^{-n} Y_n$, see Eq. (6.160). Convergence of G follows from $\|B^{-i}\| \leq cm^{-i}$. Let us prove that $B^{-n} V_n (B^{-n})'$ converges to G. Denoting $Z_n = B^{-n} Y_n Y_n' (B^{-n})'$ and $Z = YY'$, by Eq. (6.160) we have $Z_n \to Z$ a.s. and therefore $c = \sup_i \|Z_i\| < \infty$ a.s. For a given $\varepsilon > 0$ let $n(\varepsilon)$ be such that $\|Z - Z_i\| \leq \varepsilon$ for $i \geq n(\varepsilon)$. We need to prove that

$$B^{-n} V_n (B^{-n})' = \sum_{i=1}^{n} B^{i-n} B^{-i} Y_i Y_i' (B^{-i})' (B^{i-n})'$$

$$= \sum_{i=1}^{n} B^{i-n} Z_i (B^{i-n})'$$

converges to $G = \sum_{i=0}^{\infty} B^{-i} Z (B^{-i})'$. This convergence follows from the next three bounds.

The first bound is

$$\left\| \sum_{i=0}^{n(\varepsilon)-1} B^{i-n} Z_i (B^{i-n})' \right\| \leq \sum_{i=0}^{n(\varepsilon)-1} \|B^{i-n}\|^2 c$$

$$\leq c \sum_{j=n-n(\varepsilon)+1}^{\infty} \|B^{-j}\|^2 \to 0, \quad n \to \infty.$$

The second is

$$\left\| \sum_{j=n-n(\varepsilon)+1}^{\infty} B^{-j} Z (B^{-j})' \right\| \leq \sum_{j=n-n(\varepsilon)+1}^{\infty} \|B^{-j}\|^2 \|Z\| \to 0, \quad n \to \infty.$$

Finally,

$$\left\| \sum_{i=n(\varepsilon)}^{n} B^{i-n} Z_i (B^{i-n})' - \sum_{j=0}^{n-n(\varepsilon)} B^{-j} Z (B^{-j})' \right\|$$

$$= \left\| \sum_{j=0}^{n-n(\varepsilon)} B^{-j} (Z_{n-j} - Z)(B^{-j})' \right\| \leq \varepsilon \sum_{j=0}^{\infty} \|B^{-j}\|^2.$$

For these bounds to yield the desired result, $n(\varepsilon)$ is chosen first and n next.

(ii) Suppose that

$$0 = x' G x = \sum_{i=0}^{\infty} x' B^{-i} YY' (B^{-i})' x = \sum_{i=0}^{\infty} (x' B^{-i} Y)^2.$$

Then $x' B^{-i} Y = ((B^{-i})' x)' Y = 0$. By Eq. (6.162) this is an impossible event if $(B^{-i})' x \neq 0$, that is $x \neq 0$.

(iii) Denote $C_n = B^{-n}V_n(B^{-n})'$. Since $C_n \to G$ a.s. and G is positive definite, we have

$$0 < \lim_{n \to \infty} \lambda_{\min}(C_n) \le \lim_{n \to \infty} \lambda_{\max}(C_n) < \infty \text{ a.s.}$$

This relation, the equation $V_n = B^n C_n (B^n)'$ and Lemma 6.5.3 imply

$$n^{-1}\log \lambda_{\max}(V_n) = n^{-1}\log\lambda_{\max}(B^n(B^n)') + o(1). \tag{6.193}$$

However, by Lemma 6.5.2(ii) and Eq. (6.119)

$$n^{-1}\log \lambda_{\max}(B^n(B^n)') = n^{-1}\log \|B^n\|^2 = 2(1 + o(1))\log M. \tag{6.194}$$

The first equation in (iii) follows from Eqs. (6.193) and (6.194).

As a result of $V_n^{-1} = (B^{-n})'C_n^{-1}B^{-n}$, along with Eq. (6.193), we have

$$n^{-1}\log \lambda_{\min}(V_n) = -n^{-1}\log \lambda_{\max}(V_n^{-1})$$
$$= -n^{-1}\log \lambda_{\max}((B^{-n})'B^{-n}) + o(1).$$

Instead of Eq. (6.194) we need now

$$n^{-1}\log \lambda_{\max}((B^{-n})'B^{-n}) = n^{-1}\log \|B^{-n}\|^2 = -2(1 + o(1))\log m.$$

The above two relations prove the second equation in (iii).   ∎

6.7.8   Some Bounds Involving V_n

As before, we denote $V_n = \sum_{i=1}^{n} Y_i Y_i'$ and let

$$N = \inf\{n: V_n \text{ is nonsingular}\}, \quad \inf \emptyset = \infty.$$

In the lemma below, we explicitly take account of the fact that the error vectors e_n form an array

$$e_1 = (e_{11}, \dots, e_{1p}), \quad e_2 = (e_{21}, \dots, e_{2p}), \dots, e_n = (e_{n1}, \dots, e_{np})$$

[see Eq. (6.107)].

Lemma.   *Let the m.d. sequence $\{e_n, \mathcal{F}_n\}$ satisfy Eq. (6.105) and suppose that Eq. (6.179) or, equivalently, Eq. (6.180) holds. If, additionally, $M \le 1$, then*

(i) *$N < \infty$ a.s. and $\|V_n^{-1/2}\| = O(n^{-1/2})$ a.s.*

(ii) *$Y_n' V_n^{-1} Y_n \le 1$ for $n \ge N$ and $\sum_{i=N}^{n} Y_i' V_i^{-1} Y_i = O(\log n)$ a.s.*

(iii) *We have the bound*

$$\left\| V_n^{-1/2} \sum_{i=1}^{n} Y_i e_{i+1}' \right\| = O((\log n)^{1/2}) \text{ a.s.}$$

Proof.

(i) By Theorem 6.7.5 $\liminf_{n\to\infty} n^{-1}\lambda_{\min}(V_n) > 0$, and so $N < \infty$ and

$$\|V_n^{-1/2}\|^2 = \sup_{\|x\|=1} \|V_n^{-1/2}x\|^2 = \sup_{\|x\|=1} x'V_n^{-1}x$$

$$= \lambda_{\max}(V_n^{-1}) = 1/\lambda_{\min}(V_n) = O(n) \text{ a.s.}$$

(ii) As V_{n-1} is nonnegative definite and V_n is positive definite for $n \geq N$, we have $|V_{n-1}| \geq 0$, $|V_n| > 0$ and by Lemma 6.4.2 $Y_n'V_n^{-1}Y_n = 1 - |V_{n-1}|/|V_n| \leq 1$, $n \geq N$. Further, by Lemma 6.4.3

$$\sum_{i=N}^n Y_i'V_i^{-1}Y_i = O(\log \lambda_{\max}(V_n)).$$

It remains to recall that $\log \lambda_{\max}(V_n) = O(\log n)$, according to parts (ii) and (iii) of Theorem 6.7.2.

(iii) To apply Lemma 6.4.5(iii), we need to reveal in

$$\left\| V_n^{-1/2} \sum_{i=1}^n Y_i e_{i+1}' \right\|^2 = \left(\sum_{i=1}^n Y_i e_{i+1}' \right)' V_n^{-1} \left(\sum_{i=1}^n Y_i e_{i+1}' \right)$$

the structure associated with regression $y_n = X_n\beta + \varepsilon_n$. Let

$$X_n' = (Y_1, \ldots, Y_n), \quad \varepsilon_n^{(j)} = (e_{2,j}, \ldots, e_{n+1,j}),$$
$$Q_n^{(j)} = (\varepsilon_n^{(j)})'X_n(X_n'X_n)^{-1}X_n'\varepsilon_n^{(j)}, \quad j = 1, \ldots, p.$$

Then $V_n = \sum_{i=1}^n Y_i Y_i' = X_n'X_n$ and the rows of X_n are not changed as new rows are appended. For each j, $\{e_{i+1,j}, \mathcal{F}_{i+1}\}$ is a m.d. sequence and Y_i is $\mathcal{F}_i$-measurable. Further,

$$\sum_{i=1}^n Y_i e_{i+1}' = \begin{pmatrix} \sum_{i=1}^n Y_i e_{i+1,1} \\ \cdots \\ \sum_{i=1}^n Y_i e_{i+1,p} \end{pmatrix} = \begin{pmatrix} X_n'\varepsilon_n^{(1)} \\ \cdots \\ X_n'\varepsilon_n^{(p)} \end{pmatrix}.$$

So by Lemma 6.4.5(iii)

$$\left\| V_n^{-1/2} \sum_{i=1}^n Y_i e_{i+1}' \right\|^2 = ((\varepsilon_n^{(1)})'X_n, \ldots, (\varepsilon_n^{(p)})'X_n)(X_n'X_n)^{-1} \begin{pmatrix} X_n'\varepsilon_n^{(1)} \\ \cdots \\ X_n'\varepsilon_n^{(p)} \end{pmatrix}$$

$$= Q_n^{(1)} + \cdots + Q_n^{(p)} = O(\log \lambda_{\max}(V_n)) = O(\log n) \text{ a.s.} \quad \blacksquare$$

6.7.9   More Bounds Involving V_n

Lemma.   *Let the conditions of Lemma 6.7.8 hold and suppose that B is nonsingular. Then*

(i) $\|V_n^{1/2}B'V_{n+1}^{-1}BV_n^{1/2}\| \leq 1 + O(n^{-1/2}(\log n)^{1/2})$ *a.s.*

(ii) *Let $\rho > 1/\alpha$ where α is the integrability parameter from Eq. (6.105). Then*

$$\limsup_{n \to \infty} n^{1/2-\rho}(Y'_{n+1}V_{n+1}^{-1}Y_{n+1} - Y'_n V_n^{-1}Y_n) \leq 0 \text{ a.s.}$$

Proof.

(i) We intend to apply Lemma 6.5.9(i) to $A_n = V_n^{1/2}B'V_{n+1}^{-1}BV_n^{1/2}$. To obtain a recursion for V_{n+1}, consider

$$V_{n+1} = \sum_{i=1}^{n+1} Y_i Y'_i = \sum_{i=1}^{n+1} (BY_{i-1} + e_i)(Y'_{i-1}B' + e'_i)$$

$$= \sum_{i=1}^{n+1} (BY_{i-1}Y'_{i-1}B' + BY_{i-1}e'_i + e_i Y'_{i-1}B' + e_i e'_i)$$

$$= B(V_n + Y_0 Y'_0)B' + B \sum_{i=0}^{n} Y_i e'_{i+1} + \sum_{i=0}^{n} e_{i+1} Y'_i B' + \sum_{i=1}^{n+1} e_i e'_i.$$

Therefore

$$A_n^{-1} = V_n^{-1/2}B^{-1}V_{n+1}(B')^{-1}V_n^{-1/2} = I_p + B_n + \tilde{C}_n + \tilde{C}'_n \qquad (6.195)$$

where

$$B_n = V_n^{-1/2}\left[Y_0 Y'_0 + B^{-1}\left(\sum_{i=1}^{n+1} e_i e'_i\right)(B')^{-1}\right]V_n^{-1/2}$$

is nonnegative definite,

$$\tilde{C}_n = V_n^{-1/2}\left(\sum_{i=0}^{n} Y_i e'_{i+1}\right)(B')^{-1}V_n^{-1/2}.$$

By Lemma 6.7.8, parts (i) and (iii),

$$\|\tilde{C}_n\| \leq \left\|V_n^{-1/2}\sum_{i=0}^{n} Y_i e'_{i+1}\right\|\|(B')^{-1}\|\|V_n^{-1/2}\|$$

$$= O(n^{-1/2}(\log n)^{1/2}) \text{ a.s.} \qquad (6.196)$$

Noting that $C_n = \tilde{C}_n + \tilde{C}'_n$ is symmetric, we can apply Eqs. (6.195) and (6.196) and Lemma 6.5.9(i) to conclude that

$$\|A_n\| \leq 1/[1 - O(n^{-1/2}(\log n)^{1/2})] = 1 + O(n^{-1/2}(\log n)^{1/2}).$$

(ii) For $n \geq N$ we have

$$Y'_{n+1} V_{n+1}^{-1} Y_{n+1} = (BY_n + e_{n+1})' V_{n+1}^{-1}(BY_n + e_{n+1})$$

$$= Y'_n B' V_{n+1}^{-1} BY_n + Y'_{n+1} V_{n+1}^{-1} e_{n+1}$$

$$+ e'_{n+1} V_{n+1}^{-1} Y_{n+1} - e'_{n+1} V_{n+1}^{-1} e_{n+1}.$$

Remembering that V_{n+1}^{-1} is positive definite, we continue as follows:

$$Y'_{n+1} V_{n+1}^{-1} Y_{n+1} \leq (V_n^{-1/2} Y_n)' V_n^{1/2} B' V_{n+1}^{-1} B V_n^{1/2}(V_n^{-1/2} Y_n)$$

$$+ 2(C_{n+1}^{-1/2} Y_{n+1})'(C_{n+1}^{-1/2} e_{n+1})$$

[applying statement (i)]

$$\leq [1 + O(n^{-1/2}(\log n)^{1/2})] \|V_n^{-1/2} Y_n\|^2$$

$$+ 2\|V_{n+1}^{-1/2} Y_{n+1}\|\|V_{n+1}^{-1/2}\|\|e_{n+1}\|. \tag{6.197}$$

By Lemmas 6.6.1 and 6.7.8(i,ii)

$$\|e_n\| = o(n^\rho), \quad \|V_n^{-1/2}\| = O(n^{-1/2}), \quad \|V_n^{-1/2} Y_n\|^2 = Y'_n V_n^{-1} Y_n \leq 1.$$

These bounds and Eq. (6.197) give

$$Y'_{n+1} V_{n+1}^{-1} Y_{n+1} \leq Y'_n V_n^{-1} Y_n + O(n^{-1/2}(\log n)^{1/2}) + o(n^{\rho-1/2})$$

$$= Y'_n V_n^{-1} Y_n + o(n^{\rho-1/2}). \tag{6.198}$$

This proves statement (ii). ∎

6.7.10 Convergence of Certain Quadratic Forms

An important difference between purely explosive ($m > 1$) and nonexplosive ($M \leq 1$) systems is described in the theorem below.

Theorem. *Let $\{e_n\}$ be a m.d. sequence satisfying Eqs. (6.105) and (6.161), and define Y_n by Eq. (6.106).*

(i) If $m > 0$, then for $k = 0, \pm 1, \pm 2, \ldots$

$$\lim_{n \to \infty} Y'_{n-k} V_n^{-1} Y_{n-k} = (B^{-k} Y)' G^{-1}(B^{-k} Y) > 0 \text{ a.s.}$$

where G and Y are the same as in Theorem 6.7.7.

(ii) If $M \leq 1$, then

$$\lim_{n \to \infty} \max_{1 \leq j \leq n} Y_j' V_n^{-1} Y_j = 0 \text{ a.s.} \tag{6.199}$$

Proof. **Proving (i).** The random variables under consideration converge by Theorem 6.7.7:

$$Y_{n-k}' V_n^{-1} Y_{n-k} = (B^{-k} B^{k-n} Y_{n-k})' [B^{-n} V_n (B^{-n})']^{-1} (B^{-k} B^{k-n} Y_{n-k})$$
$$\to (B^{-k} Y)' G^{-1} (B^{-k} Y)$$

where G^{-1} exists.

Proving (ii). The proof is split into several steps.

Step 1. For the proof of Eq. (6.199) it suffices to show that

$$\lim_{n \to \infty} Y_n' V_n^{-1} Y_n = 0 \text{ a.s.} \tag{6.200}$$

Indeed, by Lemma 6.7.8(i) for $1 \leq j < N$

$$Y_j' V_n^{-1} Y_j \leq \max_{1 \leq j < N} \|Y_j\|^2 O(n^{-1}) = O(n^{-1}).$$

For $N \leq j \leq n$ we can use the fact that, according to Eq. (6.88), $V_j^{-1} \geq V_{j+1}^{-1}$ and therefore $Y_j' V_j^{-1} Y_j \geq Y_j' V_{j+1}^{-1} Y_j \geq \cdots \geq Y_j' V_n^{-1} Y_j$.

Step 2. *Case of a nonsingular B.* By Lemma 6.7.9(ii), in Eq. (6.198) we can choose $\rho \in (1/\alpha, 1/2)$. Denoting $a_t = Y_t' V_t^{-1} Y_t$, by Eq. (6.198) we have $a_{t+1} \leq a_t + o(t^{-\kappa})$, with $\kappa = 1/2 - \rho > 0$, whereas by Lemma 6.7.8(ii) $\sum_{t=N}^n a_t = O(\log n) = o(n^\delta)$ for any $\delta > 0$. Therefore Lemma 6.6.10 implies $a_n = o(n^{-\beta})$ for all $\beta < \min\{1, \kappa/2\}$.

Case of a singular B. In this case 0 is a root of the characteristic polynomial $\phi(\lambda)$ of B. Denote r its multiplicity, $r \leq p$.

Subcase $r < p$. In the spectrum-separating decomposition of Section 6.5.8 we can assume that M is nonsingular, B_1 is nonsingular and all eigenvalues of B_2 are zero. The error vectors ξ_n, ζ_n in Eq. (6.134) satisfy the same conditions as e_n. As we proved in the nonsingular case,

$$S_n' \left(\sum_1^n S_i S_i' \right)^{-1} S_n \to 0 \text{ a.s.} \tag{6.201}$$

Denoting $A_n = MV_nM'$, from Eqs. (6.133) and (6.135) we get

$$
Y_n'V_n^{-1}Y_n = (MY_n)'A_n^{-1}MY_n = \begin{pmatrix} S_n \\ 0 \end{pmatrix}' A_n^{-1} \begin{pmatrix} S_n \\ 0 \end{pmatrix}
$$

$$
+ \begin{pmatrix} 0 \\ T_n \end{pmatrix}' A_n^{-1} \begin{pmatrix} 0 \\ T_n \end{pmatrix} + 2 \begin{pmatrix} S_n \\ 0 \end{pmatrix}' A_n^{-1} \begin{pmatrix} 0 \\ T_n \end{pmatrix}
$$

$$
= I_{n1} + I_{n2} + 2I_{n3}, \quad \text{say.} \tag{6.202}
$$

As M is nonsingular and $\|V_n^{-1}\| = O(n^{-1})$ by Lemma 6.7.8(i), we have

$$
\|A_n^{-1}\| \leq \|(M')^{-1}\| \|V_n^{-1}\| \|M^{-1}\| = O(n^{-1}) \text{ a.s.} \tag{6.203}
$$

Lemma 6.6.4, applied to T_n, gives $\|T_n\| = o(n^{1/2})$. Consequently,

$$
0 \leq I_{n2} \leq \|A_n^{-1}\| \|T_n\|^2 = O(n^{-1})o(n) = o(1). \tag{6.204}
$$

By Lemma 6.6.9

$$
\text{tr}\left(\sum_1^n T_iT_i'\right) = \sum_1^n \|T_i\|^2 = O(n). \tag{6.205}
$$

As a result of the partitioning [Eq. (6.135)], Lemma 6.5.9(ii) can be applied to A_n. Using Eqs. (6.201), (6.203) and (6.205) we get

$$
0 \leq I_{n1} \leq S_n'\left(\sum_1^n S_iS_i'\right)^{-1} S_n\left[1 + \|A_n^{-1}\|\text{tr}\left(\sum_1^n T_iT_i'\right)\right]
$$

$$
= o(1)[1 + O(n^{-1})O(n)] = o(1). \tag{6.206}
$$

The bounds obtained allow us to estimate I_{n3} :

$$
\|I_{n3}\| \leq \left\|\begin{pmatrix} S_n \\ 0 \end{pmatrix}' A_n^{-1/2}\right\| \left\|A_n^{-1/2}\begin{pmatrix} 0 \\ T_n \end{pmatrix}\right\| = (I_{n1}I_{n2})^{1/2} = o(1). \tag{6.207}
$$

The desired conclusion Eq. (6.200) follows from Eqs. (6.202), (6.204), (6.206) and (6.207).

Subcase $r = p$. In this case S_n is empty, $Y_n = T_n$ and the bound is similar to Eq. (6.204):

$$
Y_n'V_n^{-1}Y_n = T_n'V_n^{-1}T_n \leq \|V_n^{-1}\| \|T_n\|^2 = O(n^{-1})o(n) = o(1). \qquad \blacksquare
$$

6.7.11   Another Lemma on Purely Explosive Processes

Lemma.   *Let $\{e_n\}$ be a m.d. sequence satisfying Eqs. (6.105) and (6.161). Suppose $m > 1$. Then*

$$\lim_{n \to \infty} \sum_{i=1}^{n} \|B^{-n}Y_i\| = \sum_{i=1}^{\infty} \|B^{-i}Y\| < \infty \ a.s.,$$

where Y is from Eq. (6.160).

Proof.   Obviously, for any $I > 0$

$$\sum_{i=1}^{n} \|B^{-n}Y_i\| = \left(\sum_{i=I+1}^{n} + \sum_{i=1}^{I} \right) \|B^{-(n-i)}B^{-i}Y_i\|. \tag{6.208}$$

By Theorem 6.6.7 the number I can be chosen in such a way that for $i \geq I$ we have $\|B^{-i}Y_i - Y\| \leq \varepsilon$. We handle the first sum in Eq. (6.208) using Lemma 6.5.2:

$$\left| \sum_{i=I+1}^{n} \|B^{-(n-i)}B^{-i}Y_i\| - \sum_{j=0}^{n-I-1} \|B^{-j}Y\| \right|$$

(change $j = n - i$ in the second sum)

$$= \left| \sum_{i=I+1}^{n} \left(\|B^{-(n-i)}B^{-i}Y_i\| - \|B^{-(n-i)}Y\| \right) \right|$$

$$\leq \sum_{i=I+1}^{n} \|B^{-(n-i)}(B^{-i}Y_i - Y)\| \leq \varepsilon \sum_{i=I+1}^{n} \|B^{-(n-i)}\|$$

$$\leq \varepsilon \sum_{i=0}^{\infty} \|B^{-i}\| \leq c_1 \varepsilon \sum_{i=0}^{\infty} m^{-i} = c_2 \varepsilon. \tag{6.209}$$

For the second sum in Eq. (6.208) we apply the bound $c_3 = \sup_i \|B^{-i}Y_i\| < \infty$:

$$\sum_{i=1}^{I} \|B^{-(n-i)}B^{-i}Y_i\| \leq c_4 \sum_{i=n-I}^{\infty} m^{-i} = c_5 m^{-(n-I)} \to 0, \quad n \to \infty. \tag{6.210}$$

Besides,

$$\sum_{i=n-I}^{\infty} \|B^{-i}Y\| \leq c_6 \sum_{i=n-I}^{\infty} m^{-i} \to 0, \quad n \to \infty. \tag{6.211}$$

Equations (6.208)–(6.211) prove the statement.   ∎

6.7.12   Strong Consistency of the Ordinary Least Squares Estimator

Theorem.   *Suppose that the m.d. sequence $\{e_n\}$ satisfies Eqs. (6.105) and (6.179) [or, equivalently, Eq. (6.180)]. Then for $k = 1, \ldots, p$*

$$\lim_{n \to \infty} \hat{b}_k(n) = b_k \text{ a.s.} \tag{6.212}$$

Proof.   *Setting up proper normalization.* The elements of the representation

$$\hat{b}_k(n) - b_k = \left(\sum_{i=1}^{n-1} Y_i Y_i' \right)^{-1} \sum_{i=1}^{n-1} Y_i e_{i+1,k} \tag{6.213}$$

need to be properly normalized to converge. We are assuming that for the spectrum-separating decomposition Eq. (6.132) holds and the process $\{S_n\}$ is purely explosive. Therefore, by Theorem 6.7.7(i)

$$\lim_{n \to \infty} B_1^{-n} \left(\sum_{1}^{n-1} S_i S_i' \right) (B_1^{-n})' \equiv G \text{ is positive definite a.s.} \tag{6.214}$$

Denoting

$$V_n = \sum_{1}^{n-1} T_i T_i', \quad D_n = \begin{pmatrix} B_1^{-n} & 0 \\ 0 & V_{n-1}^{-1/2} \end{pmatrix}, \quad A_{n-1} = M \left(\sum_{1}^{n-1} Y_i Y_i' \right) M', \tag{6.215}$$

from Eq. (6.213) we get the desired representation:

$$\hat{b}_k(n) - b_k = [n^{1/2} M' D_n'] [D_n A_{n-1} D_n']^{-1} \left[n^{-1/2} D_n M \sum_{i=1}^{n-1} Y_i e_{i+1,k} \right]. \tag{6.216}$$

Convergence of the denominator matrix. Here we prove that

$$D_n A_{n-1} D_n' \to \begin{pmatrix} G & 0 \\ 0 & I_r \end{pmatrix} \text{ a.s.,} \tag{6.217}$$

where r is the dimension of the process $\{T_n\}$. From Eqs. (6.135) and (6.215) we obtain the following representation for the denominator matrix:

$$D_n A_{n-1} D_n' = \begin{pmatrix} B_1^{-n} & 0 \\ 0 & V_{n-1}^{-1/2} \end{pmatrix} \begin{pmatrix} \sum_{1}^{n-1} S_i S_i' & \sum_{1}^{n-1} S_i T_i' \\ \sum_{1}^{n-1} T_i S_i' & \sum_{1}^{n-1} T_i T_i' \end{pmatrix} \begin{pmatrix} (B_1^{-n})' & 0 \\ 0 & V_{n-1}^{-1/2} \end{pmatrix}$$

$$= \begin{pmatrix} B_1^{-n} \sum_{1}^{n-1} S_i S_i' (B_1^{-n})' & B_1^{-n} \sum_{1}^{n-1} S_i T_i' V_{n-1}^{-1/2} \\ V_{n-1}^{-1/2} \sum_{1}^{n-1} T_i S_i' (B_1^{-n})' & I_r \end{pmatrix}.$$

The limit of the upper left element of this matrix is given by Eq. (6.214). To prove Eq. (6.217), it suffices to show that

$$B_1^{-n} \sum_1^{n-1} S_i T_i' V_{n-1}^{-1/2} = \sum_1^{n-1} (B_1^{-n} S_i)(V_{n-1}^{-1/2} T_i)' \to 0. \tag{6.218}$$

Since the process $\{T_n\}$ is nonexplosive, by Theorem 6.7.10(ii)

$$\max_{1 \le j \le n-1} \|V_{n-1}^{-1/2} T_j\|^2 = \max_{1 \le j \le n-1} T_j' V_{n-1}^{-1} T_j \to 0.$$

Besides, by Lemma 6.7.11 in the purely explosive case

$$\sup_n \sum_{i=1}^{n-1} \|B_1^{-n} S_i\| < \infty. \tag{6.219}$$

Clearly, Eq. (6.218) is a consequence of the above two equations.
Bounding the first factor in Eq. (6.216). By Lemma 6.7.8(i)

$$\|V_{n-1}^{-1/2}\| = O(n^{-1/2}) \text{ a.s.} \tag{6.220}$$

This bound, definition (6.215) and Lemma 6.5.2 imply

$$\|n^{1/2} M' D_n'\| \le n^{1/2} \|M'\|(\|(B_1^{-n})'\| + \|V_{n-1}^{-1/2}\|)$$
$$= O(n^{1/2})[O(m^{-n}) + O(n^{-1/2})] = O(1). \tag{6.221}$$

Bounding the last factor in Eq. (6.216). Using Eqs. (6.133) and (6.215) we get

$$n^{-1/2} D_n M \sum_{i=1}^{n-1} Y_i e_{i+1,k} = n^{-1/2} \begin{pmatrix} B_1^{-n} & 0 \\ 0 & V_{n-1}^{-1/2} \end{pmatrix} \begin{pmatrix} \sum_{i=1}^{n-1} S_i e_{i+1,k} \\ \sum_{i=1}^{n-1} T_i e_{i+1,k} \end{pmatrix}$$

$$= \begin{pmatrix} n^{-1/2} B_1^{-n} \sum_{i=1}^{n-1} S_i e_{i+1,k} \\ n^{-1/2} V_{n-1}^{-1/2} \sum_{i=1}^{n-1} T_i e_{i+1,k} \end{pmatrix}. \tag{6.222}$$

Since $\|e_n\| = o(n^{1/2})$ by Lemma 6.6.1, Eq. (6.219) implies

$$\left\| n^{-1/2} B_1^{-n} \sum_{i=1}^{n-1} S_i e_{i+1,k} \right\|$$

$$\le (n^{-1/2} \max_{1 \le i \le n-1} e_{i+1,k}) \sum_{i=1}^{n-1} \|B_1^{-n} S_i\| \to 0 \text{ a.s.} \tag{6.223}$$

From Lemma 6.7.8(iii) we know that

$$\left\| V_{n-1}^{-1/2} \sum_{i=1}^{n-1} T_i e_{i+1,k} \right\| = O((\log n)^{1/2}). \tag{6.224}$$

Combining this with Eq. (6.220) we see that

$$\left\| n^{-1/2} V_{n-1}^{-1/2} \sum_{i=1}^{n-1} T_i e_{i+1,k} \right\| = O(n^{-1/2}(\log n)^{1/2}). \tag{6.225}$$

Equations (6.222), (6.223) and (6.225) prove that

$$n^{-1/2} D_n M \sum_{i=1}^{n-1} Y_i e_{i+1,k} \to 0 \text{ a.s.} \tag{6.226}$$

The strong consistency (6.212) is a consequence of Eqs. (6.216), (6.217), (6.222), (6.226) and the fact that G is positive definite a.s. ∎

CHAPTER 7

NONLINEAR MODELS

IN THIS chapter we consider two types of nonlinear estimation techniques: NLS and the ML method. In the first case we give a full proof of the result by Phillips (2007) for the model $y_s = \beta s^\gamma + u_s$, $s = 1, \ldots, n$. This proof includes an expanded exposition of the Wooldridge (1994) approach to asymptotic normality of an abstract estimator. In the second case, we give an extension to the unbounded explanatory variables of the result of Gouriéroux and Monfort (1981) for the binary selection model. Problems arising from the unboundedness assumption are explained. Some ideas of the proof, such as obtaining and analyzing the Lipschitz constant, can be used in models other than binary logit, and others, like the link to the linear model, are specific to the binary logit model.

7.1 ASYMPTOTIC NORMALITY OF AN ABSTRACT ESTIMATOR

The theory of nonlinear estimation is complex, and some authors in this area "overcome" its complexities by hiding them under a pile of conditions. The result by Wooldridge (1994) stands out by being rigorous and applicable to nonlinear regressions for nonstationary dependent time series.

7.1.1 The Framework

We begin with an objective function $Q_n(\omega, \theta)$, where ω is the sample data and θ is the parameter in the parameter space Θ. Θ is assumed to be of dimension p and, correspondingly, all square matrices will be of size $p \times p$. Most of the time dependence on ω of Q_n and its derivatives is suppressed.

The vector of first-order derivatives

$$S_n(\theta) = \nabla_\theta Q_n(\theta)'$$

is called a *score* and the matrix of second-order derivatives

$$H_n(\theta) = \nabla_\theta S_n(\theta)$$

Short-Memory Linear Processes and Econometric Applications. Kairat T. Mynbaev
© 2011 John Wiley & Sons, Inc. Published 2011 by John Wiley & Sons, Inc.

is called a *Hessian*. By an *estimator* of the true value θ_0 we mean a maximizing or minimizing point $\hat{\theta}_n$ of the objective function $Q_n(\omega, \theta)$, which, under appropriate conditions, is a solution to the first-order condition

$$S_n(\hat{\theta}_n) = 0 \text{ a.s.} \tag{7.1}$$

Usually such an estimator exists only *asymptotically almost surely* in the sense that the probability of the sample points ω for which it exists approaches unity as $n \to \infty$. We are interested in conditions sufficient for existence and consistency of such an estimator. Once we have it, a mean value expansion about θ_0

$$0 = S_n(\hat{\theta}_n) = S_n(\theta_0) + H_n(\hat{\theta}_n, \theta_0)(\hat{\theta}_n - \theta_0) \tag{7.2}$$

can be used to investigate the asymptotic normality of $\hat{\theta}_n$. In Eq. (7.2) $H_n(\theta, \theta_0)$ denotes the Hessian with rows evaluated at mean values $\bar{\theta}$ between θ and θ_0. That is, if we denote $H_{n1}, \ldots, H_{np}$ the rows of H_n, then with some $\Delta_1, \ldots, \Delta_p \in [0, 1]$

$$H_n(\theta, \theta_0) = \begin{pmatrix} H_{n1}(\theta_0 + \Delta_1(\theta - \theta_0)) \\ \cdots \\ H_{np}(\theta_0 + \Delta_p(\theta - \theta_0)) \end{pmatrix} \tag{7.3}$$

(in fact, the argument here belongs to the cube with vertices θ and θ_0). The numbers Δ_i arise from an application of the mean value theorem to p components of S_n. It is well known that, in general, they are different (one cannot apply the mean value theorem to the whole vector S_n to produce a single Δ for $i = 1, \ldots, p$). With some abuse of notation the argument in Eq. (7.3) is denoted $\bar{\theta} = \theta_0 + \Delta(\theta - \theta_0)$ and then $H_n(\theta, \theta_0)$ can be written as $H_n(\theta, \theta_0) = H_n(\bar{\theta})$.

7.1.2   Wooldridge's Assumptions

The first assumption is a set of regularity conditions to ensure a proper smoothness of Q_n.

7.1.2.1   *Assumption W1*

1. $Q_n \colon \Omega \times \Theta \to \mathbb{R}$ is the objective function defined on the data space Ω and the parameter space $\Theta \subseteq \mathbb{R}^p$.
2. The true parameter θ_0 belongs to the interior $\text{int}(\Theta)$.
3. Q_n satisfies standard measurability and differentiability conditions:

    a. for each $\theta \in \Theta$, $Q_n(\cdot, \theta)$ is measurable,
    b. for each $\omega \in \Omega$, $Q_n(\omega, \cdot)$ is twice continuously differentiable on $\text{int}(\Theta)$.

The second assumption is about normalization of the score and Hessian at the true value θ_0.

7.1.2.2 Assumption W2   There exists a sequence of nonstochastic positive definite diagonal matrices $\{D_n\}$ such that

$$D_n^{-1} S_n(\theta_0) \xrightarrow{d} N(0, B_0)$$

and

$$D_n^{-1} H_n(\theta_0) D_n^{-1} \xrightarrow{p} A_0, \tag{7.4}$$

where A_0 and B_0 are nonrandom matrices and A_0 is positive definite.

The next assumption realizes the idea to provide a type of uniform convergence $H_n(\theta) \to H_n(\theta_0)$ of the Hessian normalized by something tending to infinity at a rate slower than D_n.

7.1.2.3 Assumption W3   There is a sequence of nonstochastic positive definite diagonal matrices $\{C_n\}$ such that

$$C_n D_n^{-1} \to 0 \text{ as } n \to \infty \tag{7.5}$$

and

$$\max_{\theta \in N_n^r(\theta_0)} \| C_n^{-1} [H_n(\theta) - H_n(\theta_0)] C_n^{-1} \| = o_p(1), \tag{7.6}$$

where the neighborhood $N_n^r(\theta_0)$ of θ_0 is defined by

$$N_n^r(\theta_0) = \{\theta \in \Theta : \| C_n(\theta - \theta_0) \| \leq r\}, \ 0 < r \leq 1.$$

Owing to this assumption, (i) we allow each element of the Hessian to be standardized by a different function of the sample size and (ii) the neighborhood $N_n^r(\theta_0)$, over which the convergence $H_n(\theta) \to H_n(\theta_0)$ must take place, uniformly shrinks to θ_0 as the sample size tends to infinity. Everywhere in Section 7.1 Assumptions W1–W3 are assumed to hold.

7.1.3 Algebraic Lemma

It is convenient to denote

$$S_n^0 = S_n(\theta_0), \ H_n^0 = H_n(\theta_0), \ A_n = D_n^{-1} H_n^0 D_n^{-1}.$$

One of Wooldridge's tricks is to use expansions about the point

$$\tilde{\theta}_n = \theta_0 - (H_n^0)^{-1} S_n^0, \tag{7.7}$$

which mimics $\hat{\theta}_n$ [from Eq. (7.2) we see that $\hat{\theta}_n = \theta_0 - (H_n(\bar{\theta}))^{-1} S_n^0)$]. This point has the properties

$$(\tilde{\theta}_n - \theta_0)' S_n^0 = -(S_n^0)'(H_n^0)^{-1} S_n^0,$$

$$(\tilde{\theta}_n - \theta_0)' H_n^0 (\tilde{\theta}_n - \theta_0) = (S_n^0)'(H_n^0)^{-1} S_n^0. \tag{7.8}$$

The purpose of the lemma below is to show that the difference $Q_n(\theta) - Q_n(\tilde{\theta}_n)$ is a quadratic function.

Lemma. *The objective function satisfies*

$$Q_n(\theta) - Q_n(\tilde{\theta}_n) = \frac{1}{2}(\theta - \tilde{\theta}_n)' H_n^0 (\theta - \tilde{\theta}_n) + R_n(\theta, \theta_0) - R_n(\tilde{\theta}_n, \theta_0), \tag{7.9}$$

where

$$R_n(\theta, \theta_0) = (\theta - \theta_0)'[H_n(\theta, \theta_0) - H_n^0](\theta - \theta_0).$$

Proof. By the second-order Taylor expansion

$$Q_n(\theta) - Q_n(\theta_0) = (\theta - \theta_0)' S_n^0 + \frac{1}{2}(\theta - \theta_0)' H_n^0 (\theta - \theta_0) + R_n(\theta, \theta_0). \tag{7.10}$$

Replacing θ by $\tilde{\theta}_n$ in Eq. (7.10) and using Eq. (7.8) we get

$$Q_n(\tilde{\theta}_n) - Q_n(\theta_0) = (\tilde{\theta}_n - \theta_0)' S_n^0 + \frac{1}{2}(\tilde{\theta}_n - \theta_0)' H_n^0 (\tilde{\theta}_n - \theta_0) + R_n(\tilde{\theta}_n, \theta_0)$$

$$= -\frac{1}{2}(S_n^0)'(H_n^0)^{-1} S_n^0 + R_n(\tilde{\theta}_n, \theta_0). \tag{7.11}$$

By Eq. (7.7) we have $-\theta_0 = -\tilde{\theta}_n - (H_n^0)^{-1} S_n^0$, so by Eq. (7.10)

$$Q_n(\theta) - Q_n(\theta_0) = [\theta - \tilde{\theta}_n - (H_n^0)^{-1} S_n^0]' S_n^0 + \frac{1}{2}[\theta - \tilde{\theta}_n - (H_n^0)^{-1} S_n^0]'$$

$$\times H_n^0 [\theta - \tilde{\theta}_n - (H_n^0)^{-1} S_n^0] + R_n(\tilde{\theta}_n, \theta_0)$$

$$= (\theta - \tilde{\theta}_n)' S_n^0 - (S_n^0)'(H_n^0)^{-1} S_n^0 + \frac{1}{2}(\theta - \tilde{\theta}_n)' H_n^0 (\theta - \tilde{\theta}_n)$$

$$- \frac{1}{2}(\theta - \tilde{\theta}_n)' H_n^0 (H_n^0)^{-1} S_n^0 - \frac{1}{2}(S_n^0)'(H_n^0)^{-1} H_n^0 (\theta - \tilde{\theta}_n)$$

$$+ \frac{1}{2}(S_n^0)'(H_n^0)^{-1} S_n^0 + R_n(\theta, \theta_0).$$

Here some terms cancel out, and the result is

$$Q_n(\theta) - Q_n(\theta_0) = -\frac{1}{2}(S_n^0)'(H_n^0)^{-1}S_n^0 + \frac{1}{2}(\theta - \tilde{\theta}_n)'H_n^0(\theta - \tilde{\theta}_n) + R_n(\theta, \theta_0). \quad (7.12)$$

Subtracting Eq. (7.11) from Eq. (7.12) we get Eq. (7.9). ■

7.1.4   Lemma on Convergence in Probability

Lemma.   *If a sequence of random vectors $\{\alpha_n\}$ satisfies* plim $\alpha_n = 0$, *then there exists a sequence of positive numbers $\{r_n\}$ such that* $\lim r_n = 0$ *and* $\lim P(\|\alpha_n\| > r_n) = 0$.

Proof.   By definition, for any $\delta > 0$ we have $P(\|\alpha_n\| > \delta) \to 0$. Hence, letting $\delta_1 = 1$ we can find n_1 such that $P(\|\alpha_n\| > \delta_1) \le \delta_1$ for all $n \ge n_1$. Similarly, for $\delta_2 = 2^{-1}$ there exists $n_2 > n_1$ such that $P(\|\alpha_n\| > \delta_2) \le \delta_2$ for all $n \ge n_2$. On the kth step we put $\delta_k = 2^{-k+1}$ and find $n_k > n_{k-1}$ such that

$$P(\|\alpha_n\| > \delta_k) \le \delta_k \text{ for all } n \ge n_k. \quad (7.13)$$

Since $\cup_{k=1}^{\infty}[n_k, n_{k+1}) = [n_1, \infty)$, for any $n \ge n_1$ there is a segment $[n_k, n_{k+1})$ containing this n. We can define $r_n = \delta_k$ for $n_k \le n < n_{k+1}$. Then from Eq. (7.13) it follows that $P(\|\alpha_n\| > r_n) = P(\|\alpha_n\| > \delta_k) \le \delta_k$. Since the conditions $n \to \infty$, $n_k \to \infty$ and $\delta_k \to 0$ are equivalent, this proves the lemma. ■

7.1.5   Bounding the Remainder in the Vicinity of θ_0

Lemma.   *One has the bound*

$$\sup_{\theta \in N_n^r(\theta_0)} |R_n(\theta, \theta_0)| \le \delta_n r^2 \text{ for all } r \le 1,$$

where δ_n are random variables satisfying

$$\delta_n = o_p(1). \quad (7.14)$$

Proof.   Denote

$$\delta_n = \sup_{\theta \in N_n^r(\theta_0)} \|C_n^{-1}[H_n(\theta) - H_n^0]C_n^{-1}\|.$$

Then Eq. (7.14) follows from Eq. (7.6). Write $R_n(\theta, \theta_0) = b_n(\theta)'B_n(\theta, \theta_0)b_n(\theta)$, where

$$b_n(\theta) = C_n(\theta - \theta_0), \quad B_n(\theta, \theta_0) = C_n^{-1}[H_n(\theta, \theta_0) - H_n^0]C_n^{-1}.$$

Since for any $r \le 1$ we have $\{\theta : \|b_n(\theta)\| \le r\} = N_n^r(\theta_0) \subseteq N_n^1(\theta_0)$ and for $\theta \in N_n^r(\theta_0)$ the argument $\bar{\theta} = \theta_0 + \Delta(\theta - \theta_0)$ of $H_n(\theta, \theta_0)$ belongs to $N_n^r(\theta_0)$,

$\|C_n(\bar{\theta} - \theta_0)\| \leq \|C_n(\theta - \theta_0)\| \leq r$, by condition (7.6) we obtain

$$\sup_{\theta \in N_n^r(\theta_0)} |R_n(\theta, \theta_0)| \leq \sup_{\theta \in N_n^r(\theta_0)} \|b_n(\theta)\|^2 \|B_n(\theta, \theta_0)\| \leq \delta_n r^2. \qquad \blacksquare$$

7.1.6 Bounding the Remainder in the Vicinity of $\tilde{\theta}_n$

Define

$$\tilde{N}_n(r) = \{\theta: \|D_n(\theta - \tilde{\theta}_n)\| \leq r\}, \quad \Omega_n = \{\omega: \|C_n(\tilde{\theta}_n - \theta_0)\| \leq r_n\}.$$

Lemma.   *There exists a sequence of positive numbers $\{r_n\}$ such that*

(i) *$P(\Omega_n) \to 1$ as $n \to \infty$.*

(ii) *For all large n we have*

$$\sup_{\omega \in \Omega_n, \, \theta \in \tilde{N}_n(r_n)} |R_n(\theta, \theta_0)| \leq 4\delta_n r_n^2 \, a.s.$$

(iii) *For $r_n \leq 1$*

$$\sup_{\omega \in \Omega_n} |R_n(\tilde{\theta}_n, \theta_0)| \leq \delta_n r_n^2 \, a.s.$$

Proof.

(i) By Assumption W2 and definition (7.7)

$$D_n(\tilde{\theta}_n - \theta_0) = -D_n(H_n^0)^{-1} S_n^0 = -A_n^{-1} D_n^{-1} S_n^0 \xrightarrow{d} N(0, A_0^{-1} B_0 A_0^{-1})$$

and, therefore,

$$D_n(\tilde{\theta}_n - \theta_0) = O_p(1). \qquad (7.15)$$

By Eq. (7.5)

$$m_n \equiv \|C_n D_n^{-1}\| \to 0. \qquad (7.16)$$

Equations (7.15), (7.16) and the bound $\|C_n(\tilde{\theta}_n - \theta_0)\| \leq m_n \|D_n(\tilde{\theta}_n - \theta_0)\|$ imply

$$\text{plim } C_n(\tilde{\theta}_n - \theta_0) = 0. \qquad (7.17)$$

According to Lemma 7.1.4, then there exists a positive sequence $\{r_n\}$ such that $\lim_{n \to \infty} r_n = 0$ and $P(\Omega_n) = P(\|C_n(\tilde{\theta}_n - \theta_0)\| \leq r_n) \to 1$. This proves (i).

(ii) Obviously, $\|D_n(\theta - \tilde{\theta}_n)\| \leq r_n$ implies $\|C_n(\theta - \tilde{\theta}_n)\| \leq m_n r_n$ so

$$\tilde{N}_n(r_n) \subseteq \{\theta: \|C_n(\theta - \tilde{\theta}_n)\| \leq m_n r_n\} \subset \{\theta: \|C_n(\theta - \tilde{\theta}_n)\| \leq r_n\} \text{ for } n \text{ large.}$$

$$(7.18)$$

By the triangle inequality

$$\|C_n(\theta - \theta_0)\| \leq \|C_n(\theta - \tilde{\theta}_n)\| + \|C_n(\tilde{\theta}_n - \theta_0)\|. \tag{7.19}$$

In view of Eqs. (7.18) and (7.19) we have the implication

$$\omega \in \Omega_n, \ \theta \in \tilde{N}_n(r_n) \ \Rightarrow \ \theta \in N_n^{2r_n}(\theta_0).$$

Therefore (ii) follows from Lemma 7.1.5 and Eq. (7.17):

$$\sup_{\omega \in \Omega_n, \theta \in \tilde{N}_n(r_n)} |R_n(\theta, \theta_0)| \leq \sup_{\theta \in N_n^{2r_n}(\theta_0)} |R_n(\theta, \theta_0)| \leq 4\delta_n r_n^2$$

if n is large.

(iii) Since $\tilde{\theta}_n \in N_n^{r_n}(\theta_0)$ for $\omega \in \Omega_n$, statement (iii) follows immediately from Lemma 7.1.5. ∎

7.1.7 Consistency of $\hat{\theta}_n$

Theorem. *There exists a sequence of sets $\{\tilde{\Omega}_n\}$ such that*

$$P(\tilde{\Omega}_n) \to 1 \ as \ n \to \infty \tag{7.20}$$

and for almost any $\omega \in \tilde{\Omega}_n$ there exists an estimator $\hat{\theta}_n \in \tilde{N}_n(r_n)$ such that

$$D_n(\hat{\theta}_n - \theta_0) = O_p(1). \tag{7.21}$$

Proof. Denote $f_n(\theta) = Q_n(\theta) - Q_n(\tilde{\theta}_n)$. Obviously, the center $\tilde{\theta}_n$ of the neighborhood $\tilde{N}_n(r_n)$ satisfies $f_n(\tilde{\theta}_n) = 0$. We want to show that on the boundary $\partial\tilde{N}_n(r_n)$ of $\tilde{N}_n(r_n)$ the function f_n is positive. Let λ_n denote the smallest eigenvalue of $A_n = D_n^{-1}H_n^0 D_n^{-1}$ and let

$$\tilde{\Omega}_n = \Omega_n \cap \{\omega: 5\delta_n \leq \lambda_n/4\}.$$

Since λ_n tends to a positive number by Assumption W2, Lemma 7.1.6(i) and Eq. (7.14) imply Eq. (7.20). By Lemmas 7.1.3 and 7.1.6 for $\omega \in \tilde{\Omega}_n$

$$\min_{\theta \in \partial\tilde{N}_n(r_n)} f_n(\theta) \geq \min_{\theta \in \partial\tilde{N}_n(r_n)} \left\{ \frac{1}{2}[D_n(\theta - \tilde{\theta}_n)]'(D_n^{-1}H_n^0 D_n^{-1})[D_n(\theta - \tilde{\theta}_n)] \right.$$

$$\left. +R_n(\theta, \theta_0) - R_n(\tilde{\theta}_n, \theta_0) \right\}$$

$$\geq \frac{1}{2}\lambda_n r_n^2 - 5\delta_n r_n^2 \geq \frac{1}{4}\lambda_n r_n^2 > 0.$$

Thus, there are points inside $\tilde{N}_n(r_n)$ where f_n takes values lower than on its boundary. Since f_n is smooth by Assumption W1, it achieves its minimum inside $\tilde{N}_n(r_n)$ and the point of minimum $\hat{\theta}_n$ satisfies the first-order condition (7.1). The inequality $\|D_n(\hat{\theta}_n - \tilde{\theta}_n)\| \leq r_n$ and Eq. (7.15) prove Eq. (7.21). $\blacksquare$

7.1.8 Asymptotic Normality of $\hat{\theta}_n$

Theorem. *Under Assumptions W1–W3 the estimator $\hat{\theta}_n$ from Theorem 7.1.7 satisfies*

$$D_n(\hat{\theta}_n - \theta_0) \xrightarrow{d} N(0, A_0^{-1}B_0A_0^{-1}). \tag{7.22}$$

Proof. By Theorem 7.1.7 for almost any $\omega \in \tilde{\Omega}_n$ we can use Eq. (7.2). Premultiplication of that equation by D_n^{-1} yields

$$
\begin{aligned}
0 &= D_n^{-1}S_n^0 + D_n^{-1}\tilde{H}_n(\hat{\theta}_n - \theta_0) \\
&= D_n^{-1}S_n^0 + A_nD_n(\hat{\theta}_n - \theta_0) + D_n^{-1}(\tilde{H}_n - H_n^0)D_n^{-1}D_n(\hat{\theta}_n - \theta_0),
\end{aligned} \tag{7.23}
$$

where we denote $\tilde{H}_n = H_n(\hat{\theta}_n, \theta_0)$.

Now we show that the end term in Equation (7.23) is negligible. Equation (7.21) implies that the mean value $\bar{\theta}_n = \theta_0 + \Delta(\hat{\theta}_n - \theta_0)$ satisfies $D_n(\bar{\theta}_n - \theta_0) = O_p(1)$. By condition (7.5) then

$$C_n(\bar{\theta}_n - \theta_0) = o_p(1). \tag{7.24}$$

Denoting $\bar{\Omega}_n = \{\omega \in \tilde{\Omega}_n : \|C_n(\bar{\theta}_n - \theta_0)\| \leq 1\}$ we have $P(\bar{\Omega}_n) \to 1$ by Eqs. (7.20) and (7.24). For $\omega \in \bar{\Omega}_n$ it holds that $\bar{\theta}_n \in N_n(1)$ for all large n and therefore, by Assumption W3

$$\|D_n^{-1}(\tilde{H}_n - H_n^0)D_n^{-1}\| \leq \|D_n^{-1}C_n\|\|C_n^{-1}(\tilde{H}_n - H_n^0)C_n^{-1}\|\|C_nD_n^{-1}\| = o_p(1)$$

$(D_n^{-1}C_n = C_nD_n^{-1}$ because these matrices are diagonal). This bound and consistency (7.21) show that the end term in Eq. (7.23) is $o_p(1)$. It follows that $0 = D_n^{-1}S_n^0 + A_nD_n(\hat{\theta}_n - \theta_0) + o_p(1)$. As a result of Assumption W2 this implies $D_n(\hat{\theta}_n - \theta_0) = -A_n^{-1}D_n^{-1}S_n^0 + o_p(1)$. It remains to apply Assumption W2 again to prove Eq. (7.22). $\blacksquare$

7.2 CONVERGENCE OF SOME DETERMINISTIC AND STOCHASTIC EXPRESSIONS

To make the exposition of the Phillips' method in Section 7.3 clearer, in Section 7.2 we collect some technical tools arising in his approach.

7.2.1 Approximation of Integrals by Integral Sums: General Statement

Lemma. *Denote*

$$R(f) = \frac{1}{n} \sum_{t=1}^{n} f\left(\frac{t}{n}\right) - \int_0^1 f(t)\, dt.$$

(i) *If f is absolutely continuous on $[0, 1]$, then $|R(f)| \leq \|f'\|_1 / n$.*

(ii) *Suppose f is continuously differentiable on $(0, 1]$, $|f|$ is monotone on $[0, \delta_0)$ for some $0 < \delta_0 < 1$ and*

$$\sup_{\delta < t < 1} |f'(t)| \leq c|f'(\delta)| \quad \text{for all } 0 < \delta \leq \delta_0/2. \tag{7.25}$$

Then

$$|R(f)| \leq 2 \int_0^{2\delta} |f(t)|\, dt + c \frac{|f'(\delta)|}{n} \quad \text{for all } 0 < \delta \leq \delta_0/2.$$

Proof.

(i) Using the Newton–Leibniz formula and changing the order of integration we have $[i_t = ((t-1)/n, t/n)]$

$$\int_{i_t} \left| f\left(\frac{t}{n}\right) - f(s) \right| ds \leq \int_{i_t} \int_s^{t/n} |f'(\tau)|\, d\tau\, ds$$

$$= \int_{i_t} \int_{(t-1)/n}^{\tau} ds |f'(\tau)|\, d\tau \leq \frac{1}{n} \int_{i_t} |f'(\tau)|\, d\tau.$$

Hence,

$$|R(f)| \leq \sum_{t=1}^{n} \int_{i_t} \left| f\left(\frac{t}{n}\right) - f(s) \right| ds \leq \frac{1}{n} \sum_{t=1}^{n} \int_{i_t} |f'(\tau)|\, d\tau = \frac{\|f'\|_1}{n}.$$

(ii) By monotonicity of $|f|$ for small t the term $\frac{1}{n}\left| f\left(\frac{t}{n}\right) \right|$ does not exceed either

$\int_{i_t} |f(s)|\, ds$ or $\int_{i_{t+1}} |f(s)|\, ds$, so for $\frac{1}{n} \leq \delta \leq \delta_0/2$

$$\left| \frac{1}{n} \sum_{t=1}^{n\delta} f\left(\frac{t}{n}\right) \right| \leq \int_0^{\delta+1/n} |f(t)|\, dt \leq \int_0^{2\delta} |f(t)|\, dt.$$

By the finite increments formula and condition (7.25)

$$\left| \frac{1}{n} \sum_{t=n\delta}^{n} f\left(\frac{t}{n}\right) - \int_{\delta}^{1} f(s)\,ds \right| \le \sum_{t=n\delta}^{n} \int_{i_t} \left| f'(\theta)\left(s - \frac{t}{n}\right) \right| ds$$

$$\le \frac{1}{n} \sup_{s \ge \delta} |f'(s)| \sum_{t=1}^{n} \int_{i_t} ds \le \frac{c|f'(\delta)|}{n}.$$

The last two bounds result in

$$|R(f)| \le \left| \frac{1}{n} \sum_{t=1}^{n\delta} f\left(\frac{t}{n}\right) \right| + \int_{0}^{\delta} |f(s)|\,ds$$

$$+ \left| \frac{1}{n} \sum_{t=n\delta}^{n} f\left(\frac{t}{n}\right) - \int_{\delta}^{1} f(s)\,ds \right| \le 2 \int_{0}^{2\delta} |f(s)|\,ds + c\frac{|f'(\delta)|}{n}. \qquad \blacksquare$$

7.2.2 Approximation of Integrals by Integral Sums: Special Cases

Lemma. *Let i be a nonnegative integer and g_0 a real number such that $g_0 > -1$. Denote $f_i(t) = t^g (\log t)^i$ where g belongs to a small neighborhood $O_\delta(g_0) \subseteq (-1, \infty)$ of g_0. Then uniformly in $g \in O_\delta(g_0)$*

$$R(f_i) = O\left(\frac{1}{n}\right) \quad \text{if } g_0 > 1, \tag{7.26}$$

$$R(f_i) = O\left(\frac{(\log n)^i}{n^{(g+1)/2}}\right) \quad \text{if } 1 \ge g_0 > -1. \tag{7.27}$$

Proof. From $f_i'(t) = g t^{g-1}(\log t)^i + i t^{g-1}(\log t)^{i-1}$ we get

$$|f_i'(t)| \le c t^{g-1}(1 + |\log t|^i). \tag{7.28}$$

Equation (7.26) follows from this bound and Lemma 7.2.1(i).

In case $g_0 \le 1$ we see from Eq. (7.28) that f_i satisfies assumptions of Lemma 7.2.1(ii). Therefore

$$|R(f_i)| \le 2 \int_{0}^{2\delta} t^g |\log t|^i\,dt + c\frac{|f_i'(\delta)|}{n}. \tag{7.29}$$

It is easy to see that with some constants c_{ij}

$$\int_0^a t^g (\log t)^i \, dt = a^{g+1} \sum_{j=0}^i c_{ij} \log^j a. \tag{7.30}$$

Indeed, for $i = 0$ one has $\int_0^a t^g dt = a^{g+1}/(g+1)$. Suppose Eq. (7.30) is true for $i = k$. Then for $i = k+1$

$$\int_0^a t^g (\log t)^{k+1} \, dt = \frac{t^{g+1} (\log t)^{k+1}}{g+1} \bigg|_0^a - \frac{k+1}{g+1} \int_0^a t^g (\log t)^k \, dt$$

$$= \frac{a^{g+1} (\log a)^{k+1}}{g+1} - \frac{k+1}{g+1} a^{g+1} \sum_{j=0}^k c_{kj} \log^j a,$$

which is of form Eq. (7.30). Equations (7.28)–(7.30) imply for small δ

$$|R(f_i)| \leq c_1 \delta^{g+1} |\log \delta|^i + c_2 \frac{\delta^{g-1} |\log \delta|^i}{n}.$$

The choice $\delta = n^{-1/2}$ yields $\delta^{g+1} = \dfrac{\delta^{g-1}}{n} = n^{-(g+1)/2}$ and finishes the proof of Eq. (7.27). ∎

7.2.3 L_p-Approximability of Power Sequences

Here we consider sequences $x_n = (1^\gamma, 2^\gamma, \ldots, n^\gamma)$. For $\gamma \geq 0$ L_p-approximability of $x_n / \|x_n\|$ is shown in Section 2.7.3, where the fact that γ is an integer did not play any role. Continuity, however, was important. Here we consider negative γ when there is no continuity.

Lemma. *Let $1 \leq p < \infty$ and $0 > \gamma > -1/p$. Then*

(i) $\|x_n\|_p^p = \dfrac{n^{\gamma p + 1}}{\gamma p + 1} + O(n^{(\gamma p + 1)/2})$,

(ii) the sequence $w_n = n^{-1/p} \left(\left(\dfrac{1}{n}\right)^\gamma, \ldots, \left(\dfrac{n}{n}\right)^\gamma \right)$ is L_p-close to $W(s) = s^\gamma$. Moreover, $\|w_n - \delta_{np} W\|_p \to 0$ uniformly in $\gamma \in (-1/p + \delta, 0)$ for any $\delta > 0$.

Proof.

(i) By Eq. (7.26)

$$\|x_n\|_p^p = \sum_{t=1}^n t^{\gamma p} = n^{\gamma p + 1} \frac{1}{n} \sum_{t=1}^n \left(\frac{t}{n}\right)^{\gamma p}$$

$$= n^{\gamma p + 1} \left[\int_0^1 s^{\gamma p} \, ds + O(n^{-(\gamma p + 1)/2}) \right] = \frac{n^{\gamma p + 1}}{\gamma p + 1} + O(n^{(\gamma p + 1)/2}).$$

(ii) By Minkowski's inequality

$$\|w_n - \delta_{np} W\|_p \leq \left(\sum_{t=1}^{n\delta} |w_{nt}|^p \right)^{1/p} + \left(\sum_{t=1}^{n\delta} |(\delta_{np} W)_t|^p \right)^{1/p}$$

$$+ \left(\sum_{t=n\delta}^{n} |w_{nt} - (\delta_{np} W)_t|^p \right)^{1/p}. \tag{7.31}$$

Here, by monotonicity

$$\sum_{t=1}^{n\delta} |w_{nt}|^p = \frac{1}{n} \sum_{t=1}^{n\delta} \left(\frac{t}{n} \right)^{\gamma p} \leq \int_0^{\delta} s^{\gamma p} ds = c\delta^{\gamma p + 1}. \tag{7.32}$$

Using Hölder's inequality and the definition $(\delta_{np} W)_t = n^{1-1/p} \int_{i_t} W(s)\, ds$ we obtain a similar bound for the second term at the right of Eq. (7.31)

$$\sum_{t=1}^{n\delta} |(\delta_{np} W)_t|^p = n^{p-1} \sum_{t=1}^{n\delta} \left| \int_{i_t} W(s)\, ds \right|^p$$

$$\leq n^{p-1} \sum_{t=1}^{n\delta} \int_{i_t} W^p(s)\, ds \left(\int_{i_t} ds \right)^{p-1}$$

$$= \int_0^{\delta} s^{\gamma p} ds = c\delta^{\gamma p + 1}. \tag{7.33}$$

By the finite increments formula

$$\sum_{t=n\delta}^{n} |w_{nt} - (\delta_{np} W)_t|^p = \sum_{t=n\delta}^{n} \frac{1}{n} \left| \left(\frac{t}{n} \right)^{\gamma} - n \int_{i_t} s^{\gamma} ds \right|^p$$

$$= \sum_{t=n\delta}^{n} \frac{1}{n} \left| n \int_{i_t} W'(\theta) \left(\frac{t}{n} - s \right) ds \right|^p$$

$$\leq \sup_{s \geq \delta} |W'(s)|^p \sum_{t=n\delta}^{n} \frac{1}{n^{p+1}}$$

$$\leq \frac{1}{n^p} \sup_{s \geq \delta} |W'(s)|^p. \tag{7.34}$$

Since W satisfies condition (7.25), Eq. (7.34) implies

$$\left(\sum_{t=n\delta}^{n} |w_{nt} - (\delta_{np}W)_t|^p\right)^{1/p} \le \frac{c}{n}\delta^{\gamma-1}. \tag{7.35}$$

Equations (7.31), (7.32), (7.33), and (7.35) yield

$$\|w_n - \delta_{np}W\|_p \le c\left(\delta^{\gamma+1/p} + \frac{\delta^{\gamma-1}}{n}\right).$$

The choice $\delta^{\gamma+1/p} = \delta^{\gamma-1}/n$ or, equivalently, $\delta = n^{-(1+1/p)}$ finishes the proof of L_p-approximability with the bound $\|w_n - \delta_{np}W\|_p = O(n^{-(p\gamma+1)/(p+1)})$. The fact that this convergence is uniform in $\gamma \in (-1/p + \delta, 0)$ follows from the observation that the constants in Eqs. (7.32), (7.33), and (7.35) are uniformly bounded. ∎

7.2.4 Definition of Auxiliary Deterministic and Stochastic Expressions

Phillips defines the matrix C_n required in the Wooldridge framework by

$$C_n = n^{\gamma_0+1/2-\delta}\text{diag}[1, \log n].$$

With this definition the neighborhood from Assumption W3 becomes

$$N_n^r(\theta_0) = \{\theta \in \Theta : \|C_n(\theta - \theta_0)\| \le r\}$$
$$= \{\theta : [n^{\gamma_0+1/2-\delta}(\beta - \beta_0)]^2 + [n^{\gamma_0+1/2-\delta}(\log n)(\gamma - \gamma_0)]^2 \le r^2\}. \tag{7.36}$$

In particular, for $\theta \in N_n^1(\theta_0)$

$$|\beta - \beta_0| \le \frac{1}{n^{\gamma_0+1/2-\delta}}, \quad |\gamma - \gamma_0| \le \frac{1}{n^{\gamma_0+1/2-\delta}\log n}. \tag{7.37}$$

We need two types of deterministic expressions:

$$D_{ni}^1 = \sum_{s=1}^{n} (\beta^i s^{2\gamma} - \beta_0^i s^{2\gamma_0})\log^i s, \quad i = 0, 1, 2, \tag{7.38}$$

$$D_{ni}^2 = \sum_{s=1}^{n} (\beta s^\gamma - \beta_0 s^{\gamma_0})\beta^i s^\gamma \log^{i+1} s, \quad i = 0, 1. \tag{7.39}$$

and two types of stochastic ones:

$$S_{ni}^1 = \sum_{s=1}^{n} u_s(\beta^i s^\gamma - \beta_0^i s^{\gamma_0}) \log^{i+1} s, \quad i = 0, 1, \tag{7.40}$$

$$S_{ni}^2(\gamma) = \frac{1}{\sqrt{n}} \sum_{s=1}^{n} u_s \left(\frac{s}{n}\right)^\gamma \log^i \frac{s}{n}, \quad i = 0, 1, 2, 3. \tag{7.41}$$

In these definitions, $(\beta, \gamma) \in N_n^r(\theta_0)$. Therefore Eqs. (7.38), (7.39), and (7.40) should converge to zero in some sense.

7.2.5   Bounding Deterministic Expressions

Lemma.   *Let $\gamma_0 > -1/2$. With some (β^*, γ^*) between (β_0, γ_0) and (β, γ) uniformly in $(\beta, \gamma) \in N_n^1(\theta_0)$ we have*

$$|D_{ni}^1| \le \frac{c}{n^{\gamma_0 - 2\gamma^* - 1/2 - \delta}} \log^i n, \tag{7.42}$$

$$|D_{ni}^2| \le \frac{c}{n^{\gamma_0 - \gamma - \gamma^* - 1/2 - \delta}} \log^{i+1} n. \tag{7.43}$$

Proof.   With some (β^*, γ^*) between (β_0, γ_0) and (β, γ) by the finite increments formula

$$\beta^i s^{2\gamma} - \beta_0^i s^{2\gamma_0} = i(\beta^*)^{i-1} s^{2\gamma^*}(\beta - \beta_0) + 2(\beta^*)^i s^{2\gamma^*}(\gamma - \gamma_0) \log s. \tag{7.44}$$

Therefore Eq. (7.38) becomes

$$D_{ni}^1 = i(\beta^*)^{i-1}(\beta - \beta_0) \sum_{s=1}^{n} s^{2\gamma^*} \log^i s + 2(\beta^*)^i(\gamma - \gamma_0) \sum_{s=1}^{n} s^{2\gamma^*} \log^{i+1} s. \tag{7.45}$$

This requires estimation of

$$T_{ni} = \sum_{s=1}^{n} s^{2\gamma^*} \log^i s, \quad i = 0, \ldots, 4. \tag{7.46}$$

Substitution of $\log s = \log(s/n) + \log n$ yields

$$T_{ni} = \sum_{s=1}^{n} s^{2\gamma^*} \sum_{j=0}^{i} C_j^i \left(\log^j \frac{s}{n}\right) \log^{i-j} n$$

$$= n^{2\gamma^*+1} \sum_{j=0}^{i} C_j^i (\log^{i-j} n) \frac{1}{n} \sum_{s=1}^{n} s^{2\gamma^*} \log^j \frac{s}{n}.$$

As a result of Eq. (7.37) for all large n we have $2\gamma^* + 1 > \delta_1$ for some $\delta_1 > 0$. Hence, by Lemma 7.2.2

$$|T_{ni}| \le c_1 n^{2\gamma^*+1} \log^i n. \tag{7.47}$$

Now Eqs. (7.37), (7.45), and (7.47) imply Eq. (7.42):

$$|D_{ni}^1| \le \frac{c_2 n^{2\gamma^*+1} \log^i n}{n^{\gamma_0+1/2-\delta}} + \frac{c_3 n^{2\gamma^*+1} \log^{i+1} n}{n^{\gamma_0+1/2-\delta} \log n} = c_4 n^{2\gamma^*-\gamma_0+1/2+\delta} \log^i n.$$

In the case of D_{ni}^2 instead of Eqs. (7.44) and (7.45) we have, respectively,

$$\beta s^\gamma - \beta_0 s^{\gamma_0} = s^{\gamma^*}(\beta - \beta_0) + \beta^* s^{\gamma^*}(\gamma - \gamma_0) \log s, \tag{7.48}$$

$$D_{ni}^2 = \beta^i(\beta - \beta_0) \sum_{s=1}^n s^{\gamma^*+\gamma} \log^{i+1} s + \beta^i \beta^*(\gamma - \gamma_0) \sum_{s=1}^n s^{\gamma^*+\gamma} \log^{i+2} s, \quad i = 0, 1.$$

Instead of Eq. (7.46) we need to estimate $T_{ni} = \sum_{s=1}^n s^{\gamma^*+\gamma} \log^i s$, $i = 1, 2, 3$. In addition to Lemma 7.2.2, in the derivation of the analog of Eq. (7.47) we have to apply the Hölder inequality

$$\left| \frac{1}{n} \sum_{s=1}^n \left(\frac{s}{n}\right)^{\gamma^*+\gamma} \log^j \frac{s}{n} \right| \le \left(\frac{1}{n} \sum_{s=1}^n \left(\frac{s}{n}\right)^{2\gamma} \left|\log^j \frac{s}{n}\right| \right)^{1/2} \left(\frac{1}{n} \sum_{s=1}^n \left(\frac{s}{n}\right)^{2\gamma^*} \left|\log^j \frac{s}{n}\right| \right)^{1/2}.$$

The result is $|T_{ni}| \le c_1 n^{\gamma^*+\gamma+1} \log^i n$ and, hence,

$$|D_{ni}^2| \le \frac{c_2 n^{\gamma^*+\gamma+1} \log^{i+1} n}{n^{\gamma_0+1/2-\delta}} + \frac{c_3 n^{\gamma^*+\gamma+1} \log^{i+2} n}{n^{\gamma_0+1/2-\delta} \log n}$$

$$= c_4 n^{\gamma^*+\gamma-\gamma_0+1/2+\delta} \log^{i+1} n. \qquad \blacksquare$$

7.2.6 Multiplication of L_p-Approximable Sequences by Continuous Functions

Suppose sequences $\{w_n(\gamma): n = 1, 2, \ldots\}$ depend on a parameter $\gamma \in \Gamma_n$. We say that $\{w_n(\gamma)\}$ is L_p-close to $W \in L_p(0, 1)$ uniformly on Γ_n if

$$\sup_{\gamma \in \Gamma_n} \|w_n(\gamma) - \delta_{np} W\|_p \longrightarrow 0.$$

The lemma below shows that this property is preserved under multiplication by continuous functions.

Lemma. *Let $f \in C[0, 1]$. Denote $M(s) = W(s)f(s)$ and consider the product sequences*

$$m_n(\gamma) = \left(w_{n1}(\gamma)f\left(\frac{1}{n}\right), \ldots, w_{nn}(\gamma)f\left(\frac{n}{n}\right)\right).$$

If $\{w_n(\gamma)\}$ is L_p-close to $W \in L_p(0, 1)$ uniformly on Γ_n, then $\{m_n(\gamma)\}$ is L_p-close to M uniformly on Γ_n.

Proof. Denote $z_n(\gamma) = m_n(\gamma) - \delta_{np}M$. We need to prove that

$$\sup_{\gamma \in \Gamma_n} \|z_n(\gamma)\|_p \longrightarrow 0. \tag{7.49}$$

As f is uniformly continuous, for any $\varepsilon > 0$ there exists $\delta > 0$ such that $|s - s'| \leq \delta$ implies $|f(s) - f(s')| \leq \varepsilon$ and $\sup_{s \in i_t} |f(t/n) - f(s)| \leq \varepsilon$ for $n \geq 1/\delta$. Now we bound the tth component of $z_n(\gamma)$:

$$|[z_{nt}(\gamma)]_t| = \left| w_{nt}(\gamma)f\left(\frac{t}{n}\right) - [\delta_{np}(Wf)]_t \right|$$

$$\leq \left| f\left(\frac{t}{n}\right) \right| \left| w_{nt}(\gamma) - n^{1/q}\int_{i_t} W(s)\, ds \right|$$

$$+ n^{1/q}\left| \int_{i_t} W(s)\left[f\left(\frac{t}{n}\right) - f(s)\right] ds \right|$$

$$\leq \|f\|_C |w_{nt}(\gamma) - (\delta_{np}W)_t| + \varepsilon(\delta_{np}|W|)_t.$$

Hence by boundedness of δ_{np}

$$\|z_n(\gamma)\|_p \leq \|f\|_C \sup_{\gamma \in \Gamma_n} \|w_n(\gamma) - \delta_{np}W\|_p + \varepsilon\|W\|_p.$$

This proves Eq. (7.49).   ∎

7.2.7   Convergence in Distribution of $S_{ni}^2(\gamma_0)$

7.2.7.1   Assumption P1   The errors u_t in the model $y_s = \beta s^\gamma + u_s$ are linear processes

$$u_t = \sum_{j \in \mathbb{Z}} \psi_j e_{t-j}, \quad t \in \mathbb{Z},$$

where $\{e_t, \mathcal{F}_t : t \in \mathbb{Z}\}$ is a m.d. array, $\sum_j |\psi_j| < \infty$, second conditional moments are constant, $E(e_t^2 \mid \mathcal{F}_{t-1}) = \sigma_e^2$ for all t and the squares e_t^2 are uniformly integrable.

Lemma. *If $\gamma_0 > -1/2$ and u_t satisfy Assumption P1, then*

$$S_{ni}^2(\gamma_0) = \frac{1}{\sqrt{n}} \sum_{s=1}^{n} u_s \left(\frac{s}{n}\right)^{\gamma_0} \log^i \frac{s}{n} \xrightarrow{d} N\left(0, \left(\sigma_e \sum_j \psi_j\right)^2 \int_0^1 s^{2\gamma_0} \log^{2i} s \, ds\right).$$

Proof. Let $\delta > 0$ be such that $\gamma_0 - \delta > -1/2$. The sequence

$$\left\{\frac{1}{\sqrt{n}} \left(\frac{s}{n}\right)^{\gamma_0-\delta} : s = 1,\ldots,n\right\}, \quad n = 1, 2, \ldots$$

is L_2-close to $W(s) = s^{\gamma_0-\delta}$ by Lemma 7.2.3(ii). Since the function $f(s) = s^\delta \log^i s$ is continuous on $[0, 1]$, the product sequence

$$\left\{\frac{1}{\sqrt{n}} \left(\frac{s}{n}\right)^{\gamma_0-\delta} \left(\frac{s}{n}\right)^\delta \log^i s\right\} = \left\{\frac{1}{\sqrt{n}} \left(\frac{s}{n}\right)^{\gamma_0} \log^i s\right\}$$

is L_2-close to $M(s) = W(s)f(s) = s^{\gamma_0} \log^i s$ by Lemma 7.2.6 (where $\Gamma_n = \{\gamma_0\}$). The conclusion of this lemma follows from Theorem 3.5.2. ∎

7.2.8 A Uniform Bound on $S_{ni}^2(\gamma)$

Lemma. *If $\gamma_0 > -1/2$ and u_t satisfy Assumption P1, then uniformly in $\gamma \in N_n^1(\theta_0)$ [see Eqs. (7.36) and (7.41) for the definitions]*

$$S_{ni}^2(\gamma) = O_p(1). \tag{7.50}$$

Proof. To make use of Lemma 7.2.7, we approximate $S_{ni}^2(\gamma)$ by $S_{ni}^2(\gamma_0)$. For the approximation to work, we need to bound γ away from $-1/2$. Therefore we write

$$S_{ni}^2(\gamma) = \frac{1}{\sqrt{n}} \sum_{s=1}^{n} u_s \left(\frac{s}{n}\right)^{\gamma} \log^i \frac{s}{n} = \frac{1}{\sqrt{n}} \sum_{s=1}^{n} u_s \left(\frac{s}{n}\right)^{\gamma-\delta} \left(\frac{s}{n}\right)^{\delta} \log^i \frac{s}{n},$$

where $\delta > 0$ is small and $\gamma - \delta$ is uniformly bounded away from $-1/2$.

By the mean value theorem there are points $\gamma_{s,n}$ between γ and γ_0 such that

$$\left(\frac{s}{n}\right)^{\gamma-\delta} - \left(\frac{s}{n}\right)^{\gamma_0-\delta} = \left(\frac{s}{n}\right)^{\gamma_{s,n}-\delta} (\gamma - \gamma_0) \log \frac{s}{n}.$$

Denoting $w_n(\gamma) = \left\{\frac{1}{\sqrt{n}} \left(\frac{s}{n}\right)^{\gamma-\delta} : s = 1,\ldots,n\right\}$ we have

$$\|w_n(\gamma) - w_n(\gamma_0)\|_2^2 = \frac{1}{n} \sum_{s=1}^{n} \left|\left(\frac{s}{n}\right)^{\gamma-\delta} - \left(\frac{s}{n}\right)^{\gamma_0-\delta}\right|^2$$

$$= |\gamma - \gamma_0|^2 \frac{1}{n} \sum_{s=1}^{n} \left(\frac{s}{n}\right)^{2(\gamma_{s,n}-\delta)} \log^2 \frac{s}{n}.$$

By Lemma 7.2.2 uniformly in n and $\gamma_{s,n}$ the estimate

$$\frac{1}{n}\sum_{s=1}^{n}\left(\frac{s}{n}\right)^{2(\gamma_{s,n}-\delta)}\log^2\frac{s}{n}\le c$$

is true. Thus, by Eq. (7.37) uniformly in $\gamma\in N_n^1(\theta_0)$,

$$\|w_n(\gamma)-w_n(\gamma_0)\|_2\le\frac{c}{n^{\gamma_0+1/2-\delta}\log n}.$$

We know from Lemma 7.2.3 that $w_n(\gamma_0)$ is L_2-close to $W(s)=s^{\gamma_0-\delta}$, so the above inequality implies

$$\sup_{\gamma\in N_n^1(\theta_0)}\|w_n(\gamma)-\delta_{n2}W\|_2\ \longrightarrow\ 0.$$

With $f(s)=s^\delta\log^i s$ then by Eq. (7.49)

$$\sup_{\gamma\in N_n^1(\theta_0)}\|m_n(\gamma)-\delta_{n2}M\|_2\ \longrightarrow\ 0,\tag{7.51}$$

where $M(s)=W(s)f(s)=s^{\gamma_0}\log^i s$ and

$$m_n(\gamma)=\left\{\frac{1}{\sqrt{n}}\left(\frac{s}{n}\right)^{\gamma-\delta}\left(\frac{s}{n}\right)^{\delta}\log^i\frac{s}{n}\right\}=\left\{\frac{1}{\sqrt{n}}\left(\frac{s}{n}\right)^{\gamma}\log^i\frac{s}{n}\right\}.$$

Now we use identity (3.25), orthogonality of m.d.'s and Lemma 2.3.2 to get

$$\|S_{ni}^2(\gamma)-S_{ni}^2(\gamma_0)\|_2^2$$

$$=\left\|\frac{1}{\sqrt{n}}\sum_{s=1}^{n}u_s\left(\frac{s}{n}\right)^{\gamma}\log^i\frac{s}{n}-\frac{1}{\sqrt{n}}\sum_{s=1}^{n}u_s\left(\frac{s}{n}\right)^{\gamma_0}\log^i\frac{s}{n}\right\|_2^2$$

$$=\left\|\sum_{s=1}^{n}u_s[m_n(\gamma)-m_n(\gamma_0)]\right\|_2^2$$

$$=\left\|\sum_{i\in\mathbb{Z}}e_i\{T_n[m_n(\gamma)-m_n(\gamma_0)]\}_i\right\|_2^2$$

$$=\sigma_e^2\|T_n[m_n(\gamma)-m_n(\gamma_0)]\|_2^2$$

$$\le\sigma_e^2\left(\sum_{i\in\mathbb{Z}}|\psi_i|\right)^2\|m_n(\gamma)-m_n(\gamma_0)\|_2^2.$$

Since $m_n(\gamma_0)$ is L_2-close to M, this bound and Eq. (7.51) imply

$$S_{ni}^2(\gamma) = S_{ni}^2(\gamma_0) + O_p(1) \tag{7.52}$$

uniformly in $\gamma \in N_n^1(\theta_0)$. Lemma 7.2.7 and Eq. (7.52) prove Eq. (7.50). ∎

7.2.9 Bounding S_{ni}^1

Lemma. *If $\gamma_0 > -1/2$ and u_t satisfy Assumption P1, then the variables (7.40) satisfy*

$$S_{ni}^1 = O_p\left(\frac{(\log n)^{i+1}}{n^{\gamma_0 - \gamma^* - \delta}}\right) \text{ uniformly in } \theta \in N_n^1(\theta_0).$$

Proof. Using Eq. (7.48) rewrite Eq. (7.40) as

$$S_{ni}^1 = i(\beta^*)^{i-1}(\beta - \beta_0) \sum_{s=1}^{n} u_s s^{\gamma^*} \log^{i+1} s + (\beta^*)^i(\gamma - \gamma_0)$$

$$\times \sum_{s=1}^{n} u_s s^{\gamma^*} \log^{i+2} s, \quad i = 0, 1. \tag{7.53}$$

Therefore we need to bound

$$U_{ni} = \sum_{s=1}^{n} u_s s^{\gamma^*} \log^i s, \quad i = 1, 2, 3.$$

Substituting $\log s = \log(s/n) + \log n$ we get

$$U_{ni} = \sum_{s=1}^{n} u_s s^{\gamma^*} \sum_{j=0}^{i} C_j^i \left(\log^j \frac{s}{n}\right) \log^{i-j} n$$

$$= \sum_{j=0}^{i} C_j^i(\log^{i-j} n) n^{\gamma^*+1/2} \frac{1}{\sqrt{n}} \sum_{s=1}^{n} u_s \left(\frac{s}{n}\right)^{\gamma^*} \log^j \frac{s}{n}$$

$$= n^{\gamma^*+1/2} \sum_{j=0}^{i} C_j^i(\log^{i-j} n) S_{nj}^2(\gamma^*).$$

By Lemma 7.2.8 $U_{ni} = O_p(n^{\gamma^*+1/2} \log^i n)$. This bound, Eqs. (7.37) and (7.53) yield

$$S_{ni}^1 = O_p\left(\frac{n^{\gamma^*+1/2} \log^{i+1} n}{n^{\gamma_0+1/2-\delta}}\right) + O_p\left(\frac{n^{\gamma^*+1/2} \log^{i+2} n}{n^{\gamma_0+1/2-\delta} \log n}\right)$$

$$= O_p(n^{\gamma^* - \gamma_0 + \delta} \log^{i+1} n)$$

uniformly in $\theta \in N_n^1(\theta_0)$. ∎

7.3 NONLINEAR LEAST SQUARES

7.3.1 The Model and History

Asymptotically collinear regressors arise in nonlinear regressions of type

$$y_s = \beta s^\gamma + u_s, \quad s = 1, \ldots, n, \tag{7.54}$$

where the trend component $\gamma > -1/2$ is to be estimated along with the regression coefficient β. Let β_0 and γ_0 denote the true values of the parameters. The first-order expansion for βs^γ is

$$\begin{aligned}
\beta s^\gamma &\approx \beta_0 s^{\gamma_0} + s^{\gamma_0}(\beta - \beta_0) + (\beta_0 s^{\gamma_0} \log s)(\gamma - \gamma_0) \\
&= \beta s^{\gamma_0} + (\gamma - \gamma_0)\beta_0 s^{\gamma_0} \log s.
\end{aligned} \tag{7.55}$$

Thus, the linearized form of Eq. (7.54) involves the regressors s^{γ_0} and $s^{\gamma_0} \log s$, which are asymptotically collinear and whose second moment matrix is asymptotically singular upon appropriate (multivariate) normalization. Wu (1981, p. 509) noted that model (7.54) failed his conditions [which require a single normalizing quantity and a positive definite limit matrix for the second moment matrix of the linearized version of Eq. (7.54) $y_s = \beta s^{\gamma_0} + (\gamma - \gamma_0)\beta_0 s^{\gamma_0} \log s + u_s$]. More precisely, Wu noted that the model (7.54) satisfies his conditions for strong consistency of the least-squares estimator $\hat{\theta} = (\hat{\beta}, \hat{\gamma})$, but not his conditions for asymptotic normality. There are two reasons for the failure:

1. the Hessian requires different standardizations for the parameters β and γ (whereas Wu's approach uses a common standardization) and
2. the Hessian is asymptotically singular because of the asymptotic collinearity of the functions s^{γ_0} and $s^{\gamma_0} \log s$ that appear in the score (whereas Wu's theory requires the variance matrix to have a positive definite limit).

Phillips (2007) derived the asymptotic distribution of the NLS estimator for Eq. (7.54). The theory is very instructive because of:

1. his choice of standardizing matrices,
2. the way he modified the Wooldridge approach to suit Eq. (7.54) and
3. the possibility to adapt the theory to models different from Eq. (7.54).

This section contains a full proof of his results using, where necessary, statements based on L_p-approximability instead of those based on Brownian motion. While it is in general a matter of taste which approach to use, in one case the Brownian motion methods do not seem adequate for applications. Phillips (2007, Lemma 6.1) is proved for smooth functions, while its purported application Phillips (2007, p. 607) is to functions which may not be continuous.

7.3.2 The Objective Function, Score and Hessian

In the NLS method, the objective function for model (7.54) is defined by

$$Q_n(\theta) = \sum_{s=1}^{n}(y_s - \beta s^{\gamma})^2, \quad \text{where } \theta = (\beta, \gamma).$$

The estimator $\hat{\theta}$, by definition, solves the extremum problem

$$\hat{\theta} = \arg\{\min_{\theta} Q_n(\theta)\}$$

(we minimize over θ the objective function and take the minimizing point as the estimator). As a result of smoothness of Q_n, the estimator satisfies the first-order condition

$$S_n(\hat{\theta}) = 0. \tag{7.56}$$

Since scaling the derivatives by $1/2$ does not change the validity of the expansion (7.2) and does not affect asymptotic conditions, we define the score by [see the derivatives of βs^{γ} in Eq. (7.55)]

$$S_n(\theta) = \frac{1}{2}\nabla_{\theta}Q_n(\theta)' = -\sum_{s=1}^{n}\begin{pmatrix} s^{\gamma} \\ \beta s^{\gamma}\log s \end{pmatrix}(y_s - \beta s^{\gamma}). \tag{7.57}$$

The Hessian for Eq. (7.57) is

$$H_n(\theta) = \nabla_{\theta}S_n(\theta) = \sum_{s=1}^{n}h_s(\theta), \tag{7.58}$$

where

$$h_s(\theta) = -\left(\frac{\partial}{\partial\beta}\begin{pmatrix} s^{\gamma}(y_s - \beta s^{\gamma}) \\ \beta s^{\gamma}(y_s - \beta s^{\gamma})\log s \end{pmatrix}, \quad \frac{\partial}{\partial\gamma}\begin{pmatrix} s^{\gamma}(y_s - \beta s^{\gamma}) \\ \beta s^{\gamma}(y_s - \beta s^{\gamma})\log s \end{pmatrix}\right).$$

Replacing y_s by its expression from the true model $y_s = \beta_0 s^{\gamma_0} + u_s$ we find the elements of $h_s(\theta)$ to be

$$h_{s11}(\theta) = -\frac{\partial}{\partial\beta}s^{\gamma}(y_s - \beta s^{\gamma}) = s^{2\gamma}, \tag{7.59}$$

$$h_{s12}(\theta) = h_{s21}(\theta) = -\frac{\partial}{\partial\beta}(y_s - \beta s^{\gamma})\beta s^{\gamma}\log s$$

$$= -y_s s^{\gamma}\log s + 2\beta s^{2\gamma}\log s$$

$$= -\beta_0 s^{\gamma_0+\gamma}\log s - u_s s^{\gamma}\log s + 2\beta s^{2\gamma}\log s$$

$$= \beta s^{2\gamma}\log s - u_s s^{\gamma}\log s + (\beta s^{\gamma} - \beta_0 s^{\gamma_0})s^{\gamma}\log s, \tag{7.60}$$

$$h_{s22}(\theta) = -\frac{\partial}{\partial\gamma}(y_s - \beta s^\gamma)\beta s^\gamma \log s$$

$$= \beta^2 s^{2\gamma} \log^2 s - (\beta_0 s^{\gamma_0} + u_s - \beta s^\gamma)\beta s^\gamma \log^2 s$$

$$= \beta^2 s^{2\gamma} \log^2 s - u_s\beta s^\gamma \log^2 s + (\beta s^\gamma - \beta_0 s^{\gamma_0})\beta s^\gamma \log^2 s. \quad (7.61)$$

7.3.3 Lemma on Convergence of the Score

Define the normalization matrix

$$D_n = n^{\gamma_0+1/2} \operatorname{diag}[1, \ \log n]. \quad (7.62)$$

Lemma. *If $\gamma_0 > -1/2$ and u_t satisfy Assumption P1, then*

$$D_n^{-1} S_n(\theta_0) \xrightarrow{d} N\left(0, \ \frac{\sigma^2}{2\gamma_0 + 1}\begin{pmatrix} 1 & \beta_0 \\ \beta_0 & \beta_0^2 \end{pmatrix}\right), \quad \sigma^2 \equiv \left(\sigma_e \sum_j \psi_j\right)^2.$$

Proof. Equations (7.57) and (7.62) imply

$$D_n^{-1} S_n(\theta_0) = -n^{-\gamma_0-1/2}\begin{pmatrix} 1 & 0 \\ 0 & 1/\log n \end{pmatrix} \sum_{s=1}^{n} \begin{pmatrix} s^{\gamma_0} u_s \\ \beta_0 s^{\gamma_0}(\log s)u_s \end{pmatrix}$$

$$= -\begin{pmatrix} \dfrac{1}{\sqrt{n}} \displaystyle\sum_{s=1}^{n} \left(\dfrac{s}{n}\right)^{\gamma_0} u_s \\[2ex] \dfrac{\beta_0}{\sqrt{n}\log n} \displaystyle\sum_{s=1}^{n} \left(\dfrac{s}{n}\right)^{\gamma_0}(\log s)u_s \end{pmatrix}. \quad (7.63)$$

Replacing $\log s = \log(s/n) + \log n$ and using notation (7.41) we get, by Lemma 7.2.7,

$$D_n^{-1} S_n(\theta_0) = -\begin{pmatrix} S_{n0}^2(\gamma_0) \\[1ex] \dfrac{\beta_0}{\log n} S_{n1}^2(\gamma_0) + \beta_0 S_{n0}^2(\gamma_0) \end{pmatrix} = -\begin{pmatrix} 1 \\ \beta_0 \end{pmatrix} S_{n0}^2(\gamma_0) + o_p(1),$$

where $S_{n0}^2(\gamma_0) \xrightarrow{d} N[0, \ \sigma^2/(2\gamma_0 + 1)]$. This proves the lemma. ∎

7.3.4 Asymptotic Representation of the Normalized Hessian

Lemma. *Suppose $\gamma_0 > -1/2$ and u_t satisfy Assumption P1. With H_n defined by Eqs. (7.58)–(7.61) from Section 7.3.2 and D_n defined by Eq. (7.62) for the matrix*

$A_n(\theta_0) = D_n^{-1} H_n(\theta_0) D_n^{-1}$, *we have asymptotically*

$$
A_n(\theta_0) = \frac{1}{\gamma_1}
\begin{pmatrix}
1 & \beta_0 \left(1 - \dfrac{1}{\gamma_1 \log n}\right) \\[2ex]
\beta_0 \left(1 - \dfrac{1}{\gamma_1 \log n}\right) & \beta_0^2 \left(1 - \dfrac{2}{\gamma_1 \log n} + \dfrac{2}{\gamma_1^2 \log^2 n}\right)
\end{pmatrix}
+ O_p(n^{-\varepsilon}),
$$

where $\gamma_1 = 2\gamma_0 + 1$ *and* ε *is some number from* $(0, \gamma_0 + 1/2)$.

Proof. By Eqs. (7.58)–(7.61) from Section 7.3.2

$$
H_n(\theta) = \sum_{s=1}^n
\begin{pmatrix}
s^{2\gamma_0} & \beta_0 s^{2\gamma_0} \log s - u_s s^{\gamma_0} \log s \\[2ex]
\beta_0 s^{2\gamma_0} \log s - u_s s^{\gamma_0} \log s & \beta_0^2 s^{2\gamma_0} \log^2 s - u_s \beta_0 s^{\gamma_0} \log^2 s
\end{pmatrix}. \tag{7.64}
$$

This equation and definition (7.62) lead to the following expressions for the elements of $A_n(\theta_0)$:

$$
A_{n11}(\theta_0) = \frac{1}{n^{2\gamma_0+1}} \sum_{s=1}^n s^{2\gamma_0} = \frac{1}{n} \sum_{s=1}^n \left(\frac{s}{n}\right)^{2\gamma_0}, \tag{7.65}
$$

$$
A_{n12}(\theta_0) = \frac{1}{n^{2\gamma_0+1} \log n} \sum_{s=1}^n (\beta_0 s^{2\gamma_0} - u_s s^{\gamma_0})\left(\log \frac{s}{n} + \log n\right)
$$

$$
= \beta_0 \sum_{j=0}^1 \frac{1}{\log^j n}\left[\frac{1}{n}\sum_{s=1}^n \left(\frac{s}{n}\right)^{2\gamma_0} \log^j \frac{s}{n}\right]
$$

$$
- \sum_{j=0}^1 \frac{1}{n^{\gamma_0+1/2} \log^j n}\left[\frac{1}{\sqrt{n}}\sum_{s=1}^n u_s \left(\frac{s}{n}\right)^{\gamma_0} \log^j \frac{s}{n}\right]. \tag{7.66}
$$

Similarly, replacing $\log s$ by $\log \frac{s}{n} + \log n$, we have

$$
A_{n22}(\theta_0) = \frac{1}{n^{2\gamma_0+1} \log^2 n} \sum_{s=1}^n (\beta_0^2 s^{2\gamma_0} - u_s \beta_0 s^{\gamma_0}) \sum_{j=0}^2 C_j^2 \left(\log^{2-j} \frac{s}{n}\right) \log^j n
$$

$$
= \beta_0^2 \sum_{j=0}^2 \frac{C_j^2}{\log^{2-j} n}\left[\frac{1}{n}\sum_{s=1}^n \left(\frac{s}{n}\right)^{2\gamma_0} \log^{2-j} \frac{s}{n}\right]
$$

$$
- \beta_0 \sum_{j=0}^2 \frac{C_j^2}{n^{\gamma_0+1/2} \log^{2-j} n}\left[\frac{1}{\sqrt{n}}\sum_{s=1}^n u_s \left(\frac{s}{n}\right)^{\gamma_0} \log^{2-j} \frac{s}{n}\right]. \tag{7.67}
$$

The bounds from Lemma 7.2.2 can be joined as

$$R(f_i) = O(n^{-\varepsilon}) \tag{7.68}$$

with some $\varepsilon \in (0, \gamma_0 + 1/2)$. It is easy to calculate that

$$\int_0^1 t^{2\gamma_0} \, dt = \frac{1}{\gamma_1}, \quad \int_0^1 t^{2\gamma_0} \log t \, dt = -\frac{1}{\gamma_1^2}, \quad \int_0^1 t^{2\gamma_0} \log^2 t \, dt = \frac{2}{\gamma_1^3}. \tag{7.69}$$

Hence, Eq. (7.65) asymptotically is

$$A_{n11}(\theta_0) = \frac{1}{\gamma_1} + O(n^{-\varepsilon}). \tag{7.70}$$

For Eq. (7.66) Lemma 7.2.7 and Eqs. (7.68) and (7.69) imply

$$A_{n12}(\theta_0) = -\frac{\beta_0}{\gamma_1^2 \log n} + \frac{\beta_0}{\gamma_1} + O(n^{-\varepsilon}) - \frac{1}{n^{\gamma_0+1/2} \log n} S_{n1}^2(\gamma_0)$$

$$- \frac{1}{n^{\gamma_0+1/2}} S_{n0}^2(\gamma_0) = \frac{\beta_0}{\gamma_1} - \frac{\beta_0}{\gamma_1^2 \log n} + O_p(n^{-\varepsilon}). \tag{7.71}$$

Finally, for Eq. (7.67), we use Eqs. (7.68) and (7.69) and Lemma 7.2.7 to obtain

$$A_{n22}(\theta_0) = \beta_0^2 \sum_{j=0}^{2} \frac{1}{\log^{2-j} n} C_j^2 \left[\int_0^1 t^{2\gamma_0} \log^{2-j} t \, dt + O(n^{-\varepsilon}) \right] + O_p(n^{-\varepsilon})$$

$$= \beta_0^2 \left(\frac{1}{\gamma_1} - \frac{2}{\gamma_1^2 \log n} + \frac{2}{\gamma_1^3 \log^2 n} \right) + O_p(n^{-\varepsilon}). \tag{7.72}$$

Equations (7.70)–(7.72) prove the lemma.   ∎

7.3.5   The Right Normalization of the Hessian

From the proof of Theorem 7.1.8 we can see that it is really not the convergence of the normalized Hessian $A_n(\theta_0)$ that is important [see Eq. (7.4)] but the convergence of the inverse $A_n^{-1}(\theta_0)$. The lemma below shows that if $H_n(\theta_0)$ is normalized by D_n this inverse does not converge. The inverse converges if D_n is replaced by

$$F_n = \frac{1}{\log n} D_n = n^{\gamma_0+1/2} \, \text{diag}[1/\log n, 1].$$

Lemma. *Suppose $\beta_0 \neq 0$, $\gamma_0 > -1/2$ and u_t satisfy Assumption P1.*

(i) The inverse of $A_n(\theta_0)$ is

$$A_n^{-1}(\theta_0) = \gamma_1^3 \log^2 n \begin{pmatrix} 1 - \dfrac{2}{\gamma_1 \log n} + \dfrac{2}{\gamma_1^2 \log^2 n} & \dfrac{1}{\beta_0} \left(\dfrac{1}{\gamma_1 \log n} - 1 \right) \\ \dfrac{1}{\beta_0} \left(\dfrac{1}{\gamma_1 \log n} - 1 \right) & \dfrac{1}{\beta_0^2} \end{pmatrix}$$

$$+ \dot{O}_p(n^{-\varepsilon})$$

and, hence, $A_n^{-1}(\theta_0)$ diverges as $n \to \infty$.

(ii) Denote $E_n = F_n^{-1} H_n(\theta_0) F_n^{-1}$. Then

$$E_n^{-1} = \frac{\gamma_1^3}{\beta_0^2} \begin{pmatrix} \beta_0^2 \left(1 - \dfrac{2}{\gamma_1 \log n} + \dfrac{2}{\gamma_1^2 \log^2 n} \right) & \beta_0 \left(\dfrac{1}{\gamma_1 \log n} - 1 \right) \\ \beta_0 \left(\dfrac{1}{\gamma_1 \log n} - 1 \right) & 1 \end{pmatrix}$$

$$+ O_p(n^{-\varepsilon})$$

$$= \frac{\gamma_1^3}{\beta_0^2} \begin{pmatrix} \beta_0^2 & -\beta_0 \\ -\beta_0 & 1 \end{pmatrix} + O_p \left(\frac{1}{\log n} \right).$$

Proof.

(i) By Lemma 7.3.4

$$\det A_n(\theta_0) = \frac{\beta_0^2}{\gamma_1^2} \left(1 - \frac{2}{\gamma_1 \log n} + \frac{2}{\gamma_1^2 \log^2 n} - 1 + \frac{2}{\gamma_1 \log n} - \frac{1}{\gamma_1^2 \log^2 n} \right)$$

$$+ O_p(n^{-\varepsilon})$$

$$= \frac{\beta_0^2}{\gamma_1^4 \log^2 n} + O_p(n^{-\varepsilon}).$$

This equation, Lemma 7.3.4 and Eq. (4.62) prove (i).

Part (ii) immediately follows from (i). ∎

7.3.6   The Order of Eigenvalues of A_n (θ_0)

Lemma. *If $\gamma_0 > -1/2$ and Assumption P1 is satisfied, then $A_n(\theta_0)$ has eigenvalues*

$$\lambda_1 = \frac{1 + \beta_0^2}{\gamma_1} + O_p \left(\frac{1}{\log n} \right), \quad \lambda_2 = \frac{\beta_0^2 (1 - \beta_0^2)}{\gamma_1^3 (1 + \beta_0^2) \log^2 n} + O_p \left(\frac{1}{\log^3 n} \right). \quad (7.73)$$

Proof. Denote $a_n = \dfrac{1}{\gamma_1 \log n}$. From Lemma 7.3.4 we see that the eigenvalues μ_1, μ_2 of $\gamma_1 A_n(\theta_0)$ are the roots of the equation

$$\det(\gamma_1 A_n(\theta_0) - \mu I) = \det\begin{pmatrix} 1 - \mu & \beta_0(1 - a_n) \\ \beta_0(1 - a_n) & \beta_0^2(1 - 2a_n + 2a_n^2) - \mu \end{pmatrix}$$

$$= \mu^2 - \mu[\beta_0^2(1 - 2a_n + 2a_n^2) + 1]$$
$$+ \beta_0^2(1 - 2a_n + 2a_n^2) - \beta_0^2(1 - 2a_n + a_n^2)$$
$$= \mu^2 - \mu[(1 + \beta_0^2) + \beta_0^2(-2a_n + 2a_n^2)] + \beta_0^2 a_n^2 = 0.$$

Hence

$$\mu_{1,2} = \frac{(1 + \beta_0^2) + \beta_0^2(-2a_n + 2a_n^2) \pm \sqrt{D}}{2}, \tag{7.74}$$

where the discriminant D is

$$D = (1 + \beta_0^2)^2 + 2\beta_0^2(1 + \beta_0^2)(-2a_n + 2a_n^2)$$
$$+ \beta_0^4(4a_n^2 - 8a_n^3 + 4a_n^4) - 4\beta_0^2 a_n^2$$
$$= (1 + \beta_0^2)^2 + 2\beta_0^2(1 + \beta_0^2)(-2a_n + 2a_n^2)$$
$$+ \beta_0^4(-8a_n^3 + 4a_n^4) + 4\beta_0^2 a_n^2(\beta_0^2 - 1).$$

Using the approximation $\sqrt{a + a_n} \approx \sqrt{a} + \dfrac{a_n}{2\sqrt{a}}$ we have

$$\sqrt{D} = (1 + \beta_0^2) + \beta_0^2(-2a_n + 2a_n^2) + \frac{2\beta_0^2 a_n^2(\beta_0^2 - 1)}{(1 + \beta_0^2)} + O_p\left(\frac{1}{\log^3 n}\right).$$

Therefore by Eq. (7.74)

$$\mu_1 = 1 + \beta_0^2 + O_p\left(\frac{1}{\log n}\right),$$

$$\mu_2 = \frac{\beta_0^2 a_n^2(1 - \beta_0^2)}{1 + \beta_0^2} + O_p\left(\frac{1}{\log^3 n}\right) = \frac{\beta_0^2(1 - \beta_0^2)}{\gamma_1^2(1 + \beta_0^2)\log^2 n} + O_p\left(\frac{1}{\log^3 n}\right).$$

Upon division by γ_1 we get Eq. (7.73).   ∎

7.3.7   Regulating Convergence of the Hessian

With Lemma 7.3.6 we have finished preparing the ingredients necessary for modifying Wooldridge's Assumption W2 (Section 7.1.2.2). In this and Section 7.3.8 we deal with definitions and statements required for his Assumption W3 (Section 7.1.2.3).

Taking some $\delta \in (0, (\gamma_0 + 1/2)/3)$ put

$$C_n = \frac{1}{n^\delta} D_n = n^{\gamma_0 + 1/2 - \delta} \, \text{diag}[1, \, \log n] \qquad (7.75)$$

and

$$\Delta_n = C_n^{-1}[H_n(\theta) - H_n(\theta_0)]C_n^{-1}.$$

Lemma.   *The elements of the matrix Δ_n are ($\gamma_1 = 2\gamma_0 + 1$),*

$$\Delta_{n11} = \frac{1}{n^{\gamma_1 - 2\delta}} \sum_{s=1}^{n} (s^{2\gamma} - s^{2\gamma_0}), \qquad (7.76)$$

$$\Delta_{n12} = \frac{1}{n^{\gamma_1 - 2\delta} \log n} \left[\sum_{s=1}^{n} (\beta s^{2\gamma} - \beta_0 s^{2\gamma_0}) \log s \right.$$

$$\left. - \sum_{s=1}^{n} u_s(s^\gamma - s^{\gamma_0}) \log s + \sum_{s=1}^{n} (\beta s^\gamma - \beta_0 s^{\gamma_0}) s^\gamma \log s \right], \qquad (7.77)$$

$$\Delta_{n22} = \frac{1}{n^{\gamma_1 - 2\delta} \log^2 n} \left[\sum_{s=1}^{n} (\beta^2 s^{2\gamma} - \beta_0^2 s^{2\gamma_0}) \log^2 s \right.$$

$$\left. - \sum_{s=1}^{n} u_s(\beta s^\gamma - \beta_0 s^{\gamma_0}) \log^2 s + \sum_{s=1}^{n} (\beta s^\gamma - \beta_0 s^{\gamma_0})\beta s^\gamma \log^2 s \right]. \qquad (7.78)$$

Proof.   Using Eqs. (7.58)–(7.61) from Section 7.3.2 and Eq. (7.64) we find the elements of the difference $G_n = H_n(\theta) - H_n(\theta_0)$:

$$G_{n11} = \sum_{s=1}^{n} (s^{2\gamma} - s^{2\gamma_0}),$$

$$G_{n12} = \sum_{s=1}^{n} (\beta s^{2\gamma} - \beta_0 s^{2\gamma_0}) \log s - \sum_{s=1}^{n} u_s(s^\gamma - s^{\gamma_0}) \log s$$

$$+ \sum_{s=1}^{n} (\beta s^\gamma - \beta_0 s^{\gamma_0}) s^\gamma \log s,$$

$$G_{n22} = \sum_{s=1}^{n} (\beta^2 s^{2\gamma} - \beta_0^2 s^{2\gamma_0}) \log^2 s - \sum_{s=1}^{n} u_s(\beta s^\gamma - \beta_0 s^{\gamma_0}) \log^2 s$$

$$+ \sum_{s=1}^{n} (\beta s^\gamma - \beta_0 s^{\gamma_0})\beta s^\gamma \log^2 s.$$

These equations and Eq. (7.7) imply Eqs. (7.76)–(7.78).   ∎

7.3.8 Verifying Wooldridge's Assumption W3

Lemma. *Provided that $\gamma_0 > -1/2$ and Assumption P1 holds we have*

$$\sup_{\theta \in N_n^1(\theta_0)} \|\Delta_n(\theta, \theta_0)\| = o_p(1).$$

Proof. To bound Eq. (7.76) we use Eq. (7.42) with $i = 0$:

$$\Delta_{n11} = O\left(\frac{1}{n^{\gamma_0 - 2\gamma^* - 1/2 - \delta + \gamma_1 - 2\delta}}\right) = O\left(\frac{1}{n^{3\gamma_0 - 2\gamma^* + 1/2 - 3\delta}}\right).$$

This tends to zero because γ^* is close to γ_0 and $\gamma_1 + 1/2 - 3\delta > 0$.

Equation (7.77) is estimated with the help of Eqs. (7.42) and (7.43) and Lemma 7.2.9:

$$\Delta_{n12} = \frac{1}{n^{\gamma_1 - 2\delta} \log n} O_p\left(\frac{\log n}{n^{\gamma_0 - 2\gamma^* - 1/2 - \delta}} + \frac{\log n}{n^{\gamma_0 - \gamma^* - \delta}} + \frac{\log n}{n^{\gamma_0 - \gamma - \gamma^* - 1/2 - \delta}}\right)$$

$$= O_p\left(\frac{1}{n^{3\gamma_0 - 2\gamma^* + 1/2 - 3\delta}} + \frac{1}{n^{3\gamma_0 - \gamma^* + 1 - 3\delta}} + \frac{1}{n^{3\gamma_0 - \gamma - \gamma^* + 1/2 - 3\delta}}\right)$$

$$= O_p\left(\frac{1}{n^\varepsilon}\right)$$

with some $\varepsilon > 0$. Here we remember that γ and γ^* are close to γ_0.

Finally, for (7.78) we use again Eqs. (7.42) and (7.43) and Lemma 7.2.9 to get

$$\Delta_{n22} = \frac{1}{n^{\gamma_1 - 2\delta} \log^2 n} \left[O\left(\frac{\log^2 n}{n^{\gamma_0 - 2\gamma^* - 1/2 - \delta}}\right) + O_p\left(\frac{\log^2 n}{n^{\gamma_0 - \gamma^* - \delta}}\right) + O\left(\frac{\log^2 n}{n^{\gamma_0 - \gamma - \gamma^* - 1/2 - \delta}}\right)\right]$$

$$= O_p\left(\frac{1}{n^{3\gamma_0 - 2\gamma^* + 1/2 - 3\delta}} + \frac{1}{n^{3\gamma_0 - \gamma^* + 1 - 3\delta}} + \frac{1}{n^{3\gamma_0 - \gamma - \gamma^* + 1/2 - 3\delta}}\right)$$

$$= O_p\left(\frac{1}{n^\varepsilon}\right)$$

with some $\varepsilon > 0$. ∎

7.3.9 Summary of Phillips' Statements

Here we review Wooldridge's assumptions in the light of the Phillips propositions proved so far. Everywhere the next two assumptions are assumed to hold.

7.3.9.1   Assumption P1   The errors u_t in the model $y_s = \beta s^\gamma + u_s$ are linear processes

$$u_t = \sum_{j \in \mathbb{Z}} \psi_j e_{j-t}, \ t \in \mathbb{Z},$$

where $\{e_t, \mathcal{F}_t : t \in \mathbb{Z}\}$ is a m.d. array, $\sum_j |\psi_j| < \infty$, the second conditional moments are constant, $E(e_t^2 \mid \mathcal{F}_{t-1}) = \sigma_e^2$ for all t, and the squares e_t^2 are uniformly integrable.

This condition, introduced in Section 7.2.7, provides convergence of stochastic expressions.

7.3.9.2   Assumption P2

(i) $\gamma_0 > -1/2$,

(ii) $\beta_0 \neq 0$ and

(iii) $|\beta_0| < 1$.

The inequality $\gamma_0 > -1/2$ is necessary for the integrability of $f(s) = s^{2\gamma_0}$. The condition $\beta_0 \neq 0$ provides the existence of $A_n^{-1}(\theta_0)$ (see Lemma 7.3.5). The inequality $|\beta_0| < 1$ is imposed to ensure positivity of the eigenvalues of $A_n(\theta_0)$ (see Lemma 7.3.6). This latter condition is missing in the Phillips paper.

Assumption W1 obviously holds for the objective function Q_n defined in Section 7.3.2. By Lemma 7.3.3 with $D_n = n^{\gamma_0+1/2}\mathrm{diag}[1, \log n]$ the first part of Assumption W2 is satisfied in the form

$$D_n^{-1} S_n(\theta_0) \xrightarrow{d} N(0, B_0), \text{ where } B_0 = \frac{\sigma^2}{2\gamma_0 + 1} \begin{pmatrix} 1 & \beta_0 \\ \beta_0 & \beta_0^2 \end{pmatrix}. \tag{7.79}$$

While the convergence (7.4) is true by Lemma 7.3.4, the part of Assumption W2 concerning positive definiteness of A_0 is not satisfied. Phillips noticed that, in fact, the inverse $H_n^{-1}(\theta_0)$ needs to be normalized. Introducing $F_n = 1/(\log n) D_n$ and $E_n = F_n^{-1} H_n(\theta_0) F_n^{-1}$ he proved [see Lemma 7.3.5(ii)]

$$E_n^{-1} \xrightarrow{p} \frac{\gamma_1^3}{\beta_0^2} \begin{pmatrix} \beta_0^2 & -\beta_0 \\ -\beta_0 & 1 \end{pmatrix}, \text{ where } \gamma_1 = 2\gamma_0 + 1. \tag{7.80}$$

The matrices C_n defined by $C_n = (1/n^\delta) D_n$ trivially satisfy the first part of Assumption W3:

$$C_n D_n^{-1} = n^{-\delta} = o(1). \tag{7.81}$$

Finally, with the neighborhood $N_n^r(\theta_0) = \{\theta: \|C_n(\theta - \theta_0)\| \leq r\}$, by Lemma 7.3.8 the second part of Assumption W3 holds:

$$\max_{\theta \in N_n^1(\theta_0)} \|C_n^{-1}[H_n(\theta) - H_n(\theta_0)]C_n^{-1}\| = o_p(1). \tag{7.82}$$

The algebraic Lemma 7.1.3 does not depend on Eq. (7.80) and continues to be true. The next lemma of the Wooldridge framework, Lemma 7.1.5, uses only Eq. (7.82) and is also true. The remaining statements, starting from Lemma 7.1.6, need a revision.

7.3.10   Bounding the Remainder in the Vicinity of $\tilde{\theta}_n$

Ω_n is the same as in Section 7.1.6, $\Omega_n = \{\omega: \|C_n(\tilde{\theta}_n - \theta_0)\| \leq r_n\}$. In the definition of $\tilde{N}_n(r)$, however, D_n is replaced by F_n:

$$\tilde{N}_n(r) = \{\theta: \|F_n(\theta - \tilde{\theta}_n)\| \leq r\}. \tag{7.83}$$

Lemma.   *Let $\gamma_0 > -1/2$ and let Assumption P1 hold. There exists a sequence of positive numbers $\{r_n\}$ such that*

(i) *$P(\Omega_n) \to 1$ as $n \to \infty$.*

(ii) *For all large n we have*

$$\sup_{\omega \in \Omega_n, \, \theta \in \tilde{N}_n(r_n)} |R_n(\theta, \theta_0)| \leq 4\delta_n r_n^2 \; a.s.$$

(iii) *For $r_n \leq 1$*

$$\sup_{\omega \in \Omega_n} |R_n(\tilde{\theta}_n, \theta_0)| \leq \delta_n r_n^2 \; a.s.$$

Proof.   By definition (7.7)

$$F_n(\tilde{\theta}_n - \theta_0) = -F_n(H_n^0)^{-1}S_n^0 = -E_n^{-1}F_n^{-1}S_n^0. \tag{7.84}$$

Here, by Eq. (7.79) and the definition of F_n we have

$$F_n^{-1}S_n^0 = (\log n)D_n^{-1}S_n^0 = O_p(\log n). \tag{7.85}$$

Therefore Eqs. (7.80) and (7.84) imply

$$F_n(\tilde{\theta}_n - \theta_0) = O_p(\log n). \tag{7.86}$$

Hence, by Eq. (7.81)

$$C_n(\tilde{\theta}_n - \theta_0) = C_n D_n^{-1} D_n(\tilde{\theta}_n - \theta_0) = (C_n D_n^{-1})[(\log n)F_n(\tilde{\theta}_n - \theta_0)] = o_p(1). \tag{7.87}$$

Lemma 7.1.4 and Eq. (7.87) prove statement (i).

Since $\|F_n(\theta - \tilde{\theta}_n)\| \le r_n$ implies $\|C_n(\theta - \tilde{\theta}_n)\| \le \|C_n D_n^{-1} \log n\| r_n \le r_n$ for large n, we have the inclusion $\tilde{N}_n(r_n) \subseteq \{\theta : \|C_n(\theta - \tilde{\theta}_n)\| \le r_n\}$ for large n. This inclusion, the triangle inequality and (7.19) lead to the implication $\omega \in \Omega_n$, $\theta \in \tilde{N}_n(r_n) \Rightarrow \theta \in N_n^{2r_n}(\theta_0)$. Therefore statement (ii) follows from Lemma 7.1.5.

As $\tilde{\theta}_n \in N_n^{2r_n}$ for $\omega \in \Omega_n$, statement (iii) follows directly from Lemma 7.1.5. ∎

7.3.11   Consistency of $\hat{\theta}_n$

Theorem.   *Let Assumptions P1 and P2 be satisfied. Then there exists a sequence of sets $\{\tilde{\Omega}_n\}$ such that*

$$P(\tilde{\Omega}_n) \longrightarrow 1 \; as \; n \longrightarrow \infty \tag{7.88}$$

and for almost any $\omega \in \tilde{\Omega}_n$ there exists an estimator $\hat{\theta}_n \in \tilde{N}_n(r_n)$ such that

$$F_n(\hat{\theta}_n - \theta_0) = O_p(\log n). \tag{7.89}$$

Proof.   By Lemma 7.1.3

$$Q_n(\theta) - Q_n(\tilde{\theta}_n) = [F_n(\theta - \tilde{\theta}_n)]' E_n[F_n(\theta - \tilde{\theta}_n)] + 2R_n(\theta, \theta_0) - 2R_n(\tilde{\theta}_n, \theta_0) \tag{7.90}$$

[the right side of Eq. (7.9) gets multiplied by two because the derivatives in Section 7.3.2 are half the usual derivatives; the notation $E_n = F_n^{-1} H_n(\theta_0) F_n^{-1}$ is from Lemma 7.3.5(ii)]. On the boundary of $\tilde{N}_n(r_n)$ [see Eq. (7.83)] we have

$$[F_n(\theta - \tilde{\theta}_n)]' E_n[F_n(\theta - \tilde{\theta}_n)] \ge \lambda_{\min}(E_n) r_n^2. \tag{7.91}$$

The numbers $\lambda_n \equiv \lambda_{\min}(E_n) = \lambda_{\min}[A_n(\theta_0) \log^2 n]$ by Lemma 7.3.6 and Assumption P2 are bounded away from zero, $\lambda_n \ge c > 0$.

Denote $f_n(\theta) = Q_n(\theta) - Q_n(\tilde{\theta}_n)$. Obviously, the point $\tilde{\theta}_n \in \tilde{N}_n(r_n)$ satisfies $f_n(\tilde{\theta}_n) = 0$. We want to show that on the boundary $\partial \tilde{N}_n(r_n)$ of $\tilde{N}_n(r_n)$ the function f_n is positive. Let $\tilde{\Omega}_n = \Omega_n \cap \{\omega : 5\delta_n \le \lambda_n/2\}$. Since $\lambda_n \ge c$, by Eq. (7.14) and Lemma 7.3.10(i) $\tilde{\Omega}_n$ satisfies Eq. (7.88).

According to Lemma 7.3.10 and Eqs. (7.90) and (7.91), for $\omega \in \tilde{\Omega}_n$

$$\min_{\theta \in \partial \tilde{N}_n(r_n)} f_n(\theta) \ge \lambda_n r_n^2 - 5\delta_n r_n^2 \ge \frac{1}{2} \lambda_n r_n^2 > 0.$$

Thus, there are points inside $\tilde{N}_n(r_n)$ where f_n takes lower values than on its boundary. Since f_n is smooth, it achieves its minimum inside $\tilde{N}_n(r_n)$ and the point of minimum $\hat{\theta}_n$ satisfies the first-order condition (7.56). The inequality $\|F_n(\hat{\theta}_n - \tilde{\theta}_n)\| \le r_n$ combined with Eq. (7.86) proves Eq. (7.89). ∎

7.3.12   Phillips' Representation of the Standardized Estimator

Lemma.   *Under Assumptions P1 and P2 the estimator from Theorem 7.3.11 satisfies*

$$F_n(\hat{\theta}_n - \theta_0) = -E_n^{-1}F_n^{-1}S_n^0 + o_p(1). \tag{7.92}$$

Proof.   Expanding $S_n(\hat{\theta}_n)$ about θ_0, we have from Eq. (7.56)

$$0 = S_n^0 + H_n^0(\hat{\theta}_n - \theta_0) + (H_n^* - H_n^0)(\hat{\theta}_n - \theta_0),$$

where the Hessian H_n^* is evaluated at mean values between θ_0 and $\hat{\theta}_n$. Scaling this condition we get

$$
\begin{aligned}
0 &= F_n^{-1}S_n^0 + (F_n^{-1}H_n^0F_n^{-1})F_n(\hat{\theta}_n - \theta_0) \\
&\quad + [F_n^{-1}(H_n^* - H_n^0)F_n^{-1}]F_n(\hat{\theta}_n - \theta_0) \\
&= F_n^{-1}S_n^0 + \{E_n + E_nE_n^{-1}[F_n^{-1}(H_n^* - H_n^0)F_n^{-1}]\}F_n(\hat{\theta}_n - \theta_0) \\
&= F_n^{-1}S_n^0 + E_n(I + E_n^{-1}\tilde{\Delta}_n)F_n(\hat{\theta}_n - \theta_0),
\end{aligned}
$$

where we have denoted

$$\tilde{\Delta}_n(\theta^*, \theta_0) = F_n^{-1}(H_n^* - H_n^0)F_n^{-1}.$$

It follows that on the set $\Xi_n = \{\omega: (I + E_n^{-1}\tilde{\Delta}_n)^{-1} \text{ exists}\}$ we have the representation

$$F_n(\hat{\theta}_n - \theta_0) = -(I + E_n^{-1}\tilde{\Delta}_n)^{-1}E_n^{-1}F_n^{-1}S_n^0. \tag{7.93}$$

Now we prove that the probability of Ξ_n approaches 1. By Lemma 7.3.8 (see also the definitions of F_n and C_n in Section 7.3.9)

$$\sup_{\theta \in N_n^1(\theta_0)} \|\tilde{\Delta}_n(\theta, \theta_0)\| = \sup_{\theta \in N_n^1(\theta_0)} \frac{\log^2 n}{n^{2\delta}}\|\Delta_n(\theta, \theta_0)\| = o_p\left(\frac{1}{n^\varepsilon}\right) \tag{7.94}$$

with some $\varepsilon \in (0, 2\delta)$. Using Eq. (7.89) we get

$$C_n(\hat{\theta}_n - \theta_0) = \frac{\log n}{n^\delta}F_n(\hat{\theta}_n - \theta_0) = O_p\left(\frac{\log^2 n}{n^\delta}\right) = o_p(1).$$

This implies that $\hat{\theta}_n$ and θ^* (which is a mean between $\hat{\theta}_n$ and θ_0) belong to $N_n^1(\theta_0)$ with probability approaching unity as $n \to \infty$. Therefore by Eq. (7.94) and Lemma 7.3.5(ii)

$$E_n^{-1} \tilde{\Delta}_n(\theta^*, \theta_0) = o_p\left(\frac{1}{n^{\varepsilon}}\right), \quad \lim_{n \to \infty} P(\Xi_n) = 1$$

and

$$(I + E_n^{-1} \tilde{\Delta}_n)^{-1} = \sum_{j=0}^{\infty} \left(-E_n^{-1} \tilde{\Delta}_n\right)^j = I + o_p\left(\frac{1}{n^{\varepsilon}}\right) \quad \text{on } \Xi_n. \tag{7.95}$$

By Eq. (7.85) and Lemma 7.3.5(ii), $E_n^{-1} F_n^{-1} S_n^0 = O_p(\log n)$. Hence, Eqs. (7.93) and (7.95) give Eq. (7.92):

$$F_n(\hat{\theta}_n - \theta_0) = -\left[I + o_p\left(\frac{1}{n^{\varepsilon}}\right)\right] E_n^{-1} F_n^{-1} S_n^0$$

$$= -E_n^{-1} F_n^{-1} S_n^0 + o_p\left(\frac{1}{n^{\varepsilon}}\right) O_p(\log n). \quad \blacksquare$$

7.3.13   Asymptotic Normality

Theorem.   *Suppose that in the model (7.54) the errors satisfy Assumption P1 and the true parameter vector satisfies Assumption P2. Then the least-squares estimator $\hat{\theta}_n$ exists with probability approaching 1, is consistent in the sense of Eq. (7.89) and has the following limit distribution:*

$$F_n(\hat{\theta}_n - \theta_0) \xrightarrow{d} \begin{pmatrix} 1 \\ -1/\beta_0 \end{pmatrix} N(0, \sigma^2(2\gamma_0 + 1)^3). \tag{7.96}$$

Proof.   We apply representation (7.92). The limit of E_n^{-1} is singular [Lemma 7.3.5(ii)] and $F_n^{-1} S_n^0$ diverges [see Eq. (7.85)]. Therefore before letting $n \to \infty$ we need to calculate the product $E_n^{-1} F_n^{-1} S_n^0$.

By Eq. (7.63) and the definition $F_n = 1/(\log n) D_n$ we have

$$F_n^{-1} S_n^0 = -\begin{pmatrix} \dfrac{\log n}{\sqrt{n}} \sum_{s=1}^{n} \left(\dfrac{s}{n}\right)^{\gamma_0} u_s \\ \dfrac{1}{\sqrt{n}} \sum_{s=1}^{n} \left(\dfrac{s}{n}\right)^{\gamma_0} u_s \beta_0 \log s \end{pmatrix} = -\frac{1}{\sqrt{n}} \sum_{s=1}^{n} \left(\dfrac{s}{n}\right)^{\gamma_0} u_s v_s, \tag{7.97}$$

where $v_s = (\log n, \beta_0 \log s)'$. With the help of the expression from Lemma 7.3.5(ii) we calculate

$$E_n^{-1} v_s \asymp \gamma_1^3 \begin{pmatrix} 1 - \dfrac{2}{\gamma_1 \log n} + \dfrac{2}{\gamma_1^2 \log^2 n} & \dfrac{1}{\beta_0}\left(\dfrac{1}{\gamma_1 \log n} - 1\right) \\ \dfrac{1}{\beta_0}\left(\dfrac{1}{\gamma_1 \log n} - 1\right) & \dfrac{1}{\beta_0^2} \end{pmatrix} \begin{pmatrix} \log n \\ \beta_0 \log s \end{pmatrix}$$

$$\asymp \gamma_1^3 \begin{pmatrix} \log n - \dfrac{2}{\gamma_1} + \dfrac{2}{\gamma_1^2 \log n} + \left(\dfrac{1}{\gamma_1 \log n} - 1\right)\log s \\ \dfrac{1}{\beta_0}\left(\dfrac{1}{\gamma_1} - \log n + \log s\right) \end{pmatrix}.$$

In this and the next two equations $\asymp$ means equality up to a term of order $O_p(n^{-\varepsilon})$. Next we replace $\log s = \log(s/n) + \log n$ and retain the terms of order $1/\log n$:

$$E_n^{-1} v_s \asymp \gamma_1^3 \begin{pmatrix} \log n - \dfrac{2}{\gamma_1} + \dfrac{2}{\gamma_1^2 \log n} + \left(\dfrac{1}{\gamma_1 \log n} - 1\right)\left(\log \dfrac{s}{n} + \log n\right) \\ \dfrac{1}{\beta_0}\left(\dfrac{1}{\gamma_1} + \log \dfrac{s}{n}\right) \end{pmatrix}$$

$$\asymp \gamma_1^3 \begin{pmatrix} \left(-\dfrac{1}{\gamma_1} - \log \dfrac{s}{n}\right) + \dfrac{1}{\gamma_1 \log n}\left(\dfrac{2}{\gamma_1} + \log \dfrac{s}{n}\right) \\ \dfrac{1}{\beta_0}\left(\dfrac{1}{\gamma_1} + \log \dfrac{s}{n}\right) \end{pmatrix}$$

$$\asymp \gamma_1^3 \begin{pmatrix} -1 \\ 1/\beta_0 \end{pmatrix}\left(\dfrac{1}{\gamma_1} + \log \dfrac{s}{n}\right) + \begin{pmatrix} \dfrac{\gamma_1^2}{\log n}\left(\dfrac{2}{\gamma_1} + \log \dfrac{s}{n}\right) \\ 0 \end{pmatrix}. \tag{7.98}$$

From Eqs. (7.97) and (7.98) we see that

$$E_n^{-1} F_n^{-1} S_n^0 \asymp \gamma_1^3 \begin{pmatrix} 1 \\ -1/\beta_0 \end{pmatrix} \dfrac{1}{\sqrt{n}} \sum_{s=1}^{n} \left(\dfrac{s}{n}\right)^{\gamma_0} u_s \left(\dfrac{1}{\gamma_1} + \log \dfrac{s}{n}\right)$$

$$+ \dfrac{1}{\log n}\dfrac{1}{\sqrt{n}} \sum_{s=1}^{n} \left(\dfrac{s}{n}\right)^{\gamma_0} u_s \left(2\gamma_1 + \gamma_1^2 \log \dfrac{s}{n}\right). \tag{7.99}$$

By Lemma 7.2.7 the second line of Eq. (7.99) is $O_p(1/\log n)$. The proof of that lemma can be easily modified to show that with $F(s) = s^{\gamma_0}(1/\gamma_1 + \log s)$

$$\dfrac{1}{\sqrt{n}} \sum_{s=1}^{n} \left(\dfrac{s}{n}\right)^{\gamma_0} u_s \left(\dfrac{1}{\gamma_1} + \log \dfrac{s}{n}\right) \xrightarrow{d} N\left(0, \sigma^2 \int_0^1 F^2(s)\, ds\right). \tag{7.100}$$

Here, by Eq. (7.69)

$$\int_0^1 F^2(s)\,ds = \int_0^1 \left(\frac{s^{2\gamma_0}}{\gamma_1^2} + \frac{2s^{2\gamma_0}}{\gamma_1}\log s + s^{2\gamma_0}\log^2 s \right) ds = \frac{1}{\gamma_1^3}. \tag{7.101}$$

Equations (7.99)–(7.101) allow us to conclude that

$$E_n^{-1}F_n^{-1}S_n^0 \xrightarrow{d} \begin{pmatrix} 1 \\ -1/\beta_0 \end{pmatrix} N(0,\sigma^2\gamma_1^3).$$

This equation and Eq. (7.92) prove Eq. (7.96).   ∎

7.4 BINARY LOGIT MODELS WITH UNBOUNDED EXPLANATORY VARIABLES

7.4.1 The Binary Logit Model and Log-Likelihood

Consider independent observations (x_t, y_t), $t = 1,\ldots,T$, where all y_t are Bernoulli variables (with values 0 and 1) and $x_t = (x_{t1},\ldots,x_{tK})'$ are vectors of explanatory variables. The Bernoulli variable is uniquely characterized by the probability $P(y_t = 1)$. In the *binary model* it is assumed that

$$P(y_t = 1|x_t) = F(x_t'b_0), \tag{7.102}$$

where F is some probability distribution function, $x_t'b_0 = \sum_{k=1}^K x_{tk}b_{0k}$ and $b_0 \in \mathbb{R}^K$ is an unknown parameter vector. The choice of the *logistic function*

$$F(x) = 1/(1 + e^{-x}), \quad x \in \mathbb{R}, \tag{7.103}$$

makes the model a binary *logit model*.

The density function of a single Bernoulli variable is $P(y) = p^y(1-p)^{1-y}$. As a result of Eq. (7.102) and the assumed independence of observations the *likelihood function* (also known as the joint density) of the sequence of observations $(x, y) = \{(x_1, y_1), (x_2, y_2), \ldots\}$ is

$$L_T(b; (x, y)) = \prod_{t=1}^T [F(x_t'b)]^{y_t}[1 - F(x_t'b)]^{1-y_t}.$$

The *log-likelihood* is, obviously,

$$\log L_T(b; (x, y)) = \sum_{t=1}^T \{ y_t \log F(x_t'b) + (1 - y_t)[1 - F(x_t'b)] \}$$

$$= \sum_{t=1}^T \left\{ y_t \log \frac{F(x_t'b)}{1 - F(x_t'b)} + \log[1 - F(x_t'b)] \right\}.$$

7.4.2   The Score and Hessian

Note that the logit function (7.103) satisfies $1 - F(x) = e^{-x}/(1 + e^{-x})$ and therefore

$$\frac{F(x)}{1 - F(x)} = e^x; \quad f(x) \equiv F'(x) = \frac{e^{-x}}{(1 + e^{-x})^2} = F(x)[1 - F(x)]. \tag{7.104}$$

Using Eq. (7.104) we find the derivatives

$$\frac{d}{db} \log \frac{F(x_t'b)}{1 - F(x_t'b)} = \frac{d}{db} x_t'b = x_t,$$

$$\frac{d}{db} \log[1 - F(x_t'b)] = \frac{-F'(x_t'b)}{1 - F(x_t'b)} x_t = -F(x_t'b)x_t$$

and the score

$$\frac{d}{db} \log L_T(b; (x, y)) = \sum_{t=1}^{T} [y_t x_t - F(x_t'b)x_t] = \sum_{t=1}^{T} [y_t - F(x_t'b)]x_t. \tag{7.105}$$

Consequently, using the notation

$$H_T(b) = \sum_{t=1}^{T} f(x_t'b)x_t x_t', \quad b \in \mathbb{R}^K, \quad T = 1, 2, \ldots$$

the Hessian can be expressed as

$$\frac{d^2 \log L_T(b; (x, y))}{db \, db'} = - \sum_{t=1}^{T} F'(x_t'b)x_t x_t' = -H_T(b). \tag{7.106}$$

7.4.3   History

The strong consistency of the ML estimator for Eq. (7.102) was studied in the context of repeated samples by Amemiya (1976) and Morimune (1959). These authors assumed that the explanatory variables can take a finite number of values and that the number of observations goes to infinity for each set of possible values of these variables. Such assumptions are appropriate in the context of controlled experiments and do not satisfy most econometric applications.

Gouriéroux and Monfort (1981) (henceforth referred to as G&M) made a significant step forward by allowing the explanatory variables to take an infinite number of values. They obtained necessary and sufficient conditions for strong consistency of the ML estimator and proved its asymptotic normality. They discovered an interesting link between the logit model and the OLS estimator for a linear model (see Section 7.4.12); such a link does not exist in case of the probit model. In their argument an important role belongs to the surjection theorem from Cartan

(1967), see Section 7.4.7. Strong consistency was proved with the help of Anderson and Taylor (1979), and asymptotic normality was obtained as an application of an asymptotic normality result for the OLS estimator due to Eicker (1966).

Let λ_{KT} and λ_{1T} denote, respectively, the largest and the smallest eigenvalues of $H_T(b_0)$, where b_0 is the true parameter vector:

$$\lambda_{KT} = \lambda_{\max}(H_T(b_0)), \quad \lambda_{1T} = \lambda_{\min}(H_T(b_0)), \quad M_T = \sup_{t \leq T} \|x_t\|, \qquad (7.107)$$

where $\|x_t\| = \left(\sum_{k=1}^{K} x_{tk}^2\right)^{1/2}$. G&M assumed that the regressors are deterministic, bounded ($\sup_T M_T < \infty$), and that the eigenvalues of $H_T(b_0)$ are of the same order: $\sup_T \lambda_{KT}/\lambda_{1T} < \infty$. We relax some or all of these assumptions, depending on the situation.

The case of unbounded explanatory variables requires an accurate estimation of the Lipschitz constant for the mapping [see Eqs. (7.105) and (7.106)]

$$\phi_T(b; (x, y)) = b + H_T^{-1}(b_0)\frac{d}{db}\log L_T(b; (x, y))$$

$$= b + H_T^{-1}(b_0) \sum_{t=1}^{T} [y_t - F(x_t'b)]x_t, \qquad (7.108)$$

which is necessary to apply the Cartan theorem. Instead of the result by Anderson and Taylor (1979) we use a more general theorem (Theorem 6.4.8) by Lai and Wei (1982). The theorem by Eicker (1966) does not apply because the squares of the error terms in the linear model are not uniformly integrable (Lemma 7.4.16); instead, we apply the Lindeberg CLT. We show that our results include, as a special case, those due to G&M.

Hsiao (1991) also addressed the issue of unbounded explanatory variables. However, since Hsiao's intention was to cover errors in variables, the resulting conditions are complex and are not directly comparable to ours. Besides, the approach by G&M generalized here gives necessary and sufficient conditions in some cases.

The main results are given in Sections 7.4.10, 7.4.13 and 7.4.21. Everywhere we maintain (without explicitly mentioning) the basic assumptions of the logit model: the observations are independent and satisfy Eq. (7.102) with the logit function (7.103). To distinguish the additional assumptions from those in the previous sections, here we provide their numbers with the prefix BL (for binary logit).

7.4.4   Uniqueness of the Maximum Likelihood Estimator

7.4.4.1   Assumption BL1   For all large T the matrix $H_T(b_0)$ is positive definite: $\lambda_{1T} > 0$.

Lemma.   *If Assumption BL1 is satisfied and the ML estimator $\hat{b}_T(x, y)$ exists, then it is unique.*

Proof. Denote

$$G(b) = \text{diag}[f(x_1'b), \ldots, f(x_T'b)], \quad X = (x_1, \ldots, x_T). \tag{7.109}$$

Then $H_T(b) = XG(b)X'$ and

$$\text{rank}H_T(b_0) \le \min[\text{rank}X, \text{rank}G(b_0)] = \text{rank}X \le K \quad \text{for } T \ge K.$$

As a result of this inequality and Assumption BL1, $\text{rank}X = K$.

Among the columns of X there are K linearly independent and the other $T - K$ are linear functions of those K columns. In the sum $\sum_{t=1}^{T} f(x_t'b)x_t x_t'$ we can relocate the terms that correspond to the linearly independent x_t to the beginning and the others to the end [this does not change $H_T(b)$] and renumber the terms correspondingly. Then $X = (Y, AY)$ where Y is $K \times K$ and nonsingular and A is some $(T - K) \times K$ matrix. Partitioning $G(b)$ correspondingly we get

$$H_T(b) = (Y, AY)\begin{pmatrix} G_1(b) & 0 \\ 0 & G_2(b) \end{pmatrix}\begin{pmatrix} Y' \\ Y'A' \end{pmatrix}$$
$$= YG_1(b)Y' + AYG_2(b)Y'A' \ge YG_1(b)Y'.$$

Since $\det[YG_1(b)Y'] = (\det Y)^2\det G_1(b) \ne 0$, $H_T(b)$ is nonsingular and the Hessian (7.106) is negative definite. This ensures uniqueness of the ML estimator. ∎

7.4.5 Lipschitz Condition for the Logit Density

Lemma. *With the notation (7.107) for any $b, b_0 \in \mathbb{R}^K$, we have*

$$|f(x_t'b_0) - f(x_t'b)| \le 4\|b - b_0\|M_T e^{\|b - b_0\|M_T}f(x_t'b_0). \tag{7.110}$$

Proof. It is convenient to use hyperbolic functions

$$\cosh x = \frac{e^x + e^{-x}}{2}, \quad \sinh x = \frac{e^x - e^{-x}}{2}, \quad \tanh x = \frac{\sinh x}{\cosh x}$$

and their obvious properties:

$$(\cosh x)' = \sinh x, \quad -\tanh x = \tanh(-x), \quad |\tanh x| \le 1. \tag{7.111}$$

The density f in Eq. (7.104) can be represented as $f(x) = [\cosh(x/2)]^{-2}/4$ and then Eq. (7.111) can be used to obtain

$$|f'(x)| = |f(x)\tanh(-x/2)| \le f(x), \quad \frac{1}{4}e^{-|x|} \le f(x) \le e^{-|x|}. \tag{7.112}$$

By the first relation in Eq. (7.112) and finite increments formula for any x, h with some $\theta \in (0, 1)$ we have

$$|f(x + h) - f(x)| = |f'(x + \theta h)h| \le f(x + \theta h)|h|. \tag{7.113}$$

Using the inequality $|x| - |x + \theta h| \le |x - (x + \theta h)| \le |h|$ and the second relation in Eq. (7.112) we bound

$$f(x + \theta h) \le e^{-|x + \theta h|} = e^{|x| - |x + \theta h|} e^{-|x|} \le e^{|h|} e^{-|x|} \le 4f(x)e^{|h|}. \tag{7.114}$$

Equations (7.113) and (7.114) imply $|f(x + h) - f(x)| \le 4|h|f(x)e^{|h|}$, which leads to the desired estimate

$$|f(x_t'b_0) - f(x_t'b)| \le 4|x_t'(b - b_0)|e^{|x_t'(b-b_0)|}f(x_t'b_0)$$
$$\le 4\|b - b_0\|M_T e^{\|b-b_0\|M_T}f(x_t'b_0).$$

∎

7.4.6 Lipschitz Condition for ϕ_T

Let $B(b_0, r) = \{b \in \mathbb{R}^K : \|b - b_0\| < r\}$ denote an open ball in $\mathbb{R}^K$ with center b_0 and radius r. The function ϕ_T is defined in Eq. (7.108).

Lemma. *If Assumption BL1 holds, then for any $r > 0$ and $T = 1, 2, \ldots$ the function ϕ_T satisfies the Lipschitz condition*

$$\|\phi_T(b; (x, y)) - \phi_T(\tilde{b}; (x, y))\| \le L(r, T)\|b - \tilde{b}\| \quad for\ b, \tilde{b} \in B(b_0, r)$$

with the Lipschitz constant

$$L(r, T) = 4rM_T e^{rM_T}\lambda_{KT}/\lambda_{1T}. \tag{7.115}$$

Proof. The finite increments formula for vector-valued functions (Kolmogorov and Fomin 1989, Ch. X, Part 1, Section 3) states that

$$\|\phi_T(b; (x, y)) - \phi_T(\tilde{b}; (x, y))\| \le \sup_{b \in B(b_0, r)} \left\|\frac{d\phi_T(b; (x, y))}{db'}\right\| \|b - \tilde{b}\|$$

and the lemma will follow if we prove

$$\sup_{b \in B(b_0, r)} \left\|\frac{d\phi_T(b; (x, y))}{db'}\right\| \le L(r, T). \tag{7.116}$$

From Eqs. (7.106) and (7.108) we get

$$\frac{d\phi_T(b; (x, y))}{db'} = I + H_T^{-1}(b_0)\frac{d^2\log L_T(b; (x, y))}{db\, db'}$$

$$= H_T^{-1}(b_0)[H_T(b_0) - H_T(b)]$$

$$= H_T^{-1}(b_0)\sum_{t=1}^{T} x_t x_t'[f(x_t'b_0) - f(x_t'b)]. \tag{7.117}$$

Equation (7.117) explains the construction of ϕ_T: when $H_T(b)$ is close to $H_T(b_0)$, the matrix $d\phi_T(b; (x, y))/db'$ should be small.

Denote

$$\alpha_t = |f(x_t'b_0) - f(x_t'b)|, \quad A = \text{diag}[\alpha_1, \ldots, \alpha_T],$$

$$\beta_t = 4\|b - b_0\|M_T e^{\|b-b_0\|M_T} f(x_t'b_0), \quad B = \text{diag}[\beta_1, \ldots, \beta_T].$$

By Lemma 7.4.5 $\alpha_t \le \beta_t$. Using the notation (7.109) we have $[(\cdot, \cdot)$ is the scalar product in $\mathbb{R}^T]$

$$\|H_T(b_0) - H_T(b)\| = \|XG(b_0)X' - XG(b)X'\|$$

$$= \sup_{\|x\|=1} ([G(b_0) - G(b)]X'x, X'x)$$

$$\le \sup_{\|x\|=1} (AX'x, X'x) \le \sup_{\|x\|=1} (BX'x, X'x)$$

$$= 4\|b - b_0\|M_T e^{\|b-b_0\|M_T} \|H_T(b_0)\|. \tag{7.118}$$

This bound and Eq. (7.117) imply

$$\left\|\frac{d\phi_T(b; (x, y))}{db'}\right\| \le \|H_T^{-1}(b_0)\|\|H_T(b_0) - H_T(b)\|$$

$$\le 4\|b - b_0\|M_T e^{\|b-b_0\|M_T} \frac{\lambda_{KT}}{\lambda_{1T}},$$

which proves Eq. (7.116) and the lemma. ∎

7.4.7 Surjection Theorem

Theorem. *(Cartan 1967, Theorem 4.4.1). If the function $\psi: B(b_0, r) \to \mathbb{R}^K$ is such that the function $\phi(b) = b - \psi(b)$ satisfies the Lipschitz condition*

$$\|\phi(b) - \phi(\tilde{b})\| \le c\|b - \tilde{b}\| \quad \text{for } b, \tilde{b} \in B(b_0, r)$$

with a constant $c < 1$, then any element of $B[\psi(b_0), (1 - c)r]$ is the image by ψ of an element of $B(b_0, r)$:

$$B(\psi(b_0), (1 - c)r) \subseteq \psi(B(b_0, r)). \tag{7.119}$$

7.4.8   Definition

Let $\{r_T\}$ be a sequence of positive numbers. We say that the ML estimator $\hat{b}_T(x, y)$ *exists a.s. and converges a.s.* to the true value b_0 *at the rate* $o(r_T)$ if for almost any (x, y)

1. there exists $T_0(x, y)$ such that $\hat{b}_T(x, y)$ exists for all $T \geq T_0(x, y)$ and
2. $\hat{b}_T(x, y) - b_0 = o(r_T)$ a.s.

7.4.9   Existence and Convergence of the Maximum Likelihood Estimator in Terms of the Inverse Lipschitz Function

The function $L(r, T)$ defined in Eq. (7.115) is continuous and monotone in r and satisfies $L(0, T) = 0$, $L(\infty, T) = \infty$ for each T. Therefore for any $c \in (0, 1)$ we can define $r_T(c)$ by $L[r_T(c), T] = c$. We call $r_T(c)$ an *inverse Lipschitz function*. By Lemma 7.4.6 for any $\varepsilon \in (0, 1)$

$$\|\phi_T(b; (x, y)) - \phi_T(\tilde{b}; (x, y))\| \leq c\|b - \tilde{b}\| \quad \text{for } b, \tilde{b} \in B(b_0, \varepsilon r_T(c)). \quad (7.120)$$

Denote [see Eq. (7.108)]

$$\psi_T(b; (x, y)) = b - \phi_T(b; (x, y)) = -H_T^{-1}(b_0) \sum_{t=1}^{T} [y_t - F(x_t'b)]x_t. \quad (7.121)$$

Lemma.   *Suppose Assumption BL1 is satisfied and let* $c \in (0, 1)$. *Then* $\hat{b}_T(x, y)$ *exists a.s. and converges a.s. to the true value* b_0 *at the rate* $o[r_T(c)]$ *if and only if*

$$\psi_T(b_0; (x, y)) = o(r_T(c)) \, a.s. \quad (7.122)$$

Proof.   **Sufficiency.** Following G&M we apply the surjection theorem. If Eq. (7.122) is true, then for almost any (x, y) and for any $\varepsilon \in (0, 1)$ there exists $T_0 = T_0(x, y, \varepsilon)$ such that

$$\|\psi_T(b_0; (x, y))\| < (1 - c)\varepsilon r_T(c) \quad \text{for all } T \geq T_0. \quad (7.123)$$

Equation (7.120) shows that Theorem 7.4.7 is applicable with $r = \varepsilon r_T(c)$. By Eq. (7.123) the null vector belongs to the ball $B[\psi_T(b_0; (x, y)), (1 - c)\varepsilon r_T(c)]$. Therefore Eq. (7.119) ensures the existence of

$$\hat{b}_T(x, y) \in B(b_0, \varepsilon r_T(c)) \quad (7.124)$$

such that $\psi_T[\hat{b}_T(x, y); (x, y)] = 0$ and, hence, $\hat{b}_T(x, y)$ is the ML estimator. (Recall that by Lemma 7.4.4 it is unique.) Since Eq. (7.124) is true for all $T \geq T_0$ and ε can be arbitrarily small, we have proved that

$$\hat{b}_T(x, y) - b_0 = o(r_T(c)) \text{ a.s.} \quad (7.125)$$

Necessity. Suppose Eq. (7.122) does not hold. Then for any (x, y) from a set of positive probability there exist $\varepsilon_1 = \varepsilon_1(x, y)$ and a sequence $\{T_n\}$ such that $T_n \to \infty$ as $n \to \infty$ and

$$\|\psi_{T_n}(b_0; (x, y))\| \geq \varepsilon_1 r_{T_n}(c) \quad \text{for all } n. \tag{7.126}$$

Letting $\varepsilon = \varepsilon_1/[2(1 + c)]$ in Eq. (7.120) we get

$$\|\psi_T(b; (x, y)) - \psi_T(b_0; (x, y))\| \leq \|b - b_0\| + \|\phi_T(b; (x, y)) - \phi_T(b_0; (x, y))\|$$

$$\leq \varepsilon r_T(c) + c\varepsilon r_T(c) = \frac{\varepsilon_1}{2} r_T(c)$$

for all $b \in B[b_0, \varepsilon r_T(c)]$. This inequality and Eq. (7.126) imply

$$\|\psi_{T_n}(b; (x, y))\| \geq \|\psi_{T_n}(b_0; (x, y))\| - \|\psi_{T_n}(b; (x, y)) - \psi_{T_n}(b_0; (x, y))\|$$

$$\geq \frac{\varepsilon_1}{2} r_{T_n}(c) \quad \text{for all } b \in B(b_0, \varepsilon r_{T_n}(c)).$$

This shows that the ML estimator $\hat{b}_{T_n}(x, y)$, if it exists, cannot belong to $B[b_0, \varepsilon r_{T_n}(c)]$ for all n. The resulting inequality

$$\|\hat{b}_{T_n}(x, y) - b_0\| \geq \varepsilon(x, y)r_{T_n}(c), n = 1, 2, \ldots,$$

is true on a set of positive probability and means that Eq. (7.125) cannot be true. ∎

7.4.10   Existence and Convergence of the Maximum Likelihood Estimator in Terms of ρ_T

Condition (7.122) is not very convenient because the inverse Lipschitz function is difficult to find explicitly. Here we show that it can be replaced by

$$\rho_T = \frac{1}{M_T} \frac{\lambda_{1T}}{\lambda_{KT}}. \tag{7.127}$$

Let $\{\alpha_T\}$, $\{\beta_T\}$ be positive sequences of constants or random variables. We write $\alpha_T \sim \beta_T$ if $c_1 \alpha_T \leq \beta_T \leq c_2 \alpha_T$ with constants $c_1, c_2 > 0$ independent of T (c_1, c_2 may depend on the point in the sample space Ω if α_T, β_T are random variables).

Theorem.   (From my drawer) *If Assumption BL1 holds, then $\hat{b}_T(x, y)$ exists a.s. and converges a.s. to b_0 at the rate $o(\rho_T)$ if and only if $\psi_T[b_0; (x, y)] = o(\rho_T)$ a.s.*

Proof.   Let us prove that for any $c \in (0, 1)$

$$r_T(c) \sim \rho_T. \tag{7.128}$$

Denoting $\tilde{r}_T(c) = r_T(c)M_T$ and $c_T = \dfrac{c\lambda_{1T}}{4\lambda_{KT}}$ we rewrite the definition

$$L(r_T(c), T) = 4r_T(c)M_T e^{r_T(c)M_T} \frac{\lambda_{KT}}{\lambda_{1T}} = c$$

of $r_T(c)$ as

$$\tilde{r}_T(c)e^{\tilde{r}_T(c)} = c_T. \qquad (7.129)$$

Now consider two cases.

1. Suppose $0 < \tilde{r}_T(c) \le 1$. Obviously, $r \le re^r \le er$ for any $0 < r \le 1$ so that $\tilde{r}_T^l(c) \le \tilde{r}_T(c) \le \tilde{r}_T^u(c)$ where the lower and upper bounds $\tilde{r}_T^l(c), \tilde{r}_T^u(c)$ are defined by $e\tilde{r}_T^l(c) = c_T$, $\tilde{r}_T^u(c) = c_T$. Thus, $\frac{1}{e}c_T \le \tilde{r}_T(c) \le c_T$ or

$$\frac{c\lambda_{1T}}{4eM_T\lambda_{KT}} \le r_T(c) \le \frac{c\lambda_{1T}}{4M_T\lambda_{KT}} \quad \text{if } r_T(c) \le \frac{1}{M_T}. \qquad (7.130)$$

2. Let $\tilde{r}_T(c) > 1$. In the range $r > 1$ we have $e^r \le re^r \le e^{2r}$. It follows that $\tilde{r}_T^l(c) \le \tilde{r}_T(c) \le \tilde{r}_T^u(c)$, where $\tilde{r}_T^l(c), \tilde{r}_T^u(c)$ are defined from $e^{2\tilde{r}_T^l(c)} = c_T$, $e^{\tilde{r}_T^u(c)} = c_T$. Hence, $\frac{1}{2}\ln c_T \le \tilde{r}_T(c) \le \ln c_T$ or

$$\frac{1}{2M_T}\left(\ln\frac{c}{4} + \ln\frac{\lambda_{1T}}{\lambda_{KT}}\right) \le r_T(c) \le \frac{1}{M_T}\left(\ln\frac{c}{4} + \ln\frac{\lambda_{1T}}{\lambda_{KT}}\right) \quad \text{if } r_T(c) > \frac{1}{M_T}. \qquad (7.131)$$

Equations (7.130) and (7.131) allow us to prove Eq. (7.128). If $\lambda_{KT}/\lambda_{1T} \to \infty$, then $c_T \to 0$ and by Eq. (7.129) $\tilde{r}_T(c) \to 0$. For all sufficiently large T Eq. (7.130) is true and Eq. (7.128) follows. If, however, $\lambda_{KT}/\lambda_{1T} = O(1)$, then $\rho_T \sim 1/M_T$ and Eq. (7.128) follows from either Eq. (7.130) or Eq. (7.131).
Now the theorem follows from Lemma 7.4.9 and Eq. (7.128). ∎

Equation (7.128) implies that $r_T(c') \sim r_T(c'')$ for any $c', c'' \in (0, 1)$, that is, the dependence of $r_T(c)$ on c is insignificant.

7.4.11 Consistency in the Case of Bounded Explanatory Variables

7.4.11.1 *Assumption BL2* The explanatory variables are bounded and the eigenvalues of $H_T(b_0)$ are of the same order: $\sup_T M_T < \infty$, $\sup_T \lambda_{KT}/\lambda_{1T} < \infty$.

Corollary. *(Gouriéroux and Monfort 1981, Lemma 3) Suppose Assumptions BL1 and BL2 are satisfied. Then $\hat{b}_T(x, y)$ exists a.s. and converges a.s. to b_0 if and only if $\psi_T[b_0; (x, y)] = o(1)$ a.s. as $T \to \infty$.*

The proof follows from the fact that under Assumption BL2 $\rho_T \sim 1$. Comparison of this corollary and Theorem 7.4.10 shows that when $M_T \lambda_{KT}/\lambda_{1T}$ is allowed to grow, convergence of $\hat{b}_T$ to b_0 is faster than just "a.s."

7.4.12 The Relationship between the Logit and Linear Models

Denote

$$z_t = x_t'\sqrt{f(x_t'b_0)}, \quad u_t = \frac{y_t - F(x_t'b_0)}{\sqrt{f(x_t'b_0)}}, \quad Z = \begin{pmatrix} z_1 \\ \cdots \\ z_T \end{pmatrix}, \quad u = \begin{pmatrix} u_1 \\ \cdots \\ u_T \end{pmatrix} \qquad (7.132)$$

and consider the model

$$g = Z\beta + u, \qquad (7.133)$$

where β is a K-dimensional parameter.

Lemma. *Under the specification of the logit model the variables u_t defined in (7.132) are independent and satisfy*

$$Eu_t = 0, \quad Eu_t^2 = 1. \qquad (7.134)$$

If, further, Assumption BL1 holds, then the OLS estimator for model (7.133) has the property

$$\hat{\beta} - \beta = (Z'Z)^{-1}Z'u = -\psi_T(b_0; (x, y)).$$

Proof. By the binary model assumption (7.102)

$$E(y_t|x_t) = 1 \cdot P(y_t = 1|x_t) + 0 \cdot P(y_t = 0|x_t) = F(x_t'b_0),$$

so

$$E(u_t|x_t) = \frac{E(y_t|x_t) - F(x_t'b_0)}{\sqrt{f(x_t'b_0)}} = 0$$

and, by the LIE, $Eu_t = 0$. Similarly, $E(y_t^2|x_t) = F(x_t'b_0)$ and Eq. (7.104) implies

$$E(u_t^2|x_t) = \frac{E(y_t^2|x_t) - 2E(y_t|x_t)F(x_t'b_0) + F^2(x_t'b_0)}{f(x_t'b_0)}$$

$$= \frac{F(x_t'b_0)[1 - F(x_t'b_0)]}{f(x_t'b_0)} = 1, \quad Eu_t^2 = 1.$$

We have proved Eq. (7.134).

Independence of u_t follows from the assumed independence of the observations (x_t, y_t). Further, using Eq. (7.121) we get

$$Z'Z = H_T(b_0), \quad Z'u = \sum_{t=1}^{T} [y_t - F(x_t' b_0)] x_t, \quad (7.135)$$

$$\hat{\beta} - \beta = (Z'Z)^{-1} Z'u = H_T^{-1}(b_0) \sum_{t=1}^{T} [y_t - F(x_t' b_0)] x_t = -\psi_T(b_0; (x, y)). $$

∎

7.4.13 Conditions for Consistency in Terms of Eigenvalues of $H_T(b_0)$

Theorem 7.4.10 and Corollary 7.4.11 supply necessary and sufficient conditions for a.s. convergence of $\hat{b}_T$ to b_0 at the rate $o(\rho_T)$. These conditions are in terms of a relatively complex function $\psi_T[b_0; (x, y)]$. Using Lemma 7.4.12 and the result by Anderson and Taylor (1979) on strong consistency of the OLS estimator, G&M obtained a simpler condition for a.s. convergence of $\hat{b}_T$ to b_0. The essence of their result is that under some circumstances the condition

$$\lim_{T \to \infty} \lambda_{1T} = \infty \quad (7.136)$$

provides a.s. convergence. That the result by Anderson and Taylor (1979) generalized by Lai and Wei (1982) allows us to prove sufficiency of Eq. (7.136) under more general conditions than in the G&M theorem (Assumption BL2 is not required in the theorem below). The next two assumptions are imposed to satisfy the conditions of the Lai and Wei theorem (Theorem 6.4.8).

7.4.13.1 *Assumption BL3* The explanatory variables x_t are deterministic.

7.4.13.2 *Assumption BL4* With some $\delta > 0$

$$(\log \lambda_{KT})^{1+\delta} = o(\lambda_{1T}), \quad \left(\frac{\log \lambda_{KT}}{\lambda_{1T}} \right)^{1/2} = o(\rho_T). \quad (7.137)$$

Theorem. (From my drawer) *If Assumptions BL3 and BL4 are satisfied and Eq. (7.136) holds, then $\hat{b}_T(x, y)$ exists a.s. and converges a.s. to b_0 at the rate $o(\rho_T)$.*

Proof. Denote $\mathcal{F}_t = \sigma(u_1, \ldots, u_t)$ the σ-field generated by $u_1, \ldots, u_t$ [for the notation see Eq. (7.132)]. By Lemma 7.4.12 $\{u_t, \mathcal{F}_t\}$ is a m.d. sequence with $\sup_t E(u_t^2 | \mathcal{F}_{t-1}) = \sup_t E u_t^2 < \infty$. z_t is deterministic and $\mathcal{F}_{t-1}$-measurable.

By Theorem 6.4.8 and Eq. (7.137)

$$\|\hat{\beta} - \beta\| = O\left(\left(\frac{\log \lambda_{KT}}{\lambda_{1T}}\right)^{1/2}\right) = o(\rho_T).$$

It remains to recall that by Lemma 7.4.12, $\hat{\beta} - \beta = -\psi_T[b_0; (x, y)]$. ∎

7.4.14 Corollary

Lemma. (Gouriéroux and Monfort, 1981, Lemma 4, sufficiency part) *Suppose Assumptions BL2 and BL3 are satisfied and condition (7.136) holds. Then the ML estimator $\hat{b}_T(x, y)$ exists a.s. and converges a.s. to b_0.*

Proof. We need to verify that Eq. (7.137) follows from the conditions of this corollary. By Assumption BL2 with some constant $c > 0$

$$\lambda_{KT} \le c\lambda_{1T}. \tag{7.138}$$

Obviously, for any $\varepsilon > 0$ there exists $c_\varepsilon > 0$ such that $\log \lambda \le \lambda^\varepsilon$ for $\lambda \ge c_\varepsilon$. Choosing $\varepsilon(1 + \delta) < 1$, by Eqs. (7.136) and (7.138) we get for all large T

$$(\log \lambda_{KT})^{1+\delta} \le \lambda_{KT}^{\varepsilon(1+\delta)} \le (c\lambda_{1T})^{\varepsilon(1+\delta)} = o(\lambda_{1T}). \tag{7.139}$$

This is the first part of Eq. (7.137). Assumption BL2 implies $\rho_T \sim 1$. Therefore the second part of Eq. (7.137) follows from Eq. (7.139):

$$\frac{\log \lambda_{KT}}{\lambda_{1T}} = \frac{o((\log \lambda_{KT})^{1+\delta})}{\lambda_{1T}} = o(1) = o(\rho_T).$$

Thus, this corollary really follows from Theorem 7.4.13. ∎

7.4.15 Example

Here is an example with one unbounded explanatory variable when Corollary 7.4.14 is not applicable and Theorem 7.4.13 is. For this example G&M established just the existence of the ML estimator (see their Remark 1 on p. 88).

EXAMPLE. Let $K = 1$, $b_0 = 1$, $x_t = \ln t$. Then

$$\hat{b}_T - b_0 = o(1/\ln T) \text{ a.s.} \tag{7.140}$$

Proof. The first several equations in the linear model asymptotically don't matter, so it suffices to find the orders of the required quantities. Thus,

$$f(x_t b_0) = \frac{e^{-\ln t}}{(1 + e^{-\ln t})^2} = \frac{1/t}{(1 + 1/t)^2} = \frac{1 + o(1)}{t},$$

$$z_t = \frac{\ln t}{\sqrt{t}}(1 + o(1)), \quad Z'Z = \sum_{t=1}^{T} \frac{\ln^2 t}{t}(1 + o(1)) \sim \ln^3 T. \quad (7.141)$$

It follows that $\lambda_{KT} = \lambda_{1T} \sim \ln^3 T$. Obviously, $M_T = \ln T$, $\rho_T = 1/\ln T$ and Assumption BL4 is satisfied:

$$(\ln \ln^3 T)^{1+\delta} = o(\ln^3 T), \quad \left(\frac{\ln \ln^3 T}{\ln^3 T}\right)^{1/2} = \left(\frac{3 \ln \ln T}{\ln T}\right)^{1/2} \frac{1}{\ln T} = o(\rho_T).$$

Application of Theorem 7.4.13 yields Eq. (7.140). ■

7.4.16 Lack of Uniform Integrability of Squared Errors

Our next goal is to provide conditions sufficient for asymptotic normality of the ML estimator. For this purpose G&M applied the theorem by Eicker (1966) for the OLS estimator for the linear model. Eicker's theorem requires uniform integrability of the squares u_t^2: $\sup_t Eu_t^2 1(u_t^2 > c) \to 0$ as $c \to \infty$. The lemma below shows that Eicker's theorem is not applicable when x_t are unbounded.

Lemma

(i) *If x_t are deterministic, then for $c > 0$*

$$Eu_t^2 1(u_t^2 > c)$$
$$= [1 - F(X_t)]1(-X_t > \ln c) + F(X_t)1(-X_t > \ln c), \quad (7.142)$$

where $X_t = x_t' b_0$.

(ii) *If, additionally, $\sup_t |X_t| = \infty$ then*

$$\sup_t Eu_t^2 1(u_t^2 > c) = 1 \text{ for any } c > 0. \quad (7.143)$$

Proof.

(i) It is convenient to collect the properties of the relevant Bernoulli variables in Table 7.1 [see Eqs. (7.102), (7.104) and (7.132)]. Based on the table data and Eq. (7.103) we note that the following equivalences hold for $c > 0$:

$$\text{if } y_t = 1 \text{ then } u_t^2 > c \iff F(X_t) < \frac{1}{1+c} \iff -X_t > \ln c$$

TABLE 7.1 Properties of Bernoulli Variables

Probabilities	Values of y_t	Values of u_t	Values of u_t^2
$F(X_t)$	1	$\dfrac{1 - F(X_t)}{\sqrt{f(X_t)}}$	$\dfrac{1 - F(X_t)}{F(X_t)}$
$1 - F(X_t)$	0	$\dfrac{-F(X_t)}{\sqrt{f(X_t)}}$	$\dfrac{F(X_t)}{1 - F(X_t)}$

and

$$\text{if } y_t = 0 \text{ then } u_t^2 > c \iff F(X_t) > \frac{c}{1+c} \iff X_t > \ln c.$$

Together with the table data these give Eq. (7.142):

$$Eu_t^2 1(u_t^2 > c) = P(y_t = 1)[u_t^2 1(u_t^2 > c)]_{y_t=1}$$

$$+ P(y_t = 0)[u_t^2 1(u_t^2 > c)]_{y_t=0}$$

$$= F(X_t)\frac{1 - F(X_t)}{F(X_t)} 1(-X_t > \ln c)$$

$$+ [1 - F(X_t)]\frac{F(X_t)}{1 - F(X_t)} 1(X_t > \ln c)$$

$$= [1 - F(X_t)]1(-X_t > \ln c) + F(X_t)1(X_t > \ln c).$$

(ii) Suppose $|X_{t_k}| \to \infty$ along a subsequence $\{t_k\}$. Then for any given $c > 0$ one has $|X_{t_k}| > \ln c$ for all large k. Since at least one of the numbers $1 - F(X_{t_k})$ or $F(X_{t_k})$ tends to 1, Eq. (7.142) implies Eq. (7.143).

∎

7.4.17 G&M Representation of the Bias

Lemma. *We have the representation*

$$H_T^{1/2}(\hat{b}_T)(\hat{b}_T - b_0) = [H_T^{1/2}(\hat{b}_T)A_T^{-1/2}][A_T^{-1/2}H_T^{1/2}(b_0)][(Z'Z)^{-1/2}Z'u], \qquad (7.144)$$

where Z and u are from Eq. (7.132),

$$A_T = \sum_{t=1}^{T} f(x_t'b_{tT}^*)x_t x_t'$$

and b_{tT}^* is some point belonging to the segment with extremities $\hat{b}_T$ and b_0.

Proof. The ML estimator $\hat{b}_T$ maximizes the log-likelihood function and, given its smoothness, is the root of the first-order condition [see Eq. (7.105)]

$$\sum_{t=1}^{T} y_t x_t = \sum_{t=1}^{T} F(x'_t \hat{b}_T) x_t.$$

Subtracting from both sides $\sum_{t=1}^{T} F(x'_t b_0) x_t$ and using Eq. (7.135) we get

$$Z'u = \sum_{t=1}^{T} [y_t - F(x'_t b_0)] x_t = \sum_{t=1}^{T} [F(x'_t \hat{b}_T) - F(x'_t b_0)] x_t.$$

Here by the finite increments formula, $F(x'_t \hat{b}_T) - F(x'_t b_0) = f(x'_t b^*_{tT}) x'_t (\hat{b}_T - b_0)$. Therefore $Z'u = A_T(\hat{b}_T - b_0)$ and

$$H_T^{1/2}(\hat{b}_T)(\hat{b}_T - b_0) = H_T^{1/2}(\hat{b}_T) A_T^{-1} H_T^{1/2}(b_0) H_T^{-1/2}(b_0) Z'u.$$

Application of the identity $Z'Z = H_T(b_0)$ [see Eq. (7.135)] finishes the proof of Eq. (7.144). ∎

7.4.18 Kadison Theorem

Let H be a Hilbert space and let $B(H)$ denote the space of all bounded operators in H. For a given set $S \subseteq \mathbb{R}$, $B(H)_S$ denotes the set of all bounded self-adjoint operators with the spectrum $\sigma(A) \subseteq S$. We are interested in conditions on a real-valued function f that provide strong continuity of $f(A)$, $A \in B(H)_S$: if $\{A_n x\}$ converges for each $x \in H$, then $\{f(A_n)x\}$ also converges for each $x \in H$. The theorem below is sufficient for our purposes:

Theorem. (Kadison, 1968, Corollary 3.7) *If S is a closed or open subset of $\mathbb{R}$, then a real-valued function defined on S is strong-operator continuous on $B(H)_S$ if and only if it is continuous on S, bounded on bounded subsets of S, and $O(x)$ at infinity.*

We need a simple case of this theorem. When $H = \mathbb{R}^n$, strong-operator continuity coincides with uniform continuity. In applications to symmetric nonnegative matrices we can put $S = [0, \infty)$ and then the desired continuity takes place if f is real-valued, continuous on $[0, \infty)$ and satisfies $f(x) = O(x)$ as $x \to \infty$.

7.4.19 Functions of Two Matrix Sequences

Lemma. *Suppose two sequences of positive, symmetric $K \times K$ matrices $\{A_T\}$, $\{B_T\}$ satisfy*

$$\sup_T \|B_T\| < \infty, \quad \|A_T - B_T\| = o(1). \tag{7.145}$$

Let f be a real-valued, continuous on $[0, \infty)$ function such that $f(x) = O(x)$ as $x \to \infty$. Then

$$\|f(A_T) - f(B_T)\| = o(1). \tag{7.146}$$

Proof.   Suppose Eq. (7.146) is wrong. Then there exist $\varepsilon > 0$ and a sequence $\{T_k\}$ such that

$$\|f(A_{T_k}) - f(B_{T_k})\| \geq \varepsilon \text{ for all } k. \tag{7.147}$$

A bounded sequence $\{B_{T_k}\}$ contains a convergent subsequence $\{B_{T_{k_n}}\}$ such that $\|B_{T_{k_n}} - B\| \to 0$ as $n \to \infty$ for some B. Hence, by Eq. (7.145) $\|A_{T_{k_n}} - B\| = o(1)$. The Kadison theorem implies

$$\|f(A_{T_{k_n}}) - f(B)\| = o(1), \ \|f(B_{T_{k_n}}) - f(B)\| = o(1)$$

and, consequently, $\|f(A_{T_{k_n}}) - f(B_{T_{k_n}})\| = o(1)$. This contradicts Eq. (7.147) and proves the statement. ∎

7.4.20   Convergence of the Elements of the G&M Representation

7.4.20.1   *Assumption BL5*   The ML estimator $\hat{b}_T$ is consistent in the sense that $\hat{b}_T - b_0 = o(\rho_T)$ a.s.

    If necessary, this assumption can be replaced by sufficient conditions from Theorem 7.4.13.

7.4.20.2   *Assumption BL6*   The largest and smallest eigenvalues of $H_T(b_0)$ are of the same order: $\sup_T \lambda_{KT}/\lambda_{1T} < \infty$.

Lemma.   *If Assumptions BL5 and BL6 hold, then*

$$A_T^{-1/2} H_T^{1/2}(b_0) \overset{a.s}{\to} I, \ H_T^{1/2}(\hat{b}_T) A_T^{-1/2} \overset{a.s}{\to} I. \tag{7.148}$$

Proof.   Let us prove the first relation in Eq. (7.148). Denote

$$\alpha_{tT} = |f(x_t'b_0) - f(x_t'b_{tT}^*)|, \ \beta_{tT} = 4\|\hat{b}_T - b_0\| M_T e^{\|\hat{b}_T - b_0\| M_T} f(x_t'b_0).$$

By Lemma 7.4.5 and the inequality $\|b_{tT}^* - b_0\| \leq \|\hat{b}_T - b_0\|$ we have $\alpha_{tT} \leq \beta_{tT}$. Then, similarly to Eq. (7.118) with $G(b_T^*) = \text{diag}[\,f(x_1'b_{1T}^*), \ldots, f(x_T'b_{TT}^*)]$, we get

$$\|H_T(b_0) - A_T\| = \|X[G(b_0) - G(b_T^*)]X'\|$$

$$\leq 4\|\hat{b}_T - b_0\| M_T e^{\|\hat{b}_T - b_0\| M_T} \lambda_{KT}. \tag{7.149}$$

By Assumption BL5 and definition (7.127)

$$\|\hat{b}_T - b_0\| M_T = o(\lambda_{1T}/\lambda_{KT}) = o(1). \qquad (7.150)$$

Equations (7.149) and (7.150) lead to

$$\|H_T(b_0)/\lambda_{KT} - A_T/\lambda_{KT}\| \le 4\|\hat{b}_T - b_0\| M_T e^{\|\hat{b}_T - b_0\| M_T} = o(1).$$

By Lemma 7.4.19, in which we put $B_T = H_T(b_0)/\lambda_{KT}$ and $f(x) = x^{1/2}$, this implies $\|(H_T(b_0)/\lambda_{KT})^{1/2} - (A_T/\lambda_{KT})^{1/2}\| = o(1)$ or

$$\|H_T^{1/2}(b_0) - A_T^{1/2}\| = o(\lambda_{KT}^{1/2}). \qquad (7.151)$$

We also need to bound $\|A_T^{-1/2}\|$. Owing to equations (7.149) and (7.150), $\|H_T(b_0) - A_T\| = o(\lambda_{1T})$. It follows that

$$\lambda_{\min}(A_T z, z) = \inf_{\|z\|=1} (A_T z, z) = \lambda_{\min}(H_T(b_0))(1 + o(1))$$

and that

$$\|A_T^{-1/2}\| \le 2\lambda_{1T}^{-1/2} \text{ for large } T. \qquad (7.152)$$

Now we combine Eqs. (7.151) and (7.152) and Assumption BL6 to get

$$\|A_T^{-1/2} H_T^{1/2}(b_0) - I\| \le \|A_T^{-1/2}\| \|H_T^{1/2}(b_0) - A_T^{1/2}\|$$
$$= o((\lambda_{KT}/\lambda_{1T})^{1/2}) = o(1) \text{ a.s.}$$

This is the first relation in Eq. (7.148). Replacing in the definition of α_{tT} the vector b_0 by $\hat{b}_T$ and making the necessary changes in the subsequent calculations, instead of Eq. (7.151) we obtain $\|H_T^{1/2}(\hat{b}_T) - A_T^{1/2}\| = o(\lambda_{KT}^{1/2})$. Combining this bound with Eq. (7.152), as above, we finish the proof of the second relation in Eq. (7.148). ∎

7.4.21 Asymptotic Normality of the Maximum Likelihood Estimator

Denote

$$\gamma_{Tt} = \|(Z'Z)^{-1/2} z_t'\|^2 = z_t(Z'Z)^{-1} z_t' = x_t' H_T^{-1}(b_0) x_t f(x_t' b_0), \quad t = 1, \ldots, T$$

and

$$\delta_T(\varepsilon) = \sum_{|x_t'b_0| > \log(\varepsilon^2/\gamma_{Tt})} \gamma_{Tt}, \quad \varepsilon > 0.$$

7.4.21.1 Assumption BL7 $\lim_{T \to \infty} \delta_T(\varepsilon) = 0$ for all $\varepsilon > 0$.

Theorem. (From my drawer) *If Assumptions BL3, BL5, BL6, BL7 and the condition* $\lim \lambda_{1T} = \infty$ *are satisfied, then*

$$H_T^{1/2}(\hat{b}_T)(\hat{b}_T - b_0) \xrightarrow{d} N(0, I), \quad T \to \infty. \tag{7.153}$$

Proof. In view of the representation (7.144), in which the first two factors in square brackets satisfy Eq. (7.148), we have to show that

$$(Z'Z)^{-1/2}Z'u \xrightarrow{d} N(0, I), \quad T \to \infty. \tag{7.154}$$

By the Cramér–Wold theorem (Theorem 3.1.53), Eq. (7.154) follows, if we prove

$$a'(Z'Z)^{-1/2}Z'u \xrightarrow{d} N(0, a'a), \quad T \to \infty, \tag{7.155}$$

for any $a \in \mathbb{R}^K$, $a \neq 0$. Denote

$$X_{Tt} = \frac{1}{\|a\|}a'(Z'Z)^{-1/2}z_t'u_t, \quad S_T = \sum_{t=1}^{T} X_{Tt} = \frac{1}{\|a\|}a'(Z'Z)^{-1/2}Z'u.$$

X_{Tt} are independent and by Eq. (7.134)

$$EX_{Tt} = \frac{1}{\|a\|}a'(Z'Z)^{-1/2}z_t'Eu_t = 0,$$

$$ES_T^2 = \frac{1}{\|a\|^2}E\left\{a'(Z'Z)^{-1/2}Z'u\left[a'(Z'Z)^{-1/2}Z'u\right]'\right\}$$

$$= \frac{1}{\|a\|^2}a'(Z'Z)^{-1/2}Z'(Euu')Z(Z'Z)^{-1/2}a = 1.$$

By the Lindeberg theorem (Davidson, 1994, p. 369) to prove Eq. (7.155) it is enough to prove that $L_T(\varepsilon) \to 0$ as $T \to \infty$, for all $\varepsilon > 0$, where

$$L_T(\varepsilon) = \sum_{t=1}^{T} EX_{Tt}^2 1(|X_{Tt}| > \varepsilon)$$

is the *Lindeberg function.* Denoting $\tilde{\gamma}_{Tt} = [a'(Z'Z)^{-1/2}z_t'/\|a\|]^2$ we have

$$\tilde{\gamma}_{Tt} \leq \left[\frac{\|a\|}{\|a\|}\left\|(Z'Z)^{-1/2}z_t'\right\|\right]^2 = \gamma_{Tt}, \quad X_{Tt}^2 = \tilde{\gamma}_{Tt}\,u_t^2 \tag{7.156}$$

and

$$L_T(\varepsilon) = \sum_{t=1}^{T} \tilde{\gamma}_{Tt}\,Eu_t^2 1(u_t^2 > \varepsilon^2/\tilde{\gamma}_{Tt}). \tag{7.157}$$

Equation (7.142) yields

$$Eu_t^2 1(u_t^2 > c) \leq [1 - F(X_t)]1(|X_t| > \ln c) + F(X_t)1(|X_t| > \ln c)$$
$$= 1(|x_t'b_0| > \ln c). \tag{7.158}$$

Now Eqs. (7.156)–(7.158) and Assumption BL7 lead to

$$L_T(\varepsilon) \leq \sum_{t=1}^{T} \gamma_{Tt}Eu_t^2 1(u_t^2 > \varepsilon^2/\gamma_{Tt})$$

$$\leq \sum_{t=1}^{T} \gamma_{Tt}1(|x_t'b_0| > \ln(\varepsilon^2/\gamma_{Tt})) = \delta_T(\varepsilon) \to 0, \quad T \to \infty,$$

for any $\varepsilon > 0$. Application of the Lindeberg theorem completes the proof of Eq. (7.155). ∎

7.4.22 Corollary

Lemma. (Gouriéroux and Monfort, 1981, Proposition 4) *If the explanatory variables satisfy Assumptions BL2 and BL3, the smallest eigenvalue of $H_T(b_0)$ goes to infinity and $\max_{1\leq t\leq T}\gamma_{Tt} \to 0$, then Eq. (7.153) is true.*

Proof. Under Assumption BL2, $\rho_T \sim 1$. By Corollary 7.4.14 $\hat{b}_T$ converges to b_0 a.s., so Assumption BL5 is satisfied with $\rho_T = 1$. Assumption BL6 is a part of BL2. Thus, to apply Theorem 7.4.21 we have to verify Assumption BL7. Take any $\varepsilon > 0$ and choose $\delta > 0$ so small that $\log(\varepsilon^2/\delta) > M\|b_0\|$, where $M = \sup_t \|x_t\|$. Let $T(\delta)$ be so large that $\max_t \gamma_{Tt} \leq \delta$ for $T \geq T(\delta)$. Then

$$|x_t'b_0| \leq M\|b_0\| < \log\left(\frac{\varepsilon^2}{\delta}\right) \leq \log\left(\frac{\varepsilon^2}{\gamma_{Tt}}\right), \quad \delta_T(\varepsilon) = 0 \text{ for } T \geq T(\delta).$$

∎

7.4.23 Example

Here is an example that satisfies the conditions of Theorem 7.4.21 but not Corollary 7.4.22.

EXAMPLE.   For K, b_0 and x_t from Example 7.4.15 one has

$$\gamma_{Tt} \sim \frac{\ln^2 t}{t \ln^3 T}, \quad \delta_T(\varepsilon) \longrightarrow 0 \quad \text{for all } \varepsilon > 0 \qquad (7.159)$$

and asymptotic normality (7.153) is true.

Proof.   From Example 7.4.15 we know that Assumption BL4 is satisfied and condition (7.136) holds. Therefore by Theorem 7.4.13, Assumption BL5 is satisfied (BL6 is trivial). To apply Theorem 7.4.21, it remains to check Assumption BL7. The expression for γ_{Tt} in Eq. (7.159) follows from Eq. (7.141). $\delta_T(\varepsilon)$ can only increase if summation over t such that $|x_t'b_0| > \log(\varepsilon^2 / \gamma_{Tt})$ is replaced by summation over t satisfying $e^{M\|b_0\|} > \varepsilon^2 / \gamma_{Tt}$. Hence,

$$\delta_T(\varepsilon) \leq c_1 \sum_{t/\ln^2 t \leq c_2/(\varepsilon^2 \ln^3 T)} \frac{\ln^2 t}{t \ln^3 T}.$$

Here the summation can be done over $\tau_T = \{t: t \geq t_0, \ t/\ln^2 t \leq c_2(\varepsilon^2 \ln^3 T)\}$ because the first several observations don't matter. The function $f(t) = t/\ln^2 t$ has a positive minimum on $[t_0, \infty)$, so for large T $\tau_T = \emptyset$ and $\delta_T(\varepsilon) = 0$.   ∎

CHAPTER 8

TOOLS FOR VECTOR AUTOREGRESSIONS

IN THIS chapter we find some technical results that proved useful in the study of VARs. The first part (Sections 8.1–8.4) is from my work. It describes algebraic properties of L_p-approximable sequences (e.g., how they can be added and multiplied). The second part (Section 8.5) is devoted to a different notion of deterministic trends originated in Johansen (2000) and developed further in Nielsen (2005). Unlike simpler approaches (e.g., polynomial and logarithmic trends), it allows us to consider periodic (seasonal) trends. The Nielsen paper contains very deep results on strong consistency of the OLS estimator for VARs with deterministic trends. My initial intention was to cover all Nielsen's results but then I realized that they would require another book.

8.1 L_p-APPROXIMABLE SEQUENCES OF MATRIX-VALUED FUNCTIONS

In this section some results from Chapter 2 concerning sequences of vectors are generalized to sequences of matrices, so as to satisfy the needs of the theory of VARs.

8.1.1 Matrix-Valued Functions

By replacing real numbers $x_1, \ldots, x_n$ with matrices $X_1, \ldots, X_n$ in the vector $x = (x_1, \ldots, x_n)$ we arrive at the following definitions. Let $\mathbb{M}_p$ denote the set of all matrices (of different sizes) equipped with the norm $\| \cdot \|_p$. Denote $\tau_n = \{1, \ldots, n\}$. $l_p(\tau_n, \mathbb{M}_p)$ stands for the set of matrix-valued functions $X \colon \tau_n \to \mathbb{M}_p$ provided with the norm

$$\|X; l_p(\tau_n, \mathbb{M}_p)\| = \begin{cases} \left(\sum_{t=1}^n \|X_t\|_p^p \right)^{1/p}, & p < \infty. \\ \max_{t=1,\ldots,n} \|X_t\|_\infty, & p = \infty. \end{cases}$$

Short-Memory Linear Processes and Econometric Applications. Kairat T. Mynbaev
© 2011 John Wiley & Sons, Inc. Published 2011 by John Wiley & Sons, Inc.

The *size* $s(A)$ of a matrix A is defined as the product of its dimensions. We consider only functions X with values X_t of the same size $s(X)$ (which may vary with X). Usual matrix algebra conventions are followed: all vectors are column vectors and all matrices in the same formula are assumed to be compatible.

8.1.2   Definition of L_p-Approximability

Let $X \in l_p(\tau_n, \mathbb{M}_p)$ be a matrix-valued function. X_{tij} denotes the (i, j)th element of X_t. For a fixed pair (i, j), the vector $T_{ij}(X) = (X_{1ij}, \ldots, X_{nij})'$ is called an (i, j)-*thread* of X or just a *thread* when the pair (i, j) is clear from the context.

Consider a sequence $\{X_n : n \in \mathbb{N}\}$ of matrix-valued functions of equal sizes $s(X_1) = s(X_2) = \cdots$. We say that $\{X_n\}$ is L_p-*approximable* if for each (i, j) the sequence of (i, j)-threads $\{T_{ij}(X_n) : n \in \mathbb{N}\}$ is L_p-approximable in the sense of Section 2.5.1. This means existence of functions $X_{ij}^c \in L_p$ satisfying $\|T_{ij}(X_n) - \delta_{np}X_{ij}^c\|_p \to 0$ for any (i, j). Applying δ_{np} element-wise to the matrix X^c composed of X_{ij}^c, we equivalently write

$$\|X_n - \delta_{np}X^c; l_p(\tau_n, \mathbb{M}_p)\| \longrightarrow 0, \quad n \longrightarrow \infty.$$

When this is true, we say that $\{X_n\}$ is L_p-*close* to X^c.

8.1.3   Convergence of Trilinear Forms

Here we generalize Lemma 2.2.2 to the case of three factors. We write $Z^c \in C[0, 1]$ if all components of the matrix Z^c belong to the space $C[0, 1]$. The notation $X^c \in L_p$ has a similar meaning.

Theorem.   *Let $1 < p < \infty$. Consider sequences of matrix-valued functions $\{X_n\}$, $\{Y_n\}$, $\{Z_n\}$ such that X_n, Y_n, Z_n are defined on τ_n for all $n \in \mathbb{N}$. Suppose $\{X_n\}$ is L_p-close to $X^c \in L_p$, $\{Y_n\}$ is L_q-close to $Y^c \in L_q$ and $\{Z_n\}$ is L_∞-close to $Z^c \in C[0, 1]$. Then*

$$\lim_{n \to \infty} \sum_{t=1}^{n} X_{nt}Y_{nt}Z_{nt} = \int_0^1 X^c(x)Y^c(x)Z^c(x)\, dx. \tag{8.1}$$

Proof.

Step 1. Let X^c, Y^c, Z^c be scalar functions. Generalizing Eq. (2.6) we get

$$\int_0^1 (P_n X^c)(P_n Y^c)(P_n Z^c)\, dx = \sum_{t=1}^{n} (\delta_{np}X^c)_t (\delta_{nq}Y^c)_t (\delta_{n\infty}Z^c)_t. \tag{8.2}$$

Further,

$$\left| \int_0^1 (P_n X^c)(P_n Y^c)(P_n Z^c)\, dx - \int_0^1 X^c Y^c Z^c\, dx \right|$$

$$= \left| \int_0^1 (P_n X^c - X^c)(P_n Y^c)(P_n Z^c)\, dx + \int_0^1 X^c (P_n Y^c - Y^c)(P_n Z^c)\, dx \right.$$

$$\left. + \int_0^1 X^c Y^c (P_n Z^c - Z^c)\, dx \right|$$

$$\leq \| P_n X^c - X^c \|_p \| P_n Y^c \|_q \| P_n Z^c \|_\infty + \| X^c \|_p \| P_n Y^c - Y^c \|_q \| P_n Z^c \|_\infty$$

$$+ \| X^c \|_p \| Y^c \|_q \| P_n Z^c - Z^c \|_\infty. \tag{8.3}$$

In the case of X^c and Y^c we can apply boundedness of Haar projectors (Lemma 2.1.7) and their convergence to the identity operator in L_p, $p < \infty$ (Lemma 2.2.1). For Z^c we use uniform continuity:

$$\| P_n Z^c - Z^c \|_\infty = \max_{1 \leq t \leq n} \max_{y \in i_t} \left| n \int_{i_t} Z^c(x)\, dx - Z^c(y) \right|$$

$$= \max_{1 \leq t \leq n} \max_{y \in i_t} \left| n \int_{i_t} (Z^c(x) - Z^c(y))\, dx \right|$$

$$\leq \sup_{|x-y| \leq 1/n} | Z^c(x) - Z^c(y) | \longrightarrow 0, \quad n \longrightarrow \infty.$$

Now Eqs. (8.2) and (8.3) lead to

$$\lim_{n \to \infty} \sum_{t=1}^n (\delta_{np} X^c)_t (\delta_{nq} Y^c)_t (\delta_{n\infty} Z^c)_t = \int_0^1 X^c(x) Y^c(x) Z^c(x)\, dx.$$

The limit at the left equals $\lim_{n \to \infty} \sum_{t=1}^n X_{nt} Y_{nt} Z_{nt}$ because

$$\left| \sum_{t=1}^n X_{nt} Y_{nt} Z_{nt} - \sum_{t=1}^n (\delta_{np} X^c)_t (\delta_{nq} Y^c)_t (\delta_{n\infty} Z^c)_t \right|$$

$$\leq \| X_n - \delta_{np} X^c \|_p \| Y_n \|_q \| Z_n \|_\infty + \| \delta_{np} X^c \|_p \| Y_n - \delta_{nq} Y^c \|_q \| Z_n \|_\infty$$

$$+ \| \delta_{np} X^c \|_p \| \delta_{nq} Y^c \|_q \| Z_n - \delta_{n\infty} Z^c \|_\infty \longrightarrow 0.$$

Here we have used the L_p-approximability assumption of the theorem and boundedness of the discretization operator (Lemma 2.1.3). The statement in the case under consideration has been proved.

Step 2. In the matrix case the matrix products at the left and right of Eq. (8.1) have elements

$$\sum_{u,v} (X_{nt})_{iu}(Y_{nt})_{uv}(Z_{nt})_{vj} \quad \text{and} \quad \sum_{u,v} X^c_{iu}Y^c_{uv}Z^c_{vj}. \qquad (8.4)$$

This means that the matrix version of Eq. (8.1) can be obtained by applying its scalar sibling to triplets of threads [the (i, u)-thread of X_n, (u, v)-thread of Y_n and (v, j)-thread of Z_n] and summing the resulting equations over all pairs (u, v). ∎

8.1.4 Refined Convergence of Trilinear Forms

Theorem. *Under the conditions of Theorem 8.1.3*

$$\lim_{n\to\infty} \sum_{t=[na]}^{[nb]} X_{nt}Y_{nt}Z_{nt} = \int_a^b X^c(x)Y^c(x)Z^c(x)\,dx$$

uniformly with respect to the intervals $[a, b] \subseteq [0, 1]$.

Proof. Since the result is not used in this book, only the main steps of the proof are indicated. Similarly to Eq. (2.7) we can obtain

$$\left| \int_0^1 P_nF \cdot P_nG \cdot P_nH\,dx - \int_0^1 FGH\,dx \right| \le c[\omega_p(F, 1/n)\|G\|_q\|H\|_\infty$$

$$+ \|F\|_p\omega_q(G, 1/n)\|H\|_\infty$$

$$+ \|F\|_p\|G\|_q\|P_nH - H\|_\infty].$$

Letting $F = 1_{[a,b]}X^c$, $G = 1_{[a,b]}Y^c$ and $H = Z^c$ and arguing as in the proof of Theorem 2.2.3, it is possible to get

$$\lim_{n\to\infty} \sum_{t=1}^n [\delta_{np}(1_{[a,b]}X^c)]_t[\delta_{nq}(1_{[a,b]}Y^c)]_t(\delta_{n\infty}Z^c)_t = \int_a^b X^c(x)Y^c(x)Z^c(x)\,dx.$$

The proof in the scalar case is completed by making obvious changes in the proof of Theorem 2.5.3. The generalization to the matrix case is straightforward. ∎

8.2   *T*-OPERATOR AND TRINITY

8.2.1   *T*-Operator Definition (Matrix Case)

The definition of the convolution operator from Section 2.3.1 needs to be modified to take into account the possibility of pre- and postmultiplication. $l_p(\mathbb{Z}, \mathbb{M}_p)$ is obtained from $l_p(\tau_n, \mathbb{M}_p)$ by way of replacing τ_n with $\mathbb{Z}$. Let $\{\psi_s^l : s \in \mathbb{Z}\}$ and $\{\psi_s^r : s \in \mathbb{Z}\}$ be two sequences of matrices intended for multiplication from the left and right, respectively. The *T-operator* $^lT_n^r : l_p(\tau_n, \mathbb{M}_p) \to l_p(\mathbb{Z}, \mathbb{M}_p)$ is defined by

$$(^lT_n^r X)_j = \sum_{t=1}^{n} \psi_{t-j}^l X_t \psi_{t-j}^r, \quad j \in \mathbb{Z}.$$

8.2.2   The Adjoint of $^lT_n^r$

Define $(^lT_n^r)^*$ by

$$[(^lT_n^r)^* X]_j = \sum_{t=1}^{n} \psi_{j-t}^r X_t \psi_{j-t}^l, \quad j \in \mathbb{Z}.$$

The formula $\langle X, Y \rangle = \operatorname{tr} \sum_{t=1}^{n} X_j Y_j$ defines a bilinear form with the argument (X, Y) from the product $l_p(\tau_n, \mathbb{M}_p) \times l_q(\tau_n, \mathbb{M}_q)$ because

$$\left| \operatorname{tr} \sum_{j=1}^{n} X_j Y_j \right| = \left| \sum_i \sum_{j=1}^{n} (X_j Y_j)_{ii} \right| = \left| \sum_i \sum_{j=1}^{n} \sum_u (X_j)_{iu} (Y_j)_{ui} \right|$$

$$\leq \sum_{j=1}^{n} \|X_j\|_p \|Y_j\|_q \leq \|X; l_p(\tau_n, \mathbb{M}_p)\| \|Y; l_q(\tau_n, \mathbb{M}_q)\|.$$

Lemma.   *The operator* $(^lT_n^r)^*$ *is the adjoint of* $^lT_n^r$ *in the sense that*

$$\langle ^lT_n^r X, Y \rangle = \langle X, (^lT_n^r)^* Y \rangle.$$

Proof.   Whenever the products AB and BA are square, the equation

$$\operatorname{tr} AB = \operatorname{tr} BA \qquad (8.5)$$

is true (see Lütkepohl, 1991, Section A.7). Change the summation order:

$$\operatorname{tr} \sum_{j=1}^{n} (^lT_n^r X)_j Y_j = \operatorname{tr} \sum_{j=1}^{n} \sum_{t=1}^{n} \psi_{t-j}^l X_t \psi_{t-j}^r Y_j$$

$$= \operatorname{tr} \sum_{t=1}^{n} X_t \left(\sum_{j=1}^{n} \psi_{t-j}^r Y_j \psi_{t-j}^l \right) = \operatorname{tr} \sum_{t=1}^{n} X_t [(^lT_n^r)^* Y]_t. \qquad \blacksquare$$

8.2.3   Boundedness of $'T_n^r$

Denote

$$\alpha_\psi = \sum_{s \in \mathbb{Z}} \|\psi_s^l\|_\infty \|\psi_s^r\|_\infty.$$

Lemma.   *If $\alpha_\psi < \infty$, then $\|'T_n^r X; l_p(\mathbb{Z}, \mathbb{M}_p)\| \le \alpha_\psi \|X; l_p(\tau_n, \mathbb{M}_p)\|$.*

Proof.   Denoting $x_t = \|X_t\|_p$, $x = (x_1, \ldots, x_n)$, $\bar{\psi}_s = \|\psi_s^l\|_\infty \|\psi_s^r\|_\infty$ we have

$$\|('T_n^r X)_j\|_p \le c \sum_{t=1}^n \|\psi_{t-j}^l\|_\infty \|X_t\|_p \|\psi_{t-j}^r\|_\infty$$

$$= c \sum_{t=1}^n x_t \bar{\psi}_{t-j} = (T_n x)_j.$$

Here c depends only on the sizes of the matrices involved. Hence, by Lemma 2.3.2

$$\left(\sum_{j \in \mathbb{Z}} \|('T_n^r X)_j\|_p^p \right)^{1/p} \le c \left(\sum_{j \in \mathbb{Z}} |(T_n x)_j|^p \right)^{1/p} = c\|T_n x\|_{l_p(\mathbb{Z})}$$

$$\le c\alpha_{\bar\psi}\|x\|_p = c\alpha_\psi \left(\sum_{t=1}^n \|X_t\|_p^p \right)^{1/p}.$$ ∎

8.2.4   The Trinity and L_p-Approximable Sequences (Matrix Case)

Here, to conserve notation, we omit the superscripts l and r and denote

$$(T_n^+ X)_j = (T_n X)_j, \quad j > n; (T_n^0 X)_j = (T_n X)_j, \ 1 \le j \le n;$$
$$(T_n^- X)_j = (T_n X)_j, \quad j < 1;$$
$$B_\psi X = \sum_{s \in \mathbb{Z}} \psi_s^l X \psi_s^r.$$

Besides, the norms in $l_p(\tau_n, \mathbb{M}_p)$, $l_p(\{j < 1\}, \mathbb{M}_p)$ and $l_p(\{j > n\}, \mathbb{M}_p)$ are denoted simply $\| \cdot \|_p$.

Theorem.   *If $\alpha_\psi < \infty$, $p < \infty$ and $\{X_n\}$ is L_p-close to $X^c \in L_p$, then*

$$\lim_{n \to \infty} \max\{ \|T_n^0 X_n - B_\psi X_n\|_p, \|T_n^- X_n\|_p, \|T_n^+ X_n\|_p \} = 0. \tag{8.6}$$

Moreover, $\{T_n^0 X_n\}$ is L_p-close to $B_\psi X^c \in L_p$.

Proof. From the generic expression (8.4) for the (i, j)th element of a product of three matrices we see that the tth coordinate of the (i, j)-thread of $T_n^0 X_n - \beta_\psi X_n$ equals

$$\sum_{s=1}^{n} \sum_{u,v} (\psi_{s-t}^l)_{iu} (X_{ns})_{uv} (\psi_{s-t}^r)_{vj} - \sum_{s\in\mathbb{Z}} \sum_{u,v} (\psi_s^l)_{iu} (X_{nt})_{uv} (\psi_s^r)_{vj}$$

$$= \sum_{u,v} \left[\sum_{s=1}^{n} (\psi_{s-t}^l)_{iu} (\psi_{s-t}^r)_{vj} (X_{ns})_{uv} - \sum_{s\in\mathbb{Z}} (\psi_s^l)_{iu} (\psi_s^r)_{vj} (X_{nt})_{uv} \right].$$

The expression in the brackets here is of the type considered in Section 2.5.4 with

$$\bar{\psi}_t = (\psi_t^l)_{iu} (\psi_t^r)_{vj}, \quad \beta_{\bar{\psi}} = \sum_{s\in\mathbb{Z}} \bar{\psi}_s.$$

Since the summation over (u, v) is finite, the L_p-norm of the (i, j)-thread of $T_n^0 X_n - \beta_\psi X_n$ tends to zero. As the number of threads is finite, we have $\|T_n^0 X_n - \beta_\psi X_n\|_p \to 0$. The other two relations in Eq. (8.6) are proved similarly.

The final statement of the theorem follows from L_p-approximability of $\{X_n\}$:

$$\|T_n^0 X_n - \delta_{np} \beta_\psi X^c\|_p \le \|T_n^0 X_n - \beta_\psi X_n\|_p + \|\beta_\psi (X_n - \delta_{np} X^c)\|_p \longrightarrow 0. \quad \blacksquare$$

8.2.5 Shift Operators

The *backward shift* (or *lag*) operator L^- and *forward shift* operator L^+ are defined by

$$(L^- X)_t = X_{t-1}, \, 2 \le t \le n, \, (L^- X)_1 = 0,$$
$$(L^+ X)_t = X_{t+1}, \, 1 \le t \le n-1, \, (L^+ X)_n = 0,$$

where $X \in l_p(\tau_n, \mathbb{M}_p)$.

Lemma. *If $\{X_n\}$ is L_p-close to $X^c \in L_p$ and $p < \infty$, then $\{L^{\pm} X_n\}$ are L_p-close to X^c.*

Proof. The lag operator obtains from $^l T_n^r$ if we choose $\psi_{-1}^l = I, \psi_s^l = 0$ for $s \ne -1$, $\psi_s^r = I$ for all s. A similar choice works for L^+. Thus the statement follows from the previous theorem. $\quad \blacksquare$

8.3 MATRIX OPERATIONS AND L_p-APPROXIMABILITY

8.3.1 Transposition and Summation of L_p-Approximable Sequences

By definition, the *transposed* matrix-valued function X' has values X_t', $t = 1, \ldots, n$. A *sum* of two functions X, Y is defined as the function with values $X_t + Y_t$.

Theorem. Let $\{X_n\}$ be L_p-close to $X^c \in L_p$. Then

  (i) $\{X_n'\}$ is L_p-close to $(X^c)'$,

  (ii) if $\{Y_n\}$ is L_p-close to $Y^c \in L_p$, then $\{X_n + Y_n\}$ is L_p-close to $X^c + Y^c$.

Proof. Statement

  (i) is obvious because transposition does not change $\| \cdot \|_p$-norms of matrices:
  $$\|X_n' - \delta_{np}(X^c)'\|_p = \|X_n - \delta_{np}X^c\|_p \to 0,$$

  (ii) follows from the triangle inequality:

$$\|(X_n + Y_n) - \delta_{np}(X_n + Y_n)\|_p \leq \|X_n - \delta_{np}X^c\|_p + \|Y_n - \delta_{np}Y^c\|_p \longrightarrow 0. \qquad \blacksquare$$

8.3.2 Multiplication of L_p-Approximable Sequences

A *product* of two functions X, Y is defined as the function with values $X_t Y_t$. The argument here is similar to that in Section 7.2.6.

Theorem. If $\{X_n\}$ is L_p-close to $X^c \in L_p$ and $\{Y_n\}$ is L_∞-close to $Y^c \in C[0, 1]$, then $\{X_n Y_n\}$ is L_p-close to $X^c Y^c$.

Proof.

Step 1. Consider the scalar case. The fact that $\{Y_n\}$ is L_∞-close to Y^c means that for any $\varepsilon > 0$ there is $n_0 > 0$ such that for $n > n_0$

$$\max_t |Y_{nt} - (\delta_{n\infty}Y^c)_t| < \varepsilon.$$

Since Y^c is uniformly continuous, we can also assert that

$$\max_t \max_{x,y \in i_t} |Y^c(x) - Y^c(y)| < \varepsilon,$$

increasing, if necessary, n_0. Therefore for all t

$$\left| Y_{nt} - Y^c\left(\frac{t}{n}\right) \right| = \left| Y_{nt} - (\delta_{n\infty}Y^c)_t + n\int_{i_t} Y^c(x)\, dx - Y^c\left(\frac{t}{n}\right) \right|$$

$$\leq |Y_{nt} - (\delta_{n\infty}Y^c)_t| + n\int_{i_t} \left| Y^c(x) - Y^c\left(\frac{t}{n}\right) \right| dx$$

$$\leq 2\varepsilon. \tag{8.7}$$

It follows that

$$|X_{nt}Y_{nt} - (\delta_{np}X^cY^c)_t| \leq \left| X_{nt}\left[Y_{nt} - Y^c\left(\frac{t}{n}\right) \right] \right| + \left| (X_{nt} - (\delta_{np}X^c)_t)Y^c\left(\frac{t}{n}\right) \right|$$

$$+ \left| \left\{ \delta_{np}\left[X^c(\cdot)\left(Y^c(\cdot) - Y^c\left(\frac{t}{n}\right) \right) \right] \right\}_t \right|$$

$$\leq 2\varepsilon|X_{nt}| + \max_{x\in[0,1]} |Y^c(x)||X_{nt} - (\delta_{np}X^c)_t| + \varepsilon(\delta_{np}|X^c|)_t.$$

Taking L_p-norms on both sides we get

$$\|X_nY_n - \delta_{np}X^cY^c\|_p \leq 2\varepsilon\|X_n\|_p + \max_{x\in[0,1]} |Y^c(x)|\|X_n - \delta_{np}X^c\|_p$$

$$+ \varepsilon\|\delta_{np}|X^c|\|_p.$$

Recalling that δ_{np} is bounded (Section 2.1.3) and $\|X_n - \delta_{np}X^c\|_p \to 0$ we see that the right-hand side here can be made arbitrarily small by increasing n.

Step 2. In the matrix case we note that the (i, j)-thread of $X_nY_n - \delta_{np}X^cY^c$ has the tth component equal to

$$(X_nY_n)_{tij} - (\delta_{np}X^cY^c)_{tij} = \sum_u \{(X_{nt})_{iu}(Y_{nt})_{uj} - [\delta_{np}(X^c)_{iu}(Y^c)_{uj}]\}.$$

Here $\{(X_{nt})_{iu} : t \in \tau_n\}$ is L_p-close to $(X^c)_{iu}$ and $\{(Y_{nt})_{uj} : t \in \tau_n\}$ is L_∞-close to $(Y^c)_{uj}$, so the expression in the curly brackets tends to 0 in L_p-norm. Since the summation over u is finite, the theorem follows. ∎

8.3.3 Functions with Constant Matrix Values

We say that a matrix-valued function $Y: \tau_n \to \mathbb{M}_p$ is *constant* if $Y_t = A$, $t = 1, \ldots, n$.

Theorem

(i) *If $\{X_n\}$ is L_∞-close to $X^c \in L_\infty$, then $\{n^{-1/p}X_n\}$ is L_p-close to X^c.*

(ii) *If $\{X_n\}$ is L_p-close to $X^c \in L_p$ and $\{Y_n\}$ is a sequence of constant functions with values $A_n \to A$, then $\{X_n + n^{-1/p}Y_n\}$ is L_p-close to $X^c + A$ and $\{X_n Y_n\}$ is L_p-close to $X^c A$.*

Proof.

(i) Since

$$\|n^{-1/p}X_n - \delta_{np}X^c\|_p = \left(\sum_{i,j} \sum_{t=1}^{n} \left| n^{-1/p}(X_{nt})_{ij} - (\delta_{np}X^c)_{tij} \right|^p \right)^{1/p},$$

it suffices to prove the statement for threads. Obviously,

$$\sum_{t=1}^{n} \left| n^{-1/p}(X_{nt})_{ij} - (\delta_{np}X^c)_{tij} \right|^p = \sum_{t=1}^{n} \left| n^{-1/p}(X_{nt})_{ij} - n^{1-1/p} \int_{i_t} X^c(x)\,dx \right|^p$$

$$\leq n \max_t \frac{1}{n} \left| (X_{nt})_{ij} - n \int_{i_t} X^c(x)\,dx \right|^p$$

$$\leq \|X_n - \delta_{n\infty}X^c; \quad l_\infty(\tau_n, \mathbb{M}_\infty)\|^p \longrightarrow 0.$$

(ii) This statement follows from part (i) of this theorem and Theorems 8.3.1 (ii) and 8.3.2. ∎

8.4 RESOLVENTS

8.4.1 Definition of Resolvents

As time series autoregressions are difference equations, difference equations resolvents should play a special role in the theory of autoregressions. Here we look at examples of three resolvents.

With a square matrix B we can associate an operator

$$(l_B X)_t = \begin{cases} \sum_{s=1}^{t-1} B^{t-1-s}X_s, & 2 \leq t \leq n, \\ 0, & t = 1, \end{cases} \qquad X \in l_p(\tau_n, \mathbb{M}_p).$$

It is easy to check that $l_B X$ satisfies the difference equation

$$(l_B X)_t - B(l_B X)_{t-1} = X_{t-1}, \quad 2 \leq t \leq n.$$

In the definition of l_B the values of X are premultiplied by powers of B, and therefore l_B can be termed a *left resolvent*.

Instead of premultiplying by powers of B and/or summing over initial values of $s = 1, \ldots, t - 1$ we can postmultiply by powers of B' and/or sum over terminal values $s = t + 1, \ldots, n$, as in

$$(r_B X)_t = \begin{cases} \sum_{s=t+1}^{n} X_s B'^{s-t-1}, & 1 \le t \le n - 1, \\ 0, & t = n, \end{cases} \qquad X \in l_p(\tau_n, \mathbb{M}_p).$$

Now the difference equation is

$$(r_B X)_t B' - (r_B X)_{t-1} = X_{t+1} B', \quad 2 \le t \le n.$$

r_B is called a *right resolvent*. Since properties of operators obtained by different combinations of pre- and/or postmultiplication and summation sets are similar, it is enough to study one example of each type. Besides, a statement on boundedness of a resolvent generates a statement on boundedness of its adjoint (Section 8.2.2). This point is not elaborated here.

The *enveloping resolvent* is defined by

$$(e_B X)_t = \begin{cases} \sum_{s=1}^{t-1} B^{t-1-s} X_s B'^{t-1-s}, & 2 \le t \le n, \\ 0, & t = 1, \end{cases} \qquad X \in l_p(\tau_n, \mathbb{M}_p).$$

It satisfies the equation

$$(e_B X)_t - B(e_B X)_{t-1} B' = X_{t-1}, \quad 2 \le t \le n.$$

8.4.2 Convergence of Resolvents

Theorem. *Suppose that all eigenvalues of B are inside the unit circle $|\lambda| < 1$ and that $\{X_n\}$ is L_p-close to $X^c \in L_p$, $p < \infty$. Then*

(i) *$\{l_B X_n\}$ is L_p-close to $(I - B)^{-1} X^c$, $\{r_B X_n\}$ is L_p-close to $X^c(I - B')^{-1}$, and*

$$\{e_B X_n\} \text{ is } L_p\text{-close to } \sum_{s=0}^{\infty} B^s X^c B'^s. \tag{8.8}$$

(ii) *If $\{Y_n\}$ is L_q-close to $Y^c \in L_q$, $q < \infty$, $1/p + 1/q = 1$, then*

$$\lim_{n \to \infty} \sum_{t=1}^{n} Y_{nt}(e_B X_n)_t = \int_0^1 Y^c(x) \sum_{s=0}^{\infty} B^s X^c(x) B'^s \, dx. \tag{8.9}$$

Proof.

(i) Comparison of definitions from Sections 8.2.1 and 8.2.4 shows that the resolvents can be obtained from T_n^0 with the following choices of the matrices ψ_s^l and ψ_s^r:

(a) choice for l_B : $\psi_s^l = \begin{cases} 0, & s \ge 0 \\ B^{-s-1}, & s < 0 \end{cases}$, $\psi_s^r = I$ for all s,

(b) choice for r_B : $\psi_s^l = I$ for all s, $\psi_s^r = \begin{cases} B'^{s-1}, & s > 0 \\ 0, & s \le 0 \end{cases}$,

(c) choice for e_B : $\psi_s^l = \begin{cases} 0, & s \ge 0 \\ B^{-s-1}, & s < 0 \end{cases}$, $\psi_s^r = \begin{cases} 0, & s \ge 0 \\ B'^{-s-1}, & s < 0 \end{cases}$.

By Eq. (6.114) the assumption about the spectrum of B ensures convergence of all series involving B, including α_ψ. By Theorem 8.2.4:

(a) $\{l_B X_n\}$ is L_p-close to $\beta_\psi X^c = \sum_{s=-\infty}^{-1} B^{-s-1} X^c = (I - B)^{-1} X^c$,

(b) $\{r_B X_n\}$ is L_p-close to $\beta_\psi X^c = \sum_{s=1}^{\infty} X^c B'^{s-1} = X^c (I - B')^{-1}$,

(c) $\{e_B X_n\}$ is L_p-close to $\beta_\psi X^c = \sum_{s=0}^{\infty} B^s X^c B'^s$.

(ii) Equation (8.8) and Theorem 8.1.3 imply Eq. (8.9).   ∎

8.5   CONVERGENCE AND BOUNDS FOR DETERMINISTIC TRENDS

8.5.1   Definition and Examples

Suppose a sequence of deterministic vectors $\{d_t : t = 0, 1, \ldots\} \subseteq \mathbb{R}^p$ satisfies the recurrent equation

$$d_t = \Delta d_{t-1}, \ t = 1, 2, \ldots, \tag{8.10}$$

where Δ is a $p \times p$ matrix. If Δ has all its eigenvalues on the unit circle and the vectors $d_1, \ldots, d_p$ are linearly independent,

$$|\lambda_j(\Delta)| = 1, \ j = 1, \ldots, p; \quad \text{rank}(d_1, \ldots, d_p) = p, \tag{8.11}$$

then $\{d_t\}$ is called a *deterministic trend*. Obviously, Eq. (8.10) is equivalent to

$$d_t = \Delta^t d_0, \ t = 1, 2, \ldots \tag{8.12}$$

EXAMPLE 8.1.   When $p = 1$, assuming that $\Delta = e^{i\varphi}$, from the Euler formula and Eq. (8.12) we get

$$d_t = e^{it\phi} d_0 = (\cos t\phi + i \sin t\phi) d_0.$$

This shows that in the 1-D case a monomial $d_t = t^k$ is not a deterministic trend, unless $k = 0$.

EXAMPLE 8.2. (Nielsen, 2005, p. 535). Let

$$\Delta = \begin{pmatrix} 1 & 0 \\ 1 & -1 \end{pmatrix}, \quad d_0 = \begin{pmatrix} 1 \\ 1 \end{pmatrix}.$$

Then

$$d_1 = \begin{pmatrix} 1 & 0 \\ 1 & -1 \end{pmatrix}\begin{pmatrix} 1 \\ 1 \end{pmatrix} = \begin{pmatrix} 1 \\ 0 \end{pmatrix}, \quad d_2 = \begin{pmatrix} 1 & 0 \\ 1 & -1 \end{pmatrix}\begin{pmatrix} 1 \\ 0 \end{pmatrix} = \begin{pmatrix} 1 \\ 1 \end{pmatrix}.$$

If the data are biannual, then the first component d_{t1} generates a constant in a regression model and the second component d_{t2} is a dummy for even-numbered years. The eigenvalues of Δ are ± 1.

EXAMPLE 8.3. In the 2-D case a linear trend is obtained as follows. Put

$$\Delta = \begin{pmatrix} 1 & 0 \\ 1 & 1 \end{pmatrix}, \quad d_t = \begin{pmatrix} 1 \\ t \end{pmatrix}$$

Then

$$\Delta d_{t-1} = \begin{pmatrix} 1 & 0 \\ 1 & 1 \end{pmatrix}\begin{pmatrix} 1 \\ t-1 \end{pmatrix} = \begin{pmatrix} 1 \\ t \end{pmatrix} = d_t;$$

$$\text{rank}(d_1, d_2) = \text{rank}\begin{pmatrix} 1 & 1 \\ 1 & 2 \end{pmatrix} = \text{rank}\Delta.$$

$\lambda(\Delta) = 1$ is an eigenvalue of multiplicity two.

EXAMPLE 8.4. (Adapted from Johansen, 2000, p. 744.) A periodical trend (biannual dummy) from Example (8.2) can be combined with a linear trend from Example (8.3). Let

$$s_1(t) = \begin{cases} 1, & t \text{ is odd;} \\ 0, & t \text{ is even;} \end{cases} \quad s_2(t) = \begin{cases} 1, & t \text{ is even;} \\ 0, & t \text{ is odd.} \end{cases}$$

Then, obviously, $s_1(t+1) = s_2(t) = 1 - s_1(t)$ and with

$$\Delta = \begin{pmatrix} 1 & 0 & 0 \\ 1 & 1 & 0 \\ 1 & 0 & -1 \end{pmatrix}, \quad d_t = \begin{pmatrix} 1 \\ t \\ s_1(t) \end{pmatrix},$$

we have

$$
\Delta d_{t-1} = \begin{pmatrix} 1 & 0 & 0 \\ 1 & 1 & 0 \\ 1 & 0 & -1 \end{pmatrix} \begin{pmatrix} 1 \\ t-1 \\ s_1(t-1) \end{pmatrix}
$$

$$
= \begin{pmatrix} 1 \\ t \\ 1 - s_1(t-1) \end{pmatrix} = \begin{pmatrix} 1 \\ t \\ s_1(t) \end{pmatrix} = d_t;
$$

$$
\mathrm{rank}(d_1, d_2, d_3) = \mathrm{rank} \begin{pmatrix} 1 & 1 & 1 \\ 1 & 2 & 3 \\ 1 & 0 & 1 \end{pmatrix} = 3 = \mathrm{rank}\Delta
$$

and the eigenvalues of Δ are 1 and -1.

8.5.2   The Jordan Representation of Δ

By assumption, Δ has eigenvalues on the unit circle. From now on we suppose that these occur at l distinct complex pairs $e^{i\theta_j}$ and $e^{-i\theta_j}$ for $0 \le \theta_j \le \pi$, which, of course, reduce to a single value of 1 or -1 if θ_j equals 0 or π. By a theorem of (Herstein, 1975, p. 308) there exists a regular, real matrix P that block-diagonalizes Δ as

$$
P\Delta P^{-1} = \mathrm{diag}[\Delta_1, \ldots, \Delta_l] \tag{8.13}
$$

where Δ_j are real Jordan matrices of the form

$$
\Delta_j = \begin{pmatrix} \Lambda_j & E_j & \ddots & 0 \\ 0 & \Lambda_j & E_j & 0 \\ 0 & \ddots & \ddots & E_j \\ 0 & 0 & \ddots & \Lambda_j \end{pmatrix} \tag{8.14}
$$

and the pair (Λ_j, E_j) is one of the pairs

$$
(1, 1), \; (-1, 1) \quad \text{or} \quad \left(\begin{pmatrix} \cos\theta_j & -\sin\theta_j \\ \sin\theta_j & \cos\theta_j \end{pmatrix}, \begin{pmatrix} 1 & 0 \\ 0 & 1 \end{pmatrix} \right) \quad \text{for } 0 < \theta_j < \pi. \tag{8.15}
$$

The numbers

$$
\delta_j = \dim \Delta_j / \dim \Lambda_j, \quad \delta = \max \delta_j \tag{8.16}
$$

are the multiplicity of the eigenvalue $\lambda_j(\Delta)$ and the largest multiplicity of the eigenvalues of Δ, respectively.

8.5.3 Normalization of d_t

The block structure (8.13) induces the block structures of the process d_t, $d_t = (d'_{t,1}, \ldots, d'_{t,l})'$, and of the initial vector, $d_0 = (d'_{0,1}, \ldots, d'_{0,l})'$. For the jth block we have the equation $d_{t,j} = \Delta_j^t d_{0,j}$, $j = 1, \ldots, l$. The partial initial vector $d_{0,j}$ itself consists of δ_j blocks that correspond to the diagonal blocks of Eq. (8.14):

$$d_{0,j} = (d'_{0,j,1}, \ldots, d'_{0,j,\delta_j})'. \tag{8.17}$$

The block $d_{t,j}$ is normalized by

$$N_{T,j} = \mathrm{diag}[(\Lambda_j/T)^{\delta_j-1}, \ldots, (\Lambda_j/T)^0] \tag{8.18}$$

and, correspondingly, d_t is normalized by

$$N_T = \mathrm{diag}[N_{T,1}, \ldots, N_{T,l}]. \tag{8.19}$$

Definitions (8.18) and (8.19) imply

$$\|N_T\| = O(1), \quad \|N_T^{-1}\| = O(T^{\delta-1}). \tag{8.20}$$

Denote $f(n, \cdot)$ the vector that consists of the first n terms of the Taylor series:

$$f(n, u) = \left(\frac{u^{n-1}}{(n-1)!}, \ldots, \frac{u^0}{0!} \right)'.$$

Lemma.   *Uniformly in* $t = 0, \ldots, T$

$$N_{T,j}d_{t,j} = (1 + o(1))f(\delta_j, t/T) \otimes (\Lambda_j^t d_{0,j,\delta_j}) + O\left(\frac{1}{T}\right), \quad as\ T \longrightarrow \infty. \tag{8.21}$$

Proof.   Using Eq. (8.14), where the pair (Λ_j, E_j) is one of those listed in Eq. (8.15), we write the powers of Δ_j as

$$\Delta_j^t = \begin{pmatrix} \Lambda_j^t & \binom{t}{1}\Lambda_j^{t-1} & \cdots & \binom{t}{\delta_j-1}\Lambda_j^{t-\delta_j+1} \\ 0 & \Lambda_j^t & \cdots & \binom{t}{\delta_j-2}\Lambda_j^{t-\delta_j+2} \\ \cdots & \cdots & \cdots & \cdots \\ 0 & 0 & \cdots & \Lambda_j^t \end{pmatrix}. \tag{8.22}$$

This is quite similar to the expression for Δ^k from Section 6.6.3, where the notation $\binom{a}{b}$ has been introduced. Upon premultiplication of Eq. (8.22) by Eq. (8.18) we get

$$
N_{T,j}\Delta_j^t =
\begin{pmatrix}
T^{1-\delta_j}\Lambda_j^{t+\delta_j-1} & T^{1-\delta_j}\binom{t}{1}\Lambda_j^{t+\delta_j-2} & \cdots & T^{1-\delta_j}\binom{t}{\delta_j-1}\Lambda_j^t \\
0 & T^{2-\delta_j}\Lambda_j^{t+\delta_j-2} & \cdots & T^{2-\delta_j}\binom{t}{\delta_j-2}\Lambda_j^t \\
\cdots & \cdots & \cdots & \cdots \\
0 & 0 & \cdots & \Lambda_j^t
\end{pmatrix}.
$$

Postmultiplying this by Eq. (8.17) we see that the first block of $N_{T,j}\Delta_j^t d_{0,j} = N_{T,j}d_{t,j}$ is

$$
(N_{T,j}d_{t,j})_1 = \frac{1}{T^{\delta_j-1}}\sum_{k=0}^{\delta_j-1}\binom{t}{\delta_j-1-k}\Lambda_j^{t+k}d_{0,j,\delta_j-k} \tag{8.23}
$$

(the blocks of $d_{0,j}$ are counted from the end).

For nonzero values of the binomial coefficients from

$$
\binom{t}{k} = \frac{t!}{k!(t-k)!} = \frac{t(t-1)\cdots(t-k+1)\,t^k}{t^k}\frac{}{k!} = \left(1-\frac{1}{t}\right)\cdots\left(1-\frac{k-1}{t}\right)\frac{t^k}{k!}
$$

we have

$$
\binom{t}{k} = (1+o(1))\frac{t^k}{k!} \quad \text{as } t\longrightarrow\infty, \quad \text{for } 0\le k\le\delta_j-1. \tag{8.24}
$$

Equations (8.23) and (8.24) imply

$$
(N_{T,j}d_{t,j})_1 = (1+o(1))\sum_{k=0}^{\delta_j-1}\frac{(t/T)^{\delta_j-1-k}}{(\delta_j-1-k)!T^k}\Lambda_j^{t+k}d_{0,j,\delta_j-k}
$$

$$
= (1+o(1))\frac{(t/T)^{\delta_j-1}}{(\delta_j-1)!}\Lambda_j^t d_{0,j,\delta_j} + O\left(\frac{1}{T}\right) \tag{8.25}
$$

(the term with $k=0$ leads; all others do not exceed c/T). Equation (8.25) is true for t large, $t\ge t_0$ and $T\ge t_0$. To extend Eq. (8.25) to values $t < t_0$, we simply bound $\binom{t}{k}\le c$ and then from Eq. (8.23) in the case $\delta_j\ge 2$

$$
(N_{T,j}d_{t,j})_1 = O\left(\frac{1}{T^{\delta_j-1}}\right) = O\left(\frac{1}{T}\right). \tag{8.26}
$$

Since also

$$\frac{(t/T)^{\delta_j-1}}{(\delta_j-1)!}\Lambda_j^t d_{0,j,\delta_j} = O\left(\frac{1}{T^{\delta_j-1}}\right),\tag{8.27}$$

Equation (8.25) follows from Eqs. (8.26) and (8.27) for $t < t_0$ in the case $\delta_j \geq 2$. Finally, if $\delta_j = 1$, then Δ_j^t consists of just one block, $N_{T,j} = I$ and

$$N_{T,j}\Delta_j^t d_{0,j} = \Lambda_j^t d_{0,j,\delta_j} = \frac{(t/T)^{\delta_j-1}}{(\delta_j-1)!}\Lambda_j^t d_{0,j,\delta_j}.$$

Equation (8.25) has been proved for all $\delta_j \geq 1$ and $0 \leq t \leq T$.

Replacing in the above argument $\delta_j - 1$ by $\delta_j - 2, \ldots, 0$ we obtain analogs of Eq. (8.25) for other blocks of $N_{T,j}d_{t,j}$. The resulting equations are collected as

$$N_{T,j}d_{t,j} = \begin{pmatrix} (1+o(1))\dfrac{(t/T)^{\delta_j-1}}{(\delta_j-1)!}\Lambda_j^t d_{0,j,\delta_j} + O\left(\dfrac{1}{T}\right) \\[2mm] (1+o(1))\dfrac{(t/T)^{\delta_j-2}}{(\delta_j-2)!}\Lambda_j^t d_{0,j,\delta_j} + O\left(\dfrac{1}{T}\right) \\[2mm] \cdots \\[2mm] (1+o(1))\dfrac{(t/T)^{0}}{0!}\Lambda_j^t d_{0,j,\delta_j} + O\left(\dfrac{1}{T}\right) \end{pmatrix}$$

$$= (1+o(1))f(\delta_j, t/T) \otimes (\Lambda_j^t d_{0,j,\delta_j}) + O\left(\frac{1}{T}\right), \quad \text{as } T \longrightarrow \infty,$$

and this relationship is uniform in t, $0 \leq t \leq T$. ∎

A slight change of this argument shows that $\max_{0\leq t\leq T} \|N_T\Delta^t\| = O(1)$.

8.5.4 Trigonometric Lemma

Lemma

(i) *Let*

$$\Lambda = \begin{pmatrix} \cos\theta & -\sin\theta \\ \sin\theta & \cos\theta \end{pmatrix}, \quad x = \begin{pmatrix} a \\ b \end{pmatrix}.$$

Then

$$\Lambda^t x(\Lambda^t x)' = \begin{pmatrix} 1 & 0 \\ 0 & 1 \end{pmatrix}\frac{a^2+b^2}{2} + A\cos 2t\theta + B\sin 2t\theta, \quad t = 1, 2, \ldots,$$

where A and B are constant 2 × 2 matrices with elements depending only on a, b.

(ii) Let

$$\Lambda_j = \begin{pmatrix} \cos\theta_j & -\sin\theta_j \\ \sin\theta_j & \cos\theta_j \end{pmatrix}, \quad x_j = \begin{pmatrix} a_j \\ b_j \end{pmatrix}, \quad j = 1, 2.$$

Then

$$\Lambda_1' x_1 (\Lambda_2' x_2)' = \sum [A^{\pm} \cos(t(\theta_1 \pm \theta_2)) + B^{\pm} \sin(t(\theta_1 \pm \theta_2))]$$

where $A^{\pm}$, $B^{\pm}$ are 2×2 matrices with elements depending only on x_1, x_2.

Proof.

(i) Since Λ is rotation by angle θ, Λ^t is rotation by angle $t\theta$ and

$$\Lambda^t x = \begin{pmatrix} \cos t\theta & -\sin t\theta \\ \sin t\theta & \cos t\theta \end{pmatrix} \begin{pmatrix} a \\ b \end{pmatrix} = \begin{pmatrix} a\cos t\theta - b\sin t\theta \\ a\sin t\theta + b\cos t\theta \end{pmatrix}. \qquad (8.28)$$

Therefore

$$\Lambda^t x (\Lambda^t x)' = \begin{pmatrix} a\cos t\theta - b\sin t\theta \\ a\sin t\theta + b\cos t\theta \end{pmatrix} (a\cos t\theta - b\sin t\theta, \; a\sin t\theta + b\cos t\theta)$$

$$= \begin{pmatrix} c_{11} & c_{12} \\ c_{21} & c_{22} \end{pmatrix}.$$

where

$$c_{11} = a^2 \cos^2 t\theta - 2ab \sin t\theta \cos t\theta + b^2 \sin^2 t\theta,$$

$$c_{12} = c_{21} = a^2 \sin t\theta \cos t\theta + ab \cos^2 t\theta - ab \sin^2 t\theta - b^2 \sin t\theta \cos t\theta,$$

$$c_{22} = a^2 \sin^2 t\theta + 2ab \sin t\theta \cos t\theta + b^2 \cos^2 t\theta.$$

Using equations $2\sin\alpha\cos\alpha = \sin 2\alpha$, $\cos^2\alpha = \frac{1}{2}(\cos 2\alpha + 1)$ and $\sin^2\alpha = \frac{1}{2}(1 - \cos 2\alpha)$ this can be rewritten as

$$c_{11} = \frac{a^2}{2}(\cos 2t\theta + 1) + \frac{b^2}{2}(1 - \cos 2t\theta) - ab \sin 2t\theta,$$

$$c_{12} = c_{21} = \frac{a^2 - b^2}{2} \sin 2t\theta + ab \cos 2t\theta,$$

$$c_{22} = \frac{a^2}{2}(1 - \cos 2t\theta) + \frac{b^2}{2}(\cos 2t\theta + 1) + ab \sin 2t\theta.$$

The result is

$$\Lambda'x(\Lambda'x)' = \begin{pmatrix} \dfrac{a^2 + b^2}{2} & 0 \\ 0 & \dfrac{a^2 + b^2}{2} \end{pmatrix} + \begin{pmatrix} \dfrac{a^2 - b^2}{2} & ab \\ ab & \dfrac{b^2 - a^2}{2} \end{pmatrix} \cos 2t\theta$$

$$+ \begin{pmatrix} -ab & \dfrac{a^2 - b^2}{2} \\ \dfrac{a^2 - b^2}{2} & ab \end{pmatrix} \sin 2t\theta.$$

(ii) This time using Eq. (8.28) we have

$$\Lambda_1'x_1(\Lambda_2'x_2)' = \begin{pmatrix} a_1 \cos t\theta_1 - b_1 \sin t\theta_1 \\ a_1 \sin t\theta_1 + b_1 \cos t\theta_1 \end{pmatrix}$$

$$\times (a_2 \cos t\theta_2 - b_2 \sin t\theta_2, a_2 \sin t\theta_2 + b_2 \cos t\theta_2).$$

The terms in the above expressions are linear combinations of the products $\cos t\theta_1 \cos t\theta_2$, $\cos t\theta_1 \sin t\theta_2$, $\sin t\theta_1 \cos t\theta_2$, and $\sin t\theta_1 \sin t\theta_2$. Using the formulas

$$\cos \alpha \cos \beta = \frac{\cos(\alpha + \beta) + \cos(\alpha - \beta)}{2},$$

$$\sin \alpha \sin \beta = \frac{\cos(\alpha - \beta) - \cos(\alpha + \beta)}{2},$$

$$\sin \alpha \cos \beta = \frac{\sin(\alpha + \beta) + \sin(\alpha - \beta)}{2}$$

these terms can be rewritten as linear combinations of $\cos(t(\theta_1 \pm \theta_2))$ and $\sin(t(\theta_1 \pm \theta_2))$. ∎

8.5.5 Sample Covariance of the Deterministic Process

Lemma

(i) With an appropriate pair (Λ_j, E_j) from Eq. (8.15) we have

$$\frac{1}{T}\sum_{t=1}^{T} (N_{T,j}d_{t-1,j})(N_{T,j}d_{t-1,j})' = (1 + o(1))\frac{\|d_{0,j,\delta_j}\|^2}{\dim\Lambda_j} \int_0^1 f(\delta_j, u)f'(\delta_j, u)\, du$$

$$\otimes E_j + O\!\left(\frac{1}{T}\right).$$

(ii) If $\|d_{0,j,\delta_j}\|^2 > 0$ then the limiting matrix in (i) is positive definite.

(iii) $\frac{1}{T}\sum_{t=1}^{T} (N_{T,i}d_{t-1,i})(N_{T,j}d_{t-1,j})' = O(\frac{1}{T})$ for $i \neq j$.

Proof.

(i) By Lemma 8.5.3

$$\frac{1}{T}\sum_{t=1}^{T}(N_{T,j}d_{t-1,j})(N_{T,j}d_{t-1,j})' = (1+o(1))\frac{1}{T}\sum_{t=1}^{T}f\left(\delta_j,\frac{t-1}{T}\right)f'\left(\delta_j,\frac{t-1}{T}\right)$$

$$\otimes(\Lambda_j^{t-1}d_{0,j,\delta_j}d'_{0,j,\delta_j}(\Lambda_j^{t-1})') + O\left(\frac{1}{T}\right) \tag{8.29}$$

(the terms corresponding to $t=1$ are of order $\frac{1}{T}$ and can be included/ excluded without affecting the result). Let $0 \le p, q \le \delta_j - 1$ be integer numbers. One block of the expression at the right of Eq. (8.29) equals

$$\frac{1}{T}\sum_{t=1}^{T}\frac{1}{p!q!}\left(\frac{t-1}{T}\right)^{p+q}\Lambda_j^{t-1}d_{0,j,\delta_j}d'_{0,j,\delta_j}(\Lambda_j^{t-1})' + O\left(\frac{1}{T}\right). \tag{8.30}$$

Consider two cases.

(a) Suppose $\dim\Lambda_j = 1$. In this case $\Lambda_j = \pm 1$, d_{0,j,δ_j} is a real number and

$$\Lambda_j^{t-1}d_{0,j,\delta_j}d'_{0,j,\delta_j}(\Lambda_j^{t-1})' = |d_{0,j,\delta_j}|^2 = E_j\frac{\|d_{0,j,\delta_j}\|^2}{\dim\Lambda_j}.$$

The limit of Eq. (8.29), therefore, is

$$\frac{1}{p!q!}\int_0^1 u^{p+q}duE_j\frac{\|d_{0,j,\delta_j}\|^2}{\dim\Lambda_j},$$

which, in combination with Eq. (8.29), proves (i).

(b) Let $\dim\Lambda_j = 2$. By Lemma 8.5.4(i), Eq. (8.30) equals

$$\frac{1}{p!q!}\frac{1}{T}\sum_{t=1}^{T}\left(\frac{t-1}{T}\right)^{p+q}E_j\|d_{0,j,\delta_j}\|^2/\dim\Lambda_j$$

$$+\frac{1}{p!q!}\frac{1}{T}\sum_{t=1}^{T}\left(\frac{t-1}{T}\right)^{p+q}(A\cos 2t\theta_j + B\sin 2t\theta_j) + O\left(\frac{1}{T}\right).$$

The desired result follows if we prove that

$$\frac{1}{T}\sum_{t=1}^{T}\left(\frac{t-1}{T}\right)^{p+q}(A\cos 2t\theta_j + B\sin 2t\theta_j) = O\left(\frac{1}{T}\right).$$

To this end, it is sufficient to prove

$$\frac{1}{T^{l+1}} \sum_{t=0}^{T-1} t^l \cos(2t\theta + a) = O\left(\frac{1}{T}\right) \tag{8.31}$$

for any nonnegative integer l and a constant $a = 0$ or $a = -\pi/2$. Direct calculation gives

$$t^{j+4k} \cos(2t\theta + a) = 2^{-j-4k} \left(\frac{\partial}{\partial\theta}\right)^{j+4k} \sin\left(2t\theta + a + \frac{\pi}{2}\right), \quad j = 0, 2,$$

$$t^{j+4k} \cos(2t\theta + a) = 2^{-j-4k} \left(\frac{\partial}{\partial\theta}\right)^{j+3k} \sin(2t\theta + a), \quad j = 1, 3,$$

for $k = 0, 1, \ldots$ These identities show that $\sum_{t=0}^{T-1} t^l \cos(2t\theta + a)$ is, up to a constant factor c_l, $\left(\frac{\partial}{\partial\theta}\right)^l \sum_{t=0}^{T-1} t^l \sin(2t\theta + a)$, where $x = a$ or $x = a + \pi/2$. By (Gradshteyn and Ryzhik 2007, Formula 1.341.1) $\sum_{t=0}^{T-1} \sin(2t\theta + x) = f(x, T, \theta)$, where $f(x, T, \theta) = \sin[x + (T - 1)\theta] \sin(T\theta)/\sin\theta$ [by definition, $f(x, T, \theta) = 0$ when $\sin\theta = 0$]. Thus,

$$\frac{1}{T^{l+1}} \sum_{t=0}^{T-1} t^l \cos(2t\theta + a) = \frac{c_l}{T^{l+1}} \left(\frac{\partial}{\partial\theta}\right)^l f(x, T, \theta).$$

It is easy to see that $\left(\frac{\partial}{\partial\theta}\right)^l f(x, T, \theta) = \sum_{m=0}^{l} a(x, T, \theta) T^m$, where $a(x, T, \theta)$ are bounded in T. Therefore Eq. (8.31) follows.

(ii) The matrix $\int_0^1 f(\delta_j, u) f'(\delta_j, u) \, du$ is positive definite as a Gram matrix of a linearly independent system (Section 1.7.5).

(iii) By Lemma 8.5.3

$$\frac{1}{T} \sum_{t=1}^{T} (N_{T,i} d_{t-1,i})(N_{T,j} d_{t-1,j})' = (1 + o(1)) \frac{1}{T} \sum_{t=1}^{T} f\left(\delta_i, \frac{t-1}{T}\right) f'\left(\delta_j, \frac{t-1}{T}\right)$$

$$\otimes \left(\Lambda_i^{t-1} d_{0,i,\delta_i} d'_{0,j,\delta_j} (\Lambda_j^{t-1})'\right) + O\left(\frac{1}{T}\right).$$

Therefore the result follows from Lemma 8.5.4(ii) and Eq. (8.31). ∎

8.5.6   Asymptotic Behavior of Normalized Deterministic Trends

Theorem.   (Nielsen, 2005, Theorem 4.1) *Suppose d_t satisfies Eqs. (8.10) and (8.11). Then*

(i) $\max_{0 \leq t \leq T} |N_T d_t| = O(1)$ *and, in particular,* $\max_{t \leq T} \|d_t\| = O(T^{\delta-1})$, *where* $\delta = \max \delta_j$ *is the largest multiplicity of eigenvalues of* Δ.

(ii) $\lim_{T \to \infty} \frac{1}{T} \sum_{t=1}^{T} (N_T d_{t-1})(N_T d_{t-1})'$ *is positive definite.*

(iii) $\max_{t \leq T} d_t' \left(\sum_{s=1}^{T} d_{s-1} d_{s-1}' \right)^{-1} d_t = O\left(\frac{1}{T}\right).$

Proof.

(i) The process $N_T d_t$ is obtained by stacking the processes $N_{T,j} d_{t,j}$:

$$N_T d_t = \begin{pmatrix} N_{T,1} & & 0 \\ & \ddots & \\ 0 & & N_{T,l} \end{pmatrix} \begin{pmatrix} d_{t,1} \\ \cdots \\ d_{t,l} \end{pmatrix} = \begin{pmatrix} N_{T,1} d_{t,1} \\ \cdots \\ N_{T,l} d_{t,l} \end{pmatrix}.$$

Therefore the first statement follows from Lemma 8.5.3 and the inequality $\|N_T d_t\| \leq l \max_j \|N_{T,j} d_{t,j}\|$. Further,

$$d_{t,j} = N_{T,j}^{-1} N_{T,j} d_{t,j} = \text{diag}[(\Lambda_j/T)^{1-\delta_j}, \ldots, (\Lambda_j/T)^0] N_{T,j} d_{t,j} = O(T^{\delta-1}),$$

which proves the statement.

(ii) The equation

$$(N_T d_{t-1})(N_T d_{t-1})' = \begin{pmatrix} N_{T,1} d_{t-1,1} \\ \cdots \\ N_{T,l} d_{t-1,l} \end{pmatrix} ((N_{T,1} d_{t-1,1})', \ldots, (N_{T,l} d_{t-1,l})')$$

$$= (N_{T,i} d_{t-1,i}(N_{T,j} d_{t-1,j})')_{i,j=1}^{l}$$

implies that the matrix

$$M \equiv \lim_{T \to \infty} \frac{1}{T} \sum_{t=1}^{T} (N_T d_{t-1})(N_T d_{t-1})'$$

$$= \lim_{T \to \infty} \left(\frac{1}{T} \sum_{t=1}^{T} N_{T,i} d_{t-1,i}(N_{T,j} d_{t-1,j})' \right)_{i,j=1}^{l}$$

has null blocks outside the main diagonal by Lemma 8.5.5(iii) and positive definite diagonal blocks by Lemma 8.5.5(ii). Thus, M itself is positive definite.

(iii) In the identity

$$
d_t' \left(\sum_{s=1}^{T} d_{s-1} d_{s-1}' \right)^{-1} d_t = \frac{1}{T} (N_T d_t)' \left[\frac{1}{T} \sum_{s=1}^{T} (N_T d_{s-1})(N_T d_{s-1})' \right]^{-1} (N_T d_t)
$$

the vector $N_T d_t$ is bounded by part **(i)**. The matrix in the brackets is positive definite by part **(ii)**. ∎

8.5.7 Corollary

Lemma. *Under the conditions of Theorem 8.5.6*

$$
\max_{t \le T} \left\| d_t' \left(\sum_{s=1}^{T} d_{s-1} d_{s-1}' \right)^{-1/2} \right\| = O(T^{-1/2}).
$$

Proof. For a vector x and symmetric matrix A we have

$$
\|x'A\| = \|A'x\| = ((A'x)'A'x)^{1/2} = (x'A^2 x)^{1/2},
$$

which implies

$$
\left\| d_t' \left(\sum_{s=1}^{T} d_{s-1} d_{s-1}' \right)^{-1/2} \right\| = \left[d_t' \left(\sum_{s=1}^{T} d_{s-1} d_{s-1}' \right)^{-1} d_t \right]^{1/2}.
$$

Now the statement follows from part (iii) of Theorem 8.5.6. ∎

REFERENCES

Aljančić, S., Bojanić, R., Tomić, M. 1955. Deux théorèmes relatifs au comportement asymptotique des séries trigonométriques. *Srpska Akad. Nauka. Zb. Rad. Mat. Inst.*, **43**(4), 15–26.

Amemiya, T. 1976. The maximum likelihood, the minimum chi-square and the nonlinear weighted least-squares estimator in the general qualitative response model. *J. Amer. Statist. Assoc.*, **71**(354), 347–351.

Amemiya, T. 1985. *Advanced Econometrics*. Oxford: Blackwell.

Anderson, T. W. 1959. On asymptotic distributions of estimates of parameters of stochastic difference equations. *Ann. Math. Stat.*, **30**, 676–687.

Anderson, T. W. 1971. *The Statistical Analysis of Time Series*. New York: John Wiley & Sons Inc.

Anderson, T. W., Kunitomo, N. 1992. Asymptotic distributions of regression and autoregression coefficients with martingale difference disturbances. *J. Multivar. Anal.*, **40**(2), 221–243.

Anderson, T. W., Taylor, J. B. 1979. Strong consistency of least squares estimates in dynamic models. *Ann. Stat.*, **7**(3), 484–489.

Anselin, L. 1988. *Spatial Econometrics: Methods and Models*. Boston: Kluwer Academic Publishers.

Anselin, L., Bera, A. K. 1998. Spatial dependence in linear regression models with an introduction to spatial econometrics. In: Ullah, A., Giles, D.E.A. (eds), *Handbook of Applied Economics Statistics*. New York: Marcel Dekker.

Barlow, W. J. 1975. Coefficient properties of random variable sequences. *Ann. Probab.*, **3**(5), 840–848.

Barro, R. J., Sala-i-Martin, X. 2003. *Economic Growth*. 2nd edn. Cambridge: MIT Press.

Bellman, R. 1995. *Introduction to Matrix Analysis*. Classics in Applied Mathematics, Vol. 12. Philadelphia, PA: Society for Industrial and Applied Mathematics (SIAM). Reprint of the 1960 original.

Beveridge, S., Nelson, C. R. 1981. A new approach to decomposition of economic time series into permanent and transitory components with particular attention to measurement of the "business cycle". *J. Monetary Econ.*, **7**, 151–174.

Billingsley, P. 1968. *Convergence of Probability Measures*. New York: John Wiley & Sons Inc.

Billingsley, P. 1995. *Probability and Measure*. 3rd edn. New York: John Wiley & Sons Inc.

Brown, B. M. 1971. Martingale central limit theorems. *Ann. Math. Stat.*, **42**, 59–66.

Burkholder, D. L. 1968. Independent sequences with the Stein property. *Ann. Math. Stat.*, **39**, 1282–1288.

Burkholder, D. L., Gundy, R. F. 1970. Extrapolation and interpolation of quasi-linear operators on martingales. *Acta Math.*, **124**, 249–304.

Cartan, H. 1967. *Calcul Différentiel*. Paris: Hermann.

Case, A. C. 1991. Spatial patterns in household demand. *Econometrica*, **59**, 953–965.

Chow, Y. S. 1965. Local convergence of martingales and the law of large numbers. *Ann. Math. Stat.*, **36**, 552–558.

Chow, Y. S. 1969. Martingale extensions of a theorem of Marcinkiewicz and Zygmund. *Ann. Math. Stat.*, **40**, 427–433.

Chow, Y. S. 1971. On the L_p-convergence for $n^{-1/p} S_n$, $0 < p < 2$. *Ann. Math. Stat.*, **42**, 393–394.

Christopeit, N., Helmes, K. 1980. Strong consistency of least squares estimators in linear regression models. *Ann. Stat.*, **8**(4), 778–788.

Chudik, A., Pesaran, M. H., Tosetti, E. 2010. *Weak and strong cross section dependence and estimation of large panels*, 45 pp. http://ideas.repec.org/p/ces/ceswps/_2689.html

Čížek, P. 2008. Robust and efficient adaptive estimation of binary-choice regression models. *J. Amer. Statist. Assoc.*, **103**, 687–696.

Cliff, A. D., Ord, K. 1981. *Spatial Processes: Models Applications*. London: Pion Ltd.

Short-Memory Linear Processes and Econometric Applications. Kairat T. Mynbaev
© 2011 John Wiley & Sons, Inc. Published 2011 by John Wiley & Sons, Inc.

Cressie, N. A. C. 1993. *Statistics for Spatial Data*. New York: John Wiley & Sons Inc.

Davidson, J. 1994. *Stochastic Limit Theory*. New York: Oxford University Press. An introduction for econometricians.

de Haan, L., Resnick, S. 1996. Second-order regular variation and rates of convergence in extreme-value theory. *Ann. Prob.*, **24**(1), 97–124.

Dvoretzky, A. 1972. Asymptotic normality for sums of dependent random variables. *Proceedings of the Sixth Berkeley Symposium on Mathematical Statistics and Probability (Univ. California, Berkeley, Calif., 1970/1971), Vol. II: Probability theory*. pp. 513–535, Berkeley: Univ. California Press.

Eicker, F. 1963. Asymptotic normality and consistency of the least squares estimators for families of linear regressions. *Ann. Math. Stat.*, **34**, 447–456.

Eicker, F. 1966. A multivariate central limit theorem for random linear vector forms. *Ann. Math. Stat.*, **37**, 1825–1828.

Gantmacher, F. R. 1959. *The Theory of Matrices*. Vols. 1, 2. New York: Chelsea Publishing Co.

Gohberg, I. C., Kreĭn, M. G. 1969. *Introduction to the Theory of Linear Nonselfadjoint Operators*. Translations of Mathematical Monographs, Vol. 18. Providence: American Mathematical Society.

Goldie, C. M., Smith, R. L. 1987. Slow variation with remainder: Theory and applications. *Q. J. Math.*, **38**, 45–71.

Gouriéroux, C., Monfort, A. 1981. Asymptotic properties of the maximum likelihood estimator in dichotomous logit models. *J. Econometrics*, **17**(1), 83–97.

Gradshteyn, I. S., Ryzhik, I. M. 2007. *Table of Integrals, Series, and Products*. 7th edn. Amsterdam Elsevier/Academic Press. Translated from the Russian, Translation edited and with a preface by Alan Jeffrey and Daniel Zwillinger, with one CD-ROM (Windows, Macintosh and UNIX).

Gundy, R. F. 1967. The martingale version of a theorem of Marcinkiewicz and Zygmund. *Ann. Math. Stat.*, **38**, 725–734.

Hahn, M. G., Kuelbs, J., Samur, J. D. 1987. Asymptotic normality of trimmed sums of mixing random variables. *Ann. Probab.*, **15**, 1395–1418.

Hall, P., Heyde, C. C. 1980. *Martingale Limit Theory and Its Application*. New York: Academic Press Inc.

Hamilton, J. D. 1994. *Time Series Analysis*. Princeton: Princeton University Press.

Hannan, E. J. 1979. The central limit theorem for time series regression. *Stoch. Proc. Appl.*, **9**(3), 281–289.

Herstein, I. N. 1975. *Topics in Algebra*. 2nd edn. Lexington: Xerox College Publishing.

Hill, J. B. 2010. Least tail-trimmed squares for infinite variance autoregressions, under review at *Journal of the Royal Statistical Society Series B*. http://www.unc.edu/~jbhill/working%20papers.htm

Hill, J. B. 2011. *Central limit theory for kernel self-normalized tail-trimmed sums of dependent data with applications*. Working paper, 30 pp. http://www.unc.edu/~jbhill/clt_tail_trim.pdf

Holly, S., Pesaran, M. H., Yamagata, T. 2008. *A spatio-temporal model of house prices in the US*, 30 pp. http://ideas.repec.org/p/cam/camdae/0654.html

Hoque, A. 1985. The exact moments of forecast error in the general dynamic model. *Sankhyā Ser. B*, **47**(1), 128–143.

Hsiao, C. 1991. Identification and estimation of dichotomous latent variables models using panel data. *Rev. Econ. Stud.*, **58**(4), 717–731.

Hurvich, C. M., Deo, R., Brodsky, J. 1998. The mean squared error of Geweke and Porter–Hudak's estimator of the memory parameter of a long-memory time series. *J. Time Ser. Anal.*, **19**(1), 19–46.

Iosida, K. 1965. *Functional Aalysis*. Berlin: Springer-Verlag.

Johansen, S. 2000. A Bartlett correction factor for tests on the cointegrating relations. *Economet. Theor.*, **16**(5), 740–778.

Jones, M. C. 1986. Expressions for inverse moments of positive quadratic forms in normal variables. *Austral. J. Stat.*, **28**(2), 242–250.

Kadison, R. V. 1968. Strong continuity of operator functions. *Pacific J. Math.*, **26**, 121–129.

Kelejian, H. H., Prucha, I. R. 1998. A generalized spatial two-stage least squares procedure for estimating a spatial autoregressive model with autoregressive disturbances. *J. Real Estate Finance*, **17**, 99–121.

Kelejian, H. H., Prucha, I. R. 1999. A generalized moments estimator for the autoregressive parameter in a spatial model. *Int. Econ. Rev.*, **40**, 509–533.

Kelejian, H. H., Prucha, I. R. 2001. On the asymptotic distribution of the Moran I test statistic with applications. *J. Econometrics*, **104**, 219–257.

Kelejian, H. H., Prucha, I. R. 2002. 2SLS and OLS in a spatial autoregressive model with equal spatial weights. *Reg. Sci. Urban Econ.*, **32**, 691–707.

Kelejian, H. H., Prucha, I. R., Yuzefovich, Y. 2004. Instrumental variable estimation of a spatial autoregressive model with autoregressive disturbances: large and small sample results. *Adv. Econometrics*, **18**, 163–198.

Kolmogorov, A. N., Fomin, S. V. 1989. *Elementy Teorii Funktsii i Funktsional'nogo Analiza*. 6th edn. Moscow: "Nauka". With a supplement, "Banach algebras", by V. M. Tikhomirov.

Kushner, H. 1971. *Introduction to Stochastic Control*. New York: Holt, Rinehart and Winston, Inc.

Lai, T. L., Wei, C. Z. 1982. Least squares estimates in stochastic regression models with applications to identification and control of dynamic systems. *Ann. Stat.*, **10**(1), 154–166.

Lai, T. L., Wei, C. Z. 1983a. Asymptotic properties of general autoregressive models and strong consistency of least-squares estimates of their parameters. *J. Multivar. Anal.*, **13**(1), 1–23.

Lai, T. L., Wei, C. Z. 1983b. A note on martingale difference sequences satisfying the local Marcinkiewicz–Zygmund condition. *Bull. Inst. Math. Acad. Sinica*, **11**(1), 1–13.

Lai, T. L., Wei, C. Z. 1985. Asymptotic properties of multivariate weighted sums with applications to stochastic regression in linear dynamic systems. In: *Multivariate Analysis VI (Pittsburgh, Pa., 1983)*. Amsterdam: North-Holland., pp. 375–393.

Lai, T. L., Robbins, H., Wei, C. Z. 1978. Strong consistency of least squares estimates in multiple regression. *Proc. Nat. Acad. Sci. USA*, **75**(7), 3034–3036.

Lai, T. L., Robbins, H., Wei, C. Z. 1979. Strong consistency of least squares estimates in multiple regression. II. *J. Multivar. Anal.*, **9**(3), 343–361.

Lee, LungFei. 2001. *Asymptotic distributions of quasi-maximum likelihood estimators for spatial autoregressive models I: spatial autoregressive processes*. Ohio State University.

Lee, LungFei. 2002. Consistency and efficiency of least squares estimation for mixed regressive, spatial autoregressive models. *Economet. Theor.*, **18**(2), 252–277.

Lee, LungFei. 2003. Best spatial two-stage least squares estimators for a spatial autoregressive model with autoregressive disturbances. *Economet. Rev.*, **22**(4), 307–335.

Lee, LungFei. 2004a. Asymptotic distributions of quasi-maximum likelihood estimators for spatial autoregressive models. *Econometrica*, **72**(6), 1899–1925.

Lee, LungFei. 2004b. *A supplement to "Asymptotic distributions of quasi-maximum likelihood estimators for spatial autoregressive models"*. http://economics.sbs.ohio-state.edu/lee/wp/sar-qml-r-appen-04feb.pdf.

Long, R. L. 1993. *Martingale Spaces and Inequalities*. Beijing: Peking University Press.

Lütkepohl, H. 1991. *Introduction to Multiple Time Series Analysis*. Berlin: Springer-Verlag.

Mann, H. B., Wald, A. 1943. On the statistical treatment of linear stochastic difference equations. *Econometrica*, **11**, 173–220.

Marcinkiewicz, J., Zygmund, A. 1937. Sur les fonctions indépendantes. *Fund. Math.*, **29**, 60–90.

Mathai, A. M., Provost, S. B. 1992. *Quadratic Forms in Random Variables*. Statistics: Textbooks and Monographs, Vol. 126. New York: Marcel Dekker Inc.

McLeish, D. L. 1974. Dependent central limit theorems and invariance principles. *Ann. Prob.*, **2**, 620–628.

Morimune, K. 1959. Comparison of normal and logistic models in the bivariate dichotomous analysis. *J. Econometrics*, **47**, 957–976.

Moussatat, M. W. 1976. *On the asymptotic theory of statistical experiments and some of its applications*. PhD thesis, Univ. of California, Berkeley.

Muench, T. J. 1974. *Consistency of least squares estimates of coefficients of stochastic differential equations*. Univ. of Minnesota Economic Department Technical Report.

Mynbaev, K. T. 1997. Linear models with regressors generated by square-integrable functions. In: *Programa e Resumos. 7a Escola de Séries Temporais e Econometria*. Porto Alegre: ABE e SBE. 6 a 8 de agosto, pp. 80–82.

Mynbaev, K. T. 2000. *Limits of weighted sums of random variables*. Discussion text No. 218/2000, Economics Department, Federal University of Ceará, Brazil.

Mynbaev, K. T. 2001. L_p-approximable sequences of vectors and limit distribution of quadratic forms of random variables. *Adv. Appl. Math.*, **26**(4), 302–329.

Mynbaev, K. T. 2006a. Asymptotic properties of OLS estimates in autoregressions with bounded or slowly growing deterministic trends. *Commun. Stat. Theor. Methods*, **35**(1-3), 499–520.

Mynbaev, K. T. 2006b. *OLS Estimator for a Mixed Regressive, Spatial Autoregressive Model: Extended Version.* http://mpra.ub.uni-muenchen.de/15153/.

Mynbaev, K. T. 2009. Central limit theorems for weighted sums of linear processes: L_p-approximability versus Brownian motion. *Economet. Theor.*, **25**(3), 748–763.

Mynbaev, K. T. 2010. Asymptotic distribution of the OLS estimator for a mixed regressive, spatial autoregressive model. *J. Multivar. Anal.*, **10**(3), 733–748.

Mynbaev, K. T. 2011. Regressions with asymptotically collinear regressors. *Economet. Journal* (forthcoming).

Mynbaev, K. T., Castelar, I. 2001. *The strengths and weaknesses of* L_2-*approximable regressors. Two Essays on Econometrics.* Vol. 1, Fortaleza, Brazil: Expressão Gráfica. http://mpra.ub.uni-muenchen. de/9056/.

Mynbaev, K. T., Ullah, A. 2008. Asymptotic distribution of the OLS estimator for a purely autoregressive spatial model. *J. Multivar. Anal.*, **99**, 245–277.

Nabeya, S., Tanaka, K. 1988. Asymptotic theory of a test for the constancy of regression coefficients against the random walk alternative. *Ann. Stat.*, **16**(1), 218–235.

Nabeya, S., Tanaka, K. 1990. A general approach to the limiting distribution for estimators in time series regression with nonstable autoregressive errors. *Econometrica*, **58**(1), 145–163.

Nielsen, B. 2005. Strong consistency results for least squares estimators in general vector autoregressions with deterministic terms. *Economet. Theor.*, **21**(3), 534–561.

Nielsen, B. 2008. *Singular vector autoregressions with deterministic terms: Strong consistency and lag order determination.* http://www.nuffield.ox.ac.uk/economics/papers/2008/w14/Nielsen08VAR explosive.pdf.

Ord, K. 1975. Estimation methods for models of spatial interaction. *J. Amer. Statist. Assoc.*, **70**, 120–126.

Pesaran, M. H., Chudik, A. 2010. *Econometric analysis of high dimensional VARs featuring a dominant unit*, 41 pp. http://ideas.repec.org/p/ces/ceswps/_3055.html

Phillips, P. C. B. 1999. *Discrete Fourier transforms of fractional processes.* Cowles Foundation discussion paper no. 1243, Yale University.

Phillips, P. C. B. 2007. Regression with slowly varying regressors and nonlinear trends. *Economet. Theor.*, **23**, 557–614.

Pötscher, B. M., Prucha, I. R. 1997. *Dynamic Nonlinear Econometric Models.* Berlin: Springer-Verlag.

Rao, C. R. 1965. *Linear Statistical Inference and its Applications.* New York: John Wiley & Sons Inc.

Rao, M. M. 1961. Consistency and limit distributions of estimators of parameters in explosive stochastic difference equations. *Ann. Math. Stat.*, **32**, 195–218.

Robinson, P. M. 1995. Log-periodogram regression of time series with long range dependence. *Ann. Stat.*, **23**(3), 1048–1072.

Rubin, H. 1950. Consistency of maximum likelihood estimates in the explosive case. In: Koopmans, T. C. (ed), *Statistical Inference in Dynamic Economic Models.* Cowles Commission Monograph No. 10. New York: John Wiley & Sons Inc., pp. 356–364.

Schmidt, P. 1976. *Econometrics.* Statistics: Textbooks and monographs. New York: Marcel Dekker, Inc.

Seneta, E. 1985. *Pravilno Menyayushchiesya Funktsii.* Moscow: "Nauka". Translated from English by I. S. Shiganov, Translation edited and with a preface by V. M. Zolotarev, With appendices by I. S. Shiganov and V. M. Zolotarev.

Smirnov, O. L., Anselin, L. 2001. Fast maximum likelihood estimation of very large spatial autoregressive models: a characteristic polynomial approach. *Comput. Statist. Data Anal.*, **35**(3), 301–319.

Smith, R. L. 1982. Uniform rates of convergence in extreme-value theory. *Adv. in Appl. Probab.*, **14**, 600–622.

Stigum, B. P. 1974. Asymptotic properties of dynamic stochastic parameter estimates. III. *J. Multivar. Anal.*, **4**, 351–381.

Stout, W. F. 1974. *Almost Sure Convergence.* Academic Press Inc., New York-London. Probability and Mathematical Statistics, Vol. 24.

Tanaka, K. 1996. *Time Series Analysis.* New York: John Wiley & Sons Inc. Nonstationary and noninvertible distribution theory.

Taylor, R. L. 1978. *Stochastic Convergence of Weighted Sums of Random Elements in Linear Spaces.* Lecture Notes in Mathematics, Vol. 672. Berlin: Springer.

Theil, H. 1971. *Principles of Econometrics.* New York: John Wiley & Sons Inc.

Trenogin, V. A. 1980. *Funktsional'nyi Analiz*. Moscow: "Nauka".

Varga, R. S. 1962. *Matrix Iterative Analysis*. Englewood Cliffs, Prentice-Hall Inc.

Vilenkin, N. Ja. 1969. *Kombinatorika*. Moscow: Nauka.

Wei, C. Z. 1985. Asymptotic properties of least-squares estimates in stochastic regression models. *Ann. Stat.*, **13**(4), 1498–1508.

White, H. 1994. *Estimation, Inference and Specification Analysis*. Econometric Society Monographs, Vol. 22. Cambridge: Cambridge University Press.

White, J. S. 1958. The limiting distribution of the serial correlation coefficient in the explosive case. *Ann. Math. Stat.*, **29**, 1188–1197.

Wooldridge, J. M. 1994. Estimation and inference for dependent processes. *Handbook of Econometrics, Vol. IV*. Handbooks in Econom., Vol. 2. Amsterdam: North-Holland., pp. 2639–2738.

Wu, Chien-Fu. 1981. Asymptotic theory of nonlinear least squares estimation. *Ann. Stat.*, **9**(3), 501–513.

Wu, W. B. 2005. Nonlinear system theory: Another look at dependence. *Proc. Natl. Acad. Sci. USA*, **102**, 14150–14154.

Wu, W. B., Min, W. 2005. On linear processes with dependent innovations. *Stochastic Process. Appl.*, **115**, 939–958.

Zhuk, V. V., Natanson, G. I. 2001. Seminorms and moduli of continuity of functions defined on a segment. *Zap. Nauchn. Sem. S.-Peterburg. Otdel. Mat. Inst. Steklov. (POMI)*, **276** (Anal. Teor. Chisel i Teor. Funkts. 17), 155–203.

AUTHOR INDEX

Short-Memory Linear Processes and Econometric Applications. Kairat T. Mynbaev
© 2011 John Wiley & Sons, Inc. Published 2011 by John Wiley & Sons, Inc.

SUBJECT INDEX

Short-Memory Linear Processes and Econometric Applications. Kairat T. Mynbaev
© 2011 John Wiley & Sons, Inc. Published 2011 by John Wiley & Sons, Inc.